Cost Accounting:
Managerial Use
of Accounting Data

The Kent Series in Accounting

Cost Accounting:
Managerial Use
of Accounting Data

Emerson O. Henke
Hankamer School of Business
Baylor University

Charlene W. Spoede
Hankamer School of Business
Baylor University

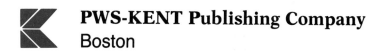
PWS-KENT Publishing Company
Boston

657.4
H51c

To my wife, Beatrice
To my husband, John Paugh

PWS-KENT
Publishing Company

20 Park Plaza
Boston, Massachusetts 02116

Sponsoring Editor: Albert Bruckner
Assistant Editor: Deirdre A. Lynch
Production Editor: Susan L. Krikorian
Interior Designer: Carol H. Rose
Cover Designer: Susan L. Krikorian
Interior Illustrator: George Nichols
Compositor: Weimer Typesetting Company, Inc.
Manufacturing Coordinator: Margaret Sullivan Higgins
Cover Printer: John P. Pow Company
Text Printer/Binder: Arcata Graphics/Halliday

PWS-KENT Publishing Company is a division of Wadsworth, Inc.

Printed in the United States of America

90 91 92 93 94 — 10 9 8 7 6 5 4 3 2 1

Library of Congress Cataloging-in-Publication Data

Henke, Emerson O.
  Cost accounting: managerial use of accounting data / Emerson O. Henke, Charlene
W. Spoede.
    p. cm.
    Includes bibliographical references.
    ISBN 0-534-92060-8
    1. Cost accounting.   I. Spoede, Charlene W.   II. Title.
HF5686.C8H413   1990
657'.42—dc20   90-7193
                                                                        CIP

Contents

v

Part III   Standard Cost Systems   365

Preface

Cost Accounting: Managerial Use of Accounting Data is designed for use in a one-semester cost accounting course. It is divided into 5 parts (24 chapters), organized to provide the instructor with flexibility in choice of materials to cover. The overriding objective of the authors was to provide a logically organized, conceptually based, easy-to-teach-from book that addresses present and future cost accounting issues.

In working toward that goal, we have developed a systems-based text in which the learning objectives to be achieved from the study of each chapter are identified at the beginning of the chapter. In Chapters 4 and 5, we develop and illustrate the accounting procedures for a basic job-order costing system. The framework and procedures associated with a process costing system are developed in Chapters 6 through 9. Chapters 11 through 13 show how those systems can be adapted to the use of standard costs. A continuing illustrated problem is used throughout all these three sets of chapters to demonstrate how the systems operate. We have carefully defined terms as they are used and have also included near the end of each chapter a glossary defining the new terms used in that chapter. A master glossary comprised of all of those terms appears at the end of the text.

To facilitate the teaching process, we have used many flowcharts and other illustrative devises that visually relate the flows of goods and costs through the production process to the accounting procedures for accumulating and allocating the cost data. Numerous questions, class exercises, and problems are included throughout the text, many adapted from past CPA and CMA examinations, thereby providing preparation for the managerial accounting parts of those exams. Also, among the end-of-chapter materials are thought-stimulation problems and cases designed to encourage students to think creatively about decisions they typically will have to make as managers or management accountants.

All of us know that managerial accounting practices will be changing to meet the challenges of manufacturing automation, just-in-time inventory practices, and synchronization of production with sales demand. We have included 4 chapters (Chapters 3, 22, 23, and 24) in which we introduce some of the changes likely to be associated with future managerial accounting systems. We also relate some of these projected changes to topics discussed in other parts of the book.

Sensing that students need to have some knowledge of the cost-accumulation and cost-allocation practices followed by service enterprises, we have included Chapter 10, "Cost Accounting Systems for Service Enterprises." We believe this chapter provides the most comprehensive coverage of the topic that can be found in any cost accounting text currently available.

The authors recognize that the time constraint associated with a one-semester course will generally limit text coverage to a maximum of 17 chapters. Twenty-four chapters are included here to provide instructors with flexibility of emphasis. We suggest the following groupings of 17 chapters each, to accommodate 4 different possible emphases.

1. Conventional cost accounting for manufacturing firms: Chapters 1–9, 11–17, and 19.
2. Conventional cost accounting for all firms (including service enterprises: Chapters 1–17.
3. Conventional cost accounting with managerial emphasis: Chapters 1, 2, 4–7, and 11–21.
4. Cost accounting with emphasis on projected future managerial accounting practices: Chapters 1–7, 14–20, and 22–24.

Because of the importance of the computer to cost accounting, a computer-applications supplement for students (authored by Dr. J. M. Hudson) has been prepared. This supplement includes LOTUS® 1-2-3® templates for selected problems in the text. A student study guide that can help students study the text materials also is provided.

We wish to thank the following individuals who took the time to review and comment on the various stages of the manuscript for this text:

Marvin L. Bouillon
Iowa State University

James M. Emig
Villanova University

LaVerne Gebhard
University of Wisconsin, Milwaukee

Donald E. Keller
California State University at Chico

Gerard A. Lange
St. John's University

Patrick M. McKenzie
Arizona State University

Richard J. Murdock
Ohio State University

Lawrence M. Ozzello
University of Wisconsin, Eau Claire

Gilroy A. Zuckerman
North Carolina State University

We also express our appreciation to Cathy Talbert, Evelyn Hupp, and Phyllis Stewart for their excellent work in typing the manuscript.

We have learned a great deal in writing this book. We are excited about the opportunities for cost accounting in the last decade of the twentieth century and the first decades of the twenty-first century.

Emerson O. Henke
Charlene W. Spoede

Part I

Introduction

Chapter 1

Objectives of Cost Accounting

Learning Objectives

When you have finished your study of this chapter, you should

1. Appreciate the importance of effort/achievement measurements and cause-and-effect relationships in cost accounting.
2. Understand the objectives of the cost-accumulation and cost-allocation process.
3. Know the steps followed in accounting for the accumulation and allocation of manufacturing costs to units produced.
4. Understand the meanings of various terms used in cost accounting.
5. Know how to prepare a statement of cost of goods manufactured.

Accounting involves the accumulation, classification, interpretation, and presentation of financial data. In **financial accounting** one accumulates and presents data primarily for use by investors, creditors, and other external parties. **Managerial accounting** involves accumulating and presenting data primarily for use by personnel within an entity's organization. *Cost accounting* is the part of the typical accounting curriculum that is responsible for helping students develop an understanding of managerial accounting.

Most professional groups have organizations through which they can work to improve the group's effectiveness. The American Institute of Certified Public Accountants (AICPA) carries out that responsibility for financial accountants. Among other things, the AICPA publishes a monthly periodical entitled *Journal of Accountancy* and sponsors certification of individuals as certified public accountants (CPAs) through an examination process. Problems in this text taken from past CPA examinations are labeled "AICPA Adapted." The National Association of Accountants (NAA) seeks to aid the effectiveness of cost accountants. This organization publishes a periodical entitled *Management Accounting* and provides a catalyst through which new ideas for cost accounting can be discussed and disseminated. Through its affiliate, the Institute of Management Accounting, the NAA sponsors the Certified Management Accounting (CMA) examination. Those problems in this text taken from past CMA examinations are labeled "ICMA Adapted." The Financial Accounting Standards Board (FASB) publishes statements of financial accounting standards that constitute a major source of **generally accepted accounting practices (GAAP)** for presenting published financial statements. These FASB standards apply only to cost accounting procedures that affect data that become a part of financial statements, such as cost of sales on the income statement and inventory on the balance sheet. Cost reports and procedures designed for internal use are not subject to the constraints of GAAP.

Because accounting data are intended to provide users of those data with quantitative measures that can be used in evaluating the efficiency and effectiveness of operations, one of the primary considerations in accumulating and presenting those data is to relate the efforts expended to earn revenue to the benefits derived from those efforts (i.e., the revenue realized). For external reporting purposes, the primary device for portraying the effort/achievement relationship is the income statement. In that statement, we match **expenses** (i.e., costs of the resources and services consumed in generating revenues) against *revenues*, defined as increases in net assets resulting from operations. The difference between revenues and expenses is called *net income* (if the difference is positive) or *net loss* (if the difference is negative).

As we develop the discipline of cost accounting, we shall see that effort/achievement relationships also can be reflected in other ways, such as by calculating the cost per unit, or **unit cost**, and comparing those data to budgeted data or similar data for prior periods or for other entities. **Cost** is defined as that which must be given up in order to acquire, produce, or effect something. In unit-cost calculations, achievements are measured in terms of units produced. Efforts are represented by the aggregate costs incurred in producing the units. To illustrate how such an effort/achievement measurement can be used, let's assume that there are two factories producing identical units. One incurs a cost of $100,000 in turning out 10,000 units; the other turns out 10,000 units with an aggregate cost of $75,000. All other things being the same, we would conclude that the second factory has operated more efficiently (had a better effort/achievement relationship) because it incurred a cost of only $7.50 per unit compared to a cost of $10.00 per unit for the first factory.

The identification of cause-and-effect relationships is an underlying requirement for relating efforts to achievements. In cost accounting, we are continually concerned with identifying cause-and-effect relationships as we accumulate and allocate costs to the goods or services being produced and as we calculate unit costs.

Cost accounting, perhaps more meaningfully described as *accounting for the flows of costs*, is concerned with the development of systems for relating costs to the products or services produced by a company. **Accounting costs** are defined as the recorded values of resources and services given up in acquiring other resources and services. Costs may be incurred for the acquisition of assets that will benefit many periods or for goods and services consumed during a single reporting period. The costs of goods and services consumed during a reporting period are appropriately characterized as *expenses*. That means that though all expenses are also costs, not all costs are expenses. Cost accounting, then, deals primarily with the accumulation and allocation of costs associated with the production of goods or services. One objective of the accumulation and allocation process is to divide those costs into asset elements and expense elements.

This aspect of cost accounting will have only limited usefulness in merchandising operations because such businesses realize revenues from providing **place utility** for merchandise. They do this by placing acquired merchandise items in counters and on shelves (or in catalogs) so that it is convenient for customers to purchase them. In such entities, there is no change in the form of the goods as they are acquired, held, and ultimately sold. Merchandise items are sold in the same form they had as when they were purchased. On the other hand, manufacturing and service enterprises earn revenue primarily by providing **form utility**—converting resources into services or into products that have different characteristics from the materials and services purchased. Manufacturing enterprises, for example, convert raw materials and other resources into products (finished goods) that have a greater sale value (are more useful) than the raw materials used in their production. Revenue is thus earned by changing the form of the goods from a raw state to a finished product. Service enterprises hire and train people to provide specialized services, such as cleaning, security, and consulting. Revenue is earned by converting "people resources" into services.

Because cost accounting produces information that is used by internal managers, it should be particularly beneficial to nonaccounting majors. Cost accounting will help future managers understand the operating reports and other data that provide the information every effective manager must use in carrying out his or her responsibilities.

In treating the discipline of cost accounting in this book, we begin by developing the systems that are used for accumulating and allocating costs to products and services (Chapters 4–13). After that, we explain how the data provided by those systems can be used by internal managers (Chapters 14–21). In the last section (Chapters 22–24), we consider some of the implications of new manufacturing and management techniques for cost accounting practices.

The Management Accounting Practices Committee of the NAA has identified five major areas of responsibility for management accounting. They include the provision of data that can be used for

1. reporting financial information to external users
2. planning future operations
3. evaluating operations
4. controlling operations
5. reflecting accountability for the uses of organizational resources.

These areas of responsibility may be summarized into the following objectives for the cost-accumulation and cost-allocation processes developed in this text. They include the provision of cost information that can be used

1. as a basis for valuing manufactured inventories and cost of goods sold in *externally presented financial reports*
2. in controlling operations through the *evaluation of operating results* and the placement of responsibilities for the *uses of organizational resources* on the shoulders of specifically identifiable persons within the organization
3. in *planning operations* through the establishment of cost and budgetary goals
4. in making day-to-day operating decisions (a part of *controlling* operations).

In this chapter, we give further attention to the implications of these objectives for a cost accounting system.

Valuation of Manufactured Inventory

Accountants use ledger accounts to accumulate the financial data relating to the various aspects of an entity's operations. The T account, an abbreviated version of a ledger account, is used for that purpose throughout the text as we develop cost-accumulation and cost-allocation procedures. Data are accumulated in various asset and equity T accounts, as shown below:

Asset Account		Equity Account	
Beginning balance + Additions	− Removals	− Removals	Beginning balance + Additions
= Ending balance			= Ending balance

Each T account will reflect a four-element equation:

$$\text{Beginning balance} + \text{Additions} - \text{Removals} = \text{Ending balance}$$

In using this equation, we can always derive the fourth element (usually removals or ending balance) if we know the amount of each of the other three elements. This basic equation, with appropriate terms inserted for each of the four elements, is used over and over again in the cost-accumulation, cost-allocation, and cost-reporting processes. As you work with the materials in Chapters 4–13, it is especially important to identify the appropriate four-element equation associated with the cost-accumulation and cost-allocation procedures being developed so you can gain better insight into and understanding of systems used to accumulate and allocate historical costs.

Inventory Valuation for a Merchandising Business

Inventory is defined as goods held for sale or for use in the production of other goods. In a merchandising business, we can accumulate the costs of acquiring inventory in a ledger account labeled "inventory." As those goods are sold, their costs will be transferred to another ledger account called "cost of goods sold" or "cost of sales." This reflects the costs allocated to the units sold. If we think of the inventory account as being a "cost-accumulation box" called "Retail Store," we may visualize both the physical flows of merchandise and the flows of the costs attributed to them as following the pattern shown in Figure 1–1. In using the cost-accumulation box, we show the beginning-of-period balance at the top of the box, the inflows on the left side, the ending balances along the bottom, and the outflows on the right side.

In addition to the costs incurred in purchasing merchandise held for sale, a merchandising firm also incurs costs in carrying out its merchandising operations, which we call **operating expenses.** Total merchandise

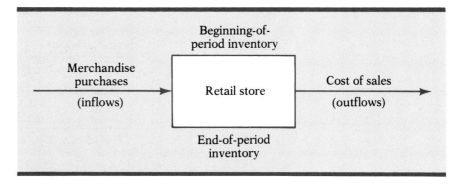

FIGURE 1–1 Typical Cost-Accumulation Box

costs (beginning inventory plus purchases) must be allocated between cost of goods sold and ending inventory to enable us to prepare an income statement and a balance sheet. In a merchandising business, we can make that allocation by assigning costs to ending inventory and allowing the rest of the cost of merchandise to go into cost of sales (**physical-inventory method** or **periodic-inventory method**), as illustrated in Figure 1–2.

Another possibility is to assign costs to the units sold as sales occur and to then accumulate cost of sales throughout the period. Doing that allows the rest of the cost of merchandise to be assigned to ending inventory (**perpetual-inventory method**), as depicted in Figure 1–3. In either instance, however, we are using the following four-element equation:

(1) Beginning merchandise inventory + (2) Purchases of inventory
− (3) Cost of sales = (4) Ending inventory

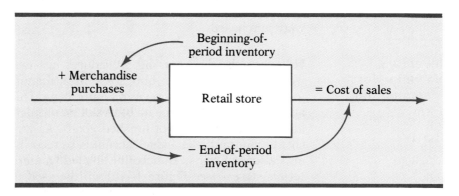

FIGURE 1–2 Physical-Inventory Method

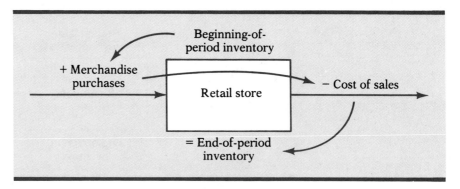

FIGURE 1–3 Perpetual-Inventory Method

These four elements are included in a merchandise inventory T account as shown below:

Merchandise Inventory

(1) Beginning balance + (2) Purchases	− (3) Costs assigned to cost of sales
= (4) Ending balance	

With a physical-inventory system, we calculate the value of ending inventory and determine cost of sales as the missing element of the four-element equation [(1) + (2) − (4) = (3)]. With a perpetual-inventory system, we assign costs to the goods as they are sold and calculate ending inventory as the missing element in the four-element equation [(1) + (2) − (3) = (4)]. In either instance, however, we can determine the costs to be associated with individual units of inventory or individual units of goods sold by reference to purchase invoices. We can do that because the form of the goods sold is the same as when the goods were purchased.

Inventory Valuation for a Manufacturing Firm

Following the flowcharting procedures just described, we can visualize the flows of goods and costs in a manufacturing enterprise as following the pattern shown in Figure 1–4a. This figure uses three cost-accumulation boxes: one for stores of materials, another for the factory, and a third for stores of finished goods. As we demonstrate later, the cost accountant uses ledger accounts to record the accumulations and allocations of costs. An account labeled "materials inventory" or "materials stores" (see Figure 1–4b) will be used to accumulate the costs relating to the "stores of materials" box (Figure 1–4a). Costs associated with goods in the "factory" box (Figure 1–4a) are accumulated in a

(a) MANUFACTURING PROCESS

(b) MANUFACTURING ACCOUNTING

Materials Inventory		Work-in-Process Inventory		Finished-Goods Inventory	
Beginning inventory Purchases	Materials used	Beginning inventory Direct materials used* Direct labor* Manufacturing overhead*	Cost of goods manufactured	Beginning inventory Cost of goods manufactured	Cost of sales
End-of-period materials inventory		End-of-period work-in-process inventory		End-of-period finished goods inventory	

*Current manufacturing costs

FIGURE 1–4 Inventory Valuation for a Manufacturing Firm. (a) Manufacturing process. (b) Associated ledger accounts. (See text for definition of terms.)

"Work-in-Process Inventory" ledger account (Figure 1–4b). Another account, labeled "finished-goods inventory," is used to accumulate the costs attached to the "stores of finished goods" box. Definitions of terms for Figure 1–4 follow.

Materials inventory   Materials held for use in manufacturing the finished product or to facilitate the production process. Most of these materials will become part of the finished product; these are called **direct materials**. However, some materials will be used to keep the factory in operation or are added to the product in such minute quantities that it is impracticable to trace the cost to the product; these are called **indirect materials**, and the costs assigned to them become part of manufacturing overhead.

Direct materials used   Materials transferred from the materials inventory to be put into the production process and become part of finished units as those units are produced.

Direct labor   Amounts paid to employees who work on the production line in the manufacture of the product.

Manufacturing overhead   Other costs incurred in keeping the factory operating over a period of time, including miscellaneous factory supplies transferred from the materials inventory (**indirect materials**); amounts paid to manufacturing employees other than those working on the production line (**indirect labor**); factory rent, or depreciation of factory building and machinery, insurance on the factory and its equipment, property taxes assessed on the factory and its equipment; payroll taxes; heat, light, and power for the factory; and other costs incidental to keeping the factory in operation.

Work-in-process inventory   Costs assigned to partially completed inventory in the factory, including the direct materials costs, direct labor costs, and manufacturing overhead costs assigned to partially completed units. Direct materials and direct labor costs (combined) are commonly referred to as **prime costs**, and direct labor and overhead (combined) are referred to as **conversion costs**.

Cost of goods manufactured   Costs assigned to the finished units produced during each operating period.

Finished-goods inventory   Costs assigned to the completely finished units that are left in inventory (unsold) at the end of an operating period.

Cost of sales (also called *cost of goods sold*)   Costs assigned to the units of finished goods sold during an operating period.

Observe in Figure 1–4b that there are three four-element equations associated with the flows of costs through a manufacturing firm. Beginning with the right side of the figure, we find we need to be able to assign values to each element of the following four-element equation to prepare the cost-of-sales section of the income statement:

$$\begin{aligned}
&\text{Beginning-of-period finished-goods inventory} \\
&+ \text{Cost of goods manufactured} \\
&- \text{End-of-period finished-goods inventory} = \text{Cost of sales}
\end{aligned}$$

All these items are included in the T account for "finished-goods inventory" in Figure 1–4b. However, we have no single direct source of costs (such as a purchase invoice) for any of these items because finished goods are in a different form from the goods that were purchased as raw materials to be used in manufacturing those goods.

If we move back to the factory-cost-accumulation segment of the figure, that is, the "work-in-process inventory" T account, we find that values must be assigned to the elements of the following four-element equation to determine the cost of goods manufactured:

$$\text{Beginning-of-period work-in-process inventory}$$
$$+ \text{ Manufacturing costs (costs of direct materials used, direct labor,}$$
$$\text{and manufacturing overhead)}$$
$$- \text{ End-of-period work-in-process inventory}$$
$$= \text{ Cost of goods manufactured}$$

All these items are included in the T account for "work in process inventory." Again, there is no single source of information that can be used to assign values to manufacturing costs (direct materials, direct labor, and overhead), work-in-process ending inventory, or cost of goods manufactured. However, we *can* determine the direct-labor and manufacturing-overhead costs by referring to the accounts in which those data will have been accumulated as part of the accounting process.

Next, we move back to the "stores of materials" segment of Figure 1–4. Assuming for the moment that all materials removed from inventory are used directly in manufacturing the product, we can observe the following four-element equation associated with arriving at a value for direct materials used:

$$\text{Beginning-of-period direct-materials inventory}$$
$$+ \text{ Purchases of direct materials}$$
$$- \text{ End-of-period direct-materials inventory}$$
$$= \text{ Cost of direct materials used}$$

All these items are included in the T account for "materials inventory." With this four-element equation, we can assign a cost to both purchases and end-of-period materials inventories by referring to the purchase invoices associated with the acquisitions of those materials. Beginning-of-period materials inventory will have been determined in a similar manner at the end of the previous period. That allows us to complete this four-element equation and calculate the cost of direct materials used.

Having computed the cost of direct materials used, let's return to the four-element equation associated with the operation of the factory, the "work-in-process inventory" T account. The critical step in completing this equation is to assign costs (**manufacturing costs**) to work-in-process inventory. Having determined the cost of direct materials used (see preceding paragraph), we could now complete the four-element equation for the factory if we had suitable procedures for assigning manufacturing costs to work-in-process inventory. Because we need those data to prepare financial statements, one of the primary objectives of cost accounting is to develop systems for allocating direct materials costs, direct labor costs, and manufacturing-overhead costs to work-in-process inventory. We make these allocations either by using a job-order costing system (see Chapter 4) or a process costing system (see Chapter 6).

Since those cost-accumulation and cost-allocation systems will be developed later in the text, we shall, at this point, illustrate only how the flows of costs for a manufacturing firm can be accounted for with arbitrarily assumed amounts allocated to the beginning and ending work-in-process inventories. Let's assume the following data and that we are expected to develop from those data the cost-of-sales element of the income statement for Hoosier Manufacturing Company.

Hoosier Manufacturing Company

Assumed Data Provided

Beginning-of-period raw-materials inventory	$ 30,000
Raw-materials purchases (25,000 units at $5 per unit)	125,000
Direct labor costs	75,000
Manufacturing overhead	150,000
Beginning-of-period work-in-process inventory	60,000
End-of-period work-in-process inventory	40,000
Beginning-of-period finished-goods inventory	30,000
End-of-period raw materials	5,000 units
Units transferred to finished-goods	25,000 units
End-of-period finished-goods inventory	3,000 units

REQUIRED: Calculate the cost of raw materials used, cost of goods manufactured, and cost of sales by using the four-element equations developed earlier in this section. Assume that all raw materials used are direct materials. The **first-in, first-out (FIFO)** method, where the costs associated with the oldest units in stock are assigned to the first units transferred out, is assumed to be used in valuing inventories.

Schedule Solution

Cost of raw materials used

Beginning-of-period inventory of raw materials	$ 30,000
+ Purchases of raw materials	125,000
Total raw materials available	$155,000
− End-of-period inventory of raw materials (see Schedule A)	25,000
= Cost of raw materials used	$130,000

Cost of goods manufactured

Beginning-of-period inventory of work in process	$ 60,000
+ Additions (total manufacturing costs added this period):	
Raw materials used	130,000
Direct labor	75,000
Manufacturing overhead	150,000
Total	$415,000
− End-of-period work-in-process inventory	40,000
= Cost of goods manufactured	$375,000

Cost of sales

Beginning-of-period finished-goods inventory	$ 30,000
+ Cost of goods manufactured	375,000
Cost of goods available for sale	$405,000
− End-of-period finished-goods inventory (see Schedule B)	45,000
= Cost of goods sold	$360,000

Schedule A

Raw materials cost per unit: $125,000 ÷ 25,000 units = $5

End-of-period raw materials inventory: 5,000 units @ $5 = $25,000

Schedule B

Cost of goods manufactured	$375,000
Units transferred to finished goods	25,000
Cost per unit ($375,000 ÷ 25,000)	$15
End-of-period finished-goods inventory (3,000 @ $15)	$ 45,000

T-Account Solution*

Materials Inventory			
	$ 30,000		
25,000 units @ $5	125,000	**$130,000 cost of raw**	
		materials used	
5,000 units @ $5	$ 25,000		

Work-in-Process Inventory			
	$ 60,000		
direct materials	**130,000**		
direct labor	75,000	**$375,000 cost of goods**	
overhead	150,000	**manufactured,**	
		25,000 units @ $15	
	$40,000		

Finished-Goods Inventory			
	$ 30,000		
cost of goods			
manufactured,			
25,000 units @ $15	375,000	**$360,000**	**cost of sales**
3,000 units @ $15	$ 45,000		

Cost of Sales	
$360,000	

*NOTE: Numbers in regular type in the T-account solution were given in the original problem data; numbers in boldface type were calculated.

Observe again in Figures 1–1 and 1–4 that we have used a rectangle or box to identify each of the cost-accumulation centers associated first with a merchandising business and then with a manufacturing business. These boxes should help you visualize the way in which the four-element equation is used to determine the cost to be assigned to the outflows from the respective cost-accumulation centers. The elements of those equations actually will be reflected in T accounts, as explained earlier. Even when amounts become very precise and details become complex, it is important to remember that this simple situation underlies the activities of each cost-accumulation center. Throughout the book, we shall use this device, which we will refer to as a *cost-accumulation box*, to visually portray various elements of the cost-accumulation and cost-allocation process.

Recall that in using the cost-accumulation box, we show the beginning balance at the top of the box, the inflows on the left side, the ending balance along the bottom, and the outflows on the right side. Thus, in applying the four-element equation, we need simply to start at the top of the box and work in a counterclockwise direction to the outflow element of the box, as shown in Figure 1–5.

For asset accounts, the relationship between the cost-accumulation box and a T account is as shown in Figure 1–6.

The Financial Accounting Connection

Although cost accounting is used primarily for the purpose of accumulating data for use by internal managers, it also provides the information for the inventory section of the balance sheet and the cost-of-sales section of the income statement included in the externally reported financial data. As we observed in the Hoosier Manufacturing Company example, the cost-of-sales section of the income statement is made up of three elements: (1) beginning-of-period inventory of finished goods, plus (2) cost of goods manufactured, minus (3) end-of-period inventory

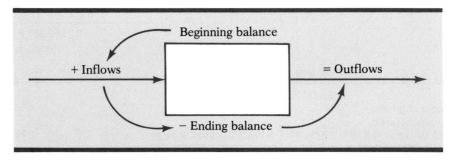

FIGURE 1–5   Cost-Accumulation Box

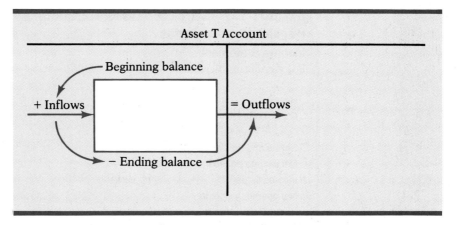

FIGURE 1–6 Relationship Between Cost-Accumulation Box and Asset T Account

of finished goods. Completion of that equation requires the preparation of a cost-of-goods-manufactured statement to support the cost-of-goods-manufactured item in the cost-of-sales section of the income statement. The formal statement reflecting those data for Hoosier Manufacturing Company is shown in Exhibit 1–1.

EXHIBIT 1–1

Hoosier Manufacturing

Statement of Cost of Goods Manufactured
For Reporting Period

Beginning-of-period work-in-process inventory		$ 60,000
Raw materials used:		
Beginning-of-period inventory	$ 30,000	
Purchases of raw materials	125,000	
Total	$155,000	
End-of-period inventory	25,000	
Raw materials used	$130,000	
Direct labor	75,000	
Manufacturing overhead	150,000	355,000
Total		$415,000
End-of-period work-in-process inventory		40,000
Cost of goods manufactured		$375,000

EXHIBIT 1–2

Hoosier Manufacturing

Income Statement

For Reporting Period

Revenue	$500,000
Cost of sales	360,000
Gross margin (or gross profit)	$140,000
Selling and administrative expenses	60,000
Net income before income taxes	80,000
Income taxes	24,000
Net operating income	$ 56,000

Having determined the cost of goods manufactured, the accountant can then prepare the cost-of-sales section of the income statement for Hoosier Manufacturing Company to reflect the following data:

Beginning-of-period finished-goods inventory	$ 30,000
+ Cost of goods manufactured	375,000
= Cost of goods available for sale	$405,000
− End-of-period finished-goods inventory	45,000
= Cost of sales	$360,000

Assuming sales of $500,000, selling and administrative expenses of $60,000, and a 30% income tax rate, Hoosier Manufacturing Company's abbreviated income statement for the period would be as shown in Exhibit 1–2.

Controlling Operations

As we observed in the introductory section of this chapter, one of the objectives of cost accounting is to accumulate, allocate, and report cost data that will help management in controlling operations. Here again, the objective is to associate costs with the causes (drivers) of those costs. However, in accumulating and reporting costs for control purposes, one must also report the data in a format that relates cost data to individuals within the organization who have been responsible for incurring the costs. Look at it this way: If we assume a very small business, one that is owned and operated by a single person (the owner), who is the only individual with authority to incur costs, then the owner would be controlling each incurrence of cost and therefore would only have to be concerned about the relationships between the costs incurred and the benefits realized from their incurrence. However, as a business becomes larger and the responsibility for the incurrence of costs is delegated to other people, it is important to have information relating the costs incurred by each of those subordinates to the benefits the business has realized from those costs. We frequently refer to the process of relating costs to those responsible for their incurrence as an element of **responsibility accounting**.

Although specific procedures and reports associated with controlling costs are developed more completely later in the text, the following list of costs and the supervisory personnel typically held accountable for them should help you understand how costs can be related to those employees responsible for their incurrence.

Cost	Supervisory Personnel Typically Held Accountable
Merchandise, or raw materials	Supervisor of purchasing
Selling expenses	Sales manager
General office expenses	Office manager
Direct labor	Foreman of the department in which the direct labor cost was incurred
Departmental maintenance costs	Departmental supervisor

The procedures for accumulating, allocating, and reporting these costs to facilitate their control will be developed in Chapter 17. These data are reported to management, where they will be compared with historical data from other periods and budgetary data for the current period in determining whether the respective subordinate supervisor has appropriately controlled the costs he or she has been responsible for incurring.

Planning Future Operations

Any business that operates effectively and efficiently must appropriately plan its operations prior to implementing them. We may visualize business operations as being made up of a repetitive operating cycle calling for the initiation of a plan for operations followed by the implementation of operations and an evaluation of the effectiveness and efficiency of those operations. The cycle then returns to the planning phase for the next operating period. This is sometimes referred to as the *plan/execute/evaluate/plan (PEEP)* cycle.

During the planning phase, management will typically project, via a budget, the revenues expected to be realized, along with the costs expected to be incurred in realizing those revenues, during the next operating period. The procedures for the preparation and development of budgetary data are discussed in Chapter 15. However, at this point, it is appropriate to recognize that the development of the cost parts of the budget depend on either historical cost data from prior periods as recorded in the cost accounting system or estimated or **predetermined costs** based on a knowledge of how costs are incurred, accumulated, and allocated. (Predetermined costs also are referred to as *standard costs*.) As we explain in Chapter 15, a **master budget** typically is developed that projects the expected results of operations all the way from expected sales in units, usually the critical constraining event, to the point of showing revenues and expenses expected to be reflected in the income statement for the budgetary period and a balance sheet showing the asset, liability, and owners' equity amounts expected to emerge at the end of the period covered by the budget.

One of the reasons for planning future operations is to determine whether management wants to pursue the planned course of action. If the initially projected results are considered unsatisfactory, an alternate operating plan typically will be developed to see whether it will produce better results. If the budgetary process is being carried out on a computer spreadsheet, it is easy to develop such alternate plans. Ultimately, the master budget for some operating plan will be adopted during the planning phase of the PEEP cycle. Later, the results of actual operations will be compared with the budgetary data as part of the evaluation phase of the PEEP cycle.

Using Cost Data in Making Operating Decisions

Elements of the cost data accumulated by the cost accounting system will be used by management in making various operating decisions. As we explain in Chapter 19, one of the major concerns in implementing this type of managerial use of accounting data is the identification of the specific cost data that are relevant to the decision to be made. Some recorded costs that relate to the specific aspect of operations being considered often must be ignored because they cannot be changed in any way by the decision. The irrelevant costs that cannot be recovered in cash regardless of which decision is made are called **sunk costs**. They are analagous to spilt milk that can be cleaned up but can't be "unspilt." Other costs exist that also will be the same regardless of which decision is made and are therefore not pertinent to the decision being made. It is imperative that management use selectively the recorded cost data available to it in making these operating decisions by isolating and concentrating on **relevant costs**, that is, the expected future costs that differ for the various alternatives being considered as a decision is being made.

While recorded costs must be used selectively, it is also important that management consider certain unrecorded **opportunity costs** in the decision-making process. These are costs represented by the sacrifice associated with a decision, such as revenue that might be earned if the contemplated action were not implemented. The opportunity cost of a decision is the net benefit of the best alternative that is foregone. For example, if management is considering purchasing a new machine, the income that could be earned on the amount to be invested in that machine were it not purchased would be a form of opportunity cost that must be considered if the right decision is to be made.

We also use selected cost data developed by the cost accounting system in the application of quantitative techniques, such as linear programming, the identification of economic order quantity, and regression analysis. These techniques are discussed in Chapter 21.

SUMMARY

We began by defining the discipline of accounting. We observed that it includes both financial accounting and managerial accounting. We then noted that while cost accounting provides some crucial data for financial accounting purposes, it is most directly associated with managerial accounting.

Next we identified the objectives of the cost-accumulation and cost-allocation process associated with cost accounting as the development of cost data that can be used in (1) valuing inventories, (2) controlling operations, (3) planning future operations, and (4) making operating decisions.

Then we explained that a business entity converting resources and services into different products or services requires a system for accumulating and allocating costs if it is to value its work-in-process and finished-goods inventories appropriately for the purpose of preparing financial statements. We then demonstrated by using assumed cost data how to prepare an operating statement for Hoosier Manufacturing Company.

Finally, we briefly introduced the general concepts underlying the accumulation and allocation of costs for the purpose of controlling operations, planning future operations, and making day-to-day operating decisions.

GLOSSARY OF TERMS INTRODUCED IN THIS CHAPTER

accounting costs   Recorded values of resources and services given up in acquiring other resources and services.

conversion costs   The sum of direct labor and manufacturing-overhead costs. These are the costs incurred in converting raw materials to finished product.

cost	That which must be given up in order to acquire, produce, or effect something.
cost of goods manufactured	Costs attached to goods transferred from the factory to finished-goods inventory. It is the total current manufacturing costs adjusted for beginning and ending work in process (WIP) (that is, plus beginning inventory of WIP and minus ending inventory of WIP).
cost of sales	The costs attached (allocated) to units of finished product delivered to customers.
direct labor	Amounts paid to manufacturing employees who work directly on changing materials to finished products and whose efforts can be economically traced to a particular unit of finished product.
direct materials	Materials that physically become a part of a finished product, that can be feasibly identified with the product, and whose amount can be economically traced to a particular unit of finished product.
expenses	Costs attached to resources and services consumed in generating revenue; sometimes referred to as *expired costs*.
financial accounting	The accumulation and presentation of financial data for use by investors, creditors, and other external parties.
finished-goods inventory	Manufactured units that have been completed and are being held for sale to customers.
first-in, first-out (FIFO) cost-flow assumption	An assumption used in assigning unit costs to goods transferred out or sold and to ending inventories whereby the costs associated with the oldest units in stock are assigned to the first units sold during a reporting period. These costs become cost of sales. That means that the most recent costs per unit will be assigned to the units remaining in inventory. The actual physical flow does not have to be first-in, first-out to use this method of assigning costs.
form utility	Increases in the usefulness of materials and other resources resulting from the conversion of resources into services or products that have different characteristics from the materials and services purchased.
generally accepted accounting practices (GAAP)	Accounting practices that conform to conventions, rules, and procedures that have general acceptability by the accounting profession.
indirect labor	Labor costs that are considered to be overhead, that is, amounts paid to manufacturing employees other than laborers working directly on the product (direct labor).
indirect materials	Materials used in keeping a factory in operation that do not become a part of the product being produced, or materials used in the product in such small quantities that it is not feasible to trace their costs to the product.
inventory	Materials and supplies (including added conversion costs) held by a firm either for use in the production of finished goods or for sale to customers.
managerial accounting	The measurement, accumulation, analysis, and presentation of financial data primarily for use by personnel within an entity's organization.

manufacturing costs	The sum of direct materials used, direct labor costs incurred, and manufacturing overhead applied to production during an operating period.
manufacturing overhead	Costs other than direct materials and direct labor costs that are incurred in keeping a factory in operation.
master budget	A document that consolidates all budgets of an organization into an overall plan including the projection of a cash-flow statement and an operating statement for the budget period and a balance sheet for the end of the budget period.
materials inventory	Materials purchased and held for use in manufacturing finished products or to facilitate the production process.
operating expenses	Expenses incurred in carrying out the selling and administrative activities of a business.
opportunity cost	Cost represented by the value of the best alternative foregone by adopting a particular strategy or employing resources in a specific manner.
periodic-inventory method	A system of assigning costs to goods transferred or sold and to ending inventory whereby balances are determined on specific dates by physical count rather than on a continuous basis.
perpetual-inventory method	A system of assigning costs to goods transferred or sold and to inventory on a continuously updated basis so that the balance in an inventory account and cumulative cost of sales is known at all times.
physical-inventory method	See *periodic-inventory method*.
place utility	The addition of usefulness (value) to goods by placing them where they can be conveniently examined and purchased, such as a merchandising business does when it places its goods in counters, on shelves, or in catalogs for customers to examine and purchase.
predetermined costs	Costs projected (that is, estimated) in advance of operations based on a knowledge of how the costs are incurred and the causes of those costs.
prime costs	The sum of the costs of direct materials used and direct labor incurred during an operating period.
relevant costs	Future costs that are expected to differ for the various alternatives being considered as a decision is being made. They highlight the essential cost differences between alternative courses of action.
responsibility accounting	A method of internal reporting that assigns costs to organizational subunits of a firm based on ability to control them. Each subunit report contains the items they have the ability to control. Therefore, they have responsibility for controlling them.
sunk costs	Costs that cannot be recovered regardless of which of the alternate decisions being considered is made.
unit cost	The cost associated with a single unit of product. It is calculated by dividing the aggregate costs of producing goods by the number of units turned out in incurring those costs.

| work-in-process inventory | Partially completed inventory. The work-in-process inventory account is used to accumulate production costs as the manufacturing process is being carried out. |

QUESTIONS FOR CLASS DISCUSSION

1—1 What is the difference between financial accounting and managerial accounting? Explain.

1—2 How is the effort/achievement relationship for a business measured in externally presented financial reports?

1—3 How can we use unit-cost data in measuring effort/achievement relationships within a business entity?

1—4 Explain the difference between the utility created by a merchandising enterprise and the utility created by a manufacturing or service enterprise.

1—5 How does the cost accounting objective of providing a basis for valuing manufactured inventories relate to external financial reporting?

1—6 What is the difference between a physical-inventory system and a perpetual-inventory system? Explain.

1—7 What special problem do we encounter in valuing the inventory for a manufacturing firm? Explain.

1—8 What are the elements included in the four-element equation for the determination of cost of sales?

1—9 What are the elements included in the four-element equation for the calculation of costs of goods manufactured? How does this equation relate to the equation used for the determination of costs of sales?

1—10 What do we mean by *responsibility accounting*? Give examples of cost–responsibility relationships.

1—11 What are the cost accountant's contributions to the plan/execute/evaluate/plan (PEEP) cycle in business operations? Explain.

1—12 What are *relevant costs* and *opportunity costs*? How do they relate to the decision-making process?

EXERCISES

1—13 **Cost Analysis** The beginning balance of materials is $7,000. Materials costing $32,000 were purchased, and $5,000 of materials are on hand at the end of the period. Calculate the amount of materials used.

1–14 **Cost Analysis** Materials costing $69,000 are used during a period. At the end of the period, $2,500 of materials are on hand. If $58,000 of materials were purchased during the period, what was the beginning inventory of materials?

1–15 **Cost Analysis** A merchandising firm sells goods with a cost of $94,000 for $131,600. At the beginning of this period, the inventory on hand amounted to $12,000. By the end of the period, inventory on hand amounted to only $7,200. How much inventory was purchased during the period?

1–16 **Multiple Choice** Items (1) through (3) are based on the following infor-
AICPA Adapted mation: Wayne Company had the following inventories at the beginning and end of March 19X3:

	3/1/X3	3/31/X3
Direct materials	$36,000	$30,000
Work in process	18,000	12,000
Finished goods	54,000	72,000

The following additional manufacturing cost data were available for the month of March 19X3:

Direct materials purchased	$84,000
Direct labor payroll	60,000
Direct labor rate per hour	7.50
Factory overhead rate per direct-labor hour	10.00

1. During March 19X3 prime cost added to production was
   a. $90,000   **b.** $140,000   **c.** $144,000   **d.** $150,000
2. During March 19X3 conversion cost added to production was
   a. $60,000   **b.** $80,000   **c.** $140,000   **d.** $150,000
3. The cost of goods manufactured for March 19X3 was
   a. $212,000   **b.** $218,000   **c.** $230,000   **d.** $236,000

1–17 **Cost of Sales** The Verde Company manufactured goods costing $832,000 during a period in which there were no beginning or ending work-in-process inventories. Assuming beginning finished goods cost $14,500 and ending finished goods cost $29,800, calculate the cost of sales for the period.

1–18 **Cost of Finished Goods** Cost of goods manufactured during January for the Rich Corp. were $642,000. At the beginning of January, Rich Corporation had finished goods on hand costing $18,700. During January, Rich sold goods costing $590,000. What was the cost of the ending inventory of finished goods on hand at the end of January?

PROBLEMS

1–19   **Unit Flows** Baker Corp. manufactures metal clips. Two feet of wire is used in each clip. During June, its first month of operation, Baker purchased 15,000 feet of wire and used 10,000 feet in production of metal clips; 4,000 metal clips are completed and transferred to finished goods. Sales during June amounted to 3,500 metal clips.

REQUIRED:

1. Complete the following T-account analysis by showing the number of units flowing through the manufacturing process and cost of sales for the month of June.

Materials Inventory		Work in Process		Finished Goods		Cost of Sales
-0- units	units	-0- units	units	-0- units	units	units
units		units		units		

Note: Two units (feet) of material are required for each unit of product (metal clip). Therefore, total material units (feet) must be divided by 2 to derive work-in-process units (metal clips).

2. If total manufacturing costs (direct materials, plus direct labor, plus overhead) amounted to $50,000, of which $8,000 was attributed to end-of-period work in process, what was the cost of goods completed during the period?
3. What was the cost per unit for finished clips?
4. What was the cost of sales for the period?

1–20   **Four Cost-Elements Equation** This chapter illustrates a general cost-accumulation box, which includes the following four elements: (a) beginning balance, (b) inflows, (c) outflows, and (d) ending balance. The normal sequence is $a + b - c = d$. Using this equation and the data provided below for the Johnathon Corp., calculate (1) the cost of raw materials used, (2) the cost of goods manufactured, and (3) the cost of sales. Of the materials issued, assume 5% are indirect.

Johnathon Corporation

Beginning-of-period raw-materials inventory	$ 2,000
Raw-materials purchases	49,000
End-of-period raw-materials inventory	3,000
Direct labor costs	70,000
Manufacturing overhead	38,000
Beginning-of-period work-in-process inventory	15,000
End-of-period work-in-process inventory	12,000
Beginning-of-period finished-goods inventory	20,000
End-of-period finished-goods inventory	30,000

1–21 **Manufacturing Statements** Garrett Company supplies NASA with electronic components for its computer systems. You are furnished the following data (in thousands of dollars):

Inventories	1/1/X1	12/31/X1
Raw materials	$10	$ 7
Work in process	20	25
Finished goods	32	12
Manufacturing costs incurred during 19X1		
Raw materials purchased		$108
Direct labor used		247
Indirect manufacturing costs		
Indirect materials used	$ 5	
Indirect labor used	87	
Utilities	4	
Depreciation—factory building and equipment	15	
Other	20	131

REQUIRED:

1. Prepare a statement of cost of goods manufactured and sold for 19X1.
2. Compute (a) prime costs, and (b) conversion costs.
3. Enter all appropriate amounts in a T account for work in process. Draw a circle around and label the amounts that would be included in total manufacturing costs for the period. Identify the amount(s) included in the calculation of cost of goods manufactured.

1–22 **Cost of Goods Manufactured and Income Statement** The Blume Company has the following balances (in millions of dollars):

Indirect labor	$ 5
Finished goods, end of period	15
Sales	600
Factory supplies used	2
Selling and administrative expenses	96
Work in process, beginning of period	8
Factory utilities	20
Direct materials, end of period	17
Finished goods, beginning of period	33
Purchases of direct materials	105
Direct labor	175
Direct materials, beginning of period	10
Work in process, end of period	4
Depreciation—factory building and equipment	70
Factory administrative salaries	3
Other factory overhead	28

REQUIRED:

1. Prepare a schedule of cost of goods manufactured and an income statement for the period.
2. If 50,000,000 units were produced during the period, what was the cost per unit?

1–23 **Cost of Goods Manufactured and Income Statement** You are provided the following information for the Birch Corporation:

Account balances	
Direct materials, 12/31/X1	$ 90,000
Accounts receivable, 12/31/X2	110,000
Accounts payable, 12/31/X1	40,000
Work in process, 12/31/X1	6,000
Direct materials, 12/31/X2	110,000
Finished goods, 12/31/X2	100,000
Finished goods, 12/31/X1	600,000
Accounts payable, 12/31/X2	30,000
Work in process, 12/31/X2	49,000
Accounts receivable, 12/31/X1	80,000
Activity during the year 19X2	
Sales	$6,000,000
Insurance on factory	20,000
Direct materials purchased	950,000
Factory utilities	28,000
Direct labor	760,000
Selling and administrative expenses	2,400,000
Factory supplies used	15,000
Indirect labor	180,000
Miscellaneous factory overhead	72,000
Depreciation–plant and equipment	38,000
Depreciation–salesmen's autos	63,000

REQUIRED: Prepare an income statement showing cost of sales and a supporting cost-of-goods-manufactured statement.

1–24 **Missing Information** Find the unknown amounts designated by alphabetical letters for each of the following cases.

	Case 1	Case 2
Sales	$20,000	$94,000
Accounts receivable, 1/1	1,000	20,000
Accounts receivable, 12/31	2,500	15,000
Cost of sales	A	79,000
Accounts payable, 1/1	1,000	1,000
Accounts payable, 12/31	500	2,000

	Case 1	Case 2
Direct materials used	3,000	A
Finished goods, 1/1	5,000	6,000
Finished goods, 12/31	B	7,000
Gross margin	9,000	B
Work in process, 1/1	2,000	5,000
Work in process, 12/31	3,000	2,500
Purchasing direct materials	C	23,000
Direct labor	8,000	30,500
Factory overhead	3,000	C
Direct materials, 1/1	1,500	5,000
Direct materials, 12/31	3,000	3,000

1–25 **Missing Information** A fire of unknown origin completely destroys the Conway Company's principal factory building and all its contents on March 15, 19X9. Records kept in the home office revealed the following information for the period December 31, 19X8, through March 15, 19X9:

Prime costs	$ 595,000
Factory overhead, 30% of conversion costs	
Direct labor	$ 350,000
Gross profit	250,000
Direct materials purchased	240,000
Cost of goods available for sale	800,000
Work in process, 12/31/X8	30,000
Direct materials, 12/31/X8	15,000
Finished goods, 12/31/X8	40,000
Sales	1,000,000

Conway's president has requested that you calculate the cost of the direct-materials, work-in-process, and finished-goods inventories destroyed so that negotiations with the insurance carrier can be initiated. What is the cost of the inventories destroyed?

1–26 **Cost Concepts** A management accountant provides vital information to assist management in controlling operations, planning future operations, and making operating decisions. A competent management accountant must possess the skills that are needed to identify problems and develop workable solutions. To do this, management accountants must be thoroughly familiar with various cost concepts.

REQUIRED:

1. Define each of the following cost terms.
   a. prime costs
   b. opportunity cost
   c. out-of-pocket costs
   d. sunk costs

2. Explain how each of the above cost terms does or does not relate to controlling operations, planning future operations, and making operating decisions.

1–27 THOUGHT STIMULATION PROBLEM. Premier Products Corporation manufactures 17 models of pleasure boats. While the firm's managers know what their total actual manufacturing costs are, they are unable to reconcile the standard (theoretical) cost of boats manufactured to the total costs incurred. Premier Products is manufacturing and selling more boats than ever before, but profits are decreasing. Management suspects that they are losing money on some of the models, but they don't know which ones.

You have been engaged to help Premier Products redesign its cost system. The president and vice president will be available to answer any questions you may have at an initial interview to be held tomorrow.

REQUIRED:

1. What effort/achievement measurements will you request management to provide for you?
2. What cause-and-effect items will you want to discuss with the president and vice president?
3. What initial recommendations might you make?

Chapter 2

Basic Concepts Underlying Cost Accumulation and Cost Allocation

Learning Objectives

When you have finished your study of this chapter, you should

1. Know the meaning of the terminology associated with accumulating and allocating costs.
2. Understand the role of cause-and-effect relationships in accumulating and allocating costs.
3. Recognize how the matching convention controls the goals associated with accounting for costs.
4. Know how to allocate general manufacturing costs to the various departments within a firm.
5. Be able to allocate manufacturing-overhead costs from manufacturing service departments to production-cost accumulation centers (departments).
6. Be able to identify the two principal cost-accumulation and cost-allocation systems used in cost accounting, and know the type of operating environment in which cash would be used.

I n Chapter 1, we observed that businesses incur costs for the purpose of producing revenues. Therefore, it is important to appropriately match those costs with the revenues produced by their incurrence to provide management and other interested parties with data that can be used in evaluating the results of operations and in planning future operations. Cost accounting, as that part of the discipline of accounting that is concerned with accounting for the flows of costs, is concerned with developing systems that can be used in accumulating and allocating costs so those costs can most effectively be related to the revenues they are instrumental in generating. In this chapter, we identify and illustrate the basic guidelines underlying the accumulation and allocation process.

Because costs are incurred for the purpose of producing revenue, they are matched against those revenues to meet the requirements of the **matching convention.** Matching underlies the entire accumulation and allocation process. For external reporting purposes (financial accounting), we are concerned with the overall matching of costs against revenues for each reporting period in the income statement. However, the managerial accountant also must be concerned with detailed elements of this matching process as they logically relate to the accumulation and allocation of costs. For example, the costs of individual products or services should be matched against the revenues realized from their sales. Also, costs must be traced (that is, matched) to individual departments and processes to facilitate an evaluation of departmental operations.

We develop the definitions and guidelines that underlie the systems used in the accumulation and allocation process by:

1. defining the cost terminology to be used throughout the remainder of the text
2. identifying the role of cause-and-effect relationships in the accumulation and allocation process
3. showing how to apply the matching convention in accounting for selected types of costs
4. identifying and discussing special cost-allocation problems, and illustrating service department allocations
5. briefly describing the systems used in accumulating and allocating manufacturing costs.

Terminology

In Chapter 1, we defined *cost* as that which must be given up in order to acquire, produce, or effect something, including both recorded costs and **imputed costs** (unrecorded hypothetical or opportunity costs). Although we will be dealing with imputed costs in Part IV of the text, our attention through Parts I–III will be on **recorded costs**, which are the recorded values of those resources and services given up in acquiring other resources and services.

Types of Costs

As the first step in developing our cost-allocation procedures, recorded costs beneficially may be divided into categories that relate to each other as shown in Figure 2–1. Observe that total recorded costs are initially subdivided into four categories based on the nature of the goods or services acquired by their incurrence. Each of the categories associated only with the current operating period (the "part used" in category 1, plus all of categories 2, 3, and 4) are, in turn, divided into fixed and variable elements.

We may visualize aggregate fixed and aggregate variable costs relating to changes in the volume of operations by plotting them as on the graphs that follow. The horizontal axes show various levels of operations (volume); the vertical axes portray aggregate dollars of costs. Within the expected range of operations (the **relevant range**), total dollars of fixed cost do not change as volume increases (left-hand graph). Variable costs, on the other hand, increase in total dollars as volume increases (right-hand graph).

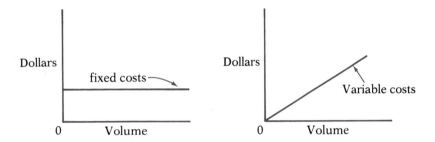

Assets are goods and services acquired with the expectation that they will help produce revenue in more than the current reporting period (category 1 in Figure 2–1). At the time of incurrence, we record such costs by debiting an asset account and crediting cash, accounts payable, or some other asset given up or liability incurred in exchange for them. As shown in Figure 2–1, these assets, if they have a limited useful life, must be amortized (charged to expense) over the periods during which they are expected to be used in producing revenues. Since these amortizations generally are based on the passage of time, we characterize this amortized portion of the assets as a **fixed cost** (costs that in the aggregate remain the same at different levels of production within some relevant range—say, from zero to 100% of current capacity). However, if such costs are amortized in relation to production (for example, the depletion of natural resources), the amortization would be a **variable cost** (a cost that in the aggregate varies directly with the level of pro-

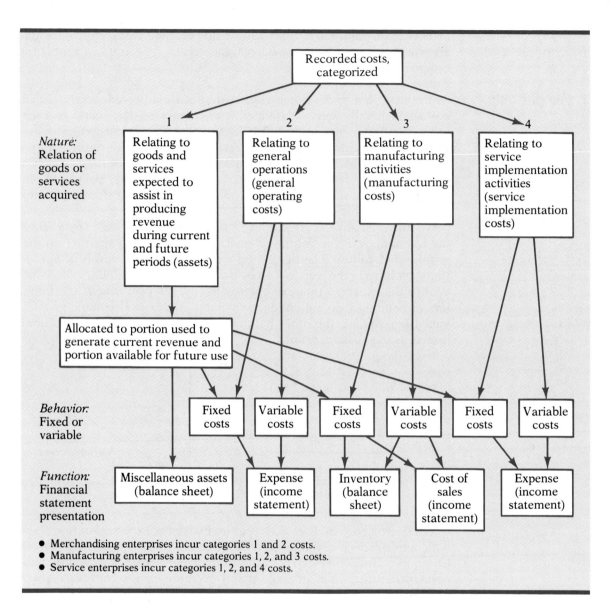

FIGURE 2–1 A Taxonomy of Costs

duction). In either case, based on the types of benefits realized from them, these costs will be allocated to general operations, to manufacturing operations, or to service implementation.

General operating costs (category 2 in Figure 2–1) are incurred in connection with the selling and administrative activities of a business. They are typically shown in the income statement as operating expenses subdivided into selling and administrative expense categories. To facilitate the evaluation of general operations, general operating costs also can be divided into fixed (period) costs (for example, straight-line depreciation on sales equipment) and variable costs (for example, sales commissions based on sales). The aggregate amounts of fixed costs, as demonstrated in the left-hand graph on page 31, remain the same at different levels of operations within a relevant range. The basic salary of the president of a company is an example of such a cost: this compensation will not change if sales increase or decrease. Because these fixed costs are related to the passage of time rather than to the level of activity of a business, they also are often characterized as **period** costs. The matching convention logically requires that these fixed costs be matched against the revenue produced in the period in which they are incurred.

Variable operating costs are those selling and administrative expenses that, in the aggregate, vary directly with changes in the level of operations. Sales commissions are good examples of a variable operating cost because they are based on the amount of sales. With a larger volume of sales, a business will incur more sales commission cost. Even though variable operating costs change according to some appropriate activity base (such as sales dollars), they always are included as an expense in the period in which they are incurred. Thus, all general operating costs, whether fixed or variable, are treated as period costs. They are *never* treated as a product cost and are therefore *never* included as an element of inventory cost because they are not associated with making a product ready for sale (that is, changing its form in some way).

Manufacturing costs (category 3 in Figure 2–1) are incurred for the production of goods. These also can be subdivided into fixed and variable costs. Because fixed costs must be incurred each period in order for the firm to be in position to produce, they are theoretically **period costs**. Thus, strictly interpreted, the matching convention seems to require that fixed manufacturing costs incurred during the period be matched against the revenues realized from the sale of goods or services during the period; however, because they are incurred in the production of goods (making them ready for sale), they are, under generally accepted accounting practices, allocated to the products produced rather than matched against the sales of their periods of incurrence. Stated another way, GAAP requires fixed manufacturing "period" costs to be treated as product costs. This cost-allocation procedure is called **absorption costing** (or *full costing* or *traditional costing*) because each unit produced absorbs a portion of all manufacturing costs incurred (both variable and fixed). Since fixed manufacturing costs, in the aggregate, remain constant over a relevant range of different production levels, the cost per unit varies inversely with the number of units produced. To illustrate, let's assume that depreciation calculated on a straight-line basis amounts to $50,000 a year. If we produce 50,000 units a year, the (depreciation) cost per unit would be $1. If production should increase to 100,000 units a year, the cost would drop to $.50 per unit. Fixed manufacturing costs allocated to units sold are included in cost of sales, whereas fixed manufacturing costs allocated to unsold units are included in work-in-process and finished-goods inventories on the balance sheet. Property taxes, factory rental costs, and time-based depreciation are examples of fixed manufacturing costs.

Since variable manufacturing costs, in the aggregate, vary directly with the volume of production, the cost per unit will remain constant. Assume, for example, that aggregate direct materials costs are $100,000 for the production of 50,000 units. That amounts to $2 per unit. If production increases to 100,000 units, aggregate direct materials costs should be $200,000, also $2 per unit. Because these costs can be directly associated with the manufacturing process, they also are considered product costs. Direct materials costs and direct labor costs are the primary examples of variable manufacturing costs. They are allocated to products as the products are produced and will be matched against sales revenue (by being included in cost of sales) in the periods when the products are sold. This also means that the amounts of these variable costs associated with the units of product remaining on hand at the end of a reporting period will be shown as part of the cost of an asset (inventory) on the balance sheet.

Some manufacturing costs, such as heat, light, and power, are neither completely fixed nor completely variable. We often call these **semivariable** (or *semifixed*) **costs**. How such costs can be divided into fixed and variable components is explained in Chapter 11. Other manufacturing costs can be thought of as **step-variable costs** because they vary in steps. For example, manufacturing supervisory costs are fixed as long as only one supervisor is required but increase immediately by the cost of an additional supervisor when the level of production reaches the point where that second supervisor must be hired.

Service implementation costs (category 4 in Figure 2–1) are incurred by a business or nonprofit organization as it converts resources into services that, in the case of business entities, are sold, or, in the case of pure nonprofit organizations, are distributed to members of society on the basis of need. Salary paid to medical professionals employed by a clinic is an example. Because such services are either sold or distributed as they are created, all service implementation costs should be matched against the revenues realized from providing the services during each reporting period. Service implementation costs also can be divided into fixed (for example, salaries of medical professionals) and variable (for example, medical supplies and drugs).

It is important to distinguish between the behavior of the cost data in the aggregate and on a per-unit basis. **Aggregate costs** are the accumulated total amount of a particular cost over a period of time, whereas

units costs are aggregate costs divided by the number of units produced in incurring those costs. The aggregate amount of fixed costs remains the same at different levels of production (within a relevant range), but the aggregate amounts of variable costs vary in direct relation to the amount of product turned out. That is:

> While fixed costs, in the aggregate, remain the same for various levels of production within a relevant range, the fixed cost per unit varies inversely with the number of units produced.

And conversely,

> While variable costs, in the aggregate, vary directly with changes in the level of production, variable costs per unit remain the same regardless of the level of production.

The following data illustrate these relationships.

Units Produced	Aggregate Fixed Cost	Fixed Cost per Unit	Aggregate Variable Cost	Variable Cost per Unit
1,000	$10,000	$10	$10,000	$10
2,000	$10,000	$ 5	$20,000	$10

Cost-Accumulation Centers

As observed earlier, generally accepted accounting practices (GAAP) require us to follow full (absorption) cost-allocation procedures, meaning that all manufacturing costs, fixed and variable, will be allocated to the units of product produced by their incurrence. That, in turn, requires extensive use of cost-accumulation and cost-allocation procedures. We also have observed that manufacturing costs should be allocated in such a way that the efficiency of operations of different segments of the factory can be evaluated, which information does *not* need to follow GAAP. To achieve both external and internal reporting objectives in allocating and accumulating costs, businesses use departments or work cells as **cost-accumulation centers**.

Although Figure 1–2 showed the factory as a cost-accumulation center, in actual practice, each of the various department or work cell heads within a factory will be responsible for carrying out the operations of its particular segment of the production process. Therefore, in order to more effectively achieve the objectives of cost accounting, it is desirable to accumulate costs by departments (or work cells) so that specific supervisors or managers can be held accountable for costs over which they exert control. This procedure leads to responsibility accounting. Also, as we shall see later, the departmental orientation helps us more accurately allocate costs to the goods and services produced by their incurrence on the basis of cause-and-effect relationships. The same procedures may be used with any segment or division of a firm. Therefore, throughout the remainder of this text, the term *department* will, in general, mean a cost-accumulation center.

Identification of Cause-and-Effect Relationships

The cost accountant, in accounting for the flows of costs, is responsible for recording the incurrence, allocation, and accumulation of costs. At each step along the way, he or she must ascertain what caused each cost and what its effect on the revenue-producing process is expected to be, so as to appropriately match those costs with the revenues produced by their incurrence.

Accounting for the Incurrence of Costs

Costs are incurred when resources or services are given up (or liabilities incurred) in exchange for other resources and services. At that time, the cause-and-effect relationship is recognized in the accounting records by appropriately labeling the cost as it is journalized.

To illustrate, Figure 2–2 lists a number of costs, what caused them to be incurred, the effect they are expected to have on the revenue-producing process, and the entries made to record them. With item 1, for example, a business incurs costs for the acquisition of assets because those assets are needed to produce revenue; the effect of such a cost incurrence is an increase in assets and is entered in a journal by debiting the asset and crediting cash, accounts payable, or whichever other resource may have been given up (or liability incurred) in acquiring the asset. The payment of sales personnel salaries (item 2) is caused by the need for people to represent the company in selling its merchandise; the effect is expected to be the sale of goods; the corresponding journal entry is a debit to sales salaries expense and a credit to accrued payroll or cash. Item 3 shows that a merchandising business purchases goods because it needs merchandise to sell to customers; the initial effect is an increase in the stock of goods on hand (inventory); the corresponding entry is a debit to either inventory (perpetual-inventory method) or purchases (periodic-inventory method) and a credit to cash or accounts payable. In the case of a manufacturing operation (item 4), a business purchases raw materials because they are needed to produce finished goods to be sold; this creates a materials inventory; the corresponding entry is a debit to materials inventory (frequently, as in Figure 2–2, raw-materials stores) and a credit to cash or accounts payable. By reviewing the other items in Figure 2–2, you can see how the payment of salaries of administrative personnel, office rent, etc., payment of salaries of factory employees, and the incurrence of costs for various items of manufacturing overhead are recorded by analyzing the cause-and-effect relationship involved in each of these cost incurrences.

Accounting for the Allocation and Accumulation of Costs

As costs are allocated in meeting the requirements of the matching convention, we again analyze cause-and-effect relationships to help us determine the journal entry required to record the allocations in the accounts.

Item	Type of Cost	Cause (Reason for Incurrence)	Effect	Journal Entry to Record Cost	Debit	Credit
1	Acquisition of assets	Assets are needed to produce revenues	Increases assets (revenue-producing capabilities)	Assets Cash, payables, etc.	XX	XX
2	Payment of sales salaries	Services of people are needed to sell merchandise	Sales people sell merchandise	Sales salaries Accrued payroll or cash	XX	XX
3	Purchase of merchandise	Merchandise is needed to sell	Creates inventory available for sale	Inventory or purchases Cash, payables, etc.	XX	XX
4	Purchase of raw materials	Materials are needed to produce finished goods for sale	Creates raw materials inventory available for production	Raw materials stores Cash, payables, etc.	XX	XX
5	Payment of administrative salaries, office rent, etc.	Management of business is needed to facilitate realization of revenue	General administrative activities are carried out	General adminis-trative expense Cash, payables, etc.	XX	XX
6	Payment of factory employees' salaries	Employees are needed to carry out manufacturing activities	Factory employees carry out manufactur-ing activities	Factory payroll Accrued payroll or cash	XX	XX
7	Manufacturing overhead costs incurred	Facilities, etc., must be maintained for pro-duction of goods	Factory operates to produce goods	Manufacturing overhead Cash, payables, etc.	XX	XX

FIGURE 2–2 Accounting for Cost Incurrence

To illustrate, Figure 2–3 lists a number of costs along with their causes, the ultimate effect they are expected to have, and the journal entry required to record each individual allocation. For example, in allocating the amortized portion of assets to expense through the medium of depreciation, the proration of prepaid expenses, and so forth, we find that the cause of the allocation is the use of the asset to produce goods that are later expected to produce revenue (item 1) or to produce revenue (item 2). The effect is to reduce the carrying value of the asset and increase either manufacturing-overhead or operating costs. This is recorded by debiting manufacturing overhead (item 1) or operating expenses (item 2) and crediting the asset account or a valuation account, such as accumulated depreciation. The disposal of merchandise (item 3) is caused by the need to deliver the merchandise to customers

Item	Cost to Be Allocated	Cause (Reason for Allocation)	Effect	Journal Entry to Record Allocation	Debit	Credit
1	Amortization of asset	Part of asset's production capability is used in the production of goods to be sold	Costs assigned to assets are reduced; manufacturing costs are increased	Manufacturing overhead	XX	
				Asset or asset valuation account		XX
2	Amortization of asset	Part of asset's value is used in the process of selling goods or in general administration	Reduces cost assigned to assets and increases general operating costs	Operating expense	XX	
				Asset or asset valuation account		XX
3	Disposal of merchandise	Need to deliver merchandise to realize revenue in form of cash or receivables	Revenues in form of asset inflows (cash or receivables) are produced; inventory is reduced; cost of sales and sales are increased	Cash or accounts receivable	XX	
				Sales (retail value)		XX
				Cost of sales (cost of units sold)	XX	
				Inventory		XX
4	Raw materials used directly in production	Raw materials are needed to produce finished products	Value is added to work in process; raw materials are reduced	Work in process	XX	
				Raw-material stores (inventory)		XX
5	Distribution of factory payroll	Need to relate labor costs to nature of work performed (direct or indirect)	Direct labor increases work in process; other factory labor increases manufacturing overhead; payroll account decreases	Work in process	XX	
				Manufacturing overhead	XX	
				Factory payroll		XX
6	Manufacturing overhead is applied to production	Manufacturing overhead is required to produce finished goods	Value is added to work in process; overhead is reduced	Work in process	XX	
				Manufacturing overhead or overhead applied		XX
7	Goods in process are finished	Work in process is completed	Finished goods are increased; work in process is decreased	Finished-goods inventory	XX	
				Work in process		XX
8	Finished goods sold	Finished goods are delivered to customers to realize revenue	Finished goods inventory is decreased; cost of sales is increased; cash or receivables are increased; sales are increased	Cost of sales (cost of units sold)	XX	
				Finished-goods inventory		XX
				Cash or receivables (sales value)	XX	
				Sales		XX

FIGURE 2–3 Accounting for Cost Allocation

in order to realize revenue in the form of cash or receivables; the effect is to produce inflows of cash or receivables that are recognized as revenues; assuming a perpetual-inventory system, this is recorded as a debit to cost of sales and a credit to inventory. For raw materials used in the production of merchandise for sale (item 4), we recognize the cause-and-effect relationship by debiting work in process and crediting raw materials inventory. To allocate the direct labor part of payroll (item 6 of Figure 2–2 and item 5 of Figure 2–3), we have another addition to work in process, which is recorded by debiting work in process and crediting the payroll account that was established at the time the payroll cost was incurred. The allocation of factory overhead items to work in process, which is more complicated, is discussed more completely in the next section of this chapter. However, the entry for that allocation is shown in item 6. The next step occurs when finished goods are produced. At that time, the costs accumulated in the work-in-process account for the units completed are transferred to finished goods (item 7) by debiting finished goods and crediting work in process for the amount of costs accumulated for those units. Later, as the finished goods are sold to customers (item 8), we debit cost of sales and credit finished goods at the time the sale is recorded (by debiting cash or receivables and crediting sales).

Figure 2–3, except for items 2 and 3, implicitly assumes a manufacturing company that is operating with one department. As observed earlier, manufacturing firms generally will be divided into departments (cost-accumulation centers) to provide for more accurate allocation of costs and to provide management with a tool for evaluating the operations of individual segments of the factory. That way, certain costs—for example, manufacturing-overhead items—will be allocated to the individual departments during the allocation process. These allocation procedures will be developed more completely later in the text.

Application of the Matching Convention

To meet the GAAP matching-convention requirement in the income statement requires that the costs incurred to generate the revenues recognized during the reporting period be offset (matched) against those revenues to arrive at the amount of net income for the period. In this way, we provide a quantitative matching of efforts (costs) with achievements (revenues) during each reporting period. This can be done most informatively by dividing costs into operating and manufacturing categories.

In accounting terminology, *cost* may refer to resources given up to acquire an asset—a resource that will benefit future operations. The part of the asset that is "used up" each period becomes an expense that should be matched against revenues earned during the period. In that way, costs of depreciable assets are systematically allowed to flow into expenses over their useful lives. Costs incurred in purchasing or producing products to be sold become expenses (cost of sales) when those products are sold.

Operating Costs

The costs incurred for the purpose of carrying out selling and general administrative activities during a reporting period should be reflected in the operating expenses section of the income statement for that reporting period. In that way, the requirements of the matching convention are met. These costs will be recognized in the same way (that is, as a current-period expense) in the income statements of merchandising as well as manufacturing firms. Regardless of whether they are variable or fixed, operating costs are matched against the revenues realized during the reporting period.

Manufacturing Costs

The application of the matching convention in reporting manufacturing costs (direct materials, direct labor, and manufacturing overhead) is more complicated because some of the goods manufactured during a particular reporting period will be held over as inventory to be sold in a future period. A strict interpretation of the matching convention would seem to call for us to allocate the fixed (time-related) manufacturing costs associated with the reporting period against the revenues earned during that period, just as are fixed operating expenses. The same line of reasoning suggests that variable manufacturing costs (primarily direct materials and direct labor) should be attached to finished goods (units completed) and then be matched against revenues of the reporting period during which those goods are sold. Variable costs associated with unsold units then would be reflected in end-of-period inventory. We refer to this cost-allocation arrangement as **variable costing** or **direct costing**. This costing procedure allocates all fixed costs (including those incurred in the manufacture of finished goods) to the periods in which they are incurred. Only variable manufacturing costs are allocated to the units produced. Although this is not a generally accepted accounting practice, it is often followed to produce data that are especially useful to management in making decisions. Procedures followed in implementing a variable (direct) costing system are developed and explained in Chapter 14.

The accounting profession does not recognize variable costing as a generally accepted practice because it also has adopted the *going-concern convention* for valuing a firm's assets, including inventory. This convention requires asset values to include all costs associated with their acquisition, based on the assumption that the firm will continue to operate into the foreseeable future unless circumstances indicate otherwise. Therefore, accountants reason that because fixed manufacturing costs are necessary to produce finished units, they should be allocated to those units rather than be matched against the revenues of the reporting period during which they were incurred. Hence, GAAP require us to follow absorption-costing procedures, meaning that all manufacturing costs (both fixed and variable) will be allocated to units produced as product costs. That, in effect, converts fixed (period) manufacturing costs into product costs.

We have identified the procedure of allocating all manufacturing costs to products as absorption costing. Direct materials costs and direct labor costs can be traced directly to the units produced as production occurs. The actual cost per unit of finished product for these elements of manufacturing costs can be determined by dividing the aggregate amounts associated with the units produced by the number of units produced. In contrast, manufacturing-overhead costs—which in general are predominantly fixed costs, or numerous individually immaterial variable costs—cannot be directly traced to units being produced on the basis of cause-and-effect relationships. As a result, we generally use a **predetermined manufacturing-overhead application rate** to allocate the approximate amount of overhead costs incurred to units produced during each reporting period. That process requires us to relate the *expected* manufacturing overhead costs to the activity that most nearly causes their incurrence. Traditionally, in most instances, the causal activity has been judged to be direct labor. The overhead rate then is generally expressed in terms of an estimated relationship between manufacturing overhead costs and direct labor costs or direct labor hours. In instances where firms are more completely automated, however, the overhead rate would logically be based on machine-hours or raw materials costs or on some combination of these items rather than on direct labor.

To illustrate the calculation of an overhead application rate, let's assume that a firm expects to incur overhead costs in the amount of $100,000 during a period in which it also expects to have 25,000 hours of direct labor. The overhead application rate would be $100,000 ÷ 25,000 hours = $4 per hour. Regardless of the activity base used in arriving at the manufacturing-overhead application rate, that rate is then used during each reporting period to allocate manufacturing-overhead costs to the units of finished product as those units are produced. For example, if 1,000 direct-labor hours were required to complete some units, then 1,000 hours × $4 = $4,000 of manufacturing overhead would be applied (allocated) to those units. We deal with the development and use of this overhead application rate more fully in Chapters 4 and 5.

Figure 2–4 illustrates the procedures followed in allocating manufacturing overhead to units produced, assuming that production for the period could be completed before one needed to determine unit costs. We assume that 10,000 units are produced during a period in which actual direct materials, direct labor, and manufacturing-overhead costs

Manufacturing Costs Assigned to Each Unit of Finished Goods

Direct materials	$\dfrac{\$200,000}{10,000}$	=	$20.00
Direct labor	$\dfrac{\$150,000}{10,000}$	=	15.00
Manufacturing overhead	$\dfrac{\$120,000}{10,000}$	=	12.00
Total cost per unit			$47.00

FIGURE 2–4   Absorption-Costing Illustration: Actual Cost Basis

of $200,000, $150,000, and $120,000, respectively, are incurred. The total cost allocated to each unit of finished-goods inventory amounts to $47.00.

Figure 2–5 shows the income statement that would result from using the data presented in Figure 2–4, plus assumed operating costs of $50,000, assumed sales of 8,000 units at $60 per unit, no beginning or ending work-in-process inventory, and no beginning finished-good inventory.

If, as is generally the case, we need the data on total cost per unit before aggregate actual overhead costs are available, we would use a *predetermined* overhead application rate to arrive at that element of unit cost. With that arrangement, the manufacturing-overhead element of total product cost would be determined by multiplying the overhead application rate by the appropriate direct-cost item (for example,

Sales (8,000 @ $60)	$480,000
Cost of sales (8,000 @ $47)	376,000*
Gross margin	$104,000
Operating expenses	50,000
Net operating income before income taxes	$ 54,000
*Cost of sales also may be calculated as follows:	
Beginning inventory	0
Cost of goods manufactured (10,000 @ $47)	$470,000
Ending finished-goods inventory (2,000 @ $47)	94,000
Cost of sales	$376,000

FIGURE 2–5   Absorption-Costing Income Statement

direct-labor hours or direct-labor costs) as units are completed during the period. When that procedure is followed, the difference between the actual manufacturing overhead incurred and the amount allocated to units produced is called **underapplied overhead** or **overapplied overhead**. Overhead-allocation procedures are dealt with more completely in Chapter 4.

Meeting Special Cost-Allocation Problems

When we allocate manufacturing-overhead costs to departmental cost centers to provide a more precise cause-and-effect allocation arrangement, and to provide management with a tool for evaluating individual departmental managers (responsibility accounting), an ultimate objective is to allocate all manufacturing costs to the products being produced. In this section, we deal with the special problems of allocating costs to cost-accumulation centers (departments) within a firm.

Standard Allocation Procedure

A common cost-allocation procedure involves the use of some base, such as square footage or machine-hours, with costs being allocated to departments on the basis of ratios of the numbers for each department to the total for all departments. For example, if the stamping, milling, and welding departments work 1,000, 2000, and 3,000 machine hours, respectively, then a total cost (maintenance, for example) of $60,000 would be allocated as follows:

Department	Hours	Ratio ×	Amount to Be Allocated =	Allocation
Stamping	1,000	1/6*	$60,000	$10,000
Milling	2,000	2/6	$60,000	$20,000
Welding	3,000	3/6	$60,000	$30,000
Total hours	6,000			

*1,000/6,000

Allocation of a Cost Benefiting More Than One Department

In any manufacturing operation, some costs will be incurred that provide benefits for more than one departmental cost center. When that happens, we must examine the cause-and-effect relationships and develop a basis for allocating those common costs to the departments benefiting from them. Figure 2–6 presents examples of such costs, the causes or reasons for their incurrence, the effect of those costs, and the allocation bases that would most likely bring about an equitable cause-and-effect relationship allocation. Study these to help you identify bases that might be used to rationally allocate various types of overhead costs to cost-accumulation centers.

Cost	Cause (Reason) for Incurrence	Effect	Allocation Basis
Factory depreciation	Need for factory building to carry out operations	Departments carry out operations	Square footage of each department in relation to total square footage
Casualty insurance	Need for insurance protection for departmental assets	Can recover value if protected assets destroyed	Valuation of assets in each department in relation to total valuation of all insured assets
Electric power	Need for power to operate machines	Machines operate in production of goods	Horsepower of equipment in each department related to total horsepower of all equipment in factory

FIGURE 2–6   Examples of Cause-and-Effect Allocations for Production Departments

Departmental Cost Allocations

Those departments within a manufacturing firm that perform work on the product being manufactured are referred to as **producing** (or *line*) **departments**. In a metals stampings plant, for example, the press, welding, finishing, and assembly departments would be producing departments. Because these departments add direct value to the product being produced, they also are referred to as *value-added* departments. As the units of the product being manufactured move through those departments, each department performs some of the work necessary to convert the raw material (rolls of steel, sheet aluminum, and so forth) into the finished units to be sold by the company.

Departments that exist for the purpose of providing services to other departments are called **service departments**. In the metal stampings plant, the maintenance department, personnel department, employee services department, and perhaps other departments that exist for the purpose of keeping the plant in operation but that don't directly add value to the product itself would be examples of service departments.

Because our ultimate objective is to allocate all manufacturing costs, including manufacturing-service-department operating costs, to the products being produced, the costs of operating these departments must be allocated to the producing departments. Thus, the total costs initially allocated to manufacturing service departments ultimately will end up as part of the overhead for the manufacturing (producing) departments. In allocating service department costs, we again try to use a basis for allocating the costs accumulated for those departments that is consistent with cause-and-effect relationships. Figure 2–7 lists typical service departments, the cause or reason for having those de-

Department	Cause (Reason) for Having Department	Effects	Allocation Basis
Maintenance	Keep machinery and equipment in proper operating condition	Equipment operates to help produce goods	Repair hours spent in each department related to total repair hours
Personnel	Provide necessary employees for each department	Employees work toward production of goods	Number of employees in each department in relation to total number of employees in plant
Employee services	Provide necessary services for employees	Employees work toward production of goods	Number of employees in each department in relation to total number of employees in plant

FIGURE 2–7 Examples of Cause-and-Effect Allocations for Service Departments

partments, the effects of the departmental operations, and the allocation basis that might be used in allocating them to the producing departments.

Some service departments, for example, an employee services department, provide services to other service departments. Since all service department costs ultimately must be allocated to the producing departments, we must determine whether part of the costs of operating an employee services department should be allocated to the maintenance department and other service departments as well as to the producing departments. Should this preliminary allocation be done, the service department providing the most service to other service departments would be allocated first. That would be followed by allocating the total costs accumulated for the service department judged to be providing the next largest amount of services to the remaining service departments, and so forth. We call this the **step method of allocating service department costs**.

The following information is assumed for Figures 2–8 and 2–9.

	Producing Departments			
	Stamping	**Welding**	**Finishing**	**Assembly**
Manufacturing overhead charged to departments	$100,000	$80,000	$90,000	$75,000
Maintenance hours	500	900	340	260
Employees	200	280	90	50

(Continues)

	Service Departments			
	Maintenance	**Personnel**	**Employee Services**	**Totals**
Manufacturing overhead charged to departments	$20,900	$19,500	$15,700	$401,100
Maintenance hours	50	20	20	2090
Employees	20	10	10	660

The personnel department costs are to be allocated first, followed by employee services and maintenance. As Figure 2–8 shows, the costs of all service departments ultimately are allocated to the producing departments, but the allocation occurs in steps. This is necessary both for determining producing department manufacturing-overhead application rates and for comparing the overhead costs applied to the products passing through each department with the actual overhead costs incurred by that department. We develop those calculation and comparison techniques in Chapter 5.

An alternate arrangement—the **direct allocation** method illustrated in Figure 2–9—involves allocating the costs of service departments only to producing departments. With this method, the service departments can be allocated in any order, but the allocation bases will include only the data for the producing departments. For example, if we are to allocate the costs accumulated for an employee services department to four producing departments (molding, drilling, finishing, and assembly) on the basis of the number of employees in those departments, we would allocate 25/100 of employee service department costs to the molding department. Observe that the direct method excludes the 25 employees in the two service departments (maintenance and employee services) from the denominator of the allocation ratio.

Department	Number of Employees
Molding	25
Drilling	40
Finishing	15
Assembly	20
Maintenance	15
Employee Services	10
Total	125

More complex systems where service department costs are allocated back and forth among the service departments at the same time also are feasible via **simultaneous allocation**. Recognition of reciprocal services

| | Producing Departments | | | | Service Departments | | | |
	Stamping	Welding	Finishing	Assembly	Maintenance	Personnel	Employee Services	Totals
Manufacturing overhead	$100,000	$ 80,000	$90,000	$75,000	$ 20,900	$ 19,500	$ 15,700	$401,100
Allocation of personnel department costs[1]	6,000[a]	8,400	2,700	1,500	600	(19,500)	300	0
Totals	$106,000	$ 88,400	$92,700	$76,500	$ 21,500	$ 0	$ 16,000	$401,100
Allocation of employee services department costs[2]	5,000	7,000	2,250	1,250	500		$(16,000)	0
Totals	$111,000	$ 95,400	$94,950	$77,750	$ 22,000	$ 0	$ 0	$401,100
Allocation of maintenance department costs[3]	5,500	9,900	3,740	2,860[b]	(22,000)			0
Totals	$116,500	$105,300	$98,690	$80,610	$ 0	$ 0	$ 0	$401,100

[1]Allocation based on number of employees in all other departments (650).
[2]Allocation based on number of employees in remaining departments (640).
[3]Allocation based on number of maintenance hours (2,000).

[a] $\frac{200}{650} \times \$19,500$

[b] $\frac{260}{2000} \times \$22,000$

FIGURE 2–8 Service Department Costs Allocated to Other Service Departments: Step Method

| | Producing Departments | | | | Service Departments | | | |
	Stamping	Welding	Finishing	Assembly	Maintenance	Personnel	Employee Services	Totals
Manufacturing overhead	$100,000	$80,000	$90,000	$75,000	$20,900	$19,500	$15,700	$401,100
Allocation of personnel department costs[1]	6,290[a]	8,806	2,831	1,573		(19,500)		0
Totals	$106,290	$88,806	$92,831	$76,573	$20,900	$0	$15,700	$401,100
Allocation of employee services department costs[2]	5,065	7,090	2,279	1,266			(15,700)	0
Totals	$111,355	$95,896	$95,110	$77,839	$20,900	$0	$0	$401,100
Allocation of maintenance department costs[3]	5,225	9,405	3,553	2,717[b]	(20,900)			0
Totals	$116,580	$105,301	$98,663	$80,556	$0	$0	$0	$401,100

[1] Allocation based on number of employees in producing departments (620); rounded to nearest whole dollar.
[2] Allocation based on number of employees in producing departments (620); rounded to nearest whole dollar.
[3] Allocation based on number of maintenance hours in producing departments (2,000); rounded to nearest whole dollar.

[a] $\frac{200}{620} \times \$19,500$

[b] $\frac{260}{2000} \times \$20,900$

FIGURE 2–9 Service Department Costs Allocated Only to Producing Departments: Direct Method between departments requires the use of simultaneous equations and so may be impractical if allocations are made manually. However, with a computer, this method of allocation can be carried out almost as easily as the step and direct methods demonstrated in Figures 2–8 and 2–9. We illustrate this method of allocation in the appendix to this chapter.

In some circumstances, it may be advisable to allocate the fixed costs of service departments on one basis (usually capacity-requirement related, such as maximum product or service that will be demanded during the period) and variable costs on another basis (usually actual use). The allocating procedures would be the same as those just illustrated, but the entire allocation process would have to be done twice—once for fixed costs and once for variable costs.

Systems for the Allocation and Accumulation of Manufacturing Costs

Our discussion, to this point, has dealt with the basic concepts underlying the allocation of manufacturing costs to the finished products being produced. The ultimate allocations of manufacturing costs to individual units of product are carried out by using either a job-order or process costing system or some combination of them. These systems are discussed in detail in Chapters 4 through 9. However, we briefly introduce them here because they are part of the overall cost accumulation and cost-allocation process.

Job-Order Costing

Manufacturing firms and service-type enterprises that produce goods or services in separately identifiable lots generally will use **job-order costing** to allocate manufacturing or service implementation costs to the individual units of finished product. A firm manufacturing different types of furniture, for example, probably would produce the furniture in job lots and therefore use a job-order system. A public accounting firm is an example of a service enterprise that might use a job-order costing system. The details of this system are developed in Chapters 4 and 5, but we will point out here that with a job-order costing system, separate job-order sheets are prepared to accumulate the direct materials, direct labor, and applied overhead costs associated with each lot of goods or services as those goods or services are being produced.

When the work on a lot of goods has been completed, the accumulated costs on the associated job-order sheet will be assigned to the individual units of finished product by dividing the total accumulated costs on the job order by the number of units of product included in the job. For example, if $19,000 of raw materials, direct labor, and applied overhead were required to produce 100 tables, the cost per table would be $19,000 ÷ 100 = $190. Work in process always will equal the costs (raw materials, direct labor, and applied overhead) accumulated on the job-order sheets for all job orders that have been started but not finished and transferred to finished goods. As jobs are completed, their costs will be transferred from work-in-process to finished-goods inventories. When the completed units are sold, the costs attached to those units will be transferred from finished-goods inventory to cost of sales, just as done in accounting for goods sold by a merchandising firm.

Process Costing

Job-order costing is unsuitable for businesses producing homogeneous goods or services on a continuing process basis, such as in the manufacture of cement, the manufacture of flour, or the refinement of crude oil. Such firms instead use **process costing**. Procedures followed in a process costing system are explained in Chapters 6–9. However, at this point, we note that costs are accumulated for periods of time by processes (or departments); unit costs are calculated by dividing the total manufacturing costs accumulated in each process (department) during that period of time by the units of output during the period for that process (department), with a unit cost generally being calculated for each of the three cost elements; direct material, direct labor, and overhead. These costs are then added together to get a total unit cost. For example, assuming total direct-materials costs of $120,000 representing 60,000 equivalent units of direct materials, direct-labor costs of $80,000 representing 50,000 equivalent units of direct labor, and manufacturing-overhead costs of $50,000 representing 50,000 equivalent units of overhead, total unit cost for a one-department plant would be:

Direct materials ($120,000/60,000)	$2.00
Direct labor ($80,000/50,000)	1.60
Overhead ($50,000/50,000)	1.00
Total unit cost	$4.60

These unit costs, then, are used in assigning values to both work-in-process and finished-goods inventories. Costs associated with completed units are transferred from work in process to finished goods in the same manner as with job-order costing. Likewise, the costs associated with units sold are transferred from finished goods to cost of sales.

SUMMARY

We first developed the basic concepts underlying cost accumulation and cost allocation for a manufacturing firm. We defined various terms, emphasizing the distinction between fixed costs and variable costs: Fixed unit costs vary inversely with changes in the level of production, while total fixed costs remain constant; variable costs per unit remain the same (constant) at different levels of production, but total variable costs vary directly with production.

After defining the various types of cost, we explained that the identification of cause-and-effect relationships, both at the time of cost incurrence and as costs are allocated, is fundamental to the appropriate allocation of costs so they can be matched against the revenues produced by them. We also demonstrated the application of cause-and-effect analysis, including the journal entries that would be made to record the incurrence and allocations of costs. We then showed how the matching convention is applied in accounting for both operating costs and manufacturing costs as those data are presented in the financial statements prepared within an absorption-costing format.

Finally, we developed the procedures for meeting special cost-allocation problems when there are departmental cost-accumulation centers. We also briefly described the characteristics of job-order and process cost-allocation and cost-accumulation systems.

APPENDIX: Simultaneous Allocations of Service Department Costs

Where service departments render considerable services to one another, it may be desirable to explicitly consider their mutual or reciprocal relationships and avoid entirely the problem of deciding (usually arbitrarily) the sequence of service department allocations required by the step method. The simultaneous allocation method often is referred to as a *reciprocal method, cross-allocation method, linear algebra method,* or *redistribution method.*

To illustrate two simultaneous allocation techniques, we will use the assumed data for Figures 2–8 and 2–9, which for convenience are repeated here.

| | Producing Departments | | | |
	Stamping	Welding	Finishing	Assembly
Manufacturing overhead charged to departments	$100,000	$80,000	$90,000	$75,000
Maintenance hours	500	900	340	260
Employees	200	280	90	50

| | Service Departments | | | |
	Maintenance	Personnel	Employee Services	Totals
Manufacturing overhead charged to departments	$20,900	$19,500	$15,700	$401,100
Maintenance hours	50	20	20	2,090
Employees	20	10	10	660

Part 1: Exact Simultaneous Allocations

Certain cost accounting purists have long recommended that formal mathematical treatment be used to simultaneously allocate reciprocal service department costs. Where the procedure is well understood and computer programs are readily available to perform the necessary calculations (Lotus® 1-2-3®, version 2.01, for example, easily will perform matrix inversion and multiplication under the DATA command), precise allocations can be determined. However, an approximate simultaneous allocation procedure, demonstrated in the next section of this appendix, will yield almost identical results and is much easier to understand (and explain to subordinates).

Simultaneous allocation requires, for each service department, a mathematical equation showing its total costs (the costs of the department itself plus its share of the costs of other service departments). For example, to determine total service department costs using the assumed data just given, letting M = maintenance department total costs, P = personnel department total costs, and ES = employee service department total costs, we would set up the following equations:

$$M = \$20,900 + \left(\frac{20}{650}\right)P + \left(\frac{20}{650}\right)ES$$

$$P = \$19,500 + \left(\frac{20}{2,040}\right)M + \left(\frac{10}{650}\right)ES$$

$$ES = \$15,700 + \left(\frac{20}{2,040}\right)M + \left(\frac{10}{650}\right)P$$

and then solve for M, P, and ES using linear algebra and matrix manipulation. There are numerous computer programs that do this efficiently. If the number of service departments is three or less, the math can be accomplished manually, as illustrated next. Still, we recommend *always* using a computer program. But here is what the math looks like: First, the equations are rearranged as follows:

$$1M - \left(\frac{20}{650}\right)P - \left(\frac{20}{650}\right)ES = \$20,900$$

$$-\left(\frac{20}{2,040}\right)M + 1P - \left(\frac{10}{650}\right)ES = \$19,500$$

$$-\left(\frac{20}{2,040}\right)M - \left(\frac{10}{650}\right)P + 1ES = \$15,700$$

Then the appropriate three matrices are identified and the information is presented in matrix multiplication form:

(1) the matrix of coefficients of the variables (which are the service department total costs), referred to as **A**

(2) the vector of service department costs before allocation, referred to as **B**

(3) the vector of total service department costs (the amounts we want to find), referred to as **X**.

$$
\begin{array}{ccccc}
\mathbf{A} & & \times & \mathbf{X} & = & \mathbf{B} \\
\begin{bmatrix}
1 & \dfrac{-20}{650} & \dfrac{-20}{650} \\
\dfrac{-20}{2{,}040} & 1 & \dfrac{-10}{650} \\
\dfrac{-20}{2{,}040} & \dfrac{-10}{650} & 1
\end{bmatrix}
& \times &
\begin{bmatrix} M \\ P \\ ES \end{bmatrix}
& = &
\begin{bmatrix} \$20{,}900 \\ \$19{,}500 \\ \$15{,}700 \end{bmatrix}
\end{array}
$$

To solve for vector **X**, matrix **A** must be inverted and multiplied by vector **B**:

$$\mathbf{X} = \mathbf{A}^{-1}\mathbf{B}$$

The procedure involves the following four steps:

1. Find the *minor* for each element in **A** by calculating the determinant of each submatrix of **A**, found by deleting the ith row and j^{th} column. For example, if the first row and first column is deleted, the submatrix is:

$$
\begin{bmatrix}
1 & \dfrac{-10}{650} \\
\dfrac{-10}{650} & 1
\end{bmatrix}
$$

The determinant then is $(+1 \times +1) - (-10/650 \times -10/650) = .9997634$. Repeating this process for all the elements in **A** results in:

$$
\begin{bmatrix}
\begin{bmatrix}
1 & \dfrac{-10}{650} \\
\dfrac{-10}{650} & 1
\end{bmatrix}
&
\begin{bmatrix}
\dfrac{-20}{2{,}040} & \dfrac{-10}{650} \\
\dfrac{-20}{2{,}040} & 1
\end{bmatrix}
&
\begin{bmatrix}
\dfrac{-20}{2{,}040} & 1 \\
\dfrac{-20}{2{,}040} & \dfrac{-10}{650}
\end{bmatrix}
\\[4ex]
\begin{bmatrix}
\dfrac{-20}{650} & \dfrac{-20}{650} \\
\dfrac{-10}{650} & 1
\end{bmatrix}
&
\begin{bmatrix}
1 & \dfrac{-20}{650} \\
\dfrac{-20}{2{,}040} & 1
\end{bmatrix}
&
\begin{bmatrix}
1 & \dfrac{-20}{650} \\
\dfrac{-20}{2{,}040} & \dfrac{-10}{650}
\end{bmatrix}
\\[4ex]
\begin{bmatrix}
\dfrac{-20}{650} & \dfrac{-20}{650} \\
1 & \dfrac{-10}{650}
\end{bmatrix}
&
\begin{bmatrix}
1 & \dfrac{-20}{650} \\
\dfrac{-20}{2{,}040} & \dfrac{-10}{650}
\end{bmatrix}
&
\begin{bmatrix}
1 & \dfrac{-20}{650} \\
\dfrac{-20}{2{,}040} & 1
\end{bmatrix}
\end{bmatrix}
$$

$$= \begin{bmatrix} .9997634 & -.0099547 & .0099547 \\ -.0312425 & .9996984 & -.0156862 \\ .0312425 & -.0156862 & .9996984 \end{bmatrix}$$

2. Convert the minors for each element in A into *cofactors* by multiplying each element by $(-1)^{i+j}$. This yields:

$$\begin{bmatrix} .9997634 & .0099547 & .0099547 \\ .0312425 & .9996984 & .0156862 \\ .0312425 & .0156862 & .9996984 \end{bmatrix}$$

3. Calculate the *determinant* of **A**, identified as $|A|$, by (a) multiplying the elements in any column (row) of the original matrix **A** by their corresponding cofactors (calculated in (2) above), and (b) summing their products. Any row or column will yield the same determinant. Using row 1, the determinant is found to be:

$$|A| = 1(.9997634) + \left(\frac{-20}{650}\right)(.0099547) + \left(\frac{-20}{650}\right)(.0099547)$$
$$= .999151$$

4. Transpose the cofactor matrix of **A** by making its row into columns. The result (called the *adjoint matrix*) then is divided by the determinant of **A** to find the inverse matrix $\mathbf{A}^{-1}$.

$$\mathbf{A}^{-1} = \frac{\begin{bmatrix} .9997634 & .0312425 & .0312425 \\ .0099547 & .9996984 & .0156862 \\ .0099547 & .0156862 & .9996984 \end{bmatrix}}{.999151}$$

$$= \begin{bmatrix} 1.0006129 & .031269 & .031269 \\ .0099631 & 1.0005478 & .0156995 \\ .0099631 & .0156995 & 1.0005478 \end{bmatrix}$$

Thus, $\mathbf{X} = \mathbf{A}^{-1}\mathbf{B}$ is:

$$\begin{bmatrix} M \\ P \\ ES \end{bmatrix} = \begin{bmatrix} 1.00066129 & .031269 & .031269 \\ .0099631 & 1.0005478 & .0156995 \\ .0099631 & .0156995 & 1.0005478 \end{bmatrix} \times \begin{bmatrix} \$20,900 \\ \$19,500 \\ \$15,700 \end{bmatrix}$$

$$= \begin{bmatrix} \$22,013.48 \\ 19,965.39 \\ 16,222.97 \end{bmatrix}$$

Figure 2–10 shows the same solution using a Lotus® 1-2-3® spreadsheet. The commands used to initiate the inversion and multiplication are printed on rows 12–14 and 20–22, but are not normally shown in this way.

Once calculated, these "artificial" total service department costs are allocated to all other departments in the agreed proportions. The se-

	A	B	C	D	E	F
1		A			X	B
2						
3	1	-20/650	-20/650		M	20900
4	-20/2040	1	10/650		P	19500
5	-20/2040	-10/650	1		ES	15700
6						
7						
8	1	-0.03076	-0.03076		M	20900
9	-0.0098	1	-0.01538		P	19500
10	-0.0098	-0.01538	1		ES	15700
11						
12	/Data Matrix Invert		(Range to Invert: A3..C5)			
13						
14	(Output Range: A16..C18)					
15						
16	1.000613	0.031269	0.031269			20900
17	0.009963	1.000548	0.015699			19500
18	0.009963	0.015699	1.000548			15700
19						
20	/Data Matrix Multiply		(First range to multiply: A16..C18)			
21			(Second range to multiply: F16..F18)			
22	(Output Range: A24..A26)					
23						
24	22013.48					
25	19965.4					
26	16222.97					
27						

FIGURE 2–10 Spreadsheet Solution for Simultaneous Allocations

quence of departmental allocations is irrelevant. Figure 2–11 presents the final results using this simultaneous allocation procedure.

It is clear from this illustration that while the simultaneous method is the most theoretically sound method to use, manual calculation is quite tedious and the results often are not significantly different from the step method (see Figure 2–8) or direct method (see Figure 2–9). Also, the simultaneous method is more difficult to understand (and explain). For example, the "artificial" total service department costs are

	Producing Departments				Service Departments			
	Stamping	Welding	Finishing	Assembly	Maintenance	Personnel	Employee Services	Totals
Manufacturing overhead	$100,000.00	$ 80,000.00	$90,000.00	$75,000.00	$ 20,900.00	$ 19,500.00	$ 15,700.00	$401,100
Allocation of maintenance*	5,395.46	9,711.83	3,668.91	2,805.64	(22,013.48)	215.82	215.82	0
Allocation of personnel**	6,143.20	8,600.47	2,764.44	1,535.80	614.32	(19,965.39)	307.16	0
Allocation of employee services**	4,991.68	6,988.36	2,246.26	1,247.92	499.17	249.58	(16,222.79)	0
	$116,530.34	$105,300.66	$98,679.61	$80,589.36	$ 0	$ 0	$ 0	$401,100

*Allocation based on number of maintenance hours in all other departments (2,040).

**Allocation based on number of employees in all other departments (650).

FIGURE 2–11 Service Department Costs Allocated to All Other Departments: Simultaneous Method

	Producing Departments				Service Departments			
	Stamping	Welding	Finishing	Assembly	Maintenance	Personnel	Employee Services	Totals
Manufacturing overhead	$100,000.00	$ 80,000.00	$90,000.00	$75,000.00	$ 20,900.00	$ 19,500.00	$ 15,700.00	$401,100
Allocation of personnel department costs[1]	6,000.00	8,400.00	2,700.00	1,500.00	600.00	(19,500.00)	300.00	0
Totals	$106,000.00	$ 88,400.00	$92,700.00	$76,500.00	$ 21,500.00	$ 0	$ 16,000.00	$401,100
Allocation of employee services department costs[1]	4,923.08	6,892.31	2,215.38	1,230.77	492.31	246.15	(16,000.00)	0
Totals	$110,923.08	$ 95,292.31	$94,915.38	$77,730.77	$ 21,992.31	$ 246.15	$ 0	$401,100
Allocation of maintenance department costs[3]	5,390.27	9,702.49	3,665.39	2,802.94	(21,992.31)	215.61	215.61	0
Totals	$116,313.35	$104,994.80	$98,580.77	$80,533.71	$ 0	$ 461.76	$ 215.61	$401,100
Allocation of personnel department costs[1]	142.08	198.91	63.94	35.52	14.21	(461.76)	7.10	0
Total	$116,455.43	$105,193.71	$98,644.71	$80,569.23	$ 14.21	$ 0	$ 222.71	$401,100
Allocation of employee services department costs[1]	68.53	95.94	30.83	17.13	6.85	3.43	(222.71)	0
Total	$116,523.96	$105,289.65	$98,675.54	$80,586.36	$ 21.06	$ 3.43	$ 0	$401,100
Allocation of maintenance department costs[2]	5.16	9.29	3.51	2.68	(21.06)	.21	.21	0
Total	$116,529.12	$105,298.94	$98,679.05	$80,589.04	$ 0	$ 3.64	$ .21	$401,100
Direct allocation of personnel department costs[3]	1.17	1.65	.53	.29		(3.64)		$ 0
Direct allocation of employee services department costs[3]	.07	.09	.03	.02			(.21)	0
Total	$116,530.36	$105,300.68	$98,679.61	$80,589.35	$ 0	$ 0	$ 0	$401,100

[1]Allocation based on number of employees in all other departments (650).
[2]Allocation based on number of maintenance hours in all other departments (2,040).
[3]Allocation based on number of employees in producing departments (620).

FIGURE 2–12 Service Department Costs Allocated "Back" to Other Service Departments (step-wise simultaneous allocation) greater than the actual costs because of the simultaneous treatment. Since different allocation systems can result in significantly different allocations, and since the simultaneous method results are fair to all departments, this method should be considered when accurate allocations are desired.

Part 2: Approximate Simultaneous Allocation

A rough estimate of the simultaneous approach, sometimes called *step-wise simultaneous allocation* because of its similarity to step-wise regression, can be obtained by applying a variation of the step method successively until the remaining service department costs are arbitrarily small enough to revert to the direct method to completely eliminate them.

The first stage of the step-wise simultaneous allocation is identical to the step method through the allocation of personnel department costs, as shown in Figure 2–8. Unlike the step method, though, the next service department cost to be allocated (employee services) would be allocated to personnel as well as the remaining departments. Maintenance department costs similarly would be allocated to personnel and employee services as well as the production departments. This approach is illustrated in Figure 2–12.

GLOSSARY OF TERMS INTRODUCED IN THIS CHAPTER

absorption costing	A system of accumulating and allocating costs in which all manufacturing costs, both fixed and variable, are allocated to the units of product being produced. Also known as *full costing* or *traditional costing*.
aggregate costs	The accumulated total amount of a particular item of cost over a period of time.
cost-accumulation centers	Departments or segments of operations that are the responsibility of specific persons within the organization and for which costs are accumulated.
direct allocation	The allocation of service department (cost-accumulation center) costs directly to producing departments (cost-accumulation centers), with no allocation to other service departments.
direct costing	See *variable costing*.
fixed costs	Costs that, in the aggregate, remain the same at different levels of operations within some relevant range.

general operating costs	Costs incurred in carrying out the selling and administrative activities of a business.
imputed costs	Hypothetical or opportunity costs assigned to a product or to an alternative in a decision-making process based on foregone alternative uses of resources. These costs are not entered into accounting records but are useful for cost analysis.
job-order costing	A cost-accumulation and cost-allocation system that accumulates the manufacturing costs (materials, direct labor, and overhead) associated with separately identifiable lots of goods as the production process is carried out.
manufacturing costs	The sum of direct materials used, direct labor costs incurred, and manufacturing overhead applied to production during an operating period.
matching convention	The overall guideline in accumulating and allocating costs that calls for relating costs to the revenues produced by those costs. Costs matched with revenues become expenses on the income statement.
overapplied overhead	The amount by which applied overhead exceeds the amount of actual overhead incurred during a reporting period.
period costs	Costs related to the passage of time and not to the products produced.
predetermined manufacturing-overhead application rate	A rate per unit of activity that is used to allocate the approximate amount of overhead costs incurred to units produced during a reporting period; calculated by dividing expected overhead costs by the expected activity base (such as direct labor, direct labor hours, or machine hours) that is most closely associated with the incurrence of overhead.
process costing	A system of cost accumulation and cost allocation in which costs are accumulated for periods of time by processes or departments that produce identical units, and those costs are then allocated to units produced during each reporting period by using unit-cost data calculated for each process or department.
producing department	A department (cost-accumulation center) in which work is performed on the product being manufactured. Also called *line department*.
product costs	Costs allocated to the products being produced. Initially recorded in inventory (asset) accounts, they become an expense (cost of sales) when the product is sold.
recorded costs	Costs recorded in accounting records.
relevant range	A range of levels of operations over which aggregate fixed costs and aggregate variable costs can be projected to behave in a linear fashion.
semivariable costs	Costs that include both variable and fixed components. Also called *semifixed costs*.
service department	A department within a business that exists for the purpose of providing services or assistance to other departments.
service implementation costs	Costs incurred by a business or nonprofit organization in providing services to the organization's clientele; comparable to cost of sales for a manufacturing or merchandising firm.

simultaneous allocation	A system for allocating service department (cost-accumulation center) costs to producing departments by the use of simultaneous equations that explicitly recognize the services provided to other service departments. Equations developed for allocating the costs of each service department to other service departments are solved simultaneously. The artificial costs resulting from the simultaneous solution are allocated to all departments benefiting from the service department's activities.
step method of allocating service department costs	A method of allocating service department costs that begins by allocating to all other departments (both service and production) the costs of that service department providing the most service to other service departments. The total costs accumulated for each of the other service departments, including those allocated in previous steps, are then allocated on a step basis to all remaining departments (producing departments and service departments that have not yet had their costs allocated), until all service department costs have been allocated to producing departments.
step-variable costs	Costs that, in the aggregate, remain fixed over a limited range of operating levels, beyond which they advance a full step upward and again remain fixed over another small range of operating levels. An example would be the additional salary cost when a second supervisor has to be added upon reaching a certain level of operations.
underapplied overhead	The amount by which actual overhead exceeds the amount of overhead applied to production.
unit cost	The costs associated with a single unit of product; calculated by dividing the aggregate cost of producing goods by the number of units turned out in incurring those costs.
variable costing	A system for accumulating and allocating manufacturing costs that allocates only variable manufacturing costs to the units produced. All fixed manufacturing costs are allocated to the periods in which the costs were incurred. Also called *direct costing*.
variable costs	Costs that in the aggregate vary directly with changes in the level of operations within a firm's relevant range. Within this range the variable cost per unit will be constant.

QUESTIONS FOR CLASS DISCUSSION

2–1 Why do businesses incur expenses? Explain.

2–2 Does *cost* include outlays for the purchase of long-term assets? Explain.

2–3 What types of costs are included in the cost assigned to finished units when using a variable costing system? How would your answer differ if the firm was using an absorption-costing system?

2–4 Are fixed manufacturing-overhead costs period costs or product costs? Explain.

2–5 How are direct-material and direct-labor costs allocated to finished units? How does the allocation process differ for manufacturing-overhead costs?

2–6 It has been said that variable costs are fixed and fixed costs are variable. What elaboration is required for this statement to be correct?

2–7 Why is the determination of cause-and-effect relationships so important in the accumulation and allocation of costs?

2–8 What is the ultimate objective in the allocation of manufacturing costs?

2–9 Why has the accounting profession adopted absorption costing rather than variable costing as a generally accepted accounting practice?

2–10 Explain how cause-and-effect relationships enter into the allocation of service department costs to producing departments.

2–11 What is the difference between the step method and the direct method of allocating service department costs to producing departments?

2–12 How do we determine the cost per unit for finished goods when using a job-order costing system?

2–13 How is the cost assigned to work-in-process inventory determined in a job-order costing system? Explain.

2–14 How are costs per unit for finished goods determined when using a process costing system?

EXERCISES

2–15 **Classification of Costs** Classify each of the following as manufacturing cost or operating cost (M or O) according to whether the cost should be matched against a product or against period revenue, and as variable (V), fixed (F), or semivariable (S), based on whether the aggregate cost changes in total as activity or volume changes. For *each* item, you should have two answers, M or O and V, F, or S.
Example: Factory rent   M, F

(a) Insurance on a factory building
(b) Rent for retail store
(c) Advertising costs
(d) Night watchman for a factory
(e) Replacement parts installed on factory machinery
(f) Lumber used in manufacturing furniture
(g) President's salary
(h) Factory supervisor's salary
(i) Electricity for factory

2–16 **Classification of Costs** Classify each of the following as manufacturing cost (M) or period cost (P), based on whether the cost should be matched against revenues from sales of a product or against period revenue, and as variable (V), fixed (F), or semivariable (S), based on whether the aggregate cost changes in total as activity or volume changes. You should have two answers, M or P and V, F, or S for *each* item.

Example: Units-of-production depreciation on factory machinery   M, V

(a) Food for a fast-food restaurant
(b) Utilities for factory
(c) Automobile expense for salespeople
(d) Security personnel for factory
(e) Factory machine operators
(f) Sales training program
(g) Maintenance costs for factory equipment
(h) Food for factory cafeteria
(i) Straight-line depreciation on factory machinery
(j) Factory janitors

2–17 **Cost Relationships** One way of classifying costs is to group them according to the reason the cost was incurred. Classify the following costs as outlays associated with:

(1) Goods and services expected to assist in producing revenue during future periods (assets)
(2) General operating costs (selling and administrative costs)
(3) Manufacturing costs
(4) Service implementation costs (i.e., the "product" costs of a service-type organization)

Note: While asset costs (1) ultimately will be allocated to categories (2), (3), and (4), do not consider this disposition in this exercise.

(a) Salary of the chief executive officer of a manufacturing firm
(b) Diagnostic examinations (test forms) for a county mental health and mental retardation clinic
(c) Direct materials used in a manufacturing process
(d) Monthly electricity for the retail showroom of a manufacturing firm
(e) Cost of a forklift truck to be used in moving materials from a storeroom to a production line
(f) Three-year insurance policy on a factory building
(g) Sales commissions for the salespeople of a manufacturing firm
(h) Supervisory salaries for manufacturing plant
(i) Salaries of university professors
(j) Production workers' pay

2–18 **Cost Relationships** All costs incurred by firms may be classified into one of the following categories:

(1) Assets costs
(2) General operating costs
(3) Manufacturing costs
(4) Service implementation costs (that is, the "product" costs of service-type organizations)

Identify the following costs as belonging to one of the preceding categories:

(a) Salary of a plant manager
(b) Purchase of raw materials to be used in a manufacturing process
(c) Factory payroll
(d) Rent on the retail showroom for a manufacturing firm
(e) Rent on a factory building
(f) Utilities for a factory
(g) Raw material used in a manufacturing process
(h) Salary for a physician in a family clinic
(i) Trade journal advertisements for a manufacturing firm
(j) Property taxes on a factory

2–19 **Unit Costs** Abbe Corp. has total fixed manufacturing costs of $66,560 and total variable costs of $104,000 during a period when 41,600 units are produced.

1. What is the total cost per unit?
2. If production is only 33,280 units, what is the total cost per unit?
3. Explain the difference in the cost per unit in questions 1 and 2.

2–20 **Unit Costs** Scott Company had an absorption cost per unit of $54 for each of the 12,400 carrying cases it constructed during a recent period. Variable manufacturing costs are $30, while fixed manufacturing costs are $24.

1. Calculate total production costs if 15,000 units are produced.
2. What would the absorption cost per unit be if 15,000 units are produced?
3. Explain the difference between $54 and your answer in question 2.

2–21
AICPA Adapted

Multiple Choice Select the *best* answer for each of the following questions.

1. Factory overhead
  a. is a prime cost.
  b. can be a variable cost or a fixed cost.
  c. can only be a fixed cost.
  d. includes all factory labor.
2. Within a relevant range, the amount of variable cost per unit
  a. differs at each production level.
  b. remains constant at each production level.
  c. increases as production increases.
  d. decreases as production increases.
3. Prime cost and conversion cost share what common element of total cost?
  a. direct materials   **c.** variable overhead
  b. direct labor   **d.** fixed overhead
4. The cost of fire insurance for a manufacturing plant is generally a
  a. nonmanufacturing cost.   **c.** semivariable cost.
  b. period cost.   **d.** conversion cost.
5. For a manufacturing company, which of the following is an example of a period rather than a product cost?

    a. depreciation on factory equipment
    b. wages of salespersons
    c. wages of machine operators
    d. insurance on factory equipment

2–22
AICPA Adapted

Multiple Choice Select the *best* answer for each of the following questions.

1. The fixed portion of the semivariable cost of electricity for a manufacturing plant is a

	Conversion Cost	Product Cost
a.	no	no
b.	no	yes
c.	yes	yes
d.	yes	no

2. Factory supplies for a manufacturing plant are generally
    a. prime costs   **c.** variable costs
    b. period costs   **d.** excluded from product costs

3. The cost of rent for a manufacturing plant is a

	Prime Cost	Product Cost
a.	no	yes
b.	no	no
c.	yes	no
d.	yes	yes

4. Indirect labor is a
    a. nonmanufacturing cost   **c.** prime cost
    b. conversion cost   **d.** period cost

5. Direct materials are a

	Conversion Cost	Manufacturing Cost	Prime Cost
a.	yes	yes	no
b.	yes	yes	yes
c.	no	yes	yes
d.	no	no	no

6. Which of the following costs is the best example of a variable cost?
    a. property taxes
    b. the corporate president's salary
    c. the controller's salary
    d. interest charges
    e. cost of material in a unit of product

PROBLEMS

2–23 **Journal Entries** S and H Corporation manufactures and sells various computer accessories. During February, the following selected transactions occurred:

(1) Purchased a new piece of equipment for $32,000. Due to installation and calibration requirements, the equipment was not put in use until March 1.
(2) Purchased plastic, lucite, and metal materials costing $164,000.
(3) Paid salespeople accrued salaries and commissions of $86,500.
(4) Paid factory utilities (electricity, water, gas, and sewage) of $16,200.
(5) Recorded payroll obligations to factory employees as follows:

Machine operators	$44,900
Materials handlers	$16,500
Supervisors and foremen	$20,750

$2,500 of the wages paid to machine operators represented idle time.
(6) Paid payroll obligations recognized in transaction 5.
(7) Issued $115,000 of materials to the production line.

REQUIRED: Prepare journal entries to record these transactions.

2–24 **Journal Entries** The Robinson Company manufactures metal clips and bearings. The following transactions occurred during a recent period:

(a) Purchased metal at a cost of $210,000.
(b) Purchased factory supplies for $15,200.
(c) Used metal with a cost of $243,000 in the production process.
(d) Factory payroll was

Direct labor	$129,000
Indirect labor	87,000

(e) Used factory supplies of $14,000.
(f) Recognized depreciation as follows:

Factory building	$22,000
Machinery	94,000

(g) Applied factory overhead of $230,000 to work in process.
(h) Incurred other factory overhead expenses of $11,800.

REQUIRED:

1. Prepare journal entries to record these transactions.
2. Post the amounts from requirement 1 to T accounts (materials inventory, work in process, factory overhead, finished goods).

2–25 **Matching** Match the following costs (a through g) with the most appropriate accounting treatment (1 through 5). The first cost item illustrates the matching required.

Cost	Usual Accounting Treatment on Date of Transaction
__5__ (a) Purchase of raw materials	(1) Cost of sales
____ (b) Payment of sales salaries	(2) General and administrative expense
____ (c) Payment of wages to factory workers	(3) Manufacturing-overhead expense
____ (d) Payment of taxes on factory building and equipment	(4) Noncurrent asset on the balance sheet
____ (e) Purchase of automobiles for sales personnel	(5) Current asset on the balance sheet
____ (f) Payment of rent for administrative offices	
____ (g) Payment of 1-year insurance policy covering goods held for sale	

2–26 **Matching** Match the following costs (a through g) with the most appropriate accounting treatment (1 through 7). You should have at least two answers for each cost, as illustrated for the first cost item.

Cost Transaction	Accounting Treatment
__5, 6__ (a) Depreciation of factory equipment	(1) Income statement operating expense increased
____ (b) Sale of manufactured product	(2) Income statement cost of sales increased
____ (c) Factory labor costs are allocated to work in process and manufacturing overhead	(3) Balance sheet asset increased
____ (d) Direct materials are used in production	(4) Income statement revenue recognized
____ (e) Manufacturing overhead is applied to production	(5) Balance sheet asset decreased
____ (f) Goods in process are completed and transferred to a warehouse	(6) Manufacturing overhead increased
____ (g) Depreciation of automobiles used by sales personnel	(7) Manufacturing overhead decreased

2–27 **Service Department Allocations—Step Method** Southwest Company has two operating (production) departments (A and B) and three service departments (X, Y, and Z). Costs incurred by the service departments are as follows:

Service Department	Total Cost
X	$165,000
Y	82,000
Z	70,000

Using various allocation bases, an assistant has provided you with the following information:

	Percentage of Service Provided To				
Department	A	B	X	Y	Z
X	36%	40%	0%	10%	14%
Y	46%	25%	9%	0%	20%
Z	40%	50%	2%	8%	0%

REQUIRED: Prepare a schedule showing the allocation of service department costs using the step method. Begin with the department that performs the largest percentage of service for other service departments.

2–28 **Service Department Allocations—Step Method** Marshall Manufacturing Company has two production departments, assembly and finishing, and three service departments, personnel, cafeteria, and utilities. The controller for Marshall has prepared the following projection of operations for the coming year:

Department	Materials	Wages and Salaries	Other Costs	Total
Assembly	$216,900	$1,250,000	$448,100	$1,915,000
Finishing	228,000	718,400	641,600	1,588,000
Personnel	0	48,000	23,000	71,000
Cafeteria	32,000	75,000	43,000	150,000
Utilities	3,000	54,000	32,000	89,000

You also are provided with the following information:

	Personnel Transactions Processed	Number of Employees	Square Footage of Space Occupied
Assembly	165	440	66,000
Finishing	275	660	66,000
	440	1,100	132,000
Personnel	22	16	4,500
Cafeteria	44	22	11,000
Utilities	66	132	—
	132	170	15,500
Total	572	1,270	147,500

You determine that personnel costs are to be allocated according to personnel transactions processed, cafeteria costs are to be allocated using number of employees, and utilities costs are to be allocated using square footage occupied. Assume that personnel costs are to be allocated first, followed by cafeteria and utilities.

REQUIRED:

1. Set up a schedule showing service department overhead allocations using the step method (round to the nearest dollar).
2. Determine overhead rates for the assembly and finishing departments assuming that direct labor hours are to be used to calculate the predetermined overhead rate. Assume that the assembly department is expected to have 300,000 hours and the finishing department to have 150,000 hours (carry rate to five decimal places).

2–29   **Service Department Allocation—Direct Method** Using the data in problem 2–27, prepare a schedule showing how the service department costs would be allocated by the direct method of allocation.

2–30   **Service Department Allocation—Direct Method** Using the data in problem 2–28, prepare a schedule showing how the service department costs would be allocated by the direct method of allocation.

2–31   **Allocating Costs of Service Departments—Step and Direct Methods** The Maness Company has prepared departmental budgets for normal activity levels before any allocation as follows (all costs in thousands of dollars):

Service Departments	Estimated Total Costs
Personnel	$ 2,500
Cafeteria	5,600
Janitorial	10,300
General factory administration	22,000
	$40,400

Production Departments	RM	DL	OH	Estimated Total Costs
Cutting	$92,500	$71,400	$54,200	$218,100
Machining	1,950	76,000	49,500	127,450
Finishing	4,850	65,000	46,800	116,650
				$462,200

Maness management has decided that each production department will have its own *overhead application rate*, to be calculated after appropriate service department costs have been allocated to the production departments. The following additional information has been compiled to aid in the allocation process:

	Personnel	Cafeteria	Janitorial	General Factory Administration	Cutting	Machining	Finishing
No. of employees	40	190	240	130	4,100	3,400	2,500
Area (square footage)	10,000	76,000	—	26,000	2,000,000	1,360,000	1,500,000
Machine hours	—	—	—	—	800,000	1,400,000	300,000
Direct-labor hours	—	—	—	—	13,000,000	7,000,000	5,000,000

You have been asked to prepare a schedule that will indicate how the service department costs are to be allocated to the production departments. You believe that cafeteria and personnel costs should be allocated first, followed by janitorial and general factory administration. General factory administration costs should be allocated on the basis of estimated total direct departmental costs. Allocate personnel costs on the basis of number of employees; janitorial costs on the basis of area; and cafeteria costs on the basis of number of employees.

REQUIRED:

1. Prepare a schedule showing how all service department costs would be allocated if the *step* method is used.
2. Prepare a schedule showing how all service department costs would be allocated if the *direct* method is used.
3. Prepare revised budgets for the three production departments after service department costs have been allocated assuming
   a. The step method of allocation is used.
   b. The direct method of allocation is used.
4. Calculate a predetermined overhead rate for each production department assuming the step method of allocating service department costs is used. Also assume the following:

Department	Activity Most Directly Associated with Overhead Costs
Cutting	Raw material costs
Machining	Machine hours
Finishing	Direct-labor hours

2–32 **Service Department Cost Allocation** EMA Corporation has one maintenance department that services four production departments. The manager of each production department schedules maintenance for his or her department. Estimated and actual maintenance hours for a recent period were as follows:

Production Department	Maintenance Provided	
	Estimated Hours	Actual Hours
1	200	250
2	400	300
3	150	140
4	100	200

The maintenance department incurs the following costs during the same period.

	Variable Costs	Fixed Costs	Total
Materials	$ 3,000	—	$ 3,000
Salaries and wages	64,000	—	64,000
Other costs	—	27,500	27,500
	$67,000	$27,500	$94,500

REQUIRED:

1. Prepare a schedule to show how maintenance department costs should be allocated to the four production departments if total maintenance costs are allocated on the basis of actual hours of maintenance provided.
2. Prepare a schedule to show how maintenance department costs should be allocated to the four production departments if variable costs are allocated on the basis of actual hours of maintenance provided and fixed costs are allocated on the basis of estimated hours of maintenance provided.
3. Which method would you recommend in this situation? Why?

2–33   **THOUGHT STIMULATION CASE—Evaluation of Assertions Made in a Dialogue.**   The following discussion was printed in the *Lybrand Journal* in 1960, as well as in numerous other sources. The original source is unknown. It is an excellent illustration of attitudes that still prevail today.

In discussing the cost associated with various types of operations, the following analogy was drawn: A restaurant adds a rack of peanuts to the counter, hoping to pick up a little additional profit in the usual course of business. Consider the actual problem faced by the restaurateur (Joe) as revealed by his accountant/efficiency expert (Eff Exp).

Eff Exp: Joe, you said you put in these peanuts because some people ask for them, but do you realize what this rack of peanuts is costing you?

Joe: It ain't gonna cost. It's gonna be a profit. Sure, I had to pay $25 for a fancy rack to hold bags, but the peanuts cost 6¢ a bag and I sell 'em for 10¢. 'Figger I sell 50 bags a week to start. It'll take 12½ weeks to cover the cost of the rack. After that I gotta clear profit of 4¢ a bag. The more I sell the more I'll make.

Eff Exp: This is an antiquated and completely unrealistic approach, Joe. Fortunately, modern accounting procedures permit a more accurate picture that reveals the complexities involved.

Joe: Huh?

Eff Exp: To be precise, those peanuts must be integrated into your entire operation and be allocated their appropriate share of business overhead. They must share a proportionate part of your expenditures for rent, heat, light, equipment depreciation, decoration, salaries for your waitresses, cook, . . .

Joe: The cook? What's he gotta do with peanuts? He don't even know I got 'em!

Eff Exp: Look, Joe, the cook is in the kitchen. The kitchen prepares the food. The food is what brings people in here, and the people ask to buy peanuts. That's why you must charge a portion of the cook's wages, as well as a part of your own salary, to peanut sales. This carefully calculated cost analysis sheet indicates the peanut operation should pay exactly $1,278 per year toward these general overhead costs.

Joe: The peanuts? $1,278 a year for overhead? The nuts?

Eff Exp: It's really a little more than that. You also spend money each week to have the windows washed and to have the place swept out in the mornings, keep soap in the washroom, and provide free cokes to the police. That raises the total to $1,313 per year.

Joe: (thoughtfully) But the peanut salesman said I'd make money. Put 'em on the end of the counter, he said, and get 4¢ a bag profit.

Eff Exp: (with a sniff) He's not an accountant. Do you actually know what the portion of the counter occupied by the peanut rack is worth to you?

Joe: Ain't worth nothing. No stool there, just a dead spot at the end.

Eff Exp: The modern cost picture permits no dead spots. Your counter contains 60 square feet and the counter grosses $15,000/year, so the square foot of space occupied by the peanut rack is worth $250 per year. Since you have taken area away from general counter use, you must charge the value of the space to the occupant.

Joe: You mean I gotta charge $250 a year more to the peanuts?

Eff Exp: Right. That raises their share of the general operation costs to a grand total of $1,563 per year. Now then, if you sell 50 bags of peanuts per week, these allocated costs will amount to 60¢ per bag.

Joe: What?

Eff Exp: Obviously, to that must be added your purchase price of 6¢ per bag, which brings the total to 66¢. So you see, by selling peanuts at 10¢ per bag you are losing 56¢ on every sale.

Joe: Somethin's crazy?

Eff Exp: Not at all! Here are the figures. They prove your peanut operation cannot stand on its own feet.

Joe: (brightening) Suppose I sell lotsa peanuts, thousand bags a week 'stead of fifty?

Eff Exp: (tolerantly) Joe, you don't understand the problem. If the volume of peanut sales increases, your operating costs will go up. You'll have to handle more bags, with more time, more depreciation, more everything. The basic principle of accounting is firm on that subject—the bigger the operation, the more general overhead costs that must be allocated. No, increasing the volume of sales won't help.

Joe: Okay. You're so smart. You tell me what I gotta do.

Eff Exp: (condescendingly) Well, you could first reduce operating expenses.

Joe: How?

Eff Exp: Move to a building with cheaper rent. Cut salaries. Wash the windows biweekly. Have the floor swept only on Thursday. Remove the soap from the washrooms. Decrease the square-foot value of your counter. For example, if you can cut your expenses 50%, you will reduce the amount allocated to peanuts from $1,563 down to $781.50 per year, reducing the cost to 36¢ per bag.

Joe: (slowly) That's better?

Eff Exp: Much, much better. However, even then you would lose 26¢ per bag if you charge only 10¢. Therefore, you must also raise your selling price. If you want a net profit of 4¢ per bag, you would have to charge 40¢.

Joe: (flabbergasted) You mean after I cut operating costs 50% I still gotta charge 40¢ for a 10¢ bag of peanuts? Nobody's that nuts about nuts! Who's gonna buy 'em?

Eff Exp: That's a secondary consideration. The point is at 40¢ you'd be selling at a price based upon a true and proper evaluation of your then-reduced costs.

Joe: (eagerly) Look! I gotta better idea. Why don't I just throw the nuts out. Put 'em in a trash can?

Eff Exp: Can you afford it?

Joe: Sure. All I got is about 50 bags of peanuts. They cost about three bucks, and I lost $25 on the rack. But I'm out of this nutsy business and no more grief.

Eff Exp: (shaking head) Joe, It isn't quite that simple. You are in the peanut business! The minute you throw those peanuts out, you are adding $1,563 of annual overhead to the rest of your operations. Joe, be realistic. Can you afford to do that?

Joe: (completely crushed) It's unbelievable! Last week I made money. Now I'm in trouble, just because I think peanuts on a counter is gonna bring me some extra profit, just because I believe 50 bags of peanuts a week is easy.

Eff Exp: (with raised eyebrow) That is the object of modern cost studies, Joe, to dispel those false illusions.

REQUIRED:

1. What is Joe's operating result on the "peanut" business? Is he losing 56¢ on the sale of every bag of peanuts? Explain.
2. Has the efficiency expert identified some relevant issues in his discussion with Joe? Explain.

3. If the volume of peanut sales is increased, does more cost have to be assigned to that aspect of operations? Explain.

4. Should Joe get out of the peanut business? Why or why not?

2–34

CMA Adapted

THOUGHT STIMULATION PROBLEM—Service Department Cost Allocation. The Independent Underwriters Insurance Co. (IUI) established a systems department two years ago to implement and operate its own data processing systems. IUI believed that its own system would be more cost effective than the service bureau it had been using.

IUI's three departments—claims, records, and finance—have different requirements with respect to hardware and other capacity-related resources and operating resources. The system was designed to recognize these differing needs. In addition, the system was designed to meet IUI's long-term capacity needs. The excess capacity designed into the system would be sold to outside users until needed by IUI. The estimated resources requirements used to design and implement the system are shown in the following schedule.

	Hardware and Other Capacity-Related Resources	Operating Resources
Records	30%	60%
Claims	50	20
Finance	15	15
Expansion (outside use)	5	5
Total	100%	100%

IUI currently sells the equivalent of its expansion capacity to a few outside clients.

At the time the system became operational, management decided to redistribute total expenses of the systems department to the user departments based on actual computer time used. The actual costs for the first quarter of the current fiscal year were distributed to the user departments as follows:

Department	Percentage Utilization	Amount
Records	60%	$330,000
Claims	20	110,000
Finance	15	82,500
Outside	5	27,500
Total	100%	$550,000

The three user departments have complained about the cost distribution method since the systems department was established. The records department's monthly costs have been as much as three times the cost experienced with the service bureau. The finance department is concerned about the costs distributed to the outside-user category because these allocated costs form the basis for the fees billed to the outside clients.

James Dale, IUI's controller, decided to review the distribution method by which the systems department's costs have been allocated for the past two years. The additional information he gathered for his review is reported in Tables 1 through 3.

Dale has concluded that the method of cost distribution should be changed to reflect more directly the actual benefits received by the departments. He believes that the hardware and capacity-related costs should be allocated to the user departments in proportion to the planned, long-term needs. Any difference between actual and budgeted hardware costs would not be allocated to the departments but remain with the systems department.

TABLE 1   Systems Department Costs and Activity Levels

| | Annual Budget | | First Quarter | | | |
| | | | Budget | | Actual | |
	Hours	Dollars	Hours	Dollars	Hours	Dollars
Hardware and other capacity related costs	—	$ 600,000	—	$150,000	—	$155,000
Software development	18,750	562,500	4,725	141,750	4,250	130,000
Operations						
Computer related	3,750	750,000	945	189,000	920	187,000
Input/output related	30,000	300,000	7,560	75,600	7,900	78,000
		$2,212,500		$556,350		$550,000

TABLE 2   Historical Utilization by Users

| | Hardware and Other Capacity Needs | Software Development | | Operations | | | |
| | | | | Computer | | Input/Output | |
		Range	Average	Range	Average	Range	Average
Records	30%	0–30%	12%	55–65%	60%	10–30%	20%
Claims	50	15–60	35	10–25	20	60–80	70
Finance	15	25–75	45	10–25	15	3–10	6
Outside	5	0–25	8	3–8	5	3–10	4
	100%		100%		100%		100%

TABLE 3 Utilization of Systems Department's Services, in Hours, First Quarter

	Software Development	Operations Computer Related	Operations Input/Output
Records	425	552	1,580
Claims	1,700	184	5,530
Finance	1,700	138	395
Outside	425	46	395
Total	4,250	920	7,900

The remaining costs for software development and operations would be charged to the user departments based on actual hours used. A predetermined hourly rate based on the annual budget data would be used. The hourly rates for the current fiscal year are as follows:

Function	Hourly Rate
Software development	$ 30
Operations	
Computer related	200
Input/output related	10

Dale plans to use first quarter activity and cost data to illustrate his recommendations. The recommendations will be presented to the systems department and the user departments for their comments and reactions. He then expects to present his recommendations to management for approval.

REQUIRED:

1. Calculate the amount of data processing costs that would be included in the claims department's first-quarter budget according to the method James Dale has recommended.
2. Prepare a schedule to show how the actual first-quarter costs of the systems department would be charged to the users if James Dale's recommended method was adopted.
3. Explain whether James Dale's recommended system for charging costs to the user departments will:
   a. Improve cost control in the systems department.
   b. Improve planning and cost control in the user departments.
   c. Be a more equitable basis for charging costs to user departments.

2–35 **Simultaneous Service Department Allocation** (based on the appendix to this chapter)

REQUIRED:

1. Use the data from problem 2–28 to set up the appropriate equations for a formal mathematical solution that will consider the reciprocal services provided by the personnel, cafeteria, and utilities departments. (*Note:* The production departments—assembly and finishing—should not appear in these equations.) Do *not* attempt the manual solution of the simultaneous equation system.
2. Use the data from problem 2–28 to find an *approximate* simultaneous allocation solution using the procedures illustrated in the appendix. (*Note:* After two complete "passes" through the service departments, use the direct method to allocate the remaining costs to the production departments—assembly and finishing.)

2–36 **Simultaneous Service Department Allocation** (based on the appendix to this chapter)

REQUIRED:

1. Use the data from problem 2–31 to set up a mathematical equation for each service department that shows its own direct costs plus its share of other service department costs. Arrange the variables and constants in a format that will facilitate a matrix solution of simultaneous allocations. If you have access to a matrix inversion computer program, invert the **A** matrix and show how service department costs would be allocated.
2. Use the data from problem 2–31 to find an *approximate* simultaneous-allocation solution using the procedures illustrated in the appendix. (*Note:* After two complete "passes" through the service departments, that is, after you have gone through the allocation sequence *twice* for each service department, use the direct method to allocate the remaining costs to the production departments—cutting, machining, and finishing.)

Chapter 3

Cost Accounting in Transition

Learning Objectives

When you have finished your study of this chapter, you should

1. Understand the theoretical and practical meanings of a JIT (just-in-time) philosophy and appreciate its limitations.
2. Have a general understanding of the characteristics of an automated factory.
3. Know what a zero-defective-goods operating policy means and the reasons such an operating goal is important.

I n Chapters 1 and 2, in addition to defining cost accounting terminology, we developed the conventional guidelines followed in accumulating and allocating manufacturing costs between cost of goods sold and inventories. We also recognized that any system used for the accumulation and allocation of manufacturing costs must give primary consideration to the operating environment in which those costs are incurred. Historically, this has called for use of either a job-order costing system or a process costing system. Job-order systems are used by firms producing goods in readily identifiable lots, whereas process costing systems are suited to situations in which one or a limited number of products are being produced on a continuous-flow basis.

As the U.S. economy has shifted from one in which manufacturers were primarily concerned with domestic competition to one in which they have had to compete internationally, American ways of producing and distributing goods have proven uncompetitive with those of certain European and Pacific rim companies. U.S. firms have lost the competitive edge in international markets, and contributed to a large foreign trade deficit in the process. In order to again become globally competitive, U.S. companies have given considerable attention to what their counterparts in Japan and other countries have been doing in taking over the international market for automobiles and certain other products. Clearly, some U.S. firms have been unable to compete with foreign companies on price or product quality, and they must change the way they operate if they are to regain a competitive position internationally.

To achieve lower unit costs and better product quality, U.S. firms are now looking for ways to (1) minimize those costs that add no value to a product, (2) lower the amount of high-priced labor, and (3) reduce the number of defective units being produced. This has produced three philosophical goals for plant operations, namely,

1. just-in-time (JIT) inventory
2. automated factories
3. zero defective goods.

In this chapter, we briefly consider these operating philosophies and the future effects they are likely to have on cost accounting systems. These topics will be discussed more completely in Chapters 22–24.

Just-in-Time Inventory Policy

In the ideal, the just-in-time (**JIT**) operating philosophy calls for raw materials and partially processed goods to be delivered precisely at the times—and to the locations—they are needed on the production line, and for finished goods to be completed at exactly the time required to meet customer orders. JIT philosophy seeks to minimize those costs associated with handling and storing inventory that add no value to the product, and to thereby reduce the cost per unit of finished product. Imagine the savings were a manufacturer not to have to own extensive warehouse facilities, incur handling costs as goods are moved into and out of storage, or suffer possible obsolescence losses from holding goods over a long storage period. Further, JIT environments are expected to shorten the required production time by reducing the handling and holding times for goods in process.

As we examine the JIT philosophy, we shall consider

1. some of the practical limitations associated with achieving a JIT environment
2. the effect that a JIT environment would have on cost accounting practices.

Practicality in Implementing a JIT Policy

As we observed, JIT requires raw materials to be delivered at exactly the points they are needed, and just when they are needed to initiate production. Partially processed goods are expected to move through the factory in such a way that goods come out of one operation just in time to be processed in the next operation. Furthermore, JIT philosophy calls for the transfer of finished goods directly to the vehicles used to deliver them to customers, rather than to storage. Such an arrangement completely eliminates the need for the extensive warehouse space that has conventionally been an expensive part of any manufacturing operation. It also significantly reduces the costs of handling, from the point of delivery of raw materials to the point where the finished product is shipped to the customer. Not only would goods be handled less often, but the smaller quantities involved might eliminate the need for expensive bulk-moving equipment (such as forklifts).

In considering the practicality of JIT, we may begin by asking why manufacturing firms have conventionally maintained sizable inventories, particularly in raw materials stores and in finished-goods stores. Historically, managers have said that a certain level of finished-goods inventory enables a firm to meet customers' needs for prompt delivery. They also have maintained that a reasonable stock of raw materials avoids having to shut down production lines due to unavailability of certain materials. Also, it has generally been believed that production runs need to be reasonably long to justify set-up costs.

As we explain in Chapter 21, the quantities of raw materials to be purchased and the number of units to be produced on a production run historically have been determined by calculating an **economical order (or production) quantity** that takes into consideration the combined costs of ordering goods (or setting up for a production run) and of holding and storing inventory items. But can such inventories be totally eliminated, as called for by a strict JIT operating philosophy?

In determining the extent to which JIT can be implemented within a particular plant, it is important to consider the potential problems to be encountered in satisfying customer needs and in arranging for the deliveries of raw materials. Consider the series of manufacturing operations required to convert a basic raw material, such as an agricultural product or a mineral ore, into a consumable finished good. Clearly, if all of the factories involved in the conversion activities are to be able to operate within a JIT environment, all production elements must be synchronized with the demand for the final consumable finished product. To illustrate, the manufacturing operations involved in converting iron ore into an automobile require, as you can see in Figure 3–1, a sequence of operations, from the mining of the ore through the delivery of the automobile to the customer.

Theoretically, the only way these operations could be carried out with zero inventories at all levels would be as follows. The automobile buyer places an order for an automobile with an auto dealer. The order is then sent to the auto manufacturer. That company, since it has no finished stock of automobiles, orders the steel parts from the steel fabricating company. Since the steel fabricator has no inventory of fabricated parts, it places an order with the smelting plant for the steel ingots needed to fabricate the steel. The smelting plant, with no steel ingots in stock because they operate with zero inventory, has to order the ore from the iron ore mining company. Finally, the complete production process can be activated. The ore is delivered to the smelter, the smelter delivers the steel ingots to the steel fabricator, which then delivers the fabricated steel parts to the auto manufacturing company for use in assembling the automobile. The auto manufacturer produces the auto and ships it to the dealer so it can be delivered to the customer. Obviously, such an operating practice would be not only highly impractical in a political environment that discourages "monopolistic" vertical integration, but perhaps impossible to implement in a consumer industry where impulse buying is of importance.

The implementation of a JIT environment throughout a series of interdependent resource conversion activities is rather idealistic at the

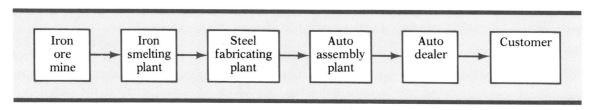

FIGURE 3–1 Automobile Production Process

present time. However, we can have practical adaptations of the JIT philosophy. JIT's more complete synchronization of the activities of various manufacturing firms involved in converting a basic raw material into a consumable finished good can help to minimize inventory levels throughout those productive processes. Certainly, the adoption of JIT goals by manufacturing firms should allow those firms to significantly reduce their inventories and thereby eliminate many of the costs that add no value to the product.

Henry Ford described a JIT scenario for an automobile assembly-line process in his book, *Today and Tomorrow* (Garden City: The Garden City Publishing Company, 1926). By controlling all operations from the moment raw material was separated from the earth to the moment when the finished product was delivered to the ultimate customer, Ford's production cycle (from the mine to the finished automobile on the freight car) was approximately 81 hours. This remarkable feat was accomplished via total standardization exemplified by Ford's famous statement, "They can have it in any color they want, so long as it's black."

Even more realistically, an individual firm in the present environment can, by careful scheduling of production based on market projections (or, even better, based on actual orders), reduce the level of finished-goods inventory. By using such production schedules and working with a limited number of suppliers of raw materials, the level of raw materials inventory also can be minimized. Processing time and the amount of work-in-process inventory also can be minimized by rearranging production facilities into **manufacturing cells** (minifactories), which include all the machines required to produce a particular part. Such an arrangement reduces the amount of movement of semiprocessed units required in the production process. Each manufacturing cell produces smaller quantities carefully orchestrated to blend into the final product at the appropriate time.

The implementation of such practices calls for more frequent setups and, therefore, the necessity of minimizing the costs of each of the individual setups. It also requires significant changes in plant layout because the emphasis is on achievement (that is, output) of the plant rather than on the achievements of individual departments (or cells) within the plant. As we explain in Chapter 23, this practical adaptation of JIT is currently being implemented by many firms.

**JIT and
Cost Allocation**

Chapter 1 emphasized the fact that a manufacturing firm has to have a system for allocating manufacturing costs to allow it to assign values to work-in-process and finished-goods inventories. A system that provides such information also enables the firm to properly assign values to cost of sales. In this part of the chapter, we briefly explore the logical effect on the cost-allocation process for a manufacturing firm operating with zero or minimum inventory.

A firm that manufactures a single product and achieves the ideal goal of a just-in-time inventory environment would have no need to allocate manufacturing costs between inventory and cost of sales. The purchase of raw materials and the incurrence of conversion costs could all be recorded by debiting cost of sales, as shown in Figure 3–2. The operating statement would match the amounts in the "cost of sales" and "operating expenses" accounts against the sales revenues for each period. As you can see, a firm with such a manufacturing environment would require no cost-allocation procedures to allow it to prepare conventional financial statements.

A firm that manufactures more than one product and is able to achieve the ideal goal of a JIT environment would still have no need to allocate costs between inventory and cost of sales. However, it would be important to allocate direct (traceable) manufacturing costs to the different products being produced for the purpose of evaluating the profitability of each of the products. Indirect materials and common conversion costs would not have to be allocated to individual products. Therefore, such a firm would need to design a cost-accumulation and cost-allocation system similar to the one shown in Figure 3–3, which would allow manufacturing costs to be allocated to the products being produced at the time raw materials were purchased and conversion costs were incurred. Logically, then, as those costs are incurred, it would be desirable to debit them to separate "cost of sales" accounts for each of the products being produced or to a common "cost of sales" account. Such an arrangement would permit the preparation of an op-

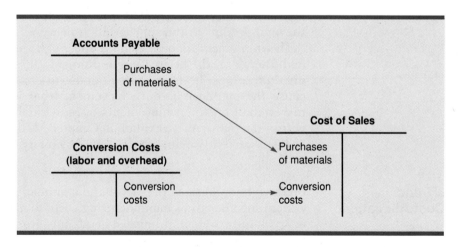

FIGURE 3–2 Accounting for JIT Production with Only One Product (no allocation required)

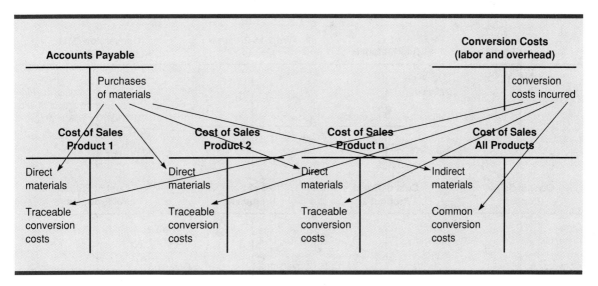

FIGURE 3–3 Accounting for JIT Production with Multiple Products (allocation to products required)

erating statement in which the sales revenue from each of the products would be matched against the direct cost of manufacturing each of those products.

A firm that is able to organize its operations so as to produce finished units just in time for delivery to customers and whose production lines are organized and synchronized so the amount of work in process at any particular instant in time is minimal must still maintain at least a limited amount of raw materials inventory to be able to achieve its goals of having no finished-goods inventory and a minimum amount of work-in-process inventory. Theoretically, such a manufacturing environment could be created by minimizing processing time and manufacturing to order. In such a situation, a raw materials inventory account would have to be maintained, to be debited when materials are purchased and credited as materials are issued into process. However, as materials are issued into process and conversion costs are incurred, the costs could be charged directly to Cost of Sales accounts, as in Figure 3–3. In such a manufacturing environment, the cost-accumulation and cost-allocation system would need to separate raw materials purchase costs into raw materials inventory and cost of sales. If more than one product was being manufactured by the firm, the cost of raw materials used and traceable conversion costs should still be allocated to individual products. Theoretically, if the firm only manufactures to fill orders, the allocation to products could be made by identifying the costs associated with the production of each order. Figure 3–4 illustrates a JIT environment with multiple products and minimal inventoried. As the

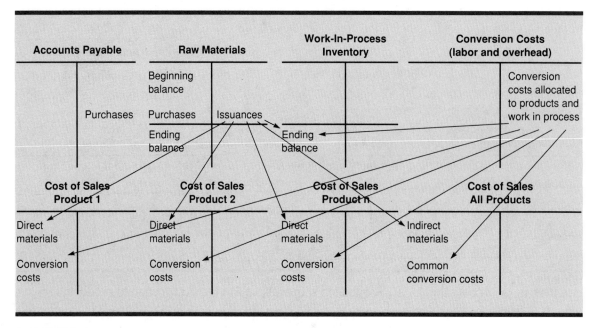

FIGURE 3–4 Accounting for JIT Production with Minimal Inventories and Multiple Products

figure shows, conversion costs of incomplete products may be inventoried along with materials in process in a Work-in-Process Inventory account. The simplified JIT accounting procedures, however, may call for all allocations to the "work-in-process" account to be made only at the end of the period, when the ending balance is determined. In its extreme form, recording of JIT manufacturing accounting cost flows may be delayed until the point of sale. This delayed-recording system has been referred to as a **backflush costing system**.[1] This term suggests cost-allocation procedures that run in the opposite direction from those followed in a conventional manufacturing cost accounting system, which "flushes" costs through the accounting records as work progresses. With a "backflush" system, completion of the manufacturing process (or sale of the finished product) triggers the recording of materials and conversion costs used rather than actual use of the resources.

To illustrate, assume a firm with no beginning inventories experienced the following transactions:

(1) purchased materials costing $16,000
(2) used materials costing $14,000
(3) incurred conversion costs during the period amounting to $32,000
(4) completed goods with a total manufacturing cost of $44,500 ($13,500 of materials and $31,000 of conversion costs)

[1] See George Foster and Charles T. Horngren, "JIT: Cost Accounting and Cost Management Issue," *Management Accounting* (June 1987): 19–25.

(5) Sold goods costing $42,000 ($12,700 of materials and $29,300 of conversion costs).

Conventional cost accounting would record these transactions as follows:

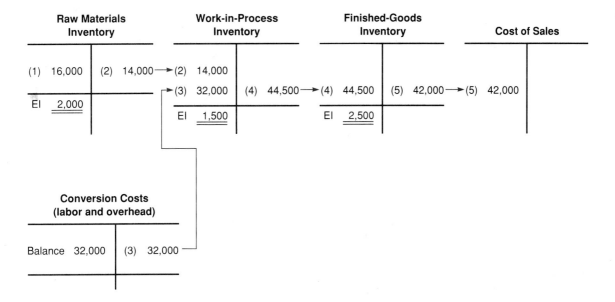

Backflush accounting would record these same transactions as follows:

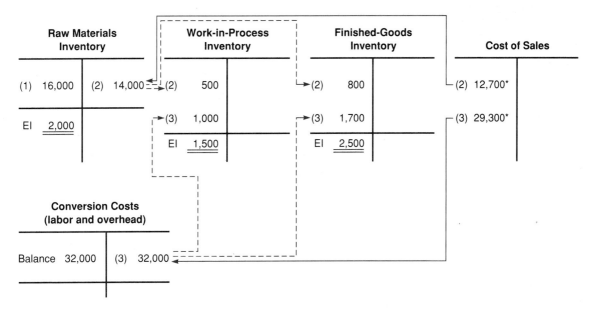

*Cost breakdown into materials and conversion cost elements for instructional purposes

Notice that as we postulated a more and more practical implementation of the JIT objective of minimum inventory, we gradually moved from a system requiring no cost-allocation procedures toward the more conventional one requiring the allocation of costs between costs of sales and inventories. As we suggested earlier, for most firms the complete implementation of the JIT philosophy is an ideal goal rather than a truly achievable one. However, as firms move toward a practicable, achievable level of JIT, the procedures for cost accumulation and allocation will have to be modified to meet the needs of that operating environment. As the discipline of cost accounting adapts itself to new manufacturing environments, it is important for cost accountants to modify conventional cost-accumulation and cost-allocation procedures so they best fit those environments. Stated another way, cost accounting systems should be designed to meet the needs of the operating environment; only then can information generated by the system be most effectively used in controlling operations.

Limitations of JIT Philosophy

Even though many firms are trying to adopt JIT operating philosophies, three significant limitations prevent most systems from achieving desired results. These limitations concern

1. applicability
2. implementation
3. lack of focus.

Applicability. JIT works best in repetitive industries and is not appropriate in a fixed continuous process environment or in plants that produce relatively small quantities of fairly unique products. Plants in continuous process environments with a set product mix are designed to produce large batches of product with minimal inventory. Therefore, the inventory control features of JIT have little to offer this type plant. Job-shop plants, even though they need help controlling inventory and quality, generally cannot benefit from JIT. To implement JIT, job shops must have protective inventory for each unique part of assembly at every work station in order to keep a smooth product flow throughout the process. This protective inventory negates any beneficial results of JIT inventory reductions. Thus, the group of firms that can benefit from JIT is fairly limited.

Implementation. Firms for which JIT is applicable face a formidable implementation process. With JIT, each work station is a link in a logistical chain and is required to coordinate its output with the needs of other elements of the system. Thus, each station or productive resource is dependent on the previous station. Statistical fluctuations in station output almost guarantee disruptions in the system resulting in lost output of completed units and lost sales. Work stoppages due to poor quality materials or machine breakdown or malfunction also can interrupt the operation of the system. Inventory may be decreased drastically, but a loss of output that could have been sold can more than offset any gain from inventory reductions. Due to the requirements of coordination and error-free operation, it may take years to implement a working JIT system.

Focus. The JIT operating philosophy developed by the Japanese treats all resources (or work stations) equally and does not focus on critical elements. There is no attempt to locate a critical resource and focus on that resource. Rather, the Japanese try to focus on everything. If the flow is disrupted, they investigate and correct the cause of the disruption. They try to improve everywhere without first knowing the impact of specific improvements. Also, protective inventory, even if only a small amount, is maintained everywhere. In spite of this protective inventory, disruptions cause shortages at some work stations. Initial benefits achieved after the introduction of JIT are often overshadowed or overwhelmed by losses resulting from shortages within the system. While the JIT methodology works, it takes an incredibly long time and a large financial commitment to achieve a smooth flow everywhere. This is not an efficient way to solve production problems.

Because of these limitations, JIT is not a sufficient solution for international competition problems facing most U.S. manufacturers. We believe the *theory of constraints*, which encompasses some elements of JIT under its synchronous manufacturing principles, is a more general solution. The theory of constraints management philosophy is described in Chapter 24.

Robotics and Cost Accounting Systems

For many years, businesspeople have contended that the high wages paid U.S. workers have been one of the main factors behind U.S. firms' losing their competitive capability in international markets. Closely associated with this contention has been the growing number of defective goods produced by U.S. firms. In recent years, many firms have been trying to solve both of these problems by increasing the use of **robotics** on their production lines.

In a sense, the introduction of the continuously moving conveyor was one of the first uses of robots in manufacturing operations. However, in recent years, the development of electronic and mechanical capabilities has led to the production of machines capable of handling almost any type of repetitive assembly-line operation. Following the pattern we used in dealing with the just-in-time philosophy, we can project robotic operations to the point where a production line is activated by pressing a button, allowing raw material to be fed into a factory at the beginning of processing and finished goods to be turned out at the end of the process, with the movements of the different elements of the robotic equipment in the plant controlled by computers—the ultimate in automation. At such a plant, you push a button, turn out the lights, and wait for the finished products to come out. Such a plant is said to be using a **computer-integrated manufacturing system (CIM).**

Just as with JIT, robotics still has practical limitations. Such equipment is, of course, very expensive. Because many of the benefits are intangible (such as customer satisfaction) and not easily quantified, it may be difficult to justify investing in such equipment by use of conventional **capital budgeting techniques.** Furthermore, inferior raw materials can be fed into the system, and robotic equipment can fail. In either case, extensive spoilage can result unless the system is closely monitored. Also, certain elements of almost any production process require on-the-spot judgment that cannot be programmed into robots.

Nevertheless, U.S. factories are moving toward the use of more robotic equipment. This too will have its effect on the cost accounting systems used by such companies. In Chapter 2, we stated that overhead costs are generally allocated on the basis of some measure of the amount of direct labor costs because the factory is presumed to be kept in operation to allow laborers to produce goods. With a highly automated factory, machine-hours or some other measure of direct input into the manufacturing of the product, such as raw materials, or some activity measure should provide a better cause-and-effect basis for allocating conversion costs than would direct labor costs. If an automated factory is combined with JIT philosophy and activity-based allocations (described in Chapter 23), many more costs may be included in conversion costs that are directly traceable to the goods being produced than is the case in more conventional manufacturing operations. Most would end up as elements of cost of sales for the period in which they are incurred.

Zero Defective Goods

Over the last several years, American firms have produced what some consumers have judged to be inferior products as compared to those produced by other industrialized countries, particularly Japan and Germany. Inferior quality is reflected in inferior performance, in extensive product recalls because of defective parts, and in excessive spoilage as goods are being produced. This has led many U.S. firms to adopt the objective of improving quality and reducing costs by setting a goal of manufacturing **zero defective goods** (reflected, for example, in Ford Motor Company's advertising slogan: "Quality is Job One").

Zero defective goods in another ideal goal. However, it is one that must be given serious consideration as plants move toward greater automation. Robots, for example, can malfunction and produce many defective parts in a short time if they are not carefully monitored. Furthermore, some of the defects in the manufacturing process can be traced to inferior raw materials. Therefore, as firms have tried to move toward the goal of zero defects, they have placed increased emphasis on monitoring the quality of incoming raw materials and on inspecting products on line as they are being produced rather than at the end of individual processes.

While the move toward the goal of zero defects should have little effect on cost-accumulation and cost-allocation procedures, it does suggest a need for measuring effort/achievement relationships insofar as quality goals are concerned. The quality of goods produced must be carefully monitored, and the causes of failures pinpointed if firms are to maintain a reasonable level of quality in their manufacturing processes. Poor quality costs firms customers. Perhaps attention must be given to more specifically identifying the full cost to a firm of a low-quality product. At the same time, a firm cannot ignore the cost of improving quality.

Logically, acceptable quality is a necessary condition for an enterprise's survival. Since quality is not free, though, zero defects may not be desirable. Some measure of need for quality improvement, perhaps in terms of additional market opportunities, would be preferable to either a dramatic decrease in sales due to unacceptable quality or unlimited expenditures in search of perfect quality.

SUMMARY

In this chapter, we considered some of the changes occurring in the manufacturing environment as U.S. firms try to become competitive once again in the international marketplace. The goals of JIT, robotics, and zero defective goods are changing the ways in which manufacturing activities are carried out. Most firms will undertake measures to minimize inventories, to increase the use of robotics, and to improve the quality of production. However, in view of the fact that these goals—taken literally—are ideals, it is safe to say that, in such environments, conventional cost accounting practices will be modified significantly but will not be abandoned. Therefore, in Chapters 4–13, as we develop systems to be used in accumulating and allocating costs to manufactured products, we shall emphasize conventional cost accounting practices. Your understanding of conventional cost accounting procedures will help you deal with any modifications required by manufacturing practices of the future. Some of the changes likely to be associated with cost accounting in automated or synchronous manufacturing environments are also explored in Chapters 22–24.

GLOSSARY OF TERMS INTRODUCED IN THIS CHAPTER

backflush costing system

A system used in accounting for cost flows in which the allocation of costs is delayed until the point when goods are manufactured or sold. Costs are allocated by *backflushing*—the opposite of allocation procedures followed in a conventional manufacturing cost accounting system, which "flushes" costs through the accounting records as work progresses. Completion of the manufacturing process or the sale of finished goods triggers recognition of the allocations of materials and conversion costs used rather than the actual uses of those resources as in a conventional cost system.

capital budgeting techniques

Techniques used in deciding whether a firm should invest in a new project or in new equipment. It involves relating the expected return from the project or equipment to the investment required to acquire it. This term is defined more completely in Chapter 20.

computer-integrated manufacturing (CIM)

Completely automated manufacturing in which all operations are performed by robots controlled by appropriately programmed computers.

economic order quantity (EOQ)

The number of units (order quantity) of a raw material that should be purchased each time an order is placed in order to minimize the total costs of ordering goods and the costs associated with holding and storing them.

just-in-time (JIT)

Just-in-time inventory policy: an operating policy that calls for materials, partially processed goods, and finished goods to be delivered to the locations where they are to be processed or sold, at exactly the time they are needed. In a perfect application, minimal inventories would be held in a JIT environment.

manufacturing cell

A plant layout whereby production equipment is arranged so all pieces of equipment required to produce a particular part are grouped together to minimize the movement of semiprocessed units during the production process. Sometimes called a *minifactory*.

robotics

The use of mechanical robots to perform various operations in the manufacture of products.

zero defective goods

A goal of having zero defective units produced by a manufacturing process. This goal is adopted for the purpose of improving quality, reducing costs, and decreasing manufacturing lead time.

QUESTIONS FOR CLASS DISCUSSION

3—1 How is the system that is used to accumulate and allocate manufacturing costs related to the operating environment? Discuss.

3—2 What is the relationship of a globally competitive market and the movement toward the use of more robotic equipment?

3—3 What is meant by the term *just-in-time*? Discuss.

3—4 What are the advantages and disadvantages of operating with JIT inventory?

3—5 What are the practical limitations of implementing a JIT inventory policy? Discuss.

3—6 How would a JIT inventory operating policy affect the cost-allocation process? Explain.

3—7 What effect is the use of robotic equipment likely to have on cost accounting practices? Discuss.

3—8 How is the use of robotic equipment expected to be related to the quality of goods produced?

3—9 What are some of the problems associated with decisions relative to the use of robotic equipment? Discuss.

3—10 What is the relationship between a slogan such as "Quality is Job One" and being internationally competitive? Discuss.

3—11 What is the cost of quality? How is opportunity cost related to the cost of quality?

EXERCISES

3—12 **Just-in-Time Manufacturing Operations** The Three-Mast Company manufactures fiberglass boats in one large facility. Because of the small size of the company's work force, each laborer is trained to perform several duties. The fiberglass is prepared in the mixing department and then immediately transferred to the molding department before the mixture cools. Since demand for its boats has decreased in the past year, Three-Mast only mixes batches of fiberglass every four or five days. Steel molds are used to shape various sizes of hull from the fiberglass mixture. When the hulls are cooled and rigid they are removed from the molds and stacked until an order requiring their use is received. When an order is received, a worker manually inspects the stock of hulls and removes the required hull(s) with a small movable winch. Each hull size can be finished into several different models, depending on the accessories added to the hull. Except for upholstered seats, which are manufactured in one corner of the plant, all accessory parts are purchased from outside manufacturers. To fill orders promptly, a rather extensive inventory of parts is maintained.

REQUIRED:

1. Make a list of the Three-Mast Company manufacturing operations that do not directly add value to its products.
2. Is a small nonautomated manufacturer such as Three-Mast a good candidate for JIT procedures?
3. What procedures would Three-Mast have to change if they desired to operate in a JIT or modified JIT environment?

3—13   **Just-in-Time Production of a Single Product—Journal Entries** ALS Corporation manufactures one model of laser printer in a strict just-in-time environment. During February, ALS completed the following transactions:

(1) purchased materials in the amount of $92,800
(2) paid factory payroll of $77,300
(3) incurred manufacturing-overhead and operating costs of $110,000
(4) recognized sales revenues of $448,200.

REQUIRED:

1. Prepare summary general journal entries to record February's transactions.
2. Calculate the net income ALS Corporation will report for the month of February.
3. What amount of inventory will ALS show on its balance sheet as of February 28?

3—14   **Modified JIT Production** Rather than implementing a strict JIT production process, Volpar Industries, a manufacturer of steel poles, desires a two-day buffer inventory of parts that feed into a machine that has been identified as a bottleneck, a two-day shipping buffer of finished goods, and a two-day supply of raw materials. The following information is available for the month of May:

Account balances, May 1	
Raw materials inventory	$ 8,400
Work-in-process inventory	16,200
Account balances, May 31	
Raw materials	$ 9,150
Work-in-process inventory	11,300*
Raw material purchases	$293,000
Factory labor	$180,900
Manufacturing overhead	$260,500

*Includes $5,500 of materials and $2,320 of labor.

REQUIRED:

1. Complete the following T accounts using conventional cost accounting procedures.
2. Prepare the appropriate T accounts to reflect these same data using backflush cost accounting procedures.

Raw Materials Inventory	Work-in-Process Inventory	Conversion Costs (labor and overhead)

Accounts Payable	Accrued Factory Payroll Payable	Miscellaneous Credits

Cost of Sales

3–15 Backflush Cost Accounting Toshim Company purchases $32,000 of materials, issues $30,500 of materials to production, incurs $64,200 of conversion costs, completes goods with a total manufacturing cost of $89,700 ($29,000 of materials and $60,700 of conversion costs), and sells goods costing $86,000 for $140,000.

REQUIRED: Assuming Toshim Company had no beginning inventory balances:

1. Prepare the general journal entries required by a conventional cost accounting system to record the transactions for Toshim Company. Post these transactions to T accounts, and indicate the flows of costs with arrows.
2. Prepare the general journal entries required in a backflush cost accounting system to record the transactions for Toshim Company. Post these transactions to T accounts, and indicate the flows of costs with arrows.

PROBLEMS

3–16 **Just-in-Time Production—Multiple Products** Seymour Company manufactures plastic molding for commercial construction projects. Their current product line includes three classes of molding—regular, special, and deluxe—which require different mixtures of raw materials. All moldings contain basic plastic, but the special and deluxe moldings also contain a porous substance, Piffer, that causes paint to adhere to the surface for long periods of time; and the deluxe line contains a sandlike material, Gryon, that simulates wood grain and resilience.

Each class of molding can be finished into three designs—modern, Greek, and arabesque. The Greek finish requires twice the conversion time of the modern finish, while the arabesque finish requires twice the conversion time of the Greek finish.

Results for the year included the following:

Material purchases	
Plastic	$2,643,000
Piffer	900,000
Gryon	675,000
Conversion costs incurred	
Labor	$1,200,000
Manufacturing overhead	4,117,500
Output (square feet)	
Regular	
Modern	1,080,000
Greek	540,000
Arabesque	180,000
Total	1,800,000
Special	
Modern	112,500
Greek	562,500
Arabesque	75,000
Total	750,000
Deluxe	
Modern	180,000
Greek	180,000
Arabesque	90,000
Total	450,000

REQUIRED:

1. Compute the cost of sales for the year for each of Seymour Company's nine products.

2. Prepare summary general journal entries for the year.

3—17 **THOUGHT STIMULATION PROBLEM.** You are sitting around with friends discussing how you would set up a manufacturing company in the United States that would compete in an international market. One of your buddies, John, is extolling the advantages of computer-controlled manufacturing operations, where direct human labor is replaced by computer-monitored robots. Another friend, Melanie, is vociferously defending a labor-intensive arrangement. It is clear that the manufacturing process being discussed could just as easily be organized in a capital-intensive manner as in a labor-intensive arrangement.

REQUIRED:

1. Summarize the advantages and disadvantages of:
   a. A capital-intensive plant as advocated by John.
   b. The labor-intensive plan supported by Melanie.
2. Which position would you support? Why?

Part II

Systems Used to Accumulate Historical Costs

Chapter 4

Job-Order Costing:
Basic Procedures

Learning Objectives

After you have finished your study of this chapter, you should

1. Be able to account for manufacturing costs (direct materials, direct labor, and applied manufacturing overhead) as they are accumulated on job-order sheets and in a work-in-process account.
2. Understand the procedures followed in transferring to finished goods the costs accumulated on completed job orders.
3. Know how to determine unit costs for goods transferred to finished-goods inventory and how to calculate and record the costs of goods sold during a reporting period.

A s explained in Chapter 2, the system used in accounting for the flows of manufacturing costs (direct materials, direct labor, and manufacturing overhead) must accommodate the operating characteristics of the firm. Firms that produce goods in separate segments or lots can most effectively account for the flows of those costs by using what is called *job-order costing*. In this chapter and Chapter 5, we explain and illustrate the procedures followed in accounting for manufacturing costs via such a system.

We describe and illustrate a **normal-cost system**, in which actual direct materials, actual direct labor, and *applied*, rather than actual, overhead costs are accumulated in a work-in-process account as goods are being produced and subsequently transferred from that account to finished goods as jobs are completed. Applied overhead is used because costs for individual job orders generally are needed before the amount of actual overhead costs are known and because of the seasonal variations normally associated with the incurrence of many overhead items. An **actual-cost system** would require the use of actual costs only. **Standard-cost systems**, in which all manufacturing costs per unit are predetermined and applied to goods as they are produced, are also used extensively. Standard costs will be described fully in Chapters 11–13.

In this chapter, we develop cost-accumulation and -allocation procedures for a simple job-order cost system. In Chapter 5, we explain the refinements that should be incorporated into such a system to most effectively meet the objectives of cost accounting described earlier, that is, to provide cost information for financial statements as well as for controlling operations, for planning future operations, and for making day-to-day operating decisions.

A job-order cost system allocates direct materials, direct labor, and applied manufacturing overhead costs generated by the production of goods to individual lots as they are being produced. A **job-order sheet**, such as the one shown in Figure 4–1, is originated for each lot of goods as it enters the manufacturing process. That sheet is then used to accumulate the direct materials, direct labor, and applied manufacturing overhead costs allocated to each lot of goods as it moves through the factory. In explaining the system, we describe and illustrate the procedures followed in accounting for the incurrence and allocation of

1. direct materials costs
2. direct labor costs
3. manufacturing overhead costs
4. work-in-process costs
5. finished-goods costs.

Assuming, for simplicity, a manufacturing operation that uses one cost-accumulation center for all goods being manufactured, the factory in the flowchart of Figure 4–2a is the cost-accumulation center for all

| Quantity and Description | 800 Gadgets | | | | Job No. | 893 |

Quantity and Description 800 Gadgets **Job No.** 893

Date Started 4/5/19XX **Date Completed** 4/15/19XX

For Finished Stock

	Direct Materials			Direct Labor		Manufacturing Overhead
Date	Requisition Number	Amount	Date	Time Card Number	Amount	Amount
4/5/19XX	2486	$360.00	4/6/19XX	L188	$ 16.00	$ 24.00
Totals		$980.00			$620.00	$930.00

Summary

	Amount	Per Unit
Materials	$ 980.00	$1.2250
Labor	620.00	0.7750
Manufacturing overhead applied	930.00	1.1625
Total	$2,530.00	$3.1625

FIGURE 4–1 Job-Order Sheet

costs associated with goods being produced. In Chapter 5, we will explain how the factory cost-accumulation center can be divided into departments to produce more accurate unit-cost data for goods in process and finished goods and to assist management in evaluating the performance of individual departmental managers. To help your understanding, we shall relate the major subtopics in this chapter to elements of the flowchart in Figure 4–2a. Basically, our discussion of the cost-allocation and -accumulation procedures moves from the left side of the flowchart through the cost-accumulation centers to cost of sales on the right side. The numbers in parentheses in the flowchart identify the T-account entries shown in Figure 4–2b to record those parts of the cost-allocation and -accumulation process. Arrows in the flowchart show the directions of cost flows.

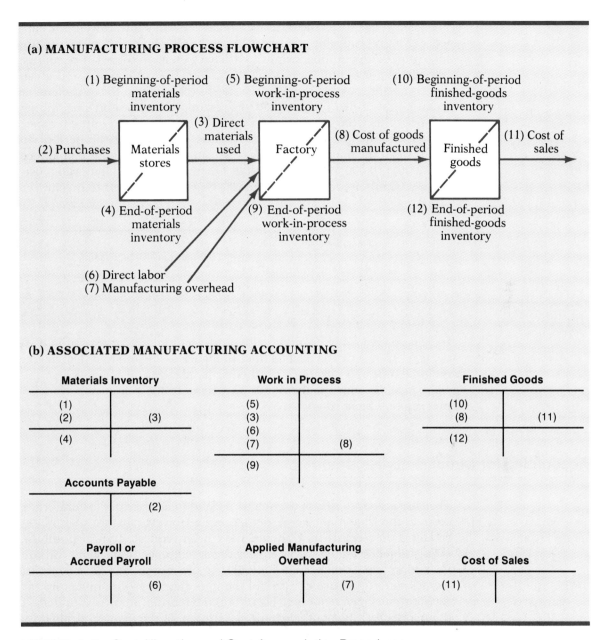

FIGURE 4–2 Cost-Allocation and Cost-Accumulation Procedures

The flowchart uses the cost-accumulation boxes introduced in Chapter 1. The relationships between those boxes and the T accounts are indicated by the numbers shown with each element of cost. T accounts, like the cost-accumulation boxes, have four basic elements; and given any three, the fourth amount can be derived by solving the four-element equation described in Chapter 1. For example, an account's beginning balance, plus what is added during the period, less the ending balance equals the amount removed from the account during the period. To illustrate, if the materials inventory account shows a beginning balance of $1,000, $10,000 worth of materials are purchased, and materials costing $9,000 are used, then materials costing $2,000 are left in inventory:

Materials Inventory

Beginning Balance	1,000	9,000 Issues (used in production)
Purchases	10,000	
Ending Balance	2,000	

It is necessary only to divide the cost-accumulation boxes into two parts, as shown by the dashed lines in Figure 4–2a, and to reflect beginning balance and additions on the left-hand side and issuances on the right side to convert them into T accounts for materials, work in process, and finished goods.

Accounting for Direct Materials Costs

The cost accountant first becomes involved in accounting for materials costs at the time materials are purchased. However, before such materials are purchased, they should have been requested via a **purchase requisition** originated by the materials storeskeeper. Some firms initiate the action to purchase an individual item of material at a *predetermined reorder point* to ensure delivery of the item shortly before inventory for the item has been depleted. Therefore, the reorder point is established at an amount equal to the expected daily use of the item multiplied by the expected number of days for delivery of the goods plus an arbitrarily determined number of units for *safety stock* to take care of possible delays in delivery of orders. As observed in Chapter 3, the JIT inventory philosophy provides no such safety stock cushion. Firms following a JIT or modified JIT philosophy would order materials as orders are received from customers. If materials stores records are maintained on computer, inventory actions can be programmed to initiate purchases automatically by a printout of the items that have been reduced to their predetermined reorder points or the items required to produce goods to fill orders received from customers. Some firms link their computer systems with the supplier's computer system so, as long as a purchase falls within designated norms, the entire purchase procedure can be accomplished electronically. Computer printouts of the acquisition-and-issuance activities also would be generated periodically.

For most firms operating with conventional cost accounting systems, the purchase requisition or computer-generated printout identifying either a low-stock position or materials required for specific customer orders will be delivered to the purchasing department, where it will be subject to scrutiny and, if approved, will cause the origination of a purchase order to be sent to the vendor. The **purchase order** is a formal document signed by the purchasing agent requesting the vendor to ship the listed goods to the purchasing company. The proposed terms of the purchase generally will be reflected on this document. If the vendor, on receipt of the purchase order, considers the proposed terms acceptable and is willing to grant credit to the purchaser, the goods will be shipped. At that time, the vendor also will send an invoice to the purchaser reiterating the terms of sale, including the amount owed to the vendor. This invoice, in effect, is a statement requesting payment for the goods shipped by the vendor.

When the purchaser receives the goods, a **receiving report** indicating the quantity of the goods received, along with notations regarding any damage to the goods, will be prepared by the receiving department of the purchasing company, validating the receipt of the goods. The individual charged with supervising the receipts of materials, generally called a *receiving clerk*, examines the materials to see they meet both the quantitative and qualitative requirements of the purchaser. A blind copy of the purchase order (one listing the items purchased but omitting the quantities ordered) generally will be provided to the receiving department to help identify goods received. The quantities ordered are omitted to force the receiving department to count the goods received and note the counts on the receiving report. Of course, the goods also should be examined to determine whether they meet the purchaser's qualitative standards. Since JIT firms rely on agreements with suppliers, rather than clerk checks, for quality assurance, a firm with a JIT operating policy might not employ a receiving clerk or generate a receiving report.

The purchasing department generally will assemble and forward a packet containing the purchase order, the purchase invoice, and the receiving report, if there is one, to the accounting department. After the accounting department has examined the packet and concluded that the purchase transaction has been appropriately carried out, it will record the cost of materials purchased by making the following kind of journal entry:

Materials inventory (stores)	XX	
Accounts payable		XX

Once the accounting department has approved the purchase, the packet, along with a voucher showing the various required approvals, will be forwarded to the cashier for payment.

In the event that materials have to be returned to the vendor, a **debit memo** will be prepared stating that the vendor's payable account is being debited (charged) for the return or for the allowance to be made for damaged goods. The following kind of entry would be made to record the return of the materials:

Accounts payable	XX	
Materials inventory (stores)		XX

If the firm desires to accumulate separately the amount of returns and allowances, a contra account entitled *materials returns and allowances* may be credited rather than materials inventory. (This account is equivalent to the purchases-returns-and-allowances account used by merchandising firms.) The materials-return-and-allowances account will be closed to materials inventory at the end of each reporting period.

As you can see from Figure 4–2, the first step in accounting for the allocation and accumulation of direct materials costs included in finished products occurs when materials are issued into process. Direct materials are charged to job orders and to work in process by use of a **materials requisition form** similar to that shown in Figure 4–3 or by

Job No. 893			Requisition No. 2486	
Authorized by James Done			Date 4/5/19XX	
Description	**Quantity Issued**	**Unit Cost**	**Amount**	
Steel Sheets 40-guage	1,200 lb	$.30	$360	
Total Issued			$360	
Issued by I. M. Stores			Received by B. J. Foreman	

FIGURE 4–3 Materials Requisition Form

use of a **bill of materials** setting out the amounts of various materials to be used for the job. The requisition in the figure shows the quantity, the type, and the cost of materials issued to the factory for use on Job No. 893. The requisition document also authorizes the storeskeeper to release the materials to the factory. It transfers accountability for the materials from the storeskeeper to the foreman of the processing department. The amount shown on the materials requisition of Figure 4–3 is posted on the job-order sheet of Figure 4–1, thus showing that it was used on Job No. 893. Other direct materials requisitions also will have been issued in support of direct materials issuances for other job orders currently in process. The following kind of journal entry is used to record the amount of direct materials charged to all jobs during an operating period:

Work in process	**XX**	
Materials inventory (stores)		**XX**

Materials Inventory	Work in Process
XX	XX

The dollar amount shown on the materials requisition depends on the cost flow assumption the firm is using in accounting for materials costs. Generally accepted accounting practices permit the use of either (1) first-in, first-out method, (2) average method, (3) last-in, first-out method, or (4) selected other methods in accounting for the flows of materials costs. To illustrate, if we assume the following regarding the purchases and issuances of 40-gauge steel sheets during a reporting period,

Beginning-of-period inventory: 15,000 lb @ $.30		$4,500
4/2/XX Purchases: 5,000 lb @ $.35		$1,750
4/5/XX Issuance to Job 893: 1,200 lb		

then the amount that should be entered on the materials issuance requisition would be one of the following:

Based on first-in, first-out cost flow:
Issuance to Job 893: 1,200 lb @ $.30 = $360.00
Based on last-in, first-out cost flow:
Issuance to Job 893: 1,200 lb @ $.35 = $420.00
Based on average cost flow:
Issuance to Job 893: 1,200 lb @ ($4,500 + $1,750)/20,000 lb = $.3125
  = $375.00

The amount to be shown on the requisition ranges from $360 to $420, depending on the cost flow assumption being used. In Figure 4–3, we used the first-in, first-out method to record the issuance on Requisition No. 2486.

Direct materials will be returned from work in process to materials inventory (stores) if they are not needed in the manufacture of a particular job, in which case a **materials return form** similar to the one shown in Figure 4–4 will be originated. The following entry would be made to record such returns:

Materials inventory (stores)	30	
Work in process		30

Materials Inventory		Work in Process	
30			30

Some materials may be requisitioned from materials inventory for use in keeping the factory in operation rather than for use on any specific job. Such things as lubricating oils and cleaning compounds constitute indirect materials costs and are included as part of manufacturing overhead. Often, minute quantities of materials such as glue and nails that are used on particular jobs also are included in indirect materials costs, either because of custom or because there is no cost–benefit advantage to including these as direct materials costs. A requisition for materials to be used for such purposes would require the following entry:

Manufacturing overhead	XX	
Materials inventory (stores)		XX

Materials Inventory		Manufacturing Overhead	
	XX	XX	

Job No. 891			Return No. 52
Returned by B. J. Foreman			Date 4/10/19XX

Description	Quantity Returned	Unit Price	Amount
Steel sheets 40-guage	100 lbs.	.30	$30.00
Total returned			$30.00
Returned by B. J. Foreman		Received by	I. M. Stores

FIGURE 4–4   Materials Return Form

Materials purchased in a particular period or in previous periods but not issued during the period constitute the end-of-period materials inventory, and the costs assigned to such goods appear on the balance sheet, along with the costs of other inventories.

The technologically advanced information systems that generate very little (or no) paper trails have not abandoned the controls discussed here. The process is speeded up dramatically, but similar checks and verifications are performed. However, because the amounts recorded in the journal entries are more aggregated, they are fewer in number.

Accounting for Direct Labor Costs

Factory employees typically are hired by the personnel department to meet the requirements expressed by the factory foremen and approved by the factory superintendent. Such employees generally are paid on an hourly basis, with the time determined by data shown on time cards maintained in the factory. The typical older factory arrangement calls for two racks of time cards, with a time clock between the two racks, at an entrance to the factory. When an employee enters the factory, he or she takes his or her time card from the rack nearer the outside of the factory, punches in at the clock, and places the card in the rack on the factory side of the clock. At the end of the day, the employee reverses this process by picking up the time card from the rack on the factory side of the time clock, punching out, and putting the card in the rack on the other side of the clock. Modern factory arrangements may permit workers to dispense with punching in and out on a time clock and allow them to keep their own logs of time worked. Whatever method is used to record time spent at the factory, at the end of each week or pay period, the time cards or other records of time worked are collected and the data on them accumulated for the purpose of preparing employee payroll checks. The following kind of entry should be made to record the payroll obligation:

Factory payroll	XX	
Factory payroll payable (accrued payroll)		XX
Payroll taxes payable		XX

The payroll account in the preceding entry is sometimes characterized as a *clearing* account. It is used to accumulate temporarily all labor costs that subsequently will be allocated to work in process and manufacturing overhead, as explained in the following paragraphs. As payroll checks are issued, the following kind of entry will be made:

Factory payroll payable (accrued payroll)	XX	
Cash		XX

Employees working on specific job orders may be expected to use **job time cards**, such as the one in Figure 4–5, to record and accumulate the amount of time spent on each job. As an employee begins work on a particular lot of goods (job order), he or she will enter on a time card the job number and insert the card in a clock to record the "time started" on the particular job or merely note manually the time work commenced. When the employee finishes work on that particular job, that time card will be either punched out or marked in the "time stopped" column to show the time work was finished. Typically, the employee then punches in on a time card with another job number (or notes the time, if a time clock is not being used) when beginning work on a new lot of goods. In all cases, the elapsed time shown on the job time card multiplied by the hourly rate of pay equals the amount of direct labor cost that should be charged to the job. The pertinent data from the job time card in Figure 4–5 is posted to the job-order sheet in Figure 4–1. Time cards will have been prepared in support of other entries in the direct labor section of each job-order sheet. The total amount shown on all job time cards for each reporting period is recorded as follows:

Work in process	XX
Factory payroll	XX

Work in Process	Factory Payroll
XX	XX

Employee Name	John Q. Worker		No.	L188
Employee No.	625		Date	4/6/19XX
Description of Work	Machine Operator		Job No.	893
Department	1			

Time Started	Time Stopped	Hours Worked	Hourly Rate	Cost
8:00	10:00	2	$8	$16.00
Total				$16.00
Approved by _____				

FIGURE 4–5 Job Time Card

Employees who do not work directly on the production line will not have their time accounted for on job time cards. Support personnel such as maintenance workers and janitorial employees perform work necessary to keep the factory in operation but do not work directly on the products being produced. Also, at times, certain direct laborers will not be assigned to specific jobs. The amounts paid for such services are characterized as *indirect labor costs*, a part of manufacturing overhead. The kind of entry to record these costs is:

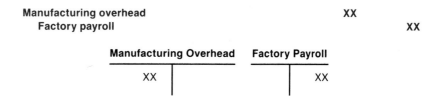

| Manufacturing overhead | XX | |
| Factory payroll | | XX |

Manufacturing Overhead	Factory Payroll
XX			XX

It is important to observe that, after the preceding entries, all factory payroll costs will have been distributed either to work in process or to manufacturing overhead.

Accounting for Manufacturing-Overhead Costs

As period (time-related) costs, most manufacturing-overhead costs cannot be directly assigned to specific lots of goods being manufactured as are direct materials and direct labor costs. In recognition of that fact, we usually allocate manufacturing overhead to job orders on the basis of a predetermined manufacturing-overhead application rate based on one or both of the direct elements of product costs (direct materials and direct labor), or on some other activity measure, such as machine-hours. As pointed out in Chapter 2, the allocation of these costs to products converts time-based (period) manufacturing costs into product costs. However, because the overhead amounts applied to job orders are based on a predetermined (estimated) application rate, they are an estimate of the amount of overhead costs to be allocated to each job order and to work in process.

Determination of Predetermined Manufacturing-Overhead Application Rates

A manufacturing-overhead application rate may be based on the historical relationship between manufacturing overhead and an appropriate activity base related to the incurrence of overhead (such as direct-labor hours, direct-labor cost, or machine-hours), or it can be based on an estimate, made prior to the beginning of a period, of what such costs and activity levels for the coming period are expected to be. In either event, consideration must be given to the expected level of operations to arrive at a reasonably accurate overhead application rate.

If there is no historical record to use in calculating the application rate, or if the volume of operations for the next period is expected to be significantly different from any past period, one can devise a reasonable overhead cost application rate by relating estimated manufacturing overhead costs to the anticipated amount of a selected activity base such as direct-labor costs, direct-labor hours, or machine-hours. This is accomplished through use of a **flexible** manufacturing-overhead **budget**, such as the one shown in Figure 4–6. A flexible manufacturing-overhead budget shows the amounts of manufacturing overhead expected to be incurred over a period of time (generally one year) at different levels of activity, measured in terms of some activity base such as direct-labor hours, direct-labor costs, or machine-hours. In Figure 4–6, we use direct-labor costs as the activity base and show a budget for four different levels of operation. Notice that the aggregate amount of fixed overhead costs is expected to remain the same regardless of the level of operations, while the total variable overhead costs is expected to vary directly with changes in the level of operations. If historical data are used, they typically are arranged in the same manner.

After a flexible budget has been prepared, management must decide, before an overhead application rate is established, the level of operations they expect to achieve during the ensuing year. For a level of operations likely to be $64,000 of direct labor cost for the next year (8,000 direct labor hours), the flexible budget of Figure 4–6 shows that the manufacturing-overhead application rate should be 150% of direct labor cost. That then becomes the factory-overhead application rate to be used during the next reporting period. Had management estimated

Illustration Company

	Possible Operating Levels			
Direct labor hours	**7,000**	**8,000**	**9,000**	**10,000**
Estimated direct labor costs	$56,000	$64,000	$72,000	$80,000
Estimated manufacturing overhead				
Variable overhead*	$17,500	$20,000	$22,500	$25,000
Fixed overhead	76,000	76,000	76,000	76,000
Total overhead	$93,500	$96,000	$98,500	$101,000
Manufacturing-overhead application rate (based on direct labor costs, nearest whole percent)	167%	150%	137%	126%

*$2.50 per direct labor hour, or 31.25% of direct labor costs

FIGURE 4–6   Flexible Manufacturing-Overhead Budget

that the firm would operate at a $72,000 direct-labor level, the firm would have used an overhead application rate of 137%.

Later, we will explain how helpful it can be to calculate separate variable and fixed manufacturing-overhead application rates as well as the total-overhead application rate. At the $64,000 level for direct labor in our illustration, the variable rate would be 31.25% and the fixed rate would be 118.75%. Following from the definition and behavior of variable and fixed costs, the variable rate would be the same for all levels of activity (31.25%), but the fixed rate would vary with the activity level chosen.

Applying Overhead Costs to Work in Process

After an overhead application rate has been determined, one records the application of manufacturing overhead to work in process and to individual job orders based on that rate. For example, if the direct labor charged to work in process during the reporting period amounts to $20,000 and the manufacturing-overhead application rate is 150%, we would record the application of manufacturing overhead as follows:

Work in process	30,000	
Applied manufacturing overhead		30,000

Manufacturing Overhead (Factory Overhead Control)	Applied Manufacturing Overhead	Work in Process
	30,000	30,000

No attention is given to the amount of actual overhead incurred in recording the amount of overhead charged to work in process. As we explain later, the actual overhead incurred is accumulated in a separate manufacturing-overhead account, frequently called *factory overhead control* because a subsidiary ledger or worksheet (or computer file) is necessary to keep track of the separate categories of overhead items.

The amount of manufacturing overhead applied to each job order also will equal 150% of the direct labor charged to that job. In Figure 4–1, observe that the amount entered in the factory-overhead part of the job-order sheet equals 150% of the direct labor charged to that job order. The same application rate will be used for all job orders being processed during the reporting period.

While manufacturing-overhead costs are being applied to job orders and to work in process as just described, actual overhead costs will be accumulating in a manufacturing-overhead account as they are incurred. Included will be such items as indirect materials and indirect labor, plus the costs incurred for insurance, property taxes, depreciation, the employer's share of payroll taxes, and so forth, that are necessary to keep the factory in operation but that cannot be allocated directly to job orders. The composite of all entries used to record actual manufacturing overhead costs during a reporting period would take the following form:

Manufacturing overhead	**XX**	
Factory payroll		**XX**
Materials inventory		**XX**
Accumulated depreciation		**XX**
Accounts payable		**XX**

At the end of each reporting period, the credit balance shown in the applied manufacturing-overhead account will be closed against the debit balance shown in the manufacturing-overhead account. The difference between these two figures is characterized as either *underapplied or overapplied overhead*. If the actual manufacturing overhead amounts to $32,000, for example, the entry to close these two accounts at the end of the reporting period would be:

Applied manufacturing overhead	**30,000**	
Underapplied or overapplied manufacturing overhead	**2,000**	
Manufacturing overhead		**32,000**

Manufacturing Overhead		Applied Manufacturing Overhead	
Balance 32,000			Balance 30,000
	(C-1) 32,000	(C-1) 30,000	

Underapplied or Overapplied Manufacturing Overhead		Cost of Sales	
(C-1) 2,000		(C-2) 2,000	
	(C-2) 2,000		

When the amount of underapplied or overapplied overhead is not material, it will be closed to cost of sales at the end of each period, as illustrated in the T accounts above. However, as we will see in Chapter 5, when the amount in the underapplied or overapplied manufacturing-overhead account is material, it should be allocated on a pro-rata basis to work in process, finished goods, and cost of sales.

Accounting for Work-in-Process Costs

Since all manufacturing costs (direct materials, direct labor, and applied manufacturing overhead) are debited to work in process as they are entered on the individual job-order sheets, the total of such costs must later be allocated either to cost of goods manufactured or to end-of-period work-in-process inventory (see Figure 4–2a). Job-order costing procedures require that all costs accumulated on completed job orders be transferred to finished-goods inventory. The amount transferred is also called *cost of goods manufactured* (see Figure 4–2a). The following kind of entry is used to transfer the costs accumulated on the finished job orders to finished goods:

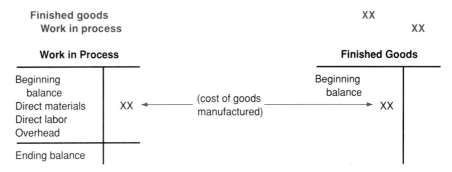

After the entry has been recorded, the balance left in the work in process account will equal the sum of the costs shown on the job-order sheets for uncompleted jobs. Those job-order sheets then constitute the subsidiary ledger supporting the work-in-process ending inventory that will appear on the balance sheet.

Accounting for Finished-Goods Costs

The costs associated with completed job orders ultimately must be allocated between the end-of-period finished-goods inventory and cost of goods sold. As job orders are completed, the cost per unit of finished product will be calculated by dividing the accumulated costs on each job-order sheet by the number of units included in the job lot (see "Summary" in Figure 4–1). That unit cost is then attached to each of the units completed for the purpose of accounting for the flows of costs through finished goods to cost of sales.

The amount to be transferred to cost of sales for units sold will depend on the cost flow assumption used in accounting for finished-goods inventory. Generally accepted accounting practices permit accountants to use any one of the cost flow assumptions described earlier in determining the amounts to be transferred from finished goods to cost of goods sold. To illustrate, we shall assume (1) that the company producing the gadgets whose costs are reflected on Job 893 (see Figure 4–1) has a beginning-of-period finished-goods inventory of 4,000 gadgets at a cost of $3 per unit, and (2) that shortly after Job 893 was completed,

500 gadgets were sold at a price of $5 per gadget. If the firm uses the first-in, first-out method, the cost of sales entry would be recorded as follows:

Cost of sales	1,500	
Finished goods (500 units @ $3 per unit)		1,500

Finished Goods				Cost of Sales	
Beginning balance	12,000				
Cost of goods manufactured	2,530	1,500		1,500	
Ending balance	13,030				

If the last-in, first-out method is used, the entry would be recorded as follows:

Cost of sales	1,581.25	
Finished goods (500 units @ $3.1625)		1,581.25

Finished goods				Cost of Sales	
Begining balance	12,000				
Cost of goods manufactured	2,530	1,581.25		1,581.25	
Ending balance	12,948.75				

If the average method is used, the entry would be recorded as follows:

Cost of sales	1,513.50	
Finished goods (500 units @ $3.027)*		1,513.50

*Cost per unit:
  4,000 @ $3.00 per unit = $12,000
    800 @ $3.1625 per unit =   2,530
                      $14,530
$14,530 ÷ 4,800 = $3.027 per unit

Finished Goods				Cost of Sales	
Beginning balance	12,000				
Cost of goods manufactured	2,530	1,513.50		1,513.50	
Ending balance	13,016.50				

The finished-goods ending-inventory balance also is affected by the cost flow assumption used in calculating cost of sales, because it equals the amount of costs left after the amount transferred to cost of sales has been removed.

Illustrative Problem

The Able Company manufactures a variety of products. It uses a job-order costing system to account for its operations. The balance sheet for the company as of 12/31/19X0 is as follows:

Able Company
BALANCE SHEET
12/31/19X0

Assets		
Cash		$ 34,000
Accounts receivable	$20,000	
Allowance for bad debts	1,000	19,000
Materials inventory		25,000
Work-in-process inventory*		15,000
Finished-goods inventory**		20,000
Equipment	$80,000	
Accumulated depreciation	7,200	72,800
Land		20,000
Total		$205,800
Liabilities and Owners' Equity		
Accounts payable		$ 35,000
Notes payable		10,000
Mortgage payable		45,000
Owners' equity		115,800
Total		$205,800

*Job 502: direct materials $9,000; direct labor $4,000; manufacturing overhead $2,000. Job is for manufacture of 10,000 units of Product A.

**Finished-goods inventory includes:

1,000 units of Product A @ $9 per unit =	$ 9,000
100 units of Product B @ $80 per unit =	8,000
500 units of Product C @ $6 per unit =	3,000
	$20,000

The following transactions occur during the month of January 19X1:

(1) Raw materials costing $80,000 are purchased on account. A perpetual-inventory system is used.

(2) Job 503 for 1,000 units of product B, Job 504 for 5,000 units of product C, and Job 505 for 20,000 units of product D are begun.

(3) Raw materials issued into process amount to $90,000, used as follows: Job 502, $38,000; Job 503, $40,000; Job 504, $7,000; Job 505, $5,000.

(4) Direct labor of $60,000 for the month is accrued. Payroll taxes amounting to $4,000 were deducted from amounts due to employees. The employer's payroll tax expense amounted to $1,200. The direct labor was charged as follows: Job 502, $26,000; Job 503, $30,000; Job 504, $3,000; Job 505, $1,000.

(5) Manufacturing overhead costs of $23,000 are incurred and paid.

(6) Depreciation on equipment (all manufacturing) should be provided on the basis of assumed life of 10 years and an estimated salvage value of $8,000.

(7) Manufacturing overhead associated with jobs in process is estimated to be approximately 50% of direct-labor costs. Manufacturing overhead should be applied on that basis to all production for the period. The difference between manufacturing overhead applied and actual manufacturing overhead incurred should be reflected on the income statement.

(8) Jobs 502 and 503 are completed during January and transferred to finished goods. The following job orders remain in process at the end of the month:

	Direct Materials	Direct Labor	Applied Manufacturing Overhead Expense	Total
Job 504	$ 7,000	$3,000	$1,500	$11,500
Job 505	5,000	1,000	500	6,500
Totals	$12,000	$4,000	$2,000	$18,000

(9) Sales for the month are $70,000. They include 1,200 units of product A and 500 units of product B. Able uses the first-in, first-out method in accounting for the cost of units sold.

REQUIRED:

a. Prepare general journal entries to record the transactions for the month of January.

b. Record the transactions for the month of January in the T accounts and job-order sheets.

c. Calculate the cost of goods manufactured during the month of January for the Able Company.

Solution to Illustrative Problem

a. Journal Entries:

(1)	**Materials inventory**	80,000	
	Accounts payable		80,000
(2)	No entry required		
(3)	**Work in process**	90,000	
	Materials inventory		90,000
	(502, $38,000; 503, $40,000; 504, $7,000;		
	505, $5,000)		
(4)	**Payroll**	60,000	
	Payroll payable (accrued payroll)		56,000
	Payroll taxes payable		4,000

The payroll account facilitates allocation of total factory payroll to work in process (direct labor) and overhead (indirect labor). Since there was no indirect labor, the $60,000 could have been debited directly to work in process. See entry 4a.

(4a)	Work in process	60,000	
	Payroll		60,000
	(502, $26,000; 503, $30,000; 504, $3,000; 505, $1,000)		
(4b)	Manufacturing overhead	1,200	
	Payroll taxes payable		1,200
(5)	Manufacturing overhead	23,000	
	Cash		23,000
(6)	Manufacturing overhead	7,200	
	Accumulated depreciation		7,200
	[($80,000 − $8,000)/10]		
(7a)	Work in process	30,000	
	Applied manufacturing overhead		30,000
	(502, $13,000; 503, $15,000; 504, $1,500; 505, $500)		
(7b)	Underapplied or overapplied overhead	31,400	
	Manufacturing overhead		31,400
	(to close the manufacturing-overhead account)		
(7c)	Applied manufacturing overhead	30,000	
	Underapplied or overapplied overhead		30,000
	(to close the applied manufacturing-overhead account)		
(7d)	Cost of sales	1,400	
	Underapplied or overapplied overhead		1,400
	(to close the underapplied or overapplied overhead to cost of sales)		
(8)	Finished goods	177,000	
	Work in process		177,000
(9a)	Accounts receivable	70,000	
	Sales		70,000
(9b)	Cost of sales	52,840	
	Finished goods		52,840

A:	1,000 @ $9	=	$ 9,000	
	200 @ $9.20	=	1,840	$10,840
B:	100 @ $80	=	$ 8,000	
	400 @ $85	=	34,000	42,000
	Total			$52,840

b. **Manufacturing cost-accumulation and -allocation accounts:**

Materials Inventory				Work in Process			
Balance	25,000	(3)	90,000	Balance	15,000	(8)	177,000
(1)	80,000			(3)	90,000		
				(4a)	60,000		
				(7a)	30,000		
	15,000				18,000		

Finished Goods		
Balance 20,000	(9b)	52,840
(8) 177,000		
144,160		

Cost of Sales		
(7d) 1,400		
(9b) 52,840		
54,240		

Payroll		
(4) 60,000	(4a)	60,000

Manufacturing Overhead		
(4b) 1,200	(7b)	31,400
(5) 23,000		
(6) 7,200		

Underapplied or Overapplied Overhead		
(7b) 31,400	(7c)	30,000
	(7d)	1,400

Applied Manufacturing Overhead		
(7c) 30,000	(7a)	30,000

Other accounts:

Cash		
Balance 34,000	(5)	23,000
11,000		

Accounts Receivable		
Balance 20,000		
(9a) 70,000		
90,000		

Allowance for Bad Debts	
	Balance 1,000

Equipment	
Balance 80,000	

Accumulated Depreciation	
	Balance 7,200
	(6) 7,200
	14,400

Land	
Balance 20,000	

Accounts Payable	
	Balance 35,000
	(1) 80,000
	115,000

Notes Payable	
	Balance 10,000

Payroll Taxes Payable			Payroll Payable		
	(4)	4,000		(4)	56,000
	(4b)	1,200			
		5,200			56,000

Mortgage Payable		
	Balance	45,000

Owners' Equity			Sales		
	Balance	115,800		(9a)	70,000
					70,000

Work-in-Process Subsidiary Ledger:

Jobs Completed

Job 502   10,000 units A

	Materials		Labor		Overhead		Total
Balance	$ 9,000		$ 4,000		$ 2,000		$15,000
	(3) 38,000		(4a) 26,000		(7a) 13,000		77,000
	Total						$92,000
	Per Unit						$9.20

(2) Job 503   1,000 units B

	Materials		Labor		Overhead		Total
	(3) $40,000		(4a) $30,000		(7a) $15,000		$85,000
	Total						$85,000
	Per Unit						$85.00

Ending Inventory

(2) Job 504   5,000 units C

	Materials		Labor		Overhead		Total
	(3) $7,000		(4a) $3,000		(7a) $1,500		$11,500

(2) Job 505   20,000 units D

	Materials		Labor		Overhead		Total
	(3) $5,000		(4a) $1,000		(7a) $ 500		$ 6,500

Finished-Goods Subsidiary Ledger

Product A

Balance 1,000 @ $9 =		$ 9,000
(8) + 10,000 @ $9.20 =		92,000
Balance		$101,000
(9b) − 1,000 @ $9 =	9,000	
− 200 @ $9.20 =	1,840	10,840
Balance		$90,160

Product B

Balance 100 @ $80 =		$ 8,000
(8) + 1,000 @ $85 =		85,000
Balance		$93,000
(9b) − 100 @ $80 =	8,000	
− 400 @ $85 =	34,000	42,000
Balance		$51,000

Product C

Balance 500 @ $6 =	$ 3,000

c. Cost of goods manufactured:

Cost of Goods Manufactured

Job 502	$92,000
Job 503	85,000
Total	$177,000

Cost of Sales

Product A	$10,840*
Product B	42,000*
Total (unadjusted)	$52,840
Adjustment for underapplied overhead	1,400
Total	$54,240

Alternate Calculation of Cost of Sales

Beginning Finished-Goods Inventory	$ 20,000
Add: Cost of Goods Manufactured	177,000
Cost of Goods Available for Sale	$197,000
Less: Ending Finished-Goods Inventory	144,160**
Cost of Sales (unadjusted)	$ 52,840
Adjustment for Underapplied Overhead	1,400
Cost of Sales (adjusted)	$54,240

*See explication of journal entry 9b.
**$90,160 + $51,000 + $3,000 = $144,160

SUMMARY

In this chapter, we developed the basic framework for a job-order costing system. We explained the procedures followed in accounting for the allocation and accumulation of costs in materials, work-in-process, finished-goods, and cost-of-sales accounts. We explained how direct materials costs, direct labor costs, and applied manufacturing-overhead costs are accumulated on job-order sheets as those costs are allocated to work in process. Then we showed how the costs accumulated on completed job orders are transferred into finished goods as the cost of goods manufactured for the period. We also demonstrated how the costs associated with units sold are transferred from finished goods to cost of sales.

We explained how direct materials requisition forms and job time cards customarily are used in allocating those costs to the job-order sheets and to the work-in-process account. We noted that such costs can be allocated to job orders in that way because direct materials and direct labor are product costs that can be related directly to specific job orders.

Next, we explained how to develop a manufacturing-overhead application rate from flexible budget data for use in allocating manufacturing-overhead costs to individual job orders and work in process. We also showed how actual manufacturing-overhead costs for each reporting period are matched against applied manufacturing-overhead costs to determine the underapplied or overapplied amount of overhead for the period. We observed that when immaterial, the underapplied or over-applied manufacturing overhead is closed directly to cost of sales.

We explained how costs accumulated in the work-in-process account are transferred to finished goods based on amounts shown on the job-order sheets for completed job orders. And we showed how the amount to be transferred from finished goods to cost of sales is determined by reference to the cost assigned to the individual units of finished goods sold. The dollar amount for that transfer was shown to be dependent on the cost flow assumption (first-in, first-out; average; or last-in, first-out) that a firm follows in its allocation of finished-goods costs. Finally, we demonstrated the procedures developed in the chapter in an illustrative problem.

GLOSSARY OF TERMS INTRODUCED IN THIS CHAPTER

actual-cost system   A cost system that accumulates and allocates actual manufacturing costs (direct materials, direct labor, and manufacturing overhead) to the units of goods produced. (Unit costs can't be determined until the end of a period, when total costs and production are known.)

bill of materials

A document listing all materials that should be used in manufacturing the units included in a job order; takes the place of a materials requisition.

debit memo

A document stating that the account payable to a vendor is being debited for the return of merchandise or for the amount of an allowance to be made for damaged goods.

flexible budget

A budget showing the amounts of costs (and/or revenues) expected to be incurred or realized over a period of time at different levels of activity (measured in terms of some activity base such as direct labor hours, direct labor costs, or machine-hours). A *flexible manufacturing-overhead budget* gives the projected costs of various manufacturing overhead items at different levels of activity.

job-order sheet

A form used to accumulate the manufacturing costs (direct materials, direct labor, and applied manufacturing overhead) allocated to a specific lot of goods as it is being produced.

job time card

A form used to accumulate the amount of time that an employee spends working on a particular job on a specified day.

materials requisition form

A form used to indicate the amount and dollar value of materials issued from materials inventory into the manufacturing process. It is a source document for recording the transfer of materials to production.

materials return form

A form used to reflect the amount and dollar values of materials returned from the factory to materials inventory.

normal-cost system

A cost system in which actual direct materials, actual direct labor, and applied, rather than actual, overhead costs are accumulated and allocated to units produced.

purchase order

Traditionally, a formal document signed by a purchasing agent and addressed to a vendor (supplier) requesting the vendor to ship the listed goods to the purchasing company. Purchase orders may be automatically generated by computer and electronically transmitted to vendors.

purchase requisition

A document generally originated by the materials storekeeper and forwarded to the purchasing department requesting that specified materials be purchased for materials inventory. If inventory records are computerized, a computer program may have the responsibility for initiating purchase orders.

receiving report

A document prepared by a person in the receiving department indicating the quantities of goods received, along with notations regarding any damage to the goods when they came into the possession of the purchasing company. (With certain approved vendors, goods may not be inspected upon receipt and a receiving report would not be completed.)

standard-cost system

A cost-accumulation and cost-allocation system in which manufacturing costs per unit are predetermined and applied to goods as they are produced. Actual costs also are accumulated and compared to standard costs to determine variances.

QUESTIONS FOR CLASS DISCUSSION

4–1 Under what circumstances is a manufacturing firm likely to use a job-order costing system? Explain.

4–2 What function does the job-order sheet perform in a job-order costing system?

4–3 What are the primary cost-accumulation T accounts used in a job-order costing system? How do these T accounts relate to the three cost-accumulation boxes used in this chapter?

4–4 What document is used to initiate a purchase of materials?

4–5 What document does a firm use to validate the quantity and quality of goods received in connection with a purchase of materials?

4–6 What are the three documents typically brought together to support the payment of an amount owed for the purchase of materials?

4–7 What document is used to support the transfer of direct materials from materials inventory to work in process?

4–8 What three cost flow assumptions may be used in determining the costs to be assigned to goods transferred from materials inventory to work in process? Explain.

4–9 How are direct labor costs allocated to individual job orders? Explain.

4–10 Are manufacturing overhead costs allocated to individual job orders on the same basis as are direct materials and direct labor? Explain.

4–11 How does a firm derive a manufacturing-overhead application rate? Explain.

4–12 What is the function of the flexible budget in the determination of a manufacturing-overhead application rate? What is meant by the term *underapplied or overapplied overhead?* What is the disposition of the balance in that account?

4–13 What documents constitute the supporting subsidiary ledger for work in process when using a job-order costing system?

4–14 What documents support the costs assigned to goods transferred from work in process to finished goods? What is the amount so transferred called?

4–15 What are the two entries typically required at the time finished units are sold? Illustrate the entries.

EXERCISES

4–16 **Materials** Rearrange the following documents (or electronic transactions) in the order in which they logically should occur:

receiving report
debit memo
requisition order
purchase order
material return
invoice

4–17 **Materials** During the month of June, Tilmore Corporation purchased raw materials for $36,000 and issued $33,000 to work in process. They had $5,000 of raw materials on hand on June 30.

REQUIRED: What was the balance of raw materials on June 1?

4–18 **Materials** Blackman Manufacturing Company began operations on January 1. During the month of October, $84,000 of materials were purchased, $6,000 of which were of inferior quality and had to be returned to the supplier. Materials requisitions in the amount of $65,000 were issued for use on jobs begun during the period. Indirect materials in the amount of $4,000 were charged to the manufacturing overhead account. An inventory of materials on October 31 revealed a balance on hand of $11,000.

REQUIRED:

1. Post the materials cost data for Blackman Manufacturing Company to a materials inventory T account.
2. Is the T account from requirement 1 complete (logically consistent)? If not, explain any amount that is missing from the account and the name of the missing item.
3. Prepare journal entries to record the materials transactions for the month of October.

4–19 **Labor** You are given the following summary information from job time cards:

Job 2119	Job 2210	Job 2233
6 hrs. @ $ 8	12 hrs. @ $7	5 hrs. @ $8
4 hrs. @ 12		3 hrs. @ 9
2 hrs. @ 4		3 hrs. @ 5

REQUIRED:

1. Calculate the total labor costs of Jobs 2119, 2210, and 2233.
2. Prepare the general journal entry to record this information.

4–20 **Labor** Ross Corporation recorded the following entry:

Payroll	158,700	
Payroll payable		124,000
Payroll taxes payable		34,700

The explanation of the entry included the following information:

Factory wages (includes $26,200 for supervisors, maintenance and security)	$112,200
General and administrative salaries	30,400
Sales salaries	16,100
Total payroll	$158,700

You find the following entry, which also was recorded:

General and administrative expense	30,400	
Selling expense	16,100	
Payroll		46,500

REQUIRED: Prepare the journal entry to complete the allocation of the balance in the payroll account.

4–21 **Overhead** Caballero Company has prepared the following flexible budget for the upcoming period:

Machine-Hours	10,000	20,000	30,000	40,000
Manufacturing overhead				
Variable	$ 62,000	$124,000	$186,000	$248,000
Fixed	94,000	94,000	94,000	94,000
	$156,000	$218,000	$280,000	$342,000

REQUIRED:

1. Assuming machine-hours are to be used as the activity base, calculate the manufacturing-overhead application rate that would be used at each activity level.
2. If the 20,000-machine-hour rate is selected for use during the period, how much overhead will be applied to work in process if 30,000 machine-hours are actually used? Will this result in underapplied or overapplied overhead? Explain.

4–22 **Overhead** White Manufacturing Corporation applied overhead to its jobs at the rate of 200% of direct labor costs. Direct labor for the period amounted to $36,000, raw materials of $74,000 were used, and actual overhead incurred was $68,000.

REQUIRED:

1. How much overhead was applied to jobs during the period?
2. Prepare the entry to close all overhead accounts.

4–23 **Work in Process** Given the following information on the activity of Walton Repair Company, record the beginning balance and post summary entries to the work-in-process inventory T account. Show the ending balance of work in process.

Job 1852			
Beginning			
balance	1,500		
Direct			
materials	10,200		
Direct labor	12,600		
Overhead	6,300		

Job 1853			
Direct			
materials	24,000		
Direct labor	15,200		
Overhead	7,600		

Job 1854			
Direct			
materials	5,280		
Direct labor	6,000		
Overhead	3,000		

Job 1855			
Direct			
materials	18,700		
Direct labor	16,800		
Overhead	8,400		

Work-in-Process Inventory	

Jobs 1852 and 1853 were completed during the period.

4–24 Work in Process Verde Company manufactures custom furniture for a small number of customers. During the month of April, the following events occurred:

(a) Job 106, which had been started in March, was completed. Costs incurred prior to April totaled $16,250 ($6,250 of materials, $8,000 of labor, and $2,000 of applied overhead). To complete the job, labor costs of $1,200 were incurred.

(b) Job 107 was started and completed. The job cost sheet reflects material costs of $18,600 and direct labor costs of $24,000.

(c) Job 108 was started but not completed. Materials of $7,300 were requisitioned and used, and time cards showed direct labor of $3,600.

Verde applied overhead on the basis of direct labor costs.

REQUIRED:

1. Calculate the total manufacturing costs of the period.
2. Calculate the cost of goods manufactured.
3. What is the ending balance of work-in-process inventory?
4. Would any of your answers to requirements 1, 2, or 3 change if you were told that actual overhead for the period was $7,100?
5. Prepare T accounts for each job and for work in process, and post the transactions for the month of April.

4–25 Finished Goods Baker Company's finished-goods inventory on September 1 was made up of the following items: 800 units of A @ $6; 400 units of B @ $10. During September, 2,000 units of A were produced at a cost of $6.50 each, and 1,000 units of B were produced at a cost of $10.20 each. Sales consisted of 2,200 units of A and 900 units of B. Baker uses the last-in, first-out method to account for finished-goods inventory.

REQUIRED:
1. Calculate Baker's cost of sales for September.
2. Prepare the journal entries to record Baker's cost of goods manufactured and cost of goods sold for September.
3. What balance will appear on Baker's September 30 balance sheet for finished goods?

PROBLEMS

4–26 **Job-Order T Accounts and Entries** Crawford Automotive Repairs, Inc., uses a job-order system, with overhead applied on the basis of direct labor cost, and has the largest operation in the state. Besides contracting with customers to repair their automobiles, Crawford occasionally purchases older automobiles, repairs and paints them, and sells them to used car dealers. The following information pertains to 19X2:

Automobile parts and supplies purchased on account	$ 400,000
Parts and supplies issued to jobs	380,000
Supplies issued to mechanics (not for use on specific jobs)	30,000
Labor used on jobs	1,235,000
Indirect labor (sweepers, assistants, car movers, etc.)	110,000
Depreciation of garage and equipment	400,000
Miscellaneous overhead (insurance, utilities, taxes, etc.)	225,000
Cost of jobs completed	2,376,000
Sales	4,000,000
Cost of sales	2,385,000
Inventories at beginning of 19X2 were:	
Parts and supplies	50,000
Work in process	30,000
Cost of automobiles awaiting sale	25,000

Overhead is applied at 60% of direct labor cost

REQUIRED:
1. Record the preceding data in T accounts for parts and supplies, work in process, units awaiting sale, cost of sales, manufacturing overhead, and manufacturing overhead applied. Number your entries.
2. Prepare general journal entries to summarize 19X2 transactions. As your final entry, dispose of the year-end overapplied or underapplied factory overhead as a direct adjustment to cost of sales. You may omit explanations. Number your entries (the numbers should match the numbers of the entries posted to the T accounts in requirement 1).
3. Prepare a detailed cost of sales report.

4–27 **Source Documents and Subsidiary Ledgers** Refer to the data in problem 4–26. For each journal entry:

a. Indicate the source document or other data that would have authorized the entry.

b. Describe how any subsidiary ledger would have been affected by the entry.

4–28 **Job Cost Sheet Detail** Presto Printing Company uses a job-order costing system and a perpetual-inventory system. The following jobs were in process at the beginning of January:

	Material	Labor	Overhead	Total
X4170	$5,980	$8,648	$4,324	$18,952
X4180	6,900	7,360	3,680	17,940
Total work in process				$36,892

A summary of materials requisitions reveals the following:

Job	Materials
X4170	$ 1,020
X4180	—
X5100	6,000
X5110	7,500
X5120	3,100
X5130	2,000
	$19,620

Time cards for the month show direct labor incurred as follows:

Job	Direct Labor
X4170	$ 2,000
X4180	3,200
X5100	8.000
X5110	6,500
X5120	2,700
X5130	1,500
	$23,900

Overhead is applied at the rate of 50% of direct labor cost. Jobs X4170, X4180, X5100, and X5110 were completed and sold. There is no beginning or ending finished-goods inventory. The jobs were sold for the estimated cost plus 30%. The estimated costs of the jobs completed were:

Job	Estimated Cost
X4170	$23,000
X4180	22,500
X5100	18,000
X5110	17,000

REQUIRED:

1. Compute the cost of completed jobs.
2. Compute the ending work in process.
3. Prepare an income statement for the month of January, assuming selling and administrative expenses are $14,500.

4–29 **Work in Process—Subsidiary and General Ledger Accounts** Wright Furniture Designs manufactures custom furniture. During November and December, three jobs were in process. The job cost sheets reflect the following information:

	T–109		C–94		S–60
	November	December	November	December	December
Materials	$8,400	—	$12,750	$6,500	$23,800
Labor	3,200	2,300	5,100	7,350	1,500
Overhead applied	4,000	?	6,375	?	?

Manufacturing overhead is applied as a percentage of direct labor costs. Selected account balances on November 30 were:

Account	Balance
Materials Inventory	$ 12,500
Finished-Goods Inventory	40,000
Accrued Payroll	1,050
Cost of Sales	505,000
Manufacturing Overhead Applied	88,400

Job T–109 was completed in December and transferred to finished goods. At the end of December, finished-goods inventory had a zero balance.

REQUIRED:

1. Calculate the overhead application rate and the overhead applied to all jobs during December.
2. Prepare a schedule showing the November 30 balance of work-in-process inventory.
3. Prepare summary journal entries for all December work-in-process transactions.
4. Prepare a work-in-process T account. Enter the beginning balance, post all transactions, and show the ending balance.
5. Prepare a schedule supporting the ending balance.

4–30 **Incomplete Data—Multiple Choice** You are applying for the position of manufacturing supervisor for Collins Manufacturing Company. Collins believes that all supervisors should understand its job cost accounting system. Therefore, all applicants for supervisory positions in manufacturing are given examinations as well as interviews. One of the questions on your examination is the following:

You are provided the following data late on Friday afternoon by the accountant who is leaving for a 2-week vacation at an undisclosed location:

Direct Materials Inventory Control		Work-in-Process Inventory Control	
Beginning		Beginning	
balance $ 84,000		balance $ 12,000	
193,200		Direct	
		materials 175,000	360,000

Finished-Goods Inventory Control		Cost of Goods Sold	
Beginning			
balance $ 58,000	370,000		

Accrued Factory Payroll	
	Beginning
	balance $ 5,500
	92,900

Notes attached to the account information include the following:

(a) Indirect manufacturing costs are applied at a rate of $6 per machine-hour.
(b) Labor cards for the month totaled 11,200 direct labor hours. The average labor cost is $8 per hour.
(c) Machine hours for the month totaled 17,500.
(d) Total manufacturing overhead incurred was $110,000.

When you get around to looking at the data on Saturday morning, you realize that much information is missing. You must have the answers to the following questions to prepare an important report that is due at 8:00 A.M. on Monday.

REQUIRED: Select the best answers to the following questions.

1. The ending balance of direct materials inventory control should be
   a. $84,000.   **b.** $277,200.   **c.** $102,200.   **d.** $175,000.
2. Direct-labor cost that should have been posted in work-in-process inventory control (and subsidiary job cost sheets) is
   a. $89,600.   **b.** $92,900.   **c.** $98,400.   **d.** $11,200.
3. Manufacturing-overhead cost that should have been posted to work-in-process inventory control (and subsidiary job cost sheets) is
   a. $67,200.   **b.** $110,000.   **c.** $3,300.   **d.** $105,000.

4. Total labor cost (direct and indirect) for the period is
   a. $98,400.   b. $92,900.   c. $89,600.   d. $812,500.
5. Cost of goods manufactured is
   a. $369,600.   b. $360,000.   c. $381,600.   d. $370,000.
   e. impossible to determine
6. The ending balance of work in process that will appear on the current period's balance sheet is
   a. $21,600.   b. $12,000.   c. $(173,000).   d. $(83,400).
7. The ending balance of finished goods that will appear on the current period's balance sheet is
   a. $48,000.   b. $312,000.   c. $58,000.   d. $68,000.
8. Cost of goods sold is
   a. $360,000.   b. $369,600.   c. $370,000.   d. $381,600.
9. For the period, manufacturing overhead was
   a. underapplied by $5,000.
   b. overapplied by $101,700.
   c. overapplied by $5,000.
   d. neither overapplied nor underapplied.
10. If factory payroll checks totaling $95,000 were issued during the period, what is the balance of accrued factory payroll at the end of the period?
    a. $193,400   b. $3,400   c. $98,400   d. $2,100

4–31   **Basic Job-Order Costing** Watson, Inc., manufactures lighting fixtures. A job-order system is used because many different models, some to customer specifications, are produced. The budget prepared for the current fiscal year ending June 30, 19X1, follows.

Annual Budget for the Year Ended June 30, 19X1

Direct materials		$2,500,000
Purchases of component kits		1,800,000
Direct labor (275,000 hours)		2,750,000
Overhead		
Supplies	$120,000	
Indirect labor	450,000	
Supervisors	162,000	
Depreciation	610,000	
Insurance	10,000	
Taxes	32,000	
Utilities	123,000	
Miscellaneous	60,500	1,567,500
		$8,617,500

Watson applied overhead on the basis of direct labor hours and uses the first-in, first-out method to account for all inventories. Through the first 11 months of the current year, operations have progressed satisfactorily. Direct labor hours through May 31, 19X1, total 238,500. Selected general ledger account balances as of 5/31/X1 are as follows:

Materials inventory	$ 20,800
Work-in-process inventory	750,000*
Finished-goods inventory	1,499,875**
Manufacturing overhead	1,470,000
Cost of sales	9,250,000

*Job 16540: Deluxe crystal chandeliers (850 units)	$ 540,000
Job 17632: Modern ranch chandeliers (1,500 units)	210,000
	$ 750,000

**Ceiling huggers, 3,200 units	$ 160,000
Deluxe crystal chandeliers, 1,032 units	645,000
Modern ranch chandeliers, 1,625 units	316,875
Outdoor lights, 5,000 units	105,000
Art deco fixtures, 1,050 units	273,000
	$1,499,875

Transactions for the month of June include the following:

(1) Purchases:

Raw materials	$270,000
Purchased parts	180,000
Supplies	8,500

(Watson, Inc., maintains only one materials inventory account.)

(2) Requisitions:

Job	Materials	Parts	Supplies	Total
16540	$ 3,000	—	—	$ 3,000
17632	65,000	$ 70,000	—	135,000
17745 (custom chandeliers)	38,000	26,000	—	64,000
17750 (economy chandeliers)	98,000	52,000	—	150,000
Overhead	—	—	13,000	13,000
	$204,000	$148,000	$13,000	$365,000

(3) Payroll for June:

Job	Hours	Cost
16540	400	$ 4,150
17632	1,600	16,200
17745	11,000	109,800
17750	300	3,000
Indirect	3,200	22,400
Supervisors	—	16,000
Administration and sales	—	78,500
		$250,050

(4) Other manufacturing overhead costs incurred during June:

Depreciation	$50,800
Insurance	850
Utilities	9,750
Miscellaneous	1,200
	$62,600

(5) Jobs completed during June:

Job	Item	Units
16540	Deluxe crystal chandeliers	850
17632	Modern ranch chandeliers	1,500
17745	Custom chandeliers	500

(6) Sales during June:

Item	Units
Ceiling huggers	2,000
Deluxe crystal chandeliers	1,200
Modern ranch chandeliers	1,600
Outdoor lights	2,100
Art deco fixtures	150

REQUIRED:

1. Prepare T accounts for materials inventory, work-in-process inventory (include subsidiary T accounts for each job), manufacturing overhead, manufacturing overhead applied, finished-goods inventory, and cost of sales. Record the 5/31/X1 balances and the June transactions.
2. Calculate the underapplied or overapplied overhead for the year ended June 30 19X1, and indicate whether it is underapplied or over-applied.
3. Determine the ending balances for:

   a. materials inventory
   b. work-in-process inventory
   c. finished-goods inventory.

4. Assuming the underapplied or overapplied overhead is closed to cost of sales, what is the adjusted cost of sales that will appear on the income statement?

4–32 THOUGHT STIMULATION PROBLEM. This text holds that the cost accounting system should be designed to most effectively account for the activities of the manufacturing or service enterprise it serves. Conventional cost accounting entries for manufacturing firms, for example, attempt to track the physical movement of products as they are being recorded in order to properly accumulate and allocate costs. Summary entries, though, provide simplicity and efficiency of record keeping. Thus, rather than recording each material requisition, one entry may be made daily (or weekly) to record all requisitions.

Suppose that Stuart Manufacturing Company, a firm that has been operating under a conventional job-order system (where a primary consideration has been the allocation of appropriate costs to ending inventories), desires to switch to a just-in-time (JIT) manufacturing arrangement. As it has in the past, the firm will continue to batch manufacture jobs, where an entire batch is sold to one customer, under the new JIT inventory policy.

In addition to minimizing inventories, Stuart Manufacturing Company desires to minimize all activities that add no value to the product or directly promote the objectives of the firm—including its record-keeping activities. Their primary focus in the future will be on *throughput*, defined as the number of products actually shipped to customers. However, management is not willing to compromise the amount of information they receive for certain decision-making purposes. For example, they still need to know the cost of each job as it is shipped to a customer. However, until the new system is fully operational, they are willing to ignore individual (departmental) measures of efficiency in the incurrence of materials, labor, and overhead costs. (In fact, a consultant has assured Stuart Manufacturing Company that the only efficiency they ever need to concentrate on is throughput.)

REQUIRED:

1. Assuming that Stuart Manufacturing Company has a reliable set of estimated materials and conversion costs for each job, design a cost accounting system for the company that will minimize the accounting entries while still maintaining control of materials and costs of jobs shipped. Your design should be in the form an annotated T account flowchart.
2. After your system (or some other system) has been implemented, what additional information would you suggest might be beneficial to management?

Chapter 5

The Job-Order System Expanded

Learning Objectives

When you have finished your study of this chapter, you should

1. Understand why manufacturing firms use departmental cost-accumulation centers.
2. Be able to prepare a schedule reflecting the allocation of service department costs to producing departments and calculate departmental manufacturing-overhead application rates.
3. Recognize the control accounts typically found in a cost accounting system and know how they relate to their respective subsidiary ledger data.
4. Know how to account for spoiled units when using a job-order costing system.
5. Be able to establish and maintain a split ledger cost accounting system.

135

C hapter 4 explained the basic procedures for installing and maintaining a job-order costing system. In this chapter, we elaborate on those basic procedures and introduce refinements that are desirable in more effectively meeting the objectives of cost accounting.[1] The procedures and practices described in this chapter are designed to make the job-order cost system produce more precise unit-cost data and provide more information relating to the various elements of the cost data in more complex manufacturing environments.

As we expand the system, we shall explain

1. how departmental cost-accumulation centers are used
2. how control accounts and subsidiary ledgers are used in accounting for manufacturing costs
3. how spoiled units affect product costs
4. how accounting records are organized when a split ledger system is used.

In addition, we present illustrated problems demonstrating how these refinements and elaborations fit into a job-order cost system.

Departmental Cost-Accumulation Centers

In developing our manufacturing overhead application rate in Chapter 4, we assumed that the entire factory was the only cost-accumulation center used. We now explore the rationale for using departmental cost-accumulation centers such as those discussed and illustrated in Chapter 2, and explain the procedures followed in accounting for the flows of costs through those centers.

Rationale for Departmental Cost-Accumulation Centers

Some parts of a factory's operations typically incur more factory overhead in relation to the activity base being used to compute the overhead rate than do other parts. For example, any part of the factory that contains a lot of sophisticated machinery requiring significant amounts of maintenance, power, and space probably incurs more manufacturing overhead in relation to direct labor (the assumed activity or allocation

---

[1] The prime objective of cost-accumulation and -allocation is to provide cost information that can be used in

1. valuing manufactured inventories and determining cost of goods sold
2. controlling operations
3. planning future operations
4. making day-to-day operating decisions.

base) than does an assembly department, which is more labor intensive and less capital intensive. Therefore, a firm that manufactures several products—some requiring more machining time and others requiring more assembly time—should use departmental cost-accumulation centers to determine more precisely the amount of overhead that should be allocated to each unit of product based on the cause-and-effect relationships underlying the incurrence of those costs.

To illustrate the hazards of using a plantwide rate when different activities are performed in different parts of a factory, let's hypothesize a manufacturing firm that produces several products, among which are product A and product B. The factory has two areas in which the manufacturing work is done: one, a machining area, contains heavy equipment that occupies a lot of space in relation to the relatively few employees working there; another area, where workers assemble the parts produced by the machines, has only a few expensive machines and requires less space, less power, and less maintenance per employee.

For the purpose of accumulating labor and overhead costs, we divide the factory into two parts—the machining department and the assembly department. The flexible budget prepared for each of these departments and for the factory as a whole shows the following data regarding the level of activity projected for the next operating period:

	Machining Department	Assembly Department	Total
Estimated direct labor	$ 20,000	$40,000	$ 60,000
Estimated manufacturing overhead	100,000	80,000	180,000
Manufacturing overhead application rate (based on direct labor dollars)	500%	200%	300%

Historically, products A and B have been produced in job lots that show the following direct materials costs and direct labor costs per unit of product:

	Product A		Product B	
Direct materials		$400		$400
Direct labor				
Machining department	$400		$100	
Assembly department	100	500	400	500
		$900		$900

Plantwide Overhead Rate.   If we apply manufacturing overhead to the job orders used to accumulate the costs of producing these units on the basis of the *overall* factory overhead percentage (300%), the costs projected for each unit of product A and of product B would be:

	Product A	Product B
Total direct costs	$ 900	$ 900
Manufacturing-overhead costs ($500 × 300%)	1,500	1,500
Total manufacturing costs	$2,400	$2,400

The total costs allocated to the manufacture of one unit of each product under this arrangement is $2,400. From this information, management would logically conclude that it could sell each product for some markup over $2,400 that would cover operating cost and provide an appropriate margin.

Departmental Overhead Rates. If we use departmental manufacturing-overhead application rates in applying overhead to the job orders used to track the costs of these products, the costs for each product would be:

		Product A	Product B	
Total direct costs		$ 900		$ 900
Manufacturing-overhead costs				
Product A: $400 × 500% = $2,000				
$100 × 200% = 200		2,200		
Product B: $100 × 500% =			$500	
$400 × 200% =			800	1,300
		$3,100		$2,200

The allocation of overhead costs on a basis that more appropriately relates overhead to the activity base (presumably adopted because it most realistically reflects cause-and-effect relationships) shows the manufacturing cost for product A to be $3,100 and for product B only $2,200. This suggests that unless the firm uses departmental cost-accumulation centers, management may be targeting the minimum selling price for product A based on a projected manufacturing cost of $2,400 when it more realistically should be based on $3,100. At the same time, they may be attempting to sell product B for a suitable markup above $2,400 of manufacturing costs when $2,200 is a more reasonable cost to be allocated to that product.

Use of a plantwide overhead rate may lead the firm to sell product A at a price lower than actual manufacturing cost, so the firm will likely beat the market competition for that product. At the same time, because of the presumed higher manufacturing cost for product B, the firm might set a price for it that is higher than the market will accept. Thus, if competitors have more precise cost information, the overall result will be for the firm to sell many units of product A at a lower-than-appropriate price and very few units of product B because management feels it cannot match the competition's price. In this type situation, in which cost information is faulty, a firm can lose money even though it is experiencing an expansion of total sales.

The use of departmental cost-accumulation centers also is important in controlling operations. As we explain in Chapter 17, detailed departmental cost information is very important in controlling certain manufacturing costs because it makes departmental supervisors responsible for the costs they incur in carrying out their department's contribution to the firm's overall operations.

Accounting for Departmental Overhead Costs

For the reasons just discussed, and also to provide a more appropriately valued inventory, most manufacturing firms should use departmental cost-accumulation centers in accounting for the accumulation and allocation of manufacturing overhead. As explained in Chapter 2, such departmental cost centers are divided into two categories—producing departments and service departments. *Producing departments*, which include the production lines, are the cost-accumulation centers in which work is performed directly on the goods being produced. On the other hand, *service departments*, which include such activities as maintenance, personnel, employee services, and the provision of heat, power, and light, are necessary for the entire factory—including the producing departments—to remain in operation.

Figures 2–8 and 2–9 demonstrated how the costs accumulated in the service department cost-accumulation centers ultimately are allocated to producing departments to allow all manufacturing-overhead costs from service as well as producing departments to be apportioned first to job orders and ultimately to the individual units being produced. These allocation procedures are followed in allocating both budgeted and actual costs. In effect, the service department costs are just other items of overhead to the producing departments, as illustrated in Figure 5–1.

After the projected or historical costs charged to service departments have been allocated to producing departments, departmental manufacturing-overhead application rates can be determined by dividing the total departmental historical or projected manufacturing-overhead costs by the selected allocation base (generally direct labor costs, direct labor hours, or machine-hours).

To illustrate, Figure 5–2 shows total manufacturing-overhead costs for the stamping, welding, finishing, and assembly departments from Figure 2–8 along with the direct labor dollars and direct labor hours for each of those departments. If the cost data are presumed to be

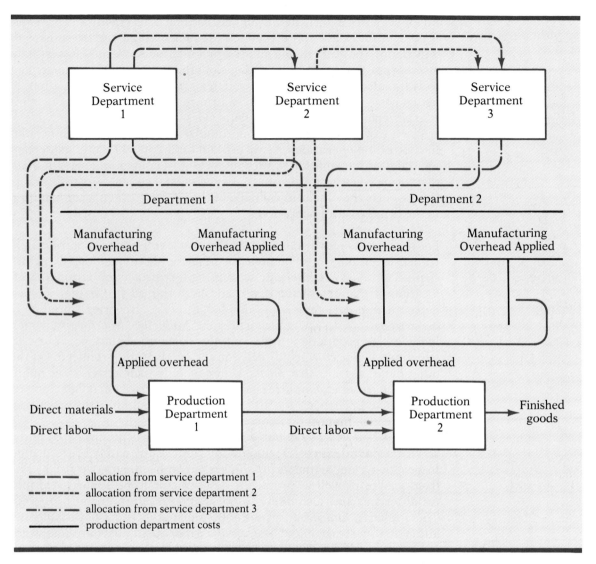

FIGURE 5–1 Service Department Allocation to Production Departments: Step Method

historical data and we use the overhead application rates calculated from them to apply overhead in a future period, we are implicitly assuming that we expect to operate at approximately the same level in that period as was achieved during the period over which the historical data were accumulated. (The manufacturing-overhead application rates shown in the last two lines of Figure 5–2 are discussed a little

	Producing Departments				
	Stamping	**Welding**	**Finishing**	**Assembly**	**Total**
Manufacturing overhead (from Figure 2–8)	$116,500	$105,300	$ 98,690	$ 80,610	$401,100
Estimated direct labor hours	10,000	5,000	20,000	10,000	45,000
Estimated direct labor costs	$80,000	$ 50,000	$120,000	$ 60,000	$310,000
Manufacturing-overhead application rate per direct labor hour	$11.65	$21.06	$4.93	$8.06	$8.91
Manufacturing-overhead application rate as percentage of direct labor costs	146%	211%	82%	134%	129%

FIGURE 5–2   Departmental Manufacturing-Overhead Application Rates

later in this chapter.) Each overhead application rate is calculated via the following formula:

$$\frac{\text{Historical or estimated manufacturing overhead}}{\text{Historical or estimated allocation base}^2} = \text{Overhead application rate}$$

If the cost and activity-level data given in Figure 5–2 are assumed to be projected amounts for the next period rather than historical data, that information will have been drawn from flexible budgets prepared for each department. Once the level of operations expected to be achieved by each department during the next period has been decided, the data in Figure 5–2 will reflect the amounts shown in the column of the flexible budget for the selected level of operations.

The cost accountant uses the calculated manufacturing-overhead application rate for each producing department to determine the amounts of manufacturing overhead to be recorded in the work-in-process account and on the job-order cost sheets. Such an arrangement enables management to determine the amount of underapplied or overapplied overhead *for each department* and to request explanations for material amounts of either underapplied or overapplied overhead from the departmental supervisors, who are in the best position to control overhead costs. To illustrate, the amounts shown as debit balances in the following manufacturing-overhead (actual overhead) T accounts reflect the actual departmental overhead costs for the reporting period. The amounts of overhead applied to production for each department are

---

[2]Direct labor hours, direct labor costs, machine-hours, or other activity.

shown as credit balances in the applied manufacturing-overhead accounts. At the end of each reporting period, manufacturing overhead is closed against applied manufacturing overhead to arrive at the underapplied or overapplied amounts shown in the last group of accounts.

Manufacturing Overhead (Actual Overhead Incurred)

Molding Department				Finishing Department			
Balance	33,500	(C1)	33,500	Balance	18,000	(C2)	18,000

Milling Department				Assembly Department			
Balance	62,000	(C3)	62,000	Balance	8,500	(C4)	8,500

Applied Manufacturing Overhead

Molding Department				Finishing Department			
(C1)	31,000	Balance	31,000	(C2)	18,500	Balance	18,500

Milling Department				Assembly Department			
(C3)	61,000	Balance	61,000	(C4)	9,000	Balance	9,000

Underapplied or Overapplied Overhead

Molding Department			Finishing Department	
(C1)	2,500		(C2)	500

Milling Department			Assembly Department	
(C3)	1,000		(C4)	500

As you can see, the molding and milling departments have underapplied overhead, while the finishing and assembly departments have overapplied overhead. If these amounts are considered material, each department manager would be asked to explain why the overhead applied did not roughly equal the overhead incurred.

A firm must decide what activity base will be used in applying its manufacturing overhead. If direct labor is judged to most appropriately meet the cause-and-effect test, a choice must still be made between using direct labor hours and using direct labor cost. If it costs about the same amount to keep the factory in operation for each employee regardless of the hourly rate of pay, and *if* the factory has a significant differential in its hourly pay rates in the different departmental cost-accumulation centers, it is generally preferable to apply overhead on the basis of a rate per direct labor hour rather than as a percentage of direct labor cost. Such an overhead application rate is calculated by dividing projected annual overhead for the department by the total estimated number of direct-labor hours to be performed *during that period* in that department. The results of such a calculation are shown in the next-to-last line of Figure 5–2; for example, the stamping department has an overhead rate of $11.65 per direct-labor hour.

If, on the other hand, the hourly rate of pay does not vary significantly, it is generally easier and almost as precise to use an overhead application rate expressed as a percentage of direct labor costs. Those rates are calculated by dividing each department's expected total overhead cost by the expected direct-labor cost for that department. The results of such a calculation are shown in the last line of Figure 5–2; for example, the welding department has an overhead rate of 211% of direct-labor cost.

In situations where machine-related costs constitute a large part of overhead, it is often more appropriate to use machine-hours as the activity base for allocating overhead costs. As we will discuss in Chapters 22 and 23, the continuing introduction of automation into manufacturing operations will reduce the amount of *direct* labor in manufacturing operations (or possibly even eliminate it altogether). In such an automated environment, most labor will be *indirect* (an overhead item), so it seems almost imperative that manufacturing overhead be allocated on some basis other than direct labor (for example, materials cost, machine-hours, or some other activity). Activity-based cost accounting, representing a further refinement of departmental cost-accumulation centers, also is discussed in Chapter 23.

When departmental cost-accumulation centers are used, job-order cost sheets must have separate columns for each department to accumulate the direct labor and applied manufacturing overhead for each job. We show the form for such a job-order sheet in Figure 5–3.

Control Accounts and Subsidiary Ledgers

As we have developed our manufacturing cost-accumulation and -allocation process, our emphasis has been on the use of the following three ledger accounts:

1. materials inventory (stores)
2. work in process
3. finished goods

Job No. 854				500 Units of Product X				
Direct Materials		**Direct Labor**						
Req. No.	Amount	**Stamping Department**	**Welding Department**	**Finishing Department**	**Assembly Department**	Total		
763	$2,400	7/1/XX $2,000	7/10/XX $1,000	7/10/XX $4,000	7/10/XX $500	$7,500		
Totals								
		Manufacturing Overhead						
		Stamping Department	**Welding Department**	**Finishing Department**	**Assembly Department**	Total		
		7/10/XX $2,920	7/10/XX $2,110	7/10/XX $3,280	7/10/XX $670	$8,980		

Summary: Totals

Direct materials   _____

Direct labor   _____

Manufacturing overhead _____   *[This part of job-order sheet will be com-*
                                                              pleted when the job is transferred to finished
Total   _____   *goods.]*

Cost per unit   _____

FIGURE 5–3 Job-Order Sheet

Since each of these requires a **subsidiary ledger** to provide the additional detailed information needed to account for and manage the individual items included in the accounts, they often are called **control accounts**.

Materials Inventory (Stores)

In a manually maintained system, the materials inventory ledger account should have a subsidiary ledger made up of individual ledger cards for each of the various items of material held in the storeroom. Each card will include the elements of the following four-element equation:

$$\text{Beginning inventory balance} + \text{Receipts} - \text{Issuances}$$
$$= \text{Ending inventory balance}$$

The amounts carried on the cards for each of these elements may be expressed both in units and in dollars, as shown in Figure 5–4. Observe

Material A								Part No. 86504			
Receipts				**Issuances**				**Balances**			
Date	Quan.	Per Unit	Amt.	Date	Quan.	Per Unit	Amt.	Date	Quan.	Per Unit	Amt.
								1/1/XX	500	$1.00	$ 500
								1/5/XX	500	$1.00	$ 500
1/5/XX	1,000	$1.20	$1,200						1,000	$1.20	$1,200
				1/10/XX	500	$1.00	$500				
					200	$1.20	$240	1/10/XX	800	$1.20	$ 960

FIGURE 5–4 Materials Inventory Ledger Card

that first-in, first-out cost flow procedures are followed in accounting for material A.

The amounts shown in the beginning-inventory and receipts portions of the cards will come from the past-period inventory records and current purchase invoices, respectively. The dollar amounts to be shown in the issuances and ending-balances sections will be determined by requisitions and the cost flow assumption being used in accounting for inventory items. The sum of the dollar amounts shown as ending balances on the cards for the individual materials items always should equal the balance in the materials inventory control account.

In today's manufacturing environment, both the control account and subsidiary ledger records are likely to be maintained on a computer, meaning the data will be stored on magnetic tapes or disks that can be accessed through terminals. Hard-copy (printed) records, if desired, can be retrieved via computer printout.

In our illustrated inventory card, we have shown dollar amounts as well as quantities for all receipts, issuances, and balances. In some instances, only quantitative records will be maintained for those items, with dollar values being inserted only as inventory values are established at the end of each reporting period.

Work in Process

As explained in Chapters 2 and 4, the uncompleted job-order cost sheets constitute the subsidiary ledger for the work-in-process account. The sum of the direct materials, direct labor, and applied manufacturing-overhead costs accumulated on these job-order sheets should equal the amount shown in the work-in-process control account. The job-order cost sheet also can be maintained as a file in a computerized system; but generally, only the largest (or newest) manufacturing firms have invested in sufficient equipment and software to set up an entirely "paperless" data system.

Finished Goods

A separate finished-goods ledger card (or file, in a computerized system) should be maintained for each type of unit carried in finished-goods inventory. Again, each of these cards will reflect the same four-element equation as the materials inventory ledger cards. The amounts shown in the beginning-balance and receipts sections will come from the past-period inventory records and the job-order sheets for completed jobs, respectively. The issuances (transfers to cost of sales) will come from the sales orders. The amounts shown for the removals (issuances) and end-of-period inventory will be determined by the cost flow assumption used in accounting for the finished goods.

Computerized Records

Computers are now used extensively in accounting for data included in cost-accumulation centers. For example, unit and cost data for the individual items of materials and finished goods are, in most instances, maintained in a computer file (magnetic tape or disk), thus eliminating the need for manually maintained records. At the same time, data are available immediately after transactions occur, with less likelihood of errors being made in the allocation and accumulation process than would be the case with manually maintained records.

Manufacturing-Overhead Costs

Manufacturing-overhead costs constitute one element of the manufacturing costs allocated to work in process and finished goods. In accumulating the actual amount of manufacturing overhead for a reporting period, we often use a **manufacturing-overhead control account**, with a subsidiary ledger showing the amounts of manufacturing overhead attributed to the individual manufacturing-overhead cost items. When that is the case, amounts will be recorded, as they are incurred or paid, in both the control account (manufacturing-overhead control) and the subsidiary ledger accounts (indirect materials, indirect labor, depreciation, power, and so forth). Data for these entries are generally summarized and recorded at the end of each month in the form shown in the following T accounts:

Manufacturing Overhead Control

(a) XX	
(b) XX	
(c) XX	
(d) XX	
(e) XX	

Indirect Materials	Indirect Labor	Factory Depreciation	Power	Misc.
(a) XX	(b) XX	(c) XX	(d) XX	(e) XX

In other instances, the individual manufacturing-overhead accounts will be included as separate accounts in the general ledger or the factory ledger to be debited as those costs are incurred. The individual overhead items will then be closed to a **manufacturing-overhead cost summary account** at the end of each period, as follows:

Indirect Materials	Indirect Labor	Factory Depreciation	Electricity	Misc.
Bal. XXX	XXX (a) Bal. XXX	XXX (a) Bal. XXX	XXX (a) Bal. XXX	XXX (a) Bal. XXX	XXX (a)

Manufacturing-Overhead Cost Summary

(a)   XXX,XXX

In either instance, the accumulated amount of actual manufacturing-overhead costs will be matched (closed) against applied overhead cost at the end of each reporting period to arrive at the underapplied or overapplied overhead for the period.

Accounting for Underapplied or Overapplied Overhead

If the amount of underapplied or overapplied overhead is insignificant, it should be closed to cost of sales. However, if the amount (the difference between actual manufacturing overhead and the total amount applied to production for the period) is material, it is inappropriate—from the point of view of the matching convention—to close the entire amount to cost of sales. Recall that the aceounting objective for manufacturing overhead is to allocate the actual manufacturing overhead incurred during a period to the units of product worked on during that period. Therefore, if there is a large amount of underapplied or overapplied overhead, that amount should be reallocated to work in process, finished goods, and cost of sales, so the total overhead amount in each of these accounts closely approximates the overhead amount that would have resulted from a direct allocation of actual overhead or from using an error-free overhead application rate.

Generally, the most equitable way of making such an allocation is to determine the amount of applied manufacturing overhead included in the work-in-process, finished-goods, and cost-of-sales accounts and to allocate the underapplied or overapplied amount to those accounts on a pro-rata basis. This pro-rata allocation (used frequently in cost accounting) begins by finding the ratio of each individual item that is to receive a portion of the underapplied or overapplied amount to the total of all items to receive an allocation (see schedule below). In allocating underapplied or overapplied overhead to work in process, finished goods, and cost of sales, the ratios have as numerators the amounts of the applied manufacturing overhead included in each of the three account balances, and as denominators the total manufacturing overhead included in all three accounts. Each ratio is then multiplied by the underapplied or overapplied amount to determine the amount to be allocated to each individual account. To illustrate, let's assume underapplied overhead of $42,000 for a reporting period and the following overhead amounts applied to goods included in end-of-period work in process and finished goods and to the goods included in cost of sales for the period.

Applied Overhead Costs Included in Ending Balances

Work in process	$ 50,000
Finished goods	90,000
Cost of sales	280,000
Total	$420,000

The $42,000 of underapplied overhead would then be allocated as follows:

Work in process

$$\frac{\$50,000}{\$420,000} \times \$42,000 = \$5,000$$

Finished goods

$$\frac{\$90,000}{\$420,000} \times \$42,000 = \$9,000$$

Cost of sales

$$\frac{\$280,000}{\$420,000} \times \$42,000 = \$28,000$$

As you can see, the allocation of underapplied overhead would yield $14,000 more net income than if all of the underapplied overhead had been closed to cost of sales (total underapplied overhead of $42,000 that would have been debited to cost of sales less the pro-rata portion of $28,000 debited to cost of sales under the allocation procedure).

For simplicity, total ending balances in work in process, finished goods, and cost of sales may be used in allocating underapplied or overapplied overhead. This will closely approximate the results of the allocation procedure just described if all three accounts contain about the same proportions of direct materials and direct labor. In many instances, however, the ratio of direct materials to total costs will be higher for work in process than for finished goods and cost of sales, because materials are generally charged to job orders at the beginning of processing.

Accounting for Spoiled Goods

Even though some firms now operate with a zero-defect objective, most of them expect to have some goods spoiled during the manufacturing process. Even if it were technically possible to produce only perfect goods, cost/benefit considerations might dictate some allowable spoilage. We refer to that expected level of spoilage as **normal-spoilage loss**. Because such spoilage is expected to occur as part of normal operations, the costs associated with these units can be removed from work in process (and individual job-order cost sheets) and debited to manufacturing overhead. To illustrate, let's assume that 10 of 100 units being produced on Job 1053 with an accumulated cost of $800 are defective. The following journal entry would be made to record the removal of those units from work in process:

Manufacturing overhead (normal spoilage)	800	
Work in process (Job 1053)		800

In instances where spoilage occurs fairly uniformly across all jobs, the costs may not be removed and the total job costs will simply be spread over the good units produced. Either method has the effect of allocating the cost of normal spoilage to the cost of producing good units. With the first treatment, manufacturing-overhead costs applied to work in process will include a provision for such spoilage.

When spoiled goods are in excess of the normally expected amount—either because of manufacturing conditions during the reporting period or because of exceptional precision requirements for goods being produced on a particular job order—the costs associated with the defective units are characterized as **abnormal-spoilage loss**. When such costs are caused by the manufacturing conditions of a particular reporting period, they should be removed from work in process (and the job-order cost sheets) and debited to a *period* cost account labeled "loss due to abnormal spoilage." At the end of the reporting period, the abnormal-spoilage loss will be shown as an additional element of cost of goods sold for the period or as a separate expense item on the income statement. However, if the abnormal spoilage is caused by stricter precision requirements relating to a particular job order, the costs associated with the spoiled units should be allowed to remain on the job-order sheet (and in work in process), to be spread over the good units produced on that particular job.

The cost of both normal and abnormal spoilage is equal to the costs associated with the spoiled units less any salvage value. For instance, if two units with accumulated costs of $900 per unit are defective but can be disposed of for $100 each, the spoilage loss would be $1,800 − $200 = $1,600.

The Split Ledger System

For a plant located some distance from the main office, or simply as a means of dividing bookkeeping responsibilities (as is now practicable with powerful personal computers), a **split ledger system** might be used. That is, the ledger accounts may be divided into two groups, labeled **general ledger** and **factory ledger.** The factory ledger will include accounts for all manufacturing cost data from the point where materials are acquired until finished goods are shipped to customers. Thus, this ledger typically includes accounts for materials, manufacturing overhead, applied manufacturing overhead, work in process, and finished goods. To preserve the balancing checks associated with the double-entry system, the sum of the balances in those accounts (a net debit) will be balanced against a reciprocal or "place-marker" credit account appearing in the factory ledger entitled **general ledger.** Also, when the factory accounts are removed from the general ledger, one inserts in their place a reciprocal, or "place-marker," account called **factory ledger.** This splitting process is illustrated in Figure 5–5.

As transactions are recorded in both of these ledgers, entries that normally would call for debits or credits to accounts appearing in the other ledger will be debited or credited to the reciprocal or "place-marker" account. For example, when materials are purchased, the normal entry would be a debit to materials inventory and a credit to accounts payable. However, since the materials inventory account now appears in the factory ledger and the accounts payable account in the general ledger, that transaction would be recorded by debiting the factory ledger account and crediting accounts payable in the general

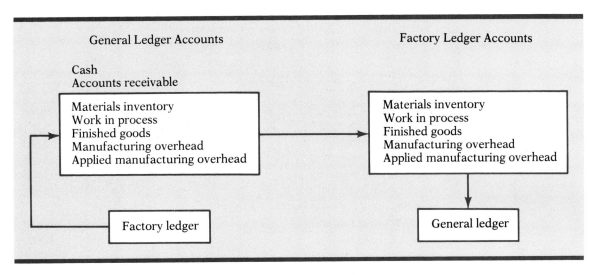

FIGURE 5–5 General Ledger Accounts and Factory Ledger Accounts

ledger and by debiting the materials inventory account and crediting the general ledger account in the factory ledger, as shown below:

General Ledger

Factory ledger	XX	
Accounts payable		XX

Factory Ledger

Materials inventory	XX	
General ledger		XX

Next, we demonstrate how this system works, in illustrative problem 1, which is a repeat of the illustrative problem in Chapter 4, with the additional assumption that the factory-related accounts are carried in a separate factory ledger.

Illustrative Problem 1

We will now show how the journal entries recorded in the illustrative problem for Able Company at the end of Chapter 4 (see pages 115–120) would be recorded in T accounts if the records were maintained in split ledgers.

Able Company

BALANCE SHEET

12/31/19X0

Assets

Cash		$ 34,000
Accounts receivable	$20,000	
Allowance for bad debts	1,000	19,000
Inventory of raw materials		25,000
Inventory of work in process*		15,000
Finished goods inventory**		20,000
Equipment	$80,000	
Allowance for depreciation	7,200	72,800
Land		20,000
Total		$205,800

Liabilities and Owners' Equity

Accounts payable	$ 35,000
Notes payable	10,000
Mortgage payable	45,000
Owners' equity	115,800
Total	$205,800

*Job 502: direct materials $9,000; direct labor $4,000; manufacturing overhead $2,000. Job is for manufacture of 10,000 units of product A.

**Finished-goods inventory includes:

1,000 units of product A @ $9 per unit =	$ 9,000
100 units of product B @ $80 per unit =	8,000
500 units of product C @ $6 per unit =	3,000
	$20,000

As in Chapter 4, the assumed transactions for the month of January 19X1 are:

(1) Materials costing $80,000 are purchased on account. A perpetual-inventory system is used.

(2) Job 503 for 1,000 units of product B, Job 504 for 5,000 units of product C, and Job 505 for 20,000 units of product D are begun.

(3) Raw materials issued into process amount to $90,000, used as follows: Job 502, $38,000; Job 503, $40,000; Job 504, $7,000; Job 505, $5,000.

(4) Direct labor of $60,000 for the month is accrued. Payroll taxes amounting to $4,000 were deducted from amounts due to employees. The employer's payroll tax expense (treated as an overhead item) amounted to $1,200. The direct labor was charged as follows: Job 502, $26,000; Job 503, $30,000; Job 504, $3,000; Job 505, $1,000.

(5) Manufacturing-overhead costs of $23,000 are incurred and paid.

(6) Depreciation on equipment (all manufacturing) should be provided on the basis of an assumed life of 10 years and an estimated salvage value of $8,000. (Depreciation expense = $7,200.)

(7) Manufacturing overhead associated with jobs in process are estimated to be approximately 50% of direct labor costs. Manufacturing overhead should be applied on that basis to all production for the period. The difference between manufacturing overhead applied and actual manufacturing overhead incurred should be reflected on the income statement.

(8) Jobs 502 and 503 are completed during January and transferred to finished goods. The following job orders remain in process at the end of the month:

	Direct Materials	Direct Labor	Applied Manufacturing Overhead	Total
Job 504	$ 7,000	$3,000	$1,500	$11,500
Job 505	5,000	1,000	500	6,500
	$12,000	$4,000	$2,000	$18,000

(9) Sales for the month are $70,000. They include 1,200 units of product A and 500 units of product B. Able uses the first-in, first-out method in accounting for the cost of units sold.

REQUIRED: Assuming a split ledger situation, where accounts for materials inventory, work in process, finished goods, factory overhead, applied factory overhead, and underapplied and overapplied overhead are kept in the factory ledger rather than the general ledger, do the following:

a. Record the transactions for the month of January in T accounts and job-order sheets.

b. Prepare general journal entries to record the transactions for the month of January.

c. Calculate the cost of goods manufactured during the month of January.

Solution to Illustrative Problem 1

a. **T-Account Entries:**

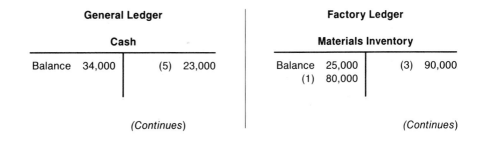

General Ledger

Cash

| Balance 34,000 | (5) 23,000 |

(Continues)

Factory Ledger

Materials Inventory

| Balance 25,000 | (3) 90,000 |
| (1) 80,000 | |

(Continues)

	General Ledger			Factory Ledger	

General Ledger

Accounts Receivable

Balance	20,000	
(9a)	70,000	

Allowance for Bad Debts

	Balance	1,000

Equipment

Balance	80,000	

Accumulated Depreciation

	Balance	7,200
	(6)	7,200

Land

Balance	20,000	

Accounts Payable

	Balance	35,000
	(1)	80,000

Notes Payable

	Balance	10,000

Mortgage Payable

	Balance	45,000

(Continues)

Factory Ledger

Work in Process

Balance	15,000	(8)	177,000
(3)	90,000		
(4a)	60,000		
(7)	30,000		

Finished Goods

Balance	20,000	(9b)	52,840
(8)	177,000		

Factory Overhead

(4b)	1,200	(7a)	31,400
(5)	23,000		
(6)	7,200		

Applied Manufacturing Overhead

(7a)	30,000	(7)	30,000

Underapplied and Overapplied Overhead

(7a)	1,400	(7b)	1,400

General Ledger Account

(7b)	1,400	Balance	60,000
(9b)	52,840	(1)	80,000
		(4a)	60,000
		(4b)	1,200
		(5)	23,000
		(6)	7,200

(Continues)

General Ledger

Owners' Equity

	Balance 115,800

Cost of Sales

(7b)	1,400	
(9b)	52,840*	

*Cost of sales:

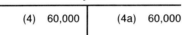

1,000 A @ $9	=	$ 9,000
200 A @ $9.20	=	1,840
100 A @ $80	=	8,000
400 B @ $85	=	34,000
		$52,840

Payroll

(4)	60,000	(4a)	60,000

Accrued Payroll

		(4)	56,000

Payroll Taxes Payable

		(4)	4,000
		(4b)	1,200

Sales

		(9a)	70,000

Factory Ledger Account

Balance	60,000	(7b)	1,400
(1)	80,000		
(4a)	60,000	(9b)	52,840
(4b)	1,200		
(5)	23,000		
(6)	7,200		

Subsidiary Factory Work-in-Process Ledger

Job 502 (10,000 units A)

Balance	15,000		
(3)	38,000		
(4a)	26,000		
(7)	13,000	(8)	92,000

Job 503 (1,000 units B)

(3)	40,000		
(4a)	30,000		
(7)	15,000	(8)	85,000

Job 504 (5,000 units C)

(3)	7,000		
(4a)	3,000		
(7)	1,500		

Job 505 (20,000 units D)

(3)	5,000		
(4a)	1,000		
(7)	500		

b. Journal Entries:

General Ledger

(1) Factory ledger account 80,000
    Accounts payable 80,000
(2) No entry required
(3) No entry required

(4) Payroll 60,000
    Accrued payroll 56,000
    Payroll taxes payable 4,000
(4a) Factory ledger account 60,000
    Payroll 60,000

(4b) Factory ledger account 1,200
    Payroll taxes payable 1,200
(5) Factory ledger account 23,000
    Cash 23,000
(6) Factory ledger account 7,200
    Accumulated depreciation 7,200
(7) No entry required

(7a) No entry required

(7b) Cost of sales 1,400
    Factory ledger account 1,400

(8) No entry required

(9a) Accounts receivable 70,000
    Sales 70,000
(9b) Cost of sales 52,840
    Factory ledger account 52,840

Factory Ledger

(1) Materials inventory 80,000
    General ledger account 80,000
(2) No entry required
(3) Work in process 90,000
    Materials inventory 90,000

(Job 502, $38,000;   Job 503, $40,000;
Job 504, $7,000;   Job 505, $5,000)
(4) No entry required

(4a) Work in process 60,000
    General ledger account 60,000

(Job 502, $26,000;   Job 503,
$30,000;   Job 504, $3,000;   Job 505,
$1,000)
(4b) Factory overhead 1,200
    General ledger account 1,200
(5) Factory overhead 23,000
    General ledger account 23,000
(6) Factory overhead 7,200
    General ledger account 7,200
(7) Work in process 30,000
    Applied manufacturing
    overhead 30,000
(7a) Applied factory overhead 30,000
    Underapplied and
    overapplied overhead 1,400
    Manufacturing overhead 31,400
(7b) General ledger account 1,400
    Underapplied and
    overapplied overhead 1,400
(8) Finished goods 177,000
    Work in process 177,000
(9a) No entry required

(9b) General ledger account 52,840
    Finished goods 52,840

Able Company

Cost of Goods Manufactured

Month of January 19X1

	Direct Materials	Direct Labor	Applied Manufacturing Overhead	Total
Job 502	$47,000	$30,000	$15,000	$ 92,000
Job 503	40,000	30,000	15,000	85,000
Totals	$87,000	$60,000	$30,000	$177,000

Illustrative Problem 2

This problem illustrates the use of control accounts and subsidiary ledgers for manufacturing overhead and the procedures followed in recording spoilage when all accounts are included in the same ledger.

The following are the assumed transactions:

(1) Manufacturing overhead costs incurred:
   (a) Indirect materials of $4,000 are used in the factory.
   (b) Indirect labor of $6,000 is allocated from the payroll account.
   (c) Depreciation of manufacturing equipment for the period is $7,000.
   (d) Heat/power/light costs of $2,000 are incurred and paid.
(2) The following costs associated with spoiled goods are removed from work-in-process inventory during the period. (No costs are recoverable from the spoiled units.)
   (a) Normal spoilage: $3,000.
   (b) Abnormal spoilage caused by operating conditions of the period: $2,000.

REQUIRED: Record these transactions in T accounts, assuming that a manufacturing-overhead control account and a subsidiary ledger for individual manufacturing-overhead items are maintained.

Solution to Illustrative Problem 2

General Ledger

Manufacturing-Overhead Control

(1a)	4,000
(1b)	6,000
(1c)	7,000
(1d)	2,000
(2a)	3,000

Manufacturing-Overhead Subsidiary Ledger

Indirect Materials

(1a)	4,000

(Continues)   *(Continues)*

Solution to Illustrative Problem 2

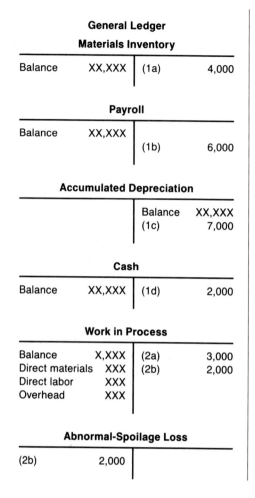

General Ledger

Materials Inventory

Balance	XX,XXX	(1a)	4,000

Payroll

Balance	XX,XXX		
		(1b)	6,000

Accumulated Depreciation

		Balance	XX,XXX
		(1c)	7,000

Cash

Balance	XX,XXX	(1d)	2,000

Work in Process

Balance	X,XXX	(2a)	3,000
Direct materials	XXX	(2b)	2,000
Direct labor	XXX		
Overhead	XXX		

Abnormal-Spoilage Loss

(2b)	2,000		

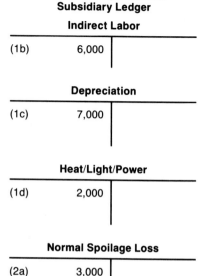

Manufacturing-Overhead Subsidiary Ledger

Indirect Labor

(1b)	6,000		

Depreciation

(1c)	7,000		

Heat/Light/Power

(1d)	2,000		

Normal Spoilage Loss

(2a)	3,000		

SUMMARY

In this chapter, we developed the refinements and elaborations that should be incorporated into a job-order costing system to make the data provided by it more precise and more useful to management. We discussed how departmental cost-accumulation centers provide more precise and more complete unit-cost data. We explained how the control accounts for materials inventory, work in process, and finished goods are supported by subsidiary ledger data. We also observed that manufacturing-overhead costs may be accounted for by using a control account with subsidiary accounts for individual manufacturing-overhead cost items, or by accumulating manufacturing-overhead costs in individual manufacturing-overhead accounts, which would then be closed into a manufacturing-overhead cost summary account at the end of each reporting period. In either case, the control account or the summary account would be matched (closed) against applied manufacturing overhead to arrive at the net underapplied or overapplied manufacturing overhead at the end of the period. We then explained how underapplied or overapplied overhead that is material in amount would be allocated to work in process, finished goods, and cost of sales.

We described how to account for the costs of spoiled goods when using a job-order cost system: Spoilage costs should be divided into normal and abnormal categories. Normal spoilage costs may be removed from work in process and charged to manufacturing overhead, or may remain as part of the total job-order costs. With either treatment, those costs would be included as part of the costs of good units. The costs associated with abnormal spoilage caused by the operating conditions of a particular period should be removed from work in process and appear as a period cost. If abnormal spoilage is caused by the exacting specifications of a particular job order, however, those costs should be allowed to remain as part of the cost of the job, to be spread over that job's good units.

Finally, we briefly explained and illustrated the accounting procedures followed in maintaining a split ledger accounting system, in which the manufacturing cost-accumulation data are accounted for in a separate factory ledger.

GLOSSARY OF TERMS INTRODUCED IN THIS CHAPTER

abnormal-spoilage loss	Loss through shrinkage or spoilage in excess of that expected to occur under normally cost-efficient operating conditions (normal spoilage).
control account	A general ledger summary account that is supported in detail by individual accounts known as a *subsidiary ledger*.
factory ledger	A separate ledger containing manufacturing-related accounts, such as materials inventory, work in process, finished goods, and manufacturing overhead, and a balancing reciprocal account generally labeled "general ledger account."
factory ledger account	The reciprocal account reflected in the general ledger as a replacement for the balances in manufacturing-related accounts transferred to a factory ledger.
general ledger	A ledger containing the accounts used by a business as part of its double-entry bookkeeping system; contains accounts for all assets, liabilities, owners' equity, income and expense items required by that system.
general ledger account	The balancing reciprocal account found in a factory ledger when using a split ledger cost accounting system. (See *factory ledger*.)

manufacturing overhead control account	The account used to accumulate actual overhead costs as they are incurred during each period.
manufacturing-overhead cost summary account	The account into which various manufacturing-overhead accounts are closed at the end of each period when accounts are maintained in the general ledger or factory ledger for each of the separately categorized overhead cost items.
normal-spoilage loss	The loss associated with the spoiled units that cannot be eliminated on a cost-effective basis and thus is included as a product cost.
split ledger system	A bookkeeping system in which the manufacturing-related accounts are removed from the general ledger and placed in a separate factory ledger. Such an arrangement requires the substitution of a reciprocal factory ledger account in the general ledger to replace the accounts transferred to the factory ledger. A general ledger reciprocal account (general ledger account) is required in the factory ledger to allow that ledger to be maintained as a self-balancing double-entry accounting system.
subsidiary ledger	A supporting ledger, consisting of a group of accounts, that provides a detailed breakdown of the contents of the control account to which it relates. The sum of the balances in the subsidiary ledger account will equal the balance in the control account maintained in either the general ledger or the factory ledger.

QUESTIONS FOR CLASS DISCUSSION

5–1 Why do manufacturing firms use departmental cost-accumulation centers? Explain.

5–2 How can the use of a general overhead application rate cause a manufacturing firm to adopt an inappropriate sales promotion policy? Explain.

5–3 What is the difference between a producing department and a service department? Explain.

5–4 What concept should underlie the base used in allocating service department costs to producing departments? Explain.

5–5 How do cause-and-effect relationships affect the allocation process?

5–6 How do actual departmental overhead costs relate to applied overhead costs? Explain.

5–7 In what kind of situation would it be appropriate to use a cost-per-machine-hour overhead application rate? Explain.

5–8 How may the subsidiary ledger for materials inventory (stores) and finished-goods inventory be maintained in a computerized environment?

5–9 What is the meaning of *underapplied or overapplied overhead*? How is it calculated? What does a debit balance in the underapplied or overapplied overhead account signify?

5—10 How should the balance in an underapplied or overapplied overhead account be disposed of at the end of a reporting period? Explain.

5—11 What is the difference between normal and abnormal spoilage? How should each be accounted for?

5—12 What is meant by a *split ledger system?* What accounts usually would be maintained in each of the subsystems? Explain.

EXERCISES

5—13 **Departmental Overhead Rates** Wichita Machine Company produces airplane parts in three departments and applies overhead according to the following schedule:

Department 1	300% of direct materials costs
Department 2	$6 per machine-hour
Department 3	200% of direct labor costs

During the first quarter of 19X3, Wichita produced three products and accumulated the following data:

	Product A–111	Product F–16A	Product X–621
Direct materials	$162,000	$88,000	$115,000
Direct labor costs			
Department 1	$ 10,500	$ 6,000	$ 9,800
Department 2	$ 8,000	$ 3,000	$ 7,500
Department 3	$ 72,000	$34,000	$ 68,000
Machine-hours			
Department 1	300	100	250
Department 2	15,000	10,000	21,000
Department 3	—	200	1,000

REQUIRED:

1. Prepare a schedule showing the total costs associated with products A–111, F–16A, and X–621 for the first quarter of 19X3.
2. If Wichita had used a single factorywide overhead application rate based on direct labor costs, how much overhead would have been applied to product X–621?

5—14 **Departmental Overhead Rates** After service department costs have been allocated, projected overhead costs in DeLynn Designs' three production departments are as follows:

	Cutting	Stitching	Finishing
Estimated Annual Overhead	$71,750	$189,900	$35,200

Each production department is to have its own overhead application rate. The cutting department's rate is to be based on direct-materials costs, estimated to be $183,750; the stitching department's rate is to be based on direct-labor costs, estimated to be $166,560; the finishing department's rate also is to be based on direct-labor costs, estimated to be $17,450. Direct-materials costs and direct-labor costs for designs constructed in the current month and traced to these departments are:

	Cutting		Stitching	Finishing
Design No.	Material	Direct Labor	Direct Labor	Direct Labor
D309	$ 8,200	$ 4,900	$ 9,000	$ 700
S940	1,500	900	2,200	200
C130	3,600	2,160	4,100	400
O22	7,200	4,840	5,800	900
	$20,500	$12,800	$21,100	$2,200

REQUIRED:

1. Calculate the overhead application rate for cutting, stitching, and finishing.
2. Compute the total overhead to be applied to designs D309, S940, C130, and O22.
3. If design O22 is sold for cost plus 125%, what would be its selling price?

5–15 Underapplied or Overapplied Overhead In the last quarter of 19X1, Tobias Corp. estimated its manufacturing overhead for the year 19X2 to be $610,000 and its direct-labor hours as 50,000. At the end of 19X2, Tobias had experienced 48,800 direct-labor hours and had incurred manufacturing-overhead costs of $609,000.

REQUIRED:

1. Compute underapplied or overapplied overhead for Tobias Corp. for 19X2.
2. Give the general journal entry to close all overhead accounts.

5–16 Materials Subsidiary Ledger SCNR, Inc., stocks four parts in its materials-inventory account. Subsidiary records reveal the following:

	Part 504	Part 809	Part 1511
Beginning balance	$ 1,250	$ 6,480	$ 3,690
Purchases	18,750	28,400	30,500
Issuances	19,250	29,680	31,190

REQUIRED:

1. Compute the beginning balance of the materials-inventory general ledger account.
2. Compute the ending balance of materials inventory.

3. If no indirect materials were issued, what is the amount of direct materials that would be debited to work-in-process inventory for the period?

5–17 **Work-in-Process Subsidiary Ledger** Nakdar Corp. worked on only four jobs during the current period. You are provided the following partial information:

Work in Process

Beginning balance	2,000
Direct materials	?
Direct labor	54,000
Overhead	48,600

Job 11101

Beginning balance	$ 1,600*
Direct materials	500
Direct labor	12,000
Overhead	10,800

* 40% of this amount is direct labor.

Job 11103

Beginning balance	?
Direct materials	$2,500
Direct labor	?
Overhead	?

Job 11105

Direct materials	$4,200
Direct labor	9,500
Overhead	?

Job 11107

Direct materials	$3,700
Direct labor	4,000
Overhead	?

REQUIRED:

1. What was the beginning balance of costs accumulated for Job 11103?
2. How much direct labor was used on Job 11103 this period?
3. Assuming overhead is applied on the basis of direct-labor cost, what is the overhead for Jobs 11103, 11105, and 11107?
4. What is the amount of materials cost in the beginning balance for Job 11101?
5. What amount of direct materials was put into work in process during the period?
6. Assume Jobs 11101 and 11103 were completed during the period. Compute the following:
   a. total current manufacturing costs
   b. cost of goods manufactured
   c. end-of-period balance in work in process.

5–18 **Finished-Goods Subsidiary Ledger** Birch Co., Inc., has a normal-cost (actual direct materials and direct labor plus applied overhead) job-order system and uses its completed job-order cost sheets as a subsidiary ledger for its finished-goods inventory accounts. The number of units on each job sheet are reduced as sales are made. At the beginning of March 19X4, the following job-order information made up the finished-goods subsidiary ledger:

Job 18256A	500 units of Part 904 @ $6.50
Job 19863J	300 units of Part 607 @ $3.60

During March, the following jobs were completed and transferred to finished goods:

Job 20584M	1,000 units of Part 301 @ $10.10
Job 21336A	3,000 units of Part 607 @ $ 3.75
Job 21457J	2,500 units of Part 904 @ $ 6.25
Job 22935A	1,500 units of Part 560 @ $ 8.20

All of the finished goods were sold during March except 200 units of part 301, 500 units of part 607, and 100 units of part 560.

REQUIRED: Assuming Birch uses first-in, first-out to account for its finished-goods inventory, and there is no underapplied or overapplied overhead:

1. What amount will appear on the March 31, 19X4, balance sheet for finished-goods inventory?
2. What is the cost-of-sales amount that will appear on the March income statement?

5–19 **Manufacturing-Overhead Subsidiary**   Northeastern Manufacturing Company incurred the following costs in January:

	Manufacturing Departments		Selling and Administrative	Total
	Forming	Finishing		
Indirect labor and factory supervision	$ 5,400	$ 5,200	—	$10,600
Supplies	2,500	700	$ 170	3,370
Utilities	4,500	1,300	850	6,650
Maintenance	4,000	1,000	80	5,080
Insurance	1,000	350	340	1,690
Depreciation on equipment	16,100	2,000	510	18,610
Rent	3,500	2,400	1,000	6,900
Property taxes	800	150	80	1,030
Miscellaneous	3,200	1,400	170	4,770
	$41,000	$14,500	$3,200	$58,700

Northeastern applied $38,900 of manufacturing overhead to work done in the forming department and $16,000 of manufacturing overhead to the work done in the finishing department.

REQUIRED:

1. Describe the subsidiary ledgers for manufacturing overhead for Northeastern for the month of January.
2. Prepare T accounts for (a) manufacturing overhead, (b) applied manufacturing overhead, and (c) underapplied and overapplied manufacturing overhead, and post all relevant January amounts.

5–20 **Allocating Underapplied or Overapplied Overhead** The chief financial officer of the Rayelene Corporation has just reviewed the 19X3 fiscal year results and is displeased with the income statement presentation. Because this is the first year of operation for Rayelene, revenues for 19X3 are low. This was not unexpected, but low sales combined with a large cost of sales and other startup costs have resulted in disappointing operating results for 19X3.

The CFO has asked you to investigate the costs included in cost of sales and report back to him. You quickly assemble the following information:

	Work in Process	Finished Goods	Cost of Sales
Direct materials used	$418,000	$220,000	$22,000
Direct labor cost	100,000	110,000	11,000
Factory overhead applied*	90,000	99,000	9,900
Total before adjustment	$608,000	$429,000	$42,900
Add underapplied overhead	—	—	33,150
Total after adjustment	$608,000	$429,000	$76,050

*Based on direct labor cost.

REQUIRED:

1. What overhead application rate was used?
2. What overhead application rate would have resulted in factory overhead applied exactly equaling factory overhead incurred?
3. Prorate the underapplied overhead to work in process, finished goods, and cost of sales on the basis of the applied overhead in each account.
4. What is the revised cost of sales that will appear on the income statement after the proration in requirement 3 is accomplished?

5–21 **Spoilage** Indiana Company manufactures machinery parts to customer specifications. During February 19X0, Job 1311 for the production of 1,000 units of part A35 was completed. The following job-order T account summarizes the costs incurred:

(Part A35) Job 1311 (1,000 units)

Direct materials	8,000
Direct labor	4,000
Applied manufacturing overhead	8,000

Upon inspection, Indiana rejected 100 units. Of the rejected units, 10 were totally worthless, 40 were sold as scrap for $100, and 50 were reworked at a total cost of $400. This spoilage was considered normal and the customer agreed to accept 950 good units. Later, when the units were delivered to the customer, 30 units were returned for reworking to meet the customer's exacting specifications. The additional processing costs for these 30 units, which the customer agreed to pay, were $190.

REQUIRED:

1. What would be the unit cost of good units produced on Job 1311?
2. Post these spoilage transactions to the Job 1311 T account.

5–22 **Split Ledger Transactions** Even though the administrative offices of Cunningham Products Company are in the same building as its manufacturing facilities, Cunningham uses a split ledger system. The accounts for materials inventory, work-in-process inventory, manufacturing overhead, and applied-manufacturing overhead are maintained by a factory clerk, while the remaining general ledger accounts are maintained by an administrative clerk.

Selected recent transactions:

(1) Materials costing $7,500 were purchased on account.
(2) Direct materials of $4,000 and indirect materials of $800 were requisitioned from materials inventory.
(3) A check for $7,500 was issued to pay accounts payable.
(4) Depreciation of $12,900 was recorded on factory equipment.

REQUIRED: Prepare general journal entries to record the transactions in (a) the general ledger, and (b) the factory ledger.

PROBLEMS

5–23 **Departmental Overhead Rates** The Oliver Company uses a predetermined overhead rate based on machine-hours in department 1 and direct-labor hours in Department 2. In October 19X4, before the current period began, Oliver projected the following amounts, among other items, in its annual budget:

	Department 1	Department 2
Direct-labor cost	$ 5,265	$84,500
Manufacturing overhead	$93,600	$97,500
Machine-hours	10,400	3,250
Direct-labor hours	650	13,000

At the end of the current period (December 31, 19X5), work-in-process and overhead accounts appeared as follows:

	Manufacturing Overhead—Department 1	
.		
.		
.		
$104,000		

	Manufacturing Overhead—Department 2	
.		
.		
.		
$99,700		

	Manufacturing Overhead Applied—Department 1	
	?	

	Manufacturing Overhead Applied—Department 2	
	?	

	Work-in-Process Inventory	
? *		

*Jobs 301, 405, 220 and 250.

Job 301

Direct materials	$106
Direct labor (25 hr)	200
Overhead	?

Job 405

Direct materials	$258
Direct labor (10 hr)	85
Overhead	?

Job 220

Direct materials	$675
Direct labor (350 hr)	2,310
Overhead	?

Job 250

Direct materials	$630
Direct labor (200 hr)	1,260
Overhead	?

During 19X5, the following actual results were achieved (includes jobs 301, 405, 220, and 250):

	Department 1	Department 2
Direct-labor hours	630	12,900**
Machine-hours	10,000*	3,000

*Includes 30 hr for job 301 and 9 hr for job 405.
**Includes 100 hr for job 220 and 60 hr for job 250.

REQUIRED:

1. Compute Oliver's predetermined overhead rates for Department 1 and Department 2, and post the appropriate amounts in the two manufacturing-overhead-applied accounts.
2. Compute the December 31, 19X5, ending balance for work-in-process inventory.
3. Assuming finished-goods inventory and cost of sales have balances of $20,000 and $270,000, respectively, allocate any underapplied or over-

applied overhead for the year to work-in-process inventory, finished-goods inventory, and cost of sales on the basis of total normal costs.

5–24   **Subsidiary Ledgers: Journal Entries** The ERAN Corporation employs a job-order cost system that uses a perpetual inventory system. ERAN began operations in April. The job cost records for April, May, and June, its first three months are:

Job 8542

	April	May	June
Direct materials	$6,000	$2,200	—
Direct labor	3,000	2,700	—
Overhead applied	4,500	4,050	—

Job 8653

	April	May	June
Direct materials	$11,200	$3,600	—
Direct labor	5,700	4,400	—
Overhead applied	8,550	6,600	—

Job 8710

	April	May	June
Direct materials	$1,800	$3,500	$7,600
Direct labor	800	2,000	3,900
Overhead applied	1,200	3,000	?

Job 8750

	April	May	June
Direct materials	—	$6,600	$4,800
Direct labor	—	3,100	5,250
Overhead applied	—	4,650	?

Job 8770

	April	May	June
Direct materials	—	$1,050	$9,200
Direct labor	—	570	4,600
Overhead applied	—	855	?

Job 8815

	April	May	June
Direct materials	—	—	$14,300
Direct labor	—	—	6,800
Overhead applied	—	—	?

Job 8845

	April	May	June
Direct materials	—	—	$12,650
Direct labor	—	—	8,200
Overhead applied	—	—	?

ERAN applied overhead on the basis of direct-labor costs. All jobs are completed in the order in which they are begun. Selected account balances accumulated at April 30 and May 31 were as follows:

	April 30	May 31
Materials inventory	$ 3,600	$21,000
Finished-goods inventory	0	14,600
Cost of goods sold	0	22,450
Payroll payable	1,670	2,554
Manufacturing overhead applied	14,250	33,405
Manufacturing overhead control	9,100	42,750

All completed jobs except 8770 were sold by June 30. Jobs 8815 and 8845 are still in process at the end of June.

REQUIRED:

1. Prepare a schedule showing the work-in-process inventory balances on (a) April 30 and (b) May 31.
2. Prepare summary general journal entries to record all changes in the work-in-process inventory account during May.
3. Prepare summary general journal entries to record all changes in the work-in-process inventory account during June.
4. Prepare a schedule showing the finished-goods inventory balance on June 30.
5. Prepare a T account for work-in-process inventory, and post all relevant June transactions.
6. Should the overhead accounts be closed at the end of June? Explain your answer.

5-25 **Manufacturing-Overhead Subsidiary Ledger** James Company produces specialized computer accessories to customer specifications, using a job-order cost system. Manufacturing overhead is applied to production using a budgeted rate set at the beginning of each year. During 19X4, the following costs were incurred:

Direct labor	$290,000
Direct materials used	230,000
Indirect labor	62,000
Depreciation—factory building	6,800
Depreciation—sales department automobiles	4,100
Liability insurance for factory	2,450
Workers' Compensation insurance (95% factory, 5% selling and	
administrative)	14,500
Overtime premium—factory (not related to individual jobs)	12,400
Property taxes—factory	3,800
Depreciation—factory equipment	12,700
Fire and casualty insurance on factory and equipment	3,600
Indirect materials used	1,540
Maintenance and repairs—factory and building	9,580
Janitorial services and supplies for factory	2,600
Security service—factory (80%) and finished-goods warehouse (20%)	10,200
Miscellaneous manufacturing overhead	8,350
Miscellaneous general and administrative overhead	5,170

REQUIRED:

1. Prepare a schedule of manufacturing-overhead costs incurred for 19X4.
2. List the accounts included in the manufacturing-overhead subsidiary ledger used to accumulate manufacturing-overhead costs during the year.
3. If the budgeted overhead rate for 19X4 were 60% of direct labor cost, how much manufacturing overhead would have been applied to work in process?
4. Compute the underapplied or overapplied overhead for James Company for 19X4. If this amount is closed to cost of sales, what will be the effect on net income (that is, net income with costs unadjusted for underapplied or overapplied overhead)?

5–26
CMA Adapted

Underapplied and Overapplied Overhead Targon, Inc., manufactures lawn equipment. A job-order system is used because the products are manufactured on a batch basis rather than a continuous basis. Targon employs a full-absorption accounting method for cost accumulation. The balances in selected general ledger accounts for the 11-month period ending August 31, 19X2, are:

Stores (materials) inventory	$ 32,000
Work-in-process inventory	1,200,000
Finished-goods inventory	2,785,000
Factory-overhead control	2,260,000
Cost of goods sold	14,200,000

The work-in-process inventory consists of two jobs:

Job No.	Units	Items	Accumulated Cost
3005–5	50,000	Estate sprinklers	$ 700,000
3006–4	40,000	Economy sprinklers	500,000
			$1,200,000

The finished-goods inventory consists of five items:

Items	Quantity and Unit Cost	Accumulated Cost
Estate sprinklers	5,000 units @ $22 each	$ 110,000
Deluxe sprinklers	115,000 units @ $17 each	1,955,000
Brass nozzles	10,000 gross @ $14 per gross	140,000
Rainmaker nozzles	5,000 gross @ $16 per gross	80,000
Connectors	100,000 gross @ $ 5 per gross	500,000
		$2,785,000

The factory cost budget prepared for the 19X1–X2 fiscal year is as follows:

Factory Cost Annual Budget
For the Year Ending September 30, 19X2

Direct materials	$ 3,800,000
Purchased parts	6,000,000
Direct labor (400,000 hours)	4,000,000
Overhead	
Supplies	190,000
Indirect labor	700,000
Supervision	250,000
Depreciation	950,000
Utilities	200,000
Insurance	10,000
Property taxes	40,000
Miscellaneous	60,000
Total factory costs	$16,200,000

The company applied factory overhead on the basis of direct-labor hours. The activities during the first 11-months of the year were quite close to the budget. A total of 367,000 direct-labor hours have been worked through August 31, 19X2.

The September 19X2 transactions are as follows:

(1) All direct materials, purchased parts, and supplies are charged to stores inventory. The September purchases were: materials, $410,000; purchased parts, $285,000; supplies, $13,000.

(2) The direct materials, purchased parts, and supplies were requisitioned from stores inventory as follows:

Job No.	Purchased Parts	Materials	Supplies	Total Requisitions
3005–5	$110,000	$100,000	$ —	$210,000
3006–4	—	6,000	—	6,000
4001–3 (30,000 gross rainmaker nozzles)	—	181,000	—	181,000
4002–1 (10,000 deluxe sprinklers)	—	92,000	—	92,000
4003–5 (50,000 ring sprinklers)	163,000	—	—	163,000
Supplies	—	—	20,000	20,000
	$273,000	$379,000	$20,000	$672,000

(3) The payroll summary for September is:

Job No.	Hours	Cost
3005–5	6,000	$ 62,000
3006–4	2,500	26,000
4001–3	18,000	182,000
4002–1	500	5,000
4003–5	5,000	52,000
Indirect	8,000	60,000
Supervision	—	24,000
Sales and administration	—	120,000
		$531,000

(4) Other factory costs incurred during September were:

Depreciation	$62,500
Utilities	15,000
Insurance	1,000
Property taxes	3,500
Miscellaneous	5,000
	$87,000

(5) Jobs completed during September and the actual output were:

Job No.	Quantity	Items
3005–5	48,000 units	Estate sprinklers
3006–4	39,000 units	Economy sprinklers
4001–3	29,500 gross	Rainmaker nozzles
4003–5	49,000 units	Ring sprinklers

(6) The following finished products were shipped to customers during September:

Items	Quantity
Estate sprinklers	16,000 units
Deluxe sprinklers	32,000 units
Economy sprinklers	20,000 units
Ring sprinklers	22,000 units
Brass nozzles	5,000 gross
Rainmaker nozzles	10,000 gross
Connectors	26,000 gross

REQUIRED:

1. **a.** Calculate the underapplied or overapplied overhead for the year ended September 30, 19X2. Be sure to indicate whether the overhead is overapplied or underapplied.
   b. What is the appropriate accounting treatment for this overapplied or underapplied overhead balance? Explain your answer.
2. Calculate the dollar balance in the work-in-process inventory account as of September 30, 19X2.
3. Calculate the dollar balance in the finished-goods inventory account as of September 30, 19X2, for the estate sprinklers using first-in, first-out.

5–27 **Overhead Entries** Assume the following information for the Starks Corporation's two divisions:

	Division 1	Division 2
Actual direct-labor hours	715	525
Factory-overhead rate per direct-labor hour	$2.70	$5.60
Actual factory-overhead costs		
Rent on factory	$325	$505
Factory supplies	180	300
Indirect labor	420	245
Utilities factory	520	860
Small tools	100	105

	Division 1	Division 2
Applied factory overhead in the end-of-period account balances:		
Cost of sales	$920	$1,400
Work-in-process inventory	325	420
Finished-goods inventory	260	280

REQUIRED: Using the information given, prepare general journal entries for each division of Stark to do the following:

1. Record the applied factory overhead.
2. Record the actual factory overhead.
3. Close applied factory overhead and actual factory overhead to under-applied or overapplied factory overhead.
4. Allocate the underapplied or overapplied overhead among ending work-in-process inventory, ending finished-goods inventory, and cost of sales for the period.

5-28 **Normal and Abnormal Spoilage** Candelabra Gourmet Delights produces gourmet casseroles that it retails in its own stores. The dishes are pre-pared in large batches and then frozen in individual containers. All items that are not sold within 2 weeks are considered substandard and are sold to an out-of-town wholesaler for $5 per container. Candelabra estimates that approximately 5 of every 100 containers will not be sold before the 2-week deadline and includes a provision for this loss in the overhead application rate. Cost information on two recently completed batches are as follows:

Beef Wellington (20 containers)		Lobster Bisque (26 containers)	
Materials	$245	Materials	$175
Labor	40	Labor	30
Overhead	49	Overhead	35
	$334		$240

Half of the Beef Wellington containers were not sealed properly by the new worker and were ruined. At the end of two weeks, one of the good Beef Wellington casseroles and two of the Lobster Bisque cartons had not been sold.

REQUIRED:

1. What is the cost per container for Beef Wellington and for Lobster Bisque?
2. What, if any, is the amount of abnormal loss for the period from these two batches? If there is an abnormal loss, prepare the general journal entry that would be required to recognize it.
3. Prepare all journal entries associated with accounting for the two batches (Beef Wellington and Lobster Bisque) from the time they are

completed (prior to their transfer to finished-goods inventory) through their disposal. Containers of Beef Wellington and Lobster Bisque are sold for $32 and $19 each, respectively.

5–29 Spoilage Recognition in Accounts Danberg Corporation produces football equipment in job lots. In the past, Danberg has estimated that spoilage costs are about 3% of the costs incurred and has chosen to ignore specific recognition of the costs of spoilage. Defective items usually are discarded. When items occasionally are reworked, the rework costs are added to the cost of the job. Even though sales have been fairly constant, costs have recently increased significantly. Danberg's president requests that the factory supervisor explain the dramatic increase in cost of goods manufactured.

The supervisor requests detailed cost information on the next batch of football jerseys being produced. She is provided the following information relating to lot 5140:

Direct materials (1,550 yards @ $2.40)	$3,720
Direct labor (210 hours @ $8)	1,680
Overhead (210 hours @ $9.50)	1,995
Total	$7,395

These were 960 good units passing inspection, and 40 yards of material (at $2.40 per yard) were ruined by an inexperienced cutter.

REQUIRED:

1. What would be the cost per jersey in lot 5140 under the current system?
2. Assuming the overhead rate includes a provision for normal spoilage, compute the amount of normal spoilage and prepare the general journal entry required to formally recognize the cost of that spoilage.
3. Compute the amount of abnormal spoilage, and prepare the general journal entry required to record this spoilage.
4. Compute the cost per unit that the 960 good units would carry in finished-goods inventory if spoilage were explicitly recognized in the accounts. Discuss.

5–30 Split Ledger System POWERAM Embroidery Company uses a job-order system and records transactions in a general journal maintained in its home office and a factory journal maintained at the manufacturing site. All inventory and factory-overhead accounts are maintained at the factory. All other accounts are maintained in the general ledger. The following transactions occurred during April 19X2:

Materials purchased on account	$ 40,800
Direct materials used	33,600
Gross wages	
Direct labor	16,000

(Continues)

Indirect labor	3,200
Office salaries	4,800
Taxes withheld	4,640
Employer taxes (80% factory)	2,400
Depreciation	
Office equipment	6,400
Factory equipment	8,000
Rent	
Factory	4,800
Office	7,500
Indirect materials used	1,650
Misc. factory expenses incurred	3,200
Cost of completed goods	40,000
Cost of sales	32,000
Sales	60,000

Factory overhead is applied at 80% of direct-labor cost.

REQUIRED:

1. Prepare summary general journal entries for the preceding transactions in (a) the general ledger and (b) the factory ledger.
2. Prepare T accounts for all overhead accounts and post the appropriate journal entries from requirement 1.
3. What is the overhead status at the end of April 19X2?

5–31 **Job-Order Costing and Split Ledgers** Blade Construction Company constructs and rebuilds highways. Job cost information is recorded on the job site in accounts for materials inventory, work-in-process inventory, finished-goods inventory, overhead incurred, and overhead applied. The main office for Blade keeps all other general ledger accounts. Transactions associated with job 895 outside of Dayton, Tennessee, during June, 19X6, the final month of construction, included the following:

Payroll	
Direct labor	$ 33,000
Indirect labor	4,400
Employee FICA taxes	660
Federal withholding taxes	2,600
Employer payroll taxes	1,500
Materials purchased	27,500
Materials used (4% indirect)	30,800
Other factory overhead items	
Rent—portable buildings and equipment	8,800
Depreciation	4,500
Miscellaneous	2,200
Cost of completed job	180,500
Sales (contract price)	217,000

Applied overhead was 50% of materials used.

REQUIRED:

1. Prepare summary journal entries for the preceding transactions for (a) the general ledger and (b) the job-site ledger.
2. What was the June 1, 19X6, balance in work in process?

5–32 **THOUGHT STIMULATION PROBLEM.** Alexander Manufacturing Company produces precision gauges in a just-in-time (JIT) environment with no tolerance for spoilage. All units produced are expected to meet or exceed a detailed set of specifications, and each worker is responsible for inspecting his or her own work as well as parts transferred from previous manufacturing cells.

Quality is a primary objective in the manufacture of Alexander's gauges. A continuous production line flows through five manufacturing cells. When a worker in a manufacturing cell discovers a defect in a part going into processing, the entire production line (backward and forward) is stopped until the cause of the defect can be located and corrected. Everyone's attention is focused on the problem. After defective units have been identified, the cause of the problem has been located, and appropriate adjustments have been made, movement of the production line is resumed. All gauges shipped to customers meet 100% of their specifications.

REQUIRED:

1. Since Alexander Manufacturing Company allows no defective units to be shipped to customers and, in fact, stops production when a defect is discovered, does it need to account for spoiled (normal and/or abnormal) goods?
2. Does Alexander incur a cost of quality? Explain.
3. Assume that Alexander uses backflush accounting, where manufacturing costs are recorded when goods are shipped. What happens to the costs incurred because of stopping the production line and investigating and correcting a production problem? Can Alexander Manufacturing Company identify any abnormal spoilage? Discuss.

Chapter 6

Process Costing:
Basic Procedures

A s we now know, one objective of cost accounting is to accumulate and allocate manufacturing costs so we can derive inventory and cost-of-sales account balances to be used in financial statements. We have shown in Chapters 4 and 5 how a job-order cost system focuses on the allocation of manufacturing costs to individual lots of goods as they move toward completion. The costs accumulated on a lot's job-order sheet are then allocated to the individual units included in the job lot as those units are completed and transferred out of work in process into finished-goods inventory. The costs accumulated on the job-order sheets of unfinished jobs constitute the subsidiary ledger in support of the work-in-process control account.

Let's review how job-order cost-accumulation and -allocation procedures relate to work-in-process and finished-goods inventories. Assume that a firm begins operations with no beginning-of-period work-in-process inventory. Four jobs are started during the period; two of them (job 1 and job 2) are completed during the period. The cost flows relating to these actions may be visualized as follows:

Job-Order Costing.

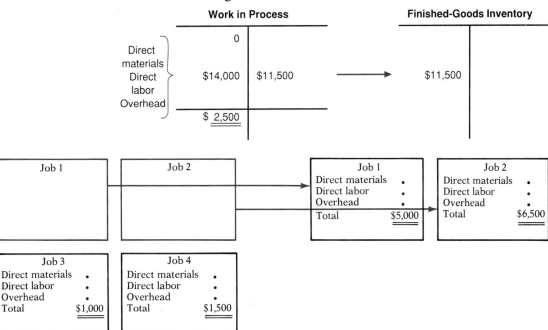

Jobs 1 and 2 were completed during the period, so the total costs accumulated for them ($11,500) were transferred from work in process to finished goods. Jobs 3 and 4, on which $1,000 and $1,500 of costs, respectively, were incurred, are incomplete at the end of the period. The total costs shown for these two jobs ($2,500) will remain as the end-of-period balance in work in process. The work-in-process T account indicates that total direct-materials, direct-labor, and manufacturing-overhead costs incurred for all jobs amounted to $14,000, while cost of goods manufactured totaled $11,500.

When a manufacturing process involves the continuous production of identical units rather than distinguishable job lots, there can be no job orientation. When there is no obvious start or finish (because the manufacturing process is endlessly repetitive), we use a *process-costing system* to accumulate and allocate manufacturing costs. In using such a system, all manufacturing costs are allocated first to departments or processes. Departmental or process costs are then allocated to units of product as units are completed. Instead of using job-cost sheets, the costs associated with each process (or department) are summarized on a **cost-of-production report**, with one report per process (or department), for a period of time. At the end of each period, the costs accumulated on each such report will be allocated between end-of-period work in process and units transferred to the next process, or, in the case of the final process, to finished goods. Again assuming no beginning-of-period work in process, these cost-allocation and -accumulation procedures may be visualized as follows:

Process Costing.

	Work in Process		Finished-Goods Inventory	
	0			
Direct materials Direct labor Overhead	$17,100	$15,000	→	$15,000
	$ 2,100			

The cost-of-production reports that provide the supporting detail relating to these cost flows would include the following data:

Process (Department) 1 Cost of Production During Period: (Direct materials, Direct labor, and Overhead)		Process (Department) 2 Cost of Production During Period: (Direct materials, Direct labor, and Overhead)		Process (Department) 3 Cost of Production During Period: (Direct materials, Direct labor, and Overhead)	
Added to process	$8,600	Added to process	$ 4,000	Added to process	$ 4,500
		Transferred in from process 1	$ 8,000	Transferred in from process 2	$11,000
Costs to be accounted for	$8,600	Costs to be accounted for	$12,000	Costs to be accounted for	$15,500
Ending inventory	$ 600	Ending inventory	$ 1,000	Ending inventory	$ 500
Transferred to Process 2	$8,000	Transferred to Process 3	$11,000	Transferred to finished goods	$15,000
Costs accounted for	$8,600	Costs accounted for	$12,000	Costs accounted for	$15,500

In this sequential manufacturing process, work is begun in process 1, transferred to process 2, where additional work is performed, then transferred to process 3, where the product is completed and finally transferred to finished goods:

End-of-period work in process consists of the sum of all costs relating to units remaining in processes 1, 2, and 3. Costs associated with units transferred from process 3 to finished goods are reflected as a reduction in the work-in-process account and a balancing addition to the finished-goods inventory account. Note that direct materials, direct labor, and manufacturing-overhead costs incurred for all three processes during the period amount to $8,600 + $4,000 + $4,500 = $17,100. The end-of-period work-in-process balance ($2,100) comprises the following amounts:

Work in process, Process 1	$ 600
Work in process, Process 2	1,000
Work in process, Process 3	500
Total	$2,100

The three cost-of-production reports constitute the subsidiary ledger for work in process for this process-costing system, just as job-cost sheets constitute the subsidiary ledger for a job-order system.

This chapter develops the specific procedures followed in installing and maintaining a process-costing system. We begin by demonstrating how these procedures would be carried out for a very simple system involving only a single product, a single process, and no work-in-process inventories. Next, we show how the procedures used in this simple system must be modified to account for the allocation and accumulation of costs when we have beginning and end-of-period work-in-process inventories. Then we explain how the cost-of-production report is organized and how the data included in it are calculated. Finally, we demonstrate the basic process-costing procedures by illustrating the preparation of a cost-of-production report.

The next three chapters continue the development of process costing. Multiprocesses are introduced in Chapter 7, and the accounting treatment of spoilage is discussed in Chapter 8. We deal with the problems of allocating costs to joint products and by-products in Chapter 9.

A Simple Process-Costing System

Let's assume we have a one-process factory that produces only one product and has no beginning or end-of-period work-in-process inventories. The appropriate cost-accumulation and -allocation boxes for such a system are shown in Figure 6–1. Since there are no work-in-process inventories, we can determine the manufacturing cost per unit of finished product by dividing the total direct-materials, direct-labor, and manufacturing-overhead costs incurred in carrying out the manufacturing process by the number of units finished and transferred to finished-goods inventory. In this special situation of zero work-in-process inventory, the number of units moving from the factory into the finished-goods inventory frequently is determined by a mechanical counter that automatically registers an additional unit each time a unit of product is completed. For example, in milling flour a packing machine is used to place the flour in bags. If a mill packs only five-pound bags of flour, a mechanical or light-sensing device can be placed on the packing machine that will automatically register the number of such bags packed during a specified period of time. With such an arrangement, we can determine the cost to assign each five-pound bag by dividing the total manufacturing cost (direct materials, direct labor, and manufacturing overhead for the reporting period) by the number of bags packed, as registered on the packing machine counter. We can then allocate the total manufacturing costs for the period between finished goods and cost of sales according to the number of units unsold and the number of units sold. If $10,000 in manufacturing costs is incurred to produce 1,000 units, the cost per unit is $10. If 100 of those units remain in finished-goods inventory at the end of the period, then end-of-period finished-goods inventory is 100 × $10 = $1,000, and the cost of sales (assuming no beginning inventory of finished goods) is $9,000.

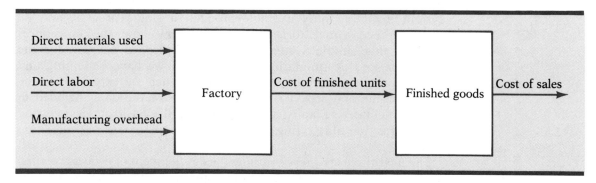

FIGURE 6–1 Cost Allocation—No Beginning or Ending Work-in-Process Inventories

Process Cost System
with Work-in-Process Inventories

We now turn to the procedures required when a firm has work-in-process inventories at the beginning and end of the reporting period. Any partially completed units in beginning work-in-process inventory will be completed during the current period, and some units started in the current period also will be completely finished. However, a portion of the units started during the period will be only partially completed at the end of the current period, thus constituting end-of-period work in process. Proper determination of how many *equivalent whole units* of work were completed during a reporting period requires the calculation of equivalent units of production, which figure is then used as divisor in computing the unit cost of manufacturing a product during the reporting period.

Calculating the Equivalent Units of Production

When we have partially processed inventories in our factory at the beginning *and* end of the period, it is no longer appropriate to divide total manufacturing costs by the number of units transferred from the factory to finished-goods inventory. Instead, we must calculate the number of whole units of product that *would have been* produced had all production efforts been devoted only to turning out completed units, rather than completing the units in process at the beginning of the period, fully completing some units put into process during the period, and partially completing other units put into process during the period. We call that figure the **equivalent units of production (EUP)** for the period.

To calculate the EUP for a reporting period, we must first determine the degree of completion of both the beginning and end-of-period work-in-process inventories. Next, we add to the number of units actually transferred from work in process to finished goods the number of equivalent whole units of production included in the end-of-period work-in-process inventory (because those units also represent production achieved during the period). Then we subtract from that total the number of equivalent whole units of work performed on beginning-of-period work-in-process inventory during the preceding reporting period (because that represents production of the prior period). After these adjustments, we have a figure that represents the equivalent whole units of production completed during the reporting period. This becomes the **equivalent-units divisor** used with the first-in, first-out cost flow method.

To illustrate the calculation of the EUP, let's assume that a factory completes and transfers 10,000 units of finished product from the factory to finished-goods inventory. There are 3,000 units still in the factory at the end of the period that are one-third complete. The factory had

4,000 units in process at the beginning of the period that were three-fourths completed during the preceding period. The equivalent whole units of production for the current period then would be calculated as follows:

Units completed and transferred to finished-goods inventory	10,000
Plus equivalent whole units in end-of-period work-in-process inventory (additional work done during current period) (3,000 × $\frac{1}{3}$)	1,000
Total	11,000
Less equivalent whole units in beginning-of-period work-in-process inventory (work done during prior period) (4,000 × $\frac{3}{4}$)	(3,000)
Equivalent units of production for the period	8,000

The equivalent units produced during the operating period also may be derived by dividing the total unit universe into three boxes: one for units included in beginning-of-period work in process, another for units started and completed during the period, and a third for units started and partially completed during the period, as shown below. Each of the partially processed boxes is divided into compartments to show the portion completed during the previous period, the portions completed during the current period, and the uncompleted portion.

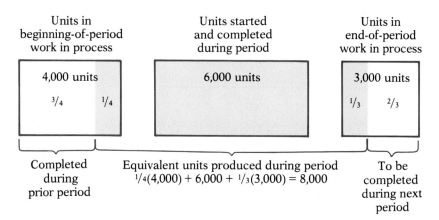

After calculating the EUP as 8,000, and assuming that all manufacturing costs were incurred as work progressed through the factory during the period (that is, direct materials, direct labor, and overhead were added at the same rate and therefore each unit showed same degree of completion for each cost element), we can determine the cost per unit of finished product produced during the period by dividing the total manufacturing costs (direct materials, direct labor, and manufacturing overhead) incurred during the period by 8,000. The only way this equivalent-units figure is used is in calculating cost per unit. All other references to units in this and future chapters will be in terms of actual physical units of product.

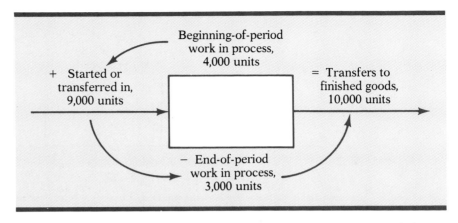

FIGURE 6–2 Units Worked on During Period (assuming no lost units)

Let us use our box illustration to show how total units are accounted for and how the equivalent-units divisor is calculated. Figure 6–2 employs the data relating to the units worked on during the reporting period. The disposition of units in beginning-of-period work-in-process inventory plus units started during the period must be explained. If no units are lost, as assumed in Figure 6–2, these units must either be in end-of-period work-in-process inventory or have been transferred to finished goods. This statement of unit accountability may be organized as follows:

Units to be accounted for:		Units accounted for:	
Beginning inventory	4,000	Transferred out	10,000
Started or transferred in	9,000	Ending inventory	3,000
Total	13,000	Total	13,000

Figure 6–3 illustrates the modifications necessary to calculate the equivalent units of production for the period. The four steps (parenthetically numbered in Figure 6–3) are worked out in the following schedule:

Transfers to finished goods	10,000	units
+ End-of-period work in process, $\frac{1}{3}(3,000)$	1,000	units
Total	11,000	units
− Beginning-of-period work in process, $\frac{3}{4}(4,000)$	3,000	units
= Equivalent units produced	8,000	units

Notice that the analysis in Figure 6–3 goes in the opposite direction from that in Figure 6–2, and also that units started during the period—because they are included either in units transferred to finished

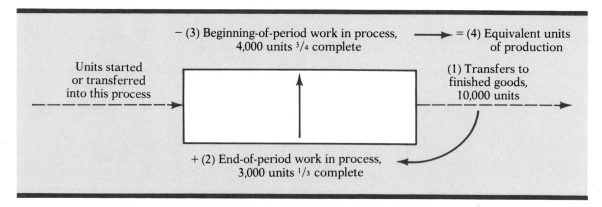

FIGURE 6–3   Equivalent Units of Production

goods or units in end-of-period work-in-process inventory—are not included in the calculation.

Different Stages of Completion for Individual Elements of Costs

Up to this point, we have assumed that the units in process at the beginning and end of the period had the same degree of completion for each element of manufacturing cost, that is, that direct materials, direct labor, and manufacturing overhead were all added at the same point(s) in time. This, however, is not usually the way manufacturing is carried out. More generally, the units in process at the end of each period will have all of the cost of materials included in them but only a portion of the total direct-labor and manufacturing-overhead costs (also called *conversion costs*) required to complete them because the process of converting raw materials to finished goods is only partially complete. When that is the case, we will have different equivalent-units figures for materials than for conversion costs. For example, if materials are added at the beginning of processing and conversion costs are incurred as those materials are processed, the units in process will be 100% complete insofar as materials are concerned and only partially complete insofar as conversion costs are concerned.

To illustrate how the equivalent-units divisors would be calculated in such a situation, let's assume that the Ajax Chemical Company shows the following production and inventory data for the current period:

Units in process at beginning of period, 100% complete as to materials, 40% complete as to labor and overhead	2,000
Units transferred to finished goods during period	5,000
Units in process at end of period, 100% complete as to materials, 25% complete as to labor and overhead	4,000

We can display these data in an *accountability box* such as the one in Figure 6–4. Following the procedures developed earlier, we can now

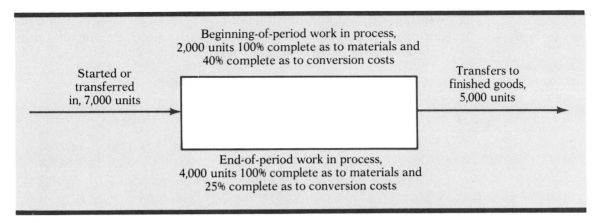

FIGURE 6–4 Unit Accountability Box (units worked on during period, assuming no lost units)

calculate the equivalent units of production (the divisors to be used in calculating costs per unit) with a first-in, first-out cost flow assumption for direct materials costs and for both direct labor and manufacturing-overhead costs:

Equivalent Units of Production

	Direct Materials	Direct Labor and Overhead
Units transferred out	5,000	5,000
Plus equivalent units of work in end-of-period work in process	+4,000	+1,000
Less equivalent units of work in beginning-of-period work in process	−2,000	− 800
Equivalent units of production for period	7,000	5,200

If direct labor and manufacturing overhead are added at different points in the production process, we would have to calculate three equivalent unit figures—one for direct materials, one for direct labor, and one for manufacturing overhead.

Calculating Unit Costs. To illustrate the calculation of unit costs in the situation just described, let's assume that the beginning-of-period work-in-process inventory of Ajax Chemical Company (2,000 units) shows a value of $7,000 (made up of materials cost of $4,000, direct labor cost of $1,300, and manufacturing-overhead cost of $1,700), that the cost of raw materials put into process during the reporting period was $14,000, and that direct-labor and manufacturing-overhead costs during the period were $7,800 and $10,400, respectively. The total costs to be accounted for then may be summarized as follows:

Costs to Be Accounted For

	Direct Materials	Direct Labor	Overhead	Total
Beginning inventory costs	$ 4,000	$1,300	$ 1,700	$ 7,000
Current period costs	14,000	7,800	10,400	32,200
Totals	$18,000	$9,100	$12,100	$39,200

The total unit cost of production for the reporting period would then be $5.50, calculated as follows:

Direct materials ($14,000/7,000 units)	$2.00
Direct labor ($7,800/5,200 units)	1.50
Manufacturing overhead ($10,400/5,200 units)	2.00
Total cost per unit	$5.50

After the unit costs have been calculated, they will be used in determining the costs to be allocated to the units transferred to finished-goods inventory and to the units remaining in work in process. This is demonstrated later in the chapter.

Materials Added During or at End of Processing. Materials may be added at points other than the beginning of manufacture. In some cases, materials may be added at the end of processing. For example, in a finishing and packaging department, packaging materials would be added to the units only when they were completed and ready to be transferred to finished-goods stores. Material added at the end of a process can be depicted as follows:

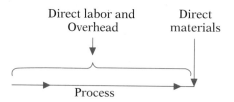

In this case, we would have 0% completion, insofar as materials added at the end of processing are concerned, for all units in process at both the beginning and end of a period. As a result, the equivalent units of production to be used as a divisor in getting packaging material cost per unit would be the number of units transferred out.

If materials are added at some point after the beginning but before the end of processing, the degree of completion for units in process depends on whether they have passed the point where the materials are added. Units beyond that point will be 100% complete as regards these materials; those that have not reached that point will be 0% complete. For example, if materials are added when processing is 25% complete, beginning inventory was 20% complete, and ending inventory is 60% complete, the process can be depicted as follows:

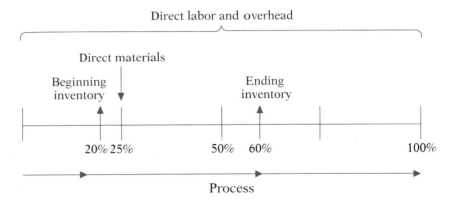

Using the data assumed in our earlier illustration (5,000 units are completed and transferred out; 2,000 units are in beginning inventory; 4,000 units are in ending inventory), with the completion percentages shown just above the equivalent-units calculations would be:

Equivalent Units of Production (Materials added when processing is 25% complete)

	Direct Materials		Direct Labor and Overhead	
Units transferred out	5,000		5,000	
Plus ending inventory work	4,000	(4,000 × 100%)	2,400	(4,000 × 60%)
Less beginning inventory work completed last period	(0)	(2,000 × 0%)	(400)	(2,000 × 20%)
	9,000		7,000	

Extreme care must be exercised in computing equivalent units of production when materials are added at points during processing. Also note that if materials are added at two (or more) points in the process, a separate equivalent-units computation should be made for each material.

In situations where production "flows through" a process on a continuing basis, the degree of completion associated with materials added during processing generally can be based on the percentage of the process that remains to be completed beyond the point where materials are added. For instance, given a "flow through" process that has 5,000 units at various stages of completion at the end of a reporting period, if materials are added 20 percent of the way through the process, we would, in the absence of other information, be justified in assuming that the equivalent units for the materials added are 5,000 × 0.8 = 4,000.

Valuation of Work-in-Process Inventory

In valuing work-in-process inventory, generally accepted accounting practices permit use of any one of three cost flow assumptions:

1. first-in, first-out method (FIFO)
2. weighted average method
3. last-in, first-out method (LIFO).

First-In, First-Out (FIFO) Costing Method

The **FIFO method** allocates costs on the basis of the physical flow of production through the factory. This means that the units in beginning-of-period work in process are assumed to be the first ones completed insofar as assignment of costs are concerned. Therefore, if the number of units transferred out of a process exceeds the number of units in beginning-of-period work in process (the usual situation), the units in process at the end of the period are presumed, for the purpose of assigning costs to them, to be units the firm began to process during the current reporting period. As a result, end-of-period work-in-process inventory should be valued at the unit cost of production during the reporting period. As illustrated earlier, that unit cost is calculated by dividing manufacturing costs incurred during the reporting period by the equivalent units of work completed during the period. In our earlier example of the Ajax Company (where materials are added at the beginning of processing, the beginning inventory is 40% complete, and the ending inventory is 25% complete), the costs assigned to work-in-process inventory at the end of the period, using the first-in, first-out method, would be calculated as follows:

Materials (4,000 × 100% × $2.00*)	$ 8,000
Labor (4,000 × 25% × $1.50*)	1,500
Manufacturing overhead (4,000 × 25% × $2.00*)	2,000
Total cost assigned to end-of-period work-in-process inventory	$11,500

*See unit-cost calculations on page 188.

Strictly interpreted, use of the FIFO method also would require us to calculate two separate unit costs for goods transferred out of the process. One of these would be the costs assigned to the 2,000 units that were in process at the beginning of the period, including the previous-period costs associated with the portion of those units completed during the prior period, plus current-period costs for the portion completed during the current period. Since the $7,000 cost associated with beginning-of-period work-in-process inventory included direct-materials costs of $4,000, direct-labor costs of $1,300, and manufacturing-overhead costs of $1,700, the strictly interpreted first-in, first-out method would show a cost of $5.60 per unit for the 2,000 units in process at the beginning of the period, calculated as follows:

Materials $4,000 ÷ 2,000 units =	$2.00
Direct labor ($1,300 + $1,800*) ÷ 2,000 units =	1.55
Manufacturing overhead ($1,700 + $2,400**) ÷ 2,000 units =	2.05
Total cost per unit	$5.60

*2,000 × 60% × $1.50 = $1,800
**2,000 × 60% × $2.00 = $2,400

A cost of $5.50 (the cost of production during the reporting period) would then be assigned to the 3,000 units that were both started and completed during the current period. The total cost of goods transferred out would be $27,700 divided into two lots as follows:

2,000 units @ $5.60 = $11,200
3,000 units @ $5.50 = $16,500
$27,700

Such an arrangement for allocating costs, however, is so laborious it is seldom used. We more generally calculate the cost to be assigned to units transferred out of the process into finished-goods inventory by subtracting the costs assigned to end-of-period work-in-process inventory from the total costs to be accounted for. In this case, that calculation would be:

Total costs to be accounted for − Ending work-in-process inventory
= Costs transferred out

That is,

$$\$39,200 - \$11,500 = \$27,700$$

Then, instead of apportioning the $27,700 to two lots of goods (the 2,000 units in process at the beginning of the period and the 3,000 processed completely during the current period), we divide the $27,700 by the 5,000 units transferred out, arriving at a cost of $5.54 to be assigned to each of the 5,000 units completed. Observe that the $27,700 is also characterized as cost of goods manufactured, which, in this one-process illustration, would be recorded by debiting finished-goods inventory and crediting work in process.

Weighted-Average Costing Method

The **weighted-average method**, as the name suggests, assigns unit costs to both transfers and end-of-period work-in-process inventory that are an average of the costs carried over from the preceding period for beginning-of-period work-in-process inventory plus the cost of processing during the current period. Because it includes the elements of costs incurred during the prior period for beginning-of-period work in process, this method of cost allocation requires use of an equivalent-units divisor consisting of the units from beginning inventory that are completed this period plus units started and finished during the current period plus the production completed on the units in end-of-period work in process. This also can be stated as the sum of units transferred out (beginning inventory units plus units started and completed) plus equivalent whole units in end-of-period work-in-process inventory. We do *not* subtract the equivalent units in beginning-of-period work in process because we include the costs associated with them in the total costs used (the numerator) in calculating unit costs. The unit cost for each element of manufacturing costs would then be calculated as follows:

$$\frac{\text{(Cost included in beginning-of-period work-in-process inventory}}{\text{(Units transferred out + Equivalent units of production}}$$

(Cost included in beginning-of-period work-in-process inventory
+ Cost incurred during current period)
÷ Weighted-average equivalent-units divisor
(Units transferred out + Equivalent units of production
in end-of-period work-in-process inventory)

Again referring to the data for the Ajax Chemical Company, unit costs for the period using the weighted-average costing method would be calculated in the following two steps:

1. Calculate the weighted-average equivalent-units divisors:

	Materials		Conversion Costs	
Units transferred out		5,000		5,000
+ End-of-period inventory units	(100%)	4,000	(25%)	1,000
Total		9,000		6,000

2. Compute weighted-average unit costs using beginning inventory costs of $4,000, $1,300, and $1,700 and current costs of $14,000, $7,800, and $10,400 for materials, labor, and overhead, respectively:

Unit cost for materials ($4,000 + $14,000)/9,000	$2.00
Units cost for direct labor ($1,300 + $7,800)/6,000	$1.51⅔
Units cost for manufacturing overhead ($1,700 + $10,400)/6,000	$2.01⅔
Total unit cost	$5.53⅓

Using these calculations, we can allocate manufacturing costs to be accounted for to end-of-period work in process and goods transferred out by calculating either the cost assigned to end-of-period work-in-process inventory or the cost assigned to units transferred to finished-goods inventory, and then attach the balance of costs to be accounted for to the other item. If we calculate the cost to be assigned to end-of-period work-in-process inventory, the balance of cost to be accounted for will be assigned to units transferred to finished-goods inventory. If we calculate the cost to be assigned to units transferred to finished-goods inventory, however, the balance of the cost to be accounted for will be assigned to end-of-period work-in-process inventory. This is analagous to calculating cost of goods sold and subtracting that figure from the cost of goods available for sale to get the cost assigned to ending inventory, or calculating ending inventory and subtracting that amount from the cost of goods available for sale to get cost of goods sold. Just as you should know how to independently calculate both cost of goods sold and ending inventory, you should also be able to calculate independently both the cost of goods transferred out of work in process and the cost of goods remaining in ending work in process. Here is how we calculate the cost assigned to Ajax Chemical Company's 4,000 units in end-of-period work in process:

Work-in-Process Inventory, End of Period

Materials (4,000 × 100% × $2)	$ 8,000
Labor (4,000 × 25% × $1.51⅔)	1,516.66⅔
Manufacturing overhead (4,000 × 25% × $2.01⅔)	2,016.66⅔
Total	$11,533.33

The costs assigned to goods transferred to finished-goods inventory would be $27,666.67, calculated as follows:

Total costs to be accounted for − Ending work-in-process inventory
= Costs transferred out

That is,

$$\$39,200 - \$11,533.33 = \$27,666.67$$

We also can calculate the costs assigned to units transferred to finished-goods inventory as follows:

Units transferred out × Weighted average cost per unit
= Costs transferred out

That is,

$$5,000 \times \$5.53⅓ = \$27,666.67$$

To avoid having to use the percentage of completion data required to calculate the costs to be assigned to end-of-period work-in-process inventory, it is simpler to calculate the cost assigned to units transferred to finished goods and determine the cost assigned to end-of-period work-in-process inventory by subtracting that amount from the total costs to be accounted for. No matter what costing method (FIFO, weighted average, or LIFO) is used, the work-in-process inventory at the end of the current period becomes the beginning inventory for the next period.

Last-In, First-Out (LIFO) Costing Method

Although it is seldom used in valuing work-in-process inventory, the **LIFO method** is a generally accepted accounting procedure and may be the most appropriate method when long periods of inflation are expected. In valuing inventory based on LIFO, we allocate costs under the assumption that all units completed during the reporting period, up to the number of units fully processed during the period (that is, the units started and finished in the current period), will be transferred to finished-goods inventory at the unit cost of production during the reporting period (the same unit cost as was calculated for the FIFO method). In this case, the cost assigned to the units transferred out would be calculated as follows:

$$\text{Units (not exceeding units started) transferred out} \times \text{Cost per unit} = \text{Costs transferred out}$$

That is,

$$5,000 \times \$5.50 = \$27,500$$

End-of period work-in-process inventory using LIFO would be calculated by subtracting the $27,500 from the total cost to be accounted for:

$$\text{Total cost to be accounted for} - \text{Costs transferred out} = \text{End-of-period work-in-process inventory}$$

That is,

$$\$39,200 - \$27,500 = \$11,700$$

Strict adherence to last-in, first-out costing would require calculating a different unit cost for the units transferred out in excess of units put into process (that is, started) during the reporting period, which would occur when the number of units in end-of-period work-in-process inventory was less than the number of units in beginning-of-period work-in-process inventory. From a practical standpoint, however, this strict LIFO procedure is unlikely to be followed. Therefore, we generally calculate the cost assigned to units transferred to finished-goods inventory by using the unit cost of production for the reporting period regardless of the change in the number of units in work-in-process inventory.

Cost-of-Production Report

Earlier, we explained that in a process-costing system manufacturing costs are accumulated and ultimately allocated to finished units through cost-of-production reports prepared for each process. We also demonstrated that the costs assigned to unfinished units of product in each process were indicated in such reports so that they constitute a subsidiary ledger for the work-in-process inventory account. Now we turn to the procedures followed in recording cost allocations and in preparing a cost-of-production report.

The entries to record the flows of costs are exactly the same as those demonstrated in Chapters 4 and 5 for job-order costing, with one exception: because costs are accounted for on a periodic basis rather than on the basis of individual lots of goods, firms *may* include actual rather than applied overhead in their cost-of-production reports. When such actual costs are used, all manufacturing costs for the period (direct materials, direct labor, and actual manufacturing overhead) will be debited to work in process as they are incurred. Observe, however, that manufacturing overhead during the period is not the same as cash paid out for overhead items. Actual manufacturing overhead will include costs associated with the recognition of prepaid and accrued balances for overhead items paid either before or after the period. When manufacturing overhead is charged to work in process by using predetermined overhead rates for each process or department, the journal entries will be essentially the same as those for a job-order system. The applied amounts, however, will be allocated to the departmental cost-of-production reports rather than to job orders. The amount of the entry to record the transfer of finished units from work in process to finished-goods inventory, which is calculated as just described, is shown on the cost-of-production report.

To demonstrate, we will show how the cost flow data given in the cost-of-production report for Ajax Chemical Company in Figure 6–5 (see page 196) would be recorded in T accounts. Observe that the first-in, first-out cost flow assumption was followed in preparing this report.

The cost-of-production report basically presents another four-element equation;

Beginning-of-period work in process
+ Additions to work in process (total manufacturing costs)
− End-of-period work in process
= Transfers to finished-goods inventory (cost of goods manufactured)

or

Beginning-of-period work in process
+ Additions to work in process (total manufacturing costs)
− Transfers to finished-goods inventory (cost of goods manufactured)
= End-of-period work in process

Ajax Chemical Company
Cost-of-Production Report
For Current Period
FIFO Costing Method

Units

Units in process beginning of period (100% direct materials, 40% conversion)	2,000
Units started during the period	7,000
Total units to be accounted for	9,000
Units remaining in end-of-period work in process (100% direct materials, 25% conversion)	4,000
Units transferred to finished goods	5,000

Costs

	Total Costs		Costs per Unit
Beginning-of-period work in process			
Direct materials costs	$4,000		
Direct labor costs	1,300		
Manufacturing-overhead costs	1,700	$ 7,000	
Direct materials costs for period		(1) 14,000	$2.00[a]
Direct labor costs for period		(2) 7,800	1.50[b]
Manufacturing-overhead costs for period		(3) 10,400	2.00[c]
Total costs to be accounted for		$39,200	$5.50
End-of-period work in process			
Direct materials costs (4,000 × $2.00)	$8,000		
Direct labor costs (4,000 × 0.25 × $1.50)	1,500		
Manufacturing-overhead costs (4,000 × 0.25 × $2.00)	2,000	11,500	
Costs transferred to finished goods		(4) $27,700	$5.54[d]

[a] $14,000 ÷ 7,000 equivalent units = $2.00
[b] $7,800 ÷ 5,200 equivalent units = $1.50
[c] $10,400 ÷ 5,200 equivalent units = $2.00
[d] $27,700 ÷ 5,000 units transferred = $5.54

Equivalent units of production:

	Direct Materials	Conversion Costs
Units transferred out	5,000	5,000
+ End-of-period inventory work	4,000	1,000
− Beginning-of-period inventory work (completed last period)	(2,000)	(800)
= FIFO equivalent units of production	7,000	5,200

FIGURE 6–5   Cost-of-Production Report, FIFO Method

The four-elements are expressed both in terms of units and in terms of dollars. Quantitatively, they are:

Units
$$2,000 + 7,000 - 4,000$$
$$= 5000 \text{ (units transferred to finished goods)}$$

Dollars
$$\$7,000 + (\$14,000 + \$7,800 + \$10,400) - \$11,500$$
$$= \$27,700 \text{ (costs transferred to finished goods)}$$

These dollar amounts also will appear in a work-in-process T account, as follows:

Work in Process

Beginning balance	7,000	Transfers to finished goods	27,700
Direct materials	14,000		
Direct labor	7,800		
Manufacturing overhead	10,400		
Ending balance	11,500		

The cost-of-production report has two sections: one for units and one for costs. The "units" section shows what has happened to all units handled by the company (or department) during the reporting period (that is, beginning inventory units and units started during the current period). Observe in Figure 6–5 that 4,000 of the 9,000 units to be accounted for are in ending work-in-process inventory and that 5,000 units were transferred to finished goods; that is, the total units to be accounted for appear either as ending inventory or as transfers to finished goods.

The "costs" section of the cost-of-production report shows what has happened to all manufacturing costs (dollars) carried over from the prior period plus those incurred by the company (department) during the reporting period. The costs that must be accounted for are the sum of beginning inventory costs and manufacturing costs of the period. In Figure 6–5, the total costs to be accounted for are $39,200. With the FIFO costing assumption, the calculated cost assigned to units remaining in ending work in process is $11,500. Subtracting this amount from the $39,200 leaves $27,700 in costs assigned to units transferred to finished goods. As discussed earlier in the chapter, the transferred-out amount in Figure 6–5 can be "proven" as follows:

Beginning work-in-process costs	$ 7,000
+ Costs to complete beginning work in process (2,000 × 60% × $3.50 conversion costs per unit)	4,200
+ Cost of units started and completed this period (5,000 units transferred out − 2,000 units in beginning inventory) × $5.50	16,500
	$27,700

Because some of the units transferred out in Figure 6–5 were begun in a previous period, when costs per unit were different from those in the current period, the cost per unit for the units transferred out ($5.54) is not the same as the cost per unit for the current period ($5.50). The important point is that the disposition of total costs to be accounted for must be shown on the cost-of-production report.

Two calculations that often are not shown on a cost-of-production report are vital to the preparation of the report: (1) equivalent units of production and (2) cost per unit (for each element of cost and in total). These calculations are given in the footnotes in Figure 6–5.

Again, we remind you that in assigning dollars to the four elements of the equation, you can calculate either the costs assigned to end-of-period work-in-process inventory or the costs assigned to goods transferred and determine the other by completing the four-element equation. The same four-element equation can be used with units. However, you must be careful never to mix units and dollars in the same equation.

We now present in T account form the journal entries that would be made to record the FIFO accumulation and allocation of costs for Ajax Chemical Company for the current period. These can be related to items in the cost-of-production report of Figure 6–5 by referring to the parenthetical journal entry numbers shown both in the T accounts and beside various items in the cost-of-production report.

Raw Materials Inventory		
Beginning balance X,XXX	(1)	14,000

Work in Process		
Beginning balance 7,000		
(1) 14,000	(4)	27,700
(2) 7,800		
(3) 10,400		
Ending balance 11,500		

Finished-Goods Inventory		
Beginning balance X,XXX		
(4) 27,700		

Payroll		
Balance X,XXX	(2)	7,800

Manufacturing Overhead		
Balance 10,400	(3) 10,400	

If a firm uses a predetermined overhead rate to apply overhead, entry (3) would show a credit to applied overhead. Later, the applied overhead account balance will be matched (closed) against manufacturing overhead to arrive at underapplied or overapplied overhead for the period, just as done in Chapters 4 and 5. The use of an applied overhead account would be appropriate where the volume of production varies significantly from month to month within an annual fiscal period or where there are numerous seasonal overhead costs.

The cost-of-production report for Ajax Chemical Company for the current period of Figure 6–5 gives the costs assigned to work in process and to units transferred to finished-goods inventory using the first-in, first-out method of allocating manufacturing costs. Figure 6–6 shows the cost-of-production report that would have been prepared had costs been allocated via the weighted-average costing method.

The weighted-average cost-of-production report in Figure 6–6 has the same two major sections, "units" and "costs," as the FIFO report in Figure 6–5. In the weighted-average report, however, the data are arranged so the cost of units transferred out is calculated and subtracted from total costs to be accounted for to find the cost assigned to ending work-in-process inventory. Proof of this ending balance is shown in footnote d in Figure 6–6. Those footnotes also include the vital equivalent-units divisors and cost-per-unit calculations used in preparing the cost-of-production report.

Figure 6–7 shows the cost-of-production report that would be prepared by using the last-in, first-out costing method.

In developing the schedule showing units to be accounted for (the first step in the preparation of every production report), we may have to calculate one of the four items in the four-element equation from three known elements. For example, if we are given the number of units in beginning and end-of-period work-in-process inventories plus the number of units placed in process during the period, we can calculate the number of units transferred to finished goods during the period with the following formula:

Beginning-of-period units in process + Units added during the period
− Units in end-of-period work in process
= Units transferred to finished-goods inventory

Illustrative Problem

The Bambino Company produces a single product in a continuing process type of manufacture. It operates its factory as a single department. At the end of the current period the company accountant develops the following data for the period.

	Units	Amount
Work in process, beginning of period	4,000	
Direct materials		$ 8,400
Direct labor and manufacturing overhead		3,900
Additions to work in process in January	8,000	
Direct materials		18,000
Direct labor and manufacturing overhead		15,000
Total		$45,300
Work in process, end of period	3,000	

Ajax Chemical Company

Cost-of-Production Report
For Current Period
Weighted-Average Costing Method

Units

Units in process beginning of period (100% direct materials, 40% conversion)	2,000
Units added	7,000
Total units to be accounted for	9,000
Units transferred to finished goods	5,000
Units remaining in end-of-period work in process (100% direct materials, 25% conversion)	4,000

Costs

	Total Costs		Costs per Unit
Beginning-of-period work in process			
Direct materials costs	$4,000		
Direct labor costs	1,300		
Manufacturing-overhead costs	1,700	$ 7,000	
Direct materials costs for period		14,000	$2.00[a]
Direct labor costs for period		7,800	1.51⅔[b]
Manufacturing-overhead costs for period		10,400	2.01⅔[c]
Total costs to be accounted for		$39,200	$5.53⅓
Transferred to finished goods (5,000 units at $5.53⅓)		27,667	
End-of-period work-in-process inventory		$11,533[d]	

[a] $\frac{\$4,000 + \$14,000}{9,000} = \$2.00$

[b] $\frac{\$1,300 + \$7,800}{6,000} = \$1.51⅔$

[c] $\frac{\$1,700 + \$10,400}{6,000} = \$2.01⅔$

[d] Proof of end-of-period work in process

4,000 × $2 =	$ 8,000	
4,000 × 0.25 × $1.51⅔ =	1,516⅔	
4,000 × 0.25 × $2.01⅔ =	2,016⅔	
	$11,533	

Equivalent-units divisors:

	Direct Materials	Conversion Costs
Units transferred out	5,000	5,000
+ End-of-period inventory units	4,000	1,000
= Weighted-average equivalent units of production	9,000	6,000

FIGURE 6–6 Cost-of-Production Report, Weighted-Average Method

Ajax Chemical Company

Cost-of-Production Report

For Current Period

LIFO Costing Method

Units

Units in process beginning of period (100% direct materials, 40% conversion)	2,000
Units added	7,000
Total units to be accounted for	9,000
Units transferred to finished goods	5,000
Units remaining in end-of-period work in process (100% direct materials, 25% conversion)	4,000

Costs

		Total Costs	Costs per Unit
Beginning-of-period work in process			
Direct materials costs	$4,000		
Direct labor costs	1,300		
Manufacturing-overhead costs	1,700	$ 7,000	
Direct materials costs for period		14,000	$2.00[a]
Direct labor costs for period		7,800	1.50[b]
Manufacturing-overhead costs for period		10,400	2.00[c]
Total costs to be accounted for		$39,200	$5.50
Transferred to finished goods (5,000 units at $5.50)		27,500	
End-of-period work in process inventory		$11,700[d]	

[a] $14,000 ÷ 7,000* equivalent units = $2.00
[b] $7,800 ÷ 5,200* equivalent units = $1.50
[c] $10,400 ÷ 5,200* equivalent units = $2.00
  *same as in Figure 6-5.
[d] Proof of end-or-period work in process inventory:

Beginning-of-period inventory				
Direct materials			$4,000	
Direct labor			1,300	
Manufacturing overhead			1,700	
			$7,000	
Work added during period				
Direct materials (2,000 × $2)			$4,000	
Direct labor				
2,000 × 0.25 × $1.50		$ 750		
less 2,000 × (0.4 − 0.25) × $1.50		− 450	300	
Manufacturing overhead				
2,000 × 0.25 × $2.00		$1,000		
less 2,000 × (0.4 − 0.25) × $2.00	− 600 =	400	4,700	
Total			$11,700	

Equivalent units of production:

	Direct Materials	Conversion Costs
Units transferred out	5,000	5,000
+ End-of-period inventory work	4,000	1,000
− Beginning of period inventory work (completed last period)	(2,000)	(800)
= LIFO equivalent units of production	7,000	5,200

FIGURE 6-7 Cost-of-Production Report, LIFO Method

You also ascertain the following regarding the accountant's report: (1) work in process at the beginning of the period is complete insofar as materials are concerned, but only 75% complete insofar as labor and manufacturing overhead are concerned; (2) work in process at the end of the period is complete insofar as materials are concerned, but only 50% complete insofar as labor and manufacturing overhead are concerned.

a. Calculate the number of units of product transferred to finished-goods inventory during the current period. Assume no units are lost in processing.
b. Calculate the number of equivalent whole units of work completed during the period.
c. Calculate the unit cost for materials during the month of January using a first-in, first-out cost flow assumption. Calculate the same unit cost using a weighted-average cost flow assumption.
d. Calculate the unit cost for labor and manufacturing overhead for the period using a first-in, first-out cost flow assumption. Calculate the same unit cost using a weighted-average cost flow assumption.
e. Calculate the work-in-process inventory at the end of the period using first the FIFO costing method and then the weighted-average costing method.
f. Calculate the total cost assigned to goods transferred to finished-goods inventory during the period using first the FIFO costing method and then the weighted-average costing method.
g. Prepare a cost-of-production report using the first-in, first-out cost flow assumption.

Solution to Illustrative Problem

a. **Units transferred to finished-goods inventory:**

$$\left(\begin{array}{c}\text{Units in beginning-}\\\text{of-period work in process}\end{array}\right) + \left(\begin{array}{c}\text{Units}\\\text{added}\end{array}\right) - \left(\begin{array}{c}\text{Units in end-of-period}\\\text{work in process}\end{array}\right)$$

$$4{,}000 \qquad + \quad 8{,}000 \quad - \qquad 3{,}000$$

$$= \left(\begin{array}{c}\text{Units transferred}\\\text{to finished goods}\end{array}\right)$$

$$= \qquad 9{,}000$$

b. **Equivalent units of production:**

	Materials	Labor and Overhead
Units transferred to finished goods	9,000	9,000
Plus equivalent units in end-of-period work in process	3,000	1,500
Total (equivalent units of production for weighted-average costing)	12,000	10,500

	Materials	Labor and Overhead
Less equivalent units in beginning-of-period work in process	4,000	3,000
Equivalent units of work completed in January (equivalent units of production for FIFO costing)	8,000	7,500

c. Unit cost, materials:

First-in, first-out method

$$\frac{\text{Direct materials costs (\$18,000)}}{\text{Equivalent units of production (8,000)}} = \$2.25$$

Weighted-average method

$$\frac{\text{Direct material costs (\$8,400 + \$18,000)}}{\text{Equivalent units (12,000)}} = \$2.20$$

d. Unit cost, direct labor and overhead:

First-in, first-out method

$$\frac{\text{Direct labor and manufacturing overhead (\$15,000)}}{\text{Equivalent units (7,500)}} = \$2.00$$

Weighted-average cost method

$$\frac{\text{Direct labor and manufacturing overhead (\$3,900 + \$15,000)}}{\text{Equivalent units (\$10,500)}} = \$1.80$$

e. End-of-period work-in-process inventory:

First-in, first-out method

Materials (3,000 × 100% × $2.25)	$ 6,750
Labor and overhead (3,000 × 50% × $2.00)	3,000
Total	$ 9,750

Weighted-average method

Materials (3,000 × 100% × $2.20)	$ 6,600
Labor and overhead (3,000 × 50% × $1.80)	2,700
Total	$ 9,300

f. Costs transferred out:

First-in, first-out method

Total cost to be accounted for	$45,300
Less end-of-period work in process	9,750
Cost assigned to units transferred to finished goods	$35,550*

Weighted-average method

Total costs to be accounted for	$45,300
Less end-of-period work in process	9,300
Cost assigned to units transferred to finished goods	$36,000**

*Direct calculation of FIFO costs transferred out:

Beginning inventory costs	$12,300
Costs required to complete beginning inventory (1,000 × $2.00)	2,000
Cost of units started and completed this period (5,000 × $4.25)	21,250
Total	$35,550

**Direct calculation of weighted-average costs transferred out:

$$9,000 \text{ units} \times \$4 = \$36,000$$

g. Cost-of-production report

Cost-of-production report
FIFO Costing Method

Units

Units in beginning-of-period work in process (75% processed)	4,000
Units added during January	8,000
Total units to be accounted for	12,000
Units transferred to finished goods	9,000
Units in end-of-period work in process (50% processed)	3,000

Costs

	Total Costs	Costs per Unit
Beginning-of-period work in process		
Direct materials	$8,400	
Direct labor and manufacturing overhead	3,900 $12,300	
Additions in January		
Direct materials	18,000	$2.25[a]
Direct labor and manufacturing overhead	15,000	2.00[b]
Total to be accounted for	$45,300	$4.25

(Continues)

	Total Costs	Costs per Unit
Total to be accounted for	$45,300	$4.25
End-of-period work in process		
Direct materials (3,000 × 100% × $2.25)	$6,750	
Direct labor and manufacturing overhead (3,000 × 50% × 2.00)	3,000 9,750	
Costs assigned to units transferred to finished goods	$35,550*	$3.95^c

NOTE: Equivalent units of production are calculated in the solution to part b.

[a] $18,000 ÷ 8,000 equivalent units of production = $2.25
[b] $15,000 ÷ 7,500 equivalent units of production = $2.00
[c] $35,550 ÷ 9,000 units transferred out = $3.95

* Independent calculation of costs transferred out:

Beginning inventory costs	$12,300	
Plus costs to complete beginning inventory (4,000 × .25 × $2.00)	2,000	
Cost of units started and completed this period [(9,000 − 4,000) × $4.25]	21,250	$35,550

SUMMARY

In this chapter, we described and illustrated the basic procedures for maintaining a simple process-costing system. The first system described was based on the assumption that the firm produces a single product through one process and has no work-in-process inventories at either the beginning or end of the reporting period. Then we explained how such procedures would be modified if the company had beginning and end-of-period work-in-process inventories requiring the calculation of equivalent units of production. We demonstrated how that figure was calculated and how it was used in arriving at unit costs under first-in, first-out, weighted-average, and last-in, first-out cost flow assumptions.

We then explained how the cost-of-production report is used in a process-costing system to support end-of-period work-in-process inventory and the cost of goods transferred (cost of goods manufactured) to finished goods, for all three cost flow assumptions. We pointed out that the cost-of-production report is, in reality, a four-element equation involving the disclosure of units as well as costs associated with beginning-of-period work-in-process inventory, plus additions during the reporting period, reduced by amounts assigned to either (1) transfers out of the process or (2) end-of-period work-in-process inventory to arrive at the other element (ending inventory or transfers out, respectively) of the four-element equation.

Finally, we presented an illustrative problem and its solution, to demonstrate the basic procedures for maintaining a simple process-costing system.

GLOSSARY OF TERMS INTRODUCED IN THIS CHAPTER

cost-of-production report
Document used in a process costing system to summarize the flows of units and costs through a process or department. Both units and dollars are accounted for via a four-element equation: Beginning balance + Additions − Removals = Ending balance.

equivalent-units divisor
The divisor used in arriving at unit costs in a process costing system. With a first-in, first-out cost flow assumption, the divisor is equal to units transferred out plus equivalent units in end-of-period work in process minus equivalent units in beginning-of-period work in process. With a weighted-average cost flow assumption, the divisor is equal to units transferred out plus equivalent units remaining in end-of-period work in process.

equivalent units of production (EUP)
The number of whole units of production that would have been turned out during a reporting period if all cost efforts had been directed only at turning out completed units. This becomes the equivalent-units divisor when using either a first-in, first-out or last-in, first-out cost flow assumption and is calculated as the units transferred out plus the equivalent units in end-of-period work-in-process minus equivalent units in beginning-of-period work-in-process. Sometimes erroneously considered a synonym for any equivalent-units divisor (see *equivalent-units divisor*).

FIFO method of process costing
The cost flow assumption in a process costing system that assumes that units and the costs assigned to them flow through a production process on a first-in, first-out basis; current period cost(s) per unit is used to value end-of-period work in process.

LIFO method of process costing
A process costing system operating under the assumption that the costs associated with the last units transferred into a process or department will be the first costs transferred out of that process or department. Thus, end-of-period work-in-process inventory is valued via a "layering" of previous periods' costs.

weighted-average method of process costing
A method of determining unit costs in a process costing system that averages costs associated with beginning inventory from the prior period with costs of the current period in arriving at the cost per unit to be used in valuing ending work-in-process inventory and goods transferred out of the department or process.

QUESTIONS FOR CLASS DISCUSSION

6–1 What operational characteristics should a manufacturing firm have for it to appropriately use a process-costing system? Explain.

6–2 What documents constitute the supporting subsidiary ledger for work-in-process inventory when using a process-costing system? Explain.

6–3 What do we mean by the term *equivalent units of production*? How is such a figure calculated?

6—4 How is the equivalent-units-of-production figure used in connection with a process-costing system?

6—5 Will we typically have a different number of equivalent units for direct materials than for conversion costs? Explain.

6—6 What cost flow assumptions may be used in assigning manufacturing costs to work in process and goods transferred out of a processing center?

6—7 How are unit costs calculated when following the first-in, first-out cost flow assumption? Explain.

6—8 How are unit costs calculated when using the weighted-average method of assigning costs to the goods produced in a department during a period? Explain.

6—9 How should the cost assigned to end-of-period work in process be calculated when using the first-in, first-out cost flow assumption? Explain.

6—10 How should the cost assigned to end-of-period work-in-process inventory be calculated when using weighted-average costing? Explain.

6—11 In what ways is the four-element equation used in the preparation of a cost-of-production report? Explain.

EXERCISES

6—12
AICPA Adapted

Multiple Choice Select the *best* answer for each of the following items.

1. An actual cost system may be used in
   a. neither process costing nor job-order costing.
   b. process costing but *not* job-order costing.
   c. job-order costing but *not* process costing.
   d. both job-order costing and process costing.
2. A nonmanufacturing organization may use
   a. job-order costing but *not* process costing.
   b. process costing but *not* job-order costing.
   c. either job-order costing or process costing.
   d. neither job-order costing nor process costing.
3. Which is the best cost-accumulation procedure to use when there is a continuous mass production of like units?
   a. actual
   b. standard
   c. job order
   d. process
4. In developing a factory-overhead application rate for use in a process-costing system, which of the following could be used in the denominator?
   a. actual factory overhead
   b. estimated factory overhead
   c. actual direct-labor hours
   d. estimated direct-labor hours

6–13   **Cost per Unit—No Beginning or Ending Work in Process** Chonko Company produces plastic glow lights that are sold by vendors at open-air events. The company uses a process-costing system. Chonko has no beginning or end-of-period work in process and no beginning finished-goods inventory for the current period. During the current period, the following data were accumulated:

Direct materials used	$20,000
Direct labor charged to work in process	$10,000
Manufacturing overhead applied	$10,000
Production	200,000 units
Sales	180,000 units

REQUIRED:

1. Compute the cost per unit of production for the current period.
2. Compute cost of sales for the period.
3. Compute the cost of ending finished-goods inventory.

6–14   **Equivalent Units of Production (EUP)—Work Completed in Current Period** Joshua Company produces toy laser guns in a one-department manufacturing process. During July 19X2, Joshua accumulated the following data:

Units in beginning-of-period work in process	3,000
Units started during the period	18,000
Units completed and transferred to finished goods	19,000

The beginning work in process was 20% completed during June and the ending work in process was 10% completed.

REQUIRED:

1. How many units were started and completed during July, 19X2?
2. Assuming first-in, first-out cost flows, compute the equivalent units of production completed during July, 19X2.

6–15   **Multiple Choice—Equivalent Units of Production** Select the *best* answer for
AICPA Adapted   each of the following items:

1. The percentage of completion of the beginning work-in-process inventory should be included in the computation of the equivalent units of production for which of the following methods of process costing?

	First-in, First-out	*Weighted Average*
a.	yes	no
b.	yes	yes
c.	no	yes
d.	no	no

2. In the computation of manufacturing cost per equivalent unit, the weighted-average method of process costing considers

    a. current costs only.
    b. current costs plus cost of ending work-in-process inventory.
    c. current costs less cost of beginning work-in-process inventory.
    d. current costs plus cost of beginning work-in-process inventory.

3. In a given process-costing system, the equivalent-units *divisor* is computed for the weighted-average method. With respect to conversion costs, the percentage of completion for the current period only is included in the calculation of the

	Beginning Work-in-Process Inventory	Ending Work-in-Process Inventory
a.	no	no
b.	no	yes
c.	yes	no
d.	yes	no

4. The first-in, first-out method of process costing differs from the weighted-average method in that the first-in, first-out method
    a. considers the stage of completion of beginning work-in-process inventory in computing equivalent units of production, whereas the weighted-average method does *not.*
    b. does *not* consider the stage of completion of beginning work-in-process inventory in computing equivalent units of production, whereas the weighted average method does.
    c. is applicable only to those companies using the first-in, first-out inventory pricing method, whereas the weighted-average method may be used with any inventory pricing method.
    d. allocates costs based on whole units, whereas the weighted-average method uses equivalent units.

6–16 **EUP—Materials Added at Beginning of Process** Arvard Corporation adds materials at the beginning of processing in Department 1, the first stage of its production cycle. Information for the month of April 19X9 for Department 1 is as follows:

Units in work in process, April 1, 19X9	2,000
Units started during April	35,000
Units completed and transferred to next department during April	33,000

April 1, 19X9, work in process was 30% complete as to direct labor and 40% complete as to overhead. April 30, 19X9, work in process was 60% complete as to direct labor and 80% complete as to overhead.

REQUIRED: Compute (a) the FIFO and (b) the weighted-average equivalent units divisors for April, 19X9, for (1) materials, (2) direct labor, and (3) overhead.

6–17 **EUP—Materials Added at Points Other Than Beginning of Process** Patrick Company assembles electric all-terrain vehicles in a factory organized as one department. The frame, suspension, steering, and wheels are assembled and inspected before the motor is installed (when processing is 25% complete). When each unit is completely assembled, a preformed, sanded, and painted fiberglass body is added to the chassis. The units are stored in an attached warehouse until they are shipped to customers. Overhead is applied on the basis of direct labor costs incurred. The factory manager reported the following activity for March:

Units started	1,500
Units from beginning inventory completed this period (entire beginning inventory was 20% complete on March 1)	500
Units partially completed (75% stage) on March 31	400

REQUIRED: Assuming all units pass inspection, and a first-in, first-out cost flow, compute the equivalent units of production for the three materials components (chassis, motor, and body) and for conversion costs for March.

6–18   **Cost per Unit—Current Period Production** Refer to the data in exercise 6–17. Costs associated with March production were:

	Total	Chassis Components	Motors	Bodies	Conversion Costs
Beginning inventory	$ 102,000	$ 75,000			$ 27,000
Added in March	1,299,000	210,000	$168,000	$435,000	486,000
	$1,401,000	$285,000	$168,000	$435,000	$513,000

REQUIRED: Compute the cost per unit for the units produced during March. Show the unit cost for each element of the total cost.

PROBLEMS

6–19   **Multiple Choice—EUP: FIFO and Weighted Average** Select the *best* answer
AICPA Adapted   for each of the following items:

1. Sussex Corporation's production cycle starts in the mixing department. The following information is available for the month of April, 19X0:

	Units
Work in process, April 1 (50% complete)	40,000
Started in April	240,000
Work in process, April 30 (60% complete)	25,000

Materials are added in the beginning of the process in the mixing department. Using the weighted-average method, calculate the equivalent-units (of production) *divisors* for the month of April, 19X0.

	Materials	Conversion
a.	240,000	250,000
b.	255,000	255,000
c.	270,000	280,000
d.	280,000	270,000

Items 2 and 3 are based on the following information:

Bronson Company had 6,000 units in work in process on January 1, 19X2, which were 60% complete as to conversion costs. During January, 20,000 units were completed. At January 31, 19X2, 8,000 units remained in work in process, which were 40% complete as to conversion costs. Materials are added at the beginning of the process.

2. Calculated using the weighted-average method, the equivalent units for January for conversion costs were
   a. 19,600.
   b. 22,400.
   c. 23,200.
   d. 25,000.
3. How many units were started during January?
   a. 18,000
   b. 19,600
   c. 20,000
   d. 22,000
4. Department A is the first stage of Mann Company's production cycle. The following information is available for conversion costs for the month of April, 19X3:

	Units
Work in process, beginning (60% complete)	20,000
Started in April	340,000
Completed in April and transferred to Department B	320,000
Work in process, ending (40% complete)	40,000

Computed using the FIFO method, the equivalent units for the conversion cost calculation are:
   a. 320,000.
   b. 324,000.
   c. 336,000.
   d. 360,000.
5. On November 1, 19X7, Yankee Company had 20,000 units of work in process in Department 1, which were 100% complete as to material costs and 20% complete as to conversion costs. During November, 160,000 units were started in Department 1 and 170,000 units were

completed and transferred to Department 2. The work in process on November 30, 19X7, was 100% complete as to material costs and 40% complete as to conversion costs. By what amount would the equivalent units for conversion costs for the month of November differ if the first-in, first-out method were used instead of the weighted-average method?

a. 20,000 less
b. 16,000 less
c. 8,000 less
d. 4,000 less

6–20 **Cost per Unit—FIFO and Weighted-Average** Information for the month of February for Sacramento Corporation's manufacturing process is as follows:

	Units	Costs Materials	Costs Conversion
Beginning-of-period work in process (40% processed)	8,000	$ 4,280	$ 861
Added during February	92,000	51,520	31,119
Total	100,000	$55,800	$31,980

There were 95,000 units completed during February. Equivalent units *divisors* were:

	Materials	Conversion
Weighted-average method	100,000	97,500
First-in, first-out method	92,000	94,300

REQUIRED:

1. Compute the cost per unit for February assuming Sacramento values its work in process inventory using: (a) the first-in, first-out cost flow method and (b) the weighted-average cost flow method.
2. What would be the cost per unit transferred out under each of the following? (a) FIFO method, (b) weighted average method.
3. How many units were in process at the end of February? What was their degree of completion?

6–21 **Cost Flows—FIFO** During August, the Halpern Company completed 5,000 units that were started during August and 1,000 units that had been started in July. Materials are added at the beginning of the process. At the end of August, 2,000 units were 25% complete as to conversion costs. The units that had been started in July were 60% complete by July 31. The Halpern Company uses the first-in, first-out method to account for all of its inventories. Cost information includes the following:

Work in process, August 1	$10,185*
Additions during August	
Materials	49,700
Conversion costs	30,975
Total costs	$90,860

*Materials costs of $6,940 and conversion costs of $3,245

REQUIRED:

1. How many units were started during August?
2. Compute the total cost of the units completed during August.
3. Compute the average unit cost for units completed.

6–22 **Cost Flows—FIFO and Weighted-Average** Information for the month of December, 19X8, for the processing department of Olympia Company is as follows:

		Costs	
	Units	Materials	Conversion
December 1 work in process	8,000	$ 2,360	$ 2,130
Added during December	100,000	43,000	40,800
Completed and transferred to finished goods	98,000		

Materials are added at the beginning of processing. The December 1 work-in-process inventory was 50% complete. The December 31 work-in-process inventory was 80% complete.

REQUIRED:

1. Assuming Olympia uses the first-in, first-out cost flow method, calculate the total cost (a) transferred to finished goods during December and (b) remaining in work in process on December 31, 19X8.
2. Assuming Olympia uses the weighted-average cost flow method, calculate the total cost (a) transferred to finished goods during the period and (b) remaining in work in process on December 31, 19X8.

6–23 **Cost-Flows—LIFO** Refer to the data in exercise 6–22, but assume that Olympia uses the last-in, first-out method to account for its work in process.

REQUIRED:

1. Compute the total costs transferred to finished goods.
2. Compute the total cost of the work-in-process inventory on December 31, 19X8.

6–24 **Memos Regarding Equivalent Units** You have just been assigned an assistant to help you prepare cost-of-production reports for your firm. You have explained the concept of equivalent units, but you suspect that the assistant does not fully understand. Since you are going to be out of the office for the next two weeks, your supervisor has suggested you write your assistant a few memos explaining equivalent-units calculations.

REQUIRED: Write three brief memos to your assistant explaining the following.

1. Why the equivalent-units calculation must be made, and why we can't merely use the number of units started during the period or the number of units completed during the period. (Do not describe the specific procedures required to calculate equivalent units of production.)
2. Why the number of equivalent units of production for materials usually is different from the number of equivalent units of production for conversion costs.
3. How equivalent-units numbers are used to compute the total cost of goods transferred out and the cost of goods remaining in ending work-in-process inventory.

6–25   **Cost-of-Production Report—FIFO** Able Corporation manufactures a single product, a telescope called Supertel, in a single department. Able uses the first-in, first-out (FIFO) process-costing method to account for the production and sales of Supertel. Data for the month of October are as follows:

(1) The beginning inventory consisted of 1,750 units, which were 100% complete as to raw material and 40% complete as to direct labor and factory overhead.
(2) An additional 7,000 units were started during the month.
(3) The ending inventory consisted of 2,000 units, which were 100% complete as to raw material and 40% complete as to direct labor and factory overhead.
(4) There were 6,750 units completed and transferred to finished goods.
(5) There was $38,640 in the work-in-process account on October 1.
(6) Actual costs added during October were:

Raw materials used	$84,000
Direct labor	74,500
Factory overhead	24,825

REQUIRED:

1. For each element of production for October (raw materials, direct labor, and factory overhead), compute (a) the equivalent units of production and (b) the cost per equivalent unit of production.
2. Prepare a cost-of-production report for Able for the month of October.

6–26   **Cost-of-Production Report—Weighted-Average Method** Casper Manufacturing Company produces a chemical agent for commercial use. Casper accounts for its production in a single cost center. Materials are placed in process at the beginning of processing, and labor costs are incurred uniformly during processing. Overhead is applied on the basis of 100% of direct-labor cost. The following information is available for the month of February:

	Costs
Work in process, February 1	
Materials	$ 3,412
Labor	320
Month of February	
Materials	63,500
Labor	21,254

Production and inventory records indicate the Casper had 1,600 gallons 60% processed on February 1 and 2,000 gallons 40% processed on February 28. There were 64,000 gallons started in production in blending and 63,600 gallons transferred to finished goods.

REQUIRED:

1. Prepare a cost-of-production report for February for Casper using the weighted-average method.
2. Prepare the journal entry needed to transfer costs from work in process to finished goods.
3. If actual overhead costs incurred during February totaled $24,500, would overhead have been underapplied or overapplied for February? If underapplied or overapplied, by how much?

6–27   **Several Raw Materials Added at Different Points of Production** The Symphony Soap Company produces a new nonallergenic soap for mature skins. The ingredients are secret, but one ingredient, called 1100, is a derivative of Retin-A. Raw materials (all direct) all placed into production as follows:

Raw material 1000: Beginning of process
Raw material 1050: When processing is 40% complete
Raw material 1100: When processing is 60% complete
Raw material 1150: When processing is 95% complete

Symphony uses the weighted-average cost flow assumption. Data for December are as follows:

Units started in process	225,000
Units transferred out	187,500
Ending units in process (30% are 20% complete, 25% are 56% complete, 20% are 70% complete, and 25% are 96% complete)	37,500

Costs incurred, including work-in-process inventory on December 1, were:

Direct Materials		Conversion Costs	
1000	$ 6,750	Direct labor	$77,250
1050	4,275	Overhead	48,300
1100	16,350		
1150	7,875		

REQUIRED:

1. Calculate the equivalent-units divisors for direct materials and conversion costs.
2. Calculate the cost of ending work-in-process inventory.

6–28 Cost-of-Production Report—Weighted-Average Method Collins Company manufactures digital watches. All materials are added to production at the beginning of the manufacturing process, and overhead is applied to each product at the rate of 80% of direct-labor costs. There was no finished-goods inventory on September 1. Work-in-process inventory on September 30 was 40% complete. A review of Collins' inventory and cost records disclosed the following:

	Units	Costs	
		Materials	Conversion
September 1 work in process	100,000	$100,000	$152,500
Added during September	1,000,000	670,000	997,700
Completed and transferred to finished goods	450,000		

REQUIRED:

1. Prepare a cost-of-production report for Collins Company for September using the weighted-average method.
2. If 300,000 watches were sold during September, what amount would be shown for finished-goods inventory on the September 30 balance sheet?

6–29 Cost Flows Through Accounts—FIFO Magic Grains Company processes feeds in a system in which all materials are added at the beginning of processing. Because costs are quite volatile due to the price fluctuations for basic commodities, Magic Grains uses FIFO process costing to account for its manufacturing costs. The feeds are processed through a single department. Overhead is applied on the basis of direct labor costs. The work-in-process inventory account showed the following costs for the 57,200 tons of cereal in process at the beginning of the current period:

Direct materials	$ 72,050
Direct labor	143,000
Overhead applied	200,200

During the period, 166,000 tons were transferred to finished goods, and 70% of this amount was sold. There was no finished-goods inventory at the beginning of the period. Actual manufacturing overhead for the period was $563,000.

Total equivalent units of production for materials for the period was 155,000 tons (using FIFO). This total included 46,200 equivalent tons of materials in ending work-in-process inventory. Material costs in the amount of $193,750 were added during the period.

Conversion costs of $975,000 were added during this period, and there were 130,000 equivalent tons of production (FIFO) as regards conversion, including 9,760 equivalent tons in ending inventory.

REQUIRED:

1. Prepare T accounts to show the flow of costs through Magic Grains Company's manufacturing process. Any difference between actual and applied overhead should be debited or credited to cost of sales.
2. What amount of cost of sales should appear on Magic's income statement?
3. What inventory cost should appear on Magic's balance sheet?

6–30 **Cost-of-Production Report—LIFO** Turnage Corporation manufactures dolls encased in lighted lucite boxes. The lucite boxes are added when processing has been completed. All other materials are added at the start of processing. Turnage has been constantly upgrading the quality of materials going into the manufacturing process and has elected to use the last-in, first-out method to account for manufacturing costs. May operations are summarized as follows:

Units
    Work in process, April 30, 6,000 units, 40% completed as regards
        conversion costs
    Units started during May, 35,200
    Units completed during May, 33,600
    Work in process, May 31, 8,000 units, 80% completed as regards
        conversion costs

Costs

Work in process, April 30 ($37,120 doll material costs, $5,888 conversion costs)	$ 43,008
Doll materials added during May	169,100
Conversion costs added during May	78,584
Lucite boxes added during May	40,320
Total costs to account for	$331,012

REQUIRED:

1. Prepare a cost-of-production report for Turnage Corporation for the month of May using the LIFO method.
2. Prepare the general journal entry required to transfer the finished units out of work-in-process inventory into finished-goods inventory.

6–31 **THOUGHT STIMULATION CASE.** This chapter has discussed actual or modified actual (normal) cost systems designed for use with process-type manufacturing of identical or fungible goods. A primary objective of this type of system is the allocation of costs between goods transferred out of the process and goods remaining in the ending inventory of work in process.

The latest manufacturing techniques call for minimizing or eliminating ending inventories. If there were no ending inventories, allocation of manufacturing costs between goods transferred out of work in process and ending inventory of work in process no longer would be a problem. All manufacturing costs incurred would be transferred out of work in process, and one of the major reasons for accumulating actual costs by process (or department) would be eliminated.

Reliable Disk Corporation manufactures 3.5-inch microdisks for personal computers. This corporation operates in a highly automated environment. Reliable uses computer-aided design (CAD) techniques to design its product and produces its disks on computer-controlled equipment (computer-aided manufacturing, or CAM).

REQUIRED:

1. Assuming that Reliable Disk Corporation maintains negligible inventories, list the reasons why it might want to accumulate actual costs by process or department.
2. Suppose Reliable Disk Corporation engineers could accurately estimate the expected manufacturing cost of its disks. How would the use of these estimated costs per unit modify the cost-of-production reports presented in this chapter?
3. Would the combination of CAD/CAM manufacturing techniques and costs projected by precise engineering estimates nullify the necessity for accumulating actual costs? Discuss.

Chapter 7

Process Costing:
Refinement of the System

Learning Objectives

When you have finished your study of this chapter, you should

1. Know the elements included in transferred-in costs and how to account for them in a cost-of-production report.
2. Understand how to calculate and use transferred-in unit-cost data.
3. Be able to journalize the transfers of costs for a multiprocess company.
4. Know how to calculate and use transferred-in unit-cost data when materials are added that increase the number of units produced.

C hapter 6 introduced the basic procedures for maintaining a process-costing system. And just as with job-order costing, the basic process-costing system must be expanded and refined in situations involving processing complexities to arrive at more precise unit-cost and inventory data. Those refinements are described in this chapter and in Chapter 8. This chapter examines the refinements that should be introduced into the system to account for

- multiprocess companies
- direct materials additions subsequent to the first manufacturing process.

The final part of the chapter presents a problem illustrating the calculations and journal entries required in systems having these refinements.

In Chapter 8, the procedures followed in accounting for lost units are explained and illustrated. In Chapter 9, we discuss the refinements required to account for the costs allocated to joint products and by-products.

Accounting for Multiprocess Operations

In Chapter 6, we assumed that finished units were produced from a single process. Most continuing-process operations put raw materials through a sequence of processes to convert them into finished goods. In the manufacture of flour, for example, the wheat is first crushed, then sifted (to separate the wheat husks from the flour), then refined, and finally packaged. Each of these operations is a separate process, and together they make up a **multiprocess operation**.

As we expand our process-costing procedures to include the production of goods through multiple processes, we shall

1. define transferred-in costs and explain how to account for them
2. describe and illustrate the journal entries used in accounting for costs in multiprocess operations.

Transferred-in Costs

In accounting for a one-process operation, we are concerned with accumulating and allocating the three basic elements of manufacturing costs (direct materials, direct labor, and manufacturing overhead). As we observed in Chapter 6, direct labor and manufacturing overhead are often combined into one category, *conversion costs*. When a production unit moves from one processing department to another, we must account for the accumulation and allocation of another element of total cost commonly referred to as **transferred-in costs**, which include the total accumulated amounts of direct materials, direct labor, and manufacturing-overhead costs allocated to the units before they were transferred from prior processing departments into the current department. Thus, total cost of completed units in a second process will include, as part of transferred-in costs, all manufacturing costs of the first process. As production reaches the third process, transferred-in costs will include the transferred-in costs from the first process plus the costs of materials, labor, and manufacturing overhead incurred in process two.

Insofar as unit-cost calculations are concerned, transferred-in costs for any process are treated the same as the costs of direct materials added at the beginning of a process. The work represented by transferred-in costs will be 100% complete for all units in a process subsequent to that in which the costs were originally added. When preliminary processing has been subcontracted to an outside firm, the costs associated with the partially completed units enter the first processing department as direct materials. Thus, we may think of transferred-in costs as those costs allocated to materials that have been previously processed by our own workers rather than by an outside firm. All transferred-in costs are merged together; thus, previous department contributions toward completion of the product (direct materials, direct labor, and overhead) are not separately identified.

When finished units are produced through more than one process or department, a cost-of-production report should be prepared for *each* process or department. The transferred-in costs, as well as the reporting department's costs allocated to the units remaining in process, will be shown on the cost-of-production report as part of ending work-in-process inventory for the reporting department. The amounts shown for transferred-in costs, direct materials costs, and conversion costs on the various departmental cost-of-production reports for end-of-period work-in-process inventory constitute the subsidiary ledger supporting the balance shown in the work-in-process control account. Cost-of-production reports relate to total work-in-process inventory in the same way that uncompleted job-order cost sheets relate to the balance in the work-in-process inventory for a job-order cost system. In some instances, however, the general ledger for a multiprocess manufacturing firm may include separate work-in-process accounts for each department or process.

We now illustrate the procedures followed in accounting for the flows of costs through a two-process manufacturing operation. The data relating to the flows of units and the incurrence of costs are given in the manufacturing flowchart (Figure 7–1). We assume that all direct materials are put into process at the beginning of the first process (process A). Figure 7–2 shows how costs are accumulated and allocated when using the first-in, first-out cost flow assumption. Figure 7–3 illustrates the accumulation and allocation process for the same data using weighted-average costing.

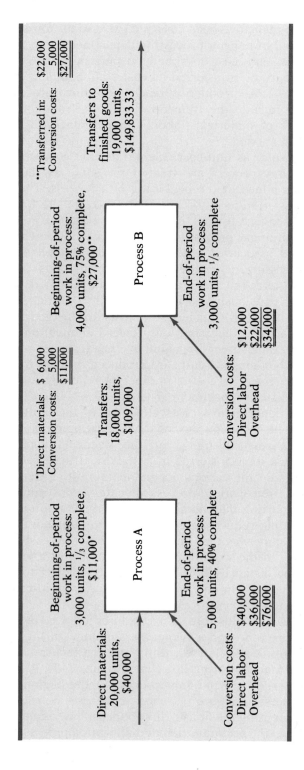

FIGURE 7-1 Two-Process Manufacturing Operation (FIFO cost flow assumptions)

Process A
Cost-of-Production Report

Units

Beginning-of-period work in process	3,000
Added	20,000
Total	23,000
Transferred to process B	18,000
End-of-period work in process	5,000

Costs	Amounts	Per Unit
Beginning-of-period work in process	$ 11,000	
Costs added		
Direct materials costs	40,000	$2.00[a]
Conversion costs	76,000	4.00[a]
Totals	$127,000	$6.00
End-of-period work in process		
5,000 x 100% x $2	$ 10,000	
5,000 x 40% x $4	8,000	
Transferred to process B	$109,000	$6.056

Process B
Cost-of-Production Report

Units

Beginning-of-period work in process	4,000
Transferred in	18,000
Total	22,000
Transferred to finished goods	19,000
End-of-period work in process	3,000

Costs	Amounts	Per Unit
Beginning-of-period work in process	$ 27,000	
Costs added		
Transferred-in costs	109,000	$6.056[b]
Conversion costs	34,000	2.000[b]
Totals	$170,000	$8.056
End-of-period work in process		
3,000 x 100% x $6.056	$ 18,166.67	
3,000 x $1/3$ x $2.000	2,000	
	$ 20,166.67	
Transferred to process B	$149,833.33	$7.386

[a] Equivalent units

	Direct Materials Cost	Conversion Costs
Transferred out	18,000	18,000
End-of-period work in process	5,000	2,000
Total	23,000	20,000
Beginning-of-period work in process	3,000	1,000
Equivalent units	20,000	19,000

Direct materials: $40,000/20,000 = $2.00 per unit
Conversion costs: $76,000/19,000 = $4.00 per unit

[b] Equivalent units

	Transferred-in Costs	Conversion Costs
Transferred out	19,000	19,000
End-of-period work in process	3,000	1,000
Total	22,000	20,000
Beginning-of-period work in process	4,000	3,000
Equivalent units	18,000	17,000

Transferred in: $109,000/18,000 = $6.0555+ per unit
Conversion costs: $34,000/17,000 = $2.00 per unit

FIGURE 7–2 Subsidiary Ledger for Work in Process (FIFO method)

Process A
Cost-of-Production Report

Units

Beginning-of-period work in process	3,000
Added	20,000
Total	23,000
Transferred to process B	18,000
End-of-period work in process	5,000

Costs	Amounts	Per Unit
Beginning-of-period work in process	$ 11,000[a]	
Costs added		
Direct materials costs	40,000	$2.00[b]
Conversion costs	76,000	4.05[b]
Totals	$127,000	$6.05
Transferred to process B (18,000 units)	108,900	$6.05
End-of-period work in process	$ 18,100[c]	

[a] Materials $ 6,000
   Direct labor 5,000
   $11,000

[b] Equivalent units

	Materials Costs	Conversion Costs
Transferred out	18,000	18,000
End-of-period work in process	5,000	2,000
Totals	23,000	20,000

Direct materials: ($6,000 + $40,000)/23,000 = $2.00 per unit
Conversion costs: ($5,000 + $76,000)/20,000 = $4.05 per unit

[c] Materials (5,000 × 100% × $2.00) $10,000
   Conversion costs (5,000 × 40% × $4.05)   8,100
            $18,100

Process B
Cost-of-Production Report

Units

Beginning-of-period work in process	4,000
Transferred in	18,000
Total	22,000
Transferred to finished goods	19,000
End-of-period work in process	3,000

Costs	Amounts	Per Unit
Beginning-of-period work in process	$ 27,000[d]	
Costs added		
Transferred-in costs	108,900	$5.95[e]
Conversion costs	34,000	1.95[e]
Totals	$169,900	$7.90
Transferred to finished goods (19,000 units)	$150,100	$7.90
End-of-period work in process	19,800[f]	

[d] Transferred-in costs $22,000
   Conversion costs 5,000
   $27,000

[e] Equivalent units

	Transferred-in Costs	Conversion Costs
Transferred out	19,000	19,000
End-of-period work in process	3,000	1,000
Totals	22,000	20,000

Transferred-in: ($22,000 + $108,900)/22,000 = $5.95 per unit
Conversion costs: ($5,000 + $34,000)/20,000 = $1.95 per unit

[f] Transferred-in costs (3,000 × 100% × $5.95) $17,850
   Conversion costs (3,000 × 1/3 × $1.95)   1,950
   Total $19,800

FIGURE 7–3 Subsidiary Ledger for Work in Process (weighted-average method)

The accounting procedures for process A are exactly the same as those described and illustrated in Chapter 6. However, the cost-of-production report for process B shows transferred-in costs ($109,000 in Figure 7–2 and $108,900 in Figure 7–3) as part of the costs added during the period. These amounts are shown as transferred to process B in the cost-of-production report for process A. Also, both beginning and ending inventories in process B include transferred-in costs. Notice that the transferred cost per unit for units transferred from process A to process B is the same in both cost-of-production reports in Figure 7–2, which assumes FIFO costing ($6.056), while it differs in Figure 7–3 ($6.05 vs. $5.95). That difference is because of the use of weighted-average rather than FIFO costing in Figure 7–3. The calculation of unit costs in Figure 7–3 includes costs in beginning-of-period inventory. Transferred-in cost per unit in process B is calculated as follows:

$$\frac{\$22,000 + \$108,900}{22,000} = \$5.95$$

It should be clear that a multiprocess company follows the same cost-accumulation and -allocation procedures for *each* process as those followed for the single-process firm discussed in Chapter 6. All steps up to and including the preparation of the cost-of-production report must be repeated for each process. However, the additional item of transferred-in costs must be accumulated and allocated for *all* processes subsequent to the first one, in addition to the direct-materials, direct-labor, and manufacturing-overhead costs incurred within the process (department) during the period.

Journal Entries

The journal entries required to account for the flows of costs for a one-department process cost system are illustrated in Chapter 6. When one accounts for work-in-process inventory in a single control account, then these same journal entries are used to account for cost flows in a multiprocess operation. The entries required to account for the data in the cost-of-production reports in Figure 7–2 are as follows:

Materials Inventory		Work in Process			Finished Goods	
Balance XXX,XXX	(1) 40,000	Balance 38,000	(3) 149,833.33	(3) 149,833.33	
		(1) 40,000			
		(2) 110,000			
		Balance 38,166.67			

Manufacturing Overhead, Process A		Manufacturing Overhead, Process B		Payroll	
Balance 36,000	(2) 36,000	Balance 22,000	(2) 22,000	Balance 52,000	(2) 52,000

Work-in-process ending balance:

Process A	$18,000.00
Process B	20,166.67
	$38,166.67

Explanation of entries:

(1) To record transfer of direct materials from materials inventory to work in process.
(2) To record conversion costs for the period.
(3) To record the transfer of costs assigned to completed units (from work in process to finished goods).

If the firm had used predetermined manufacturing-overhead rates in allocating overhead to production, entry (2) would show a credit to *applied* manufacturing overhead rather than to manufacturing overhead.

If the system calls for maintenance of separate work-in-process accounts for each process or department, the entries to record the flows of costs through the two departments and into finished goods would be as follows:

Materials Inventory				Work in Process, Process A				Work in Process, Process B			
Balance		(1)	40,000	Balance	11,000	(3)	109,000	Balance		(5)	149,833.33
XXX,XXX									27,000		
				(1)	40,000			(3)	109,000		
				(2)	76,000			(4)	34,000		
				Balance	18,000			Balance			
									20,166.67		

Finished Goods			Payroll			
Balance	XX,XXX		Balance	52,000	(2)	40,000
(5)	149,833.33				(4)	12,000

Manufacturing Overhead, Process A				Manufacturing Overhead, Process B			
Balance	36,000	(2)	36,000	Balance	22,000	(4)	22,000

These T-account entries use the amounts shown in the Figure 7–2 cost-of-production reports. Entry (1) records the direct materials costs added to process A; entry (2) reflects the conversion costs added to process A. The costs transferred to process B (entry 3) are shown at the bottom of the cost-of-production report for process A and in the "costs added" part of the cost-of-production report for process B. Entry (4) shows the addition of conversion costs in the cost-of-production report for process B. End-of-period work-in-process inventory balances are also reflected in the respective cost-of-production reports. Again, if predetermined manufacturing-overhead application rates had been used, the credits for entries (2) and (4) would be to *applied* manufacturing overhead rather than manufacturing overhead.

All of the processes (departments) through which a product moves as it is converted from raw materials to finished product are *producing* processes (or departments), as defined in Chapter 5. Continuous-processing firms also have *service* departments like the ones described in that chapter. The costs of operating such service departments will be allocated to producing processes or departments, just as was done in the job-order costing system. The procedures for allocating those costs to producing departments are the same as those illustrated in Chapter 2.

We have accounted for manufacturing-overhead costs in the illustrations in this chapter by charging (debiting) the actual costs incurred by the department or process during the period (including service department costs allocated to it) to work in process. Firms may use an overhead application rate to determine the amount of overhead to be charged to work in process, just as illustrated for a job-order cost system. This practice may be preferable if actual overhead costs are incurred sporadically during the year. If overhead is applied to production by using an overhead application rate, the credit offsetting the debit to work in process will be to applied manufacturing overhead for the process. At the end of each period, the balance in the applied manufacturing-overhead account for the process will be closed against the actual manufacturing overhead included in the manufacturing-overhead account for the same process, to arrive at the underapplied or overapplied overhead for the process for that period. The net underapplied or overapplied overhead amount for all processes, in turn, generally will be transferred to cost of sales. However, when actual overhead differs from applied overhead by a material amount, the underapplied or overapplied amount should be allocated to work in process, finished goods, and cost of sales.

Accounting for Materials Added During Processing

So far we have assumed that all direct materials were added at the beginning of the first process. That is the way operations occur in most situations. One common exception, cited in Chapter 6, is the addition of packing materials at the end of the final process. However, materials can be added at other stages of processing, for example, when a motor is added to the automobile chassis as an automobile is being produced. In accounting for such added materials, we need to determine whether the addition of the materials increases the number of units being processed.

Number of Units Remains Unchanged When Materials Are Added

If direct materials are added to units *after* the initial process without changing the number of units (for example, when a part is added to an appliance, or paint is applied to a unit), the cost of those materials is considered a direct materials cost in that department, and we calculate the unit costs for materials exactly as done in Chapter 6. Keep in mind that the direct materials costs from the initial processing department will have become part of transferred-in costs as those costs are accounted for in subsequent departments (see Figure 7–2 or 7–3). Therefore, when additional materials are added in a second or later process, there will be at least three components of total unit cost in that process: (1) transferred-in cost (including raw materials costs from previous departments), (2) materials cost, and (3) direct labor and overhead (conversion) cost.

Adding materials in subsequent departments without changing the number of units being processed typically occurs when the finished unit is assembled from various components. The unit of production is the completed assembly—for example, an appliance. The unit-cost calculations and allocations for the direct-materials costs in such situations are exactly the same as those followed in accounting for other manufacturing costs.

To illustrate, let's track the handling of costs of materials added in the second department of a three-department process where the number of units being processed is not increased, using the following unit data for the month of May 19X6:

Department 2

Units	
Beginning inventory	8,000
Transferred in from Department 1	22,000
	30,000
Transferred to Department 3	25,000
Ending inventory	5,000

We assume that the FIFO method is used to account for costs in Department 2, that materials are added when processing is 60% complete in the department, that beginning inventory is 90% complete and ending inventory 40% complete, and that the following costs are incurred:

	Transferred-in Costs	Direct Materials Costs	Conversion Costs	Total
Beginning inventory	$ 96,000	$25,600	$ 64,800	$186,400
Current costs	268,400	55,250	162,360	486,010
Total costs to account for	$364,400	$80,850	$227,160	$672,410

Using these assumptions, the cost-of-production report for Department 2 would be organized as shown in Exhibit 7–1 (page 232).

Number of Units Increases When Materials Are Added

In some instances the addition of materials will increase the number of units. In the manufacture of chemicals, for example, where the units of production often are accounted for in terms of pounds or gallons, adding materials during production increases the number of units. This practice also is followed in the manufacture of certain foods. For example, the manufacture of vanilla extract begins with the processing of the vanilla beans; at later stages, sugar and water are added, greatly increasing the quantity of mixture being processed.

If the number of units is increased as materials are added in processes subsequent to the first one, it is necessary to recalculate the transferred-in unit cost, to spread that cost over the larger number of units. Figure 7–4 illustrates the cost-calculation and -allocation procedures in accounting for materials in such a situation. We assume two processing departments, with materials added at the beginning of processing in the first and second departments. Both departments use the first-in, first-out cost flow assumption. In process A, we have 10,000 equivalent units (EUP) for materials (11,000 transferred out + 2,000 in ending work in process − 3,000 in beginning work in process) and $20,000 of materials costs added this period. Therefore, the unit cost of materials is $2.00. However, the unit cost of materials transferred out—because they include units in process at the beginning of the period—is $1.973 ($21,700 ÷ 11,000 units transferred). As the transferred-in cost is accounted for in process B, the unit cost becomes $1.669 because of the addition of 2,000 gallons of material ($21,700 ÷ new EUP of 13,000). The divisor can be calculated as shown in the footnotes to the partial production report for process B, or by simply adding the 2,000 gallons of new material to the 11,000 gallons transferred in.

Illustrative Problem

Assume the following operating data for Multi-Process Chemical Company, a continuous processing operation that produces a chemical through three processes. All units are measured in gallons. We use the

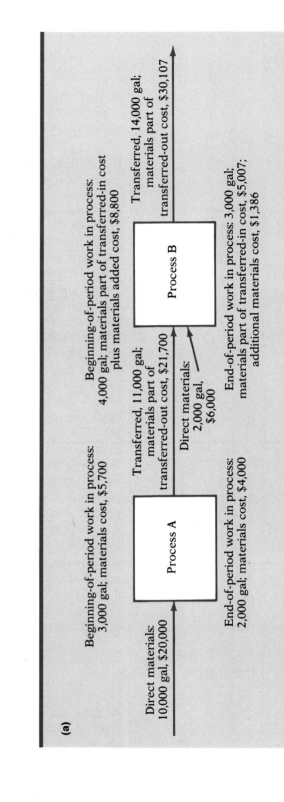

Direct materials:
10,000 gal, $20,000

Beginning-of-period work in process:
3,000 gal; materials cost, $5,700

Process A

End-of-period work in process:
2,000 gal; materials cost, $4,000

Transferred, 11,000 gal;
materials part of
transferred-out cost, $21,700

Direct materials:
2,000 gal,
$6,000

Beginning-of-period work in process:
4,000 gal; materials part of transferred-in cost
plus materials added cost, $8,800

Process B

End-of-period work in process: 3,000 gal;
materials part of transferred-in cost, $5,007;
additional materials cost, $1,386

Transferred, 14,000 gal;
materials part of
transferred-out cost, $30,107

(a)

(b)

Process A
Partial Cost-of-Production Report (materials only)

Gallons

Beginning-of-period work in process	3,000
Added	10,000
Total	13,000
End-of-period work in process	2,000
Transferred	11,000

Dollars

	Amounts	Per Unit
Beginning-of-period work in process, materials	$ 5,700	
Added	20,000	$2.00[a]
Total materials cost	$ 25,700	
End-of-period work in process (2,000 × 100% × $2)	4,000	
Transferred to process B (11,000 units)	$ 21,700	$1.973[b]

Equivalent units of production

	Direct materials
Transferred-out	11,000
Ending inventory	2,000
Beginning inventory	(3,000)
	10,000

Process B
Partial Cost-of-Production Report (materials only)

Gallons

Beginning-of-period work in process	4,000
Transferred in	11,000
Added	2,000
Total	17,000
End-of-period work in process	3,000
Transferred to finished goods	14,000

Dollars

	Amounts	Per Unit
Beginning-of-period work in process, materials part of transferred-in cost and cost of materials added to beginning inventory	$ 8,800	
Transferred-in materials cost (now 13,000 units)	21,700	$1.669[c]
Materials added (to units transferred-in during period)	6,000	.462[d]
Totals	$36,500	$2.131
End-of-period work in process (3,000 × 100% × $2.131)	$ 6,393	
Transferred to finished goods (14,000 units)	$30,107	$2.151[e]

Equivalent units of production

	Transferred-in	Direct materials
Transferred-out	14,000	14,000
Ending inventory	3,000	3,000
Beginning inventory	(4,000)	(4,000)
	13,000	13,000

[a] Cost per unit: $20,000/10,000 = $2.00
[b] Cost per unit: $21,700/11,000 = $1.973
[c] Cost per unit: Transferred-in: $21,700/13,000 = $1.669
[d] Cost per unit: Direct materials: $6,000/13,000 = $.462
[e] Cost per unit: $30,107/14,000 = $2.151

FIGURE 7–4 Number of Units Increases When Materials Are Added. (**a**) Manufacturing process. (**b**) Subsidiary Ledger for Work in Process (FIFO method).

EXHIBIT 7–1 ▬▬▬▬▬▬▬▬

Department 2

Cost-of-Production Report
For the Month of May 19X6
FIFO Method

Units

Beginning-of-period work in process (90% processed)	8,000
Additions during period	
Transfers from Department 1	22,000
Total	30,000
Transfers to Department 3	25,000
End-of-period work in process (40% processed)	5,000

Costs

Beginning-of-period work in process		
Transferred-in cost	$96,000	
Direct materials cost	25,600	
Conversion cost	64,800	$186,400
Current period		
Transferred-in cost		268,400
Direct materials cost		55,250
Conversion cost		162,360
Total costs to be accounted for		$672,410
End-of-period work in process		
Transferred-in cost (5,000 × 1 × $12.20)*	$61,000	
Conversion cost (5,000 × .4 × $8.20)*	16,400	77,400
Transfers to Department 3		$595,010**

*Equivalent units of production (EUP)

	Transferred-in Costs	Direct-Materials Costs	Conversion Costs
Transferred out to Department 3	25,000	25,000	25,000
End-of-period work in process	5,000	0	2,000
	30,000	25,000	27,000
Less Beginning-of-period work in process	8,000	8,000	7,200
FIFO EUP	22,000	17,000	19,800

Unit costs

Transferred in cost $268,400/22,000	$12.20	per unit
Direct-materials cost $55,250/17,000	3.25	
Conversion cost $162,360/19,800	8.20	
Total	$23.65	per unit

**Direct calculation of costs transferred out

Beginning inventory costs	$186,400
Costs to complete beginning inventory (8,000 × .1 × $8.20)	6,560
Cost of units started and completed this period [(25,000 − 8,000) × $23.65]	402,050
	$595,010

weighted-average cost flow assumption and assume that materials are added at the beginning of process A and at the beginning of process C.

Process A

	Units	Amounts
Beginning-of-period work in process (1/3 complete)	3,000	$ 11,000[a]
Additions during period		
Materials	17,000	34,300
Conversion costs		79,300
Totals to be accounted for	20,000	$124,600
End-of-period work in process (40% complete)	2,000	
Transferred to process B	18,000	
Total	20,000	

Process B

	Units	Amounts
Beginning-of-period work in process (75% complete)	4,000	$28,800[b]
Transferred in from process A	18,000	*
Conversion costs		34,000
Total to be accounted for	22,000	$ *
End-of-period work in process (1/3 complete)	3,000	
Transferred to process C	19,000	
Total	22,000	

Process C

	Units	Amounts
Beginning-of-period work in process (40% complete)	2,000	$19,430[c]
Additions during period		
Transfers from process B	19,000	*
Materials added	3,000	6,000
Conversion costs		54,000
Totals to be accounted for	24,000	$ *
End-of-period work in process (2/3 complete)	2,400	
Transferred to finished goods	21,600	
Total	24,000	

[a] Materials cost	$ 5,700	[b] Transferred-in cost	$23,800	[c] Transferred-in cost	$16,550
Conversion cost	5,300	Conversion cost	5,000	Materials cost	1,200
Total	$11,000	Total	$28,800	Conversion cost	1,680
				Total	$19,430

* amounts to be calculated

REQUIRED: Record the allocation and accumulation of costs from these operating data. (Multi-Process Chemical Company accounts for its flows of costs using the weighted-average cost flow method.)

Solution to Illustrative Problem

In solving a process-costing problem of this type, it is generally helpful to summarize the data in a manufacturing process flowchart such as the one in Figure 7–5. Then we use the flowchart data to prepare cost-of-production reports for each process (Exhibits 7–2, 7–3, and 7–4). In preparing these reports, we calculate the equivalent units of production and costs per unit as shown in the footnotes to the production reports.

All of the assumed data—as well as data included in the cost-of-production reports, would be recorded as shown in the following T accounts (assuming the use of one work-in-process account):

Materials Inventory		
Balance XXX,XXX	(3)	34,300
	(5)	6,000

Work-in-Process Inventory			
Beginning		(6)	216,000
balance (1)	59,230		
(3)	34,300		
(4)	167,300		
(5)	6,000		
Balance (7)	50,830		

Finished Goods Inventory	
Balance XX,XXX	
(6) 216,000	

Conversion Costs (Payroll and Manufacturing Overhead)			
Balance (2) 167,300		(4)	167,300

Cash and Miscellaneous Payables	
(2)	167,300

Explanation of balances and entries:

(1) The sum of balances in process at beginning of period: process A, $11,000; process B, $28,800; process C, $19,430.
(2) Amount incurred for direct labor and manufacturing overhead during period.
(3) To record transfer of direct materials costs to process A.
(4) To record conversion costs incurred in the three processes ($79,300, $34,000, and $54,000 for processes A, B, and C, respectively).
(5) To record transfer of direct materials costs to process C.
(6) To record transfer of cost of finished units to finished goods.
(7) End-of-period work in process:

Process A	$ 7,600
Process B	21,150
Process C	22,080
Total	$50,830

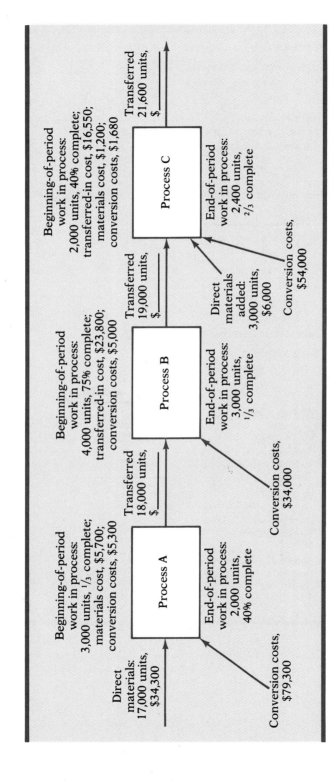

FIGURE 7–5 Manufacturing Process for Illustrative Problem

235

EXHIBIT 7–2 ████████████████████████████

Process A

Cost-of-Production Report
Weighted-Average Method

Units

Beginning-of-period work in process (1/3 complete)	3,000
Additions during period	17,000
Total	20,000
Transferred to process B	18,000
End-of-period work in process (40% complete)	2,000

Costs

Beginning-of-period work in process		
Materials	$5,700	
Conversion costs	5,300	$ 11,000.00
Additions		
Materials		34,300.00
Conversion costs		79,300.00
Total costs to be accounted for		$124,600.00
Costs accounted for:		
Transfers to process B (18,000 @ $6.50)[a]		117,000.00
End-of-period work in process		$ 7,600.00[b]

[a] **Equivalent units:**

	Materials Costs	Conversion Costs
Transferred out to process B	18,000	18,000
End-of-period work in process	2,000	800
Totals	20,000	18,800

Unit costs

Material cost [($5,700 + $34,300)/20,000]	$2.00
Conversion cost [($5,300 + $79,300)/18,800]	4.50
Total cost per unit	$6.50

[b] **Direct calculation of ending inventory**

Direct materials cost (2,000 × 100% × $2.00)	$4,000
Conversion cost (2,000 × 40% × $4.50)	3,600
Total	$7,600

EXHIBIT 7–3
Process B

Cost-of-Production Report
Weighted-Average Method

Units

Beginning-of-period work in process (75% complete)	4,000
Additions during period	
Transfers from process A	18,000
Total	22,000
Transfers to process C	19,000
End-of-period work in process (1/3 complete)	3,000

Costs

Beginning-of-period work in process		
Transferred-in costs	$23,800	
Conversion costs	5,000	$ 28,800
Transferred-in cost this period		117,000
Conversion costs		34,000
Total costs to be accounted for		$179,800
Costs accounted for:		
Transfers to process C (19,000 @ $8.35)[a]		158,650
End-of-period work in process		$ 21,150[b]

[a] **Equivalent units:**

	Transferred-in Costs	Conversion Costs
Transferred out to process C	19,000	19,000
End-of-period work in process	3,000	1,000
Totals	22,000	20,000

Unit costs

Transferred-in cost [($23,800 + $117,000)/22,000]	$6.40
Conversion cost [($5,000 + $34,000)/20,000]	1.95
Total cost per unit	$8.35

[b] **Direct calculation of ending inventory**

Transferred-in cost (3,000 × 100% × $6.40)	$19,200
Conversion cost (3,000 × 1/3 × $1.95)	1,950
Total	$21,150

EXHIBIT 7–4

Process C

Cost-of-Production Report
Weighted-Average Method

Units

Beginning-of-period work in process (40% complete)	2,000
Additions during period	
Transfers from process B	19,000
Materials added	3,000
Total	24,000
Transferred to finished goods	21,600
End-of-period work in process (2/3 complete)	2,400

Costs

Beginning-of-period work in process		
Transferred-in cost	$16,550	
Materials cost	1,200	
Conversion costs	1,680	$ 19,430
Transferred-in cost this period		158,650
Materials added		6,000
Conversion costs		54,000
Total costs to be accounted for		$238,080
Transfers to finished goods (21,600 @ $10.00[a])		216,000
End-of-period work in process		$ 22,080[b]

[a] **Equivalent units:**

	Transferred-in and Materials Costs	Conversion Costs
Transferred out to finished goods	21,600	21,600
End-of-period work in process	2,400	1,600
Totals	24,000	23,200

Unit costs

Transferred-in cost [($16,550 + $158,650)/24,000]	$ 7.30
Materials cost [($1,200 + $6,000)/24,000]	.30
Conversion cost [($1,680 + $54,000)/23,200]	2.40
Total cost per unit	$10.00

[b] **Direct calculation of ending inventory**

Transferred-in cost (2,400 × 100% × $7.30)	$17,520
Direct materials cost (2,400 × 100% × $.30)	720
Conversion cost (2,400 × 2/3 × $2.40)	3,840
Total	$22,080

SUMMARY

In this chapter, we dealt with two refinements to the process-costing system. We began by recognizing that most continuous-processing operations involve more than one process. This requires that work-in-process cost accumulation be divided into separate processes, with each process being accounted for in much the same way as for the single-process factory in Chapter 6, except that work-in-process balances for processes subsequent to the first one will include the additional element of transferred-in costs. We explained and demonstrated the accounting procedures for multiprocess operations, including the entries used to record the allocation and accumulation of costs, and the cost-of-production reports prepared for each of the different processes.

Next, we explained how to account for the costs of materials added in processes subsequent to the initial process. Such additions of materials were divided into two types: (1) when the addition of materials leaves the number of units unchanged and simply increases the total cost of production; (2) when the addition of materials also increases the number of units. We explained that when units are increased because additional materials are added to a process, a new equivalent-units divisor must be derived, which includes the quantity of materials added (as well as the quantity of units transferred in), and this revised divisor must be used in calculating a new transferred-in cost per unit.

An illustrative problem at the end of the chapter demonstrated how those two refinements to the process-costing system should be handled in the accounting records.

GLOSSARY OF TERMS INTRODUCED IN THIS CHAPTER

multiprocess operation   The division of a factory into sequential processes through which products must pass as they are being produced. Costs (direct materials, direct labor, and manufacturing overhead) are accumulated separately for each process and allocated to the products as they pass through the process.

transferred-in costs   The sum of direct-materials, labor, and manufacturing-overhead costs allocated to units in prior departments before the units are transferred to the current processing department.

QUESTIONS FOR CLASS DISCUSSION

7–1   What is meant by the term *transferred-in costs* as found on cost-of-production reports for multiprocess companies? Explain.

7–2 How are the equivalent units that should be used in arriving at transferred-in cost per unit calculated? Explain.

7–3 What element of cost would you expect to find in a cost-of-production report for processes other than the first one that is not found in the report for the first process? Explain.

7–4 What journal entry typically is made to charge manufacturing overhead to work in process in a process-costing system? Are there circumstances in which the credit included in that entry might be different from the one you have just given? Explain.

7–5 How many work-in-process accounts are likely to be found among the accounts of a process-costing system? Explain.

7–6 Is it possible to have an underapplied or overapplied overhead account in a process-costing system? Explain

7–7 How do we account for the addition of materials after the initial process if the number of units remains unchanged? Give examples of situations in which this could occur.

7–8 What special complication do we have when the quantity of units being produced increases because of the addition of materials after the initial process? Explain.

7–9 Given a two-process operation, in what situations will the transferred-in cost per unit *not* be the same on the cost-of-production report for the second process as was shown for goods transferred out of the first process? Explain.

EXERCISES

7–10
AICPA Adapted
Multiple Choice—Process-Costing Concepts Select the *best* answer for each of the following items.

1. What are transferred-in costs as used in a process cost accounting system?
   a. labor that is transferred from another department within the same plant instead of hiring temporary workers from the outside
   b. cost of the production of a previous internal process that is subsequently used in a succeeding internal process
   c. supervisory salaries that are transferred from an overhead-cost center to a production-cost center
   d. ending work-in-process inventory of a previous process that will be used in a succeeding process
2. Purchased materials added in the second department of a three-department process that do not increase the number of units produced in the second department would
   a. not change the dollar amount transferred to the next department.

    b. decrease total work-in-process inventory.

    c. increase the factory overhead portion of the ending work-in-process inventory.

    d. increase total unit cost.

3. The units transferred in from the first department to the second department should be included in the computation of the equivalent-units divisor for the second department for which of the following methods of process costing?

	First-In, First-Out	*Weighted Average*
a.	yes	yes
b.	yes	no
c.	no	yes
d.	no	no

4. Purchased materials added in the second department of a three-department process that increase the number of units produced in the second department would always

    a. change the direct labor cost percentage in the ending work-in-process inventory.

    b. cause no adjustment to the unit cost transferred in from the first department.

    c. increase total unit costs.

    d. decrease total ending work-in-process inventory.

7–11
AICPA Adapted

Multiple Choice—Weighted Average Select the *best* answer for each of the two following questions, based on the following information.

    On April 1, 19X7, the Collins Company had 6,000 units of work in process in Department B, the second and last stage of its production cycle. The costs attached to these 6,000 units were $12,000 of costs transferred in from Department A, $2,500 of material costs added in Department B, and $2,000 of conversion costs added in Department B. Materials are added at the beginning of the process in Department B. Conversion was 50% complete on April 1, 19X7. During April, 14,000 units were transferred in from Department A at a cost of $27,000; material costs of $3,500 and conversion costs of $3,000 were added in Department B. On April 30, 19X7, Department B had 5,000 units of work in process, 60% complete as to conversion costs. The costs attached to these 5,000 units were $10,500 of costs transferred in from Department A, $1,800 of material costs added in Department B, and $800 of conversion costs added in Department B.

1. Using the weighted-average method, what were the equivalent units for the month of April?

	Transferred in from Department A	*Materials*	*Conversion*
a	15,000	15,000	15,000
b.	19,000	19,000	20,000
c	20,000	20,000	18,000
d.	25,000	25,000	20,000

2. Using the weighted-average method, what was the cost per equivalent unit for conversion costs?
   a. $4,200/15,000
   b. $5,800/18,000
   c. $5,800/20,000
   d. $5,000/18,000

7-12   Missing Information—FIFO Determine the information requested for each of the following independent cases, using the FIFO method. Assume that each cost element (materials, labor, and overhead) is added evenly throughout the production process.

	Case 1	Case 2	Case 3
Beginning inventory units	2,000	1,000	?
Degree of completion	?	40%	60%
Units started or transferred in	?	?	35,500
Units started and completed this period	9,000	?	?
Units transferred out	?	8,000	38,500
Ending inventory units	6,000	1,400	10,000
Degree of completion	30%	70%	?
FIFO equivalent units of production	12,400	?	35,800

7-13   Missing Information—Weighted Average Determine the information requested for each of the following independent cases, using the weighted-average method. Assume that each cost element (materials, labor, and overhead) is added evenly throughout the production process.

	Case 1	Case 2	Case 3
Beginning inventory units	500	3,000	?
Degree of completion	30%	80%	75%
Units started or transferred in	8,200	?	?
Units started and completed this period	?	21,000	14,000
Units transferred out	8,000	?	15,200
Ending inventory units	?	5,000	1,500
Degree of completion	50%	70%	?
Weighted-average equivalent-units divisor	?	?	16,100

7-14   Additional Materials Added in Third Department—No Change in Units The GROGREEN Company produces a liquid plant fertilizer in three processes—mixing, cooking, and packaging. During the last process, just before the completed units are transferred to finished-goods inventory, the liquid fertilizer is poured into spray bottles constructed of a new biodegradable plastic. Labor and overhead costs are uniformly added throughout this final stage of processing. Data for the current accounting period for the packaging process are as follows:

	Units	Costs
Work in process, beginning inventory (labor and overhead 60% complete)	1,000	$ 9,450*
Transferred in	11,000	82,500
Materials		9,856
Labor and overhead		28,600
Work in process, ending inventory (labor and overhead 50% complete)	800	

*Transferred-in costs, $7,510; labor and overhead, $1,940

REQUIRED:

1. Compute transferred-in, materials, and labor and overhead equivalent units of production for the cooking process for GROGREEN for the current period, using the first-in, first-out method of process costing.
2. Compute the cost per unit for transferred-in, materials, and labor and overhead for the packaging process.
3. Prepare a cost-of-production report for the packaging process for GROGREEN for the current period.

7–15 **Additional Materials Added in Second Department—Units Increased** Fastgrow Corporation manufactures a granular plant fertilizer, using three departments. The active ingredients are combined in the first department; inert ingredients are added to provide bulk in the second department; the fertilizer is packaged for shipping in the third department. Information pertaining to the second department for the month of March is:

	Units	Costs
Work in process, beginning inventory (materials 40% complete; labor and overhead 60% complete)	3,000	$16,400*
Transferred in	24,000	94,950
Materials		14,860
Labor and overhead		68,210
Increase in units from added materials	4,000	
Work in process, ending inventory (materials 50% complete; labor and overhead 50% complete)	2,500	

*Transferred-in costs, $11,380; materials, $640; labor and overhead, $4,380

Fastgrow Corporation uses the weighted-average method to account for its work in process.

REQUIRED:

1. Compute transferred-in, materials, and conversion equivalent-units divisors for Fastgrow Corporation for March.
2. Compute the cost per unit for transferred-in, materials, and conversion for Fastgrow's second department for March.
3. Prepare a cost of production report for the second department for March.

PROBLEMS

7–16 **Equivalent Units of Production—Multiple Departments** The Felix Manufac-
AICPA Adapted turing Company uses a process cost system to account for the costs of its
only product, known as "Nino." Production begins in the fabrication department, where units of raw material are molded into various connect-
ing parts. After fabrication is complete, the units are transferred to the
assembly department. No material is added in the assembly department.
After assembly is complete, the units are transferred to the packaging
department, where the units are packaged for shipment. At the end of
this process, the units are complete and are transferred to the shipping
department.

At year end, December 31, 19X7, the following inventory of Ninos is on
hand:

- no unused raw material or packing material
- fabrication department: 6,000 units, 25% complete as to raw materials
  and 40% complete as to direct labor
- assembly department: 10,000 units, 75% complete as to direct labor
- packaging department: 3,000 units, 60% complete as to packing materials and 75% complete as to direct labor
- shipping department: 8,000 units

REQUIRED: Prepare, in proper form, schedules showing the following at
December 31, 19X7:

1. The number of equivalent units of raw materials in all inventories
2. The number of equivalent units of fabrication department direct labor
   in all inventories
3. The number of equivalent units of packaging department materials
   and direct labor in the packaging department inventory.

7–17 **Multiple Choice—Weighted Average and FIFO** Select the *best* answer for
AICPA Adapted each of the following items.

1. Maurice Company adds materials at the beginning of the process in
   the forming department, which is the first of two stages of its production cycle. Information concerning the materials used in the forming
   department in April 19X9 is as follows:

	Units	Materials Costs
Work in process on April 1, 19X9	12,000	$ 6,000
Units started during April	100,000	$51,120
Units completed and transferred to next department during April	88,000	

Using the weighted-average method, what was the materials cost of
the work in process on April 30, 19X9?

a. $6,120
b. $11,040
c. $12,000
d. $12,240

2. The cutting department is the first stage of Mark Company's production cycle. Conversion costs for this department were 80% complete as to the beginning work-in-process and 50% complete as to the ending work-in-process. Information as to conversion costs in the cutting department for January 19X0 is as follows:

	Units	Conversion Costs
Work in process on January 1, 19X0	25,000	$ 22,000
Units started and costs incurred	135,000	$143,120
Units completed and transferred to next department during January	100,000	

Using the FIFO method, what was the conversion cost of the work in process in the cutting department on January 31, 19X0?
a. $33,000
b. $38,100
c. $39,000
d. $45,000

3. Roy Company manufactures product X in a two-stage production cycle in Departments A and B. Materials are added at the beginning of the process in Department B. Roy uses the weighted-average method. Conversion costs for Department B were 50% complete as to the 6,000 units in the beginning work in process and 75% complete as to the 8,000 units in the ending work in process. During February 19X0 12,000 units were completed and transferred out of Department B. An analysis of the costs relating to work in process (WIP) and production activity in Department B for February 19X0 is as follows:

	Costs		
	Transferred In	Materials	Conversion
WIP, February 1: Costs attached	$12,000	$2,500	$1,000
February activity: Costs added	29,000	5,500	5,000

The total cost per equivalent unit of product X, transferred out for February 19X0 rounded to the nearest penny, was
a. $2.75
b. $2.78
c. $2.82
d. $2.85

7–18 **Cost-of-Production Report: Multiple Departments—Weighted Average** The C-Clear Optical Company manufactures eyeglass frames out of a new light-weight, heat-resistant plastic that molds to the wearer's face.

C-Clear performs the manufacturing process in three departments—forming, shaping, and finishing. Initial materials are added at the start of processing in the forming department. All additional materials except ornamental decorations are added to the frames in the finishing department when units have been 75% processed through the department. Direct labor and factory overhead (conversion) are incurred evenly throughout the manufacturing process in each department. The following information is available for the month of June:

	Department		
Units	**Forming**	**Shaping**	**Finishing**
Opening work in process			
Forming (all materials, 30% conversion)	13,000		
Shaping (60% conversion)		23,400	
Finishing (40% conversion)			6,900
Started in process or transferred in	117,000	?	?
Transferred out	?	?	?
Completed and still on hand	5,200	2,600	2,500
Forming (all materials, 75% conversion)	9,100		
Shaping (35% conversion)		10,400	
Finishing (all materials, 80% conversion)			11,500

	Department		
Costs	**Forming**	**Shaping**	**Finishing**
Opening work in process			
Materials	$ 9,425		$ 1,040
From preceding department		$31,122	12,282
Labor	936	700	280
Overhead	1,248	3,250	830
Total	$11,609	$35,072	$14,432
Added during the period			
Materials	$ 90,675		$ 9,600
Labor	29,718	$ 5,917	12,790
Overhead	39,624	49,686	38,380
Total	$160,017	$55,603	$60,770

REQUIRED: Prepare cost-of-production reports for all three departments of C-Clear for the month of June, using the weighted-average costing method.

7–19 **Journal Entries and Cost Flows** Using the data from problem 7–18, and assuming that C-Clear maintains one work-in-process account,

1. Prepare the summary general journal entries for the month of June.
2. Prepare T accounts for work in process and finished goods. Post all relevant costs for June to these accounts.

7–20 **Journal Entries and Cost Flows** Using the data from problem 7–18, and assuming that C-Clear maintains a separate work-in-process account for each department,

1. Prepare the summary general journal entries for the finishing department for the month of June.
2. Prepare T accounts for work in process, mixing; work in process, shaping; work in process, finishing; and finished goods. Post all relevant costs for June to these accounts.

7–21 **Cost-of-Production Report: Multiple Processes—FIFO** Harrison Company produces a nausea-relief pill, using two departments: (1) mixing, and (2) compounding and packaging. Chemicals are added in the mixing department. The only other materials added to the production process are packaging materials added in the compounding and packaging department when processing is complete, just prior to transfer to the finished-goods storeroom.

Harrison uses the FIFO method to account for its work in process. On January 1, the work-in-process inventory in the mixing department was complete as to materials and 25% complete as to labor and factory overhead. On January 31, the work-in-process inventory in the mixing department is complete as to materials and 40% complete as to labor and factory overhead. The January 1 work-in-process inventory in the compounding and packaging department was 60% complete as to labor and factory overhead, while the ending inventory is 80% complete as to labor and factory overhead.

January production and cost data are as follows:

Production Data	Mixing Department	Compounding and Packaging Department
Beginning inventory	1,600 units	800 units
Started in process	24,000	0
Received from prior department	0	20,000
Transferred out	20,000	18,400
Ending inventory	5,600	2,400

Cost Summary	Mixing Department	Compounding and Packaging Department
Beginning inventory		
Costs from prior department	0	$ 1,345
Materials	$ 1,568	0
Labor	96	154
Factory overhead	184	255
Costs for January		
Materials	22,800	2,208
Labor	5,187	5,952
Factory overhead	10,374	10,912

REQUIRED: Prepare a cost-of-production report for the mixing department and for the compounding and packaging department for January for the Harrison Company.

7-22 **Journal Entries and Cost Flows** Refer to the data in problem 7-21. Assume that Harrison maintains a separate work-in-process inventory account for each processing department.

REQUIRED:

1. Prepare the summary general journal entries for the compounding and packaging department for the month of January.
2. Prepare T accounts for work in process, mixing; work in process, compounding and packaging; and finished goods. Post all relevant costs for June to these accounts.

7-23 **Journal Entries and Cost Flows** Refer to the data in problem 7-21. Assume that Harrison maintains one general ledger work-in-process inventory account.

REQUIRED:

1. Prepare the summary general journal entries for the month of January.
2. Prepare T accounts for work in process and finished goods. Post all relevant costs for June to these accounts.

7-24 **Cost-of-Production Reports: Two Departments, Two Periods** Myers Corporation operates a rocking horse manufacturing firm in Tennessee. Myers purchases wooden component parts from small suppliers, assembles the parts in the construction department, and packages the completed units for shipping in the shipping department. A process-costing system is used to account for the goods manufactured.

Operating data for July and August are:

July

Construction Department: One hundred units were in work-in-process inventory on July 1. Costs incurred for these partially completed units included materials (100% complete), $940; conversion (30% complete), $195. During the month, 1,000 units were put into process and $10,500 was charged to this department for direct materials. Conversion costs incurred during the month were $7,605. Nine hundred rocking horses were finished and transferred to shipping. The work in process on July 31 was one-half completed.

Shipping Department: There was no work in process on July 1. The rocking horses transferred in from the construction department were received, and materials costing $765 were used to package rocking horses. Labor and overhead of $1,424 were used to operate the department during July. On July 31, 100 rocking horses were still in the department. All packing material had been added, and shipping department processing was 90% complete on these units.

August

Construction Department: Nine hundred rocking horses were put into process at a total material cost of $9,536. Conversion costs incurred were $6,015. At the end of August, 300 units one-third finished remained in process.

Shipping Department: Materials charged to this department in August were $685; conversion costs incurred were $1,556. On August `31, there were 200 rocking horses still in the department, of which all but 20 had received packing material. Three-fourths of the shipping department processing had been completed on the units in the ending inventory.

There is no spoilage in either of the departments, and all units unfinished (in either of the departments) at the beginning of the month are completed before new units are begun.

REQUIRED: Prepare a cost-of-production report for each process for July and for each process for August, using the weighted-average method. (*Hint:* Complete the July reports—construction, then shipping—before attempting the August reports.)

7–25 **Two Departments, Two Periods—FIFO** Refer to the data in problem 7–24. Prepare a cost-of-production report for each process for July and for each process for August, using the FIFO method to account for work-in-process inventories.

7–26
ICMA Adapted

Multiple Departments and Manufacturing Overhead Upton, Inc., manufactures a line of home furniture. The company's single manufacturing plant consists of the cutting, assembly, and finishing departments. Upton uses departmental rates for applying manufacturing overhead to production and maintains separate manufacturing-overhead control and manufacturing-overhead applied accounts for each of the three production departments.

The following predetermined departmental manufacturing-overhead rates were calculated for Upton's fiscal year ending May 31, 19X6:

Department	Rate
Cutting	$2.40 per machine-hour
Assembly	$5.00 per direct-labor hour
Finishing	$1.60 per direct-labor dollar

Information regarding actual operations for Upton's plant for the six months ended November 30, 19X5, is:

	Department		
	Cutting	Assembly	Finishing
Manufacturing-overhead costs	$22,600	$56,800	$98,500
Machine-hours	10,800	2,100	4,400
Direct-labor hours	6,800	12,400	16,500
Direct-labor dollars	$40,800	$62,000	$66,000

Based on this experience and updated projections for the last six months of the fiscal year, Upton revised its operating budget. Projected data regarding manufacturing overhead and operating activity for each department for the six months ending May 31, 19X6, are as follows:

	Department		
	Cutting	**Assembly**	**Finishing**
Manufacturing-overhead costs	$23,400	$57,500	$96,500
Machine-hours	9,200	2,000	4,200
Direct-labor hours	6,000	13,000	16,000
Direct-labor dollars	$36,000	$65,000	$64,000

Diane Potter, Upton's controller, plans to revise departmental manufacturing-overhead rates so they are more representative of efficient operations for the current fiscal year ending May 31, 19X6. To do this she has decided to include the actual results for the first six months. She then plans to adjust the manufacturing-overhead applied accounts for each department through November 19X5 to recognize the revised application rates. The following analysis was prepared by Potter from general ledger account balances as of November 30, 19X5.

Account	Direct Material	Direct Labor	Manufacturing Overhead	Account Balance
Work-in-process inventory	$ 53,000	$ 95,000	$ 12,000	$ 160,000
Finished goods	96,000	176,000	48,000	320,000
Cost of goods sold	336,000	604,000	180,000	1,120,000
	$485,000	$875,000	$240,000	$1,600,000

REQUIRED:

1. Determine the balance of the manufacturing-overhead applied accounts as of November 30, 19X5, before any revision for the
   a. cutting department
   b. assembly department
   c. finishing department.
2. Calculate the revised departmental manufacturing-overhead rates that Upton, Inc., should use for the remainder of the fiscal year, ending May 31, 19X6.
3. Prepare an analysis that shows how the manufacturing-overhead applied account for each production department of Upton, Inc., should be adjusted as of November 30, 19X5, and prepare the adjusting entry to correct all general ledger accounts affected.

7–27   Multiple Processes and LIFO Cost Flows Refer to this chapter's illustrative problem for Multi-Process Chemical Company (page 229).

REQUIRED:

1. Under what circumstances would Multi-Process Chemical Company desire to use a LIFO cost flow assumption for its cost-of-production reports?
2. Using the data provided for process A, and the LIFO cost flow assumption, prepare a cost-of-production report for that process.
3. Assuming Multi-Process Chemical Company has a work-in-process account for each process, prepare general journal entries to record the activity for process A during the period.

7–28 THOUGHT STIMULATION PROBLEM. Athletics, Incorporated, produces athletic uniforms. One of its products is basketball jerseys. Basic garments are produced through sequential processes of cutting and sewing, after which they are stored in a semifinished state until specific team orders are received. When orders are received, the basic garments are removed from storage and finished by adding team logos, numbers, and so forth.

REQUIRED:

1. What kind of cost accounting system should Athletics, Incorporated, use? Discuss.
2. How would the operations and cost accounting system be changed if Athletics adopted a JIT inventory policy?

Chapter 8

Process Costing:
Accounting for Lost Units

Learning Objectives

When you have finished your study of this chapter, you should

1. Understand what is meant by the terms *normal spoilage*, *abnormal spoilage*, and *reworking costs*.
2. Know how to account for normal spoilage using both the no-specific-recognition and specific-recognition methods.
3. Recognize the procedures followed in accounting for cost recovery from spoilage.
4. Know how to account for abnormal spoilage.
5. Know how to account for reworking spoiled units.

I n this chapter, we explain the procedures to follow in accounting for lost units. **Lost units** are defined as units that either disappear or have defects caused by processing that keep them from being transferred to finished stock as normal, saleable products. Units that are lost by shrinkage simply disappear as goods are processed. Defective units, on the other hand, may be removed from work in process and sold as scrap or as "seconds," or they may be reworked to eliminate the defects, then transferred to finished goods as good units.

We first develop and illustrate the procedures to follow in accounting for

- normal spoilage
- abnormal spoilage
- the reworking of defective units.

In the latter part of the chapter, we present a problem illustrating how to carry out the accounting procedures for shrinkage and spoilage.

Normal Spoilage

Manufacturing firms, almost without exception, expect some units to be lost during processing. Units lost through **shrinkage** simply disappear and therefore have no recoverable value. Such shrinkage generally occurs gradually during processing. **Spoiled units**, which are lost as good units, still exist physically, however, and may be reworked or sold as **scrap** or as "seconds." Such units are determined to be defective at specified points (when they are inspected) in the production process. When the number of spoiled units or the amount of shrinkage is within the range of what is normally expected in the manufacturing process, we characterize the unrecovered costs accumulated on those units as **normal-spoilage costs** (loss). We can divide our discussion of the procedures to follow in accounting for normal-spoilage losses into spoilage with (1) no cost recovery and (2) some cost recovery.

Accounting for Normal-Spoilage Costs—No Cost Recovery

Spoilage costs are defined as the unrecovered costs attached to the units lost at the time they either disappear due to shrinkage or are withdrawn from the production process because they fail to meet company inspection standards. If the number of units lost in processing is considered normal, the unrecovered costs associated with them generally will be included as part of the total manufacturing costs of good units, either by (1) eliminating the spoiled units from the equivalent-units divisors (**no-specific-recognition method**) or (2) by transferring the cost of the spoiled units from work in process to the cost of good units passing the inspection point or to manufacturing overhead (**specific-recognition**).

To contrast the two methods, let's assume that a mixing department in which all materials are added at the beginning of processing has 3,000 units in beginning work-in-process inventory, 70% complete. During the reporting period, 7,000 units are added and 8,000 units are transferred to the next department. There are 1,500 units in end-of-period work in process, 60% complete. These assumed data are reflected in the following "Units" section of the cost-of-production report:

Units

Beginning inventory (70% complete)	3,000
Started during period	7,000
Total units to be accounted for	10,000
Transfers to next department	8,000
Ending inventory (60% complete)	1,500
Lost units	*500*
Total units accounted for	10,000

If we assume that lost units are not discovered until the completion of processing in the mixing department, the equivalent units of production for the two alternative treatments would be calculated as follows:

	Specific Recognition of Lost Units		No Specific Recognition of Lost Units	
	Direct Materials Costs	Conversion Costs	Direct Materials Costs	Conversion Costs
Transfers out	8,000	8,000	8,000	8,000
Ending inventory	1,500	900	1,500	900
Lost units	500	500	—	—
Weighted-average EU	10,000	9,400	9,500	8,900
Less beginning inventory	3,000	2,100	3,000	2,100
FIFO EUP	7,000	7,300	6,500	6,800

Observe that the cost per unit using the no-specific-recognition method, because of smaller equivalent-units divisors, always will be larger than with the specific-recognition method. Thus, all units being costed in the current period (ending inventory as well as transfers out) will bear a portion of the cost of lost units when lost units are not included in the calculation of equivalent units of production. However, because units spoiled by defective processing will be identified at the point of inspection in each process or department, the loss more appropriately should be allocated only to those units that have passed the inspection point. If the inspection point is at the end of the process, the loss associated with the spoiled units should be allocated only to units transferred out of the process. Simple elimination of the normally spoiled units from the equivalent-units divisor (that is, not "counting" the work performed on the spoiled units) spreads spoilage losses over units in process, as well as units transferred out, by means of a higher unit cost. Also, because it is difficult to isolate abnormal losses if normal losses are not specifically identified, we can conclude that the no-specific-recognition treatment of loss theoretically would be appropriate only in accounting for shrinkage losses. In spite of that fact, however, the no-specific recognition method (sometimes called the *method of neglect*) is often used in accounting for losses associated with spoiled units identified at the end of a process.

Accounting for Shrinkage. When spoilage loss results from shrinkage in the volume of goods produced, most firms almost certainly will allocate the costs associated with those units to the good units produced by including only good units in the equivalent-units divisor used in determining unit costs. The smaller divisor automatically will cause an increase in unit costs over what they would have been had the spoiled units been included in the equivalent-units divisor. Problems in accounting for the costs of units determined by inspection to have been spoiled during processing center around (1) the costs accumulated on the units when they were removed from production and (2) how much spoilage cost should be included as part of good-unit costs.

A precise determination of the cost to assign to the lost units could be accomplished by accumulating and allocating to lost units all costs incurred in the production of those units up to the point they were removed from processing. In the case of shrinkage, however, the loss in volume generally occurs gradually during a particular process, such as cooking. It is impractical in such a situation to separately identify the part of the departmental processing costs incurred prior to the shrinkage that should be associated with the lost units. As a result, in a normal-shrinkage situation, we calculate the unit costs for good units by dividing total production costs by the equivalent number of good units produced, thereby allowing the loss to be absorbed by the good units (both in process and transferred out) through an increased unit cost.

To illustrate, let's assume the following about the *first* process in the manufacture of a liquid chemical (first-in, first-out cost flow assumed):

	Units	Costs
Beginning-of-period work in process	5,000	
Materials, 100% complete		$ 6,500
Labor and overhead, 40% complete		6,000
Totals	5,000	$ 12,500
		(Continues)

	Units	Costs
Additions to work in process	20,000	
Materials		34,000
Labor and overhead		65,120
Totals to be accounted for	25,000	$111,620
Units transferred to next process	16,000	
Units remaining in process—complete as to materials,		
60% complete as to labor and overhead	6,000	
Units lost in processing	3,000	
Total units accounted for	25,000	

With the no-specific-recognition method of allocating the shrinkage loss, we would calculate the equivalent units of production for the period as follows:

Equivalent Units

	Materials	Labor and Overhead
Transferred out	16,000	16,000
End-of-period work in process	6,000	3,600
Weighted-average EU for period		
(equivalent-units divisors)	22,000	19,600
Less beginning-of-period work in process	5,000	2,000
FIFO EUP for period (equivalent-units divisors)	17,000	17,600

(Observe that in calculating the numbers of equivalent units to be used as divisors, we have simply omitted the units lost in processing.) We would then calculate unit costs of production for the period:

Costs per Unit, FIFO Method

Materials ($34,000/17,000)	$2.00
Labor and overhead ($65,120/17,600)	3.70
Total unit cost	$5.70

The total costs to be accounted for ($111,620) would be divided between end-of-period work in process and transfers to the next process, as shown on the next page.

Costs to be accounted for		$111,620
Costs accounted for, FIFO method		
End-of-period work in process		
Materials (6,000 × 100% × $2.00)	$12,000	
Labor and overhead (6,000 × 60% × $3.70)	13,320	$ 25,320
Transfers to next process ($111,620 − $25,320)		86,300*
Total costs accounted for		$111,620

*The amount allocated to transfers to the next process can be confirmed as follows:

Beginning-of-period work-in-process costs	$12,500
Cost to complete beginning-of-period work in process (5,000 × 60% × $3.70)	11,100
Units started and completed this period [(16,000 transferred out − 5,000 in beginning inventory) × $5.70]	62,700
Total costs transferred to next process	$86,300

The $5.70 per unit cost includes the cost of the spoiled units because the equivalent-units divisors do not include the lost units. Such an arrangement simply adds the costs associated with the lost units to the cost per good unit of production.

Weighted-average costing procedures would yield the following unit costs and dollar values assigned to goods transferred out and end-of-period work in process. (Although, in practice, unit-cost data would be limited to no more than three decimal places, we have extended them to seven to permit proof of the figure "plugged in" for end-of-period work-in-process inventory.)

Cost per unit, weighted-average method		
Materials [($6,500 + $34,000)/22,000]	$1.8409090	
Labor and overhead [($6,000 + $65,120)/19,600]	3.6285714	
Total unit cost	$5.4694804	
Costs to be accounted for		$111,620.00
Costs accounted for, weighted-average method		
Transferred to next process (16,000 × $5.4694804)	$87,511.69	
End-of-period work in process ($111,620 − $87,511.69)	24,108.31*	
Total costs accounted for		$111,620.00

*This figure can be confirmed as follows:

Materials (6,000 × 100% × $1.8409090)	$11,045.45
Labor and overhead (6,000 × 60% × $3.6285714)	13,062.86
Total end-of-period work in process	$24,108.31

Now let's suppose the shrinkage occurs in a process *subsequent* to the first one. This creates a special problem because we will have costs transferred in from the previous department showing both an aggregate amount and an amount per unit as an element of the cost of the product. Remember that this transferred-in cost is similar to direct materials cost added at the beginning of a process. In the data just described, we calculated the materials costs per unit by dividing materials costs by equivalent-units figures that excluded units lost in processing. We do the same thing with costs transferred in from a previous process. To illustrate, let's assume the following regarding the manufacture of a product that sustains shrinkage in a department subsequent to the initial process:

	Units	Costs
Beginning-of-period work in process		
Transferred in	7,500	$ 12,850
Labor and overhead, 40% complete		12,056
Totals	7,500	$ 24,906
Additions to work-in-process		
Transferred in	30,000	68,000
Labor and overhead		130,240
Totals to be accounted for	37,500	$223,146
Units transferred to next process	24,000	
Units remaining in process—completely transferred in,		
60% complete as to labor and overhead	9,000	
Units lost in process (normal spoilage)	4,500	
Total units accounted for	37,500	

Equivalent Units of Production

	Transferred In	Labor and Overhead
Transferred out to next process	24,000	24,000
End-of-period work in process	9,000	5,400
Weighted-average equivalent-units divisor	33,000	29,400
Beginning-of-period work in process	7,500	3,000
FIFO equivalent-units divisor (equivalent units of production for period)	25,500	26,400

The costs per unit using the FIFO cost method would be calculated as follows:

Costs per Unit, FIFO Method

Transferred-in cost ($68,000/25,500)	$2.66\frac{2}{3}
Labor and overhead ($130,240/26,400)	$4.93\frac{1}{3}
Total cost per unit	$7.60

The total cost to be accounted for ($223,146) would be allocated as follows:

Costs Accounted For, FIFO Method

End-of-period work in process	
Transferred-in cost (9,000 × 100% × $2.66\frac{2}{3}$)	$ 24,000
Conversion cost (9,000 × 60% × $4.93\frac{1}{3}$)	26,640
	$ 50,640
Transferred-out costs ($223,146 − $50,640)	172,506*
Total costs accounted for	$223,146

*Beginning-of-period work in process costs	$ 24,906
Costs to complete beginning-of-period work in process (7,500 × 60% × $4.93\frac{1}{3}$)	22,200
Units started and completed this period [(24,000 − 7,500) × $7.60]	125,400
Total costs transferred out	$172,506

The cost per unit using the weighted-average method in a department subsequent to the first that sustains shrinkage would be calculated as follows:

Cost per Unit, Weighted-Average Method

Transferred-in cost [($12,850 + $68,000)/33,000]	$2.45
Labor and overhead [($12,056 + $130,240)/29,400]	4.84
Total cost per unit	$7.29

The total cost to be accounted for ($223,146) would be allocated as follows:

Costs Accounted For, Weighted-Average Method

End-of-period work-in-process	
Transferred-in cost (9,000 × 100% × $2.45)	$ 22,050
Conversion cost (9,000 × 60% × $4.84)	26,136
	$ 48,186
Transferred-out costs (24,000 × $7.29)	174,960
Total costs accounted for	$223,146

We have treated shrinkage for transferred-in costs exactly as we treated shrinkage for material costs in the first department.

In some instances, it may be desirable to calculate the lost-unit charge associated with costs transferred in:

Weighted-Average Method

Transferred-in cost before accounting for lost units
= ($12,850 + $68,000)/37,500 = $2.156
Units lost (4,500) × Transferred-in cost ($2.156) = $9,702
Lost-unit charge per good unit = $9,702 ÷ 33,000 = $.294

We can now reconcile this with the unit cost calculated earlier ($7.29):[1]

Transferred-in cost before lost-unit charge ($80,850/37,500)	$2.156
Lost-unit charge	.294
Labor and overhead	4.840
Total cost per unit	$7.290

As you can see, the determination of a separate lost-unit charge per unit simply requires division of the transferred-in cost per unit into two parts: one ($2.156) showing the amount before giving effect to the costs associated with the lost units, and the other ($.294) being a lost-unit charge.

Accounting for Spoiled Units. Earlier, we observed that a more precise determination of spoilage loss requires inclusion of the costs associated with the spoiled units up to the point within the department where those units were identified as defective. If, for example, the spoilage is detected by inspection at the *end* of the process, we can find those costs by including the spoiled units as part of the equivalent-units divisor used to arrive at unit cost for each element of cost and then multiplying the number of defective units by the calculated unit cost to get the aggregate cost of spoiled units. If we then add the aggregate cost of normally spoiled units to the cost of good units transferred out, we will be allocating the cost of spoiled units only to those units passing the inspection point (because the inspection point is at the end of the process). Using the previously assumed data, supplemented by the assumptions that the spoiled units have no sales value and the firm uses the weighted-average cost flow assumption, unit costs would be calculated as in Figure 8–1. (Recall that the spoiled units are identified by an end-of-process inspection.)

Another possible arrangement is to transfer the cost of the spoiled units from work in process to manufacturing overhead. When we follow that procedure, the normal spoilage cost is still allocated to good units but is considered as part of the overhead cost of all units rather than as a separate increase to the unit cost of good units produced during each reporting period. This method is particularly appropriate when manufacturing-overhead costs are allocated to production with a predetermined overhead application rate based on projected overhead

---

[1] A similar reconciliation for the FIFO method would be:

Transferred-in cost before lost-unit charge ($68,000/30,000)	$2.26\frac{2}{3}
Lost-unit charge [($2.26\frac{2}{3} \times 4,500)/25,500]	.40
Labor and overhead	4.93\frac{1}{3}
Total cost per unit	$7.60

	Transferred In	Conversion	
Equivalent units divisors, including 4,500 lost units	37,500*	33,900*	
Total costs to be accounted for			$223,146.00
Unit costs			
Transferred-in cost [($12,850 + $68,000)/37,500]		$2.1560000	
Conversion cost [($12,056 + $130,240)/33,900]		4.1975221	
Total		$6.3535221	
Costs assigned to units transferred out			
Good units (24,000 × $6.3535221)		$152,484.53	
Normal spoiled units (4,500 × $6.3535221)		28,590.85	
Total		$181,075.38**	
End-of-period work-in-process inventory			
9,000 × 100% × $2.156	$19,404.00		
9,000 × 60% × $4.1975221	22,666.62	42,070.62	
Total costs accounted for			$223,146.00

*Equivalent-units divisors:

	Transferred In	Conversion
Transferred out	24,000	24,000
Ending inventory	9,000	5,400
Normal spoilage	4,500	4,500
	37,500	33,900

**Cost per good unit transferred out $= \dfrac{\$181,075.38}{24,000} = 7.5488$

FIGURE 8–1 Specific Recognition of Normal Spoilage, Weighted-Average Method

costs that include normal-spoilage losses. With this arrangement, the spoilage costs shown in Figure 8–1 would be recorded as follows:

Manufacturing overhead (loss from spoilage)	28,590.85	
Work in process		28,590.25

Accounting for Normal-Spoilage Costs with Some Cost Recovery

The preceding illustrations assumed we were dealing with defective units that had no cost recovery value. Let's now consider situations in which spoiled units can be sold as seconds or as scrap. If defective units have some disposal value, we may treat the amount realized from their sale either as miscellaneous income or as a reduction of the costs included in work in process. If the proceeds are treated as *miscellaneous revenue*, the procedures followed in accounting for the spoiled units will be the same as those just described for normally spoiled units with no cost recovery. If, on the other hand, we treat the net proceeds from disposal of the spoiled units as a *reduction of processing costs*, only the difference between their costs and the amounts recovered from their sale will be recognized as a loss from spoilage. For example, using the previous data for the specific recognition of normal spoilage (weighted-average method), but assuming that the spoiled units can be sold for $2 per unit (a total recovery of $9,000), total costs to be accounted for would be:

Costs to be accounted for	
Beginning-of-period work in process	$ 24,906
Additions to work in process	
Transferred in	68,000
Labor and overhead	130,240
	$223,146
Less cost recovery on spoiled units	9,000
Total costs to be accounted for	$214,146

Calculation of equivalent units of production and cost per unit would be the same as before ($2.156 for transferred-in cost per unit and $4.1975221 for conversion cost per unit). However, we would also realize a recovery of $9,000 ÷ 24,000 units = $.375 per good unit transferred out from sale of the spoiled units, resulting in a cost of $172,075.38 ÷ 24,000 = $7.1698 per good unit transferred out (see schedule below). Total processing costs would be accounted for as follows:

Costs to be accounted for		$214,146.00
Costs accounted for		
Costs assigned to units transferred out		
Good units (24,000 × $6.3535221)		$152,484.53
Normal spoiled units:		
4,500 × $6.3535221	$28,590.85	
Less 4,500 × $2.00	9,000.00	19,590.85
		$172,075.38
End-of-period work-in-process inventory		
Transferred in (9,000 × 100% × $2.156)	$19,404.00	
Conversion cost (9,000 × 60% × $4.1975221)	22,666.62	42,070.62
Total costs accounted for		$214,146.00

The work-in-process T account would appear as follows:

Work-in-Process, This Department

Beginning balance	24,906.00		
Transferred in	68,000.00	Transferred out	172,075.38
Conversion costs	130,240.00	Sale of spoiled units	9,000.00
Ending balance	42,070.62		

(*Note*: If the cost recovery did not occur until *after* the cost of good units had been transferred out at $181,075.38, the $9,000 recovery could be credited to the next department. In any event, production costs would be decreased by any amount recovered from the sale of the spoiled goods.)

As observed earlier, we may also account for normally spoiled units by removing the costs associated with them from work in process and adding them to manufacturing overhead. When we have partial recovery of the cost of spoiled units, we remove only the *unrecovered* portion from work in process. The offsetting debit should be a manufacturing-overhead account. Assuming the overhead portion of conversion costs charged to work in process included an amount for normal spoilage, the entry to recognize net spoilage costs for our weighted-average example would be:

Manufacturing overhead (loss from spoilage)	**19,590.85**	
Work in process		**19,590.85**

A firm following this practice of including net normal-spoilage costs as part of manufacturing overhead incurred will charge work in process with manufacturing overhead that includes either the actual normal-spoilage loss (with an actual-cost system) or a provision for normal-spoilage loss (with a normal-cost system).

Abnormal Spoilage

Abnormal spoilage occurs when more units are lost than the firm would normally expect to lose, either because of special precision limits associated with a particular lot of goods being manufactured or because of the operating conditions associated with the period during which the goods were produced. We dealt with the first of these situations in Chapter 5. When a firm using a process-costing system has abnormal spoilage, we determine the costs associated with those spoiled units and account for them as separate period costs (**abnormal-spoilage costs**). Such costs should *not* be spread over good units produced. To demonstrate how to handle abnormal spoilage, we shall use the following data. We assume the firm has 2,000 units of abnormal spoilage and that all spoiled units, which have no recovery value, are discovered at the end of the process as they were being inspected prior to being transferred to the next process.

	Units	Costs
Beginning-of-period work-in-process inventory	5,000	$ 14,500
Additions during period		
Materials	19,000	34,200
Conversion costs		62,720
Totals to be accounted for	24,000	$111,420
Transferred out	16,000	
Normal spoilage	0	
Abnormal spoilage	2,000	
End-of-period work-in-process inventory	6,000	
Total units accounted for	24,000	

All materials are added at the beginning of processing. Beginning-of-period inventory is 40% complete as to conversion costs. End-of-period inventory is 60% complete as to conversion costs. Costs attached to beginning-of-period inventory are:

Work-in Process Beginning Inventory

Materials	$ 7,500
Conversion costs	7,000
Total	$14,500

The "Units" section of a cost-of-production report would appear as follows:

Units

Beginning-of-period work in process (40% complete)	5,000
Started during period	19,000
Total units to be accounted for	24,000
Transferred out	16,000
Normal spoilage	0
Abnormal spoilage	2,000
End-of-period work in process (60% complete)	6,000
Total units accounted for	24,000

To complete the "costs" section of the cost-of-production report, we first calculate equivalent units and unit costs and then determine how total costs should be allocated. Our cost data in this illustration are based on a first-in, first-out cost flow assumption.

Equivalent Units	Materials	Labor and Overhead
Transferred out	16,000	16,000
Abnormal spoilage	2,000	2,000
End-of-period work in process	6,000	3,600
Totals (weighted-average equivalent-units divisor)	24,000	21,600
Less beginning-of-period work in process	5,000	2,000
FIFO equivalent units of production for the period	19,000	19,600

Cost per Unit, FIFO

Materials ($34,200/19,000)	$1.80
Conversion cost ($62,720/19,600)	3.20
Total cost per unit	$5.00

Costs Accounted For, FIFO

End-of-period work in process		
Materials cost (6,000 × 100% × $1.80)	$10,800	
Conversion cost (6,000 × 60% × $3.20)	11,520	$22,320
Abnormal spoilage (2,000 × 100% × $5)		10,000
Transferred out to next process ($111,420 − $32,320)		79,100*
Total costs accounted for		$111,420

*Proof of costs transferred out:

Beginning-of-period work in process	$14,500
Cost to complete beginning work in process (5,000 × 60% × $3.20)	9,600
Cost of units started and completed during period [(16,000 − 5,000 × $5)]	55,000
Total	$79,100

The following entry would then be made to record the allocation of costs, assuming separate work-in-process accounts are maintained for each department.

Work in process, next department	79,100	
Abnormal spoilage loss	10,000	
Work-in-process, this department		89,100

The T account for "Work-in-Process, This Department," would include the following:

Work-in-Process, This Department

Beginning balance	14,500	Transferred to next department	79,100
Additions		Transferred to abnormal-spoilage-	
Materials	34,200	loss account	10,000
Conversion cost	62,720		
Ending balance	22,320		

To appropriately account for the costs of spoiled units, it is vital to know exactly where the inspection point is located. If, for example, the abnormally spoiled units in our example (2,000) were discovered when the units were 40% complete, the equivalent units for labor and overhead would show only 40% × 2,000 = 800 units for abnormal spoilage. That would make the equivalent-units divisor for labor and overhead 18,400 instead of 19,600:

Equivalent Units

	Labor and Overhead
Transferred out	16,000
Abnormal spoilage	800
End-of-period work in process	3,600
Total (weighted-average equivalent-units divisor)	20,400
Less beginning-of-period work in process	2,000
FIFO equivalent units of production (equivalent-units divisor) for the period	18,400

This brings the unit cost for labor and overhead to $62,720 ÷ 18,400 = $3.409, rather than $3.00. The amount charged to abnormal spoilage would then be:

Abnormal Spoilage Cost, Inspection After 40% of Processing Is Completed

Direct materials (2,000 × 100% × $1.80)	$3,600.00
Conversion costs (2,000 × 40% × $3.409)	2,727.20
Total	$6,327.20

Note that all materials costs are lost, even though processing in this department was less than half completed. The $3.409 conversion cost per unit also would be used to calculate the conversion costs of the transferred-out units and the 3,600 equivalent units of conversion work in the ending work-in-process inventory.

Reworking Defective Units

If spoiled units can be reworked and made into good units (**reworked units**), the **reworking costs** may be allowed to remain as processing costs (no-specific-recognition method), thereby increasing the cost of all units produced during the period. However, management often will want to know the amount of reworking costs incurred during *each period*, which requires a separate determination of the reworking costs. Assuming reworking costs are normal, the following kind of journal entry would isolate the additional direct labor and manufacturing-overhead costs required to convert the defective units to good units:

Manufacturing overhead (reworking costs)	XX	
Work in process (direct labor)		XX
Work in process (manufacturing overhead)		XX

Reworking costs treated this way are assumed to be a normal part of the manufacturing process and so should become a part of manufacturing overhead.

After the spoiled units have been reworked, they will be included in the calculation of equivalent units and there will be no increase in unit costs due to spoilage. However, we will have incurred reworking costs that will be included as part of manufacturing overhead.

When reworking costs are considered abnormal, they will be treated as an abnormal loss for the period. The reworking costs then would be credited to (removed from) work-in-process inventory and debited to an expense account.

Illustrative Problem

Able Company manufactures a product through cooking and refining processes. As the product is cooked, some shrinkage occurs. Final inspection at the end of the refining process always discloses some defective units. Occasionally, the number of such units exceeds the normally expected level. The following data relate to the current month's operations. Able uses the weighted-average costing method in both departments.

Cooking Process

	Units	Costs
Beginning work-in-process inventory	500	$ 1,600
Added		
Materials	10,000	19,920
Conversion costs		14,243
Transferred to refining	8,000	
Ending work-in-process inventory	800	

Both beginning and ending inventories are 40% complete insofar as processing costs are concerned. Beginning inventory includes materials costs of $1,200 and conversion costs of $400.

Refining Process

	Units	Costs
Beginning inventory	1,000	$ 5,720
Added		
Transfers from Cooking	8,000	?
Conversion costs		16,400
Transferred to finished goods	7,000	
Normal spoilage	6% of units entering inspection	
Abnormal spoilage	?	
Ending inventory	500	

Beginning inventory of work-in-process in refining includes transferred-in costs of $4,520 and conversion costs of $1,200. Both inventories are 60% complete as to conversion costs.

REQUIRED:

1. Prepare cost-of-production reports for both processes.
2. Show in T accounts how the data in the cost-of-production reports would be recorded.

Solution to Illustrative Problem

Figure 8–2 is a flowchart of the manufacturing process.

Exhibits 8–1 and 8–2 present the cost-of-production reports for the two processes, as requested in requirement 1.

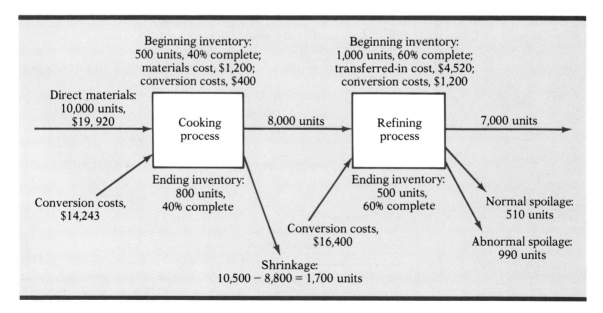

FIGURE 8–2 Manufacturing Process for Illustrative Problem

EXHIBIT 8–1

Cooking Process

Cost-of-Production Report
Weighted-Average Method

Units

Beginning inventory		500
Added during period		10,000
Total units to be accounted for		10,500
Transfers to process B	8,000	
Shrinkage	1,700	9,700
Ending inventory		800
Total units accounted for		10,500

Costs

	Total	Per Unit
Beginning inventory		
Materials	$ 1,200	
Conversion costs	400	
Total	$ 1,600	
Added during period		
Materials	19,920	$2.40
Conversion costs	14,243	1.76
Total costs to be accounted for	$35,763	$4.16
Transfers to refining process (8,000 × $4.16)	$33,280	
Ending inventory		
Materials cost (800 × 100% × $2.40) $1,920		
Conversion cost (800 × 40% × $1.76) 563	$ 2,483	
Total costs accounted for	$35,763	

	Material	Conversion Costs
Equivalent-units divisors:		
Transferred out to refining process	8,000	8,000
Ending inventory	800	320
Weighted-average equivalent-units divisor	8,800	8,320

Costs per unit:

Materials cost [($1,200 + $19,920)/8,800]	$2.40
Conversion costs [($400 + $14,243)/8,320]	$1.76
Total unit cost	$4.16

EXHIBIT 8–2
Refining Process

Cost-of-Production Report
Weighted-Average Method

Units

Beginning inventory		1,000
Transfers from process A		8,000
Total units to be accounted for		9,000
Transfers to finished goods	7,000	
Normal spoilage [(9,000 − 500) × .06]	510	
Abnormal spoilage [(9,000 − 7,500) − 510]	990	8,500
Ending inventory		500
Total units accounted for		9,000

Costs

	Total	Per Unit
Beginning inventory		
Transferred-in costs	$ 4,520	
Conversion costs	1,200	
Total	$ 5,720	
Added during period		
Transferred-in costs	33,280	$4.20
Conversion costs	16,400	2.00
Total costs to be accounted for	$55,400	$6.20

Transferred to finished goods (7,000 @ $6.20)	$43,400		
Normal spoilage (510 @ $6.20)	3,162	$46,562	
Abnormal spoilage (990 @ $6.20)		6,138	
Ending inventory			
Transferred-in cost (500 × 100% × $4.20)	$2,100		
Conversion cost (500 × 60% × $2.00)	600	2,700	
Total costs accounted for		$55,400	

	Transferred-in Cost	Conversion Costs
Equivalent-units divisors:		
Transferred out to finished goods	7,000	7,000
Normal spoilage	510	510
Abnormal spoilage	990	990
Ending Inventory	500	300
Weighted-average equivalent units of production	9,000	8,800

Costs per unit:		
Transferred-in cost [($4520 + $33,280)/9,000]	$4.20	
Conversion cost [($1,200 + $16,400)/8,800]	2.00	
Total unit cost	$6.20	

Materials Inventory			
Balance		(1)	19,920
XXX,XXX			

Work in Process			
Balance	7,320	(4)	46,562
(1)	19,920	(5)	6,138
(2)	14,243		
(3)	16,400		
Balance	5,183*		

* Cooking	$2,483
Refining	2,700
Total	$5,183

Finished Goods		
(4)	46,562	

Payroll and Manufacturing Overhead			
Balance	30,643	(2)	14,243
		(3)	16,400

Abnormal Spoilage Loss		
(5)	6,138	

Explanation of entries:

(1) Cost of direct materials transferred to cooking.

(2) Conversion costs for cooking process recorded.

(3) Conversion costs for refining process recorded.

(4) Costs assigned to good units transferred to finished goods (cost of goods manufactured).

(5) Costs assigned to abnormal spoilage removed from work in process and charged to abnormal spoilage (income statement account).

SUMMARY

In this chapter, we explained and demonstrated the accounting procedures for costs associated with lost or defective units, generally characterized as spoilage losses or reworking costs. We began by defining normal spoilage and explaining how losses of that type are treated. We noted that such losses might be removed from work in process and added to the costs of the good units being transferred to the next process or to finished goods, or they might be charged to manufacturing overhead (provided the overhead applied to work in process includes a provision for normal spoilage). In the case of shrinkage, normal losses are simply absorbed in the cost of good units by using an equivalent-units divisor that excludes lost units.

Next, we defined abnormal spoilage and demonstrated how those losses should be removed from work in process and transferred to an income statement expense account labeled "loss from abnormal spoilage." We gave some attention to the importance of the position of the inspection point in determining the amount of costs to be assigned to spoiled units.

Finally, we discussed reworking costs and presented an illustrative problem demonstrating the accounting procedures for spoiled units.

GLOSSARY OF TERMS INTRODUCED IN THIS CHAPTER

abnormal-spoilage costs	Costs associated with units lost in excess of those a firm normally expects to lose in its manufacturing operations on a regularly recurring basis. Such costs, which are considered avoidable, are expensed in the period incurred and are *not* allocated to good units.
lost units	Units that either disappear through shrinkage or have defects caused by processing that keep them from being transferred to the next process or to finished stock as good units.
normal-spoilage costs	Costs associated with units that either disappear through shrinkage or are found to be defective that are not in excess of the losses expected to occur on a repetitive basis during the manufacturing process. Such costs are considered unavoidable and are allocated to good units.
no-specific-recognition method	A method of accounting for spoilage losses by eliminating the spoiled units from the equivalent-units divisors so the spoilage loss automatically will be reflected in increased costs per unit; also, the method of accounting for reworking costs when those costs are not removed from work in process.
reworked units	Defective units recycled through certain production processes to correct the defects and thus allow them to pass inspection as good units.
reworking costs	Costs associated with the recycling of defective units through specified production processes to remedy a defective condition.
scrap	Materials coming out of the productive process that have no value other than as salvage, such as metal trimmings from stamping operations and spoiled units salvaged for the value of the metal or other materials included in them.
shrinkage	Spoilage losses that result from shrinkage in the volume of goods being produced—for example, the shrinkage that generally occurs when liquids go through a cooking process.
specific-recognition method	A method of accounting for defective (lost) units in which the costs associated with the units are separately determined and allocated either to good units produced or to abnormal-spoilage loss; also, the method of accounting for reworking costs when those costs are removed from work in process and labeled as reworking costs. (Reworking costs removed from work in process are debited either to manufacturing overhead or to abnormal loss for the period.)

spoilage costs   Costs of production associated with defective units in excess of amounts recovered from their sales.

spoiled units   Units that are damaged, do not meet specifications, or are otherwise unsuitable for further processing or sales as good output; includes normal as well as abnormal spoilage.

QUESTIONS FOR CLASS DISCUSSION

8—1   What is the difference between normal spoilage and abnormal spoilage? Explain.

8—2   What costs are associated with spoiled units? How are those costs related to the point at which units are judged to be defective?

8—3   Should there be a difference between the cost-allocation procedures followed for units lost due to shrinkage compared to units judged to be defective as a result of inspection? Explain.

8—4   If costs associated with normal spoilage are separately determined, what disposition should be made of them? Explain.

8—5   If spoiled units are identified at an end-of-process inspection point, what amount of costs should be attributed to the spoiled units? If the spoiled units are considered normal spoilage, how would you dispose of those costs?

8—6   If units are spoiled in the first process, what are the possible treatments of the costs associated with those units? Explain.

8—7   If spoilage is identified in a process subsequent to the first, what costs should be attributed to the spoiled units? How would you dispose of that cost?

8—8   What effect does the recovery of part of the cost of spoiled units as a result of their being sold as seconds have on the cost-accumulation and -allocation procedures for spoilage loses? Explain.

8—9   What are the likely causes of abnormal spoilage? For each cause, explain how the costs associated with the abnormal spoilage would be disposed of.

8—10   Are normally spoiled units ever included in the calculation of equivalent units? Explain.

8—11   Should abnormally spoiled units be included in the calculation of equivalent units? Explain.

8—12   How does the occurrence of abnormal spoilage affect the organization and content of the cost-of-production report for the process in which the spoilage occurs?

8–13   What is the difference between losses from spoilage and losses occurring as the result of reworking defective units? Explain.

8–14   How should we account for the cost of reworking defective units?

EXERCISES

8–15   **Multiple Choice—Normal and Abnormal Spoilage**

AICPA Adapted

1. Normal spoilage is properly classified as a (an)
   a. extraordinary item.
   b. period cost.
   c. product cost.
   d. deferred charge.
2. Which of the following is always an inventoriable cost?

	Abnormal Spoilage	*Normal Spoilage*
a.	no	no
b.	no	yes
c.	yes	no
d.	yes	yes

3. If the amount of spoilage in a manufacturing process is abnormal, in most instances, it should be classified as a
   a. deferred charge.
   b. joint cost.
   c. period cost.
   d. product cost.
4. Cargain Company has noticed that more spoiled units seem to occur in their manufacturing process on Monday than on any other day of the week. The plant is closed on Saturday and Sunday. If appropriate data to determine the relationship between spoiled units and the day of the week are collected, the resultant number
   a. provides a measure of the extent to which the day of the week accounts for the variability in the spoiled units.
   b. provides a measure of the extent to which the spoiled units account for the variability in the day of the week.
   c. establishes that one variable is the cause of another variable.
   d. establishes that the day of the week is the cause of the spoiled units.

8–16   **Equivalent Units—Normal Loss and Normal Spoilage** Stanley, Inc., manufactures a chemical compound via a continuous process in which units pass first through the infusion department and then through the distillation department. Materials and conversion costs are added uniformly during processing in the distillation department, and normal losses incurred as goods were processed amounted to 400 units during the current month.

There were 12,800 units of the chemical compound transferred from the infusion department to the distillation department during the month.

All units that were completed in distillation were transferred to finished goods. The following information is available for the distillation department for the current month:

| | | Percentage Completed | | |
	Units	Prior Department	Materials Added This Department	Conversion Work This Department
Beginning work in process	2,000	100%	20%	50%
Ending work in process	3,000	100%	40%	60%

REQUIRED: For the distillation department,

1. assuming that lost units are to be treated as normal shrinkage (that is, no specific recognition of lost units),
   a. compute the equivalent units divisor for the current period using the weighted-average method.
   b. compute the equivalent units of production for the current period using the FIFO method.
2. assuming that lost units are to be treated as normal spoilage (that is, specific recognition of lost units) discovered halfway through processing in the distillation department,
   a. compute the equivalent-units divisor for the current period using the weighted-average method.
   b. compute the equivalent units of production for the current period using the FIFO method.

8–17 **Transferred-in Cost per Unit** Refer to the data in exercise 8–16. The following cost information is available for the distillation department for the current period:

	Prior Department Costs	Materials Added This Department	Conversion Costs This Department
Beginning work in process	$12,372	$ 5,978	$ 9,188
Current period	42,780	63,196	49,288

REQUIRED: For the distillation department,

1. assuming that lost units are to be treated as normal shrinkage (that is, no specific recognition of lost units), compute the transferred-in cost per unit to be used on the current period's cost-of-production report using
   a. weighted-average costing.
   b. first-in, first-out costing.
2. assuming that lost units are to be treated as normal spoilage (that is, specific recognition of lost units), compute the transferred-in cost per

unit to be used on the current period's cost-of-production report using
a. weighted-average costing.*
b. first-in, first-out costing.*

*Round off your answers to three decimal points.

8–18 **Multiple Choice—Normal Loss and Normal Spoilage**

AICPA Adapted

1. Materials are added at the start of the process in Cedar Company's blending department, the first stage of the production cycle. The following information is available for the month of July 19X1:

	Units
Work in process, July 1 (60% complete as to conversion costs)	60,000
Started in July	150,000
Transferred to next department	110,000
Lost in production	30,000
Work in process, July 31 (50% complete as to conversion costs)	70,000

Under Cedar's cost accounting system, the costs incurred on the lost units are absorbed by the remaining good units, with no specific recognition of lost-unit costs. Using the weighted-average method, what are the equivalent units for the materials unit-cost calculation?
a. 120,000
b. 145,000
c. 180,000
d. 210,000

2. Barkley Company adds materials at the beginning of the process in Department M. Data concerning the materials used in March 19X3 production are as follows:

	Units
Work in process at March 1	16,000
Started during March	34,000
Completed and transferred to next department during March	36,000
Normal spoilage incurred	4,000
Work in process at March 31	10,000

Using the weighted-average method, the equivalent units for the materials unit-cost calculation are
a. 50,000.
b. 34,000.
c. 40,000.
d. 46,000.

3. Read, Inc. instituted a new process in October 19X7. During October, 10,000 units were started in Department A. Of the units started, 1,000 were lost by shrinkage in the process, 7,000 were transferred to Department B, and 2,000 remained in work in process at October 31,

19X7. The work in process at October 31, 19X7, was 100% complete as to materials costs and 50% complete as to conversion costs. Materials costs of $27,000 and conversion costs of $40,000 were charged to Department A in October. What were the total costs transferred to Department B?

a. $46,900
b. $53,600
c. $56,000
d. $57,120

4. Milton, Inc., had 8,000 units of work in process in its Department M on March 1, 19X0, which were 50% complete as to conversion costs. Materials are introduced at the beginning of the process. During March, 17,000 units were started, 18,000 units were completed, and there were 2,000 units of normal spoilage. Milton had 5,000 units of work in process at March 31, 19X0, which were 60% complete as to conversion costs. Under Milton's cost accounting system, spoiled units reduce the number of units over which total cost can be spread. Using the weighted-average method, the equivalent units for March for conversion costs were

a. 17,000.
b. 19,000.
c. 21,000.
d. 23,000.

8–19 **Multiple Choice—Abnormal Spoilage**

AICPA Adapted

1. Dex Co. had the following production for the month of June:

	Units
Work in process at June 1	10,000
Started during June	40,000
Completed and transferred to finished goods	33,000
Abnormal spoilage incurred	2,000
Work in process at June 30	15,000

Materials are added at the beginning of the process. As to conversion costs, the beginning work in process was 70% completed and the ending work in process was 60% completed. Spoilage is detected at the end of the process. Using the weighted-average method, the equivalent units for June, with respect to conversion, were

a. 42,000.
b. 44,000.
c. 45,000.
d. 46,000.

2. Tooker Company adds materials at the beginning of the process in Department A. Information concerning the materials used in April 19X2 production is as follows:

	Units
Work in process at April 1	10,000
Started during April	50,000
Completed and transferred to next department during April	36,000
Normal spoilage incurred	3,000
Abnormal spoilage incurred	5,000
Work in process at April 30	16,000

Under Tooker's cost accounting system, costs of normal spoilage are treated as a part of the costs of the good units produced and are not specifically identified. However, the costs of abnormal spoilage are charged to factory overhead. Using the weighted-average method, what are the equivalent units for the materials unit-cost calculation for the month of April?

a. 47,000
b. 52,000
c. 55,000
d. 57,000

8–20   Normal and Abnormal Spoilage and Reworking Costs of Defective Units
Shaw Corporation manufactures anatomical bicycle seat covers. All materials are added at the start of processing in process 1. Finished units are inspected twice—once at the end of process 1 (cutting and initial stitching) and again at the end of process 2 (when the units are completed). Shaw's engineers have predicted that 1% of the units entering the first inspection point will be rejected and 2% of the units entering the final inspection point will be rejected. Defective units from the first inspection are scrapped with no recovery value, but approximately half of the units failing the final inspection can be reworked and made into good units. The remaining defective units are scrapped.
The following results are reported for October:

	Process 1 Units	Process 1 Costs	Process 2 Units	Process 2 Costs
Beginning inventory	800	$ 674	1,100	$ 5,403
Added this period				
Materials	8,200	6,970		
Conversion		21,306		27,726
Prior process			8,100	
Transferred out to next process or finished goods	8,100		8,040	
Ending inventory	800		1,000	

The October 1 work in process for process 1 was 40% complete as to conversion and for process 2 was 30% complete as to conversion. The stages of completion of October 31 work-in-process inventories (as regards conversion) were 20% and 50%, respectively.

Shaw uses the first-in, first-out method to account for its work in process. The costs associated with normal lost units (those expected to be rejected) are added to the costs of good units transferred out of the departments. The costs of lost units in excess of those normally expected are expensed immediately.

One-half of the defective units discovered at the final inspection point were reworked during October and transferred to finished goods. (These units are not included in the 8,040 units transferred out.) Reworking costs in the amount of $105 are included in process 2 conversion costs.

REQUIRED:

1. Compute the equivalent units of production for
   a. process 1
   b. process 2.
2. Compute the total cost per unit for
   a. process 1
   b. process 2.
3. Prepare the general journal entry to record the recognition of reworking costs.

PROBLEMS

8–21 **Equivalent Units of Production—Lost Units** Dexter Designs, Inc., produces plastic cases for personal computers via three departments. Molds are prepared in Department 1 and transferred uninspected into Department 2. In Department 2, three separate inspections occur. The molds from Department 1 are inspected as soon as they arrive in Department 2. Then the good molds are cleaned and oiled while plastic is heated to a liquid consistency. When processing in Department 2 is 40% completed, the plastic material is poured into the molds. The units are inspected a second time after the molds have cured, at the point where processing in Department 2 is 60% complete. Units that pass the second inspection are removed from the molds, cleaned, and sanded. A final inspection in Department 2 is made just before the units are transferred to Department 3, where they are packed for shipping. Units rejected by the inspection process have no recovery value. A diagram of the Department 2 manufacturing process is given in Figure 8–3.

During September, the following data were reported for Department 2:

	Units
Beginning inventory, 75% processed	2,200
Received from Department 1	14,300
Total	16,500

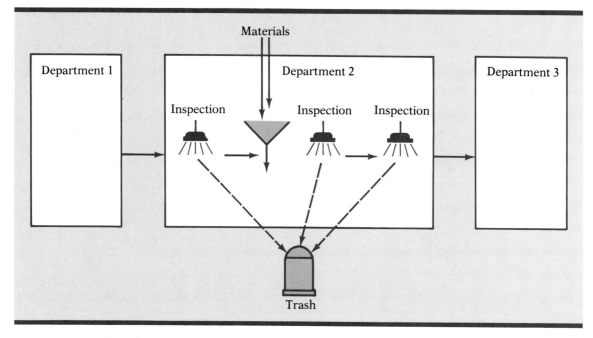

FIGURE 8–3 Manufacturing Process, Dexter Designs, Inc.

Completed and transferred to Department 3	13,700
Lost—failed inspection	900
Ending inventory	1,900
Total	16,500

Manufacturing overhead is allocated to production by use of a predetermined overhead application rate that includes a provision for normal spoilage.

REQUIRED: For Department 2, for *each* of the following independent situations, (a) compute equivalent-units divisors for transfers in, materials, and conversion, using the weighted-average method, and (b) explain what should happen to the cost of lost units.

1. All losses are normal, 450 defective units are discovered at the first inspection, and 450 at the final inspection; ending inventory is 55% processed.
2. All losses are abnormal, 200 defective units are discovered at the first inspection, 200 at the second inspection, and 500 at the final inspection; ending inventory is 70% processed.

3. Ending inventory is 25% processed and detected losses are as follows:

Inspection Point	Department 2 Processing Point	Normal-Spoilage Units	Abnormal-Spoilage Units
First inspection	0%	150	50
Second inspection	60%	225	75
Third inspection	100%	300	100

8–22
ICMA Adapted

Manufacturing Costs with Normal and Abnormal Spoilage The following data apply to items 1–5. JC Company employs a process cost system. A unit of product passes through three departments—molding, assembly, and finishing—before it is completed.

The following activity took place in the finishing department during May:

	Units
Work-in-process inventory, May 1	1,400
Units transferred in from the assembly department	14,000
Units spoiled	700
Units transferred out to finished goods	11,200

Raw material is added at the beginning of the processing in the finishing department without changing the number of units being processed. The work-in-process inventory was 70% complete as to conversion on May 1 and 40% complete as to conversion on May 31. All spoilage was discovered at final inspection before the units were transferred to finished goods; 560 of the units spoiled were within the limit considered normal.

JC Company employs the weighted-average costing method. The equivalent units and the current costs per equivalent unit of production for each cost factor are as follows:

Cost Factor	Equivalent Units	Current Costs per Equivalent Unit
Cost of prior departments	15,400	$5.00
Raw materials	15,400	1.00
Conversion cost	13,300	3.00
		$9.00

Select the *best* answer for each of the following items.

1. The cost of production transferred to the finished goods inventory is
  a. $100,800.
  b. $105,840.
  c. $107,100.
  d. $102,060.

2. The cost assigned to the work-in-process inventory on May 31 is
   a. $28,000.
   b. $31,000.
   c. $25,200.
   d. $30,240.
3. If the total costs of prior departments included in the work-in-process inventory of the finishing department on May 1 amounted to $6,300, the total cost transferred in from the assembly department to the finishing department during May is
   a. $70,000.
   b. $62,300.
   c. $70,700.
   d. $63,700.
4. The cost associated with the abnormal spoilage is
   a. $6,300.
   b. $1,260.
   c. $560.
   d. $840.
5. The cost associated with abnormal spoilage ordinarily would be charged to
   a. inventory.
   b. goods transferred out.
   c. manufacturing overhead.
   d. a special loss account.

8–23
ICMA Adapted

Cost-of-Production Report—Normal and Abnormal Spoilage APCO Company manufactures various lines of bicycles. Because of the high volume of each type of product, the company employs a process cost system, using the weighted-average method to determine unit costs. Bicycle parts are manufactured in the molding department. The parts are consolidated into a single bike unit in the molding department and transferred to the assembly department, where they are partially assembled. After assembly, the bicycle is sent to the packing department.

Costs per unit for the 20-inch dirt bike have been compiled through the molding department. Annual cost-and-production figures for the assembly department are presented in the following tables:

Assembly Department Cost Data

	Transferred in from Molding Department	Assembly Materials	Assembly Conversion Costs	Total Cost of Dirt Bike Through Assembly
Prior period costs	$ 82,200	$ 6,660	$ 11,930	$ 100,790
Current period costs	1,237,800	96,840	236,590	1,571,230
Total costs	$1,320,000	$103,500	$248,520	$1,672,020

Assembly Department Production Data

| | | Percentage Completed | | |
	Bicycles	Transferred in	Assembly Material	Assembly Conversion
Beginning inventory	3,000	100	100	80
Transferred in from molding department during year	45,000	100	—	—
Transferred out to packing department during year	40,000	100	100	100
Ending inventory	4,000	100	50	20

Defective bicycles are identified at an inspection point when the assembly labor process is 70% complete. All assembly materials have been added by this point. The normal rejection percentage for defective bicycles is 5% of the bicycles reaching the inspection point. Any defective bicycles over and above the 5% quota are considered abnormal. All defective bikes are removed from the production process and destroyed.

Costs of lost units are specifically recognized. A provision for normal spoilage is included in departmental overhead.

REQUIRED:

1. Compute the number of defective bikes that are considered to be:
   a. a normal number of defective bikes.
   b. an abnormal number of defective bikes.
2. Compute the equivalent-units divisors for the year for:
   a. bicycles transferred in from the molding department.
   b. bicycles produced with regard to assembly materials.
   c. bicycles produced with regard to assembly conversion.
3. Compute the cost per equivalent unit for the fully assembled dirt bike.
4. Compute the amount of the total production cost of $1,672,020 that will be associated with the following items:
   a. normal defective units
   b. abnormal defective units
   c. good units completed in the assembly department
   d. ending work-in-process inventory in the assembly department.
5. Describe how the applicable dollar amounts for the following items would be presented in the financial statements.
   a. normal defective units
   b. abnormal defective units
   c. completed units transferred into the packing department
   d. ending work-in-process inventory in the assembly department

8–24
ICMA Adapted

Cost-of-Production Report—Normal and Abnormal Shrinkage West Corporation is a divisionalized manufacturing company. A product called Aggregate is manufactured in one department of the California division. At a predetermined price, Aggregate is transferred on completion to the Utah division, where it is used in the manufacture of other products.

Raw materials are added at the beginning of the process. Labor and overhead are added continuously throughout the process. Shrinkage of 10–14%, all occurring at the beginning of the process, is considered normal. In the California division, all departmental overhead is charged to the departments and divisional overhead is allocated to the departments on the basis of direct labor hours. The divisional overhead rate for 19X9 is $2 per direct labor hour.

The following relates to production during November 19X9:

(1) Work-in-process, November 1 (4,000 pounds—75% complete):

Raw materials	$22,800
Direct labor @ $5.00 per hour	24,650
Departmental overhead	12,000
Divisional overhead	9,860

(2) Raw materials:

Inventory, November 1, 2,000 pounds	$10,000
Purchases, November 3, 10,000 pounds	51,000
Purchases, November 18, 10,000 pounds	51,500
Released to production during November, 16,000 pounds	

(3) Direct labor costs @ $5.00 per hour: $103,350
(4) Direct departmental overhead costs: $52,000
(5) Transferred to Utah division: 15,000 pounds
(6) Work in process, November 30: 3,000 pounds, $33\frac{1}{3}$% complete

The FIFO method is used for materials inventory valuation, and the weighted-average method is used for work-in-process inventories.

REQUIRED:

1. Prepare a cost-of-production report for the department of the California division producing Aggregate for November 19X9 that
   a. presents the equivalent units of production by cost factor of Aggregate (for example, raw materials, direct labor, overhead).
   b. shows the calculation of the equivalent-units costs for each cost factor of Aggregate.
   c. presents the cost of Aggregate transferred to the Utah division.
   d. presents the cost of abnormal shrinkage, if any.
   e. presents the cost of the work-in-process inventory at November 30, 19X9.
2. The California division intends to implement a flexible budgeting system to improve cost control over direct labor and departmental overhead. The basis of the flexible budget will be the production that occurs in the budget period. For the department producing Aggregate, what amount reflects the best measure of production activity for the November 19X9 flexible budget? Explain your answer.

8–25 **Cost-of-Production Report—Units Lost During a Process** The Half Earth Pottery Company produces pottery in two processes. Most materials are added in process 1. Materials added in process 2 are added at the beginning of the process.

The following information was accumulated for process 2 during the month of July:

	Units	Costs
Beginning work in process (40% complete as to conversion costs)	350	
Transferred in		$ 2,450
Materials		1,400
Conversion		613
Added during July		
Transferred in	1,400	10,850
Materials		7,700
Conversion		5,723
Totals to account for	1,750	$28,736
Transferred out	1,100	
Ending work in process (50% complete as to conversion costs)	500	

Half Earth Pottery uses the weighted-average method to account for its work in process.

REQUIRED:

1. Prepare a cost-of-production report for Half Earth Pottery under each of the following assumptions.
   a. All units lost are normal losses, and inspection occurs when units are 60% complete as to conversion costs. Normal spoilage costs are allocated to good units transferred out.
   b. Of the lost units, 60% are normal losses and 40% are abnormal, and inspection occurs when units are 20% complete as to conversion costs. Normal spoilage costs are allocated to good units transferred out. Abnormal spoilage costs are transferred to an income statement expense account.
2. Using the assumption of requirement (b) above, prepare the appropriate journal entry or entries for July to transfer costs out of the process 2 work-in-process account.

8–26 **Cost-of-Production Report—Two Periods** Instant Replay Company manufactures miniature video cameras. In the final processing department, Department 3, cases are added to the camera components at the beginning of processing and direct labor and factory overhead are incurred evenly throughout processing.

Units are inspected in Department 3 just before they are transferred to finished goods. Instant Replay expects that normal spoilage will not exceed 1% (rounded to the nearest whole unit) of the units entering inspection. Department 3 uses weighted-average costing to account for its work in process.

Information accumulated for May and June is as follows:

Units	May	June
Beginning inventory of work in process: 100% materials, 40% conversion cost	400	
Units received from preceding department	1,420	1,260
Units transferred to finished goods	1,500	1,400
Ending inventory of work in process		
100% materials; 50% conversion	300	
100% materials; 20% conversion		150

Costs	May	June
Beginning inventory of work in process		
From preceding department	$149,600	
Materials	1,335	
Direct labor	280	
Factory overhead (applied)	350	
Costs transferred in during the period	460,100	$429,900
Costs added during the period		
Materials	4,125	3,936
Direct labor	2,392	2,128
Factory overhead (applied)	2,990	2,660

REQUIRED: Prepare cost-of-production reports for May and June for Department 3.

8–27 **Cost-of-Production Report—Normal Spoilage with Recovery Value** Marshall Processing Company manufactures a fuel additive in two processes. Material A (one gallon per gallon of output) is put in at the start of processing in process 1; material B (three cans per gallon of output) is added at the end of processing in process 2. Spoilage is detected in process 2 when processing is approximately 50% complete. The company uses FIFO costing for process 1 and weighted-average costing for process 2.

Data for April included the following:

(1) Units transferred:

From process 1 to process 2	1,980 gallons
From process 2 to finished goods	1,620 gallons
From finished goods to cost of goods sold	1,080 gallons

(2) Materials unit costs: A, $6 per gallon; B, $1 per can
(3) Conversion costs: process 1, $6,400; process 2, $7,578
(4) Spoilage recovery: $180
(5) Work-in-process inventory:

	Process 1		Process 2	
	Beginning	**Ending**	**Beginning**	**Ending**
Gallons	360	600	360	540
Fraction complete (conversion cost)	$\frac{1}{2}$	$\frac{1}{3}$	$\frac{1}{2}$	$\frac{2}{3}$
Costs				
Materials	$1,008			
Conversion	$ 195		$ 702	
Prior department			$4,143	

(6) There is no spoilage in process 1.

(7) Net spoilage cost is charged to good units transferred out of process 2.

REQUIRED: Prepare a cost-of-production report for April for process 1 and for process 2

8–28 **THOUGHT STIMULATION PROBLEM.** L.L. Christopher Company manufactures a line of expensive collector's dolls. Each basic doll is identical, but in the final department—dressing—20 different costumes are placed on the doll bodies. Each model has its own accessories and display stand, which are packaged in a trunk with the dressed doll prior to shipment. A subcontractor provides the fully equipped trunks according to a daily schedule prepared by the marketing department.

Production begins in the construction department, where a purchased plastic skeletal form is covered with simulated muscles and tendons. Skin covering of a new synthetic, porous, flesh-colored material then is added in the derma department. Each unit is inspected for flaws, and defective units are scrapped.

Blank dolls are transferred to the color department, where artists hand paint faces and add subtle shading to other parts of the doll bodies. Different-colored wigs (60% blond, 30% brunette, and 10% auburn) are attached to the dolls just before they are inspected and transferred to the dressing department. Units that fail to pass inspection are reprocessed through the color department.

L.L. Christopher sells its dolls by catalog and to specialty toy stores. In the past, prices have been set based on estimated costs of production and demand. However, L.L. Christopher's new chief executive officer, Benjamin Brown, desires to know the total production cost of each of the 20 dolls in the company's complete line.

REQUIRED:

1. Prepare a flowchart of the manufacturing process showing each department, inspection points, and materials-addition points.

2. L.L. Christopher obviously has a combination job-order and process costing system. Design a cost system that will track the complete manufacturing cost of each doll in the company's line. For simplicity, you may show detailed information in T-account form for only one doll. (You may assume that all doll costs are the same through the color department.)

Chapter 9

Process Costing:
By-Products and Joint Products

Learning Objectives

When you have finished your study of this chapter, you should

1. Know the difference between a joint product and a by-product.
2. Be able to account for by-products as they are removed from a joint process, are subjected to further processing, and are sold.
3. Know how to allocate joint-processing costs to joint products.
4. Be able to journalize the flows of costs associated with the production of joint products.

Our discussion of process costing up to this point has assumed that no more than one product was transferred out of any process. In this chapter, we deal with the special accounting problems associated with the allocation of departmental costs when *two or more* products are produced from one process. We refer to such products as either **by-products** or **joint products**.

By-products and joint products are an automatic result of certain manufacturing processes, such as oil refining and lumber production, in which the producer has limited control over the quantities of each product emerging from a joint manufacturing process. This is not to be confused with the situation in which a manufacturer elects to use a single factory or process to produce multiple products each of which could be produced alone.

The distinction between a by-product and a joint product hinges primarily on the importance of the product to the revenues produced by the company. If the market value of one of the multiple products produced by a process is relatively insignificant, such that it would be economically impractical to carry out the manufacturing process for the purpose of producing it, we call it a *by-product*. Its production occurs incidental to the production of one or more other products. For example, a large part of the inert ingredients constituting much of the volume of cleansing powder comes from the operations of meat packing plants. For those plants, cleansers are products that would not be manufactured except for the major processing objective of producing various cuts of meat. Therefore, cleansing powder is a by-product for a meat packing plant.

A *joint product*, on the other hand, is produced in conjunction with one or more other products, each earning revenue sufficient to justify its production. The various cuts of meat produced by a meat packing plant are joint products. Figure 9–1 distinguishes by-product A from joint products B and C by portraying the manufacturing process as a straight line with the individual products branching off. Observe that the direction of the line does not change with the splitting off of the by-product (product A), suggesting that the objective of the joint process is to produce products B and C. The firm would not carry out the process just to manufacture product A; instead, its primary efforts are directed toward producing products B and C.

It is not always easy to decide whether to treat a product as a by-product or as a joint product. Some products coming from a joint process will be such insignificant revenue producers that they obviously are by-products. Other products may be somewhat, but not critically, important to the overall revenue of a company; some of these could be classified as either by-products or joint products. The decision rests on the judgment of management working with the controlling accountant. Prior to the widespread use of computers, the detailed computations and additional work required to treat as joint products those products

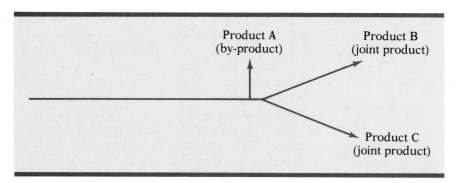

FIGURE 9–1   By-Product Versus Joint Product

that might be classified either way was not economical. Nowadays, treating a product as a joint product is not so costly. As a result, some products that might have been treated as by-products with a manual accounting system now can be (and *should* be) accounted for as joint products in a computer-maintained system.

The primary problem associated with accounting for by-products and joint products centers around the joint-processing costs that should be allocated to each product as it comes out of the joint process. The first step in allocating such **joint costs** is to classify each product coming out of a joint-process cost-accumulation center as either a by-product or a joint product. Then we apply the appropriate accounting procedures in allocating these jointly incurred costs to the products produced.

Our discussion will be divided into two parts:

1. accounting for by-products
2. accounting for joint products.

We then will illustrate how such cost-allocation procedures are applied in accounting for the processing costs of a hypothetical company (Multi-Prod).

Accounting for By-Products

A by-product, by definition, does not produce sufficient revenue to justify the incurrence of costs of producing it apart from the other products. As a result, by-products generally will be accounted for by using one of the following procedures:

1. allocating no joint processing costs to them at the point of split-off
2. allocating to them at the split-off point joint-processing costs equal to their anticipated net realizable values (anticipated sales values re-

duced by estimated or actual additional processing and selling costs), which has the effect of reducing the joint-processing costs allocated to joint products

3. allocating to them at the split-off point joint-processing costs equal to **net realizable value less a normal profit margin**, which also has the effect of reducing the joint-processing costs allocated to joint products.

Method 1:
No Joint
Cost Allocation

When a by-product is accounted for by allocating no costs to it at the point at which it comes out of the joint production process, we are concerned only with matching against the revenues realized from its sale the *additional* costs incurred after it has been transferred out of the joint production process. By-products awaiting sale in finished-goods inventory would be valued at an amount equal to their additional processing costs. The difference between the revenues realized from the sale of such by-products and the additional processing and selling costs can appear as *net revenue from sale of by-products*.

Using this method, the accounting procedures for the additional processing costs of by-products are exactly the same as those followed for any other process-costing department, except that no cost is associated with the materials transferred from the joint process. Additional processing costs (materials and conversion costs) would be assigned to the units of by-product by calculating the equivalent units of production and determining unit costs, which can then be used in allocating the additional processing costs between units transferred to by-product finished-goods inventory and those remaining in by-products-in-process inventory. As by-products are sold, cost of by-product sales will be determined on the basis of the costs assigned to the finished units of by-product in the by-product inventory (that is, costs incurred after the split-off point).

For example, if (1) a by-product with a sales value of $1,000 is produced from a joint process, (2) no additional processing is performed, and (3) the entire amount is sold, then the first accounting entry, at the time of sale, would be:

Cash	1,000	
By-product revenue		1,000

If the by-product is processed further (after split-off) for $900 ($400 of labor and $500 of overhead) and then sold for $2,000, the following entries would be recorded:

By-product inventory	900	
Payroll or accrued wages payable		400
Manufacturing overhead applied		500
Cash	2,000	
Cost of sales, by-product	900	
By-product inventory		900
By-product revenue		2,000

This simple method is easy to use but may cause internal control problems, especially if no additional processing is required. Under those conditions, the by-product would not enter the accounting records until it was sold, which might implicitly convey the idea to employees that the by-product units do not need much care or attention. If controls over such products are weak, proceeds from their sales may be embezzled by employees responsible for disposing of them, or the units may be allowed to deteriorate before they are sold.

Method 2: Net Realizable Value Assigned to By-Products

By another line of reasoning, an amount equal to the expected **net realizable value** from the sale of by-products (sales price less additional processing costs and selling costs) should be allocated from the joint-processing costs to the by-product as it is removed from the joint process. This is based on a "recovery of cost" concept similar to the situation (discussed in Chapter 8) wherein the disposal value of spoiled goods reduces the cost of spoilage. The costs to be allocated to the joint products would then equal total joint-processing costs less costs allocated to (or recovered by) the by-products. If, for example, expected by-product net revenue is significant enough to influence the decision as to whether or not to incur the processing costs for the other product or products being produced by the joint-processing center, it is logical to allocate to the by-product joint costs equal to its net realizable value. This may be thought of as a partial recovery of joint-processing costs. When a portion of the joint costs is allocated to a by-product, the costs allocated to the other product or products coming out of the joint process will be reduced. That, in turn, will cause the income statement to show a larger margin realized from the sale of the joint products than if no costs had been allocated to the by-product at the point of split-off.

For example, given a joint process costing $62,000 that results in three products—joint products 1 and 2 and a by-product (which must undergo additional processing at a cost of $2,100 before it can be sold for $4,100), the journal entry to allocate joint costs to the by-product at the split-off point, using net realizable value, would be:

Work in process, by-product	2,000	
Work in process, joint process		2,000

Where inventories are negligible or unchanging, a firm may elect to reduce cost of sales rather than the joint process work-in-process account as costs are allocated to the by-product. As the additional processing is completed the additional costs are recorded as follows:

Work in process, by-product	2,100	
Factory payroll and factory overhead applied		2,100

The remaining joint-processing costs of $60,000 ($62,000 less $2,000 allocated to by-product) will be allocated to joint products 1 and 2. Upon completion of by-product processing, the cost of by-products manufactured is transferred from by-product work in process to by-product finished goods:

Finished goods, by-product	4,100	
Work in process, by-product		4,100

When the by-product is sold, the total inventory cost of $4,100 is matched against by-product revenues:

Cash or accounts receivable	4,100	
Cost of sales, by-product	4,100	
Finished goods, by-product		4,100
By-product revenues		4,100

Removing the difference between the expected sales price of a by-product and its expected additional processing costs (and selling costs, if any) from joint-processing costs has the effect of recognizing that amount as a cost recovery *before* the product is sold. That, in turn, causes the inventory of the by-product to be stated at its anticipated net realizable value (a revenue-based amount) rather than at the additional processing cost (a cost-based amount) as is the case when using no joint cost allocation. This may be theoretically sound if the by-product is readily marketable without much sales effort. However, this procedure will yield a by-product inventory value that includes unrealized profit. On the other hand, the inventory values of the joint products will be more conservatively stated (that is, lower) than if a zero value had been assigned to the by-product at its split-off point.

Methods 1 and 2 Compared. To illustrate the differences between the two methods discussed, let's assume a joint-process cost-accumulation center that produces products A, B, and C at a total cost of $40,000. Product A is a by-product expected to yield sales revenue of $8,000 after additional processing costs of $3,000. If no joint cost is allocated to product A, the entire joint-processing cost of $40,000 will be allocated to products B and C. Product A, after additional processing, will be valued at $3,000. On the other hand, if the anticipated net realizable value ($8,000 − $3,000) is allocated from joint costs to by-product A, the costs allocated to products B and C will amount to $40,000 − $5,000 = $35,000. Product A, after additional processing, will be valued at its expected sales value ($8,000). If it is sold at this price, no profit would be recognized at the time of sale.

Observe that total net income for a reporting period will be the same under either method *if* all products are sold. However, as shown in Figure 9–2, the net income can be different for the two methods if a firm has inventories on hand at the end of the period. Figure 9–2 assumes the total sales value for the joint products is $60,000. Under the headings "Method 1" (no joint cost allocation to by-products) and "Method 2" (net realizable value of by-product allocated to by-product from joint costs), we illustrate the results of three alternative assump-

	Method 1 Assumptions			Method 2 Assumptions		
	a	b	c	a	b	c
Joint product sales	$60,000	$36,000[a]	$60,000	$60,000	$36,000[a]	$60,000
By-product sales	8,000	8,000	4,800[c]	8,000	8,000	4,800[c]
Total sales	$68,000	$44,000	$64,800	$68,000	$44,000	$64,800
Joint product cost of sales	$40,000	$24,000[b]	$40,000	$35,000	$21,000[e]	$35,000
By-product cost of sales	3,000	3,000	1,800[d]	8,000	8,000	4,800[f]
Total cost of sales	$43,000	$27,000	$41,800	$43,000	$29,000	$39,800
Gross margin	$25,000	$17,000	$23,000	$25,000	$15,000	$25,000

[a]0.6($60,000) = $36,000   [d]0.6($ 3,000) = $ 1,800
[b]0.6($40,000) = $24,000   [e]0.6($35,000) = $21,000
[c]0.6($ 8,000) = $ 4,800   [f]0.6($ 8,000) = $ 4,800

Assumptions:
(a) No ending inventory of by-product or joint products.
(b) No ending inventory of by-product; 40% of joint products in ending inventory.
(c) 40% of by-product in ending inventory; no ending inventory of joint products.

FIGURE 9–2   Comparison of Methods of Accounting for By-Products

tions regarding inventories of by-products and joint products. In all instances, we assume no beginning inventory. Under each method, we assume: (a) no ending inventory for either the by-product or joint product, (b) 40% of the joint products remain in ending inventory, or (c) 40% of the by-product remains in inventory. Assumption (a) yields the same gross margin for both methods. However, gross margin varies by $2,000 between method 1 and method 2 when ending inventories exist [assumptions (b) and (c)]. Either method 1 or 2, as well as method 3 (discussed next), is acceptable in accounting for the removal, processing, and sale of by-products.

Method 3: Net Realizable Value Less Normal Profit Allocated to By-Product

To avoid the recognition of profit before it has been earned, as can occur with the net-realizable-value method, expected normal profit, plus additional processing costs and expected selling costs, can be deducted from expected by-product revenue to find the amount of joint costs to allocate to the by-product. For example, if the expected by-product profit margin is 20% and there are no selling expenses associated with disposal of the by-product, the joint costs allocated to the by-product, using the data from Figure 9–2, would be:

By-product sales value	$8,000
Less	
Additional processing costs	3,000
Normal profit ($8,000 × 20%)	1,600
Net realizable value less normal profit	$3,400

The entry to record this cost allocation would be:

Work in process, by-product	3,400	
Work in process, joint process		3,400

As the additional processing costs are incurred, the work-in-process by-product account would be increased. A summary general journal entry would be:

Work in process, by-product	3,000	
Factory payroll payable and factory overhead		3,000

When the by-product is completed, it would be transferred to finished goods with the following summary entry:

Finished goods, by-product	6,400	
Work in process, by-product		6,400

Then, when the by-product is sold, a profit of $1,600 ($8,000 revenue less the $6,400 cost of sales) would be recognized on the income statement.

By definition, a by-product has no material effect on a firm's revenues and very little effect on its profit. Also, a "normal" profit margin on the by-product may be difficult to estimate. Therefore, in spite of the theoretical merits of this procedure, few firms carry their by-product inventories at net realizable value less normal profit.

Accounting for Joint Products

When a single process produces more than one product having significant revenue-producing capability, we are faced with the problem of allocating the costs accumulated in that process to all the units coming out of it. These *joint costs* must be allocated to the products so a value can be assigned to each product as it is placed in inventory, transferred to another department, or sold. This is a problem because we cannot divide such costs among the two or more joint products on the basis of *directly determinable* cause-and-effect relationships. Therefore, we must *arbitrarily* allocate such costs to the joint products in one of the following ways:

1. on the basis of relative volumes produced
2. on the basis of relative sales values
3. so as to produce the same gross margin for each product.

Other methods of allocating joint costs have been suggested. A particularly interesting one, involving the use of shadow prices from a linear programming solution of an optimal-production problem, is discussed in Chapter 21.

Joint Costs Allocated on the Basis of Relative Volumes (Physical Units)

If the joint products of a process are measured in the same kind of units, such as pounds, there is some justification for arbitrarily allocating the joint costs on the basis of the quantities of each product turned out in relation to the total production for all products. To illustrate, let's assume that Ash Company produces 10,000 pounds of product X, 15,000 pounds of product Y, and 5,000 pounds of product Z as joint products of a process with accumulated processing costs of $60,000, as depicted below. Let's also assume there is no work-in-process inventory at either the beginning or the end of the period.

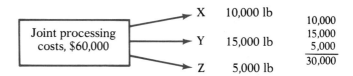

X	10,000 lb	10,000
Y	15,000 lb	15,000
Z	5,000 lb	5,000
		30,000

Joint processing costs, $60,000

If the processing costs are to be allocated on the basis of the quantities (volumes) of each product produced, we would allocate 10/30 × $60,000 = $20,000 to product X; 15/30 × $60,000 = $30,000 to product Y; and 5/30 × $60,000 = $10,000 to product Z. We would then divide each of these costs by their respective poundage to arrive at a cost of $2 per pound for each of the three products as they are transferred to finished goods or to the next process.

This method of allocating joint costs has some justification if the processing costs are volume related. For example, if the jointly incurred costs are caused largely by the need to move the products through the process, it is reasonable to assume that it costs as much to move one pound of product A as to move one pound of either of the other two products. Observe that this process allocates the same amount of joint cost to each pound of all products, regardless of their final sales values, and so can cause a joint product to show a negative margin when the sales values of joint products differ significantly.

Joint Costs Allocated on the Basis of Relative Sales Value

A much more widely used method of allocating joint costs is called the **relative-sales-value method**. Even though this method also is arbitrary, there is some logic to support it. Remember that costs are incurred for the purpose of producing revenues. Also, in a joint production process, management has little or no control over the proportionate amounts of the different joint products produced. For example, since in a meat packing plant each hog yields two hams, two shoulders, and so forth, the amount of joint costs allocated to each joint product should have the same percentage relationship to total joint costs as its revenue has to total revenue for all products.

With the relative-sales-value method we multiply the number of units of each of the joint products by its respective sales price at the point at which the products are removed from the joint process (split-off point) and use those amounts as the basis for allocating the joint costs. To illustrate, let's return to our previous illustration and assume the following sales prices at split-off:

Product X: $4.00 per pound
Product Y: $2.00 per pound
Product Z: $10.00 per pound

Using the previous data regarding production volumes, the sales values at split-off would be:

Product X (10,000 pounds at $4.00 per pound)	$40,000
Product Y (15,000 pounds at $2.00 per pound)	$30,000
Product Z (5,000 pounds at $10.00 per pound)	$50,000
Total	$120,000

Using the relative-sales-value method, we would then allocate the $60,000 of joint costs as follows:

Product X ($40,000/$120,000 × $60,000)	$20,000
Product Y ($30,000/$120,000 × $60,000)	$15,000
Product Z ($50,000/$120,000 × $60,000)	$25,000
Total	$60,000

This method of allocating joint costs would produce the following costs per pound:

Product X ($20,000/10,000)	$2.00 per pound
Product Y ($15,000/15,000)	$1.00 per pound
Product Z ($25,000/5,000)	$5.00 per pound

Observe that when the relative-sales-value method is used, the percentage relationship between joint cost per unit allocated to each type of unit and its sales price per unit at split-off will be *exactly the same* for all jointly produced products. In this case, the joint cost allocated to each of the products equals 50% of its sales price. With this method, the relationship between the allocated joint cost per unit and sales price per unit at split-off always will be the same for all types of units because we use sales prices per unit in arriving at our basis for allocation. The markup percentage at split-off based on the allocated costs, therefore, will be exactly the same for all of the different units produced by a joint process. In this case, that markup is 100% of allocated costs.

A problem can occur with this method if one or more of the joint products does not have a sales price at the point of split-off. For instance, when a joint product has to go through further processing before it can be sold, we must reduce the sales value after further processing by the additional processing cost to arrive at an **imputed sales value at split-off** for the product. That figure is then used with the sales values at split-off of the other joint products in allocating the joint costs.

To illustrate, let's assume that product X in our previous illustration has no quoted sales value at split-off but can be sold for $6.00 per pound after additional processing costing $10,000, and that there are no beginning or end-of-period work-in-process inventories in the additional-processing cost-accumulation center. The processing and cost data can be visualized as follows:

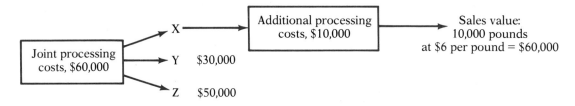

A sales value at split-off would be imputed for product X by subtracting the additional processing costs from the sales value after additional processing:

Sales value of product X after additional processing (10,000 units @ $6.00 per unit)	$60,000
Less additional processing costs	10,000
Imputed sales value at split-off for product X	$50,000

That figure then would be used, along with the $30,000 for product Y and $50,000 for product Z, to arrive at ratios for allocating the $60,000 of joint costs (50/130, 30/130, and 50/130 for products X, Y, and Z, respectively). Imputed sales values also are referred to as net realizable values.

In this illustration, we assumed no work in process in the department performing the additional processing of product X, which allowed us to subtract the total additional processing (conversion) costs of $10,000 from the total sales value after processing ($60,000) to get an imputed sales value for the 10,000 units of product X as they emerged from the joint process. If the additional-processing cost-accumulation center has beginning or ending work-in-process inventories, it will be necessary to determine the unit cost of additional processing (using the procedures for calculating the equivalent units and costs per unit described in Chapters 6–8) and subtract that from the unit sales price after processing, to arrive at a per-unit imputed sales value at the split-off point.

That figure then can be multiplied by the number of units of product coming out of the joint process, to yield an imputed sales value for that product at split-off.

To illustrate, let's assume that the additional-processing cost-accumulation center just discussed has a beginning-of-period work-in-process inventory of 5,000 pounds, 80% complete, and an end-of-period work-in-process inventory of 3,000 pounds, one-third complete as to additional processing. Since 10,000 pounds were transferred from the joint-process costing center to the additional processing department, and assuming no spoilage, we can calculate that 12,000 pounds were transferred out of the additional processing center:

	Units (pounds)		Units (pounds)
Beginning work in process	5,000	Transfers out to finished goods	**12,000**
Transfers in from joint process	10,000	Ending work in process	3,000
Total units to account for	15,000	Total units accounted for	15,000

With these assumptions we begin our calculation of the imputed sales value at split-off by determining the equivalent-units divisor for the additional processing department. Using the FIFO cost flow assumption, we get 9,000 units, calculated as follows:

Additional Processing Department EUP	
Units transferred out	12,000
Units in end-of-period work in process (3,000 $\times \frac{1}{3}$)	1,000
Less beginning-of-period work-in-process inventory (5,000 $\times$ 0.8)	(4,000)
FIFO equivalent units	9,000

If we assume that the additional processing (conversion) costs for the period amount to $10,800, rather than the $10,000 used previously, the additional processing costs are $10,800 ÷ 9,000 = $1.20 per unit. The imputed sales value at split-off for product X then would be 10,000 × ($6.00 − $1.20) = $48,000. It is important to recognize that any time the additional-processing cost-accumulation center has work-in-process inventory at either the beginning or the end of the reporting period, it will be necessary to calculate an *additional* processing (conversion) cost per unit and to subtract that from the sales price per unit after additional processing to get an imputed sales value per unit at split-off. As previously stated, that figure is then multiplied by the number of units transferred out of the joint process to arrive at the imputed sales value at split-off for the product.

End-of-period work-in-process inventory in the additional processing department would be valued at the joint cost per unit plus the additional processing cost per unit. If we assume a joint-cost allocation of $2.25 per unit for the product just described, the end-of-period work-in-process inventory for the additional processing department would amount to $7,950, calculated as follows:

**End-of-Period Work-in-Process Inventory,
Additional Processing Department**

Joint cost (3,000 units × $2.25 per unit)	$6,750
Additional processing cost (3,000 units × $\frac{1}{3}$ × $1.20 per unit)	1,200
Total end-of-period work-in-process	$7,950

In this illustration, we assumed FIFO cost flow. If we had used weighted-average costing, the equivalent-units divisor would have been 13,000 and the additional processing cost per unit would have been:

$$\text{Cost per unit} = \frac{\text{Beginning-of-period inventory of additional processing costs} + \$10,800}{13,000}$$

Joint Costs Allocated to Produce the Same Gross Margin for Each Product

When additional processing is required before products can be sold, joint costs allocated on the basis of relative sales value cause joint products to have different gross margins. For example, in the earlier illustration involving products X, Y, and Z produced from a joint process, where product X did not have a sales value at split-off, we found joint cost-allocation ratios of 50/130, 30/130, and 50/130 for products X, Y, and Z, respectively, when there was no work-in-process in the joint-processing department or in the department performing the additional processing of product X. Using these ratios, the joint costs of $60,000 would be allocated as follows:

Product X (50/130 × $60,000)	$23,077
Product Y (30/130 × $60,000)	$13,846
Product Z (50/130 × $60,000)	$23,077
	$60,000

Gross margins and gross margin percentages would be as follows:

	Total	Product X	Product Y	Product Z
Sales	$140,000	$60,000	$30,000	$50,000
Allocated joint costs	(60,000)	(23,077)	(13,846)	(23,077)
Additional processing costs	(10,000)	(10,000)	(0)	(0)
Gross margin	$ 70,000	$26,923	$16,154	$26,923
Gross margin percent	50%	44.87%	53.85%	53.85%

Inasmuch as all three products emerge from the same process, all three joint products might be expected to earn the same companywide gross profit of 50%. The constant gross margin method assures this equality by deducting a gross margin equal to the total gross margin percentage (50% in this case), as well as additional processing costs, from the sales values in arriving at the joint costs to allocate to each product. Using the previously assumed data, this approach would yield joint-cost allocations of $20,000, $15,000, and $25,000, respectively, for products X, Y, and Z:

		Total	Product X	Product Y	Product Z
	Sales	$140,000	$60,000	$30,000	$50,000
(1)	Gross margin (50%)	70,000	30,000	15,000	25,000
(2)	Adjusted sales value	$ 70,000	$30,000	$15,000	$25,000
(3)	Additional processing costs	(10,000)	(10,000)	(0)	(0)
(4)	Allocated joint costs	$ 60,000	$20,000	$15,000	$25,000

The four steps followed in applying the constant gross margin method in this example are:

(1) Calculate the overall gross margin and gross margin percentage for all joint products (together) and apply that percentage to the sales value of each product to find the projected absolute gross margin for each product.
(2) Subtract the absolute gross margin from each joint product's sales value.
(3) Subtract additional processing costs from the result of step (2).
(4) The amounts left after step (3) are the joint costs to allocate to each product.

Of course, if there is no compelling reason to believe that joint products should have the same profit margin, this method would not be used. The primary agreement for its use is that it does not penalize products that have no sales value at the point of split-off from a joint process.

Work-in-Process Inventories in a Joint-Processing Department. As we allocated costs to joint products, we have so far assumed that the process that produced the joint products had no work-in-process inventories. If the joint-processing department *does* have end-of-period work-in-process inventory, it will be necessary to allocate the total costs of the joint process (costs assigned to beginning inventory plus costs added during the period) between the joint products transferred out of the process and end-of-period work-in-process inventory. That can be done by applying previously explained process-costing procedures to the allocation of the joint-processing costs. To illustrate, let's assume the following for a joint-process cost-accumulation center:

Beginning-of-period work in process		$ 0
Additions during the period		
Materials	$41,925	
Direct labor and manufacturing overhead	59,040	100,965
Total costs to be accounted for		$100,965

	Product C	Product D
Units completed and transferred out:	4,000	8,000

Ending work in process (900 undivided units) is assumed to be complete as to materials and one-third complete as to conversion costs.

The equivalent-units divisors and costs per unit of undivided (joint) units then would be calculated as follows:

	Materials	Conversion
Transferred out		
Product C + product D	12,000	12,000
End-of-period work in process	900	300
Total equivalent units	12,900	12,300
Materials cost per unit ($41,925/12,900)		$3.25
Conversion cost per unit ($59,040/12,300)		4.80
Total cost per unit of undivided product		$8.05

The total joint-processing costs then would be allocated as follows:

Total cost to be accounted for		$100,965
End-of-period work in process		
900 units @ $3.25	$2,925	
900 units ($\frac{1}{3}$) @ $4.80	1,440	4,365
Costs allocated to joint products during this period		$96,600
Proof of joint costs transferred out: 12,000 units @ $8.05		$96,600

If we assume that the sales prices per unit for products C and D are $15 and $12, respectively, the following journal entry would be made to record the costs transferred out of the joint process:[1]

[1] Product C: $15 × 4,000 = $60,000   60/156 × $96,600 = $37,154
Product D: $12 × 8,000 = 96,000   96/156 × $96,600 = $59,446
Total $156,000

Finished-goods product C (or work in process, next process)	37,154	
Finished-goods product D (or work in process, next process)	59,446	
Work in process, joint process		96,600

Work in Process, Joint Process

Balance	100,965	Transfers	$96,600
Balance	4,365		

Illustrative Problem

Multi-Prod Refining Company operates a joint-processing department that produces by-product A and joint products B and C. Both by-product A and product C require further processing before they can be sold. However, product B is sold as it comes out of the joint-processing department. Multi-Prod allocates no joint-processing department costs to by-product A. Joint-processing costs are allocated to products B and C by use of the relative-sales-value method. The joint-processing department has no work-in-process inventory at either the beginning or the end of the period. Multi-Prod uses the first-in, first-out method in valuing its inventories. Other facts relating to one period's operations are:

Joint-process manufacturing costs (direct materials, direct labor, manufacturing overhead)		$66,000
Additional processing costs, product A		900
Additional processing costs, product C		22,800

Units transferred out of joint process

Product A	500
Product B	4,000
Product C	8,000

Beginning-of-period work-in-process inventories for additional processing departments

By-product A processing: 100 units, 30% complete		$ 40
Joint product C processing: 2,000 units, 40% complete	$2,500	
Transferred-in costs from joint process	8,000	10,500
Total		$10,540

End-of-period inventories of work in process in additional processing departments

By-product A processing: 200 units, 40% complete
Joint product C processing: 4,000 units, 60% complete

Sales price per unit

Product A	$ 3.00
Product B	10.00
Product C	9.00

REQUIRED:

1. Calculate:
   a. additional processing costs per unit for product A and for product C.
   b. relative sales values to be used in allocating joint costs.
   c. joint costs assigned to each joint product.
   d. costs associated with units transferred to inventories.
2. Prepare T accounts showing beginning-of-period balances and the entries required to record the cost accumulations and cost allocations for the period. By-product data are to be shown in separate accounts. Multi-Prod maintains one work-in-process account for the joint process and the additional processing department for joint product C.

Solution to Illustrative Problem

We begin by summarizing the given data in the form of a flowchart, as depicted in Figure 9–3.

Solution to Requirement 1.

a. Product A additional processing costs

Transferred out	400
End-of-period work in process (200 × 0.4)	80
Beginning-of-period work in process (100 × 0.3)	(30)
FIFO equivalent units of production	450

$$\frac{\$900}{450} = \$2 \text{ per unit}$$

Product C additional processing costs

Transferred out	6,000
End-of-period work in process (4,000 × 0.6)	2,400
Beginning-of-period work in process (2,000 × 0.4)	(800)
FIFO equivalent units of production	7,600

$$\frac{\$22,800}{7,600} = \$3 \text{ per unit}$$

b.

Product B (4,000 units @ $10)	$40,000
Product C [8,000 units @ ($9 − $3)]	48,000
Total	$88,000

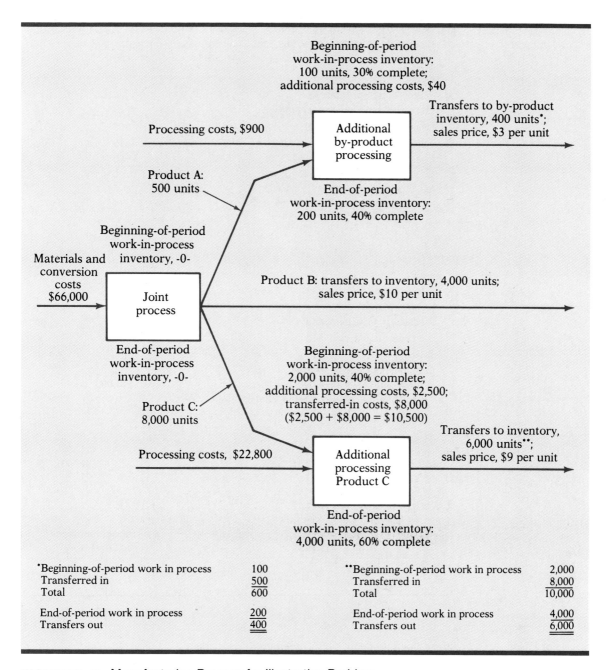

Beginning-of-period
work-in-process inventory:
100 units, 30% complete;
additional processing costs, $40

Transfers to by-product
inventory, 400 units*;
sales price, $3 per unit

Processing costs, $900

Additional
by-product
processing

Product A:
500 units

End-of-period
work-in-process inventory:
200 units, 40% complete

Beginning-of-period
work-in-process
inventory, -0-

Materials and
conversion
costs
$66,000

Joint
process

Product B: transfers to inventory, 4,000 units;
sales price, $10 per unit

End-of-period
work-in-process
inventory, -0-

Product C:
8,000 units

Beginning-of-period
work-in-process inventory:
2,000 units, 40% complete;
additional processing costs, $2,500;
transferred-in costs, $8,000
($2,500 + $8,000 = $10,500)

Transfers to inventory,
6,000 units**;
sales price, $9 per unit

Processing costs, $22,800

Additional
processing
Product C

End-of-period
work-in-process inventory:
4,000 units, 60% complete

*Beginning-of-period work in process	100	
Transferred in	500	
Total	600	
End-of-period work in process	200	
Transfers out	400	

**Beginning-of-period work in process	2,000	
Transferred in	8,000	
Total	10,000	
End-of-period work in process	4,000	
Transfers out	6,000	

FIGURE 9–3 Manufacturing Process for Illustrative Problem

c. Product B (40,000/88,000 × $66,000) $30,000 ($30,000/4,000 = $7.50 cost/unit)
  Product C (48,000/88,000 × $66,000) 36,000 ($36,000/8,000 = $4.50 cost/unit)
  Total $66,000

d. **By-Product (product A)**

Beginning-of-period work in process	$ 40
Processing costs for period	900
Total	$940
End-of-period work in process (200 × 0.4 × $2)	160
Costs associated with by-products transferred to inventory	$780*

*Beginning inventory $ 40
 To complete beginning inventory (100 × 0.7 × $2)   140 $180
 Started and completed this period (300 × $2)   600
                             $780

Joint Product (product B) $30,000

Joint Product (product C)

Beginning-of-period work-in-process inventory		$10,500
Processing costs for period		22,800
Joint costs transferred in		36,000
Total		$69,300
End-of-period work-in-process inventory		
Transferred-in costs [4,000($4.50)]	$18,000	
Additional processing costs [4,000(0.6)($3)]	7,200	(25,200)
Costs associated with units transferred to inventory		$44,100*

*Beginning inventory $10,500
 To complete beginning inventory (2,000 × 0.6 × $3)   3,600 $14,100
 Started and completed this period [4,000 × ($4.50 + $3)]   30,000
                               $44,100

Solution to Requirement 2.

By-Product Work in Process				By-Product Finished- Goods Inventory	
Beginning balance 40	(4)	780		(4) 780	
(2) 900					
Ending balance 160					

Joint Process and Additional Joint Product Processing Work in Process			Joint Products B and C Finished-Goods Inventory			Various Accounts	
Beginning balance 10,500	(5)	30,000	(5)	30,000		(1)	66,000
(1) 66,000	(6)	44,100	(6)	44,100		(2)	900
(3) 22,800						(3)	22,800
Balance 25,200							

Explanation of entries:

(1) To record joint-process direct materials, direct labor, and manufacturing-overhead costs for the period.
(2) To record additional processing (conversion) costs for further processing of by-product A.
(3) To record additional processing (conversion) costs for further processing of product C.
(4) To record the transfer costs assigned to completed units of by-product A to by-product inventory.
(5) To record the transfer of costs assigned to completed units of product B to finished-goods inventory.
(6) To record the transfer of costs assigned to completed units of product C to finished-goods inventory.

SUMMARY

In this chapter, we explained the cost-allocation procedures used in accounting for by-products and joint products. We explained that there are three generally accepted accounting procedures for by-products. One of these allocates no costs to the by-product at the point of split-off and values by-product inventory at the cost of additional processing. The consequent difference between the sales price and the additional processing costs is reflected in the income statement as net income from the sale of by-products in the period when the products are sold.

The second procedure allocates a value to the by-product that approximates its net realizable value. That amount then is subtracted from (credited to) work in process for the joint process and included as part of the inventory value of the by-product. This method has the effect of reducing the joint-processing department work-in-process balance by the amount of the margin expected to be realized from the sale of the by-product, rather than allowing that figure to be shown as net income from the sale of by-products. A variation of this method allocates to the by-product at the split-off point joint costs equal to the by-product's net realizable value less expected normal profit.

In accounting for joint products, the most widely used procedure for allocating joint-processing costs to the individual products is the relative-sales-value method, which allocates joint costs by using a ratio composed of the sales value at split-off for each of the joint products over the sum of their sales values at split-off. The sales value ratio for each product is then multiplied by total joint costs to get the costs assigned to each product.

When one of the joint products has no quoted sales value at the point at which it comes out of the joint process, an imputed sales value must be developed for the product by subtracting the additional processing cost from the sales value after additional processing. That net realizable value is then used, along with the sales values of the other joint products at split-off, to allocate the joint costs to the different joint products.

In situations in which there is no reason for joint products to have different profit margins, it might be appropriate to use the constant gross margin method to allocate joint costs. This procedure subtracts gross margin plus additional processing costs from the sales value of each product to arrive at, as a residual number, the joint costs allocated to it.

We also discussed how to handle situations in which the additional processing department or the joint-processing department has ending balances of work in process.

GLOSSARY OF TERMS INTRODUCED IN THIS CHAPTER

by-product

A product that emerges from a joint process and whose sales value is relatively insignificant when compared with the sales value of the major products, therefore making it economically impractical to carry out the manufacturing process to produce the by-product independent of the major products (if that were possible).

imputed sales value at split-off

A value assigned to a joint product that has no sales value at the point of split-off. The assigned amount is calculated by subtracting additional processing costs from the sales value of the product after additional processing, net of selling expenses. That figure is then used with the sales values at split-off of other joint products in allocating joint costs by use of the relative-sales-value method. Also called *net realizable value*.

joint costs

The common costs of two or more simultaneously produced products before the point at which the joint products become individually identifiable, accumulated in a joint-processing cost-accumulation center.

joint product

A product produced in conjunction with one or more other products, each earning revenue sufficient to justify joint production.

net realizable value

A value equal to a product's sales value less its cost of completion and disposal. In this chapter, it refers to a value that may be assigned to a joint product or by-product equal to its anticipated sales value less the sum of disposal cost and the cost of processing beyond the point at which the product is removed from the joint process.

net realizable value less normal margin

A value equal to a product's sales value less the sum of additional processing costs, disposal cost, and normal profit margin. In this chapter, it refers to a value that may be assigned to a joint product or by-product equal to its anticipated sales value less the sum of additional processing costs, disposal cost, and normal profit margin.

relative-sales-value method

A method of allocating joint costs on the basis of the aggregate sales value of each of the joint products in relation to the total aggregate sales value of all joint products at the point of split-off. (The numerator in each ratio is the aggregate sales value at the split-off point of the individual product; the denominator is the sum of the aggregate sales values at the split-off point of *all* of the joint products.)

QUESTIONS FOR CLASS DISCUSSION

9—1 What is the difference between a joint product and a by-product? Explain.

9—2 Why is it important to distinguish between products characterized as by-products and products characterized as joint-products?

9—3 Are costs always allocated to by-products as they are removed from a joint-processing center? Explain.

9—4 If no costs are allocated to by-products as they are removed from the joint-processing center, what value will be assigned to by-products held in inventory?

9—5 If costs equal to the expected net realizable value are assigned to by-products as they are removed from work in process, what value will be assigned to by-product inventory that is ready to be sold?

9—6 Which of the first two methods of assigning costs to by-products is more conservative? Explain.

9—7 What method is most commonly used for allocating joint-processing costs to joint products? Explain.

9—8 What procedures are followed when using the relative-sales-value method of allocating joint costs if one of the joint products requires further processing before it can be sold? Explain.

9—9 What costs are assigned to joint-products as they emerge from an additional processing center prior to being sold? Explain.

9—10 How are joint-processing costs allocated between work-in-process inventory and joint products completed when the joint-processing center has end-of-period work-in-process inventory? Explain.

9—11 How are the accounting procedures in this chapter related to the process-costing procedures in Chapters 6–8? Explain.

EXERCISES

9—12 **By-Product Valuation** Diamond Company produces joint products Alpha and Beta from a process that also yields a by-product, Omega. Products Alpha, Beta, and Omega all require additional processing before they can be sold. Joint costs are allocated to joint products by use of the relative-sales-value method.

During April 19X2, Diamond's information system produced the following data:

(1) Costs incurred in joint-processing department: $72,000

(2)

Product	Units Produced	Sales Value	Additional Processing Costs
Alpha	1,120	$61,600	$5,600
Beta	1,000	45,000	5,000
Omega	700	5,600	1,400

(3) Sales during April:

Product	Units
Alpha	1,000
Beta	900
Omega	680

(4) There are no beginning or end-of-period work-in-process inventories.

(5) There is no beginning-of-period finished-goods (Alpha and Beta) or by-product (Omega) inventory.

REQUIRED:

1. Assuming Diamond allocates none of the joint-processing costs to Omega, what is the cost per unit of product Omega in finished-goods inventory?

2. Assuming Diamond uses the net-realizable-value method to value Omega at point of split-off from Alpha and Beta, what will be the cost per unit of product Omega in finished-goods inventory?

9–13 **By-Product Journal Entries** Refer to the data in exercise 9–12. Prepare general journal entries to record the transactions involving Omega during April 19X2, assuming:

1. Diamond allocates no joint costs to Omega.

2. Diamond allocates joint costs equal to Omega's net realizable value to Omega at point of split-off.

9–14
AICPA Adapted

By-Product Affect on Gross Margin Earl Corporation manufactures a product that gives rise to a by-product called Zafa. The only separable costs associated with Zafa are selling costs of $1 for each unit sold. Earl accounts for Zafa sales by deducting its separable costs from such sales, and then deducting this net amount from cost of sales of the major product. In 19X1, 1,000 units of Zafa were sold at $4 each.

Select the *best* answer for each of the following items.

1. If Earl changes its method of accounting for Zafa sales to showing the net amount as additional sales revenue, then Earl's gross margin would
  a. be unaffected.

        b. increase by $3,000.
        c. decrease by $3,000.
        d. increase by $4,000.
    2. If Earl changes its method of accounting for Zafa sales to showing the net amount as "other income," then Earl's gross margin would
        a. be unaffected.
        b. increase by $3,000.
        c. decrease by $3,000.
        d. decrease by $4,000.

9–15 **By-Product—Net Realizable Value Less Normal Profit** Crowley Chemical Company manufactures products A and B from a joint process that also yields a by-product, Q. Crowley has been assigning no costs to Q at point of split-off but is considering switching to the method of net realizable value less normal profit to value by-product Q. Additional processing costs of $0.50 a unit must be incurred before Q can be sold for $2.00 a unit. Selling expenses for Q amount to $0.10 a unit.

    Crowley earns a gross profit margin of 40% on products A and B. Because of the market for by-product Q, however, Crowley estimates that it should be sold at a gross profit margin of 20%.

    During September, 1,000 units of Q were produced from a joint process that cost $40,000. During that period, 900 units of Q were sold for $1,800. There was no beginning-of-period inventory of product Q.

REQUIRED:

1. Compute the joint costs that should be allocated to by-product Q if Crowley uses net realizable value less normal profit to value by-product Q at point of split-off.
2. Assuming no beginning inventory of by-product Q, and assuming that Crowley uses net realizable value less normal profit to allocate joint costs to by-product Q, compute the value of ending finished-goods inventory of by-product Q.

9–16 **Allocation of Joint-Processing Costs** Baily Company produces joint products X and Y in Department 1 from a process that also yields by-product P. Product X and by-product P are sold after separation, but product Y must be further processed in Department 2 before it can be sold. The cost assigned to the by-product is its market value less $0.40 per pound for delivery expense (net-realizable-value method). Information relating to a batch produced in July 19X3 is as follows:

(1)

Product	Production (in pounds)	Sales-Price per Pound
X	4,000	$4.50
Y	8,000	9.00
P	1,000	1.50

(2) Joint cost in Department 1: $36,000
(3) Product Y additional-processing cost in Department 2: $20,000
(4) There are no work-in-process inventories on July 1 or July 31.
(5) Joint processing costs are to be allocated by use of the relative sales value method.

REQUIRED:

1. Determine the imputed sales value at split-off for product Y.
2. Calculate the amount of Department 1 costs that should be allocated to the joint products.
3. Show how Department 1 costs should be allocated.

9–17 **Joint-Cost Allocation and Total Cost per Unit** Refer to the data in exercise 9–12. Compute the cost per unit of Alpha and Beta in ending finished-goods inventory under each of the following assumptions regarding Omega:

(1) Diamond allocated none of the joint-processing costs to Omega.
(2) Diamond uses the net-realizable-value method to value Omega at point of split-off from Alpha and Beta.

9–18 **Imputed Sales Value with Work-in-Process Inventory** Great Lakes Fertilizer Company manufactures liquid fertilizers F and G from a joint process. Joint costs are allocated on the basis of relative sales values at split-off. It costs $1,752 to process 850 gallons of product F and 1,700 gallons of product G to the split-off point. Product G is sold at split-off for $1.50 a gallon, but product F must be processed further before it can be sold for $2.20 a gallon.

The additional processing department for F reported the following information for March:

	Gallons	Costs
Work in process, March 1, 70% processed	90	
Transferred in		$ 71
Conversion		25
Transferred in from joint process	850	
Conversion added during March		339
Work in process, March 31, 60% processed	75	

Great Lakes uses the relative-sales-value method to allocate joint costs and the weighted-average method to account for its work in process.

REQUIRED: Compute the joint costs to be allocated to product F and product G during March.

9–19 **Allocation of Joint Costs** Shaw, Inc., manufactures products A, B, and C from a joint process. Joint product costs were $132,000. Additional information for a recent period is as follows:

			Sales Values and Additional Processing Costs If Processed Further	
Product	Units Produced	Sales Value at Split-off	Sales Values	Additional Costs
A	13,200	$88,000	$121,000	$19,800
B	8,800	77,000	99,000	15,400
C	4,400	55,000	66,000	11,000

There are no beginning or end-of-period work-in-process inventories.

REQUIRED:

1. Assuming that joint product costs are allocated on the basis of volume (physical units), compute the joint costs allocated to products A, B, and C.

2. Assuming that joint product costs are allocated on the basis of relative sales value at split-off, compute the joint costs allocated to products A, B, and C.

9–20
ICMA Adapted

Multiple Choice: Joint Products—Allocation of Joint Processing Costs
Hovart Corporation manufactures two products out of a joint process— Compod and Ultrasene. The joint (common) costs incurred are $250,000 for a standard production run that generates 120,000 gallons of Compod and 80,000 gallons of Ultrasene. Compod sells for $2.00 per gallon, while Ultrasene sells for $3.25 per gallon.
Select the best answer for each of the following items.

1. If there are no additional processing costs incurred after the split-off point, the amount of joint costs of each production run allocated to Compod on a physical-quantity basis is
   a. $100,000.
   b. $120,000.
   c. $130,000.
   d. $150,000.

2. If there are no additional processing costs incurred after the split-off point, the amount of joint cost of each production run allocated to Ultrasene on a net-realizable-value (relative sales value) basis is
   a. $100,000.
   b. $120,000.
   c. $130,000.
   d. $150,000.

3. If additional processing costs beyond the split-off point are $0.10 per gallon for Compod and $1.10 per gallon for Ultrasene, the amount of joint cost of each production run allocated to Ultrasene on a physical quantity basis is
   a. $100,000.
   b. $148,000.
   c. $142,500.
   d. $150,000.

4. If additional processing costs beyond the split-off point are $0.10 per gallon for Compod and $1.10 per gallon for Ultrasene, the amount of joint cost of each production run allocated to Compod using the relative-sales-value method is
   a. $100,000.
   b. $107,500.
   c. $142,500.
   d. $150,000.

9–21

Missing Information Tracktuf Corporation manufactures products L, M, and N from a joint process. Joint costs are allocated by use of the relative sales value method. The following information is available:

	Product			
	L	M	N	Total
Joint costs	$ 48,000	?	?	$ 90,000
Units produced	5,000	3,000	2,000	10,000
Sales value at split-off	?	?	$50,000	$150,000
Additional processing costs	$ 22,000	$11,000	$ 7,000	$ 40,000
Sales value after additional processing	$105,000	$35,000	$60,000	$200,000

REQUIRED:

1. Compute the sales values at split-off for products L and M.
2. Compute the joint costs allocated to products M and N.

PROBLEMS

9–22   **Journal Entries—Joint Products and By-Product** Lares Confectioners, Inc.,
AICPA Adapted makes a candy bar called Rey, which sells for $0.50 per pound. The man-
ufacturing process also yields a product known as Nagu. Without further
processing, Nagu sells for $0.10 per pound. With further processing, Nagu
sells for $0.30 per pound. During the month of April, total joint manufac-
turing costs up to the point of separation consisted of the following
charges to work in process:

Raw materials	$150,000
Direct labor	120,000
Factory overhead	30,000

   Production for the month aggregated 394,000 pounds of Rey and 30,000
pounds of Nagu. To complete Nagu during the month of April and obtain
a selling price of $0.30 per pound, further processing of Nagu during
April would entail the following additional costs:

Raw materials	$2,000
Direct labor	1,500
Factory overhead	500

REQUIRED: Prepare the April journal entries for Nagu, if Nagu is:

1. Transferred as a by-product at sales value to the warehouse without
further processing, with a corresponding reduction of Rey's manufacturing costs.
2. Further processed as a by-product and transferred to the warehouse
at net realizable value, with a corresponding reduction of Rey's manufacturing costs.
3. Further processed and transferred to finished goods, with joint costs
being allocated between Rey and Nagu based on relative sales value
at the split-off point.

9–23 **Joint Costs, Joint Products, By-Products, and Evaporation Losses** Speciality Chemical Company produces cosmetic dyes. Processing begins in the mixing department, where chemicals are combined and processing is begun. At the end of processing in the mixing department, two products emerge, N-4H and I-17, plus a by-product of chemical residues. These products are produced in the ratio of 6:8:1.

N-4H is transferred into Processing Department 2, where it is heated and combined with additional materials to produce a hair dye called Newglow, which is packaged in 8-ounce bottles. As a result of the heating and curing processes prior to bottling, however, 25% of the good output is lost to evaporation.

I-17 is transferred into Processing Department 3, where it is refined and further processed. The output of Department 3 is an eyebrow and eyelash dye called Eye Enhancer and a by-product, Colorglow, that, when further processed, becomes a powder used to dye cosmetics. Ten percent of the material entering Processing Department 3 is lost to evaporation. Eye Enhancer represents 70% of the output of Processing Department 3 and is transferred to Department 4, where it is packaged in 4-ounce bottles. Colorglow accounts for the remaining 30% of the output of Processing Department 3 and is transferred to Processing Department 5 for drying and bulk packaging.

Chemical residues from the mixing department are sold without further processing to clothing dyers.

Records of the past month's production processes reveal the following:

(1) The mixing department produced 12,000 pounds of output at a cost of $26,400. Joint costs are allocated on a relative sales value basis.

(2) Additional processing costs were:

Department	Costs
Processing Department 2	$1,920
Processing Department 3	3,888
Processing Department 4	2,016
Processing Department 5	432

(3) Sales prices were:

Mixing department chemical residues—$0.20 per pound
Newglow—$2.00 per 8-ounce bottle
Eye Enhancer—$1.75 per 4-ounce bottle
Colorglow—$0.75 per pound

(4) There are no work-in-process inventories.

REQUIRED: Prepare a schedule showing the allocation of the $26,400 joint costs of the mixing department. Net revenues from sales of by-products should be credited to the manufacturing costs of the related main product(s).

9–24 **Joint Cost Allocation—Net-Realizable-Value Method** Doe Corporation
ICMA Adapted grows, processes, cans, and sells three main pineapple products—sliced pineapple, crushed pineapple, and pineapple juice. The outside skin is

cut off in the cutting department and processed as animal feed. The skin is treated as a by-product. Doe's production process goes as follows:

1. Pineapples first are processed in the cutting department. The pineapples are washed and the outside skin is cut away. Then the pineapples are cored and trimmed for slicing. The three main products (sliced, crushed, juice) and the by-product (animal feed) are recognizable after processing in the cutting department. Each product is then transferred to a separate department for final processing.
2. The trimmed pineapples are forwarded to the slicing department, where they are sliced and canned. Any juice generated during the slicing operation is packed in the cans with the slices.
3. The pieces of pineapple trimmed from the fruit are diced and canned in the crushing department. The juice generated during this operation is packed in the can with the crushed pineapple.
4. The core and surplus pineapple generated from the cutting department are pulverized into a liquid in the juicing department. There is an evaporation loss equal to 8% of the weight of the good output produced in this department that occurs as the juices are heated.
5. The outside skin is chopped into animal feed in the feed department.

The Doe Corporation uses the relative sales value method to assign costs of the joint process to its main products. The by-product is inventoried at its market value.

A total of 270,000 pounds was entered into the cutting department during May. The following schedule shows the costs incurred in each department, the proportion by weight transferred to the four final processing departments, and the selling price of each end product.

Processing Data and Costs
May 19X1

Department	Costs Incurred	Percentage of Product by Weight Transferred to Departments	Selling Price per Pound of Final Product
Cutting	$60,000	0%	none
Slicing	4,700	35	$0.60
Crushing	10,580	28	0.55
Juicing	3,250	27	0.30
Animal Feed	700	10	0.10
Total	$79,230	100%	

REQUIRED:

1. The Doe Corporation uses the relative sales value method to determine inventory values for its main products and market value to determine by-product inventory value. Calculate
   a. the pounds of pineapple that result as output for pineapple slices, crushed pineapple, pineapple juice, and animal feed.

b. the imputed sales value at the split-off point of the three main products.

c. the amount of the cost of the cutting department assigned to each of the three main products and to the by-product in accordance with corporate policy.

d. the gross margins for each of the three main products.

2. Comment on the significance to management of the gross margin information by main product.

9–25 **Alternative Methods of Joint-Cost Allocation** Natura Soap Company manufactures three cleansing products, a liquid facial soap called Elegance, a bath gel called Squeeky, and a bar soap called Miteesoft. The basic ingredients for all three products, Top, Mid, and Lo, are produced in a joint process in Natura's first processing department, C-1.

From each batch processed in C-1, 20% becomes Top and is transferred to Department E-2 for further processing into Elegance; 70% becomes Mid and is transferred to Department S-2 for further processing into Squeeky; and 10% becomes Lo and is transferred to Department M-2 for further processing into Miteesoft. A by-product from Department M-2 is sold to another company as the raw material for an industrial hand cleaner. Natura credits Department M-2 costs for the net realizable value of this by-product.

Each gallon of Top transferred into Department E-2 furnishes enough material for 32 bottles of Elegance, and each gallon of Mid transferred into Department S-2 provides the raw material for 16 bottles of Squeeky. One gallon of product Lo transferred into Department M-2 provides the raw material for sixty 2-ounce bars of Miteesoft and 8 ounces of by-product. Sales prices are:

Product	Sales Price
Elegance	$0.75 per bottle
Squeeky	.50 per bottle
Miteesoft	.30 per bar
By-product	.50 per ounce with packaging cost of $.10 per ounce

Information for the month of December 19X5 is:

Department	Unit Output	Direct Materials	Labor	Overhead
			Costs	
C-1	5,000 gallons	$13,500	$3,300	$6,200
E-2	32,000 bottles	1,430	5,150	2,748
S-2	56,000 bottles	2,160	4,824	5,464
M-2	30,000 bars plus 4,000 ounces of by-product	815	566	1,543

All products produced during the month were sold.

REQUIRED:

1. Assuming joint costs are allocated on the basis of volume (physical units), compute, for December 19X5, Natura's
   a. gross profit for each joint product.
   b. gross profit for the entire firm.
2. Assuming joint costs are allocated on the basis of relative sales values, compute, for December 19X5, Natura's
   a. gross profit for each product.
   b. gross profit for the entire firm.
3. Assuming Natura uses the constant gross margin method to allocate joint costs to joint products, compute the joint costs that will be allocated to Elegance, Squeeky, and Miteesoft during December 19X5.

9–26   **Joint-Cost Allocation—Relative-Sales-Value Method** Multiproduct Corpo-
ICMA Adapted   ration is a chemical manufacturer that produces two main products (Pepco-1 and Repke-3) and a by-product (SE-5) from a joint process. If Multiproduct had the proper facilities, it could process SE-5 further into a main product. The ratio of output quantities to input quantity of direct materials used in the joint process remains consistent with the processing conditions and activity level.

Multiproduct currently allocates joint costs to the main products on the basis of quantities produced. The FIFO inventory method is used to value the main products. The by-product is inventoried at its net realizable value, and the net realizable value of the by-product is used to reduce the joint production costs before the joint costs are allocated to the main products.

Jim Simpson, Multiproduct's controller, wants to implement the relative-sales-value method of joint-cost allocation. He believes that inventoriable costs should be based on each product's ability to contribute to the recovery of joint production costs. The net realizable value of the by-product would be treated in the same manner as with the physical method.

Data regarding Multiproduct's operations for November 19X6 follow. The joint cost of production amounted to $2,640,000 for November 19X6.

	Main Products		
	Pepco-1	**Repke-3**	**By-Product SE-5**
Finished-goods inventory, in gallons, on November 1, 19X6	20,000	40,000	10,000
November sales, in gallons	800,000	700,000	200,000
November production, in gallons	900,000	720,000	240,000
Sales value per gallon at split-off point	$2.00	$1.50	$0.55*
Additional processing after split-off costs	$1,800,000	$720,000	
Final sales value per gallon	$5.00	$4.00	

*Disposal and selling costs of $0.05 per gallon will be incurred in order to sell the by-product.

REQUIRED:

1. Describe the relative-sales-value method, and explain how it accomplishes Jim Simpson's objective.
2. Assuming Multiproduct Corporation adopts the relative-sales-value method for internal reporting purposes,
   a. calculate how the joint production cost for November, 19X6, would be allocated.
   b. determine the dollar values of the finished-goods inventories for Pepco-1, Repke-3, and SE-5 as of November 30, 19X6.
3. Multiproduct Corporation plans to expand its production facilities to enable the further processing of SE-5 into a main product. Discuss how the allocation of the joint production costs under the relative-sales-value method would change when SE-5 becomes a main product.

9–27 **Missing Information** You have just been employed by the Oakdale Manufacturing Company and have been assigned to make a presentation to departmental supervisors on the firm's processing costs. You have been briefed on the manufacturing process and gathered all the data you thought you would need to prepare your presentation. After everyone leaves the office, you realize there are some gaps in your knowledge. The missing items of information (labeled *a* through *k*) and the information you have gathered are shown in Figure 9–4 (on page 320) and the following notes.

(1) Products A, B, and C are joint products; X is a by-product.
(2) Joint costs are allocated based on relative sales values.
(3) All products can only be sold at the end of all processing.
(4) The total gross margin for all products is $9,068.

REQUIRED:

1. Determine the amounts for items *a* through *k*. *Hint:* These can best be calculated in alphabetical order from *a* through *g*.
2. Identify each of the items of cost calculated in requirement 1.
3. Calculate the total costs allocated to each joint product.

9–28 **Joint Products—Allocation of Joint-Processing Costs with Work-in-Process Inventory** Hansen Company buys cedar scraps from a lumber company that makes cedar fence posts. Hansen processes the cedar scraps, including bark, in Department 1. At the end of processing in Department 1, two identifiable products emerge—cedar garden chips, which are packaged in 25-pound bags and sold to nurseries, home improvement, and discount stores, and powdered cedar residue, which is further processed in Department 2 to produce fireplace logs. Department 1 produces chips and the powdered residue in a 3:2 ratio, with no spoilage. Each pound of powdered residue entering Department 2, when combined with additional materials, produces one 2-pound fireplace log.

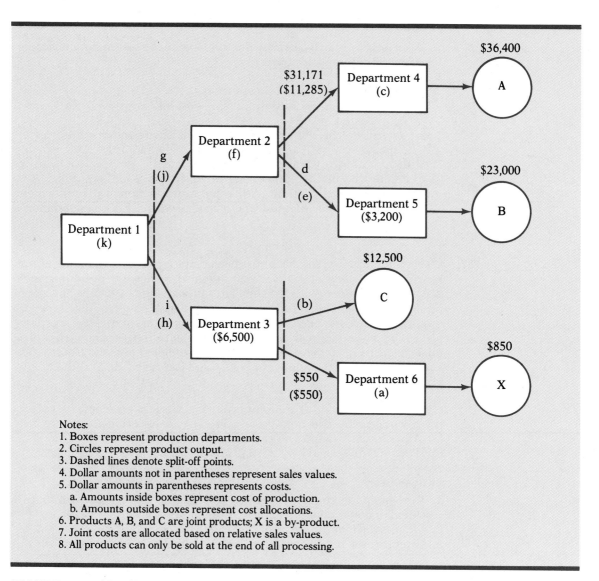

Notes:
1. Boxes represent production departments.
2. Circles represent product output.
3. Dashed lines denote split-off points.
4. Dollar amounts not in parentheses represent sales values.
5. Dollar amounts in parentheses represents costs.
   a. Amounts inside boxes represent cost of production.
   b. Amounts outside boxes represent cost allocations.
6. Products A, B, and C are joint products; X is a by-product.
7. Joint costs are allocated based on relative sales values.
8. All products can only be sold at the end of all processing.

FIGURE 9–4 Manufacturing Process, Oakdale Manufacturing Company

Information accumulated for February 19X9 includes the following:

	Department 1		Department 2
	Pounds	**Costs**	**Costs**
Beginning work in process: all materials, 50% labor and overhead	5,000	$ 540	
Direct materials used	50,000	$2,500	$2,040
Factory payroll		$3,650	$1,200
Overhead (applied)		$2,530	$1,800
Ending work in process: all materials, 75% labor and overhead	4,000		

The 25-pound bags of cedar chips sell for $8.50 per bag. Each fireplace log sells for $0.55.

Hansen Company uses relative sales values to allocate the joint costs of Department 1. All inventories are valued by use of the first-in, first-out cost flow assumption.

There was no finished-goods inventory of either product on February 1. Finished-goods inventory on February 28 included 66 bags of cedar chips and 400 fireplace logs. Department 2 had no work-in-process inventory on either February 1 or February 28.

REQUIRED:

1. Compute the Department 1 costs allocated to cedar chips and fireplace logs during February.
2. Compute the total gross margin and gross margin percents for
   a. cedar chips.
   b. fireplace logs.

9–29
ICMA Adapted

Joint-Cost Allocation—Physical Volume Versus Relative Sales Value Talor Chemical Company is a highly diversified chemical processing company. The company manufactures swimming pool chemicals, chemicals for metal processing companies, specialized chemical compounds for other companies, and a full line of pesticides and insecticides.

Currently, the Noorwood plant is producing two derivatives, RNA-1 and RNA-2, from the chemical compound VDB developed by Talor's research labs. Each week 1,200,000 pounds of VDB is processed, at a cost of $246,000, into 800,000 pounds of RNA-1 and 400,000 pounds of RNA-2. The proportion of these two outputs is fixed and cannot be altered because this is a joint process. RNA-1 has no market value until it is converted into a product with the trade name Fastkil. The cost to process RNA-1 into Fastkil is $240,000. Fastkil wholesales at $50 per 100 pounds.

RNA-2 is sold as is for $80 per hundred pounds. However, Talor has discovered that RNA-2 can be converted into two new products through further processing. The further processing would require the addition of 400,000 pounds of compound LST to the 400,000 pounds of RNA-2. The joint process would yield 400,000 pounds each of DMZ-3 and Pestrol—the two new products. The additional raw materials and related processing costs of this joint process would be $120,000. DMZ-3 and Pestrol would each be sold for $57.50 per 100 pounds. Talor management has decided not to process RNA-2 further based on the analysis presented in the following schedule. Talor uses the physical method to allocate the common costs arising from joint processing.

| | RNA-2 | Process Further | | |
		DMZ-3	Pestrol	Total
Production in pounds	400,000	400,000	400,000	
Revenue	$320,000	$230,000	$230,000	$460,000
Costs				
VDB	$ 82,000	$ 61,500	$ 61,500	$123,000
Additional raw materials (LST) and processing of RNA-2	0	60,000	60,000	120,000
Total	$ 82,000	$121,500	$121,500	$243,000
Weekly gross profit	$238,000	$108,500	$108,500	$217,000

A new staff accountant who was to review the preceding analysis commented that it should be revised, stating, "Product costing of products such as these should be done on a relative sales value basis, not a physical-volume basis."

REQUIRED:

1. Discuss whether the use of the relative sales value method would provide data more relevant for the decision to market DMZ-3 and Pestrol.
2. Critique the Talor Company's analysis, and make any revisions that are necessary. Your critique and analysis should indicate:
   a. whether Talor Chemical Company made the correct decision
   b. the gross savings (loss) per week of Talor's decision not to process RNA-2 further, if different from the company-prepared analysis.

9–30 THOUGHT STIMULATION PROBLEM. Brune Candy Company manufactures a toffeelike chocolate-covered bar called Synergy. A batch of 5,000 bars costs $700 to produce. In the process of removing bars from molds, approximately 300 bars in each batch are broken. The broken bars are unsuitable as livestock feed. Prior to a year ago, Brune paid a subcontractor to haul off the broken bars along with the sludge residual from cooking vats.

At a party last year, Paul Brown, the president of Brune Candy Company, met Samantha Sands, the founder of a chain of frozen yogurt stores called Yummy Yogurt, and discovered a market for the broken Synergy candy bars as topping for frozen yogurt. Brune Candy Company subsequently contracted to sell all its broken bars to Yummy Yogurt for $.10 a bar and immediately began shipping them to the Yummy Yogurt central distribution center in Minneapolis.

New Yummy Yogurt franchises, along with a new yogurt manufacturing process that allows the crushed candy to be blended into the yogurt mixture as it is being produced so that it can be frozen and packaged for sale in grocery stores, have increased the demand for broken Synergy bars beyond the supply occurring from Brune's normal operations. To fill Yummy Yogurt's current order, Brune Candy Company would have to deliberately break 20% of the 4,700 good bars produced in each batch.

REQUIRED:

1. Evaluate the product status, prior to the Yummy Yogurt contract, of
   a. broken Synergy bars
   b. sludge residue from cooking vats.
2. Evaluate the product status of naturally occurring broken Synergy bars *after* sales were initiated with Yummy Yogurt.
3. Will the product status of broken bars change if they are purposely broken to fill Yummy Yogurt's order?
4. What information would Paul Brown need before making a decision to divert unbroken Synergy bars to a crusher to fill Yummy Yogurt's demand?

Chapter 10

Cost Accounting Systems for Service Enterprises

Learning Objectives

When you have finished your study of this chapter, you should

1. Be familiar with the terminology associated with the operations of service enterprises.
2. Understand how cost-allocation and -accumulation systems are useful to service enterprises.
3. Recognize the fundamental differences between a cost accounting system for a manufacturing firm and a cost accounting system for a profit-motivated service enterprise.
4. Realize the importance of identifying direct and indirect costs in planning for service enterprises.
5. Appreciate the differences between expense-oriented financial statements of service organizations that have some profit motivation and expenditure-oriented statements of pure nonprofit service enterprises.

hapters 4–9 covered cost accounting for *manufacturing* enterprises. Systems for cost accumulation and cost allocation also are important in the effective management of *service* enterprises.

Service enterprises convert resources into services, much as manufacturing firms convert resources and services into finished products. Some service enterprises produce goods as well as provide services (for example, country clubs that provide food). In this chapter, we shall identify the special considerations involved in allocating and accumulating costs associated with the providing of services.

There are two important differences between the cost accounting systems previously discussed and those needed to account for the costs of producing services. First, with services, we have no direct materials costs to allocate. Also, with the exception of public accounting firms, law firms, and certain other firms that perform services on what can best be characterized as a job-order basis, service enterprises are not concerned with accounting for inventories other than those of miscellaneous supplies. Firms providing services on a job-order basis *will* be concerned with accounting for work-in-process inventory (called services-in-process inventory) because such services often will be billed (sold) only after the job has been completed. However, no service enterprise will be concerned with accounting for finished-services inventories (analogous to finished-goods inventories) because services are delivered as they are performed. Thus, cost accounting systems for service enterprises (with the exceptions just noted) must primarily assist management in meeting the last three of the four objectives described in Chapter 1:

1. planning future operations
2. controlling operations
3. making day-to-day operating decisions.

To effectively meet these objectives, we need data that properly relate operating results to the operating objectives of the resource-conversion entities. Service enterprises (one type of resource-conversion entity) may be categorized according to ownership of the enterprise to more specifically identify their operating objectives. Those objectives then can be used to identify the data that should be presented to help management make planning, controlling, and operating decisions. We then can develop the accumulation and allocation procedures to follow for each type of service enterprise (see Figure 10–1):

- pure-profit service enterprises
- quasi-profit service enterprises
- quasi-nonprofit service enterprises
- pure-nonprofit service enterprises.

First we will divide all service enterprises according to the sources of equity funding. After that, the operating objectives associated with each

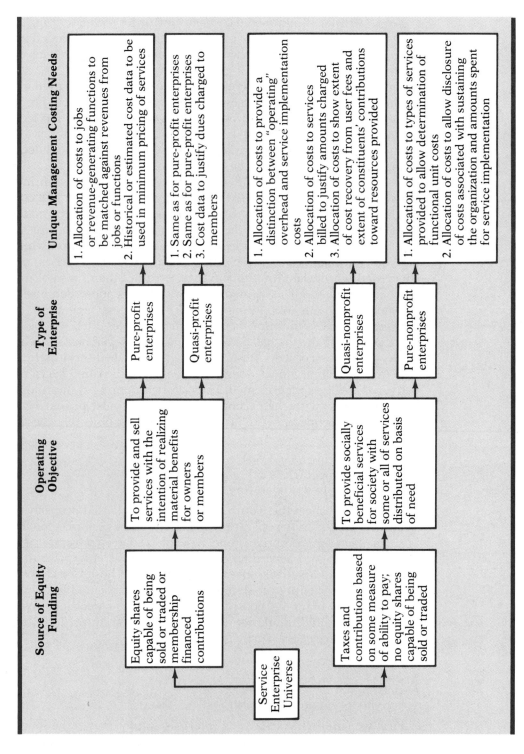

FIGURE 10–1 Types of Service Enterprises and Their Operating Characteristics

funding source will be identified. (The profit objective drives the operations of pure-profit enterprises and quasi-profit enterprises; the service objective motivates the operations of quasi-nonprofit enterprises and pure-nonprofit enterprises.) Then we will project the logical accounting information needs for effectively managing each type of enterprise. The operating objectives listed in Figure 10–1 range from the conversion of resources into services to be sold for the purpose of earning net income for owners (pure-profit enterprises) to the conversion of resources into services to be distributed on the basis of need for the services (pure-nonprofit enterprises).

Even though many nonprofit organizations could probably improve the efficiency of their operations by paying careful attention to cost data, few of them—other than hospitals—have formal cost accounting systems. Moreover, even though many profit-oriented service enterprises use cost accumulation and allocation techniques, their use of formal cost accounting systems appears to be limited. The development of detailed systems for service enterprises is organization specific and beyond the scope of this text. Our coverage is limited to some of the important general considerations.

Pure-Profit Service Enterprises

Pure-profit service **enterprises** convert resources into services sold for the purpose of realizing net income for the owners. This includes public accounting firms, law firms, consulting firms, household moving and storage firms, banks, and other similar business entities.

Some service enterprises, such as public accounting, law, and consulting firms, should have a job-order cost system (see Chapters 4 and 5), so the accumulated and allocated costs of completing each job can be matched against the revenues earned from the job.

Other service enterprises, such as banks and other financial institutions, should employ a process cost system (see Chapters 6–9), so costs can be accumulated in departmental cost centers and ultimately allocated to the types of services provided by those centers. For example, for a bank to know the costs of processing a deposit, processing a customer's check, and providing monthly statements for customers, it is critical to trace the bank's clerical costs to these and the other services provided by the bank. The resulting data then can be used to determine what interest to pay on customer accounts and what service charges to levy.

Firms using a job-order system should originate job-order sheets, similar to those illustrated in Chapters 4 and 5, to accumulate the costs incurred in carrying out each separately identifiable project. In the case of public accounting firms, for example, this could involve the performance of an audit or the installation of an accounting system for a particular client. The job-order sheet should be organized to accumulate the directly chargeable professional costs for *each* job. This can be thought of as the equivalent of direct-labor costs incurred in the production of a separately identifiable lot of goods by a manufacturer.

Most public accounting firms generate revenues by charging clients a specified rate per hour for each professional that works on the job, ranging from the lowest rate for a staff person to the highest rate for a partner. The direct costs per hour of providing those services would be the rates a firm pays those professionals, calculated by dividing annual salaries by the number of hours employees are expected to work each year. The costs of unbilled time become part of overhead. In addition to accumulating the direct professional (labor) costs associated with each job, the system should periodically compare the billable time provided by each professional to a predetermined goal for billable time (which may be different for each professional staff level).

Other specialized (nonroutine) direct costs of a public accounting firm, such as travel, printing, and subcontracted work, also would be charged to individual job-order sheets. Routine job costs, such as photocopying and proofing, may be either traced to individual jobs or included in overhead.

The other element of conversion cost will be a percentage add-on for the overhead incurred in operating the accounting firm's office. This generally involves the establishment of an *operating-overhead application rate* based on the expected relationship between the costs of operating the office and the direct professional (labor) costs, possibly derived from the historical relationship between direct professional costs and all other costs or from budgetary data developed for the reporting period.

For example, for a professional firm with the following condensed operating budget for the current year:

Revenue	$10,000,000
Direct professional (labor) costs	3,000,000
Contribution margin	$ 7,000,000
All other costs (overhead)	6,000,000
Operating income	$ 1,000,000

the overhead application rate would be:

$$\frac{\$6,000,000}{\$3,000,000} = 200\%$$

If one job shows direct professional charges of $30,000, then overhead of $30,000 × 200% = $60,000 would be added to the job to arrive at the total cost. This total cost would then be matched against the revenue realized from the job to determine the operating income realized from that engagement. Ultimately, the actual overhead incurred will be closed against the overhead applied to all jobs worked on during the reporting period to arrive at the amount of underapplied or overapplied overhead for the period. This amount normally will be reflected in the income statement as an adjustment to costs of jobs completed and sold during the period, just as for a manufacturing firm.

Service enterprises sometimes have a *services-in-process inventory*, whose account balance will be the accumulated costs associated with jobs not yet completed. As jobs are completed and billed, the costs accumulated on the related job-order sheets should be transferred to a cost-of-services-provided account to be matched against the revenues from services rendered in the income statement. Some engagements may be carried out under an arrangement calling for partial billing prior to completion of the engagement (*progress billing*), in which case it is appropriate to show amounts billed in advance as a subtraction from the services-in-process inventory in the balance sheet or to include the partial payments in an advances-from-customers account in the current-liability section.

A comparison of the accounts required for a manufacturing firm using a job-order system and those for a service enterprise using a job-order system follows.

Manufacturing Firm (Job-Order-System) T Accounts

Materials	
Purchases	Uses (Direct materials used) (Indirect materials used)
Ending balance	

Work in Process	
Beginning balance Direct materials Direct labor Overhead applied	Cost of goods manufactured
Ending balance	

Finished Goods	
Beginning balance Cost of goods manufactured	Cost of goods sold
Ending balance	

Cost of Goods Sold	
Cost of goods sold (Overhead adjustment)	(Overhead adjustment)

Factory Payroll	
(Actual accrued wages)	Direct labor Indirect labor

Manufacturing Overhead	
Indirect materials, indirect labor, and other actual overhead costs incurred	(Close)*
0	

Manufacturing Overhead Applied	
(Close)*	Overhead applied
	0

*The difference in these two amounts, either a debit or a credit, is the overhead adjustment to cost of goods sold.

Subsidiary Work-in-Progress Accounts.

Job A		Job B		Job C		Job D	
Beginning balance Direct materials Direct labor Overhead applied		Direct materials Direct labor Overhead Applied		Direct materials Direct labor Overhead applied		Direct materials Direct labor Overhead applied	
Ending balance		Ending balance		Ending balance		Ending balance	

Service Firm (Job-Order-System) T Accounts

Services in Progress	
Beginning balance Direct job costs (travel, etc.) Professional labor Overhead applied	Completed jobs
Ending balance	

Cost of Services Rendered	
Completed jobs (Overhead adjustment)	(Overhead adjustment)

Overhead Incurred	
Indirect professional labor & other actual overhead incurred	(Close)*
0	

Overhead Applied	
(Close)*	Overhead applied
	0

Accounts Receivable, Engagements in Progress	
Progress billings	

Professional Salaries	
Actual accrued salaries	Direct professional labor Indirect professional labor

*The difference in these two amounts, either a debit or a credit, is the overhead adjustment to cost of services rendered.

Subsidiary Service-in-Progress Accounts.

Company A Engagement		Company B Engagement		Company N Engagement	
Beginning balance Travel Professional labor Overhead applied		Professional labor Overhead applied		Subcontract work Professional labor Overhead applied	
Ending balance		Ending balance		Ending balance	

Other firms, such as banks, provide services to customers on a *continuing* basis that cannot be conveniently divided into separately identifiable jobs (by customer, for example). The operating policies of such institutions may call for charging customers for some or all of such services. In the banking industry, for example, revenue is realized primarily from the investment of the funds deposited by customers for whom the banks provide checking and other services. The costs of providing those services, as well as interest paid on deposits and funds borrowed, is part of the cost of having funds available to loan. All costs of acquiring funds, including the cost of providing banking services, should be matched against the revenue realized from investing the funds.

When customers are charged fees for services, it is important to accumulate and allocate the costs of providing the services so they can be appropriately matched against the revenues realized from them. This involves the analysis of cause-and-effect relationships associated with the incurrence of costs and the use of allocation bases consistent with those relationships. For example, the salaries of check-processing clerks, depreciation on check-processing equipment (or fees paid for check processing), plus a reasonable allocation of overhead for space occupied, bank teller time required to accept and process deposits, and executive management time absorbed by the checking account division could be accumulated and allocated to checking accounts on the basis of transactions processed. Several *pools of costs*, each with its own allocation basis, may be desirable. Then each checking account transaction (deposit, checks cleared, insufficient funds checks, and so forth) can be separately costed.

In the case of banks, if we look on the interest paid to depositors as a direct cost of acquiring the money banks loan or invest, then it is important to match the direct costs incurred in the form of interest paid to depositors, plus the costs of providing services not charged to customers, against the revenues realized from the investment of those funds. As a means of more specifically determining what should be done regarding interest and services, customers may be divided into classes based on the average balance maintained and number of transactions. Then different service charge and interest arrangements may be provided for each class of customer.

A comparison between the accounts required for a manufacturing firm using a process cost system and a service enterprise using process costing follows.

Manufacturing Firm (Process Cost System) T Accounts

Materials	
Beginning balance Purchases	Uses
Ending balance	

Work in Process	
Beginning balance Direct materials Direct labor Overhead applied	Cost of goods manufactured
Ending balance	

Finished Goods

Beginning balance Cost of goods manufactured	Cost of goods sold
Ending balance	

Cost of Goods Sold

Cost of goods sold (Overhead adjustment)	(Overhead adjustment)

Manufacturing Overhead*

Actual overhead costs incurred	(Closed)**
0	

Manufacturing Overhead Applied*

(Closed)**	Overhead applied
	0

*There may be multiple overhead accounts.
**The difference in these two amounts, either a debit or a credit, is the overhead adjustment to cost of goods sold.

Subsidiary Work-in-Process Accounts.

Cost-of-Production Report, Department A

Beginning balance Direct materials Direct labor Overhead applied	Transfers to Department B*
Ending balance*	

Cost-of-Production Report, Department B

Beginning balance Transfers from Department A Direct materials Direct labor Overhead applied	Transfers to finished goods*
Ending balance*	

*Requires calculation of equivalent-units divisors and cost per unit.

Service Firm (Process Cost System) T Accounts

Cost of Services Rendered

Professional labor Overhead applied (Overhead adjustment)	Fees charged for service* (Overhead adjustment)

Overhead Incurred

Indirect professional labor and other actual overhead costs incurred	(Closed)**
0	

Overhead Applied

(Closed)**	Overhead applied
	0

Customers' Accounts

Fees charged for services	

Professional Salaries

Actual accrued salaries	Direct professional labor Indirect professional labor

*May be reflected as revenues rather than as a reduction of costs.
**The difference in these two amounts, either a debit or a credit, is the overhead adjustment to cost of services rendered.

Subsidiary Cost-of-Services-Rendered T Accounts.

Cost of Services Rendered, Department A		Cost of Services Rendered, Department B	
Professional labor Overhead applied	Fees charged for services*	Professional labor Overhead applied	Fees charged for services*

*May be reflected as revenues rather than as a reduction of costs.

The cost per unit of services rendered can be calculated by dividing the balances in the subsidiary ledger accounts by the number of units of service provided by the respective departments. The balances in the costs-of-services-rendered accounts would be closed at the end of each fiscal period, along with all other income-statement accounts.

Quasi-Profit Service Enterprises

Quasi-profit service **enterprises** provide services to a select group of fee-paying members who have certain exclusive rights to the services of the organization. Profits from the operation of quasi-profit service enterprises may be distributed in a number of ways, including some distribution to members as well as no distribution to members (the more typical situation). Quasi-profit service enterprises include country clubs, athletic clubs, and various associations that provide services for people who have purchased membership shares. For example, a country club may provide golfing, swimming, tennis, and social activities for its members in exchange for periodic dues payments, and also may allow members and invited guests to participate in activities on payment of established fees; it also may sell some services to members on a user-fee basis. Such an organization would need procedures for allocating the costs of operating the club to the various types of services provided. Such data could be used to inform members about how their dues are being used to support each of the activities and to set equitable guest fees. Management also will be expected to judge whether such services are being rendered efficiently, based, to some extent, on cost data. Again, all costs should be allocated, as far as practicable, on the basis of cause-and-effect relationships. This necessitates distinguishing between *direct* costs of the specific services provided and indirect operating (*overhead*) costs. General operating or overhead costs may be allocated to types of service provided on the basis of a percentage of one or more of the directly charged costs, so all operating costs (both direct and general) ultimately will be allocated to the various types of services provided. Some of the more important costs to be charged *directly* to the service provided would be amortization of the costs of facilities required to provide the services, the costs of maintaining those facilities, and the cost of personnel directly engaged in providing the services. General operating (*overhead*) costs would include the amortization of the costs of general facilities, maintenance of those facilities, and salaries paid to management and other general operations personnel. The accounting records for a quasi-profit country club that uses a process cost system could include the following service T accounts.

Service Firm (Process Cost System) T Accounts for a Country Club

Cost of Services Rendered		General Operating Overhead Incurred		General Operating Overhead Applied	
Direct costs of activities	Fees received*	Actual overhead incurred			Overhead applied
Overhead applied (Overhead adjustment)	(Overhead adjustment)		Closed**	Closed**	
		0			0

*May be reflected as revenues rather than as a reduction of cost.
**The difference between these two amounts is the overhead adjustment to cost of services rendered.

Subsidiary Cost-of-Services-Rendered Accounts.

Golf		Swimming		Tennis	
Direct cost of golf course operations	Greens fees* Lesson fees*	Direct costs of swimming pool operation	Swimming lesson fees*	Direct costs of tennis	Tennis lesson fees*
Golf pro wages		Depreciation of pool and equipment		Depreciation of courts	
Depreciation of course		Overhead applied		Depreciation of equipment	
Overhead applied					

Special Clubhouse Activities		Restaurant	
Director	Activity fees*	Food	Meals receipts*
Orchestra and band costs		Cooks and waitresses	
Decorating costs		Manager	
Space charges		Depreciation—Equipment	
Overhead applied		China and silverware depreciation	
		Depreciation—space occupied	
		Overhead applied	

*These items may be shown as revenues rather than as reductions of costs.

The cost per unit of service rendered can be calculated by dividing the total debits in each of the subsidiary ledger accounts by the number of units of service rendered for that activity. The balances in these cost-of-services-rendered accounts would be closed at the end of each fiscal period when other income statement accounts are closed.

Quasi-Nonprofit Service Enterprises

Unlike quasi-profit enterprises, **quasi-nonprofit** enterprises exist for the purpose of providing socially desirable services to the general public in exchange for fees covering *less than* all of the costs of providing those services. This category includes colleges, universities, and most hospitals, which provide services to clientele in exchange for fees established to cover some of the costs of providing the services but do not attempt to earn a profit for the benefit of nonclientele "owners." Here again, the cost accounting system needs to include procedures for allocating operating costs to the individual types of services being provided on a user-fee basis. In the case of colleges and universities, tuition charges generally are based on semester hours of services provided. In the case of hospitals, patients are billed for room service, drugs, operating room charges, X ray services, and other services provided during their stays.

Even though the only way colleges and universities can develop useful and meaningful cost data is for them to account for costs on the full accrual basis, the purchases of assets from current fund resources traditionally have been recorded as expenditures with no depreciation recognized as long-term assets. That practice will be changed with the implementation of FASB 93,[1] requiring the capitalization of long-term assets and the subsequent recognition of depreciation as an expense as those assets are used. This should encourage the use of accrual-based costs per unit of service (generally a student credit hour) for various university subdivisions.

When organizations use expenditure-oriented rather than expense-oriented (full accrual basis) accounting procedures, they are forced to use data on *expenditures per unit of service* rather than the more meaningful costs per unit of service. *Expenditures* measure *outflows of spendable resources* relating to the provision of services rather than the resources and services consumed in providing services. When programs are initiated, expenditures include costs of assets that will be used for a long time, perhaps years. Later, after a program is established, expenditures during a period may be significantly less than the cost of services and resources consumed. *Expenses,* on the other hand, reflect goods and services *consumed* during a reporting period in rendering services. When we divide expenses by the number of units of service provided we get a meaningful cost per unit of service.

In accumulating and allocating costs for colleges and universities, we should determine the *cost per credit hour* for services provided by each of the various academic disciplines. Appropriate cost-allocation and -accumulation procedures typically will disclose higher costs for pro-

---

[1]Statement of Financial Accounting Standards No. 93, "Recognition of Depreciation by Not-for-Profit Organizations, August 1987. The effective date of this standard, as amended by FASB 99, is January 1, 1990.

viding a credit hour of educational services in some disciplines than in others because of differences in needs (laboratories, practice areas, and so forth) and in effective class size. An appropriate expense-allocation system for a college or university allocates direct and indirect costs to separate programs, providing information justifying either differential tuition rates or the recognition that the institution is providing a much larger subsidy per credit hour in some areas of study than in others.

Hospitals are service enterprises that, because of the need for accurate cost data to support insurance and other patient service claims, have developed cost accounting systems, the primary objective being to relate costs to the various services billed to patients. That requires the identification and use of cause-and-effect relationships in the allocation process. The need for a sophisticated cost-accumulation and -allocation system for hospitals became even more acute with the enactment of the Medicare Prospective Payment Plan, which set maximum reimbursable charges Medicare will accept for various types of services. This forced hospitals to become more cost conscious, which in turn demanded sophisticated cost-accumulation and -allocation systems to improve operating efficiency.

Cost-accumulation and -allocation procedures for hospitals should be directed primarily toward matching the costs of providing billable services against the revenues realized from those services. However, patient accounts must be charged for services as they are dispensed. To meet both of these information needs, a hospital accounting system may incorporate elements of both job-order and process costing. The matching of revenue-producing departmental revenues and expenses can best be accomplished by accumulating the costs of providing each type of billable service over periods of time in revenue-producing cost center accounts within a process-costing format. As charges to patients (revenues) are recorded, they may be credited to the revenue producing cost centers (as shown below) or to patient service revenues. At the same time, subsidiary records, in the nature of job order sheets, should be maintained to accumulate the charges to individual patients. The T accounts that typically would be used in such a system follow.

Service-Charge-Accumulation T Accounts for a Hospital

Charges for Services Provided		**Accounts Receivable**	
Detailed patient charges (rooms, surgery, etc.)	Transfer to accounts receivable	Transfers from charges for services provided	

Subsidiary Charges for Services-Provided Account.

Patient 1		**Patient 2**		**Patient M**	
Detailed charges	Transfer to accounts receivable	Detailed charges	Transfer to accounts receivable	Detailed charges	Transfer to accounts receivable

Cost-of-Services-Provided Accounts

Revenue-Producing Cost Centers.

Rooms	

Direct costs
Allocated service
    department
    costs
Overhead applied
	Charges to
	    patients*

Surgery	

Direct costs
Allocated service
    department
    costs
Overhead applied
	Charges to
	    patients*

Emergency	

Direct costs
Allocated service
    department
    costs
Overhead applied
	Charges to
	    patients*

Pharmacy	

Direct costs
Allocated service
    department
    costs
Overhead applied
	Charges to
	    patients*

Laboratory	

Direct costs
Allocated service
    department
    costs
Overhead applied
	Charges to
	    patients*

Pathology	

Direct costs
Allocated service
    department
    costs
Overhead applied
	Charges to
	    patients*

Overhead Incurred	
Actual overhead incurred	(Closed)***
0	

Overhead Applied	
(Closed)***	Overhead applied
	0

Underapplied or Overapplied Overhead**	
Underapplied	Overapplied

*These items may also be shown as revenues rather than credits to departmental cost accounts.

**The balance in this account will be closed to the income statement.

***The difference between these amounts becomes either underapplied overhead (if overhead incurred is greater than overhead applied) or overapplied overhead (if overhead incurred is less than overhead applied).

Supporting-Service Cost Centers.

Laundry	

Direct costs	Transfers to
	    revenue-
	    producing
	    centers

Cleaning	

Direct costs	Transfers to
	    revenue-
	    producing
	    centers

Food	

Direct costs	Transfers to
	    revenue-
	    producing
	    centers

Building Maintenance	

Direct costs	Transfers to
	    revenue-
	    producing
	    centers

Security	

Direct costs	Transfers to
	    revenue-
	    producing
	    centers

Nursing	

Direct costs	Transfers to
	    revenue-
	    producing
	    centers

The charges-for-services-provided account may be thought of as a type of work-in-process account supported by individual patient job-order sheets. As patients are billed for services rendered, the amounts accumulated on those patients' job-order sheets should be transferred from the charges-for-services-provided account to accounts receivable. Balances in the accounts for the **revenue-producing cost centers** then will reflect the extent to which costs incurred by each revenue-producing center have been covered by patient service revenues (charges to patients). Hospitals can relate these costs to the revenues realized from their incurrence to arrive at *ratios of costs to charges* (*RCC*) for each type of service and for the hospital as a whole. The costs allocated to each revenue-producing-cost-center account also can be divided by the units of service provided to arrive at a cost per unit of service. The underapplied-or-overapplied-overhead account should be transferred to the income statement as an additional expense (if underapplied) or a reduction in expense (if overapplied).

A typical hospital cost accounting system divides its cost-accumulation centers into two categories: (1) revenue-producing cost centers and (2) supporting-service cost centers. The procedures for allocating costs to these centers should be based on cause-and-effect relationships and should be essentially the same as those for manufacturing firms. The costs of operating the **supporting-service cost centers** should be allocated to the revenue-producing centers just as service department costs are allocated to producing departments of manufacturing firms (see Chapter 4). We give more specific attention to that allocation process for hospitals in Exhibit 10–1, which shows how the costs of operating Hypothetical Hospital are allocated (using the direct method) to four revenue-producing cost centers. In that exhibit, one of the key elements of data is the *cost per unit of service*, which becomes the basis for determining the billing price for the services provided by each of the departments, if the hospital is to base fees on some relationship to the costs incurred.

The use of a flexible budget is important in developing the data in Exhibit 10–1. Recall that a *flexible budget* is a schedule projecting the probable costs of operating a department at different levels of activity by giving appropriate recognition to the ways that fixed and variable costs are expected to behave in relation to changes in the level of operations. To illustrate, Exhibit 10–2 presents an assumed flexible budget for Hypothetical Hospital, Department 1, showing the costs expected to be incurred at four different levels of activity. The data in Exhibit 10–1 for Department 1 are the same as those in Exhibit 10–2's flexible budget column for the 80% level of operations. The determination of the cost per unit (billing unit) of service is the same as that for arriving at the overhead application rate in job-order costing: expected total costs of the department divided by the expected activity base expressed in billing units equals the estimated cost per unit of the activity. These data can be used by hospitals in establishing the billing price for each unit of service and in evaluating the results of departmental operations.

EXHIBIT 10–1

Hypothetical Hospital

Allocation of Costs

	Revenue-Producing Cost Centers				Supporting Cost Centers			Total
	Dept. 1	Dept. 2	Dept. 3	Dept. 4	Dept. 5	Dept. 6	Dept. 7	
Direct costs	$400,000	$ 800,000	$300,000	$600,000	$200,000	$ 80,000	$100,000	$2,480,000
Allocated general costs	80,000	120,000	100,000	150,000	40,000	30,000	30,000	550,000
Totals	$480,000	$ 920,000	$400,000	$750,000	$240,000	$110,000	$130,000	$3,030,000
Allocation of Dept. 6 costs[a]	20,000	60,000	10,000	20,000		$110,000		
Allocation of Dept. 7 costs[b]	60,000	30,000	25,000	15,000			$130,000	
Allocation of Dept. 5 costs[c]	100,000	50,000	30,000	60,000	$240,000			
Totals	$660,000	$1,060,000	$465,000	$845,000				$3,030,000
Billing units (quantity)	66,000	10,600	93,000	42,250				
Cost per unit of service	$10	$100	$5	$20				

[a]Dept. 6 costs are building-related costs allocated on the basis of square footage as follows: Dept. 1, 4,000; Dept. 2, 12,000; Dept. 3, 2,000; Dept. 4, 4,000.

[b]Dept. 7 costs are employee-related costs allocated on the basis of number of employees as follows: Dept. 1, 60; Dept. 2, 30; Dept. 3, 25; Dept. 4, 15.

[c]Dept. 5 costs are equipment-related costs allocated on the basis of cost of equipment in each department as follows: Dept. 1, $1,000,000; Dept. 2, $500,000; Dept. 3, $300,000; Dept. 4, $600,000.

339

EXHIBIT 10–2

Hypothetical Hospital

Flexible Budget

For Department 1

	Level of Operations (related to capacity)			
	70%	80%	90%	100%
Direct costs (variable)	$262,500	$300,000	$337,500	$375,000
Direct costs (fixed)	100,000	100,000	100,000	100,000
Total direct costs	$362,500	$400,000	$437,500	$475,000
Allocated general costs (fixed)	80,000	80,000	80,000	80,000
Allocated service dept. costs				
Dept. 6 (fixed)	20,000	20,000	20,000	20,000
Dept. 7 (semifixed)	55,000	60,000	65,000	70,000
Dept. 5 (fixed)	100,000	100,000	100,000	100,000
Total costs	$617,500	$660,000	$702,500	$745,000
Billing units	57,750	66,000	74,250	82,500
Cost per unit of service	$10.69	$10.00	$9.46	$9.03

In evaluating the efficiency of operations for a reporting period, the expected costs developed from the flexible budget data should be compared with actual costs incurred in providing services during the period. Exhibit 10–3 shows a budget performance schedule for Hypothetical Hospital, Department 1, with assumed actual costs for the reporting period (the costs accumulated in the ledger account for the department) and the budget allocation based on the actual operating level of 85% of capacity. This type of budget performance schedule is used in evaluating the efficiency with which individual departments or cost centers have been managed. The footnotes to Exhibit 10–3 suggest actions management might take if the variances shown for the individual items of cost are considered material. In Chapters 11–13, we will explain how to prepare and use this type of analytical schedule for the departments of a manufacturing firm.

Pure-Nonprofit Service Enterprises

Pure nonprofit enterprises realize their revenues by collecting taxes or soliciting contributions from constituents based on some measure of ability to pay or willingness to give (social consciousness). These re-

EXHIBIT 10–3

Hypothetical Hospital

Budget Performance Schedule
For Department 1
(Actually Operating at 85% of Capacity)

	Actual Costs	Budget Allocation	Variances
Direct costs (variable)	$320,000	$318,750	$1,250[a] — unfavorable
Direct costs (fixed)	101,000	100,000	1,000[b] — unfavorable
Allocated general costs (fixed)	78,000	80,000	2,000[c] — favorable
Allocated service dept. costs			
Dept. 6 (fixed)	20,500	20,000	500[d] — unfavorable
Dept. 7 (semifixed)	65,000	62,500	2,500[e] — unfavorable
Dept. 5 (fixed)	101,500	100,000	1,500[f] — unfavorable
Totals	$686,000	$681,250	$4,750 — unfavorable

[a]This unfavorable variance should be explained by the Dept. 1 supervisor. It appears that the supervisor failed to properly control variable costs in relation to the actual level of operations. Individual items of cost should be reviewed.

[b]This variance suggests that the departmental supervisor has "overspent" the allocation for fixed costs.

[c]This favorable variance indicates less was paid for general costs than anticipated. Perhaps staff positions are not completely filled. The general manager should review individual cost items.

[d] and [f]These variances have probably been caused by inadequate cost controls in Service Depts. 6 and 5. Costs should be reviewed with departmental supervisors.

[e]This variance could have been caused either by Dept. 1 having relatively more employees than were expected or by inadequate cost controls in Dept. 7.

sources are then converted to services to be distributed to recipients on the basis of their needs. Governmental entities and volunteer health and welfare agencies are examples of pure-nonprofit service enterprises.

In allocating the costs of operating a governmental entity, the objective is to arrive at **functional-unit cost** (cost per person or per household) of providing each of the various governmental services. Generally accepted accounting practices for governmental entities currently require use of the *modified accrual* (expenditure-oriented) *basis* of accounting, rather than the full accrual (expense-oriented) basis used by business entities. The modified accrual basis recognizes inflows of resources as revenues in the accounting period in which they become available and are measurable; outflows of spendable resources are recognized as expenditures in the accounting period in which a fund liability is incurred and measurable. This means that the revenue and expenditure data shown in the operating statement of a governmental entity will include expenditures for fixed assets and will include no provision for depreciation. So, unless those data are converted to the full accrual basis, the functional-unit data will be **functional-expenditure data** rather than true functional-cost data.

Recognizing the limitations associated with the operating data produced by following generally accepted accounting practices for governmental entities, we shall now identify the procedures to follow in arriving at functional expenditures per unit of service. The first step is to allocate total expenditures to the different types of services being provided by the governmental entity, frequently referred to as an *allocation to programs*. For example, a city will generally provide at least the following types of services (programs) for its citizens:

- general government
- police
- sanitation
- recreation
- street maintenance.

In some instances, school services also will be provided directly by the city. In other instances, a separate tax-receiving entity will be established to account for resources earmarked for educational services.

After all expenditures have been allocated to the service programs on the basis of cause-and-effect relationships, we can derive the **functional-expenditures-per-unit data** by dividing the expenditures allocated to each type of service by the population or by the number of households in the city, to arrive at expenditures per capita or per household. Per capita data, for example, give the expenditures per person incurred in carrying out each governmental service, information important to city management and to taxpayers in determining whether an appropriate balance is being maintained among the various services and whether the level of total services is appropriate. Exhibit 10–4 shows how these data for Model City (population 20,000) may be presented for use by management and the voters. We also include some relationships between revenues and expenditures that may be helpful both to management and external users of the data.

The distinction between *sustentation costs* and *service implementation costs* is the most critical part of the cost-allocation and -accumulation process for health and welfare agencies. **Sustentation costs** are those costs incurred in sustaining the agency, including fund-raising costs as well as general operating costs allocable to the fund-raising efforts. **Service implementation costs**, on the other hand, are costs incurred in providing the services the agency was originated to provide. Thus, in effect, we allocate the costs of operating the agency into two categories: (1) the cost of keeping the entity in operation (sustentation or supporting costs) and (2) the costs of rendering agency services (service implementation costs). Again, the allocation of costs should be made on the basis of cause-and-effect relationships, which may call for some creative techniques. For example, some cause-and-effect relationships can be

EXHIBIT 10–4
Model City

Analysis of Expenditure-Based Data

Items	Expenditures	Percentage	Expenditures per Capita (population 20,000)
General administration	$ 409,800	16.1%	$ 20.49
Police services	293,200	11.6	14.66
Sanitation services	188,400	7.4	9.42
Recreation services	90,300	3.6	4.51
Street maintenance services	1,115,800	43.9	55.79
School services	441,550	17.4	22.08
Total expenditures	$2,539,050	100.0%	$126.95

Relationship Between Revenues and Expenditures
(values not shown above are assumed)

Excess revenues over expenditures	$81,875
Ratio of revenues to expenditures ($2,620,925 ÷ $2,539,050)	1.032
General long-term debt per capita ($500,000 ÷ 20,000)	$25
Tax assessment to market value of property ($1,460,000 ÷ $90,625,000)	1.6%
Expenditures per person ($2,539,050 ÷ 20,000)	$126.95

established by observing the amount of time spent by various operating personnel on sustaining activities (fund-raising, for example) and each of the service implementation activities over a short period of time and using that as a basis for the allocation of salary costs.

After the allocations have been made, it is helpful to show the net results of the allocations on a common-size (percentage) basis. Such a schedule will reflect the percentage of total expenses incurred for sustaining the organization (keeping it in position to render services) and for implementing the services the organization was created to provide. Those data are important because they allow current and potential contributors to know what part of every dollar contributed was used in sustaining the organization and what part eventually was used for implementing services.

Where multiple services are provided by health and welfare agencies, it is also important to allocate the service implementation costs to the different categories of services provided and to convert those to common-size data. To demonstrate, Exhibit 10–5 presents certain of those common-size data for Standard Voluntary Health and Welfare Agency. Note that $.28 of every expense dollar was used to sustain the organization. That also tells contributors that $.72 of every dollar con-

EXHIBIT 10–5
Standard Voluntary Health and Welfare Agency
Common-Size Operating Statement
19X2

		Percentage
Revenues, by source		
Public support		91.9%
Revenues earned		8.1
Total		100.0%
Expenses		
Sustentation		28.0%
Service implementation		
Research	32.3%	
Public health education	12.4	
Professional education and training	14.1	
Community services	13.2	72.0
Total		100.0%

tributed was spent in implementing services. Exhibit 10–6, which presents functional-cost data for the same agency, tells us that functional-unit costs amount to slightly more than $14,000 per research project. The agency also is spending $54.40 per person on public health education, $1,030 per person on professional education and training, and $5.78 per person on community services.

EXHIBIT 10–6
Standard Voluntary Health and Welfare Agency
Functional Cost Data
19X2

Assumptions regarding services rendered	
Research projects completed	100
Public health education (persons served)	10,000
Professional education and training (persons served)	600
Community services (population of community)	100,000
Service implementation costs	
Average research costs per completed project	$14,140.00
Public health education per participant	54.40
Professional education and training per participant	1,030.00
Community services per person	5.78

Even though generally accepted accounting principles dictate an expenditure-oriented modified accrual basis of accounting for published financial statements for governmental entities, there is no reason why accrual-basis data cannot be accumulated for management decision making and planning. Pure-nonprofit service enterprises need to know the *costs* of services rendered, even if the data must be accumulated in an accounting system parallel to the one that results in published financial statements. With proper planning, both sets of information (expenditure and cost) can be gleaned from one accounting database. If pure-nonprofit service enterprises gather expense rather than expenditure data, the appropriate cost system would be similar to those already discussed for quasi-nonprofit enterprises.

SUMMARY

In this chapter, we summarized the general considerations associated with the development of cost accounting systems for service enterprises. Except for public accounting firms, consulting firms, law firms, and other such firms that require a service-in-progress "inventory" account, we are not concerned with accounting for inventories of services rendered. There is no inventory account for service firms equivalent to finished-goods inventory for a manufacturing firm. That means that the systems should be designed primarily to help management in controlling operations, planning future operations, and making day-to-day operating decisions.

We divided the service enterprise universe into four categories: pure profit, quasi-profit, quasi-nonprofit, and pure-nonprofit enterprise units, to identify more specifically the considerations that should underlie the systems for accumulating and allocating costs for each type. With the exception of pure-nonprofit enterprises, the basic cost structure for all service enterprises is quite similar.

We pointed out that in some instances job-order systems that follow cost-accumulation and -allocation procedures described in Chapters 4 and 5 should be used. In other situations, process cost systems designed to arrive at unit costs for each of the various types of services provided over a period of time should be used. This can be accomplished by using cost-accumulation and -allocation procedures like those described in Chapters 6–8. The primary objective of such a system is to determine costs per unit of service provided during each reporting period. Some enterprises, for example, hospitals, may want to use some elements of both job-order and process cost systems.

Expenditure-based pure-nonprofit enterprises were discussed in the final portion of the chapter. We noted that even these organizations can benefit from expense-oriented (accrual) cost data.

GLOSSARY OF TERMS INTRODUCED IN THIS CHAPTER

functional-expenditure data	In governmental accounting, the amounts of expenditures allocated to various functions performed by a governmental entity.
functional-expenditure-per-unit data	An amount equal to the total expenditures allocated to each function performed divided by the number of functional activity units provided.
functional-unit cost	An amount equal to total costs allocated to each function performed divided by the number of functional activity units provided.
pure-nonprofit enterprises	Service enterprises that realize substantially all of their resources from taxes or voluntary contributions and distribute the services funded by those resources on the basis of need for the services.
pure-profit enterprises	Enterprises financed by owners and creditors that operate for the purpose of producing net income to be distributed to owners on the basis of ownership interests.
quasi-nonprofit enterprises	Enterprises that have some but not all of the characteristics of pure-nonprofit enterprises. They are financed by contributions and/or taxes but also realize a significant part of their resource inflows in the form of payments (revenues) for services rendered.
quasi-profit enterprises	Enterprises that have some but not all of the characteristics of profit enterprises. They are financed by member contributions, but they distribute benefits or services, rather than earnings, to their members.
revenue-producing cost centers	Cost-accumulation centers that provide billable services to an organization's clientele.
service enterprises	Enterprises engaged in converting resources into services rather than into finished goods.
service implementation costs	Costs incurred by a business or nonprofit organization in providing services to the organization's clientele; comparable to cost of sales for a manufacturing or merchandising firm.
supporting-service cost centers	Cost-accumulation centers that provide services to revenue-producing cost centers; comparable to service department cost centers for a manufacturing firm.
sustentation costs	Costs incurred by a nonprofit organization in sustaining itself, primarily fund-raising costs and certain administrative costs.

QUESTIONS FOR CLASS DISCUSSION

10–1 In what ways can a cost accounting system be useful to the management of a service enterprise? Explain.

10–2 What are the two most important differences between the cost accounting systems discussed in previous chapters and the ones that should be used for a service enterprise? Explain.

10–3 What is the operational difference between profit service enterprises and nonprofit service enterprises?

10–4 Do all service enterprises fall into either a pure-profit or pure-nonprofit category? Explain.

10–5 What type of cost accounting system should be used by a public accounting firm? Briefly explain the elements of such a system.

10–6 Why is it important for a service enterprise such as a bank to know the costs of providing each of the various customer services?

10–7 What would be the most important data a college or university cost accounting system could provide for a manager of such an institution? Explain.

10–8 Could a country club beneficially use a cost accounting system? Explain.

10–9 Why have hospitals been inclined to develop better cost-accumulation and -allocation techniques than most other nonprofit organizations? Explain.

10–10 What is the primary objective in accumulating and allocating the operating costs of a hospital? Briefly explain how that allocation is achieved.

10–11 What procedures can be followed in evaluating the efficiency of a service-providing department in a hospital? Explain.

10–12 What is the difference between expenditures per unit and cost per unit? Explain.

10–13 What data should a governmental cost accounting system provide for the use of managers and voters?

10–14 What is the difference between sustentation costs and service implementation costs for a health and welfare organization? Why is it important to divide the expenses of such an organization into these two categories? Explain.

EXERCISES

10–15 **Journal Entries** During July, the TL Management (TLM) Group worked 200 hours for COARM Steel, 100 hours for the Computer Information Institute, and 40 hours for Western Steel. TLM bills clients at the rate of $110 an hour, while professional fees earned by freelance consultants used by TLM average $50 an hour. Overhead is charged to clients on the basis of 80% of professional fees paid. The billing rate is intended to provide net operating income to the firm equal to 20% of fees charged.

Actual overhead expenses amounted to $14,000. There is no service in progress on either July 1 or July 31.

REQUIRED:

1. Prepare general journal entries for all July transactions.
2. Prepare an income statement for TLM Group for the month of July.
3. Comment on the results of operations for July.

10–16 **Pricing Services** American Cleaning Company, Inc., is preparing to bid on a contract to furnish janitorial services to a university. American projects the following estimates of annual costs of providing the services:

Direct labor	$1,000,000
Fringe benefits	230,000
Supervision	150,000
Office and administration	80,000
Cleaning supplies	3,200
Depreciation of equipment	25,000
	$1,488,200

REQUIRED:

1. Assume American's policy is to quote a fixed contract price that is 20% above the total costs expected to be incurred. What annual fee would American Cleaning Company quote?
2. Assume American obtains the contract and that actual costs for the first year are the same as those projected. Prepare an income statement for the first year's operations.

10–17 **Planning** Personal Financial Counselors, Inc., which conducts seminars and performs personal financial counseling, estimates its overhead for the coming year will be $760,000. The firm estimates that 20,000 hours of professional services costing $50 per hour will be provided. Other direct costs of engagements are expected to be $40,000 for the year. Clients are billed on the basis of hours of services provided. The hourly billing rate is established at a level designed to produce net operating revenues equal to 20% of billings.

REQUIRED:

1. Calculate the billing rate per hour.
2. Prepare a projected income statement for Personal Financial Counselors for the next year.
3. Assume the firm wishes to realize operating income of $500,000. Compute the average billing rate per hour that Personal Financial Counselors will have to use in order to achieve that operating income objective.

10–18 **Cost per Unit of Service** Metropolitan International Bank has a department that issues letters of credit for its own customers and, upon the request and recommendation of other banks, for selected individuals who are not regular customers.

During January, the International Letter of Credit Department incurred the following costs:

Salaries	$7,580
Credit investigation costs	415
Depreciation, equipment	220
Telephone, Telex, and electronic funds transfer fees	310
Miscellaneous costs	90

January general costs of $1,800, including charges for space occupied, utilities, security, and cleaning, are allocated to the International Letter of Credit Department.

Interest and fees earned on 25 letters of credit, representing $8,680,000 in confirmed (guaranteed) funds, issued and outstanding during the period (including net interest earned on funds required to be deposited at Metropolitan) totaled $12,750.

REQUIRED:

1. Compute the total cost of service provided by Metropolitan's International Letter of Credit Department.
2. What is the cost of service provided:
   a. per $100,000 guaranteed?
   b. per letter of credit?

10–19 **Quasi-Profit Enterprise Costs** The Northern Direct Marketing Trade Association provides a central organization to conduct direct marketing research and publish research reports and a monthly trade magazine for its members. Annual dues are $175 for each of its 1,500 members. During 19X6, the association's operating results included the following items:

Item	Amount
Research grants	$ 43,750
Publishing expenses	
Research projects	5,480
Magazine	156,000
General and administrative expenses	51,200
Advertising income (magazine)	(36,000)

For fiscal year 19X6, management spent 20% of its time monitoring research projects. Approximately 65% of management's time was spent on the publication of the association's magazine. The remaining 15% was spent on keeping the organization functioning.

REQUIRED: Based on 19X6 results, compute the following:

1. cost per member of Northern's research program
2. cost of each magazine, assuming 1,500 copies are printed each month
3. cost per member for maintaining the organization.

Then prepare an income statement for the year. Comment on the operating results reflected in the statement.

10–20 **Club Costs** The Ballroom Dance Club is an organization committed to the preservation and furtherance of ballroom dancing. Club officers and the board of directors serve without compensation. Membership fees of $125 per person per year entitle members to attend 10 dances each year. Average membership was 258 during the 19X5–19X8 period. The club began fiscal year 19X9 with $7,500 in surplus funds and the expectation that it would have 250 paid members during that year. The following costs were incurred during 19X9:

Orchestras	$25,300
Room rentals	4,550
Postage and clerical costs	1,950
Miscellaneous expenses	385

Paid members during 19X9 totaled 178, and the club netted $1,225 from the sale of drinks at the dances.

REQUIRED:

1. What would have been the cost incurred per member in 19X9 if the Ballroom Dance Club had enrolled a membership of 250?
2. What was the actual cost per member in 19X9?
3. What action would you recommend to the Ballroom Dance Club's board of directors?

10–21 **Hospital Ratio of Costs to Revenues** Crestview Hospital allocates all costs to revenue-producing departments and uses past experience, adjusted for expected changes, to bill patients. Patients are assigned to departments based on space available and degree of care required. To evaluate the productivity (number of discharged patients) and efficiency (profitability) of each department, Crestview calculates a ratio of departmental costs to revenues realized from services provided for patients.
  Data for a recent period included the following:

	Department			
	1	2	3	4
Direct costs	$4,500	$16,800	$ 7,300	$12,400
Indirect costs	4,725	17,640	7,665	13,020
Patient revenues	8,487	32,718	17,958	26,691
Billing units	100	500	1,000	50

REQUIRED:

1. Compute the ratio of costs to revenues for each of Crestview's revenue-producing departments.
2. Calculate the average billing price per unit of service.

3. How is Crestview Hospital's cost system similar to a process cost system for a manufacturing firm? How is it dissimilar? Explain.

10–22 **Cost Information for a Pure-Nonprofit Organization** Neighbors, United is a nonprofit civic organization established to serve as a conduit between individuals and food merchants who are willing to donate surplus and damaged but usable food items to needy individuals in the community. With the exception of one paid employee, all labor is donated. Neighbors, United received a $30,000 grant from the United Way and reported the following operating information for the fiscal year just ended:

Expenses	
Salary	$29,700
Rent and utilities	6,600
Truck	1,950
Postage	390
Number of meals served	40,250

REQUIRED:

1. Compute the amount of funds Neighbors, United had to raise from donations during the past fiscal year.
2. What was Neighbors, United's cost per meal served?

PROBLEMS

10–23 **Cost per Unit of Service: T Accounts** Instant Pest Control Company has three departments: residential contract, commercial contract, and specialty. Two employees are assigned to each department. Residential contract employees have a predetermined schedule of houses to spray each day, and they earn $8 an hour. Because of problems in coordinating times with homeowners, the average number of homes sprayed per day is six. Commercial contract employees also have a predetermined schedule of businesses to service, earn $9 per hour, and usually do not have idle time.

One of the two employees handling specialty assignments also is the office supervisor and goes out on calls (locking the office and activating an answering machine to take incoming telephone calls) only when the other specialty employee gets overloaded or a customer complaint needs to be handled. The office supervisor earns $2,000 a month, while the specialty employee earns $10 per hour.

Detailed time and expense records are kept for each department, reflecting the following information for October:

	Residential Contract	Commercial Contract	Specialty Office Manager	Other
Sales revenue	$8,300	$12,700	$625	$3,500
Hours on service calls	260	340	30	104
Hours not on service calls	84	0	143	69

Departmental Overhead Costs	Residential Contract	Commercial Contract	Specialty
Chemicals	$1,300	$1,750	$574
Truck operation (allocated cost)	240	210	190
Equipment Depreciation	350	350	350

Other overhead (common costs) incurred during October totaled $1,200.

REQUIRED:

1. Compute the direct cost per service call hour for Instant Pest Control's three departments for the month of October.
2. Assuming there were no service-in-progress inventories on October 1 or 31, show the flow of costs through T accounts.
3. Prepare an income statement for Instant Pest Control for October showing operating results by department. Instant Pest Control does not allocate common costs to departments.

10–24 The legal firm of Winget and Winget has the following staff:

Category	Number
Attorneys	6
Paraprofessionals	3
Office staff	4

The three senior attorneys bill their time at $126.50 per hour. The other three attorneys have a billing rate of $80.50 an hour. Paraprofessional time is charged to clients at a rate of $41.25 an hour. The rates include a provision for overhead and a 25% markup on direct-labor cost (cost of professional time of attorneys and paraprofessionals) for profit. The overhead rate for attorneys is 105% of direct-labor cost and for paraprofessionals is 150% of direct-labor cost.

Information on open cases on August 1, 19X1, included the following unbilled amounts:

Case	Filing Fees	Miscellaneous Expense	Professional Fees	Total
JN-15110	$220	$50	$910	$1,180
KR-26100	75	20	240	335

During August, the following time was logged on cases in progress:

	Hours		
Case Number	Senior Attorneys	Attorneys	Paraprofessionals
JN-15110	30	50	60
KR-26100	80	90	30
BB-03972	50	70	75
CP-69000	60	80	20

Costs incurred on behalf of clients during August included filing fees of $160 paid in connection with case CP-69000 and miscellaneous expenses recorded for the following cases:

Case Number	Miscellaneous Expense, August
JN-15110	$25
KR-26100	40
BB-03972	90
CP-69000	30

Overhead for August, including all office staff salaries, amounted to $21,300. Statements were sent out to clients on August 31 for the following amounts:

Case Number	Statement Amount
JN-15110	$11,395
KR-26100	17,655
BB-03972	14,015
CP-69000	14,645

Service in progress (unbilled) on August 31 included:

Case Number	Professional Time	Overhead	Total
KR-26100	$480	$540	$1,020
BB-03972	400	465	865
CP-69000	120	135	255

REQUIRED:

1. Prepare T accounts for service in progress, cost of services rendered, overhead incurred, overhead applied, and each open case. Post all August transactions to the T accounts. Underapplied and overapplied overhead will not be formally recognized and closed until the end of the current fiscal year (June 30, 19X2).
2. Prepare summary general journal entries for the month of August.
3. Prepare an income statement for Winget and Winget for the month of August.

10–25 **T Account: Cost per Service Unit** Handyman for Hire, Inc., provides maintenance personnel that perform all types of routine maintenance and minor home repairs for residential customers. In return for a set monthly fee, homeowners may subscribe to a schedule of benefits consisting of a set number of nonchargeable service calls and a predetermined fixed rate for various types of repairs and maintenance.

Because of a lack of qualified applicants for maintenance positions, Handyman has decided to conduct classes for trainees that will provide a pool of applicants for the firm. Initially, no charge will be made for attending the classes.

During an experimental four-week training session, the following information was accumulated:

Cost	Amount
Instruction	$3,950
Rental of facilities	600
Books and supplies	900
Depreciation of equipment	730
Number of trainees starting classes	10
Number of trainees completing classes	6
Number of class graduates hired	3

Handyman has found that the average maintenance employee works for the firm approximately two years. Because of this high employee turnover rate, Handyman needs to run three training sessions each year to meet their employee needs.

During the past year, Handyman paid 25 maintenance personnel $420,000 in wages and salaries and incurred the following other costs:

Item	Amount
Rent	$12,000
Office staff salaries	44,600
Payroll taxes	53,300
Other taxes and insurance	9,100
Depreciation, vehicles	37,500
Depreciation, equipment	3,580
Advertising	3,250
Supplies	900
Miscellaneous	1,100

Overhead equal to 40% of direct maintenance personnel costs is applied to services rendered during the year.

Handyman maintenance personnel responded to 35,000 calls during the past year.

REQUIRED:

1. Show the flow of costs through T accounts for Handyman for the past year.
2. Compute the cost per service call for Handyman for the past year, ignoring the training session costs.
3. If Handyman decides to continue the training program, what will be the cost per service call?
4. What other factors should Handyman consider in connection with its employee-retention problem?

10–26 **Service Process Flowchart: Service Department Allocation** Each region of the North American Fire and Casualty Company is organized into five divisions: sales, underwriting, policy service, claims, and office service (supplies and mail). Agents have their own offices in various locations within a three- to five-state region and send applications for insurance to their regional office. Commissions are paid monthly to the agents on the policies that have been issued during the previous month.

The sales division is managed by a sales director who maintains an office in the regional office but spends most of his time in the field recruiting and training agents and managers.

Applications received by a regional office are sent to the underwriting department for acceptance, rejection, or further study (pending the arrival of additional information). Rejected applications are processed separately, and appropriate rejection letters are sent to the applicants. Approved and rejected applications are then forwarded to the policy service department.

The policy service department enters the information into a computer located in the home office in California. This computer prints the appropriate policy for approved applications, prepares statements, and updates agent commission records. Detailed information from rejected applications also is stored on the computer. At the end of each day, the main computer downloads active file information processed that day for each region to computers located in the regional office. Agents within each region can then access their policy information through links to their regional computer. Policies are mailed in bulk from the printing office in California to the appropriate regional office for distribution to local agents.

Policy service personnel also correct errors, make changes, and handle complaints. The claims department handles all claims.

Because claims can be made on an insurance policy after the policy has expired for events occurring during the policy period, North American sets up reserves for claims based on detailed actuarial information.

Results for the Utah region of North American Fire and Casualty Company for the previous year are as follows:

Premiums written	$310,860,000
Claims paid	134,033,140
Claims pending	53,157,100
Reserves for claims incurred but not reported	20,651,600
Interest earned on premiums	930,500
Underwriting department direct costs	1,400,800
Sales department direct costs (excluding agent commissions)	210,700
Agent commissions	46,629,000
Policy service department direct costs	4,400,000
Claims department direct costs	15,543,000
Office service department direct costs	308,300
Building costs (depreciation, maintenance, security, taxes, etc.)	203,200
Regional general and administrative costs	248,400
Home office costs (primarily computer costs)	6,217,200

Building costs are allocated on the basis of square feet of space occupied. General and administrative costs are allocated to departments based on number of employees. Service department costs are allocated 80% to sales, 8% to underwriting, 6% to policy service, and 6% to claims. The Utah region uses the direct method to allocate common costs, allocating building costs first, then general and administrative costs, then service department costs. The following data are used for common cost allocation:

	Department				
	Sales	Underwriting	Policy Service	Claims	Total
Square footage occupied	1,000	10,000	40,000	2,000	53,000
Number of employees	625*	45	200	30*	900

*Includes personnel not officed at the regional office.

REQUIRED:

1. Prepare a service process flowchart for the Utah region of North American Fire and Casualty Insurance Company. Use the following boxes in your flowchart.

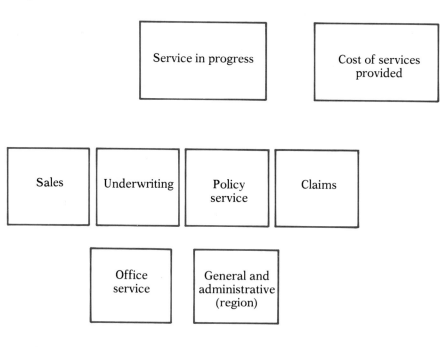

2. Show the Utah region flow of costs through T accounts.
3. Compute the operating income for the Utah region of North American Fire and Casualty Company for the previous year.

10–27   **Cost per Facility: Tracing Direct Costs**   The Diamond Athletic Club has 850 members who paid an average initiation fee of $200 and who pay dues of $50 per month. Facilities provided to members include tennis courts, racquetball courts, an indoor and an outdoor swimming pool, two weight rooms (one of which has an indoor jogging track), an outdoor jogging track, and locker rooms equipped with Jacuzzis and saunas. Club policy currently does not permit members to bring guests.

Costs incurred in 19X9 include the following:

Lifeguards	$14,980
Pool supplies	790
Pool maintenance and repairs	420
Tennis net replacement	675
Refinishing racquetball courts	1,750
Salaries	
Club director	62,500
Weight room director	32,600
Club employees	110,000
Clerical/administrative employees	34,300
Janitorial/cleaning employees	44,670
Depreciation	
Building	22,200
Equipment	37,500
Swimming pools	14,500
Tennis courts (including lights)	33,300
Tracks	3,200
General building maintenance	3,000
Taxes	4,200
Insurance	28,400
Miscellaneous	1,860
Advertising	6,850

The club is considering changing its policy regarding guests. In determining the fees to be charged for guest services, Jane Jones, the club director, has decided she needs information about operating costs for each of the club's service facilities (tennis courts, racquetball courts, swimming pools, weight rooms, and tracks). The club operates 300 hours per month.

The following information has been accumulated to be used in allocating costs of operation to each of the club's facilities:

Cost	Basis Used to Trace Cost	Detail						
		Tennis Court	Racquetball Court	Pools	Weight Room	Track	Locker Room	General Operations
Club employees' salaries	Time spent in area	23%	10%	20%	17%	3%	2%	25%
Janitorial employees' salaries	Time spent in area	3%	8%	19%	20%	5%	30%	24%
Depreciation, building	Square footage occupied	0	4,000	6,000	9,000	1,000	5,000	3,000

(Continues)

		Detail						
Cost	Basis Used to Trace Cost	Tennis Court	Racquetball Court	Pools	Weight Room	Track	Locker Room	General Operations
Depreciation, equipment	Investment in equipment (percentage of total)	8%	0%	4%	85%	0%	2%	1%
General building maintenance	Square footage occupied	0	4,000	6,000	10,000	0	5,000	5,000
Taxes	Square footage occupied	0	4,000	6,000	10,000	0	5,000	5,000
Insurance	Square footage occupied	0	4,000	6,000	10,000	0	5,000	5,000

Common costs include salaries for the club director and clerical/administrative employees, costs associated with locker rooms and general operations, miscellaneous costs, and advertising costs. It is felt these costs cannot beneficially be traced to any particular club service facility, so they are to be allocated, arbitrarily, on the basis of the following estimated average member hours of usage each month:

	Area of Club				
	Tennis Court	Racquetball Court	Pools	Weight Room	Track
Average member hours of usage per month	7,400	3,900	1,800	6,500	2,400

1. Compute Diamond Athletic Club's overall cost per member per month.
2. Compute the cost per member, per month, for operating the
    a. tennis courts
    b. racquetball courts
    c. swimming pools
    d. weight rooms
    e. tracks.
3. What additional calculations might be useful to Ms. Jones? Discuss.

10–28   Using Cost Data for Fund-Raising Purposes The School of Music of Wright University, which occupies one of the oldest buildings on campus, is planning a campaign to raise funds to build a new music building and provide endowment for scholarships for music majors. Because music instruction requires very small classes or one-on-one instruction and individual practice rooms, the cost per student credit hour is assumed to be much higher for the School of Music than for the rest of Wright University. However, there are no hard data to support this assumption.

In order to have the necessary information to complete proposals to various foundations and to prepare solicitation letters to be used in the campaign, the dean of the School of Music has secured the following data from the university controller:

	Average Annual Amounts for Previous Three Years			
	School of Business	School of Education	Arts and Sciences	School of Music
Direct operating costs excluding depreciation	$6,240,000	$2,496,000	$11,024,000	$1,040,000
Facilities costs	$3,200,000	$160,000	$2,900,000	$35,000
Student hours enrolled	49,800	21,248	106,000	3,320

University administration costs of $12,400,000 are allocated to the above university divisions on the basis of direct operating costs.

REQUIRED:

1. Compute the average cost per student credit hour, excluding depreciation, for the School of Business, School of Education, Arts and Sciences, and School of Music.
2. Discuss the impact of facilities costs on the analysis.
3. As an outside consultant, what recommendation(s) would you make to the university administration concerning the allocation of general university costs?

10–29 Allocation of Hospital Operating Costs Maley Memorial Hospital has followed the procedure of matching revenues and expenses at the revenue-producing departmental level because reimbursement from insurance companies and the government (Medicare) has been tied to the billing rates for those departments. Maley is now in the process of refining its budgets for the year 19X6. It will use a variety of information, including the following actual data for the year ending December 31, 19X5:

	Revenue-Producing Cost Centers			**Supporting Cost Centers**	
	Dept. 1	Dept. 2	Dept. 3	Dept. 4	Dept. 5
Direct costs	$327,908	$655,940	$491,848	$82,000	$164,000
Allocated general costs	65,600	98,400	123,000	24,600	32,800
Totals	$393,508	$754,400	$614,848	$106,600	$196,800
Billing units	54,120	8,692	34,645		
Charges (revenues)	$468,768	$901,692	$767,050		

Department 4 costs are allocated to revenue-producing departments on the basis of number of employees. Department 5 costs are allocated on the basis of square footage. Relevant allocation data are:

	Dept. 1	Dept. 2	Dept. 3	Dept. 4	Dept. 5
Employees	50	30	10	15	10
Square footage	3,280	9,840	3,280	1,040	1,280

Maley uses the step method to allocate supporting center costs to revenue-producing departments. Department 4 costs are to be allocated first. The level of operations for 19X6 is expected to be approximately the same as for 19X5 (approximately 83% of capacity).

REQUIRED:

1. Prepare a schedule showing the total costs expected to be incurred by the three revenue-producing cost centers in 19X6.
2. Based on your answers to requirement 1, compute for each revenue-producing department the
   a. cost per unit of service
   b. billing rate per unit of service
   c. ratio of costs to charges (revenues).
3. Which department(s) appear(s) to be most profitable?

10–30   Nonprofit Counseling Center Costs The Golden Triangle Family Counseling Center is preparing budget requests for the coming year to be submitted to three municipalities and the state. Inasmuch as benefits of the Family Counseling Center to the community are impossible to measure objectively, the center has decided to analyze the cost of its various treatment programs to provide information to substantiate its request for funds for the coming year. The center engages in family counseling, substance abuse counseling and psychological testing and evaluation of individuals referred by various governmental or educational units.

Total costs expected to be incurred in the coming year included the following:

Professional salaries	
Psychologists (2 full time)	$120,000
Counselors (LPC) (10 full time)	300,000
Registered nurses (2 full time)	50,000
General and administrative salaries (1 director, 5 staff)	150,000
Rent, utilities, supplies	98,000
Test forms and grading	49,000

Based on previous experience, the time of the professional staff is expected to be allocated to the three programs and administrative tasks as follows:

	Professional Staff Time			
	Family Counseling	Substance Abuse Counseling	Testing and Evaluation	Administration
Psychologists	25%	35%	20%	20%
Counselors	28%	42%	25%	5%
Nurses	5%	45%	0%	50%

The Golden Triangle Family Counseling Center estimates it will treat 15,000 persons in the family counseling program, 6,100 in the substance abuse counseling program, and 7,500 in its testing and evaluation program. General and administrative costs are to be allocated to the three programs on the basis of number of persons going through the three programs.

REQUIRED: Prepare a schedule showing costs expected to be allocated to the family counseling, substance abuse counseling, and testing and evaluation programs for the coming year. The projection for each program should show: (a) a listing of operating costs; (b) the percentage of total cost represented by each individual item of cost; and (c) the cost per person treated.

10–31 **THOUGHT STIMULATION PROBLEM—United States Government Facility.** The Missouri River Project is a facility constructed by the United States Government over a 30-year period to produce refined uranium and other nuclear materials for government use. Management of the operation is contracted out to a private firm. A simplified diagram of the project's power sources is shown in Figure 10–2.

Since a total loss of power could be catastrophic in a nuclear reaction process, the Missouri River Project includes numerous power plants designed to supply the minimum amount of critical power to reactors, to the refinery, and to certain administration and maintenance buildings in the event of total failure of its outside power source. All reactors have their own power plants. To provide an appropriate power distribution, power in excess of the critical minimum amount required to maintain a reactor is transferred to a power grid that routes the power from the on-site power plants, as well as power from the outside supplier, to all facilities in the complex. The power plants were constructed over a 30-year period, and the newer plants are far more efficient than the older plants. The larger power plants also have some economies of scale not available to the smaller power plants.

The cost-allocation system for power has been modified extensively over the years, but currently involves the proration of actual costs incurred by a power plant between the facilities served and the power grid. The actual cost of all power coming into the power grid is averaged and charged to users at an average rate per kilowatt hour.

Managers of some of the reactors serviced by older, smaller power plants object to the allocation system. They claim their costs of operation are higher because of the inefficient power plants they are forced to use.

The current management company has decided to redesign the power cost-allocation system.

REQUIRED:

1. Since this is a nonprofit operation, is there a need to be concerned about specific allocations of costs?
2. What general allocation procedure would you recommend?

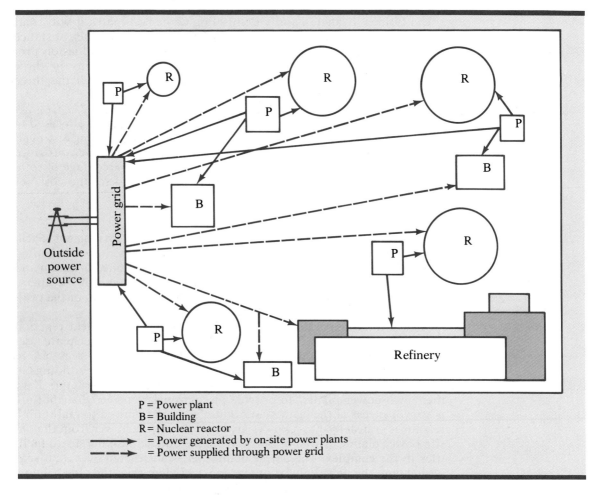

P = Power plant
B = Building
R = Nuclear reactor
———▶ = Power generated by on-site power plants
– – –▶ = Power supplied through power grid

FIGURE 10–2   Missouri River Project Power Sources

10–32   THOUGHT PROJECTION PROBLEM—University Cost Accounting. Central
States University is involved in providing educational and research services. Because of its world-renowned faculty, Central States University
conducts a considerable number of research projects for the United
States government. Most of these projects include a provision for overhead costs associated with them. Almost inevitably, there is disagreement
between the university and the government regarding the proper amount
of add-on percentage to be included for overhead. In the past, this disagreement has been negotiated from somewhat polarized positions, with
Central States University administrators seeking the largest percentage
add-on that could be realized and representatives of the government attempting to settle for a lower percentage. The university has no cost
accounting system that can be used to justify any specific overhead application rate.

The university operates with the following organizational units:

Maintenance Department
Food Services Department
Utilities Department
Computation Center
University Administration
Schools
Libraries
Laboratories
Buildings and Grounds Department

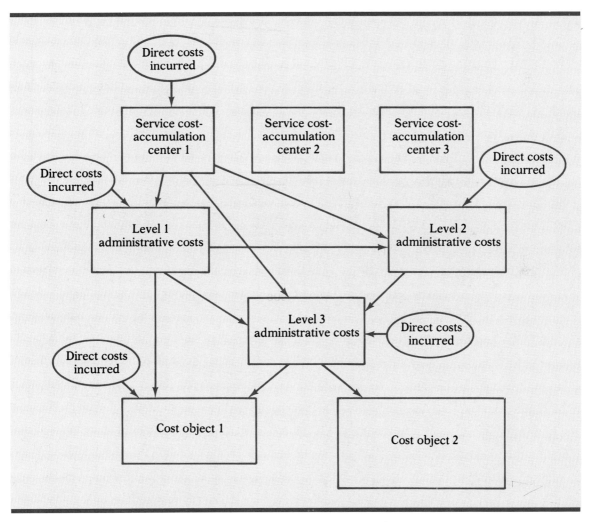

FIGURE 10–3 Suggested Flowchart Approach to Accompany Problem 10–32.

Note: Schools perform the administrative tasks of development of school policy, approval of curriculum, authorization of faculty positions (subject to university approval), and so forth. Each school is organized into departments that perform administrative tasks of scheduling classes, recruiting faculty, and so on.

REQUIRED: Assuming that the *products* provided by Central States University are (a) student credit hours (organized by department) and (b) completed research projects, design a logical cost accounting system to reasonably allocate all costs as closely as possible on a cause-and-effect basis to productive output. Your design should be in the form of a flowchart with a box for each cost-accumulation center. An example of the general flowchart approach suggested is Figure 10–3.

Part III

Standard Cost Systems

Chapter 11

Installing the System and Estimating Costs

Learning Objectives

When you have finished your study of this chapter and its appendix, you should:

1. Know what a standard cost card is and how it is used in a standard cost system.
2. Know how quantitative and dollar amounts shown on standard cost cards are derived.
3. Be able to use the scattergraph and high–low, two-point methods to determine the fixed and variable elements of semivariable costs, and be able to use the output of regression analysis to determine the fixed and variable elements of semivariable costs.
4. Understand the three different levels of expectations that may be incorporated into standard costs and how they affect expected variances.
5. Know how to convert production measured in units into standard hours of production.

C hapters 4–10 described two systems (job order and process cost) used to accumulate and allocate **historical costs** of manufacturing (which include actual direct materials, actual direct labor, and actual or applied overhead) for the purpose of meeting the four objectives of cost accounting. These systems meet the first of those objectives very well—the development of cost data that can be used in assigning values to work-in-process and finished goods inventories. They do not, however, always provide the most useful information for meeting the other three objectives (planning, controlling, and decision making). In using these cost systems or some variation of them, management must plan operations, control operations, and make day-to-day operating decisions on the basis of historical costs. Therefore, if the historical (that is, **actual**) **cost** data are derived from inefficient operations, management may be planning, controlling, and making operating decisions that incorporate those same inefficiencies. A more satisfactory arrangement, particularly for firms producing long-life-cycle products, calls for the *predetermination* of what costs should be and the subsequent use of those data in carrying out planning, controlling, and decision making. Such projected cost data can be in the form of *estimated costs* or in the form of *standard costs*.

Estimated costs generally are based on historical cost data adjusted for expected changes in operations; therefore they have some of the same weaknesses historical costs have. **Standard costs**, however, are carefully projected theoretical costs that reflect a combination of quantity and unit-cost goals that are expected to be met in the efficient production of goods or services. They are based on what *should be* achieved if operations are carried out effectively and efficiently.

The following example regarding unit costs should help you understand the differences between historical costs, estimated costs, and standard costs. Recall that many elements of overhead costs are fixed. As a result, cost per unit will be affected by the level of operations achieved. Because of fixed costs, all other things being the same, cost per unit will be lower with a higher volume of production and higher with a lower level of operations. Therefore, as we cite different kinds of unit costs for illustrative purposes, we are implicitly assuming the same level of production for each type (historical, estimated, or standard) cost.

Suppose the actual cost of producing one unit of product is determined from the cost-of-production report or job-order cost sheet to be:

Actual Cost per Unit	
Direct materials	$ 4.20
Conversion cost (direct labor and overhead)	6.10
Total	$10.30

Using this historical information, plus the fact that a new piece of equipment should reduce conversion costs by 20%, the estimated cost per unit for the next period would be:

Estimated Cost per Unit

Direct materials	$4.20
Conversion cost ($6.10 × 0.80)	4.88
Total	$9.08

However, an industrial engineer reports (based on a thorough investigation and analysis of operations) that the cost per unit using the new equipment *should* be as follows:

Standard Cost per Unit

Direct materials	$4.10
Conversion cost	4.25
Total	$8.35

Observe that the targeted standard cost per unit ($8.35) apparently has eliminated certain inefficiencies incorporated into the historical cost data. It is based on an analysis of operations to determine what the costs should be rather than on what costs have been in the past.

The use of standard (predetermined) costs can provide more useful information for planning, controlling, and decision making by setting out specific goals to be met and by incorporating into those activities the principle of **management by exception**. As long as standards are being met (or variances that are generated are immaterial), management does not need to take any action. When significant variances occur, however, the exception is reported to management and an investigation launched. A standard cost system is designed primarily to call attention to the variances from standard and secondarily to generate the values to be assigned to inventories and cost of sales.

The budgeting (planning) process is especially facilitated by the use of standard cost data. If the standard (predetermined) costs are carefully set, they will represent goals the firm can expect to achieve if operations are carried out as they should be. Also, by measuring the differences between those standards and actual achievements (**variances**), management needs give attention only to those situations in which actual accomplishments deviate significantly from original expectations. If a standard cost per unit is achieved, or nearly achieved, management attention can be given to other problem-solving or planning activities. Because standard costs per unit include fixed costs, deviations from standards may be caused by either operational inefficiencies or by an unexpected change in the volume of operations. We deal with the calculations of variances and identification of the causes of deviations from standards in Chapters 12 and 13.

Standard (predetermined) costs, in a variety of formats, can be used with a traditional absorption-costing system or a direct (variable) costing system. Direct costing, defined earlier, is discussed further in Chapter 14. Problem 14–31 (page 540) demonstrates the use of standard costs in such a direct cost system. Standard costs also can be used within either a job-order or process-costing format. The system to be used (job order or process) is determined by the operating characteristics of the firm, regardless of whether historical or standard costs are used. Whichever system is used, however, projected costs must be very carefully established if they are to be effective in meeting the planning, controlling, and decision-making objectives. Because standard cost systems are more often installed within a process-costing format, most of our illustrations pertain to process costing.

In this chapter, we explain the basic considerations that underlie the establishment of a cost accounting system using standard cost data. We shall

- describe standard cost data and illustrate how the data on materials and direct labor included in the standard cost cards are derived
- show how mixed costs that are partly variable and partly fixed can be divided into pure variable and fixed components
- illustrate how standard overhead rates are derived
- discuss the types of standards that may be incorporated into a standard cost system
- explain how production is measured when using a standard cost system
- deal with the problem of assigning values to inventories
- describe the records required for implementing a standard cost system
- summarize the unique characteristics of a job-order standard cost system.

The Standard Cost Card

The foundation of any standard cost system is the **standard cost card** (or standard cost sheet). One of these cards or sheets is prepared for each item of materials and for each product being manufactured. The information on these cards also can be stored in a computer file. The standard cost cards for products being manufactured must be organized so standard cost values can be assigned to partially completed units as well as to completed units. To demonstrate, we shall return to the Ajax Chemical Company illustration from Chapter 6 and explain how a standard cost system could be established for Ajax to replace the historical cost system described in that chapter. In Chapters 12 and 13, we describe and illustrate the operation of Ajax's standard cost system.

For this chapter, we make the following changes in the assumed data for Ajax Chemical Company: (1) The term *units* will be changed to *pounds*. (2) The units placed in process will be changed to show an assumed number of pounds of each of three raw materials placed in process (material A, material B, and material C).

Establishing Standard Costs for Direct Materials

As we have already observed, the standard cost system requires predetermination of the standard cost per unit for each item of materials that will be used in the manufacturing process. This may be reflected on individual cards for each item of materials inventory or on a list of items in inventory showing a standard cost for each of the items. To facilitate the handling of these data, it is important to assign part numbers to each item in materials inventory so the items will not be confused with one another and to facilitate computerization of the inventory record. Even with a just-in-time inventory system, where the ideal situation involves a zero materials inventory, materials pass, at least momentarily, through "materials inventory" status prior to entering the manufacturing process (and the work-in-process inventory account).

Generally speaking, the purchasing department of a firm should provide the primary information leading to the establishment of standard costs per unit for each of the individual materials inventory items. These costs must take into consideration the qualitative standards to be met for each item as well as the quantities likely to be purchased on each order. In our illustration, these costs are assumed to be $2.00, $2.20, and $1.70 per pound for raw materials A, B, and C, respectively (see Figure 11–1).

To arrive at the standard cost of direct materials for each finished product, we must next project the quantities of each element of raw material required to produce the finished product. Those quantities are assumed to be 0.3, 0.3, and 0.4 pounds for raw materials A, B, and C, respectively (see Figure 11–2). These standard quantities are then multiplied by the standard cost per unit (pound) of raw material to arrive at the total standard cost of each element of direct materials required for one unit of finished product (see Figure 11–2). The projected cost for the individual direct materials items are then added together to determine the $1.94 total standard cost of direct materials for the finished product (see Figure 11–2).

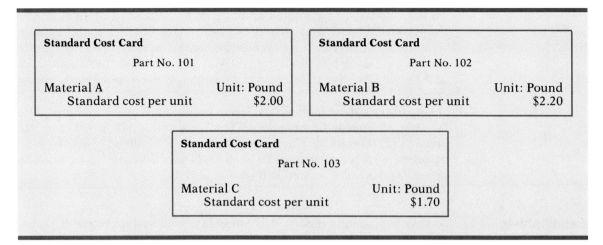

FIGURE 11–1   Standard Cost Cards for Materials A, B, and C

Standard Cost Card

Finished Product No. 5001

	Quantity	Cost per Pound	Total Cost
Direct materials			
Material A (part 101)	0.3 pound	$2.00	$ .60
Material B (part 102)	0.3 pound	$2.20	$ .66
Material C (part 103)	0.4 pound	$1.70	$ .68
Total standard cost of direct materials			$1.94
	Hours	**Rate per Hour**	
Direct labor	0.2 hour	$8.00	1.60
Manufacturing overhead	0.2 hour	$9.50	1.90
Total standard cost per pound of finished product			$5.44

FIGURE 11–2   Standard Cost Card for Finished Product No. 5001

Establishing Standard Costs for Direct Labor

In determining the cost to be shown on the standard cost card for direct labor, the operations or processes required to produce the product must be studied carefully to arrive at the amount of time that should be spent in carrying out each operation or process. This is generally done by conducting engineering time studies of each of those operations or processes as they are performed by employees who have an appropriate level of expertise. This yields the *predetermined (standard) hours* of direct labor required to produce the finished product. In Figure 11–2 this was determined to be 0.2 hours per unit. If a product requires multiple operations, a separate standard time would be determined for each operation.

Next the accountant, establishing a standard cost system, must determine a *standard rate of pay per hour* for each of the operations. In some instances, the standard rate may be set in the union labor contract. In other instances, the accountant may have to work with the personnel department in determining the rate per hour that the company should expect to pay for labor to perform each of the operations. In Figure 11–2 that is assumed to be $8 per hour. The total amount of standard direct labor cost per unit, then, can be calculated by multiplying the standard hours allowed (0.2 hours for Ajax) by the standard rate per hour ($8 per hour for Ajax).

Establishing Standard Manufacturing-Overhead Costs

In our earlier discussion of the allocation of manufacturing overhead to the units of product being manufactured, we explained how an overhead application rate (that is, a predetermined overhead rate) could be developed by relating the projected amount of manufacturing overhead shown in the flexible budget for the expected level of operations to some activity base—generally direct labor in a labor-intensive manufacturing operation. The flexible budget also is used in establishing a standard overhead rate for a standard cost system. In standard cost systems where overhead is "caused" by direct labor, the amount of projected overhead for a period of time (generally one year) is divided by the projected number of total standard labor hours for the period to get the *standard (predetermined) overhead rate per direct labor hour*. Total standard labor hours is calculated by multiplying the number of units *expected* to be produced by the standard time (hours) shown on the standard cost cards for those units. The rate per standard hour is then calculated as follows:

$$\frac{\text{Estimated total overhead}}{\begin{array}{c}\text{Estimated total units}\\\text{to be produced}\end{array}} \times \begin{array}{c}\text{Standard direct}\\\text{labor hours per unit}\end{array} = \begin{array}{c}\text{Standard overhead}\\\text{rate per standard}\\\text{direct labor hour}\end{array}$$

The predetermined (standard) overhead rate per standard direct-labor hour is then multiplied by the standard labor hours required to produce one unit of product to arrive at the standard manufacturing-overhead cost per unit of product ($1.90 in Figure 11–2).

In Chapter 4, we pointed out that all manufacturing-overhead costs should be classified as either fixed or variable so we could predict their behaviors in relation to changes in the level of operations. In the process of predetermining a standard cost per hour or per unit for overhead, we must examine the behavior of individual items of overhead more carefully. We will typically find that some overhead costs are *semivariable* rather than completely variable or completely fixed. These costs will vary to some extent with changes in the level of operations but not directly in relation to those changes. Utility costs, for example, might be $2,200 when 3,000 units are produced ($.7333 per unit) but increase to only $2,800 when 4,000 units are produced ($.70 per unit). If utility costs were totally variable, the cost per unit would be the same within a relevant range of activity levels.

Because of the importance of separating semivariable (mixed) costs into their variable and fixed elements for purposes other than establishing standard overhead costs, we shall cover the separation techniques in the following major section, after which we will return to our discussion of standard overhead costs. You will need to refer to these separation techniques anytime a cost has to be separated into variable and fixed elements—for example, when you want to prepare a variable- (direct-) costing income statement (Chapter 14), when you want to prepare a detailed master budget (Chapter 15), or when you want to perform cost–volume–profit analysis (Chapter 16).

Allocation of Semivariable (Mixed) Costs

Semivariable, or *mixed*, *costs* vary with the level of production, though not in direct relation to it, presumably because part of the cost is fixed while the rest is variable. The problem, then, becomes one of identifying the fixed and variable portions of the mixed cost, so the fixed part can be included as part of fixed costs and the variable portion included with the other variable costs. The cost of electricity where there is a basic minimum charge plus a specified cost per kilowatt hour above the minimum is an example of such a semivariable cost.

One of the most important steps in estimating the variable and fixed components of a mixed cost is to examine the cause-and-effect relationships between activities that affect costs (independent variables) and the cost to be estimated (dependent variable). We may logically assume, for example, that electricity cost (dependent variable) increases as direct-labor hours (independent variable) increases.

If we wish to relate those costs to direct-labor hours, we can consider the total cost of electricity as being a combination of fixed- and variable-cost elements, as shown in Figure 11–3.

We will now illustrate four methods of separating mixed costs into fixed and variable components: (1) scattergraph, (2) high–low, two-point, (3) modified high–low, two-point method, and (4) regression analysis.

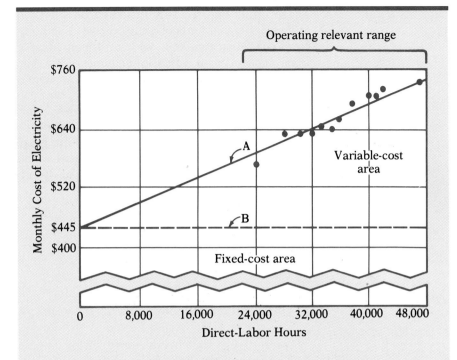

FIGURE 11–3 Scattergraph and Table of Historical Data Showing the Division of a Mixed Cost into Variable and Fixed Elements *Source: Emerson O. Henke, Roderick Holmes, and Lucian Conway,* Managerial Use of Accounting Data *(Houston, TX: Gulf Publishing, 1978), p. 123. Used with permission.*

Summary within figure:

Summary of Electricity Costs and Direct Labor Hours

Month	Direct Labor Hours	Cost of Electricity
January	28,000	$ 625
February	24,000	565
March	30,000	630
April	33,000	640
May	38,000	685
June	34,000	640
July	35,000	655
August	40,000	700
September	42,000	715
October	47,000	730
November	41,000	700
December	32,000	630
Totals	424,000	$7,915

Scattergraph Method

The graph in Figure 11–3 illustrates one method of arriving at the fixed and variable elements of a mixed cost. The points on the graph plot the costs that historically have been incurred at various levels of operations, measured in direct-labor hours. Line A has been drawn so as to place approximately the same number of dots on each side of the line; it represents projected total electricity costs at different levels of operations, based on historical experience. We refer to this method of analyzing semivariable costs as the **scattergraph method**. The point at which line A intersects the cost axis of the graph, provided it is within the feasible range of operations, indicates the amount of fixed cost ($445). The variable cost of electricity per direct-labor hour can then be calculated as follows:

Total annual cost of electricity	$7,915
Less annual fixed cost of electricity ($445 × 12)	− 5,340
Annual variable cost of electricity	$2,575

$$\frac{\text{Annual variable cost of electricity}}{\text{Total direct labor hours for the year}} = \frac{\$2,575}{424,000} = \$.006$$

Alternatively, the variable cost can be calculated by selecting an activity point on the line and reading the total costs associated with that activity. For instance, for 32,000 direct-labor hours:

$640	Total cost of electricity
− 445	Total fixed costs
$195	Total variable costs

$$\frac{\$195}{32,000} = \$.006 \text{ variable rate per direct-labor hour}$$

We can then project the electricity cost per month to be $445 plus $.006, multiplied by the expected direct-labor hours for the month. If we let x be the expected number of direct-labor hours, the equation for determining the projected total electricity costs for any month, using the scattergraph approach, is

$$\text{Total electricity cost} = \$445 + \$.006x$$

High–Low, Two-Point Method

Another often-used method of separating the variable and fixed elements of semivariable costs is called the **high–low, two-point method**. Using the data from Figure 11–3, the fixed and variable elements of total electricity cost would be calculated as follows:

	Direct-Labor Hours	Cost
Highest month (October)	47,000	$730
Lowest month (February)	24,000	565
Difference	23,000	$165

$$\frac{\$165}{23,000} = .0071739, \text{ or } \$.0072 \text{ variable rate per direct-labor hour.}$$

Fixed cost can be found using either the high or low data.

	High	Low
Total cost of electricity	$730	$565
Less variable portion		
($.0072 × 47,000)	338	
($.0072 × 24,000)		173
Monthly fixed cost	$392	$392

The formula for projecting the total monthly cost of electricity based on these data would be $392 plus $.0072 multiplied by the direct-labor hours expected to be worked during the period. The equation for projecting total electricity costs for any month derived from the high–low, two-point method is

$$\text{Total electricity cost} = \$392 + \$.0072x$$

The high–low method has the advantage of being a simple and quick way to identify the variable and fixed elements of a mixed cost. However, it should be used with caution because distortions may result when the high and/or low data for the period are not representative of all the data points. With the exception of two pieces of information (the highest level and the lowest level), this method ignores all other data gathered from past experience. Special care must be taken to ensure that the high and low points are not aberrations (*outliers*). In general, any aberrations should be eliminated from historical data before they are used for projections. This may be interpreted to mean that if the high activity level does not also show the higher cost for the data being examined (or if the low activity level does not show the lower cost), those data should not be used and the nearest high and low activity levels that meet those criteria should be used instead.

Modified High–Low, Two-Point Method

To avoid the distortions that might result from using outlier data, and also to avoid discarding most of the historical cost data as we do with the traditional high–low method, a **modified high–low, two-point method** may be used. This calls for dividing the data into two equal subsets, one containing the higher data points and the other containing the lower data points. Then we take an average of each subset (in terms of dollars and activity levels) and use those data as the "high" and "low" points. Using this method, for the data in Figure 11–3, we find the variable cost per hour and aggregate fixed cost to be $.0073387 and $400.28, respectively, as follows. (This also is known as the *semi-averages method*.)

	High Points			Low Points	
	Direct Labor Hours	Cost of Electricity		Direct Labor Hours	Cost of Electricity
	38,000	$ 685.00		28,000	$ 625.00
	35,000	655.00		24,000	565.00
	40,000	700.00		30,000	630.00
	42,000	715.00		33,000	640.00
	47,000	730.00		34,000	640.00
	41,000	700.00		32,000	630.00
	243,000	$4,185.00		181,000	$3,730.00
Averages	40,500	$ 697.50		30,166⅔	$ 621.66⅔

$$\frac{\text{Cost}}{\text{Direct-labor hours}} = \frac{\$697.50 - \$621.66\frac{2}{3}}{40,500 - 30,166\frac{2}{3}} = \frac{75.83\frac{1}{3}}{10,333\frac{1}{3}}$$

$$= .0073387 \text{ variable rate per direct-labor hour}$$

Total cost of electricity	$697.50	$621.67
Less variable portion		
($.0073387 × 40,500)	297.22	
($.0073387 × 30,166⅔)		221.38
	$400.28*	$400.29*

*0.01 difference due to rounding

The equation for total monthly electricity costs using this modified high–low, two-point method would be:

$$\text{Total electricity cost} = \$400.28 + \$.0073387x$$

Regression Analysis

Line A in Figure 11–3 may be drawn mathematically with the greatest degree of precision by using the **least-squares method**, also known as **regression analysis**. This procedure positions the total-cost line so the sum of the squares of the deviations of all the actual data points from the line are at a minimum. No other method more efficiently uses the historical data to estimate the slope of the total-cost line (variable cost per unit) and cost-axis intercept point (total fixed cost).

This method of determining the total-cost line (Line A in Figure 11–3), which is best accomplished with a programmable or specialized calculator or a computer, is explained more completely in the appendix to this chapter (page 391). Besides precision, the biggest advantage of the least-squares method of separating mixed costs into fixed and variable elements is that statistics easily can be generated on the potential error of the estimate and confidence intervals can be constructed. These statistical concepts also are discussed in the appendix. Once the parameters (a, the intercept with the vertical cost axis, which is interpreted as fixed cost, and b, the slope of the total-cost line, which is interpreted as variable cost per unit of activity) are estimated using regression analysis, total projected costs can be found as follows (see appendix):

$$\text{Total electricity cost} = a + bx$$
$$= \$409.4723 + \$.00707861x$$

We can now summarize the four separate estimates of the intercept (or fixed cost) and slope (variable cost per unit) developed for our 12 months of data for electricity costs and direct labor hours:

Method	Intercept (Fixed Costs)	Slope (Variable Cost per Direct-Labor Hour)
Scattergraph	$445	$.006
High–low, two-point	392	.0072
Modified high–low, two-point	400.28	.0073387
Regression analysis	409.4723	.00707861

For a firm expecting to work 45,000 direct-labor hours, for example, the four methods would produce the following estimates of total electricity cost:

Method	Formula	Estimated Electricity Cost
Scattergraph	$445 + $.006(45,000)	$715
High–low, two-point	$392 + $.0072(45,000)	$716
Modified high–low, two-point	$400.28 + $.0073387(45,000)	$730.52
Regression analysis	$409.47 + $.00707861(45,000)	$728.01

All of these methods are based on historical data and therefore may predict future costs incorrectly, especially outside the relevant range of past experience (24,000–47,000 direct-labor hours in our example). Management must decide which estimate to use. For example, it may decide to use all four estimates, to see how sensitive the data are to the various estimation methods. In any event, the data should be graphed so the general behavior of costs and possible unrepresentative outliers can be observed.

Standard Overhead Cost Rates

In developing a standard overhead application rate to be used on standard cost cards, particular attention must be given to the level of accuracy achieved in dividing semivariable costs into fixed and variable elements. This may call for the repeated use of one of the more sophisticated allocation procedures described earlier (such as regression analysis) on the separate components of total overhead cost before deciding on the estimated total variable-overhead cost and estimated total fixed-overhead cost to be used in calculating the standard variable-overhead and fixed-overhead rates per hour. (These two overhead rates are lumped together as $9.50 per direct-labor hour in manufacturing overhead costs in Figure 11–2.)

Because all of the methods described rely on historical cost data to project future costs, they incorporate past inefficiencies into projected costs. In some cases, that weakness may be important enough to lead us to start from scratch to project individual items of manufacturing-overhead costs for different levels of operations. This is comparable to the **zero-base budgeting** concept used by some governmental entities. It involves extensive analysis of the needs to be met by each element of overhead cost and the ultimate assignment of dollar values to those needs. An important advantage of starting over is that an intense examination of the reasons for incurring overhead costs will help to trace those costs to products or departments incurring them. Thus, products or departments could have individualized overhead rates. More precise information on overhead can yield better decisions by managers and helps avoid dysfunctional shifts of costs among products.

Step-Variable Costs. Some manufacturing-overhead items may be considered *step-variable costs*—costs that remain fixed over a certain range of operating levels but jump (step up) to another level as operations rise above that relevant range. For example, a single employee may be able to handle an assigned responsibility over a range of different levels of operations (say, from zero to 2,000 units of production); but when that range is exceeded (that is, production is greater than 2,000 units—even if only by a few units), an additional employee must be hired. Thus, supervisory costs probably provide the best example: perhaps with one shift of laborers a single person can handle the supervisory responsibilities; but when activity increases to the point of working another shift of direct laborers, another supervisor must be hired. As a result, the graphically projected cost for supervision will show the cost of the added supervisory employee as a vertical increase in costs at the activity level where a second shift is added, after which the cost will again remain fixed over another series of operating levels. (See Figure 11–4.)

We often call the range of possible operating levels the *relevant range*. If a flexible budget is being prepared for a relevant range of operations

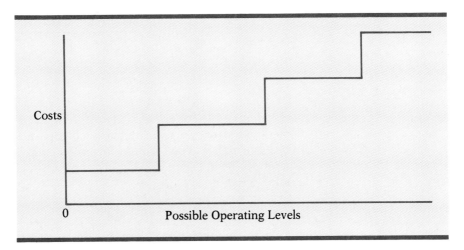

FIGURE 11–4 Step-Variable Costs

presumed to include only one shift, supervisory costs would be treated as a fixed cost. However, if a flexible budget is to include a range of operations that extend beyond the one shift, we must show project supervisory cost as an item separate from either fixed or variable costs, to incorporate the appropriate level of precision into the flexible budget. For example, the flexible budget for a firm that must employ one supervisor (at $20,000 per year) for each 1,000 standard hours beyond 10,000 would be projected in the following format:

Standard hours	10,000	11,000	12,000
Variable overhead costs	$ XXX	$ XXX	$ XXX
Step-variable (supervisory) overhead costs	20,000	40,000	60,000
Fixed overhead costs	XXX	XXX	XXX
Total overhead costs	$ XXX	$ XXX	$ XXX

Calculating Standard Manufacturing- Overhead Costs

To illustrate how a standard overhead rate is derived, let's assume that the flexible manufacturing-overhead budget for Ajax Chemical Company involves no step-variable costs but shows the following projected data for three operating levels:

	Aggregate Hour and Manufacturing Overhead Data		
Standard hours per reporting period	800	1,000	1,200
Variable overhead costs	$2,000	$2,500	$ 3,000
Fixed overhead costs	7,000	7,000	7,000
Total overhead	$9,000	$9,500	$10,000

	Manufacturing-Overhead Rate		
Variable	$ 2.50	$2.50	$2.50
Fixed	8.75	7.00	5.83
Total	$11.25	$9.50	$8.33

The $9.50 standard overhead rate per hour (see Figure 11–2) has been selected based on an expected level of operations of 1,000 standard direct labor hours. The formula for projecting what the total overhead costs should be at any level of operations within the range shown in the flexible budget is

$$\text{Total manufacturing overhead cost} = \$7,000 + \$2.50x$$

where x is the anticipated number of standard direct-labor hours of production. This is presented graphically in Figure 11–5.

With a process-costing system, the standard direct-labor hours of production over a period of time would equal the number of equivalent units of production for the period multiplied by the standard hours allowed for each unit. In the case of the Ajax Chemical Company, the number of standard hours of production *achieved* for the reporting period was 5,200 equivalent units × 0.2 hour per unit = 1,040.

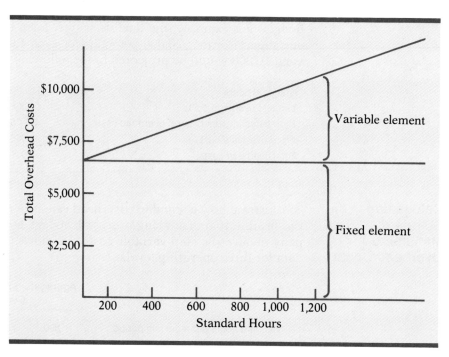

FIGURE 11–5 Projecting Total Overhead

As we explain later in this chapter, the amount of production, when a firm manufactures more than one product, is generally measured in standard hours. Such an arrangement allows the firm to directly compare production levels for various periods using a single measuring unit.

Types of Standards

Standard costs may be based on at least three different levels of expectations:

1. best attainable (ideal) standards
2. normal standards
3. currently attainable (expected actual) standards.

Best Attainable (Ideal) Standards

If standard costs are based on the highest level of efficiency that can be achieved in the production of the goods or services, the standards are described as **best attainable standards** (or **ideal standards**). These standards will project material costs, for example, based on the assumption that the firm will have no spoilage and that the best possible prices will be obtained in the acquisitions of materials. In setting the standards for labor, the best attainable standard would assume the amount of labor as that projected from time study analyses, with no provision for lost time or inefficiencies in carrying out the operations required to produce the product. The labor rate would be the basic required rate, with no provision for overtime pay. The standard overhead rate per hour would be based on the assumption that the firm would operate at the most efficient level of production—generally, 100% of capacity.

If best attainable standards are used, the firm should expect to see unfavorable variances from those standards. As actual operations are carried out, the variances from the standard should reflect the extent to which the actual operations have deviated from perfection. Since some unfavorable variance would be expected on all items, management would be concerned with only those variances that are exceptionally large.

While best attainable standards *may* serve to inspire employees to achieve as close to the ideal as possible, these standards are not so useful for other purposes, such as the preparation of realistic budgets and evaluation of performance. And standards that are impossible to achieve in the normal work environment might discourage employees from doing their best. For these and other reasons, few firms use best attainable standards.

Normal Standards

Normal standards are based on the quantities of materials, costs per unit of material, the number of hours of labor, cost per hour of direct labor, and cost per hour of manufacturing overhead that can be *expected* to be achieved over a long period of time (sometimes the length of the business cycle—perhaps three to five years). Like best attainable standards, normal standards make no provision for either expected spoilage of materials or expected idle (nonproductive) labor time. Overhead is applied using a rate based on an *expected average* level of capacity utilization over a longer period of time (sometimes several years).

Just as with best attainable standards (and for the same reasons), a firm should expect unfavorable overhead variances during the bad years of the business cycle. Other variances should fluctuate between favorable and unfavorable over the years in the business cycle. In general, with normal standards we can expect to have favorable overhead variances in periods when the volume of production is high, but unfavorable variances in periods when production is low. Normal standards reflect the realization that businesses operate within the constraints of a business cycle that allows firms to operate at a high level of production in some periods but forces them to operate at a low level during other periods.

While normal overhead standards may be achieved during certain periods, the numbers must be carefully scrutinized, and generally adjusted, before they can be used for budgeting purposes. The negative effect on employee morale of best attainable standards also applies to normal standards. Few firms actually use either ideal or normal standards; but you should be aware of their existence.

Currently Attainable Standards

Currently attainable standards (also known as **expected actual standards**) are the most widely used approach in establishing standard costs. These standards are based on currently achievable efficient operations, that is, on the level of efficiency and production expected to be achieved during the next fiscal period. The direct materials standard costs, for example, allow for a normal amount of spoilage and scrap, along with some expected inefficiencies in purchasing. Attainable standards also provide for some lost labor time in establishing the standard times allowed for various operations. When the standard labor rate is established, currently attainable standards assume that some overtime will have to be paid and less than prefect utilization of facilities is assumed in establishing the standard overhead rate per hour.

With current attainable standards, a firm should expect to have both favorable and unfavorable variances from those standards as actual operations are carried out. In controlling operations, significant unfavorable variances should be investigated, so appropriate remedial action can be taken. The cause of significant favorable variances should also be investigated, so their repetition can be consciously promoted.

Besides furnishing an attainable goal for employees, these standards may be used to most effectively predict purchase requirements and cash flows. Currently attainable standards can be achieved consistently (and sometimes even surpassed) with efficient operations. In most instances, therefore, they also will provide, without allocation of variances, reasonable values for inventories.

Measurement of Production

The job-order and process-costing procedures discussed in Chapters 4– 10 measured production in terms of units and dollar amounts shown on completed job-order sheets or cost-of-production reports. We determined unit costs by dividing the total costs incurred on the job or during the period by the number of units produced on the job or the number of equivalent units produced during the period. When we use standard costs, we generally measure overall production in terms of number of **standard hours of production** during the period—either machine-hours or, more conventionally, labor hours.

Although standard costs can be used with job-order costing, they are more often used within what is basically a process-costing format. That means that the standard hours of production must be calculated by taking into consideration not only the number of whole units transferred out of the process during the period, but also the partially completed units in process at both the beginning and end of the period, just as was done in calculating the equivalent units of production for the period with historical cost process costing (see Chapter 6). The equivalent whole units of production for each type of unit being manufactured is multiplied by the standard direct-labor hours allowed for it, to convert the units produced to standard hours of output. The sum of the standard hours for all products is then the total standard hours of production for the period. For example, let's suppose that a firm produces three types of units—product A, product B, and product C—and the standard labor hours allowed for the production of one unit of each product are 0.5 hour, 0.15 hour, and 3 hours, respectively. If the firm produces 1,000, 2,000, and 500 equivalent units of products A, B, and C, respectively, then total standard hours of production during the period can be calculated as follows:

Product A (1,000 × 0.5)	500	standard hours
Product B (2,000 × 0.15)	300	standard hours
Product C (500 × 3)	1,500	standard hours
Total production for period	2,300	standard hours

For a highly automated firm, we can measure production in terms of machine-hours. (See Chapter 23.)

The use of standard hours to measure the level of production achieved allows us to relate the actual level of production for a reporting period to that projected for the period in the establishment of the standard manufacturing overhead rate per hour, regardless of how many different products the firm makes or how the level of production varies among the types of units being produced.

Observe that we do not have to divide production costs by the number of units to get unit costs because all units will be valued at their respective standard costs as they move through the factory to finished-goods inventory and are sold to customers. However, if the variances from standard are significant, they must be allocated to materials inventory, work in process, finished goods, and cost of sales, to meet the GAAP requirement that inventory be valued at actual cost or the lower of cost or market. (This was illustrated in Chapter 5 for underapplied or overapplied overhead.) It is important to recognize that standard costs do not constitute an acceptable basis for valuing inventories and cost of sales, except where the variances from actual are considered immaterial.

Assigning Values to Inventories

In some standard-costing systems, materials inventory may be accounted for at actual costs, with standard costs being used in valuing work-in-process and finished-goods inventories. More generally, however, a standard cost system will use unit costs from standard cost cards or standard cost sheets in assigning values to all inventories, including materials inventory, at the end of each period. However, as we just observed, generally accepted accounting practices do not allow the use of standard costs in valuing inventories and cost of sales for external reporting purposes, except where the deviations (variances) from actual costs are immaterial. Therefore, if a firm follows the practice of routinely valuing all inventories and cost of sales at standard costs, variances considered material must be allocated as additions to or subtractions from those standard costs when those items are presented in the published financial statements. However, with the use of currently attainable standards, variances generally are not expected to be material enough to require allocation.

In allocating variances from standard costs, the objective is to "correct" the standard cost numbers so they approximate actual costs. In doing that, the variances associated with the *purchases* of raw materials should be allocated to all three categories of inventory (materials inventory, work in process, and finished goods) and cost of sales, because direct materials costs are included in the account balances of all four of those accounts at standard amounts per unit. On the other hand, the variances associated with the *usage* of materials, the direct-labor costs, and the manufacturing-overhead costs will be allocated only to work-in-process inventory, finished-goods inventory, and cost of sales. The procedures followed in allocating those variances are explained further in Chapters 12 and 13.

Records Required in Maintaining a Standard Cost System

As we said earlier, the establishment of a standard cost system requires the development of predetermined (standard) costs for all items of raw materials, work in process, and finished goods, and the reflection of those costs on standard cost cards. The establishment of these records involves a significant amount of clerical effort, but it significantly reduces the other records required to maintain the system once it is established. Thus, another major advantage of standard costs is that a firm need maintain a record showing only the *quantities* of individual items included in various inventories and transferred from process to process and ultimately to finished goods and to cost of sales. Those quantities can be converted to dollar amounts by referring to the appropriate standard cost cards and multiplying the quantities by the standard cost(s) per unit. These standard amounts are then used in record keeping when transfers of goods are recorded and to calculate values assigned to inventories.

With a standard cost system, standard costs are moved through the entire cost-accumulation and -allocation system, usually beginning with materials inventory. Actual cost amounts are recorded as the offsetting credits to cash and various payable accounts as costs are incurred. The differences between the actual and standard amounts are then reflected in variance accounts. For example, the general journal entry for recording materials purchases, which will be developed in detail in Chapter 12, is

Materials inventory	(Standard cost)	
Materials price variance		(Favorable price variance)
Accounts payable		(Actual cost)

Job-Order Standard Cost System

The precise makeup of a job-order standard cost systems may vary significantly, depending on the nature of a firm's operations. Generally, however, standard costs will be established for each type of material carried in materials inventory. The standard quantity of direct materials to be used on each job typically will be determined by analyzing the specifications for the job and converting the results of those analyses to the quantities of direct materials that should be required for the job. Those data are then converted to dollar amounts by reference to the materials standard cost cards.

A standard rate per hour for direct labor will be established in exactly the same manner as for a process cost system. Again however, the quantity of direct labor required for each job will depend on the nature of the job. Generally, the work of direct laborers will be divided into specific operations, and the standard time allowed for each operation determined by time studies. Then the specific operations required for individual jobs will be identified, to permit a total standard labor cost to be projected for each job.

A standard manufacturing-overhead rate per direct-labor hour (or machine-hour) will be established exactly as was explained and illustrated earlier in the chapter, thus allowing a projection of the total standard cost of producing each job before it is placed in process. Such standard cost data can be particularly helpful in bidding on jobs and in deciding the selling price that will be sought in disposing of stock (that is, finished goods) items.

Variances from standard costs can be associated with individual jobs in a job-order costing system. However, those variances also may be subdivided into price and efficiency (quantity) amounts for materials, labor, and overhead, to provide additional information for management to use in controlling costs. Each of those variances then can be accumulated to arrive at separate total cost variances for materials, labor, and overhead during each reporting period. This information may be used to control operations, help eliminate inefficiencies, or even justify a revision of the standards when appropriate.

Illustrative Problem: Part 1

To illustrate the installation and operation of a standard cost system, we now introduce certain assumptions relating to the operations of Illustration Company. In this part of our illustration, we show how standard cost cards are prepared and how inventories are valued when using a standard cost system. Parts 2 and 3 of Illustration Company operations are presented in Chapters 12 and 13, respectively.

Illustration Company produces two products, M and N. Product M requires two units of raw material A and two units of raw material B. Product N requires three units of raw material C and two units of raw material D. Other assumptions are as follows. Standard costs per unit of raw materials: A, $.50; B, $.25; C, $1.00; D, $.75. Direct labor in the amount of 0.6 hour and 0.8 hour are expected to be required to produce products M and N, respectively. The standard cost for direct labor has been set at $6 per hour. A standard overhead rate of $10 per direct-labor hour is expected to be incurred in producing both products.

All materials are added at the beginning of processing. Inventories and transfers to finished goods of products M and N are as follows:

Beginning-of-Period Work in Process

Product M	300 units, $\frac{1}{3}$ complete as to conversion costs
Product N	200 units, 40% complete as to conversion costs

End-of-Period Work in Process

Product M	100 units, 75% complete as to conversion costs
Product N	400 units, 20% complete as to conversion costs

Transfers to Finished Goods

Product M	1,000 units
Product N	1,200 units

REQUIRED:

1. Prepare standard cost cards for products M and N.
2. Compute the standard costs of end-of-period work-in-process inventory and transfers to finished goods.
3. Compute the number of standard direct-labor hours of production achieved during the period.

Solution to Illustrative Problem, Part 1

1. Standard Cost Cards.

Product M

Direct materials	
2 units of raw material A @ $.50	$ 1.00
2 units of raw material B @ $.25	.50
Total	$ 1.50
Direct labor (0.6 hour @ $6 per hour)	3.60
Overhead (0.6 hour @ $10 per hour)	6.00
Total standard cost	$11.10

Product N

Direct materials	
3 units of raw material C @ $1.00	$ 3.00
2 units of raw material D @ $.75	1.50
Total	$ 4.50
Direct labor (0.8 hour @ $6 per hour)	4.80
Overhead (0.8 hour @ $10 per hour)	8.00
Total standard cost	$17.30

2. Work-in-Process Inventory.

Product M

Raw materials (100 units × 100% × $1.50)	$ 150
Direct labor and overhead	
100 units × 75% × 0.6 hours = 45 hours	
45 hours @ $6 + $10 = $16 per hour	720

Product N

Raw materials (400 units × 100% × $4.50)	1,800
Direct labor and overhead	
400 units × 20% × 0.8 hours = 64 hours	
64 hours @ $6 + $10 = $16 per hour	1,024
Total	$ 3,694

Transfers to Finished Goods

Product M (1,000 units @ $11.10)	$11,100
Product N (1,200 units @ $17.30)	20,760
Total	$31,860

3. Standard Direct Labor Hours of Production.

Production for the Period

	Product M	Product N	Total
Units transferred to finished goods	1,000	1,200	
End-of-period work in process (equivalent whole units)	75	80	
Total	1,075	1,280	
Units included in beginning-of-period work in process (equivalent whole units)	(100)	(80)	
Equivalent units of production	975	1,200	
Standard hours allowed per unit	× 0.6	× 0.8	
Standard hours of production	585	960	1,545

SUMMARY

In this chapter, we explained the basic elements of a standard cost system and how such a system would be established. We began by identifying the standard cost card (or sheet) as the basic document underlying the system. We then explained how standard costs are determined for direct materials, direct labor, and manufacturing overhead and illustrated how those data would appear on standard cost cards for

Ajax Chemical Company, to show how standard costs can be used in a previously illustrated (Chapter 6) process-costing system based on historical costs.

We discussed four methods of separating semivariable (mixed) costs into fixed and variable components: (1) scattergraph, (2) the high–low, two-point method, (3) modified high–low, two-point method, and (4) least-squares (regression) analysis.

We explained that standard costs reflect operating goals a company desires to achieve in converting raw materials into finished products. Such standard costs can be those that are the best attainable, those expected to be *normal* over a longer period of time, or those that are currently attainable (expected actual standards) during the next fiscal period. We briefly explained the differences in the variances from standards that could be expected when using each of these standards.

We then explained that, in using a standard cost system, overall production can most effectively be measured in standard hours of work turned out rather than in terms of the number of units produced. This allows us to convert the production of many different types of units into one common measurement (standard hours of production). In measuring the overall level of production achieved during any particular operating period, the standard hours of production will equal the sum of the equivalent units of production of each of the different types of units produced multiplied by the standard hours allowed for that type of unit. Standard hours of production may be measured using direct labor hours or machine-hours, depending on whether a process is labor intensive or capital intensive.

We explained how, in general, dollar values are assigned to inventories and the cost flow transactions when using a standard cost system. We also pointed out that generally accepted accounting practices do not permit inventories to be valued at standard costs unless those standard costs are not significantly different from actual costs. Therefore, if the variances from standard costs are significant, they must be allocated to the various inventory and cost of sales accounts before those items are displayed in the financial statements. We also observed that because all valuations and transfers will be based on standard costs, we need maintain only quantitative records relating to materials, work in process, transfers, finished goods, and cost of sales. Those quantities can then be multiplied by data shown on the standard cost cards to convert them to dollar amounts. We also discussed the unique characteristics associated with a job-order standard cost system.

APPENDIX: Simple Linear Regression Analysis

When a line is drawn through data points plotted on a scattergraph, the relationship of a data point and the line may be expressed as follows:

$$\text{Observed data point } (y)_t = a + bx_t + e_t$$

where a and b are the intercept and slope, respectively, e represents the distance between the observed data point and the line (error term), x represents the independent variable, and t denotes the tth observation.

The line of best fit through the data, therefore, mathematically will occur when the sum of the errors, squared (in recognition of positive and negative errors), is minimized. This may be written as

$$\min \Sigma e_t^2 = \min \Sigma(y_t - a - bx_t)^2$$

The solution to this minimization problem may be found through calculus by taking the first derivative of the function with respect to a and the first derivative with respect to b, and setting each resultant equation equal to zero.

This procedure, after rearranging terms and dividing through by 2, results in the following two *normal equations*:

$$\Sigma y_t = na + b(\Sigma x_t)$$
$$\Sigma x_t y_t = a(\Sigma x_t) + b(\Sigma x_t^2)$$

These equations can be expressed as

$$a = \frac{(\Sigma y_t)(\Sigma x_t^2) - (\Sigma x_t)(\Sigma x_t y_t)}{n(\Sigma x_t^2) - (\Sigma x_t)(\Sigma x_t)}$$

$$b = \frac{n(\Sigma x_t y_t) - (\Sigma x_t)(\Sigma y_t)}{n(\Sigma x_t^2) - (\Sigma x_t)(\Sigma x_t)}$$

where n refers to the number of observations and Σ signifies summation over all t observations.

Using the data from the electricity cost example in the chapter, the following computations would be made:

Independent Variable x	Dependent Variable y	xy	x²
28,000	625	17,500,000	784,000,000
24,000	565	13,560,000	576,000,000
30,000	630	18,900,000	900,000,000
33,000	640	21,120,000	1,089,000,000
38,000	685	26,030,000	1,444,000,000
34,000	640	21,760,000	1,156,000,000
35,000	655	22,925,000	1,225,000,000
40,000	700	28,000,000	1,600,000,000
42,000	715	30,030,000	1,764,000,000
47,000	730	34,310,000	2,209,000,000
41,000	700	28,700,000	1,681,000,000
32,000	630	20,160,000	1,024,000,000
424,000	7,915	282,995,000	15,452,000,000

$$\bar{x} = 35,333.3333 \qquad \bar{y} = 659.583333$$

$$a = \frac{(7,915)(15,452,000,000) - (424,000)(282,995,000)}{(12)(15,452,000,000) - (424,000)(424,000)}$$

$$= 409.4724$$

$$b = \frac{(12)(282,995,000) - (424,000)(7,915)}{(12)(15,452,000,000) - (424,000)(424,000)}$$

$$= .00707861$$

The resulting cost equation is

$$\text{Total electricity cost} = \$409.4724 + \$.00707861x$$

Rather than performing these calculations manually, however, a computer program should be used to estimate the intercept (a) and slope (b). LOTUS®1-2-3®, for example, has a regression option under the "DATA" menu. Microsoft® EXCEL® also has a linear estimation subroutine under the "Formula" menu (submenu item "Paste Function"). Many regression packages, such as SPSS or SAS, are available on a mainframe computer, and quite a few regression packages are available for personal computers. The formulas also easily can be inserted (that is, typed) into any spreadsheet.

Unfortunately, this powerful tool of regression can be misused and misinterpreted. The assumptions of regression analysis (linearity of the data, constant variance of residuals, independence of residuals, and normality of residuals), if met, ensure that the regression sample values of a and b are the best available efficient, unbiased estimates of the population values A and B. Cost data routinely violate these assumptions, however. Most computer regression programs include tests that indicate whether these assumptions hold for the data set being analyzed. Those tests are described in textbooks on regression analysis and some familiarity with them is strongly recommended before reliance is placed on regression output. Familiarity with a good book on econometrics or access to expert guidance also is recommended before multiple regression analysis (where there is more than one independent variable) is performed.

Reliability of Estimation

Even if all regression assumptions are met, management will want to know how "good" an estimated relationship is before decisions are made.

Correlation Analysis. The coefficient of determination (R^2) measures the variability in the dependent variable that can be explained by the independent variable. If no independent variable were used to try to explain changes in the dependent variable, the method of least squares would give the mean of the dependent variable as the sample value to

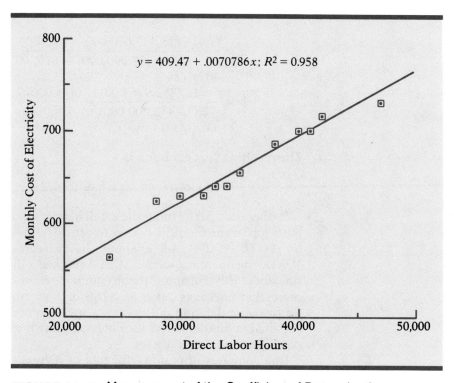

FIGURE 11–6   Measurement of the Coefficient of Determination

estimate the dependent variable. Thus, we are interested in the ability of the independent variable to explain variations of the dependent variable from its mean. Figure 11–6 illustrates the measurement of the coefficient of determination.

The total variance of electricity cost is measured by the sum of the squared values of the difference of each observed electricity cost from the average electricity cost, $\Sigma(y - \bar{y})^2$. The portion of the variance of electricity cost not explained by direct labor hours is the sum of the squared values of the difference of each observed electricity cost from the estimated (sample) point predicted by the regression equation, $\Sigma(y - y')^2$. The coefficient of determination indicates the proportion of the variance in electricity cost that is explained by direct-labor hours, which is equivalent to 1 minus the proportion of total variance that is not explained.

$$\text{Coefficient of determination } (R^2) = \frac{\text{Explained variance}}{\text{Total variance}}$$
$$= 1 - \frac{\text{Unexplained variance}}{\text{Total variance}}$$

The information necessary to calculate R^2 for our electricity cost example is shown below:

y Value Predicted from x Value $(y' = a + bx)$	Total Variance of y $(y - \bar{y})^2$	Unexplained Variance $(y - y')^2$	Total Variance of x $(x - \bar{x})^2$
607.673513	1,196.00694	300.20716	53,777,777.78
579.359065	8,946.00694	206.18275	128,444,444.44
621.830737	875.17361	66.73686	28,444,444.44
643.066572	383.50694	9.40386	5,444,444.44
678.459632	646.00694	42.77641	7,111,111.11
650.145184	383.50694	102.92476	1,777,777.78
657.223796	21.00694	4.94526	111,111.11
692.616856	1,633.50694	54.51082	21,777,777.78
706.774079	3,071.00694	67.66577	44,444,444.44
742.167139	4,958.50694	148.03926	136,111,111.11
699.695467	1,633.50694	0.09274	32,111,111.11
635.987960	875.17361	35.85566	11,111,111.11
	24,622.91670	1,039.34136	470,666,667.67

Using the values calculated above, the coefficient of determination is

$$R^2 = 1 - \frac{1039.34136}{24622.91670} = .9577896732$$

This is an extremely high value. Calculated values of R^2 can range from zero (indicating that the dependent variable has no ability to explain the variance in the dependent variable) to 1 (indicating that the independent variable is able to explain all of the variance in the independent variable). The word "explain" means that the variations in the dependent variable are related to, but not necessarily caused by, the variations in the independent variable. Thus, the mathematically derived coefficient of determination measures covariation; it does not establish a cause-and-effect relationship between the dependent variable and the independent variable. Such a relationship must be theoretically developed or physically observed.

The adjusted R^2, $\bar{R}^2$, is the coefficient of determination adjusted for the number of independent variables and observations used to make the estimate. This adjustment recognizes that as the number of independent variables increases, and the number of observations remains unchanged, the unadjusted R^2 increases. For example, if there are as many independent variables as there are observations, R^2 (unadjusted) would be 1. The adjusted coefficient of determination, $\bar{R}^2$, is computed as

$$\overline{R}^2 = 1 - \frac{(n-1)(1-R^2)}{n-k}$$

where k = the number of independent variables (one with simple linear regression).

While this adjustment can be extremely important in multiple regression analysis, it has a minimal effect in simple linear regression. In our example, for instance, the adjusted R^2 would be

$$\overline{R}^2 = 1 - \frac{(11)(1-.9577896732)}{10} = .9535686405$$

The square root of the coefficient of determination, or R, is called the coefficient of correlation and represents the proportion of the total variation in the dependent variable (electricity cost) that is accounted for by differences in the independent variable (number of direct-labor hours). For our example,

$$R = \sqrt{.9577896732} = .9786673$$

Correlation of two variables can range from -1 (perfect negative correlation) to $+1$ (perfect positive correlation), with 0 indicating no correlation. The sign of R is the same as the sign of b in the equation $y = a + bx$. Direct-labor hours and total electricity cost, as indicated by their correlation coefficient, are almost perfectly positively correlated.

Standard Error of the Estimate. Because we used a limited sample of historical data to estimate the regression equation ($y = a + bx$), and a variable(s) not included in the regression equation may have some influence on the cost being predicted, the calculated cost usually will be different from the actual expense at the same level of activity (see Figure 11–6). The dispersion (standard deviation) of observed values of y from the predicted regression line can be measured by calculating the standard error of the estimate. A small value for the standard error of the estimate indicates a good fit. If the R^2 value were one (perfect explanation), the standard error would equal zero. The formula is

$$\text{Standard error of the estimate} = S_e = \sqrt{\frac{\text{Unexplained variance}}{\text{Degrees of freedom}}}$$

where degrees of freedom = sample size − the parameters being estimated.

For our data, since we are estimating two parameters, a and b, the standard error of the estimate would be

$$S_e = \sqrt{\frac{1039.34136}{12-2}} = 10.194809$$

Since the prediction errors usually are assumed to follow a standard normal distribution or a student's t-distribution (for small samples), a confidence interval can be constructed around a predicted value using the standard error of the estimate and an appropriate distribution table value.

A table of selected t values (based on the assumption that two tails of the distribution are of concern, that is, that positive and negative deviations are of equal concern) is shown below:

Degrees of Freedom	Desired Confidence Level		
	90%	95%	99%
10	1.812	2.228	3.169
11	1.796	2.201	3.106
12	1.782	2.179	3.055
13	1.771	2.160	3.012
14	1.761	2.145	2.977
15	1.753	2.131	2.947
20	1.725	2.086	2.845
25	1.708	2.060	2.787
30	1.697	2.042	2.750
40	1.684	2.021	2.704
60	1.671	2.000	2.660
120	1.658	1.980	2.617
∞	1.645	1.960	2.576

The expected range of actual expense around the predicted expense would be computed for a sample size of n by multiplying the standard error of the estimate by the t value for $n - 2$ degrees of freedom at the desired confidence level, and by a correction factor for small samples as shown below:

$$y' \pm t_p S_e \sqrt{1 + \frac{1}{n} + \frac{(x' - \bar{x})^2}{\Sigma(x_i - \bar{x})^2}}$$

where

t_p = Desired confidence level
S_e = Standard error of the regression
n = Number of observations
x' = Value of x for which the estimate is desired
$\bar{x}$ = Mean of the x values in the data set
x_i = Value of each x in the data set

Continuing our electricity cost example, assume that the actual level of activity for a period is 45,000 direct-labor hours. The electricity cost computed for the budget from the regression equation is $728 [$409.4724 + $.00707861(45,000)]. If management wants to be 95% confident that the actual electricity expense is within the limits implied by past experience, the range of expected electricity cost when direct-labor hours are 45,000 would be calculated as follows:

$$y' \pm t_{95\%}S_e\sqrt{1 + \frac{1}{n} + \frac{(x' - \bar{x})^2}{\Sigma(x_i - \bar{x})^2}}$$

$$\$728 \pm (2.228)(\$10.194809)\sqrt{1 + \frac{1}{12} + \frac{(45,000 - 35,333.33)^2}{470,666,667}}$$

$$\$728 \pm \$25.72$$

Management can expect the actual electricity cost to be between $753.72 ($728 + $25.72) and $702.28 ($728 − $25.72) about 95% of the time when direct labor hours are 45,000. This *confidence interval* can be used in budgeting or in controlling operations. For example, if actual electricity cost is greater than $753.72 or less than $702.28 when 45,000 direct labor hours are worked, management might want to investigate

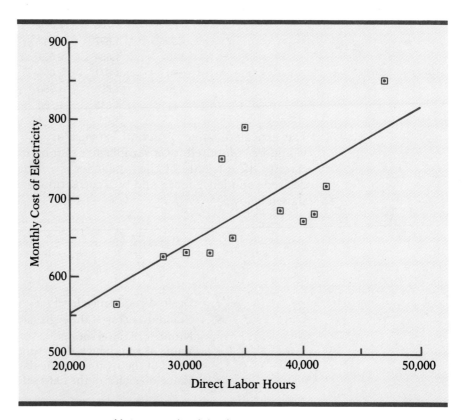

FIGURE 11–7 Heteroscedasticity (nonconstant variance of residuals)

the cause and take indicated corrective action. Or, when a cash budget is being prepared, the upper limit of electricity cost might be used to determine the adequacy of available cash.

Caution: While the *a* and *b* regression coefficients are still unbiased, the standard error of the estimate and confidence intervals based on the standard error are unreliable measures if the variance differs at different points on the regression line (referred to as heteroscedasticity), as illustrated in Figure 11–7, or the observations appear to be correlated with one another (serial correlation), as illustrated in Figure 11–8.

With less than twenty observations, computer tests for constant variance are not very powerful, but heteroscedasticity can be observed in graphed data, as shown in Figure 11–7.

Serial correlation in the estimated residuals can be measured with the Durbin-Watson statistic which is available with most computer regression programs. For a small sample of 10 to 20 observations, a Durbin-Watson statistic of 1.30 to 2.70 is consistent with the residuals being independent (nonserially correlated). Serial correlation also can be observed in graphed data as shown in Figure 11–8.

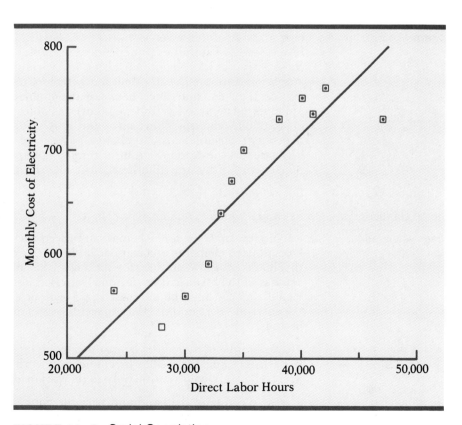

FIGURE 11–8 Serial Correlation

GLOSSARY OF TERMS INTRODUCED IN THIS CHAPTER

actual costs	The actual dollar values of resources given up to acquire goods and services; also known as *historical costs*. In this chapter, the term describes the dollar amounts of resources given up for direct materials, direct labor, and manufacturing overhead.
best attainable standards	Standard costs based on the highest level of efficiency that can be achieved in the production of goods or services.
currently attainable standards	Standard costs based on the level of efficiency and production expected to be achieved during the next fiscal period. Such standards allow for normal-spoilage and/or normal-scrap losses as well as expected lost labor time and ordinary equipment failure. Also known as *expected actual standards*.
estimated costs	Predetermined costs usually based on historical cost data adjusted for expected changes in operations.
expected actual standards	See *currently attainable standards*.
high–low, two-point method	A way to estimate the fixed and variable components of a semivariable cost. Uses the differences between the historical amounts for highest and lowest levels of activities (independent variable) and the costs relating to those activities (dependent variable). The variable component per unit of activity is estimated by dividing the difference between the high cost and low cost by the difference between the high-activity and low-activity amounts. [The activity (independent) variable may be stated in terms of units or some other measure, and it is treated as if it "causes" the dependent variable, cost, to change.] The fixed component then can be estimated as the amount left after removing the aggregate variable component from either the high-level or low-level total cost figures.
historical costs	See *actual costs*.
ideal standards	See *best attainable standards*.
least-squares method	Regression analysis: a mathematical procedure for estimating the variable and fixed elements of a semivariable cost. It develops an equation (in this book, a *linear* equation) for total cost that minimizes the sum of the squares of the historical deviations from that equation or line. Total projected cost can then be expressed as a sum of aggregate fixed cost plus the variable cost per unit (the slope of the line) multiplied by the number of units.
management by exception	The technique of managing operations by giving attention only to exceptions from expected goals. In connection with standard costs, this is achieved by giving attention only to the variances from standards.
modified high–low, two-point method	A way to estimate the fixed and variable components of a semivariable cost. Historical cost and activity data are divided into two equal subsets, one containing the higher data points and the other the lower data points.

The data in each of the two subsets are then averaged and used as the high and low points in the high–low, two-point formula.

normal standards Standard costs based on the quantity of materials, cost per unit of material, the number of hours of labor, cost per hour of direct labor, and cost per unit of manufacturing overhead that can be expected to be achieved over a longer period of time, such as the length of the business cycle (perhaps three to five years).

regression analysis See *least-squares method*.

scattergraph method Used in estimating the fixed and variable components of a semivariable cost. Historical costs and activity data are plotted on a graph, with dollar amounts (dependent variable) along the vertical axis and activity levels (independent variable) along the horizontal axis. The total cost line is then drawn so as to place approximately the same number of data points on each side of the line. The fixed element of the semivariable cost can be determined by reference to the intercept of that line with the vertical axis of the graph. Variable cost per unit of activity can be determined by subtracting the fixed costs from total costs at any activity level and dividing that figure by the number of units of activity associated with that cost. The projected total cost then can be stated as the sum of the aggregate fixed cost plus the variable cost per unit multiplied by the projected number of units of activity.

standard cost card The card or sheet that indicates the amounts of standard costs expected to be incurred to acquire or produce a single unit.

standard costs Predetermined costs, based on a careful projection of quantity and unit-cost goals, that are expected to be met in the production of goods or services.

standard hours of production An amount equal to the number of equivalent units of production multiplied by the number of standard hours allowed for the production of each unit; measures the amount of production achieved during a reporting period when using a standard-cost system.

variance The difference between the actual cost and the cost that was expected to be incurred.

zero-base budgeting A budget procedure, used primarily by governmental entities, in which managers are required to justify each budgetary expenditure anew, as if the budget were being initiated for the first time, each year rather than basing it on an adjustment of prior-year data.

QUESTIONS FOR CLASS DISCUSSION

11–1 What is the difference between standard costs and estimated costs? Explain.

11–2 How do standard costs facilitate the application of the principle of management by exception?

11–3 How is the standard cost card used in a standard cost system? Explain.

11–4 What are the two elements used to determine the standard cost of direct materials for a finished product?

11–5 What are the two elements used to determine the standard costs of direct labor for a product?

11–6 Are standard manufacturing-overhead costs per unit of finished product determined in the same manner as are direct materials and direct labor? Explain.

11–7 What is a semivariable cost? How is it separated into fixed and variable elements? Explain.

11–8 How may a scattergraph be used in determining what total semivariable expenses should be at different levels of production? Explain.

11–9 What is the high–low, two-point method of projecting semivariable costs for different levels of production? Explain how a total-cost equation can be developed from such a calculation.

11–10 How may the high–low, two-point method be modified to avoid ignoring available data?

11–11 Explain how the output of a simple regression program may be used to estimate total costs at a particular level of activity.

11–12 What is meant by the term *step-variable costs*? Give an example of such a cost.

11–13 What is the difference between best attainable and currently attainable standard costs? Which is more generally used? Explain.

11–14 How is production for a reporting period generally measured when using a standard cost system? Explain.

11–15 How are costs assigned to inventories when using a standard-cost system? Explain.

11–16 Is it appropriate to value inventories at standard costs for the purposes of external financial reporting? Explain.

11–17 How may standard-costing procedures be applied when using a job-order cost system? Explain.

EXERCISES

11–18 **Multiple Choice—Standard Cost Concepts** Select the *best* answer to each
AICPA or ICMA Adapted of the following independent items.

    1. A standard cost system may be used in
      a. job-order costing but *not* process costing.
      b. either job-order costing or process costing.

    c. process costing but *not* job-order costing.

    d. neither process costing nor job-order costing.

2. A flexible budget

    a. classifies budget requests by activity and estimates the benefits arising from each activity.

    b. presents a statement of expectations for a period of time but does not present a firm commitment.

    c. presents the plan for only one level of activity and does not adjust to changes in the level of activity.

    d. presents the plan for a range of activity so that the plan can be adjusted for changes in activity levels.

3. When a flexible budget is used, an increase in production levels within a relevant range would

    a. not change fixed costs per unit.

    b. change total fixed costs.

    c. not change variable costs per unit.

    d. not change total variable costs.

4. When production levels are expected to decline within a relevant range, and a flexible budget is used, what effects would be anticipated with respect to each of the following?

	Fixed Costs per Unit	Variable Costs per Unit
a.	increase	increase
b.	increase	no change
c.	no change	no change
d.	no change	increase

5. The best basis on which to set cost standards to measure controllable production inefficiencies is

    a. engineering standards based on ideal performance.

    b. normal capacity.

    c. recent average historical performance.

    d. engineering standards based on attainable performance.

6. Which of the following methods can be used to determine the fixed and variable elements of a semivariable expense?

    a. statistical scattergraph method

    b. linear programming

    c. input–output analysis

    d. program-evaluation-review technique

11–19 Computing the Direct Material Standard Costs Dean Company is in the process of installing a standard cost system for its principal product, Omni. Each finished unit of Omni contains 1.996 pounds of powdered plastic material. This material is mixed with water and poured into molds for cooking and curing. Some of the material is lost when the mix is poured into the molds, and some of the formed units are ruined when they are removed from the molds. This molding process results in a loss of 20% of material put in the molds, which is discarded.

Finished units are inspected when the molding process has been completed, just prior to transfer to the finished-goods warehouse. Previous experience and engineering analysis indicate that for each 1,000 units inspected two will be irretrievably spoiled and discarded.

The powdered plastic material costs $3.10 per pound.

REQUIRED: Prepare the direct materials portion of a standard cost card for Product Omni.

11—20   **Computing Direct Labor Standard Costs** The Golinda Company is preparing to begin manufacturing a new product and is setting up standard costs for it. Several options are available for the addition of the labor component to the manufacturing process, but management has rejected all but two. The labor activity will be performed by teams under one of the following options:

(1) Eight-person teams organized as follows:

	Skill Category		
	Level I	Level II	Level III
Number of laborers	4	3	1

(2) Nine-person teams organized as follows:

	Skill Category		
	Level I	Level II	Level III
Number of laborers	6	2	1

The eight-person team is expected to complete 200 units per month (160 hours), while the nine-person team is expected to complete 190 units per month. Wage rates for each level of worker will be the same regardless of which labor standard is adopted. Those rates are: Level I, $7.80 per hour; Level II, $9.75 per hour; Level III, $14.95 per hour.

REQUIRED:

1. Prepare the labor portion of the standard cost card for
   a. the eight-person team option
   b. the nine-person team option.
2. Besides total direct-labor cost per unit, what other factors should Golinda consider before adopting a labor standard?

11—21   **Manufacturing Overhead Standard Cost** Coker Company uses a standard cost system and produces two models, regular and deluxe, of a pump used in pipelines. For the month of March 19X5 total overhead is budgeted at $100,000 based on the normal capacity of 20,000 machine-hours. At standard, each finished regular pump requires 0.5 machine-hours and each finished deluxe pump requires 0.8 machine-hours. The following data are available for the March 19X5 production activity:

Equivalent units of production	
Regular pumps	15,000
Deluxe pumps	20,000
Machine-hours worked	20,500
Direct-labor hours worked	21,500
Actual total overhead incurred	$102,000

REQUIRED:

1. Compute Coker's standard overhead application rate at normal capacity.
2. What amount should Coker credit to the applied factory-overhead account for the month of March, 19X5?

11–22 **Standard Overhead Rate at Normal Capacity** Weber Company is preparing a flexible budget for 19X3 and the following maximum capacity estimates for Department Q are available:

	At Maximum Capacity
Direct labor hours	102,000
Variable factory overhead	$255,000
Fixed factory overhead	$408,000

Weber is planning to operate at 80% of maximum capacity for 19X3.

REQUIRED: Compute the total standard factory-overhead rate, based on direct-labor hours, in a flexible budget at 80% of maximum capacity.

11–23 **Estimating Fixed and Variable Costs** Johnson Corporation is preparing a flexible budget and desires to separate its electricity expense, which is semivariable and fluctuates with total machine-hours, into its fixed and variable components. Information for the first three months of 19X7 is as follows:

	Machine-Hours	Electricity Expense
January	3,500	$31,500
February	2,000	20,000
March	4,000	35,600

REQUIRED: Compute the fixed portion of Johnson's electricity expense.

11–24 **High–Low, Two-Point Method of Computing Fixed and Variable Costs** Beal Company is preparing a flexible budget for 19X3 and must separate its maintenance cost into fixed and variable elements. The following data on the cost of maintenance and direct-labor hours worked are available for the last six months of 19X2:

	Maintenance Cost	Direct-Labor Hours
July	$11,000	4,100
August	9,200	3,300
September	11,422	3,920
October	13,840	6,200
November	12,322	4,540
December	12,950	4,500
Total	$70,734	26,560

REQUIRED:

1. Assuming Beal uses the high–low, two-point method of analysis, compute the flexible budget equation for predicting maintenance cost.
2. Assuming Beal uses the modified high–low, two-point method of analysis (using an *average* low point and an *average* high point), compute the flexible budget equation for predicting maintenance cost.

11–25   **Use of Scattergraph to Analyze Mixed Costs** A scattergraph of maintenance cost as a function of direct labor hours is shown in Figure 11–9.

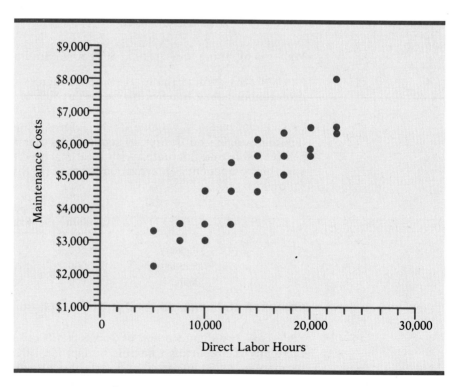

FIGURE 11–9   Scattergraph of Maintenance Cost as a Function of Direct Labor Hours

REQUIRED:

1. Describe the relationship between maintenance cost and direct labor hours.
2. Use the data on the graph to prepare a flexible budget equation showing fixed cost and variable cost per direct labor hours.

11–26 **Estimating Overhead Costs (Appendix)** Arnold Company has developed the following regression equation to analyze the behavior of its maintenance cost (dependent variable, y) based on machine-hours worked (independent variable, x).

$$y = \$9{,}600 + \$8x; \qquad R^2 = 90$$

Monthly data from the previous 36 months were used to develop this equation.

REQUIRED: What total maintenance cost would Arnold estimate for a month in which it plans to operate 2,000 machine-hours?

PROBLEMS

11–27
ICMA Adapted

Developing Standard Costs Ogwood Company is a small manufacturer of wooden household items. Al Rivkin, Corporate Controller, plans to implement a standard cost system for Ogwood. Rivkin has information from several coworkers that will assist him in developing standards for Ogwood's products.

One of Ogwood's products is a wooden cutting board. Each cutting board requires 1.25 board feet of lumber and 12 minutes of direct labor time to prepare and cut the lumber. The cutting boards are inspected after they are cut. Because the cutting boards are made of a natural material that has imperfections, one board is normally rejected for each five that are accepted. Four rubber foot pads are attached to each good cutting board. A total of 15 minutes of direct labor time is required to attach all four foot pads and finish each cutting board. The lumber for the cutting boards costs $3.00 per board foot, and each foot pad costs $.05. Direct labor is paid at the rate of $8.00 per hour.

REQUIRED:

1. Develop the standard cost for the direct cost components of the cutting board. For each direct cost component of the cutting board, the standard cost should identify the (a) standard quantity, (b) standard rate, and (c) standard cost per unit.
2. Identify the advantages of implementing a standard cost system.
3. Explain the role of each of the following persons in developing standards:

a. purchasing manager
b. industrial engineer
c. cost accountant.

11–28
ICMA Adapted

Flexible Budgets and Evaluation of Operations The University of Boyne offers an extensive continuing education program in many cities throughout the state. For the convenience of its faculty and administrative staff and also to save costs, the university operates a motor pool. Until February, the motor pool operated with 20 vehicles. However, an additional automobile was acquired in February, increasing the total to 21 vehicles. The motor pool furnishes gasoline, oil, and other supplies for the cars, and hires one mechanic who does routine maintenance and minor repairs. Major repairs are done at a nearby commercial garage. A supervisor manages the operations.

Each year the supervisor prepares an operating budget for the motor pool. The budget informs university management of the funds needed to operate the pool. Depreciation on the automobiles is recorded in the budget in order to determine the costs per mile.

Exhibit 11–1 presents the annual budget approved by the university. The actual costs for March are compared to one-twelfth of the annual budget.

The annual budget was constructed on the following assumptions:

(1) 20 automobiles in the pool
(2) 30,000 miles per year per automobile

EXHIBIT 11–1 ▬▬▬▬▬▬▬▬▬▬▬▬▬▬▬▬▬▬▬▬▬▬▬▬▬▬▬▬

University Motor Pool

Budget Report
For March 19X6

	Annual Budget	One-Month Budget	March Actual	(Over) or Under
Gasoline	$ 24,000	$2,000	$ 2,800	($800)
Oil, minor repairs, parts and supplies	6,600	550	630	(80)
Outside repairs	4,320	360	185	175
Insurance	7,800	650	675	(25)
Salaries and benefits	39,000	3,250	3,250	—
Depreciation	36,900	3,075	3,185	(110)
	$118,620	$9,885	$10,725	($840)
Total miles	600,000	50,000	63,000	
Cost per mile	$0.1977	$0.1977	$0.1702	
Number of automobiles	20	20	21	

(3) 25 miles per gallon per automobile
(4) $1.00 per gallon of gas
(5) $0.011 per mile for oil, minor repairs, parts and supplies
(6) $216 per automobile in outside repairs

The supervisor is unhappy with the monthly report comparing budget and actual costs for March. He claims it presents unfairly his performance for March. His previous employer used flexible budgeting to compare actual costs to budgeted amounts.

REQUIRED:

1. Employing flexible budgeting techniques, prepare a report that shows budgeted amounts, actual costs, and monthly variation for March.
2. Explain briefly the basis of your budget figure for outside repairs.

11–29
ICMA Adapted

Flexible Budget for a Service Enterprise Service enterprises face many of the same problems confronting manufacturing firms. Pearsons, a successful regional chain of moderate-price restaurants, each with a carryout delicatessen department, is planning to expand into a nationwide operation. As the chain gets larger and the territory covered widens, managerial control and reporting techniques become more important.

The company management believes that a budget program for the entire company as well as each restaurant–deli unit is needed. The budget shown in Exhibit 11–2 has been prepared for the typical unit in the chain. A new unit, once it is in operation, is expected to perform in accordance with the budget.

EXHIBIT 11–2
Typical Pearsons Restaurant–Deli

Budgeted Income Statement
For the Year Ending December 31
(000 omitted)

	Delicatessen	Restaurant	Total
Gross sales	$1,000	$2,500	$3,500
Purchases	$ 600	$1,000	$1,600
Hourly wages	50	875	925
Franchise fee	30	75	105
Advertising	100	200	300
Utilities	70	125	195
Depreciation	50	75	125
Lease expense	30	50	80
Salaries	30	50	80
Total	$ 960	$2,450	$3,410
Net income before income taxes	$ 40	$ 50	$ 90

EXHIBIT 11–3

Pearsons Restaurant–Deli—Akron, Ohio

Net Income

For the Year Ended December 31, 19X8

	Actual Results				Over (Under) Budget
	Delicatessen	**Restaurant**	**Total**	**Budget**	**Budget**
Gross Sales	$1,200	$2,000	$3,200	$3,500	$(300)
Purchases	$ 780	$ 800	$1,580	$1,600	$ (20)
Hourly wages	60	700	760	925	(165)
Franchise fee	36	60	96	105	(9)
Advertising	100	200	300	300	—
Utilities	76	100	176	195	(19)
Depreciation	50	75	125	125	—
Lease expense	30	50	80	80	—
Salaries	30	50	80	80	—
Total	$1,162	$2,035	$3,197	$3,410	$(213)
Net income before income taxes	$ 38	$ (35)	$ 3	$ 90	$ (87)

All units are of approximately the same size, with the amount of space devoted to the carryout delicatessen similar in each unit. The style of the facilities and the equipment used are uniform in all units. The unit operators are expected to carry out the advertising program recommended by the corporation. The corporation charges a franchise fee (a percentage of gross sales) for the use of the company name, the building and facilities design, and the advertising advice.

The Akron, Ohio, unit was selected to test the budget program. The Akron restaurant–deli performance for the year ended December 31, 19X8, compared to the typical budget, is presented in Exhibit 11–3.

A careful review of the report and a discussion of its meaning were carried out by company management. One conclusion was that a more meaningful comparison would result if a flexible budget analysis for each of the two lines was performed rather than just the single budget comparison as in the test case. Food inventories are approximately the same at both the beginning and end of the period.

REQUIRED:

1. Prepare a schedule that compares a flexible budget for the deli line of the Akron restaurant–deli to its actual performance.
2. Would a complete report, comparing a flexible budget to the performance of each of the two operations, make the problems of the Akron operation easier to identify? Explain, using an example from the problem and your answer to requirement 1.

3. Should a flexible budget comparison to actual performance become part of the regular reporting system for the following? Explain your answer.
- **a.** the annual review
- **b.** a monthly review

11–30
ICMA Adapted

Using Regression Analysis to Formulate a Flexible Budget Equation (Appendix) The Alma Plant manufactures the industrial product line of CJS Industries. Plant management wants to be able to get a good, yet quick, estimate of the manufacturing-overhead costs that can be expected to be incurred each month. The easiest and simplest way to accomplish this appears to be to develop a flexible budget formula for the manufacturing-overhead costs.

The plant's accounting staff suggested that simple linear regression be used to determine the cost behavior pattern of the overhead costs. The regression data can provide the basis for the flexible budget formula. Sufficient evidence is available to conclude that manufacturing-overhead costs vary with direct-labor hours. The actual direct-labor hours and the corresponding manufacturing-overhead costs for each month of the last three years were used in the linear regression analysis.

The three-year period contained various occurrences not uncommon to many businesses. During the first year, production was severely curtailed during two months due to wildcat strikes. In the second year, production was reduced in one month because of material shortages and materially increased (overtime scheduled) during two months to meet the units required for a one-time sales order. At the end of the second year, employee benefits were raised significantly as the result of a labor agreement. Production during the third year was not affected by any special circumstances.

Alma's accounting staff raised the following issues regarding the historical data collected for the regression analysis:

(1) Some members of the accounting staff believed that the use of data from all 36 months would provide a more accurate portrayal of the cost behavior. While they recognized that any of the monthly data could include efficiencies and inefficiencies, they believed these efficiencies/inefficiencies would tend to balance out over a longer period of time.
(2) Other members suggested that only those months considered normal should be used, so the regression would not be distorted.
(3) Still other members felt that only the most recent 12 months should be used, because they were the most current.
(4) Some members questioned whether historical data should be used at all as the basis for a flexible budget formula.

The accounting department ran two regression analyses of the data—one using the data from all 36 months and the other using only the data from the last 12 months. The information derived from the two linear regressions follows.

	Least-Squares Regression Analyses	
	Data from All 36 Months	Data from Most Recent 12 Months
Coefficients of the regression equation		
Constant	$123,810	$109,020
Independent variable (direct-labor hours)	$1.6003	$4.1977
Coefficient of correlation	.4710	.6891
Standard error of the estimate	13,003	7,473

REQUIRED:

1. From the results of Alma Plant's regression analysis that used the data from all 36 months:
   a. Formulate the flexible budget equation that can be employed to estimate monthly manufacturing-overhead costs.
   b. Calculate the estimate of overhead costs for a month when 25,000 direct labor hours are worked.
2. Using *only* the results of the two regression analyses, explain which of the two results (12 months versus 36 months) you would use as a basis for the flexible budget formula.
3. How would the four specific issues raised by the members of Alma's accounting staff influence your willingness to use the results of the statistical analyses as the basis for the flexible budget formula? Explain your answer.

11–31 THOUGHT STIMULATION PROBLEM. The use of a standard cost system requires that all costs be capable of being divided by behavior into variable or fixed categories. Because they are strictly variable, direct materials and direct labor meet this requirement. Manufacturing overhead, because it includes fixed elements, poses a major problem.

PC-Synergy is a new firm organized to manufacture the hardware for networking personal computers. Management has projected all costs for the first year of operation and desires to use a standard cost system.

REQUIRED:

1. Since PC-Synergy has no historical data it can use to apply the fixed/variable cost separation techniques discussed in this chapter (see "Allocation of Semivariable (Mixed) Costs" section, page 374), how can it divide its overhead into variable and fixed components?
2. If PC-Synergy decides to implement a just-in-time manufacturing environment, will it have any need for standard costs?

11–32
ICMA Adapted

Regression Analysis (Appendix) Regression analysis is a procedure used to measure the relationship of one variable with one or more other variables. Regression provides a rational statement rather than a causal statement with regard to the relationship. The basic formula for a regression equation is:

$$Y_i = \alpha + \beta_1 X_{i1} + E_i$$

For a regression equation to provide meaningful information, it should comply with the basic criteria of goodness of fit and specification analysis. Specification analysis involves examining the population relationships for (1) linearity within a relevant range, (2) constant variance (homoscedasticity), and (3) independence of observations (serial correlation).

REQUIRED:

1. Explain what is meant by the following sentence: "Regression provides a rational statement rather than a causal statement."
2. Explain the meaning of each of the following symbols, which appear in the basic formula for a regression equation.
   a. Y_i
   b. α
   c. β_1
   d. χ_{i1}
   e. E_i
3. Identify the statistical factors used to test a regression equation for goodness of fit and, for each item identified, indicate whether a high or low value describes a "good" fit.
4. Explain what each of the following terms means with respect to linear regression.
   a. linearity within a relevant range
   b. constant variance (homoscedasticity)
   c. serial correlation

CASE STUDIES

11–33
ICMA Adapted

Establishing a Standard-Cost System to Evaluate Performance Associated Media Graphics (AMG) is a rapidly expanding company involved in the mass reproduction of instructional materials. Ralph Boston, owner and manager of AMG, has made a concerted effort to provide a quality product at a fair price, with delivery on the promised due date. Expanding sales have been attributed to this philosophy. Boston is finding it increasingly difficult to supervise personally the operations of AMG and is beginning to institute an organizational structure that would facilitate management control.

One recent change was the designation of operating departments as cost centers, with control over departmental operations transferred from Boston to each department manager. However, quality control still reports directly to Boston, as do the finance and accounting functions. A materials manager was hired to purchase all raw materials and to oversee the inventory handling (receiving, storage, and so forth) and record-keeping functions. The materials manager also is responsible for maintaining an adequate inventory based on planned production levels.

The loss of personal control over the operations of AMG caused Boston to look for a method of efficiently evaluating performance. Dave Cress, a new cost accountant, proposed the use of a standard cost system. Variances for material, labor, and manufacturing overhead could then be calculated and reported directly to Boston.

REQUIRED:

1. Assume that AMG is going to implement a standard cost system and establish standards for materials, labor, and manufacturing overhead. Identify and discuss for each of these cost components:
   a. who should be involved in setting the standards
   b. the factors that should be considered in establishing the standards.
2. Describe the basis for assignment of responsibility under a standard cost system.

11—34
ICMA Adapted

Behavioral Impacts of Standard Costs The Kristy Company has grown from a small operation of 50 people in 19W0 to 200 employees in 19X1. Kristy designs, manufactures, and sells environmental support equipment. In the early years, each item of equipment had to be designed and manufactured to meet each customer's requirements. The work was challenging and interesting for the employees as innovative techniques were often needed in the production process to complete an order according to customers' requirements. In recent years, the company has been able to develop several components and a few complete units that can be used to meet the requirements of several customers.

The early special design and manufacture work has given the Kristy Company a leadership position in its segment of the pollution control market. Kristy takes great pride in the superior quality of its products, and this quality has contributed to its dominant role in this market segment. To help ensure high-quality performance, Kristy hires the most highly skilled personnel available and pays them salaries above the industry average. This policy has resulted in a labor force that is very efficient, stable, and positively motivated toward company objectives.

The recent increase in government regulations requiring private companies to comply with specific environmental standards has made this market very profitable. Consequently, several competitors have entered the market segment once controlled by Kristy. While Kristy still maintains a dominant position in its market, it has lost several contracts to competitors that offer similar equipment to customers at a lower price.

The Kristy manufacturing process is very labor intensive. The production employees have played an important role in the early success of the company. As a result, management gave employees a great deal of freedom to schedule and manufacture customers' orders. For instance, when the company increased the number of orders accepted, more employees were hired rather than pressuring existing employees to produce at a faster rate. In management's view, the intricacy of work involved required employees to have ample time to ensure the work was done right.

Management introduced a standard cost system they believed would be beneficial to the company. They thought it would assist in identifying the most economical way to manufacture much of the equipment, would give management a more accurate picture of the costs of the equipment, and could be used in evaluating actual costs for cost control purposes.

Consequently, the company should become more price competitive. Although the introduction of standards would likely lead to some employee discontent, management was of the opinion that the overall result would be beneficial. The standards were introduced on June 1, 19X1.

During December, 19X1, the production manager reported to the president that the new standards were creating problems in the plant. The employees had developed bad attitudes, and absenteeism and turnover rates had increased. As a result, standards were not being met. In the production manager's judgment, employee dissatisfaction outweighed any benefits management thought would be achieved by the standard cost system. The production manager supported this contention with the following data for 19X1, during which monthly production volume was at normal levels.

19X1

	J	F	M	A	M	J	J	A	S	O	N
Absenteeism rates	1%	1%	1%	1%	0.5%	1%	2%	4%	6%	8%	11%
Turnover rate	0.2%	0.5%	0.5%	0.5%	0.3%	0.8%	0.7%	1.4%	1.9%	2.5%	2.9%
Direct-labor-efficiency variance (unfavorable)	—	—	—	—	—	$(10,000)	$(11,500)	$(14,000)	$(17,000)	$(20,500)	$(25,000)
Direct-materials-usage variance (unfavorable)	—	—	—	—	—	$(4,000)	$(5,000)	$(6,500)	$(8,200)	$(11,000)	$(14,000)

REQUIRED:

1. Explain the general features and characteristics associated with the introduction and operation of a standard cost system that make it an effective cost control tool.
2. Discuss the apparent impact of Kristy Company's costs system on:
   a. cost control
   b. employee motivation.
3. Discuss the probable causes for employee dissatisfaction with the new cost system.

Chapter 12

Accounting for Direct Materials Costs and Direct Labor Costs

Learning Objectives

When you have finished your study of this chapter, you should

1. Understand the meanings of *price variance* and *quantity variance*.
2. Know how to calculate and record materials price variance and quantity (efficiency) variance.
3. Know how to calculate and record labor rate variance and efficiency variance.
4. Be able to journalize the flows of materials costs and labor costs through the manufacturing process.
5. Recognize what causes materials variances and labor variances, how they are used by management, and how they may relate to each other.
6. Understand how variances are disposed of at the end of each reporting period.

As you know, direct materials and direct labor are prime costs of producing a finished product that, in the aggregate, should vary directly with the volume of production. This means that we can expect the quantities of both materials and labor per finished unit and costs per finished unit to remain constant at all levels within a relevant range of outputs. That allows us to project the total anticipated amounts for each of these elements of production costs for any level of operations: the number of units of direct materials and hours of direct labor expected to be used in producing a unit of finished goods multiplied by their respective projected costs per unit (unit of direct materials or hour of direct labor) equals total standard direct materials and direct-labor costs of producing a unit of finished goods. That calculation is shown on the standard cost cards for each of the different products being manufactured by any firm using a standard cost system (see, for example, Figure 11-2).

Because of the strictly variable linear relationship just described, management, in planning and controlling materials and labor costs, will be especially interested in information showing the parts of the difference between total actual costs and total standard costs of materials and labor that are caused by

- deviations of actual costs from standard costs per unit (*price variances*)
- deviations of actual quantities used from standard quantities allowed for the production achieved (*quantity variances*).

These variances become the primary devices used by management for controlling the prime costs (direct materials and direct labor) of producing finished units because they point up the causes of exceptions from standard costs. Management can then focus attention on determining why the price and quantity variances from standards have occurred in controlling those costs. Because of its complexity, the calculation and use of manufacturing-overhead variances are treated separately in Chapter 13.

In this chapter, we explain how prime costs (materials and labor) should be accounted for when the cost system utilizes standard costing procedures. We do that by developing and illustrating the procedures followed in

1. recording the acquisitions and uses of direct materials
2. recording the incurrence and allocation of direct-labor costs
3. calculating, recording, and disposing of variances.

We will give particular attention to calculating, recording, and using data showing quantity variances and price variances. To set the stage, we present, in Figure 12–1, a three-box flowchart showing the points in the cost-accumulation and -allocation process at which quantity and price variances for direct materials and direct labor are recognized.

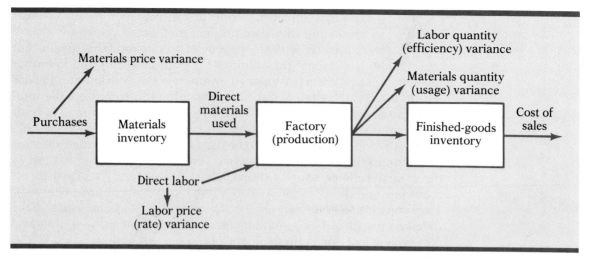

FIGURE 12–1 Recognition of Prime Cost Variances in the Production Process

In a standard cost system, we project the total costs of both direct materials and direct labor required to produce each unit of finished goods as the product of the quantity that should be used to produce one unit multiplied by the expected (that is, standard) costs per unit (unit of direct materials or hour of direct labor). **Price variances** for both direct materials and direct labor then may be calculated by using the following formula:

$$
\begin{aligned}
&\text{Actual price paid per unit} \\
&\underline{-\ \text{Standard cost expected to be paid per unit}} \\
&=\text{Price variance per unit} \\
&\underline{\times\ \text{Actual quantity (either purchased or used)}^1} \\
&=\text{Total price variance}
\end{aligned}
$$

The standard costs expected to be paid per unit of direct materials and per hour of direct labor is obtained from the appropriate standard cost cards, such as those illustrated in Figures 11–1 and 11–2. The actual costs per unit of direct materials will be found on purchase invoices, while the actual costs per hour of direct labor will be found in the payroll records. The actual quantities of the materials element of this

---

[1] Because they can be stored, materials may be purchased at one time and used at another time. The price variance can be calculated at either the point of acquisition or the point of use. Direct labor, however, cannot be stored and thus the price variance must always be calculated at the point at which it is used.

formula will be obtained from either the purchase invoices or materials requisitions. The actual quantities of direct labor will be found in the payroll records showing the hours worked during the reporting period.

The dollar amounts for **quantity variances** (variances caused by the differences between the actual quantities used and those that should have been used according to the standard cost cards) are calculated by using the following formula:

$$
\begin{aligned}
&\text{Actual quantity used}\\
-\ &\underline{\text{Standard quantity expected to be used for output achieved}}\\
=\ &\text{Quantity variance (in units)}\\
\times\ &\underline{\text{Standard cost per unit}}\\
=\ &\text{Quantity variance (in dollars)}
\end{aligned}
$$

We have just cited the sources of actual quantities and standard costs per unit for direct materials and for direct labor. The standard quantities of these items expected to be used is determined by multiplying the number of equivalent finished units produced (that is, output achieved) during a reporting period by the standard quantity per unit (units of material or hours of labor) shown on the appropriate standard cost cards. In the next two sections, we describe and illustrate the procedures followed in accounting for direct materials and direct labor in a standard cost system. The appendix at the end of this chapter illustrates the use of "Triangles" in calculating materials and labor variances.

Accounting for Direct Materials

Accounting for the flow of direct materials through the manufacturing process begins with the purchase of materials and extends to the transfer of the cost of materials included in completed units transferred to finished goods.

Accounting for Materials Purchases

The flow chart in Figure 12–1 presumes that all materials will be valued at standard cost. Although this is generally true for cost accounting systems using standard costs, we may, in some instances, find materials inventory valued at actual cost instead. When that practice is followed, the materials price variance will be determined as materials are issued into process rather than at the time materials are purchased. Recognition of price variances at the time of purchase is preferable because that allows management to react to the exceptions sooner than if they were not identified until the point of use. Therefore, virtually all our attention in this text will be focused on the identification of materials price variances at the time materials are purchased.

When materials are valued at standard cost, the **materials price variance** should be calculated and recorded as materials are *purchased*. The entry to record such purchases requires a debit to the materials-inventory account for the actual quantity of materials purchased multiplied by the standard cost per unit shown on the standard cost cards. Accounts payable will be credited for the amount shown on the purchase invoice (actual quantity × actual price). The difference between those two figures then will be recorded as either a debit or a credit to an account called "materials price variance." It will be equal to the difference between the actual and standard cost per unit multiplied by the actual number of units shown on the purchase invoice. For example, if 1,000 units of a raw material are purchased for $1,300, and the standard cost card for the raw material shows a predetermined (standard) cost of $1.20 per unit, the $100 unfavorable price variance is calculated by multiplying the 1,000 units by the difference between the $1.30 per unit actual cost and the $1.20 per unit standard cost:

Actual price paid per unit	$ 1.30	
− Standard price per unit	1.20	
= Price variance per unit	$ .10	Unfavorable
× Actual quantity purchased	× 1,000	
= Total materials price variance	$ 100	Unfavorable

The purchase should be recorded as follows:

Materials inventory	1,200	
Materials price variance	100	
Accounts payable		1,300

This entry shows that the firm has purchased 1,000 units of raw materials at a total cost of $100 more than should have been paid based on predetermined standards. The debit to the variance account shows it to be an unfavorable (U) variance.

If the invoice for raw materials carried a price of $1.15 per unit ($1,150 total), the materials price variance would be calculated as follows:

Actual price paid per unit	$ 1.15	
− Standard price per unit	1.20	
= Price variance per unit	($ .05)	Favorable
× Actual quantity purchased	× 1,000	
= Total materials price variance	($50.00)	Favorable

The journal entry to record the purchase would be:

Materials inventory	1,200	
Accounts payable		1,150
Materials price variance		50

This entry shows that the firm purchased 1,000 units of raw materials at a total cost of $50 less than the materials should have cost based on predetermined standards. The credit to the variance account shows it to be a favorable (F) variance.

Let's now use an assumed purchase transaction for the Ajax Chemical Company (part of our continuing illustration), whose standard cost cards were presented in Figures 11–1 and 11–2 (see page 372), to show how the data from standard cost cards are used in recording materials purchases and calculating the materials quantity variance. We will use the following data from Ajax Chemical Company's standard cost cards:

Material A, standard cost per pound	$2.00
Material B, standard cost per pound	$2.20
Material C, standard cost per pound	$1.70

Finished Product Part No. 5001	
Materials	
Material A (0.3 pound @ $2.00)	$ .60
Material B (0.3 pound @ $2.20)	.66
Material C (0.4 pound @ $1.70)	.68
Total	$1.94

Assume that Ajax had invoices showing the following purchases of direct materials A, B, and C:

2,500 pounds of direct material A (@ $2.16)	$ 5,400
3,000 pounds of direct material B (@ $2.10)	6,300
3,200 pounds of direct material C (@ $1.80)	5,760
Total	$17,460

The materials price variance would be calculated as follows:

Material A

Invoice cost per unit	$2.16
Standard cost per unit	2.00
Price variance per unit	$ .16 (U)
Actual quantity purchased	× 2,500 lb
Material A price variance	$ 400 (U)

Material B

Invoice cost per unit	$2.10
Standard cost per unit	2.20
Price variance per unit	($ .10) (F)
Actual quantity purchased	× 3,000 lb
Material B price variance	($300) (F)

Material C

Invoice cost per unit	$1.80
Standard cost per unit	1.70
Price variance per unit	$ .10 (U)
Actual quantity purchased	× 3,200 lb
Material C price variance	$ 320 (U)
Total price variance	$ 420 (U)

Ajax's purchases should be recorded as follows:

Materials inventory	$17,040	
Materials price variance	420	
Accounts payable		$17,460

The debit to materials inventory was calculated as follows:

Material A [2,500 pounds at standard cost ($2.00)]	$ 5,000
Material B [3,000 pounds at standard cost ($2.20)]	$ 6,600
Material C [3,200 pounds at standard cost ($1.70)]	$ 5,440
	$17,040

The credit to accounts payable is equal to the sum of the three invoices. This analysis informs management about the materials that cost more than was expected (A and C in this situation) and the material that cost less than expected (B). Observe that we labeled the unfavorable variances (U) and the favorable variances (F). We shall follow that practice throughout this chapter and Chapter 13. After making the preceding calculations, we may, as an alternative to the preceding journal entry, want to record the materials purchase as follows:

Materials inventory	17,040	
Material A price variance	400	
Material C price variance	320	
Material B price variance		300
Accounts payable		17,460

Accounting for Materials Used in Production

We have shown how the materials price variance is determined and recorded at the point at which materials are purchased. All other variances, including the **direct materials quantity variance**—more generally called **direct materials usage variance**—are recognized as we account for the flows of manufacturing costs through the production process (see Figure 12–1).

To illustrate how the direct materials quantity (usage) variance is calculated and recorded, let's assume that 5,000 units of direct materials have been used to produce 2,250 finished units, that the standard cost card for the finished product shows the firm should expect to use 2 units of direct materials for each finished product turned out, and that the standard cost of each unit of direct materials is $1. In this situation, we calculate the standard quantity of direct materials that should have been used by multiplying the number of finished units turned out (output achieved) by 2 units of material: $2,250 \times 2 = 4,500$ units. Since the actual quantity used was 5,000 units, the direct material usage variance is $500 (U):

Actual quantity of materials used	5,000
− Standard quantity of materials for output achieved (2,250 × 2)	4,500
= Quantity variance (in units)	500 (U)
× Standard cost per unit	× $1
= Total materials quantity variance	$500

The following entry should be made to record the material usage variance:

Material quantity (usage) variance	**500**	
Work-in-process inventory		**500**

We will show, as we carry through our illustration of the Ajax Chemical Company, that this entry generally is included as part of the monthly, or more frequent, entry that records the transfer of the materials costs allocated to finished products from work in process to finished-goods inventory.

We will now discuss and illustrate the handling of materials price variance and quantity variance based on the purchases and production data previously assumed for the Ajax Chemical Company. Figure 12–2 shows a production cost-accumulation box using the data from the Ajax Chemical Company illustration in Chapter 6 plus assumptions in Chapter 11 (see page 371). These data will be used in this chapter and Chapter 13 as we explain and illustrate the procedures to follow in accounting for the manufacturing operations of Ajax with the installation of a standard cost system.

We now demonstrate the procedures followed in accounting for the flows of direct materials costs for Ajax. No dollar values are shown for beginning-of-period work in process or for materials put into process because all of these items will be valued at standard costs. As you can see in Figure 12–2, we also have made the following assumptions regarding direct materials put into process:

Material A, 2,200 pounds
Material B, 2,050 pounds
Material C, 3,000 pounds

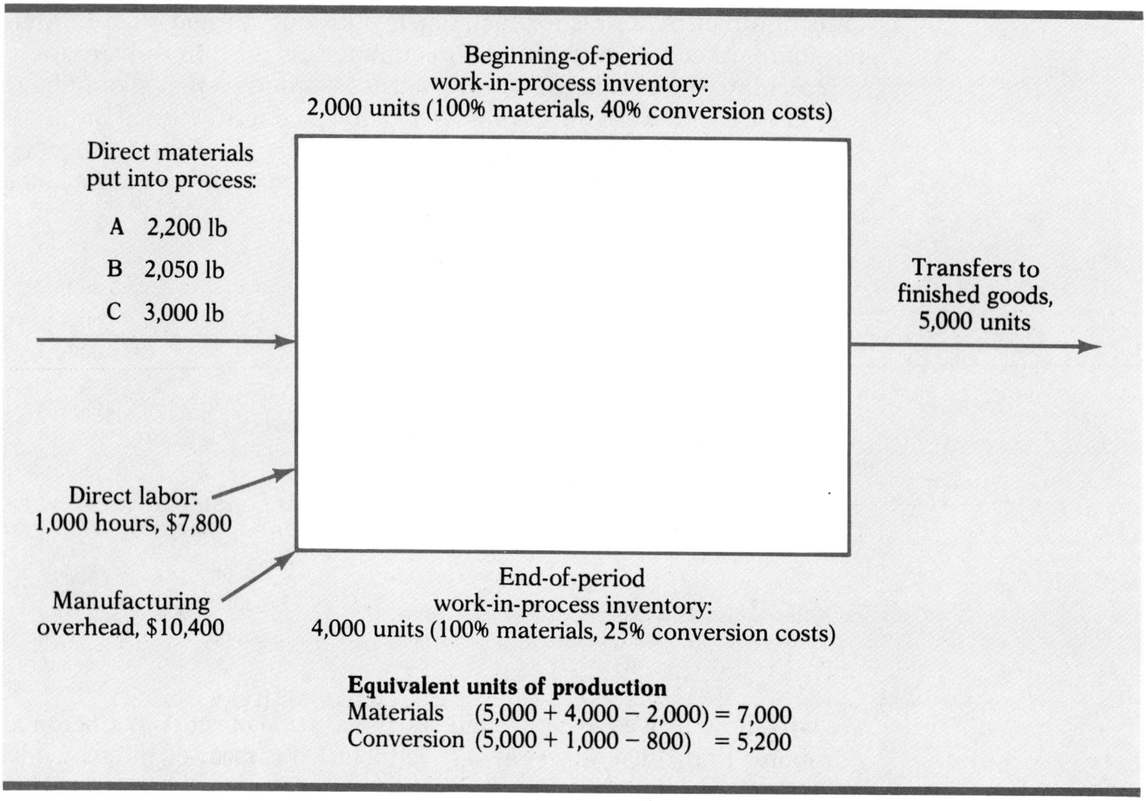

Beginning-of-period
work-in-process inventory:
2,000 units (100% materials, 40% conversion costs)

Direct materials
put into process:

A   2,200 lb

B   2,050 lb

C   3,000 lb

Transfers to
finished goods,
5,000 units

Direct labor:
1,000 hours, $7,800

Manufacturing
overhead, $10,400

End-of-period
work-in-process inventory:
4,000 units (100% materials, 25% conversion costs)

Equivalent units of production
Materials   (5,000 + 4,000 − 2,000) = 7,000
Conversion (5,000 + 1,000 − 800)   = 5,200

FIGURE 12–2   Ajax Chemical Company: Manufacturing Cost-Accumulation Box, Finished Product No. 5001

The following entry should be made to record the issuance of direct materials into work in process:

Work-in-process inventory	14,010 (1)	
Materials inventory		14,010

Explanation:

(1)

2,200 pounds of Material A @ $2.00	$ 4,400
2,050 pounds of Material B @ $2.20	4,510
3,000 pounds of Material C @ $1.70	5,100
Total	$14,010

As direct materials costs are allocated between end-of-period work-in-process inventory and transfers to finished goods, we will assign a dollar value to the difference between the quantities of materials that should have been used, according to the standard cost cards, and the amounts actually issued into in the process by using the following equation:

> Actual quantities of materials used
> — Standard quantities of materials expected to be used
> = Quantity variance (in units)
> × Standard cost per unit of materials
> = Materials quantity (usage) variance

The actual quantities of direct materials A, B, and C used were, as assumed, 2,200, 2,050, and 3,000 pounds, respectively. For materials, the output was 5,000 units transferred to finished goods + 4,000 units in end-of-period work in process − 2,000 units in beginning-of-period work in process = 7,000 equivalent finished units, which should have required 2,100, 2,100, and 2,800 pounds of direct materials A, B, and C, respectively, calculated as follows:

Material A (7,000 × 0.3 pound)	2,100 pounds
Material B (7,000 × 0.3 pound)	2,100 pounds
Material C (7,000 × 0.4 pound)	2,800 pounds

We can now calculate the materials usage (quantity) variance:

Material A (2,200 − 2,100) × $2	$200 (U)
Material B (2,050 − 2,100) × $2.20	(110) (F)
Material C (3,000 − 2,800) × $1.70	340 (U)
Total	$430 (U)

The units transferred to finished goods would include materials valued at $9,700, calculated as follows:

> 5,000 units @ $1.94 (see standard cost data on Part. No. 5001, page 421) = $9,700

The following entry should be made at the end of the period to record the transfer of direct materials costs into finished-goods inventory:

Finished goods	9,700	
Materials usage variance	430	
Work in process		10,130

As you can see, the credit to work in process equals the sum of materials costs transferred to finished goods and the materials usage variance.

To complete our illustration and prove the correctness of our credit to work in process, we will now show that the end-of-period work-in-process inventory also is valued at standard cost. In doing that, we reproduce the following T account showing the materials element of work in process at the beginning of the period, the entry made earlier to show the issuance of direct materials into process, and the preceding credit to work in process to transfer completed units to finished goods. We then show a calculated proof of the ending balance of work in process:

Work-in-Process Inventory (materials element only)

Beginning-of-period balance	3,880 (1)	9,700 (3)	Transfer to finished goods
Added during period	14,010 (2)	430 (3)	Transfer to variance account
End-of-period balance	7,760 (4)		

Explanation:

(1) 2,000 units @ $1.94 (see standard cost card information, page 421.) = $3,880.

(2) Raw materials added to work in process (see entry on page 424):

Raw material A (2,200 × $2)	$ 4,400
Raw material B (2,050 × $2.20)	4,510
Raw material C (3,000 × $1.70)	5,100
Total	$14,010

(3) See entry on page 425.

(4) 4,000 units × $1.94 (see standard cost card information, page 421).

Of course, the earlier a variance is recognized, the sooner appropriate corrective action can be taken. With a standard cost job-order system, requisitions can be prepared for the standard amount of materials required in advance of the issuance of direct materials. If additional materials are then required to complete the job, an additional requisition would be prepared; this special requisition would trigger the immediate recognition of an unfavorable materials usage (quantity) variance. Excess materials from a standard issuance would be returned to stores with an accompanying materials-returned form, signaling a favorable materials usage variance. In the preceding illustration, if we followed that procedure, a special requisition would call for an additional 100 pounds of material A and an additional 200 pounds of material C. Fifty pounds of material B would be returned to stores.

Accounting for Direct Labor

As you can observe in Figure 12–1, both the labor price (rate) and the labor quantity (efficiency) variances are recognized as the labor costs flow into and through the department or the manufacturing cost-accumulation center. The **direct labor rate variance** is recognized at the

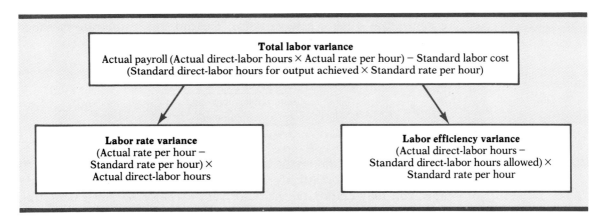

FIGURE 12–3   Labor Variances

point at which the direct labor charge to work in process is recorded. The **direct labor efficiency variance** is recognized as we account for the cost of goods transferred from work in process into finished goods. It may be helpful to visualize labor variances as shown in Figure 12–3.

Accounting for Payroll Costs

As we have seen in the case of both job-order and process-costing systems, the flow of direct labor costs into work in process is recognized at the point at which a company incurs a responsibility for paying its direct laborers. The incurrence of the payroll obligation and the distribution of payroll costs under an actual or normal cost system, as explained and illustrated earlier in the text, is recognized through the following journal entries:

Manufacturing payroll	XXXX	
Payroll taxes payable		XX
Accrued payroll		XXXX
Work in process	XXXX	
Manufacturing overhead	XXX	
Manufacturing payroll		XXXX

The debit to work in process is for the direct labor part of payroll, calculated as the actual direct labor hours worked multiplied by the actual rate(s) per hour. Manufacturing overhead is charged for the indirect labor costs included in the payroll account.

When using standard costs, we debit work in process for an amount equal to the actual direct labor hours multiplied by the standard rate(s) per hour shown on the standard cost cards. The difference between that figure and the amount of direct labor included in the payroll account is recognized as a labor rate variance. The amount of the rate variance also can be calculated by using the following formula:

$$
\begin{array}{l}
\text{Actual labor rate per hour} \\
- \text{ Standard labor rate per hour} \\
\hline
= \text{Rate variance per hour} \\
\times \text{ Actual hours worked} \\
\hline
= \text{Direct-labor rate variance}
\end{array}
$$

However, because the credit to accrued payroll for amounts owed to direct laborers automatically will be actual hours multiplied by actual rates, you may determine the labor rate variance by first calculating the debit to work in process as the actual hours worked by the direct laborers multiplied by the standard rate per hour. The debit or credit to labor rate variance then will be the balancing (plug) amount required in the entry to remove actual direct-labor cost from the payroll account.

To illustrate, let's assume the following data regarding direct labor for Alpha Company:

Direct-labor payroll: 8,200 hours, $58,000
Standard direct labor rate: $7.00 per hour

The incurrence of the direct-labor payroll with those assumed data would be recorded as follows:

Direct-labor payroll	58,000	
Accrued payroll (and other payroll-related		
obligations)		58,000
Work in process	57,400 (1)	
Direct-labor rate variance	600 (2)	
Direct-labor payroll		58,000

Explanation:

(1) 8,200 hours at $7 = $57,400.
(2) $58,000 − $57,400 = $600 (amount required to complete, or plug, the entry).

The debit to the labor rate variance reflects an unfavorable (U) variance. It shows that a higher rate per hour ($58,000/8,200 = $7.0731707) was paid than was anticipated when the standard cost per hour for labor was established.

We now return to the Ajax Chemical Company illustration to demonstrate the procedures followed in accounting for the flows of direct-labor costs from the point at which those costs are incurred through their transfer to finished goods. Observe from Figure 12–2 that the actual direct-labor payroll for the period was 1,000 hours, costing the company $7,800, an actual labor rate per hour of $7,800 ÷ 1,000 = $7.80. We then use the following data from the standard cost card for

Finished Product No. 5001 (Figure 11–2): direct labor = 0.2 hour @ $8 per hour = $1.60. The direct labor rate variance then would be:

Actual labor rate per hour	$7.80
− Standard labor rate per hour	8.00
= Rate variance per hour	($ .20) (F)
× Actual hours worked	× 1,000
= Direct labor rate variance	($ 200) (F)

The flow of direct-labor costs into work in process would be recorded as follows:

Direct labor payroll	7,800	
Accrued payroll (and other payroll-related obligations)		7,800
Work in process (1,000 hours @ $8)	8,000	
Direct labor payroll		7,800
Direct labor rate variance		200

The favorable (F) rate variance indicates that the actual rate of pay was less than was anticipated when the standard rate per hour was established.

Accounting for the Transfer of Direct-Labor Cost to Finished Goods

As explained during our discussion of both job-order and process cost systems, using actual costs are allocated to completed units transferred to finished goods by making the following entry:

Finished goods	XXX	
Work in process		XXX

One element of those costs in all instances would be the amount of direct labor allocated to the finished units.

When we use standard costs, all units transferred to finished-goods inventory should be valued at standard cost. The direct labor portion of standard cost of goods manufactured (the total cost of units transferred from work in process to finished goods) would be equal to the standard hours of direct labor allowed for the production of completed units multiplied by the standard rate per hour. The labor element of the end-of-period work-in-process inventory should be valued at the standard hours of direct labor allowed for units in process (that is, standard equivalent units of work completed) multiplied by the standard rate per hour.

Earlier, as we demonstrated the procedures for recording the labor rate variance for Alpha Company (see page 428), we debited work in process for $57,400, representing 8,200 actual hours multiplied by the company's standard rate of $7 per hour. Let's now assume that the standard cost card for Alpha's product shows one hour of direct labor allowed for each unit, that 7,000 finished units are transferred to finished goods, that the end-of-period work-in-process inventory includes 2,000 units 50% complete (as to direct labor), and that the company had no beginning-of-period work-in-process inventory. This means that Alpha has turned out 8,000 standard hours of production, calculated as follows:

7,000 units finished × 1 hour per unit	7,000 hours
2,000 units in process × 50% × 1 hour	1,000 hours
Total	8,000 hours

The direct labor efficiency variance can then be calculated:

Actual direct labor hours	8,200
− Standard direct labor hours	8,000
= Quantity variance (in hours)	200 (U)
× Standard labor rate per hour	× $7
= Direct labor efficiency variance	$1,400 (U)

The transfer of labor costs associated with finished units would be recorded as follows:

Finished goods	**49,000 (1)**	
Direct labor efficiency variance	**1,400**	
Work in process		**50,400**

Explanation:

(1) 7,000 standard hours × $7 per hour = $49,000.

This entry automatically allows the labor element of end-of-period work-in-process inventory to be valued at its standard cost. We demonstrate that fact in the following T account:

Work in Process (direct-labor element)

Beginning balance	0	49,000	Transfer to finished goods
Payroll entry	57,400	1,400	Transfer to variance account
Ending balance	$ 7,000 (1)		

Explanation:

(1) 1,000 standard hours (2,000 units × 50% completion) × $7 per hour = $7,000.

Returning to Ajax Chemical Company, we find that 5,200 equivalent units of direct-labor production of Finished Product No. 5001 were turned out during the reporting period (see equivalent units of production in Figure 12–2). The standard cost card for a finished unit shows that this also could be expressed as 1,040 standard direct-labor hours of production (0.2 hours × 5,200 units). When we refer to the payroll data (see Figure 12–2), we find that the company used 1,000 actual hours of direct labor during the period. We can now calculate the labor efficiency variance:

Actual direct-labor hours	1,000	
− Standard direct-labor hours	1,040	
= Quantity variance (in hours)	(40)	(F)
× Standard direct-labor rate per hour	× $8	
= Direct-labor efficiency variance	$(320)	(F)

During the reporting period, the company transferred 5,000 units to finished-goods inventory. From these data, we would make the following journal entry to record the labor efficiency variance and the transfer of the labor element of work in process to finished goods:

Finished goods	8,000 (1)	
Direct labor efficiency variance		320
Work in process		7,680

Explanation:

(1) 5,000 units × 0.2 hour × $8; or, 5,000 units × $1.60 = $8,000.

The net reduction of work in process is equal to the difference between the transfer to finished goods and the favorable labor efficiency variance. This entry also will cause the labor element of end-of-period work in process to be reflected in the work-in-process account at its standard cost. We demonstrate that fact in the following T account:

Work in Process (direct-labor element)

Beginning balance	1,280 (1)	Transfer to finished goods	$8,000 (4)
Payroll entry	8,000 (2)		
Transfer to variance account	320 (3)		
Ending balance	1,600 (5)		

Explanation:

(1) 2,000 units × 40% × $1.60 = $1,280 or
    2,000 units × 40% × 0.2 hour = 160 standard hours
        160 standard hours × $8 = $1,280
(2) See entry on page 429 (1,000 actual hours @ $8 per hour).
(3) See entry on page 429 (1,000 actual hours − 1,040 standard hours × $8 per hour).

(4) See entry on page 431 (5,000 units $\times$ 0.2 hour $\times$ \$8 per hour).
(5) 1,000 equivalent units (4,000 $\times$ 0.25) $\times$ \$1.60 = \$1,600 or
    1,000 units $\times$ 0.2 hour = 200 standard hours
       200 standard hours $\times$ \$8 = \$1,600

Use and Disposal of Variances

Parts I, II, and III of this text are devoted primarily to the explanation and discussion of systems used to accumulate and allocate manufacturing costs to products being produced and the use of those data in valuing inventories. Managerial use of cost data is covered in Part IV. However, it seems appropriate to discuss briefly some of the ways in which management can use the data provided by variance calculations in controlling the costs of manufacturing in this chapter and Chapter 13. We begin our discussion of variance analysis by describing how data on direct-materials variances and direct-labor variances are used. After that, we explain how the variance account balances are disposed of at the end of each reporting period.

Using Variance Data

The managers of a firm that uses standard costs control manufacturing costs by giving their attention to the *exceptions* from standards that appear in the variance accounts; that is, they follow up on significant favorable or unfavorable exceptions (variances) from standards. Typically, they communicate those data to the appropriate responsible persons in the organization, who then are expected to investigate the situation, find what has caused the variances and take appropriate action to correct any problems, show that the established standards are inappropriate, or try to perpetuate favorable situations.

Materials Price Variances.   The purchasing department is held primarily responsible for direct materials price variances. However, before the person in charge of that department can act to correct the causes of those variances, the total price variance must be related to either individual items or categories of items. On pages 421–422 we showed how that was done for the three materials purchased by Ajax Chemical Company. Having made that allocation, the person in charge of the purchasing department is expected to explain why the variances have occurred and to take necessary corrective action. A firm should investigate significant *favorable* variances as well as significant unfavorable ones. A favorable price variance might occur, for example, because materials of lower quality than specified were purchased. The firm could then incur an unfavorable usage variance because of the number of spoiled units produced from inferior materials.[2]

---

[2]Even if there is no problem with quality, an investigation into the possibility of sustaining the favorable variance (or changing the standard) should be initiated.

Materials price variances cannot be evaluated blindly in terms of favorable and unfavorable variances from standard because of their possible impact on overall firm operations. For example, if, for whatever reason, materials required to produce goods that are immediately saleable are unavailable, the purchasing department should acquire the materials. The cost purchasing should be prepared to pay depends on the additional income that could be earned had the materials been available rather than on the standard cost of the materials.

Labor Rate Variances. *Unfavorable* labor rate variances can be created by utilizing employees whose base hourly rates exceed the standard rate, or by incurring more overtime hours than were projected in establishing the standard rate per hour. The person responsible for assigning employees to jobs—in most instances the departmental supervisor—is generally held responsible for explaining this variance. For excess overtime, improper scheduling may be an appropriate explanation. Management must then take corrective action or, in the event the variance has been created by an unexpectedly large volume of work, simply acknowledge that the variance is part of the price paid for the higher level of operations. If employees paid higher rates per hour have been utilized for work expected to be done by employees earning lower rates, the supervisor is expected to take corrective action by being more selective in assigning employees to specific tasks. A *favorable* labor rate variance could result from employing workers who are not as experienced as called for by the standard. This situation may in turn be associated with an unfavorable labor efficiency variance.

Materials Usage Variances. *Unfavorable* materials usage variances can result from improper processing of raw materials, using inferior grades of materials, or improper handling or theft of materials as they are being processed. The processing supervisor is generally held responsible for all of these causes, except the use of inferior grades of materials, for which responsibility goes back to the purchasing department or the person approving the purchase. *Favorable* material usage variances can be created by using higher-quality materials than the standard calls for (most likely associated with an unfavorable price variance) or by having less than normal scrap or spoilage.

In a multidepartment firm, it is important to allocate the total materials usage variance to the individual items of materials used. Those variances then can be related to the departments in which those materials are processed, to establish responsibilities for specific elements of the total variance and permit the initiation of appropriate corrective action.

Labor Efficiency Variances. Labor efficiency variances can be created by assigning too many or too few employees in relation to the work turned out; by employees not being fully assigned to productive work; by the assignment of more experienced (and expensive) employees than the standard calls for; or by employees not meeting (or exceeding) time study expectations for work turned out. In other instances, unfavorable labor efficiency variances may have been caused by the use of inferior materials, which may have been corroborated by favorable materials price variances.

Again, the departmental supervisor generally is held responsible for all of these, except possibly for employees not meeting expectations and the use of inferior materials, and even these can be a result of inadequate monitoring or instructions from the supervisor. It also is possible that the standard, which is not controlled by the supervisor, needs to be changed. Therefore, the *total* labor efficiency variance should be allocated to individual departments, to allow the production manager to relate the segments of the total variance to the appropriate departmental supervisors. Discussions with the individual supervisors should then lead to explanations permitting appropriate action.

Disposal of Variances

Although we have been saying, both in Chapter 11 and this chapter, that direct materials, work-in-process, and finished-goods inventories are valued at standard costs, it is important to realize that this is a generally acceptable basis for valuing inventories *only* when those values are not significantly different from actual costs. Therefore, when variances resulting from the differences between standard and actual costs are immaterial, they can be closed to cost of sales, just as immaterial amounts of underapplied or overapplied overhead are disposed of when using historical costs.

When variances are significant, however, they must be appropriately allocated to the various inventory and cost-of-sales accounts to meet the requirements of generally accepted accounting practices for external reporting purposes. The allocation generally will be based on the relationship of the standard cost of the element (direct materials or direct labor) associated with the variance included in each of the ending inventories and the cost-of-sales accounts to the total amount of the element included in all inventories and cost of sales. Recall that we allocated underapplied or overapplied overhead on the basis of the relationship between the applied overhead shown in work in process, finished goods, and cost of sales to the total applied overhead included in all of those accounts. That standard format, where a ratio is formed from the relationship of the amount in one account to the total in all accounts, should be followed in allocating all significant variances to inventory and cost-of-sales accounts.

Materials Price Variances. Following that line of reasoning, a materials price variance recognized at the point at which materials are purchased would be allocated to all accounts containing direct materials: materials inventory, work-in-process inventory, finished-goods inventory, and cost of sales. This allocation arrangement is based on the assumption that the amount of the price variance associated with the direct material usage variance will not significantly affect the results of total material variances allocated to the various inventory and cost of sales accounts. A more precise allocation would include material usage variance as a fifth element in the allocation process. That would increase (unfavorable) or decrease (favorable) the balance in the material usage variance to be allocated, as shown below. The amount of standard materials costs included in each of those account balances divided by total standard materials costs shown in all of those accounts would be used to allocate that variance. For example, assume an unfavorable materials price variance of $6,000 is to be allocated to the following accounts:

Material Inventory	**Work in Process**	**Finished Goods**	**Cost of Sales**
$7,000	$27,000	$65,000	$185,000
All direct materials	Direct materials $ 3,000	Direct materials $13,000	Direct materials $37,000
	Direct labor 12,000	Direct labor 26,000	Direct labor 74,000
	Overhead 12,000	Overhead 26,000	Overhead 74,000

The allocation of the materials price variance should then be computed as follows:

Accounts with Direct Materials Costs	Direct Materials Costs	Ratio	× Price Variance to Be Allocated	= Unfavorable Variance to Be Debited to Each Account
Materials inventory	$ 7,000	7/60	$6,000	$ 700
Work in process	3,000	3/60	6,000	300
Finished goods	13,000	13/60	6,000	1,300
Cost of sales	37,000	37/60	6,000	3,700
	$60,000			$6,000

Using this information, the journal entry to record the allocation of the $6,000 unfavorable materials price variance is:

Materials inventory	700	
Work-in-process inventory	300	
Finished-goods inventory	1,300	
Cost of sales	3,700	
Materials price variance		6,000

After this entry has been recorded, the materials price-variance account balance will be zero and the other accounts in the entry will reflect the approximate *actual*, rather than standard, costs of materials included in them.

Because, as a normal operating procedure, we want to carry our inventory accounts at standard rather than actual costs, we should *reverse* the inventory parts of the preceding entry by making the following reversing journal entry after financial statements have been prepared at the end of the reporting period. (As an alternate procedure, the preceding entry can be made only on a worksheet used to adjust the accounts prior to preparing financial statements.)

Materials price variance	2,300	
Materials inventory		700
Work-in-process inventory		300
Finished-goods inventory		1,300

Direct Materials Usage Variances. The direct materials usage (quantity) variance would be allocated to work-in-process inventory, finished-goods inventory, and cost of sales on the basis of the standard cost of direct materials shown in each of those accounts. Using the data from the previous example, the allocation of a $4,717 *favorable* material usage variance would be calculated as follows:

Accounts with Materials-Used Costs	Materials-Used Costs	Ratio ×	Quantity Variance to Be Allocated	=	Favorable Variance to Be Credited to Each Account
Work in process	$ 3,000	3/53	$4,717		$ 267
Finished goods	13,000	13/53	4,717		1,157
Cost of sales	37,000	37/53	4,717		3,293
	$53,000				$4,717

Note: Materials inventory is not included here because the usage variance relates only to materials that have been issued to the factory.

The entry to allocate the $4,717 materials usage variance to inventories and cost of sales would be:

Materials usage variance	4,717	
Work-in-process inventory		267
Finished-goods inventory		1,157
Cost of sales		3,293

Again, the inventory parts of this entry should be reversed by making the following reversing journal entry after statements have been prepared at the end of the reporting period. (Also, as with the allocation of a price variance, the allocation entry could be recorded in a worksheet rather than in the formal accounting records.)

Work-in-process inventory	267	
Finished goods inventory	1,157	
Material usage variance		1,424

For both direct materials variances (price and usage), unfavorable variances would be added to the standard costs, and favorable variances would be subtracted from standard costs. In that way, the amounts shown for materials cost in the three inventory accounts and the cost-of-sales account will approximate *actual* costs after the variances have been allocated.

Direct Labor Rate and Efficiency Variances. Both the direct labor rate variance and the direct labor efficiency variance should be allocated to work-in-process inventory, finished-goods inventory, and cost of sales on the basis of the standard costs of direct labor included in each of those accounts in relation to the total direct-labor cost included in all of those accounts.

To illustrate the allocation of labor variances, let's assume a $5,600 unfavorable direct-labor rate variance and a $6,720 favorable direct-labor efficiency variance. We then use the direct-labor data given on page 435 to arrive at the following entry to allocate the $5,600 Unfavorable Direct Labor Rate Variance and $6,720 Favorable Direct-Labor Efficiency Variances):

Direct labor efficiency variance	6,720	
Work-in-process inventory		
($600 debit + $720 credit)*		120
Finished goods inventory		
($1,300 debit + $1,560 credit)*		260
Cost of sales ($3,700 debit + $4,440 credit)*		740
Direct-labor rate variance		5,600

*Accounts with Direct Labor Costs	Labor Costs	Ratio ×	Labor Rate Variance to Be Allocated =	Unfavorable Variance to Be Debited to Each Account
Work in process	$ 12,000	12/112	$5,600	$ 600
Finished goods	26,000	26/112	5,600	1,300
Cost of sales	74,000	74/112	5,600	3,700
	$112,000			$5,600

Accounts with Direct Labor Costs	Labor Costs	Ratio ×	Labor Efficiency Variance to Be Allocated =	Favorable Variance to Be Credited to Each Account
Work in process	$ 12,000	12/112	$6,720	$ 720
Finished goods	26,000	26/112	6,720	1,560
Cost of sales	74,000	74/112	6,720	4,440
	$112,000			$6,720

Again, the inventory parts of the allocation entry should be reversed, as follows (unless that entry has been recorded in a worksheet rather than in the formal accounting records):

Direct-labor rate variance	1,900	
Work-in-process inventory	120	
Finished-goods inventory	260	
Direct-labor efficiency variance		2,280

Illustrative Problem: Part 2

We now continue our Illustration Company problem (originated in Chapter 11) by adding the following assumptions regarding the costs of direct materials and direct labor:

Purchases of Materials

Material A (2,000 units @ $.55)	$1,100
Material B (1,200 units @ $.291$\frac{2}{3}$)	350
Material C (4,000 units @ $.975)	3,900
Material D (3,000 units @ $.80)	2,400
Total	$7,750

Materials Used

Material A: 1,650 units
Material B: 1,620 units
Material C: 4,210 units
Material D: 2,820 units

Direct Labor Payroll

1,625 hours @ average rate of $5.9692308 = $9,700

The standard cost cards for the two products of Illustration Company are reproduced in Figure 12–4 from the solution to Part 1 in Chapter 11.

All materials are added at the beginning of processing. Inventories and transfers to finished goods of products M and N are as follows:

Beginning of Period Work-in-Process Inventory

Product M: 300 units, $\frac{1}{3}$ complete as to conversion costs
Product N: 200 units, 40% complete as to conversion costs

```
┌─────────────────────────────────────────────────────────────────────┐
│  Standard Cost Card                                                   │
│                                                                       │
│                          Product M                                    │
│                                                                       │
│  Direct materials                                                     │
│      2 units of raw material A @ $.50                       $ 1.00    │
│      2 units of raw material B @ $.25                          .50    │
│      Total                                                  $ 1.50    │
│                                                                       │
│  Direct labor (0.6 hour @ $6 per hour)                        3.60    │
│  Overhead (0.6 hour @ $10 per hour)                           6.00    │
│  Total standard cost                                        $11.10    │
└─────────────────────────────────────────────────────────────────────┘
```

```
┌─────────────────────────────────────────────────────────────────────┐
│  Standard Cost Card                                                   │
│                                                                       │
│                          Product N                                    │
│                                                                       │
│  Direct materials                                                     │
│      3 units of raw material C @ $1.00                      $ 3.00    │
│      2 units of raw material D @ $.75                         1.50    │
│      Total                                                  $ 4.50    │
│                                                                       │
│  Direct labor (0.8 hour @ $6 per hour)                        4.80    │
│  Overhead (0.8 hour @ $10 per hour)                           8.00    │
│  Total standard cost                                        $17.30    │
└─────────────────────────────────────────────────────────────────────┘
```

FIGURE 12–4 Standard Cost Cards for Products M and N

End-of-Period Work-in-Process Inventory

Product M: 100 units, 75% complete as to conversion costs
Product N: 400 units, 20% complete as to conversion costs

Transfers to Finished-Goods Inventory

Product M (1,000 units @ $11.10)	$11,100
Product N (1,200 units @ $17.30)	20,760
Total	$31,860

REQUIRED:

1. Record the purchases of direct materials.
2. Record the incurrence of direct-labor payroll costs.
3. Record the raw materials used.
4. Record the transfers of direct-material and direct-labor costs to finished goods.

Solution to Illustrative Problem, Part II

1. **Purchase of Direct Materials.**

Direct materials inventory	7,550 (1)	
Materials price variance	200 (2)	
Accounts payable		7,750

(1)

2,000 units @ $.50	$1,000
1,200 units @ $.25	300
4,000 units @ $1.00	4,000
3,000 units @ $.75	2,250
Total	$7,550

(2)

Invoice cost of materials purchased		$7,750
Standard cost of materials purchased		
Material A (2,000 units @ $.50)	$1,000	
Material B (1,200 units @ $.25)	300	
Material C (4,000 units @ $1.00)	4,000	
Material D (3,000 units @ $.75)	2,250	7,550
		$ 200 (U)

or

Material A [($.55 − $.50) × 2,000]	$100 (U)
Material B [($.291⅔ − $.25) × 1,200]	50 (U)
Material C [($.975 − $1.00) × 4,000]	100 (F)
Material D [($.80 − $.75) × 3,000]	150 (U)
	$200 (U)

2. **Direct-Labor Payroll Costs.**

Work-in-process inventory	9,750 (3)	
Labor rate variance		50 (4)
Direct-labor payroll		9,700

(3) Actual hours × standard cost per unit: (1,625) × $6 = $9,750
(4) Actual payroll − (actual hours × standard cost per unit):
($9,700 − $9,750) = $50 (F)

3. **Raw Materials.**

Work-in-process inventory	7,555 (5)	
Direct materials inventory		7,555

(5) Actual units at standard cost

1,650 units @ $.50	$ 825
1,620 units @ $.25	405
4,210 units @ $1.00	4,210
2,820 units @ $.75	2,115
Total	$7,555

4a. Transfer of Direct-Materials Costs from Work in Process to Finished Goods.

Finished-goods inventory	6,900 (6)	
Materials usage variance	55 (7)	
Work-in-process inventory		6,955

(6)

Product M (1,000 × $1.50)	$1,500
Product N (1,200 × $4.50)	5,400
Total	$6,900

(7) Equivalent units of production (materials)

Product M (1,000 + 100 − 300)	800
Product N (1,200 + 400 − 200)	1,400

Standard materials cost for equivalent units of production

800 × $1.50	$1,200
1,400 × $4.50	6,300
Total	$7,500
Actual materials used at standard cost per unit (see 3 above)	7,555
Materials usage variance	$ 55 (U)

or

Material A [1,650 − (800 × 2)] × $.50	$25	(U)
Material B [1,620 − (800 × 2)] × $.25	5	(U)
Material C [4,210 − (1400 × 3)] × $1.00	10	(U)
Material D [2,820 − (1400 × 2)] × $.75	15	(U)
	$55	(U)

4b. Transfer of Direct-Labor Costs from Work in Process to Finished Goods.

Finished goods inventory	9,360 (8)	
Labor efficiency variance	480 (9)	
Work-in-process inventory		9,840

(8) Transfers to finished goods

Product M (1,000 units @ $3.60, or 600 hours @ $6.00)	$3,600
Product N (1,200 units @ $4.80, or 960 hours @ $6)	5,760
Total	$9,360

(9) Equivalent units of production

	M	N
Transferred out	1,000	1,200
End-of-period work in process	+ 75	+ 80
Total	1,075	1,280
Beginning-of-period work in process	− 100	− 80
Equivalent units of production	975	1,200
Standard hours per unit	× 0.6	× 0.8
Production, in standard hours	585	960

Total for period	1,545
Actual hours of direct labor	1,625
Standard hours of direct labor	1,545
Excess hours	80

Labor efficiency variance = 80 hours × $6 = $480 (U)

SUMMARY

In this chapter, we explained how to account for direct-materials costs and direct-labor costs when using a standard cost system. Since these are prime costs that, in the aggregate, vary directly in relation to production, the amounts of each of these cost elements that should be incurred in manufacturing one finished unit can be stated as a product of the quantity of materials or labor expected to be used to produce one unit of finished goods multiplied by the expected costs per unit of direct materials or per hour of direct labor. As a result, the standard cost card for each finished unit will reflect the quantities of materials or hours of labor expected to be used to produce the unit multiplied by its respective projected (standard) costs per unit or per hour to arrive at the standard costs of materials and labor for one unit of finished product.

Materials price variances, generally calculated and recognized as purchases are recorded, will equal the actual units purchased multiplied by the difference between the actual and standard costs per unit. Materials usage variances, generally recognized as manufacturing costs are transferred from work in process to finished goods, will equal the standard cost per unit of material multiplied by the difference between the actual number of units of materials used and the number of units of materials that should have been used for the production achieved. The number of units of material that should have been used will equal the equivalent units of finished product multiplied by the standard quantities of raw materials per unit.

The labor rate variance, calculated and recorded at the time direct labor is charged to work in process, is equal to the actual direct-labor hours multiplied by the difference between the actual rate(s) paid per hour and the standard rate(s) per hour shown on the standard cost cards. The labor efficiency variance, calculated and recorded as the cost of finished units is transferred from work in process to finished goods, will equal the standard cost per hour multiplied by the difference between the actual hours worked and the standard hours that should have been worked for the output achieved, which itself equals the equivalent units produced multiplied by the standard labor hour(s) per unit shown on the standard cost cards.

Finally, we pointed out that the valuation of inventories and cost of sales at standard cost is not a generally accepted accounting practice unless the differences between standard costs and actual costs are immaterial. Therefore, when the amount of a standard cost variance is significant (that is, a material amount), it should be allocated to inventories and cost of sales. In connection with the allocation of variances, we observed that materials price variances originating at the point of purchase would be allocated to materials inventory, work-in-process inventory, finished-goods inventory, and cost of sales. All other variances would be allocated to work-in-process inventory, finished-goods inventory, and cost of sales.

APPENDIX: Alternative "Triangle" Variance Analysis

A triangle model may be used to calculate materials variances and labor variances. (This format also may be used, without change, to calculate the variable overhead variances discussed in Chapter 13.) The general triangle model is shown at the top of page 444. Actual costs are shown on the lower left base of the triangle, while standard costs are shown on the right. The outside portions of each of the base formulas [actual quantity (AQ) and standard cost per unit (S$/unit)] are moved to the peak and combined to create the formula for the total actual/standard cost.

Variances then may be calculated as the differences between each of the totals. If the "actual" cost (on the left-hand side) is greater than the "standard" cost (on the right-hand side), the variance is unfavorable. For example, if the total actual cost is $1,200 and the total actual/standard cost is $1,150, the price variance is $50 unfavorable. Further, if the actual/standard cost is $1,150 and the total standard cost is $1,000, the quantity or efficiency variance is $150 unfavorable. The total variance is the sum of the price and quantity variances ($50 + 150 =

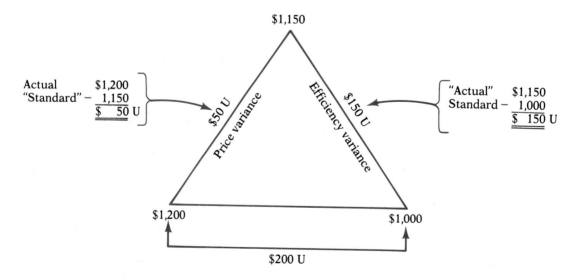

$200). Alternatively, the total variance may be calculated as the difference between the total actual cost of $1,200 and the total standard cost of $1,000:

Since materials may be purchased and stored before being used, the triangle for direct materials must be separated and the price variance calculated using data on materials *purchased*, whereas the quantity variance is calculated using data on materials *used*. This separation technique for direct materials can be illustrated as follows:

Direct materials

AQ purchased × S$/unit
= Total actual/standard cost

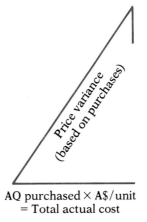

AQ purchased × A$/unit
= Total actual cost

AQ used × S$/unit
= Total actual/standard cost

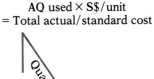
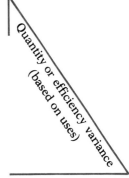

SQ for output achieved × S$/unit
= Total standard cost

When one quantity of materials is purchased and another quantity used, there is no meaningful total materials variance.

The Ajax Chemical Company illustration in this chapter is complex because three different materials were involved and purchases did not equal uses. A price and quantity variance may be calculated for each material (requiring three separate "triangle" analyses), or all materials may be treated together, as illustrated next:

Direct Materials

2,500 lb of material A × $2.00	$ 5,000	
3,000 lb of material B × $2.20	6,600	
3,200 lb of material C × $1.70	5,440	
Total actual/standard costs purchased	$17,040	

2,200 lb of material A × $2.00	$ 4,400	
2,050 lb of material B × $2.20	4,510	
3,000 lb of material C × $1.70	5,100	
Total actual/standard costs used	$14,010	

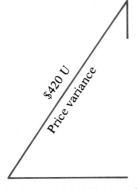
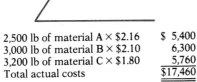
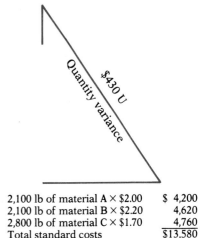

2,500 lb of material A × $2.16	$ 5,400	
3,000 lb of material B × $2.10	6,300	
3,200 lb of material C × $1.80	5,760	
Total actual costs	$17,460	

2,100 lb of material A × $2.00	$ 4,200	
2,100 lb of material B × $2.20	4,620	
2,800 lb of material C × $1.70	4,760	
Total standard costs	$13,580	

Direct labor variances for the Ajax Chemical Company follow.

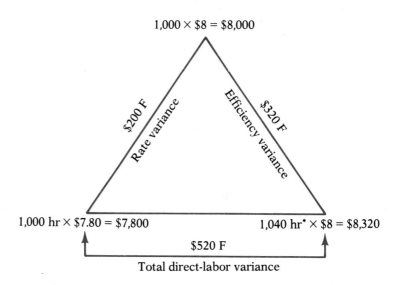

Direct Labor

$1,000 \times \$8 = \$8,000$

$200 F
Rate variance

$320 F
Efficiency variance

$1,000 \text{ hr} \times \$7.80 = \$7,800$ $1,040 \text{ hr}^* \times \$8 = \$8,320$

$520 F
Total direct-labor variance

*5,200 equivalent units of production $\times$ 0.2 direct-labor hours

The appendix to Chapter 13 applies this triangle analysis to manufacturing overhead.

GLOSSARY OF TERMS INTRODUCED IN THIS CHAPTER

direct labor efficiency variance
An amount equal to the difference between the actual direct labor hours used and the standard hours allowed for the production achieved multiplied by the standard labor rate per hour. Also called *direct labor quantity variance*.

direct labor rate variance
An amount equal to the difference between the standard and actual direct-labor rates per hour multiplied by the actual number of direct-labor hours used during a reporting period. Also called *direct labor price variance*.

direct materials quantity variance
An amount equal to the difference between the actual quantity of materials used and the standard quantity of materials allowed to produce a given output multiplied by the standard cost per unit. Also called *direct materials usage variance*.

direct materials usage variance
See *direct materials quantity variance*.

materials price variance	An amount equal to the difference between the standard and actual prices per unit multiplied by the actual number of units either purchased (preferred treatment) or issued into process.
price variance	The difference between the actual and standard costs or prices per unit multiplied by the actual number of units; considered a direct materials price variance when used in relation to materials and a direct-labor rate variance when used in relation to labor. Also, the difference between actual sales of one period and budget sales for the same period (or actual sales of one period and actual sales of another period) attributable to a change in price.
quantity variance	A variance caused by the difference between the standard quantity allowed for output achieved and actual quantity used multiplied by the standard cost or price per unit. Often called *material usage variance* when used in connection with the analysis of direct material variances, or *labor efficiency variance* when used in connection with the analysis of variances in direct labor.

QUESTIONS FOR CLASS DISCUSSION

12–1 Why can the component elements of the standard costs of direct materials and direct labor for a finished unit be stated as the product of the quantities of those items expected to be used and their standard costs per unit? Explain.

12–2 At what points may the direct-materials price variance be recognized? How does the point of recognition relate to the valuation of materials inventory?

12–3 What is meant by the term *price variance*? How is it calculated?

12–4 What is meant by the term *quantity variance*? How is it calculated?

12–5 What are the component elements of the entry used to record a direct materials purchase if the items in materials inventory are valued at standard costs? Explain.

12–6 At what point in the cost-accumulation and -allocation process are materials quantity variances generally recognized? What entry is made to record them?

12–7 How may the total materials price variance accumulated during a reporting period best be analyzed? Explain.

12–8 At what point is the direct-labor rate (price) variance recognized? What journal entry is made to record its recognition?

12–9 At what point in the cost-accumulation and -allocation process is a direct-labor efficiency (quantity) variance recognized? What journal entry is made to record its recognition?

12–10 How does the use of the standard-cost-variance accounts facilitate the process of management by exception? Explain.

12–11 What person in a firm's organization ordinarily is held accountable for materials price variances?

12–12 What person within a firm's organization ordinarily is held accountable for most materials usage variances? Explain.

12–13 What are the typical causes of labor rate variances? Explain.

12–14 What are the typical causes of labor efficiency variances? Explain.

12–15 What are the two possible procedures that may be followed in disposing of balances in variance accounts at the end of a reporting period? Explain.

EXERCISES

12–16 **Multiple Choice—Definitions and Concepts** Select the *best* answer to each
AICPA Adapted of the following items.

1. If the total materials variance (actual cost of materials used compared with the standard cost of the standard amount of materials required) for a given operation is favorable, why must this variance be further evaluated as to price and usage?
   a. There is *no* need to further evaluate the total materials variance if it is favorable.
   b. Generally accepted accounting principles require that all variances be analyzed in three stages.
   c. All variances must appear in the annual report to equity owners for proper disclosure.
   d. To allow management to evaluate the efficiency of the purchasing and production functions.

2. The difference between the actual labor rate multiplied by the actual labor hours worked and the standard labor rate multiplied by the standard labor hours is the
   a. total labor variance.
   b. labor rate variance.
   c. labor usage variance.
   d. labor efficiency variance.

3. An unfavorable price variance occurs because of
   a. price increases on raw materials.
   b. price decreases on raw materials.
   c. less-than-anticipated levels of waste in the manufacturing process.
   d. more-than-anticipated levels of waste in the manufacturing process.

4. If the actual hours worked exceed the standard hours allowed, what type of variance will occur?

a. favorable labor usage (efficiency) variance
b. favorable labor rate variance
c. unfavorable labor usage (efficiency) variance
d. unfavorable labor rate variance
5. The standard unit cost is used in the calculation of which of the following variances?

	Materials Price Variance	Materials Usage Variance
a.	no	no
b.	no	yes
c.	yes	no
d.	yes	yes

6. Which of the following is the most probable reason a company would experience an unfavorable labor rate variance and a favorable labor efficiency variance?
    a. The mix of workers assigned to the particular job was heavily weighted toward the use of higher-paid, experienced individuals.
    b. The mix of workers assigned to the particular job was heavily weighted toward the use of new, relatively low-paid, unskilled workers.
    c. Because of the production schedule, workers from other production areas were assigned to assist this particular process.
    d. Defective materials necessitated more labor in order to produce a standard unit.
7. How is labor rate variance computed?
    a. The difference between standard and actual rate is multiplied by actual hours.
    b. The difference between standard and actual rate is multiplied by standard hours.
    c. The difference between standard and actual hours is multiplied by actual rate.
    d. The difference between standard and actual hours is multiplied by the difference between standard and actual rate.

12–17 **Materials Price Variance** Information on Nhan Company's production costs and direct materials costs for October 19X5 is as follows:

Units produced	7,250
Actual quantity of direct materials purchased and used	30,000 lb
Actual cost of direct materials	$84,000
Unfavorable direct materials usage variance	$3,000
Standard quantity of direct materials per unit	4 lb

REQUIRED: Compute the October 19X5 materials price variance for Nhan Company.

12–18 **Materials Variances and Journal Entries** Hatchett Company, which has a standard cost system, had 800 gallons of raw material Q in its inventory on January 1, 19X2. This material had been purchased in December, 19X1, for $2.05 per gallon and is carried at the standard cost of $2.00 per gallon. The following information pertains to raw material Q for the month of January, 19X2:

Actual gallons purchased	2,900
Actual gallons used	3,200
Standard gallons allowed for actual production	3,160
Actual cost per gallon	$2.10

There is no work in process at either the beginning or end of the period.

REQUIRED:

1. Compute Hatchett Company's January, 19X2, raw materials
   a. price variance
   b. quantity or efficiency variance.
2. Prepare all general journal entries associated with raw materials for January, 19X2, including the raw materials portion of costs transferred to finished goods.

12–19 **Missing Information—Materials** You are given the following information on direct materials for the Finch Company:

Standard unit price	$2.70
Actual quantity purchased	1,200
Standard quantity allowed for actual production	1,090
Materials purchase price variance, favorable	$180
Materials quantity variance, unfavorable	$27

REQUIRED:

1. What was the actual purchase price per unit?
2. What was the actual quantity used?

12–20 **Missing Information—Labor** Data on Brence Company's direct labor costs are:

Standard direct-labor hours	20,000
Actual direct-labor hours	19,800
Direct-labor usage (efficiency) variance	$2,000 Favorable
Direct-labor rate variance	$990 Favorable
Total payroll	$197,010

REQUIRED: Compute Brence Company's

1. actual direct labor rate
2. standard direct labor rate.

12–21 **Missing Information—Labor** Find the missing amounts for each of the following independent cases.

	Case 1	Case 2	Case 3
Actual direct-labor rate	$8.00	$10.50	_____
Actual direct-labor hours	12,000	_____	30,000
Standard direct-labor rate	_____	$10.00	$9.00
Standard direct-labor hours allowed for output achieved	11,000	5,000	31,000
Direct-labor rate variance	$3,000 F	_____	$1,500 U
Direct-labor efficiency variance	_____	$2,500 F	_____
Total direct-labor payroll	$96,000	_____	_____

12–22 Materials Variances and Labor Variances Sandhoff Company prepared the following production budget for March 19X5:

Output	30,000 units
Materials (37,500 square feet of vinyl @ $2.10)	$ 78,750
Direct labor (18,000 hours @ $8.00)	144,000
Overhead (18,000 hours @ $10)	180,000
	$402,750

Actual results for March were:

Output	32,000 units
Materials used	42,000 square feet
Materials purchased (42,000 square feet of vinyl @ $2.05)	$ 86,100
Direct-labor payroll (19,150 hours)	$157,030

REQUIRED: For March, 19X5, compute Sandhoff's

1. materials price and quantity (usage) variances
2. direct-labor rate (price) and efficiency variances.

12–23 Allocation of Standard Cost Variances Hartberg Corporation has the following standard cost card for its one product :

Standard Cost Card	
Direct materials	$ 5.60
Direct labor (0.5 hour @ $8)	4.00
Manufacturing overhead	8.00
Total standard cost	$17.60

At the end of the current fiscal year, the following account balances are reported:

Work in process	0
Finished goods ending inventory	$ 17,600
Cost of goods sold	$193,600
Labor rate variance (debit)	$ 6,336
Labor efficiency variance (credit)	$ 4,224

REQUIRED:

1. Based on the standard cost and other information just given, prepare a schedule to allocate the labor rate variance and the labor efficiency variance.
2. After all allocations have been completed, what amount will appear on the income statement for cost of goods sold?

PROBLEMS

12–24 **Materials Variances and Labor Variances** The following information pertains to Karla Company's manufacturing activity during the month of July:

Materials purchased	4,000 board-feet of lumber
Cost of materials purchased	$3.10 per board-foot
Materials consumed for manufacture of 10,000 units	32,000 board-feet of lumber
Actual direct-labor hours required for 10,000 units	31,500
Actual direct-labor cost per hour	$10.25

Karla's standard materials and labor costs per unit are:

Standard Materials and Labor Cost per Unit	
Materials (3 board-feet of lumber @ $3.20)	$ 9.60
Labor (3 hours @ $10)	30.00
	$39.60

The materials price variance is recognized when materials are purchased.

REQUIRED: Compute, for the month of July, Karla's

1. materials price and quantity (usage) variances
2. labor rate and efficiency variances.

12–25 **General Journal Entries** Refer to the data for Karla Company in problem 12–24. Assume there is no beginning or end-of-period work in process.

REQUIRED: Prepare general journal entries for the month of July. All variances should be assumed immaterial.

12–26
ICMA Adapted

Prime Cost Variances The Lonn Manufacturing Company produces two primary chemical products to be used as base ingredients for a variety of products. The 19X8 budget for the two products was (000 omitted):

	X-4	Z-8	Total
Production output, in gallons	600	600	1,200
Direct-materials cost	$1,500	$1,875	$3,375
Direct-labor cost	900	900	1,800
Total prime manufacturing cost	$2,400	$2,775	$5,175

The following planning assumptions were used for the budget:

(1) Direct materials yield of 96%
(2) Direct labor rate of $6 per hour

The actual direct production data for 19X8 was (000 omitted):

	X-4	Z-8	Total
Production output, in gallons	570	658	1,228
Direct-materials cost	$1,368.00	$2,138.50	$3,506.50
Direct-labor cost	936.00	1,092.00	2,028.00
Total prime manufacturing cost	$2,304.00	$3,230.50	$5,534.50

The actual production yield was 95% for X-4 and 94% for Z-8. The direct-labor cost per hour for both products was $6.50.

REQUIRED:

1. Calculate for product X-4
   a. the direct-materials price variance
   b. the direct-materials quantity (yield) variance.
2. Calculate for product Z-8
   a. the direct-labor rate variance
   b. the direct-labor efficiency variance.

12–27
ICMA Adapted

Multiple Choice The following data apply to all questions in problem 12–27.
Arrow Industries employs a standard cost system in which direct-materials inventory is carried at standard cost. Arrow has established the following standards for the prime costs of one unit of product:

	Standard Quantity	Standard Price	Standard Cost
Direct materials	8 pounds	$1.80 per pound	$14.40
Direct labor	0.25 hour	$8.00 per hour	2.00
			$16.40

During May, Arrow purchased 160,000 pounds of direct materials at a total cost of $304,000. The total factory wages for May were $42,000, 90% of which was for direct labor. Arrow manufactured 19,000 units of product during May using 142,500 pounds of direct materials and 5,000 direct-labor hours.

Select the *best* answer to the following items.

1. The direct-materials purchase price variance for May is
   a. $16,000 favorable.
   b. $16,000 unfavorable.
   c. $14,250 favorable.
   d. $14,250 unfavorable.
   e. some amount other than those given above.
2. The direct-materials usage (quantity) variance for May is
   a. $14,400 unfavorable.
   b. $1,100 favorable.
   c. $17,100 unfavorable.
   d. $17,100 favorable.
   e. some amount other than those given above.
3. The direct-labor price (rate) variance for May is
   a. $2,200 favorable.
   b. $1,900 unfavorable.
   c. $2,000 unfavorable.
   d. $2,090 favorable.
   e. some amount other than those given above.
4. The direct-labor usage (efficiency) variance for May is
   a. $2,200 favorable.
   b. $2,000 favorable.
   c. $2,000 unfavorable.
   d. $1,800 unfavorable.
   e. some amount other than those given above.

12–28 **Materials and Labor Standards and Variance Analysis** NuLathe Company
ICMA Adapted produces a turbo engine component for jet aircraft manufacturers. A standard cost system has been used for years, with good results. Unfortunately, NuLathe has recently experienced production problems. The source for its direct materials went out of business. The new source produces a similar but higher-quality material. The price per pound from the original source has averaged $7.00, while the price from the new source is $7.77. The use of the new materials results in a reduction in scrap. This scrap reduction reduces the actual consumption of direct materials from 1.25 to 1.00 pounds per unit. In addition, the direct labor

is reduced from 24 to 22 minutes per unit, because there is less scrap labor and machine setup time.

The direct materials problem was occurring at the same time that labor negotiations resulted in an increase of over 14% in hourly direct-labor costs. The average rate rose from $12.60 per hour to $14.40 per hour. Production of the main product requires a high level of labor skill. Because of a continuing shortage in that skill area, an interim wage agreement has to be signed.

NuLathe started using the new materials on April 1, the same date the new labor agreement went into effect. NuLathe has been using standards that were set at the beginning of the calendar year. The direct materials and direct-labor standards for the turbo engine component are as follows:

Direct materials (1.2 lb @ $6.80/lb)	$ 8.16
Direct labor (20 min @ $12.30/direct-labor hour)	4.10
Standard prime cost per unit	$12.26

Howard Foster, cost accounting supervisor, had been examining the performance report (shown in Exhibit 12–1) that he had prepared at the close of business on April 30. Jane Keene, assistant controller, came into Foster's office, and Foster said, "Jane, look at this performance report. Direct-materials price increased 11% and the labor rate increased over

EXHIBIT 12–1
NuLathe Company
Analysis of Prime Costs

Standard Cost Variance Analysis for April 1985

	Standard	Price Variance	Quantity Variance	Actual
Direct materials	$ 8.16	($.97 × 1.0) $.97 U	($6.80 × 0.2) $1.36 F	$ 7.77
Direct labor	4.10	($2.10 × $\frac{22}{60}$) $.77 U	($12.30 × $\frac{2}{60}$) $ .41 U	5.28
	$12.26			$13.05

Comparison of 19X5 Actual Costs

	First Quarter Costs	April Costs	Percentage Increase (Decrease)
Direct materials	$ 8.75	$ 7.77	(11.2)%
Direct labor	5.04	5.28	4.8%
	$13.79	$13.05	(5.4)%

14% during April. I expected greater variances, yet prime costs decreased over 5% from the $13.79 we experienced during the first quarter of this year. The proper message just isn't coming through."

"This has been an unusual period," said Keene. "With all the unforeseen changes, perhaps we should revise our standards based on current conditions and start over."

Foster replied, "I think we can retain the current standards but expand the variance analysis. We could calculate variances for the specific changes that have occurred to direct materials and direct labor before we calculate the normal price and quantity variances. What I really think would be useful to management right now is to determine the impact the changes in direct materials and direct labor had in reducing our prime costs per unit from $13.79 in the first quarter to $13.05 in April—a reduction of $.74."

REQUIRED:

1. Discuss the advantages of
   a. immediately revising the standards
   b. retaining the current standards and expanding the analysis of variances.
2. Prepare an analysis that reflects the impact the new direct material and new labor contract had on reducing NuLathe Company's prime costs per unit from $13.79 in the first quarter to $13.05 in April. The analysis should show the changes in prime costs per unit that are due to the:
   a. use of new direct material
   b. new labor contract.

Your analysis should be in sufficient detail to identify the changes due to

- direct-materials price
- direct-labor rate
- the effect of direct-materials quality on direct-materials usage
- the effect of direct-materials quality on direct-labor usage.

12–29
ICMA Adapted

Analysis of Labor Variances The Felton Company manufactures a complete line of radios. Because many models have plastic cases, the company has its own molding department for producing the cases. The month of April was devoted to the production of the plastic case for one of the portable radios—Model SX76.

The molding department has two operations—molding and trimming. There is no interaction of labor in these two operations. The standard labor cost for producing 10 plastic cases for Model SX76 is:

Molders (0.50 hr @ $6.00)	$3.00
Trimmers (0.25 hr @ $4.00)	1.00
	$4.00

During April, 70,000 plastic cases were produced in the molding department. However, 10% of these cases (7,000) had to be discarded because they were found to be defective at final inspection. The purchasing department had changed to a new plastics supplier to take advantage of a lower price for comparable plastic. The new plastic turned out to be of a lower quality and resulted in the rejection of completed cases.

Direct-labor hours worked and direct-labor costs charged to the molding department were:

Direct Labor Charged to the Molding Department

Molders (3,800 hr @ $6.25)	$23,750
Trimmers (1,600 hr @ $4.15)	6,640
Total labor charges	$30,390

As a result of poor scheduling by the production scheduling department, the supervisor of the molding department had to shift molders to the trimming operation for 200 hours during April. The company paid the molding workers their regular hourly rate even though they were performing a lower-rated task. There was no significant loss of efficiency caused by the shift. In addition, the department supervisor indicated that 75 hours and 35 hours of idle time occurred in the molding and trimming operations, respectively, as a result of unexpected machinery repairs required during the month.

REQUIRED:

1. The monthly report that compares actual costs with standard cost of output for the month of April shows the following labor variance for the molding department:

Actual labor costs for April	$30,390
Standard labor cost of output (63,000 × $4.00/10)	25,200
Unfavorable labor variance	$ 5,190

This variance is significantly higher than normal, and management would like an explanation. Prepare a detailed analysis of the unfavorable labor variance for the molding department that shows the variance resulting from (a) labor rate, (b) labor substitution, (c) materials substitution, (d) operating efficiency, and (e) idle time.

2. The supervisor of the molding department is concerned with the large variances charged to her department. She feels the variances due to labor substitution and change in raw materials should not be charged to the department. Does the supervisor have a valid argument? Briefly justify your position.

12–30 **Standard Cost Variance Disposition** Brown Company began operations on July 1, 19X2, with a process standard cost system. All inventories are carried at standard cost.

The standard cost of Brown's product is:

Standard Cost Card	
Direct materials	$ 3
Direct labor (1 hour @ $12)	12
Manufacturing overhead	15
Total standard cost	$30

Brown sold 6,000 units during their first year of operation. Selected account balances on June 30, 19X3, are as follows:

Raw materials	$ 3,000
Work in process	$ 8,250
Finished goods	$24,000
Materials price variance	$ 1,095 Unfavorable
Materials quantity variance	$ 1,224 Unfavorable
Labor rate variance	$ 1,632 Favorable
Labor efficiency variance	$ 4,080 Unfavorable

Detail from the work-in-process inventory account reveals the following:

Materials	$1,500
Labor	$3,000
Overhead	$3,750

All variances are considered material and should be allocated to the inventories and cost of goods sold at the end of fiscal year for financial statement purposes. After allocation of variances, inventories and cost of goods sold should be stated at actual cost.

1. Prepare schedules to allocate all variances on June 30, 19X3, to the appropriate accounts.
2. Compute the amounts that should be shown on the June 30, 19X3, balance sheet for:
   a. raw materials inventory
   b. work-in-process inventory
   c. finished-goods inventory.
3. What amount will be shown on the income statement for cost of goods sold for the year ending June 30, 19X3?

12–31   **THOUGHT STIMULATION PROBLEM.** Antaeus Manufacturing Company produces a variety of communication equipment, including portable two-way radios produced in a new plant equipped with semiautomated equipment operated by skilled technicians. In anticipation of receiving a government contract, Antaeus has decided to try to increase its radio production by following a new manufacturing *constraint* theory.

Constraint procedure requires that the company's primary constraint be identified so it can be utilized to the maximum extent possible. To increase production, Antaeus will focus its attention on the assembly department, which it has identified as the major constraint in its production line. All other cost centers are to subordinate their production to the assembly department. That means the parts needs of the assembly department will be assured by scheduling production in other departments so the assembly department can operate at 100% of capacity.

The new scheduling procedure also will require that all cost centers supplying the assembly department operate only when parts are needed by the assembly department. A buffer (a small quantity of work-in-process inventory) of two hours of parts for the assembly department is to be maintained at all times. Experiments have shown that the new procedure can increase production by more than 22%. Supervisors of cost centers have been instructed to make sure workers conform to production schedules so the buffer is kept filled. Workers should work like crazy when their parts are needed and should perform maintenance or housekeeping chores when parts are not needed. However, they are always expected to be alert and ready to resume production when a need is signaled by the assembly department.

Antaeus's supervisors are concerned about the effect of the new production system on their firm's standard cost system because direct labor efficiency measures will be unreliable measures of performance.

REQUIRED:

1. Is a standard cost system relevant in this situation?
2. In what ways can a standard cost system benefit Antaeus's operations?
3. If labor efficiency variances cannot be measured in the usual way, how can labor performance be evaluated?

CASE STUDIES

12–32
ICMA Adapted

Variance Analysis Design Maidwell Company manufactures washers and dryers on a single assembly line in its main factory. The market has deteriorated over the last five years, and competition has made cost control very important. Management has been concerned about the materials cost of both washers and dryers. There have been no model changes in the past two years, and economic conditions have allowed the company to negotiate price reductions in many key parts.

Maidwell uses a standard cost system in accounting for materials. Purchases are charged to inventory at a standard price, with purchase discounts considered an administrative cost reduction. Production is charged at the standard price of the materials used. Thus, the price variance is isolated at time of purchase as the difference between gross contract price and standard price multiplied by the quantity purchased. When a substitute part is used in production rather than the regular part, a price variance equal to the difference in the standard prices of the materials is recognized at the time of substitution in the production process. The quantity variance is the actual quantity used compared to the standard quantity allowed, with the difference multiplied by the standard price.

The materials variances for several of the parts Maidwell uses are unfavorable. Part no. 4121 is one such item. Maidwell knows that some of these parts will be defective and fail. Failure is discovered during production. The normal defective rate is 5% of normal input. The original contract price of this part was $.285 per unit; thus, Maidwell set the standard unit price at $.285. The unit contract purchase price of part no. 4121 was increased $.04 to $.325 from the original $.285 due to a parts specification change. Maidwell chose not to change the standard, but instead to treat the increase in price as a price variance. In addition, the contract terms were changed from n/30 to 4/10, n/30, as a consequence of negotiations resulting from changes in the economy.

Data regarding the usage of part no. 4121 during December are as follows:

Purchases of part no. 4121	150,000 units
Unit price paid for purchases of part no. 4121	$.325
Requisitions of part no. 4121 from stores for use in products	134,000 units
Substitution of part no. 5125 for part no. 4121 to use obsolete stock (standard unit price of part no. 5125 is $.35)	24,000 units
Units of part no. 4121 and its substitute (part no. 5125) identified as being defective	9,665 units
Standard allowed usage (including normal defective units) of part no. 4121 and its substitute based on output for the month	153,300 units

Maidwell's materials variances related to part no. 4121 for December were reported as follows:

Price variance	$7,560.00 U
Quantity variance	1,339.50 U
Total materials variances for part no. 4121	$8,899.50 U

Bob Speck, the purchasing director, claims the unfavorable price variance is misleading. Speck says his department has worked hard to obtain price concessions and purchase discounts from suppliers. In addition, Speck has indicated, engineering changes have been made in several parts increasing their price, even though the part identification has not changed. These price increases are not his department's responsibility. Speck declares that price variances simply no longer measure the purchasing department's performance.

Jim Buddle, the manufacturing manager, thinks responsibility for the quantity variance should be shared. Buddle states that manufacturing cannot control quality arising from less expensive parts, substitutions of material to use up otherwise obsolete stock, or engineering changes that increase the quantity of materials used.

The accounting manager, Mike Kohl, has suggested that the computation of variances be changed to identify variations from standard as well as the causes and functional areas responsible for the variances. The following system of materials variances and the method of computation for each was recommended by Kohl:

Variance	Method of Calculation
Economics variance	Quantity purchased times the changes made after setting standards that were the result of negotiations based on changes in the general economy
Engineering change variance	Quantity purchased times change in price due to parts specifications changes
Purchase price variance	Quantity purchased times change in contract price due to changes other than parts specifications or the general economy
Substitutions variance	Quantity substituted times the difference in standard price between parts substituted
Excess usage variance	Standard price times the difference between the standard quantity allowed for production minus actual parts used (reduced for abnormal scrap)
Abnormal failure rate variance	Abnormal scrap times standard price

REQUIRED:

1. Discuss the appropriateness of Maidwell Company's current method of variance analysis for materials, and indicate whether the claims of Bob Speck and Jim Buddle are valid.
2. Compute the materials variances for part no. 4121 for December using the system recommended by Mike Kohl.
3. Indicate who would be responsible for each of the variances in Mike Kohl's system of variance analysis for materials.

12–33
ICMA Adapted

Standard Costs and Decision Making The Lenco Company employs a standard cost system as part of its cost control program. The standard cost per unit is established at the beginning of each year. Standards are not revised during the year for any changes in materials or labor inputs or in the manufacturing processes. Any revisions in standards are deferred until the beginning of the next fiscal year. However, in order to recognize such changes in the current year, the company includes planned variances in the monthly budgets prepared after such changes have been introduced.

The following labor standard was set for one of Lenco's products effective July 1, 19X9, the beginning of the fiscal year:

Class I labor (4 hr @ $6.00)	$24.00
Class II labor (3 hr @ $7.50)	22.50
Class V labor (1 hr @ $11.50)	11.50
Standard labor cost per 100 units	$58.00

The standard was based on the quality of materials that had been used in prior years and what was expected to be available for the 19X9–19Y0 fiscal year. The labor activity is performed by a team consisting of four persons with class I skills, three persons with class II skills, and one person with class V skills. This is the most economical combination for the company's processing system.

The manufacturing operations occurred as expected during the first five months of the year. The standard costs contributed to effective cost control during this period. However, there were indications that changes in the operations would be required in the last half of the year. The company had received a significant increase in orders for delivery in the spring. There was an inadequate number of skilled workers available to meet the increased production. As a result, the production teams, beginning in January, would be made up of more class I labor and less class II labor than the standard required. The teams would consist of six class I persons, two class II persons, and one class V person.

This labor team would be less efficient than the normal team. The reorganized teams work more slowly, so only 90 units are produced in the same time that 100 units normally would be produced. No raw materials will be lost as a result of the change in the labor mix. Completed units have never been rejected in the final inspection process as a consequence of faulty work; this is expected to continue.

In addition, Lenco was notified by its materials supplier that a lower-quality material would be supplied after January 1. One unit of raw material normally is required for each good unit produced. Lenco and its supplier estimated that 5% of the units manufactured would be rejected on final inspection due to defective material. Normally, no units are lost due to defective material.

REQUIRED:

1. How much of the lower-quality material must be entered into production in order to produce 42,750 units of good production in January with the new labor teams? Show your calculations.
2. How many hours of each class of labor will be needed to produce 42,750 good units from the materials input? Show your calculations.
3. What amount should be included in the January budget for the planned labor variance due to the labor team and materials changes? What amount of this planned labor variance can be associated with (a) the materials change, and (b) the team change? Show your calculations.

Chapter 13

Accounting for Manufacturing Overhead

Learning Objectives

When you have finished your study of this chapter,
you should

1. Understand how to determine the standard
   manufacturing-overhead cost per unit.
2. Be able to record both actual and applied manufacturing-
   overhead costs when using a standard cost system.
3. Know how to determine and record total overhead
   variance.
4. Be able to allocate total overhead variance into: (a) two
   variances (controllable and volume); (b) three variances
   (spending, efficiency, and volume); or (c) four variances
   [variable spending, variable efficiency, fixed spending
   (budget), and volume].
5. Know how to record the accumulation and allocation of
   all manufacturing costs when using a standard cost
   system (that is, be able to integrate the procedures
   developed in Chapters 11–13).

C hapter 12 explained how the differences (variances) between total standard and actual costs of materials and labor are subdivided to show the amounts caused by the differences between actual and standard prices (price variances) and the differences between actual and standard quantities (quantity variances). Such a price/quantity breakdown is the most useful way of allocating those variances because both materials and labor are prime costs that, in the aggregate, should vary directly with the level of production. These allocations help management, in controlling direct materials costs and direct labor costs, and in placing the responsibility for explaining the variances on specific people within the organization.

The standard cost of manufacturing overhead per unit of finished product is shown on the standard cost card as the product of the standard activity (for example, direct labor hours, direct labor dollars, machine-hours, or units of raw material) allowed to produce one unit of the product multiplied by the standard overhead rate per unit of activity. Because the **activity base** in conventional cost systems generally is direct labor hours, we shall use that base in this chapter. This means we shall show the total standard overhead cost per unit to be the product of standard direct labor hours allowed for the production of one finished unit multiplied by the standard overhead rate per direct labor hour (see standard cost card in Figure 11–2). When the activity base is direct labor hours, manufacturing overhead is applied to production by multiplying the total equivalent standard direct labor hours allowed for production achieved during each reporting period by the standard overhead rate per hour. The **total overhead variance** is then equal to the difference between this standard amount, called *applied overhead*, and the overhead costs actually incurred. Thus, the difference between actual manufacturing overhead and standard manufacturing overhead applied to production could be analyzed by computing price and quantity variances in a manner similar to the procedures followed for materials and labor. However, since only a minor part of manufacturing-overhead costs generally is directly variable with the level of production, such an analysis of the total overhead variance would not be especially useful to management in controlling those costs.

To provide a more useful analysis of the total overhead variance, we begin by identifying the part of the total overhead variance associated with each manufacturing-overhead cost-accumulation center. Next, we determine what part of each departmental overhead variance has been caused by the department's spending more than should have been spent based on the amount allowed for the production turned out. That part of the total variance is called **controllable variance** or **budget variance**, and it includes the amount "overspent" for both fixed and variable overhead cost items.

The rest of the difference between the amount of overhead actually incurred and the amount applied to production can be attributed to the department operating at a different level of activity than was anticipated when the standard overhead rate was established. To understand this variance, recall that part of the standard manufacturing-overhead rate per unit of activity (that is, direct labor hours, direct labor dollars, machine-hours, and so forth) will be made up of fixed costs. As observed earlier, the aggregate amounts of such costs are expected to remain the same within the relevant range of production used in establishing the manufacturing-overhead rate. Therefore, the *actual* rate per hour is expected to vary inversely with the level of production. As a result, a failure to produce enough finished units to allow the firm to operate at the level anticipated when the standard overhead rate was established will cause the amount of fixed overhead applied to production to be less than was anticipated when the rate was established. We refer to that difference as an unfavorable *production volume variance*. The opposite would be true if a firm operated at a level in excess of that anticipated when the standard overhead rate was set. Thus, to be most useful to management, the analysis of the total manufacturing-overhead variance should show, as one element, the amount of overhead that was underapplied or overapplied simply because production was different from that anticipated when the overhead rate was established. The part of the total overhead variance caused by such a deviation from the expected level of operations generally is called a **volume variance**, but is sometimes referred to as an "uncontrollable" variance—somewhat of a misnomer. Because production schedules must be based on sales, we generally can attribute this variance to the firm's marketing department.

As we continue our analysis of the procedures followed in accounting for manufacturing overhead in a standard cost system, we shall

1. explain how standard manufacturing-overhead costs are calculated and recorded when using a standard cost system
2. demonstrate how the overall manufacturing-overhead variance should be analyzed to assist management in controlling manufacturing-overhead costs
3. demonstrate the procedures followed in accounting for the manufacturing overhead incurred in Ajax Chemical Company's operations.

In the last part of the chapter, we will show, in Illustrative Problem, Part 3, how manufacturing-overhead accounting procedures would be carried out for Illustration Company. To summarize the materials covered in the three chapters on standard costs (Chapters 11–13), we will repeat the procedures illustrated in earlier chapters to account for materials costs and labor costs.

Accounting for Manufacturing-Overhead Costs

When using a standard cost system, *actual* manufacturing-overhead costs will be accumulated in the same manner as with either a job-order or a process-costing system based on historical costs. We typically use either a manufacturing-overhead cost-control account with a supporting subsidiary ledger or a manufacturing-overhead cost-summary account to accumulate those costs (see Chapter 5).

Total applied (standard) overhead cost for the operating period will equal the volume of production, measured in terms of some standard activity (such as standard labor hours), multiplied by the standard overhead rate per unit of activity (labor hour). It is important to recognize when using a standard cost system that applied manufacturing overhead will be different from the applied amount when using a historical cost system. In a historical cost system, applied overhead is calculated by multiplying *actual* labor hours (or actual labor dollars or actual machine-hours, depending on the selected activity base) by an overhead application rate. With a standard cost system, overhead is applied on the basis of a standard measure of activity (for example, **standard hours of production**—the direct labor hours that *should* have been required for actual output) rather than actual activity (for example, direct labor hours actually used). This difference can be seen in the following comparative T accounts, in which manufacturing-overhead control and manufacturing-overhead applied have been merged into one composite overhead account:

<table>
<tr><td colspan="2" align="center">**Actual or Normal Cost System**</td><td colspan="2" align="center">**Standard Cost System**</td></tr>
<tr><td colspan="2" align="center">**Manufacturing Overhead**</td><td colspan="2" align="center">**Manufacturing Overhead**</td></tr>
<tr><td align="center">*Debit*</td><td align="center">*Credit*</td><td align="center">*Debit*</td><td align="center">*Credit*</td></tr>
<tr><td>Actual dollars incurred for overhead items</td><td>*Actual* activity (e.g., direct labor hours) × Overhead application rate = Overhead applied</td><td>Actual dollars incurred for overhead items</td><td>*Standard* activity (e.g., direct labor hours that should have been used for production achieved) × Overhead application rate = Overhead applied</td></tr>
</table>

Recognize also that the standard overhead application rate includes both fixed and variable elements. To illustrate, let's assume that Don Company (which operates as one department) has developed its **standard overhead application rate** per hour from the flexible-budget data shown in Figure 13–1. Let's also assume that Don Company expects to

	Level of Operations			
Standard hours	7,000	8,000	9,000	10,000
Variable costs	$5,600	$ 6,400	$ 7,200	$ 8,000
Fixed costs	3,600	3,600	3,600	3,600
Manufacturing costs allowed	$9,200	$10,000	$10,800	$11,600
Variable overhead application rate	$ .80	$ .80	$ .80	$ .80
Fixed overhead application rate	.51	.45	.40	.36
Total application rate (per standard hour)	$ 1.31	$ 1.25	$ 1.20	$ 1.16

FIGURE 13–1 Don Company Flexible-Budget Overhead Data

operate at the level of 8,000 standard hours, that is, to produce a volume of goods requiring 8,000 standard hours of direct labor. Total overhead then will be applied at a rate of $1.25 per standard hour, regardless of the level of operation actually achieved.

The manufacturing cost allowed for each of the four possible levels of production listed in the flexible budget can be read directly from Figure 13–1. The amounts of overhead costs allowed for other levels of production can be either interpolated from the flexible budget or calculated by use of the following equation:

$$\text{Cost allowed} = \text{Fixed cost} + (\text{Variable overhead rate per hour} \times \text{Standard hours allowed for production achieved})$$

Don's variable overhead rate per hour for all levels of activity then is:

$$\frac{\$5,600}{7,000} = \frac{\$6,400}{8,000} = \frac{\$7,200}{9,000} = \frac{\$8,000}{10,000} = \$.80$$

Therefore, the expected or allowed overhead cost for 9,500 hours, for example, can be calculated as follows:

$$\text{Cost allowed} = \$3,600 + \$.80(9,500) = \$11,200$$

This also can be stated as:

$$\text{Cost allowed} = a + bx$$

where a = fixed cost, b = variable cost per unit used to measure the level of operations (in this case, standard hours), and x = number of units of activity base (in this case, standard labor hours) expected to be achieved.

In establishing its standard overhead rate at $1.25 per hour, the firm anticipates that it will operate at 80% of capacity (produce goods requiring 8,000 standard hours of labor). If the firm were to actually achieve 8,000 standard hours of production during a reporting period, the amount of overhead applied would be 8,000 × $1.25 per hour = $10,000, the amount budgeted for that level of production. However, the actual amount of production almost certainly will be either higher or lower than the 8,000 hours on which the manufacturing-overhead application rate was based. That, in turn, will result in the application of more or less than $10,000 of overhead to production.

To illustrate the effect of higher- or lower-than-expected levels of production on the application of overhead, let's assume Don Company produces goods equivalent to 9,000 standard hours of labor during a reporting period. The overhead applied then would be 9,000 hours × $1.25 per hour = $11,250. In Figure 13–1, that amount is $450 in excess of what would have been applied had we based our standard overhead rate on the flexible-budget allowance for the 9,000-hour level of production ($10,800). That is because the firm applied fixed overhead at the **fixed manufacturing overhead application rate** of $3,600 ÷ 8,000 = $.45 per hour rather than the $3,600 ÷ 9,000 = $.40 per hour that would have been used had we known that production was going to be 9,000 standard hours. This excess application of overhead is attributed to the fact that the firm was able to operate at a higher volume than was anticipated at the time the standard overhead rate was established. We characterize the amount of that variance as a *volume variance*. These relationships are presented graphically in Figure 13–2.

Some might argue, with justification, that any overhead application rate in excess of $1.16 per hour in our illustration (see Figure 13–1) improperly includes **idle-capacity costs** in the valuation of inventory (in our illustration, $.09 per standard hour). However, that argument fails to recognize that it is impractical for a firm to operate at capacity on a continuing basis. Therefore, we do not conventionally recognize as a separate item idle-capacity costs caused by operating at less than capacity.

To illustrate how the deviation from the expected volume of operations can cause an underapplication of overhead, let's assume that Don Company produces output that should require 7,000 standard hours during a reporting period, rather than the 8,000 that was anticipated when the overhead application rate of $1.25 per hour was established. Under those circumstances, the firm would have applied 7,000 × $1.25 = $8,750 of manufacturing overhead, rather than the $9,200 that is expected to be incurred at that level of production according to the flexible budget (see Figure 13–1). The difference of $9,200 − $8,750 = $450 arises because the firm applied fixed manufacturing overhead at the rate of $.45 per hour of production when it would have been applied at the rate of $3,600 ÷ 7,000 hours = $.51429 had the firm known

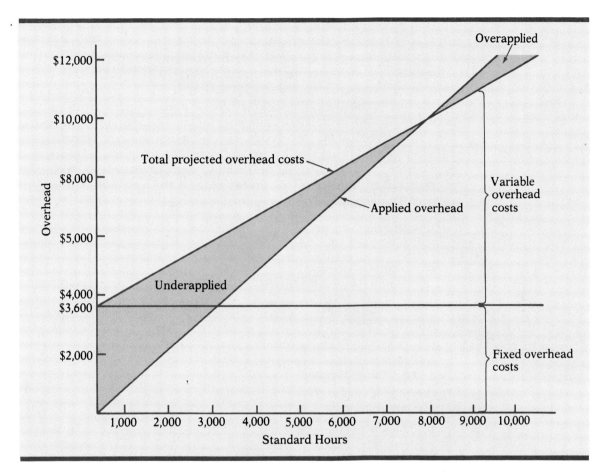

FIGURE 13–2 Applied Versus Projected Overhead

at the time the standard overhead application rate was established that it was going to achieve only 7,000 hours of production. Thus, underapplied or overapplied overhead can result from the failure of the company to achieve the volume of production that was expected to be achieved when the standard overhead rate per hour was established as well as by incurring more overhead costs than should have been incurred for the level of operations actually achieved. Regardless of the cause of the variance, it should be recognized as the balances in the manufacturing-overhead (control) account and the applied manufacturing-overhead accounts are closed, just as in accounting for manufacturing overhead when using a normal cost system.

When completed units are transferred from the factory to finished-goods inventory, we debit finished goods and credit work in process for an amount equal to the number of units, or standard hours of production represented by those units, multiplied by the standard overhead rate (per unit or per hour) shown on the standard cost card.

To illustrate, let's assume that actual overhead costs for Don Company for the reporting period are $11,700, that production (total equivalent units) equal to 9,000 standard labor hours occurred during the period, and that completed units equivalent to 8,700 standard hours were transferred to finished goods. The following summary journal entries then would be used to record the incurrence of overhead costs, the application of manufacturing overhead to work in process, the transfer of overhead to finished-goods inventory, and the amount of overhead variance (underapplied or overapplied overhead):

Manufacturing overhead	11,700	
Misc. payables, etc.		11,700
Work-in-process inventory	11,250 (1)	
Manufacturing overhead applied		11,250
Finished goods inventory	10,875 (2)	
Work-in-process inventory		10,875
Manufacturing overhead applied	11,250	
Underapplied or overapplied overhead	450	
Manufacturing overhead		11,700

Explanations:

(1) 9,000 standard hours × $1.25
(2) 8,700 standard hours × $1.25

After recording manufacturing-overhead activities, we are ready to divide the total overhead variance (underapplied overhead of $450 in this case) into different parts based on factors causing the variance. How that is done is explained in the next section.

Analysis of the Manufacturing-Overhead Variance

After having determined the amount of underapplied or overapplied manufacturing overhead (overhead was underapplied by $450 in the Don Company illustration), we are ready to apportion that amount to detailed variance accounts that show what has caused it. As we have observed, this total overhead variance could be attributed to either or both of two elements of operations: (1) spending more than should have been spent for the level of production achieved, and (2) achieving greater or fewer standard hours of production than was anticipated when the overhead application rate was established. When we divide the total overhead variance into the amounts caused by these two operational deviations, we are using a *two-variance analysis*. As we shall explain, however, one of these two variances may be subdivided to show more specifically what has caused it. When we do that we are using either a *three-variance* or a *four-variance analysis*.

Two-Variance Analysis

Probably the most widely used method of analyzing the total overhead variance is to divide that variance into two categories: controllable, or budget, variance, and volume variance.

A *controllable*, or *budget, variance* always will equal the difference between the actual manufacturing overhead incurred and the manufacturing overhead that should have been incurred for the level of production actually achieved (that is, the budgeted overhead for the level of production achieved). Continuing the Don Company illustration, we first determine what part of the $450 total unfavorable overhead variance was caused by incurring more overhead costs than should have been incurred based on the flexible-budget data. We assumed that the Don Company completed 9,000 standard hours of production during an operating period in which the firm incurred total actual manufacturing-overhead costs of $11,700. According to the flexible budget in Figure 13–1 the manufacturing overhead allowed for 9,000 standard hours of production is $10,800, so we can compute the amount of the controllable (budget) variance by subtracting that figure from the $11,700 of manufacturing overhead actually incurred to arrive at a $900 unfavorable variance:

Actual manufacturing overhead	$11,700
− Overhead allowed for 9,000 hours of production	− 10,800
= Controllable (budget) variance	$ 900 (U)

This controllable (budget) variance means that the company incurred $900 more overhead costs than should have been incurred in turning out 9,000 standard hours of production.

The difference between the total variance [$450 (U)] and the budget variance [$900 (U)] is caused by the difference between the level of production achieved and the level projected at the time the overhead application rate was established. We call the difference a *volume variance*, which is the difference between the amount of manufacturing overhead applied to production and the amount of manufacturing overhead that should have been incurred for the level of production actually achieved (that is, the flexible-budget amount that would have been projected for the output achieved).

Don Company will have applied manufacturing overhead of 9,000 standard hours of work turned out × $1.25 per hour = $11,250. Given the $10,800 of manufacturing overhead costs that should have been incurred to achieve 9,000 standard hours of production (see Figure 13–1), the volume variance would then be calculated as follows:

Manufacturing overhead allowed for 9,000 standard hours of work	$10,800
− Manufacturing overhead applied	− 11,250
= Volume variance	$ 450 (F)

The volume variance shows the part of the total overhead variance caused by producing 9,000 standard hours of work instead of the 8,000 contemplated when the manufacturing-overhead rate was established. The firm has applied $450 more manufacturing overhead to units produced during the period than would have been applied had the firm used the $1.20 overhead application rate based on the 9,000-hour option of its flexible budget (Figure 13–1).

Because the differences between the overhead application rates at various levels of operation and the amounts allowed for those levels are entirely caused by differences between the amounts of fixed costs per unit allowed and fixed cost per unit applied, the volume variance also can be calculated in two other ways:

1. Multiply the difference between the budgeted hours of production (8,000) and the actual number of standard hours of work turned out (9,000) by the fixed part of the manufacturing-overhead application rate ($.45):

Budgeted (expected) hours	8,000
− Standard hours allowed for output achieved	− 9,000
= Volume variance in hours	(1,000) (F)
× Fixed overhead application rate	× $ .45
= Total volume variance	($ 450) (F)

2. Multiply the difference between the fixed overhead application rates at the 8,000-hour level ($.45) and the 9,000-hour level ($.40) by the total standard hours of production:

Fixed overhead application rate for expected volume	$ .45
− Fixed overhead application rate that would have been used if firm had known in advance the correct volume (9,000 hours) for the period	− .40
= Fixed overhead rate variance	$ .05 (F)
× Standard hours of production achieved	× 9000
= Volume variance	$ 450 (F)

Using a two-variance analysis of manufacturing overhead, we would then distribute the total overhead variance amount recorded earlier as underapplied overhead (see page 470) with the following entry:

Controllable (budget) variance	900	
Manufacturing-overhead volume variance		450
Underapplied or overapplied manufacturing		
overhead		450

On receiving this information, management would expect the person in charge of the production activities for Don Company to provide reasons for the $900 unfavorable controllable (budget) variance. At the same time, management should recognize that the marketing division of the business, by providing the opportunity for a greater volume of production than was anticipated, has enabled the firm to have a $450 favorable volume variance.

Three-Variance Analysis

The controllable (budget) variance will have been caused by two operating deviations. Since, as observed earlier, manufacturing overhead is incurred to provide the space and facilities required to produce finished goods, having to keep the factory or department in operation for more or fewer hours than were allowed for the production achieved will cause the firm to incur more or less overhead than was anticipated. In addition, spending more or less for individual items of overhead than was allowed by the flexible budget also will cause actual overhead to deviate from the budgeted amount. We call the first of these an **overhead efficiency variance** (or a **manufacturing overhead efficiency variance**), and the second an **overhead spending variance** (or a **manufacturing-overhead spending variance**).

The *overhead efficiency variance* is calculated by multiplying the difference between the actual hours worked and the standard hours allowed for production achieved by the **standard variable manufacturing-overhead rate** per hour. To illustrate, let's assume that Don Company required 9,500 actual hours to turn out 9,000 standard hours of production. The manufacturing-overhead efficiency variance then would be calculated as follows:

Actual hours of labor	9,500
− Standard hours of labor for output achieved	− 9,000
= Efficiency variance in hours	500 (U)
× Standard variable overhead rate	× $ .80
= Overhead efficiency variance	$ 400 (U)

The manufacturing-overhead efficiency variance also can be calculated as the difference between the flexible-budget amount for *actual hours* worked (9,500) and the flexible budget for *standard hours* that should have been worked for output achieved (9,000):

Flexible budget based on actual hours worked [(9,500 × $.8) + $3,600]	$11,200
− Flexible budget based on standard hours that should have been worked for output achieved	− 10,800
Efficiency variance	$ 400 (U)

The *overhead spending variance* equals the difference between the actual overhead costs incurred in keeping the factory in operation and the amount that the flexible budget shows should have been spent for the *actual hours* the factory was in operation. In our situation, that amounts to $500 (U), calculated as the difference between the $11,700 actual overhead costs and the $11,200 of overhead costs that should have been incurred, according to the flexible budget, to operate the plant for 9,500 hours:

Actual overhead costs	$11,700
− Flexible-budget amount based on actual hours worked	
[(9,500 × $.8) + $3,600]	− 11,200
= Spending variance	$ 500 (U)

Thus, $500 of the $900 unfavorable controllable (budget) variance was caused by the firm spending more than was anticipated for various manufacturing-overhead items (both fixed and variable). The other $400 is attributed to the extra variable overhead required because the firm had to operate 500 more hours than was allowed for the production turned out. Thus, the total controllable (budget) variance of $900 (U) has been caused by a spending variance of $500 (U) and an efficiency variance of $400 (U).

A spending variance can be analyzed further by comparing the actual expenditures for individual manufacturing-overhead items with those projected in the flexible budget for the actual hours worked. To illustrate, let's assume that the fixed and variable costs shown in the flexible budget for Don Company (Figure 13–1) are made up of the following manufacturing-overhead cost items:

Don Company Manufacturing-Overhead Budget Detail

	Level of Operations			
Standard hours	7,000	8,000	9,000	10,000
Variable costs				
Item 1	$1,400	$ 1,600	$ 1,800	$ 2,000
Item 2	700	800	900	1,000
Item 3	3,500	4,000	4,500	5,000
Fixed costs				
Item A	1,200	1,200	1,200	1,200
Item B	2,400	2,400	2,400	2,400
Totals	$9,200	$10,000	$10,800	$11,600

Let's further assume that actual manufacturing overhead includes the following items and amounts:

Don Company Actual Manufacturing Overhead

Item 1	$ 2,100
Item 2	1,000
Item 3	4,700
Item A	1,300
Item B	2,600
Total	$11,700

We can now relate the spending variance of $500 to the individual overhead expense items:

	Actual	Flexible Budget for 9,500 Hours	Variance
Item 1	$ 2,100	$ 1,900	$200 (U)
Item 2	1,000	950	50 (U)
Item 3	4,700	4,750	50 (F)
Item A	1,300	1,200	100 (U)
Item B	2,600	2,400	200 (U)
Total	$11,700	$11,200	$500 (U)

Such an analysis allows management to determine the specific overhead items that have been overspent (U) or underspent (F).

Our calculation of the manufacturing-overhead efficiency variance by using only the variable portion of the overhead application rate recognizes that the aggregate amount of fixed manufacturing overhead should not vary with the number of hours of operation. As a result, we can think of that manufacturing-overhead efficiency variance as being the marginal cost of keeping the plant in operation for the 500 excess hours required to turn out 9,000 standard hours of production.

The third element of the three-variance analysis recognizes that the planned utilization of the manufacturing facilities (8,000 hours) was exceeded, resulting in a favorable volume variance. This is the same volume variance [$450 (F)] calculated earlier as part of the two-variance analysis.

The entry to record the distribution of the total manufacturing-overhead variance using the three-variance method would be:

Manufacturing-overhead spending variance	500	
Manufacturing-overhead efficiency variance	400	
Manufacturing-overhead volume variance		450
Underapplied or overapplied manufacturing overhead		450

Four-Variance Analysis

The four-variance analysis of underapplied or overapplied manufacturing overhead is, in reality, an extension of the three-variance analysis.

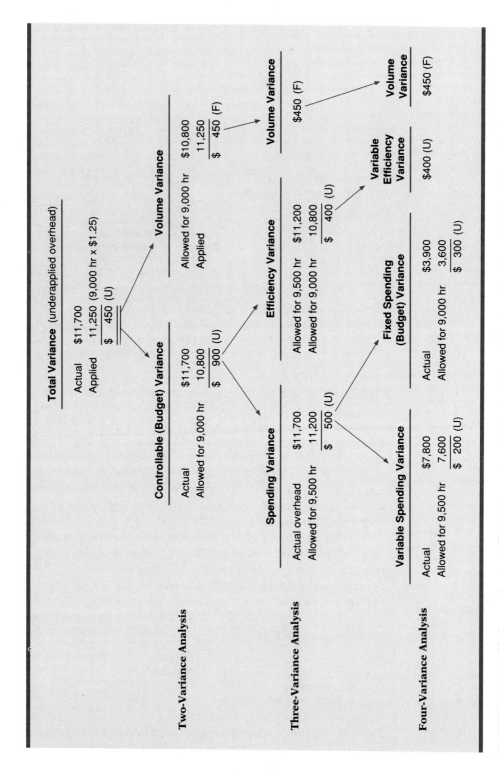

FIGURE 13—3 Variance Analysis Techniques Applied to the Manufacturing-Overhead Costs of Don Company

It divides the spending variance into fixed and variable portions while retaining the same efficiency and volume variances. According to our assumed actual expenses for Don Company (page 475), actual overhead costs included $7,800 of variable costs and $3,900 of fixed costs. Thus, we can allocate the total spending variance [$500 (U)] to variable and fixed overhead categories as follows:

Actual variable overhead	$7,800
− Variable overhead allowed for 9,500 hours (9,500 × $.80)	− 7,600
= Variable spending variance	= $ 200 (U)

Actual fixed overhead	$3,900
− Allowed (budgeted) fixed overhead	− 3,600
= Fixed overhead spending variance	= $ 300 (U)

This four-variance analysis would call for the following entry to be made to distribute the underapplied overhead:

Variable overhead spending variance	200	
Fixed overhead spending (budget) variance	300	
Variable overhead efficiency variance	400	
Fixed manufacturing-overhead volume variance		450
Underapplied or overapplied overhead		450

Techniques for Calculating Manufacturing-Overhead Variances

Manufacturing-overhead variances can be calculated logically if their definitions, as we have just described, are clearly understood. However, it may be helpful to visualize the calculations in a flowchart such as the one in Figure 13–3, which relates the overhead data for Don Company to the variance definitions used to calculate the variances. The flowchart shows how the $450 total underapplied overhead is allocated using two-, three-, and four-variance analyses, and how those variance analyses are related to each other.

Another approach to the mechanical calculation of variances is to use triangles and lines. We demonstrate those techniques in the appendix to this chapter.

Accounting for Ajax Company Manufacturing Overhead

Chapter 11 explained how to establish a standard cost system for Ajax Chemical Company, a hypothetical company first introduced in Chapter 6 to show how a company's historical costs would be accumulated and allocated when using a process cost system. Chapter 12 explained how the direct materials costs and direct labor costs of Ajax would be

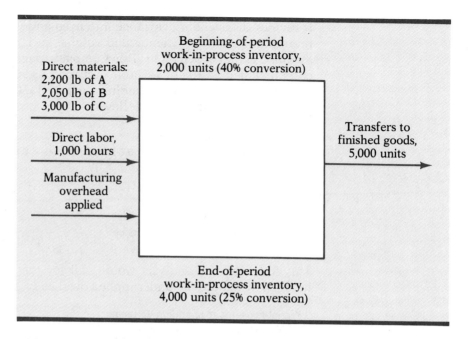

FIGURE 13–4 Manufacturing Cost-Accumulation Box for Ajax Chemical Company's Finished Product No. 5001

accounted for when using the newly installed standard cost system. Now we demonstrate, through the use of T accounts and journal entries, the accounting procedures to follow in accumulating and allocating manufacturing-overhead costs for Ajax using its newly installed standard cost system. Figure 13–4 summarizes the unit information previously presented for Ajax.

We shall assume that Ajax uses a two-variance analysis of manufacturing overhead. The equivalent units of direct labor and overhead production for the period again would be calculated as follows:

Units transferred out	5,000
+ End-of-period work in process (4,000 × 0.25)	+ 1,000
	6,000
− Beginning-of-period work in process (2,000 × 0.4)	− 800
= Equivalent units of production	= 5,200

The standard cost card for Product No. 5001 (see Figure 11–2, page 372) shows that each unit should require 0.2 hour of overhead at $9.50, for a total unit cost of $1.90. This standard is based on Ajax's flexible-budget formula:

Total projected manufacturing-overhead cost =
$7,000 + ($2.50 × standard direct labor hours)

The company expected to produce 1,000 standard labor hours of production for the period. Equivalent production is 5,200 units. Therefore, overhead applied to production will amount to:

5,200 units × 0.2 hr × $9.50 per hr = $9,880

These data are recorded as follows:

Manufacturing-Overhead Control		
Balance 10,400	(c)	10,400

Work in Process (overhead element only)		
Beginning balance 1,520 (1) (a) 9,880 (2)	(b)	9,500 (3)

Finished Goods (overhead element only)	
(b) 9,500 (3)	

Manufacturing Overhead Applied		
(c) 9,880	(a)	9,880 (2)

Underapplied or Overapplied Overhead		
(c) 520	(d)	520

Controllable Variance	
(d) 800 (4)	

Volume Variance	
	(d) 280 (5)

Explanation of Amounts:

(1)   2,000 units × 40% × $1.90 = $1,520
    or

        2,000 units × 40% × 0.2 hr = 160 standard hours
        160 standard hours × $9.50 = $1,520

(2) 5,200 equivalent units × 0.2 hr per unit × $9.50 per hour = $9,880
(3) 5,000 units × 0.2 hr × $9.50 per hour = $9,500
(4) Controllable (budget) variance

Actual overhead incurred	$10,400
Overhead allowed for 5,200 units × 0.2 hr = 1,040 hr [$7,000 + ($2.50 × 1,040)]	9,600
Controllable (budget) variance	$ 800 (U)

(5) Volume variance

Overhead allowed for 5,200 units × 0.2 hr = 1,040 hr [$7,000 + ($2.50 × 1,040)]	$9,600
Overhead applied (5,200 × 0.2 × $9.50)	9,880
Volume variance	$ 280 (F)

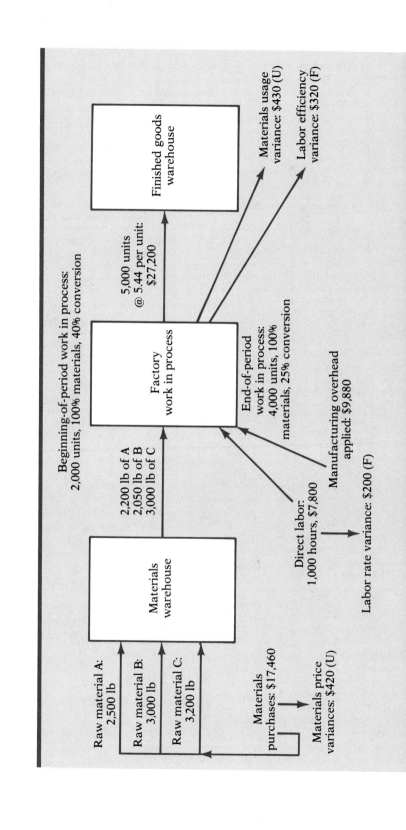

Materials Inventory

17,040	(2) 14,010 (3)

Accrued Payroll

	7,800 (4)

Accounts Payable

	17,460 (2)

Work-in-Process Inventory

Beginning balance 6,680 (1)	(X) 27,200
Direct materials 14,010 (3)	(X) 110
Direct labor 8,000 (4)	
Overhead 9,880 (5)	
Ending balance 11,260 *	

Manufacturing Overhead

Balance 10,400	10,400 (6)
9,880 (6)	

Manufacturing Overhead Applied

	9,880 (5)
9,880 (6)	

Finished-Goods Inventory

(X) 27,200	

Material Price Variance

420 (2)	

Labor Rate Variance

200 (4)	

Under- or Overapplied Overhead

520 (6)	520 (7)

Materials Usage Variance

(X) 430	

Labor Efficiency Variance

	(X) 320

Overhead Controllable Variances

800 (7)	

Overhead Volume Variance

280 (7)	

*See calculated proof on page 483.

(1) 2,000 × 100% × $1.94 = $3,880
2,000 × 40% × $3.50 = 2,800
$6,680

(2) See entry on page 422
(3) See entry on page 424
(4) See entry on page 429

(5) See entry (a) on page 482
(6) See entry (c) on page 482
(7) See entry (d) on page 482

FIGURE 13–5 Ajax Chemical Company: Summary of Cost Flows

Manufacturing-Overhead Journal Entries:

(a) Work-in-process inventory   9,880
      Manufacturing overhead applied   9,880

Overhead is applied to work in process.

(b) Finished-goods inventory   9,500
      Work-in-process inventory   9,500

Standard overhead associated with completed units (5,000) is transferred to finished goods. (This would be part of an entry to transfer the *total* standard cost of units completed to finished-goods inventory.)

(c) Manufacturing overhead applied   9,880
    Underapplied or overapplied overhead   520
      Manufacturing overhead control   10,400

Manufacturing overhead control and manufacturing overhead applied are closed to the underapplied or overapplied overhead account.

(d) Controllable variance   800
    Volume variance   280
    Underapplied or overapplied overhead   520

The total underapplied overhead is transferred to the controllable-variance and volume-variance accounts.

We now summarize the accumulation and allocation of *all* manufacturing costs for Ajax Chemical Company using the standard cost system established in Chapter 11 and the historical-cost data assumed in Chapters 6, 11, and 12. Those data are presented in the flowchart and T accounts of Figure 13–5 on pages 480–481.

The entries given in Chapter 12 and this chapter to transfer standard direct materials costs, direct labor costs, and manufacturing-overhead costs to finished-goods inventory would be combined into the following entries labelled (X) in Figure 13–5:

Finished-goods inventory   27,200 (1)
    Work-in-process inventory   27,200

To transfer the standard cost of completed units from work in process to finished-goods inventory.

Materials usage variance   430 (2)
    Labor efficiency variance   320 (3)
    Work-in-process inventory   110

To transfer materials and labor production variances from work in process to appropriate variance accounts.

Explanation:

(1) 5,000 units @ $5.44 $27,200
  or, Materials (5,000 @ $1.94) $9,700
        Labor (5,000 × $1.60)   8,000
        Overhead (5,000 × $1.90)   9,500 $27,200

(2) Raw material A [(2,200 − 2,100) × $2.00] $200 (U)
  Raw material B [(2,050 − 2,100) × $2.20]   110 (F)
  Raw material C [(3,000 − 2,800) × $1.70]   340 (U) $430 (U)

(3)   1,000 actual hours − 1,040 standard hours × $8 = $320 (F)

The journal entry to distribute the underapplied overhead to the variance accounts is the same as previously illustrated in the manufacturing-overhead journal entries (see T accounts on page 482).

Controllable variance	800	
Underapplied or overapplied overhead		520
Volume variance		280

To close the underapplied or overapplied overhead account and recognize two overhead variances.

The controllable-variance and volume-variance accounts are closed at the same time and in the same way as the other variance accounts. That is, they may be closed directly to cost of sales or allocated to the inventory and cost of sales accounts.

Proof of Work-in-Process Inventory Ending Balance:

Balance shown in ledger account (see page 481)	$11,260
Calculated balance	
Materials costs (4,000 × $1.94)	7,760
Conversion costs (4,000 × 25% × $3.50*)	3,500
Total	$11,260

*$1.60 direct labor plus $1.90 manufacturing overhead.

Illustrative Problem: Part 3

In Chapter 11, we demonstrated the installation of a standard cost system for Illustration Company, a firm assumed to manufacture two finished products, M and N, from raw materials A, B, C, and D. In Chapter 12, we showed how raw materials costs and direct labor costs should be recorded for the company within the framework of the standard cost system established in Chapter 11 and additional assumed data for materials and labor costs. Now we add an additional assumption: manufacturing overhead costs amounting to $15,800 ($11,600 fixed + $4,200 variable) were incurred during the operating period. The $10 standard overhead rate per hour was determined from the following flexible-budget data (projected level of operations is 1,600 labor hours):

	Level of Operations			
Labor Hours	1,400	1,600	1,800	2,000
Variable costs	$ 3,500	$ 4,000	$ 4,500	$ 5,000
Fixed costs	12,000	12,000	12,000	12,000
Total	$15,500	$16,000	$16,500	$17,000
Total application rate	$11.07	$10.00	$9.17	$8.50
Variable overhead application rate	$ 2.50	$ 2.50	$2.50	$2.50
Fixed overhead application rate	8.57	7.50	6.67	6.00
Total	$11.07	$10.00	$9.17	$8.50

From these data, we can develop the following overhead cost projection formula:

$$\text{Total projected overhead cost} =$$
$$\$12,000 + (2.50 \times \text{standard hours of production})$$

Illustration Company expected to operate at 1,600 labor hours and therefore used $16,000 ÷ 1,600 = $10 per hour as its standard overhead application rate. Actual direct labor hours for the period, however, were 1,625. Production for the period was equal to 975 equivalent units of M at 0.6 hour per unit + 1,200 equivalent units of N at 0.8 hour per unit = 1,545 standard hours.

The standard cost cards for products M and N as presented in Chapter 11 are repeated here:

Standard Cost Card	
Product M	
Direct materials	
2 units of raw material A @ $.50	$ 1.00
2 units of raw material B @ $.25	.50
	$ 1.50
Direct labor (0.6 hour @ $6 per hour)	3.60
Overhead (0.6 hour @ $10 per hour)	6.00
Total standard cost per unit	$11.10

Standard Cost Card

Product N

Direct materials	
3 units of raw material C @ $1.00	$ 3.00
2 units of raw material D @ $.75	1.50
	$ 4.50
Direct labor (0.8 hour @ $6 per hour)	4.80
Overhead (0.8 hour @ $10 per hour)	8.00
	$17.30

REQUIRED:

1. Record the application of manufacturing overhead to production for the period and determine the underapplied or overapplied overhead.
2. Record the allocation of underapplied or overapplied overhead to variance accounts using two-variance, three-variance, and four-variance analyses.
3. Prepare journal entries to summarize the accumulation and allocation of all manufacturing costs for the period. Use a two-variance analysis for manufacturing overhead.

Solution to Illustrative Problem, Part 3

We begin by summarizing in the flowchart in Figure 13–6 the assumptions made in Chapters 11 and 12.

1. Application of Manufacturing Overhead to Production.

Work-in-process inventory	15,450	
Applied manufacturing overhead		15,450 (1)
Applied manufacturing overhead	15,450	
Underapplied or overapplied overhead	350 (2)	
Manufacturing overhead control		15,800

Explanation:

(1)	975 equivalent units of M @ $6* per unit	$ 5,850
	1,200 equivalent units of N @ $8** per unit	9,600
	Total	$15,450

(or, 1,545 hours × $10 per hour = $15,450)

*0.6 direct labor hour per unit × $10 per hour
**0.8 direct labor hour per unit × $10 per hour

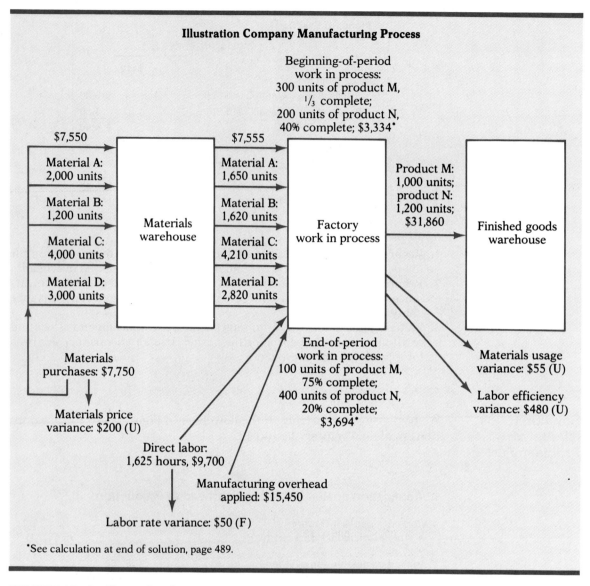

FIGURE 13–6 Illustration Company Manufacturing Process

(2) Actual overhead incurred		$15,800
Applied overhead		
Standard hours for		
M (975 equivalent units × 0.6)	585	
N (1,200 equivalent units × 0.8)	960	
Total	1,545	
or, 1,545 hours @ $10 per hour		15,450
Underapplied overhead		$ 350

2. Allocation of Overhead to Variance Accounts.

Two-Variance Analysis

Volume variance	$412.50 (1)	
Underapplied or overapplied overhead		350.00
Controllable variance		62.50 (2)

Explanation:

(1) Overhead allowed for 1,545 hours

[$12,000 + (1,545 × $2.50)]	$15,862.50
Applied overhead (1,545 hr. @ $10)	15,450.00
Volume variance	$ 412.50 (U)

(2)

Actual overhead	$15,800.00
Overhead allowed for 1,545 hours	15,862.50
Controllable variance	$ 62.50 (F)

Three-Variance Analysis

Efficiency variance	200.00 (3)	
Volume variance	412.50 (1)	
Underapplied or overapplied overhead		350.00
Spending variance		262.50 (4)

Explanation:

(1) Same as for two-variance analysis.

(3)

Actual hours	1,625
Standard hours	1,545
Excess hours	80

$$80 \text{ hours @ } \$2.50 = \underline{\$200} \text{ (U)}$$

(4) Overhead allowed for actual hours

[$12,000 + (1,625 × $2.50)]	$16,062.50
Actual overhead	15,800.00
Total spending variance (variable + fixed)	$ 262.50 (F)

Four-Variance Analysis

Efficiency variance	200.00 (3)	
Volume variance	412.50 (1)	
Variable overhead spending variance	137.50 (5)	
Underapplied or overapplied overhead		350.00
Fixed overhead spending variance		400.00 (6)

Explanation:

(1) Same as for two-variance analysis.
(3) Same as for three-variance analysis.

(5) Actual variable overhead · $4,200.00

Variable overhead allowed (1,625 hours @ $2.50) · · · · · · · · · · · · · · · · 4,062.50

Variable spending variance · $ 137.50 (U)

(6) Actual fixed overhead · $11,600

Fixed overhead allowed (budgeted) · 12,000

Fixed overhead spending variance · $ 400 (F)

3. Journal Entries.

Materials inventory	7,550.00	
Material price variance	200.00	
Accounts payable		7,750.00

(See page 440.)

Work-in-process inventory	7,555.00	
Materials inventory		7,555.00

(See page 440.)

Work-in-process inventory	9,750.00	
Labor rate variance		50.00
Accrued payroll		9,700.00

(See page 440.)

Work-in-process inventory	15,450.00	
Applied manufacturing overhead		15,450.00

Applied manufacturing overhead	15,450.00	
Underapplied or overapplied overhead	350.00	
Manufacturing overhead		15,800.00

Finished-goods inventory	31,860.00 (1)	
Work-in-process inventory		31,860.00

Materials usage variance	55.00 (2)	
Labor efficiency variance	480.00 (3)	
Work-in-process inventory		535.00

Explanation:

(1)
1,000 units of N @ $11.10	$11,100
1,200 units of M @ $17.30	20,760
Total	$31,860

(2) See page 441.
(3) See page 441.

Volume variance	412.50 (4)	
Underapplied or overapplied overhead		350.00
Controllable variance		62.50 (5)

Explanation:

(4) See explanation (1) under two-variance analysis.
(5) See explanation (2) under two-variance analysis.

Proof of work-in-process account balance:

Work-in-Process Inventory

Beginning balance	3,334 (1)	31,860 (see page 488)
Materials	7,555	535 (see page 488)
Labor	9,750	
Overhead	15,450	
Balance	3,694 (2)	

Explanation:

(1) Materials
   300 units of Product M (300 × $1.50) $ 450
   200 units of Product N (200 × $4.50)   900
Labor
   300 units of Product M (300 × 1/3 × 0.6)   60 hr
   200 units of Product N (200 × 0.4 × 0.8)   64 hr
Total   124 hr
Total labor (124 hr @ $6)   744
Overhead (124 hr @ $10)   1,240
Total $3,334

(2) Materials
   100 units of Product M (100 × $1.50) $ 150
   400 units of Product N (400 × $4.50)   1,800
Labor
   100 units of Product M (100 × 0.75 × 0.6)   45 hr
   400 units of Product N (400 × 0.2 × 0.8)   64 hr
Total   109 hr
Total labor (109 hr @ $6)   654
Overhead (109 hr @ $10)   1,090
Total $3,694

SUMMARY

In this chapter, we explained how manufacturing-overhead costs are accumulated and allocated when using a standard cost system. Because of the nature of manufacturing-overhead costs, an analysis of variances from standard in terms of price and quantity elements would not provide the same useful information as those variances provide for materials costs and labor costs. Therefore, instead of following the price/quantity approach, the total overhead variance should be analyzed to show the part that was controllable within the period and the part that has occurred because of the difference between the actual volume of production achieved and the volume anticipated at the time the standard manufacturing-overhead rate was established.

We emphasized that manufacturing overhead is applied on the basis of standard hours allowed for output achieved rather than on the basis of actual hours (as is the case when using historical costs). Thus, the total overhead variance equals the difference between actual manufacturing costs and the manufacturing costs applied to production, and can be characterized as underapplied or overapplied manufacturing overhead.

After demonstrating the way in which the underapplied or overapplied overhead should be calculated and recorded, we focused on the analysis of the underapplied or overapplied amount using either a two-variance, a three-variance, or a four-variance approach. The two-variance analysis divides the total overhead variance into two parts: controllable (or budget) variance, and volume variance. The three-variance analysis divides the total overhead variance into spending, efficiency, and volume variances. The four-variance analysis also includes the spending, efficiency, and volume variances, but it divides the three-variance method's spending variance into variable and fixed elements.

Finally, we continued our illustration of the accounting procedures followed by Ajax Chemical Company under the assumption that a standard cost system had been established to replace the historical-cost process-costing system illustrated in Chapter 6. We also concluded our standard cost example of Illustration Company, begun in Chapter 11.

APPENDIX: Alternative "Triangle" Overhead Analysis

Triangles and lines may be used to calculate overhead variances. Once you understand the logic of overhead variance analysis, the triangles are a convenient way to recall overhead relationships. This approach is illustrated in Figure 13–7 (pages 492–493) using data from the Don Company. Just as in the triangle approach for materials and labor (see appendix to Chapter 12), actual costs anchor the lower left base of the triangles and standard (or applied) costs anchor the lower right bases. The variable portion of the overhead analysis follows the same "rules" as the materials and labor models. That is, the actual quantity from the lower left base and the standard cost per unit from the lower right base are moved to the "peak" of the triangle and combined there. For example, under the variable overhead portion of the four-variance overhead analysis, the actual number of hours (9,500) from the left base and standard cost per hour ($0.80) from the right base form the "peak" actual/standard components that, when multiplied together, total $7,600. The fixed overhead, however, is treated differently. For fixed overhead in the two-, three-, and four-variance approaches, all "peak" amounts are the same—budgeted fixed overhead.

To determine whether the variance is favorable or unfavorable, we recommend that the calculation of variances proceed clockwise from the lower left-hand corner of the triangle, using two amounts for each variance comparison. If the first ("actual") amount is greater than the second ("standard") amount, the variance is unfavorable.

GLOSSARY OF TERMS INTRODUCED IN THIS CHAPTER

activity base
Measure of output or performance that is highly correlated with the amount of cost incurred; used as a basis for allocating manufacturing-overhead costs.

applied overhead
See *total applied (standard) overhead costs*.

budget variance
The difference between actual overhead costs and the costs allowed in the flexible budget for the level of activity actually achieved; also known as *controllable variance*.

controllable variance
See *budget variance*.

fixed overhead application rate
Budgeted fixed overhead for a period of time divided by the number of units of the activity base (generally direct labor hours) expected to be achieved during that period. The calculation is made for the purpose of establishing an overhead application rate used in both historical and standard cost systems.

idle-capacity costs
A variance attributable to failure to utilize facilities at their practical capacity. Idled capacity may be planned (for future expansion) or unplanned (erroneous demand estimates).

manufacturing-overhead efficiency variance
See *overhead efficiency variance*.

manufacturing-overhead spending variance
See *overhead spending variance*.

overhead efficiency variance
An amount equal to the difference between standard hours of work produced and actual hours used for that production multiplied by the variable overhead application rate; measures how efficiently the activity base (direct labor hours, machine-hours, raw materials cost, and so forth) was utilized.

Two-Variance Overhead Analysis (Variable Overhead and Fixed Overhead Combined)

Flexible-Budget Overhead (based on output achieved)
Variable (9,000 × $.80) $ 7,200
Plus fixed (budgeted) + 3,600*
Total flexible budget $10,800

Alternate Calculation of Volume Variance
Denominator hours* (hours used to calculate fixed overhead rate/hour) 8,000
Less standard hours allowed −9,000
"Excess" hours of operation −1,000 F
Fixed overhead rate/hour × $.45
  $450 F

Total Standard (Applied) Overhead
Variable (9,000 × $.8) $ 7,200
Plus fixed (9,000 × $.45*) + 4,050
Total standard (applied) overhead $11,250

Alternate Calculation of Controllable Variance as a "Missing Information" Item
Total overhead variance $450 U
Less volume variance −450 F
Controllable variance $900 U

Total Actual Overhead
Variable $ 7,800
Plus fixed + 3,900
Total actual overhead $11,700

$900 U — Controllable (budget) variance
$450 F — Volume variance
Total overhead variance = $450 U

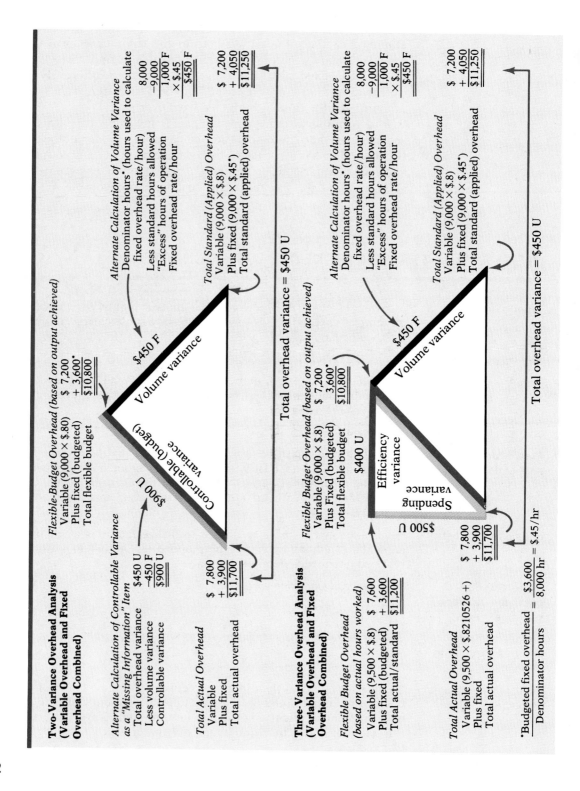

Three-Variance Overhead Analysis (Variable Overhead and Fixed Overhead Combined)

Flexible Budget Overhead (based on output achieved)
Variable (9,000 × $.8) $ 7,200
Plus Fixed (budgeted) 3,600*
Total flexible budget $10,800

Alternate Calculation of Volume Variance
Denominator hours* (hours used to calculate fixed overhead rate/hour) 8,000
Less standard hours allowed −9,000
"Excess" hours of operation −1,000 F
Fixed overhead rate/hour × $.45
  $450 F

Total Standard (Applied) Overhead
Variable (9,000 × $.8) $ 7,200
Plus fixed (9,000 × $.45*) + 4,050
Total standard (applied) overhead $11,250

Flexible Budget Overhead
(based on actual hours worked)
Variable (9,500 × $.8) $ 7,600
Plus fixed (budgeted) + 3,600
Total actual/standard $11,200

Total Actual Overhead
Variable (9,500 × $.8210526 +) $ 7,800
Plus fixed + 3,900
Total actual overhead $11,700

$500 U — Spending variance
$400 U — Efficiency variance
$450 F — Volume variance
Total overhead variance = $450 U

*Budgeted fixed overhead / Denominator hours = $3,600 / 8,000 hr = $.45/hr

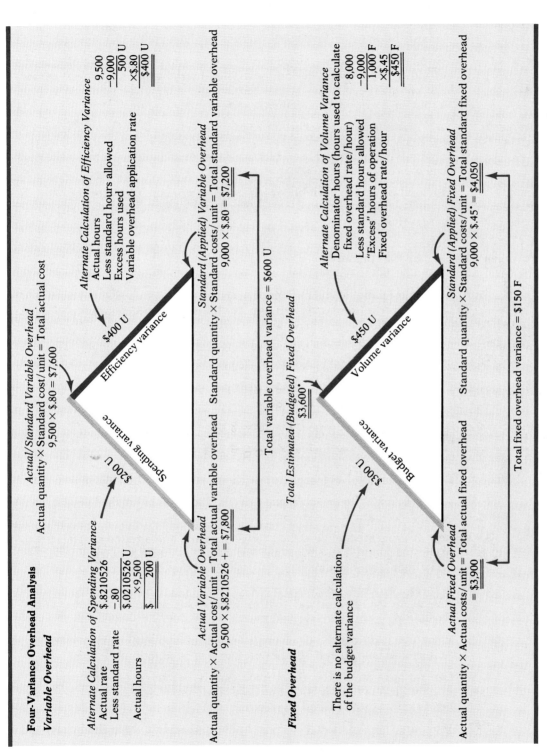

FIGURE 13–7 Overhead Variance Analysis for the Don Company

493

overhead spending variance	An amount equal to the difference between actual overhead incurred and the costs allowed in the flexible budget for the actual hours worked.
standard hours of production	An amount equal to the number of equivalent units of production turned out during a reporting period multiplied by the standard hours allowed for each unit; used to describe the amount of production achieved during a reporting period when using a standard cost system.
standard overhead application rate	Total manufacturing overhead projected in a flexible budget for the level of activity expected to be achieved divided by the number of units of the activity base (generally direct labor hours) associated with the projected level of production.
standard variable manufacturing-overhead rate	The total projected variable overhead for a projected level of production divided by the activity base (generally direct labor hours) associated with that level of activity.
total applied (standard) overhead cost	An amount equal to the standard hours of production achieved multiplied by the standard overhead rate per hour.
total overhead variance	An amount equal to the difference between actual overhead incurred and applied overhead for a reporting period; also called *underapplied or overapplied overhead.*
volume variance	An amount equal to the difference between the flexible budget overhead cost for the actual level of production achieved and the overhead applied at that level of production.

QUESTIONS FOR CLASS DISCUSSION

13–1 How is a standard overhead application rate established? Explain.

13–2 How is manufacturing overhead allocated to units of finished goods when using a standard cost system?

13–3 Can we separate the difference between actual and applied overhead into price and quantity variances as we did in accounting for direct materials and direct labor? Explain.

13–4 Is there a difference between manufacturing overhead applied to production when using an actual cost system versus a standard cost system? Explain.

13–5 What equation can be used in projecting the manufacturing overhead that should be incurred at different levels of production?

13–6 Can we have an overhead variance simply because a firm operates at a different level of production than was anticipated when a standard overhead rate was established? Explain.

13–7 What are the two basic causes of underapplied or overapplied overhead when a firm is using a standard cost system? Explain.

13—8   How is total overhead variance calculated?

13—9   How is the controllable (budget) variance calculated? What is its significance?

13—10   How is the volume variance calculated? What does it represent?

13—11   What are the two possible causes of a controllable (budget) variance?

13—12   What is a spending variance? How may a spending variance be further analyzed for use in controlling manufacturing-overhead expenses?

13—13   What causes a manufacturing-overhead efficiency variance? Explain.

13—14   How is the manufacturing-overhead efficiency variance calculated?

13—15   How is the manufacturing-overhead spending variance calculated? What causes such a variance?

13—16   Can the manufacturing-overhead spending variance relate to both fixed and variable manufacturing-overhead items? Explain.

13—17   What is the relationship between two-variance overhead analysis and three-variance overhead analysis?

13—18   What is the relationship between a three-variance and a four-variance analysis of total overhead variance?

EXERCISES

13—19   **Multiple Choice—Standard Overhead Costs** Select the *best* answer to each
AICPA Adapted   of the following independent items.

1. Under the two-variance method for analyzing factory overhead, the controllable (budget) variance is the difference between the
   a. budget allowance based on standard hours allowed and the factory overhead applied to production.
   b. budget allowance based on standard hours allowed and the budget allowance based on actual hours worked.
   c. actual factory overhead and the factory overhead applied to production.
   d. actual factory overhead and the budget allowance based on standard hours allowed.
2. Under the two-variance method for analyzing factory overhead, the volume variance is the difference between the
   a. budget allowance based on standard hours allowed and the budget allowance based on actual hours worked.
   b. budget allowance based on standard hours allowed and the factory overhead applied to production.
   c. actual factory overhead and the budget allowance based on standard hours allowed.
   d. actual factory overhead and the factory overhead applied to production.

3. Under the three-variance method of analyzing factory overhead, the difference between the actual factory overhead and the budget allowance based on actual hours is the
   a. efficiency variance.
   b. spending variance.
   c. volume variance.
   d. idle-capacity variance.
4. Under the three-variance method for analyzing factory overhead, which of the following is used in the computation of the spending variance?

	Actual Factory Overhead	Factory Overhead Applied to Production
a.	yes	yes
b.	yes	no
c.	no	yes
d.	no	no

13–20 **Two-Variance Analysis of Overhead** Mandy Company uses a flexible-budget system and prepared the following information for 19X2:

	Normal Capacity	Maximum Capacity
Percentage of capacity	80%	100%
Direct labor hours	48,000	60,000
Variable factory overhead	$72,000	$90,000
Fixed factory overhead	$180,000	$180,000
Total factory overhead rate per direct labor hour	$5.25	$4.50

Mandy planned to operate at normal capacity, but actually operated at 90% of maximum capacity during 19X2. The actual factory overhead for 19X2 was $273,000.

REQUIRED: Compute the following for Mandy Company:
1. total overhead applied during 19X2
2. budget (controllable) overhead variance for the year
3. volume variance for the year.

13–21 **Total Overhead Variance** Wilcox Company uses a flexible-budget system and prepared the following information for 19X0:

Percentage of capacity	90%	95%
Direct labor hours	45,000	47,500
Variable factory overhead	$135,000	$142,500
Fixed factory overhead	$213,750	$213,750
Total factory overhead rate per direct labor hour	$7.75	$7.50

Wilcox operated at 90% of capacity during 19X0, but applied factory overhead based on 95% capacity.

REQUIRED:

1. Assuming that actual factory overhead was $339,750, compute the total overhead variance for the year.
2. How much of the variance computed in the first requirement can be attributed to overutilization or underutilization of factory facilities (i.e., volume variance)?

13–22 **Missing Information** Fancher Company had total underapplied overhead of $15,000. Additional information is as follows:

Variable Overhead

Applied, based on standard direct labor hours allowed	$105,000
Budgeted	$ 95,000

Fixed Overhead

Applied, based on standard direct labor hours allowed	$ 75,000
Budgeted, based on standard direct labor hours	$ 67,500

REQUIRED: Compute Fancher Company's actual total overhead.

13–23 **Two-Variance Analysis of Overhead** Information on Arnold Company's overhead costs for January 19X0 production activity is as follows:

Budgeted fixed overhead	$150,000
Standard fixed overhead rate per direct labor hour	$3
Standard variable overhead rate per direct labor hour	$5
Standard direct labor hours allowed for actual production	49,000
Actual total overhead incurred	$395,500

Arnold has a standard absorption and flexible-budgeting system, and uses the two-variance method (two-way analysis) for overhead variances.

REQUIRED: Compute the following for Arnold Company for January 19X0:

1. budget (controllable) variance
2. volume variance.

13–24 **Three-Variance Analysis of Overhead** The following information is available from the Trey Company:

Actual factory overhead	$33,000
Fixed overhead expenses, actual	$15,840
Fixed overhead expenses, budgeted	$15,000
Actual hours	4,500
Standard hours for output achieved	4,800
Budgeted hours	5,000
Variable overhead rate per direct labor hour	$3.60

Trey uses a three-way analysis of overhead variances.

REQUIRED: Compute the following overhead variances for the Trey Company:

1. total spending variance
2. efficiency variance
3. volume variance.

13–25 **Four-Variance Analysis of Overhead** Hannahan Company employs a standard absorption system for product costing. The standard cost of its product is:

Raw materials	$ 8.70
Direct labor (2 hours @ $9)	18.00
Manufacturing overhead (2 hours @ $12)	24.00
Total standard cost	$50.70

The manufacturing-overhead rate is based on a normal annual activity of 600,000 direct labor hours. Hannahan planned to produce 25,000 units each month during 19X3. The budgeted manufacturing overhead for 19X3 is as follows:

Variable	$2,400,000
Fixed	4,800,000
	$7,200,000

During March 19X3, Hannahan Company produced 26,000 units. Hannahan used 53,500 direct labor hours in March at a cost of $483,200. Actual manufacturing overhead for the month was $403,200 fixed and $220,420 variable. The total manufacturing overhead applied during March was $624,000.

REQUIRED: Compute the following variances for March:

1. variable manufacturing-overhead spending variance
2. variable manufacturing-overhead efficiency variance
3. fixed manufacturing-overhead spending (budget) variance
4. fixed manufacturing-overhead volume variance.

13–26 **Four-Variance Analysis of Overhead** Kraus Company has developed standard overhead costs based on an annual expected operating level of 300,000 direct labor hours. That projected level produced the following data in the overhead part of the standard cost card.

Standard Overhead Costs per Unit	
Variable portion (3 hours @ $6)	$18
Fixed portion (3 hours @ $10)	30
	$48

During June, 8,500 units were scheduled for production; however, only 8,000 units were actually produced. The following data relate to June operations:

(1) Actual direct labor cost incurred was $358,800 for 23,000 actual hours of work.
(2) Actual overhead incurred totaled $394,600: $141,600 variable and $253,000 fixed.
(3) All inventories are carried at standard cost.

REQUIRED:

1. Compute the following variances for June:
   a. variable overhead spending variance
   b. variable overhead efficiency variance
   c. fixed overhead budget (spending) variance
   d. fixed overhead volume variance.
2. Prepare general journal entries to close overhead control and overhead applied to the four overhead-variance accounts.

13–27 **Two-, Three-, and Four-Variance Analysis of Overhead** Simon Company estimates it will operate its manufacturing facilities at 400,000 direct labor hours for the year. The estimate for total budgeted overhead is $2,000,000. The standard variable overhead rate is estimated to be $2 per direct labor hour, or $4 per unit. The actual data for the year are:

Actual finished units	205,000
Actual direct labor hours	415,000
Actual variable overhead	$810,000
Actual fixed overhead	$1,210,000

REQUIRED: Prepare a complete overhead analysis via each of the following methods:

1. two-way analysis of overhead variances
2. three-way analysis of overhead variances
3. four-way analysis of overhead variances.

PROBLEMS

13–28 **Actual and Applied Manufacturing Overhead** Gore Company's flexible-budget formula for annual factory-overhead cost is:

Total factory overhead costs = $90,000 + ($7 × direct labor hours)

The standard overhead application rate is based on 180,000 hours per year. Two standard direct labor hours are allowed for each unit produced.

In November, 7,600 units were produced. An analysis of the factory overhead indicates that, in November, Gore had an unfavorable budget (controllable) variance of $1,000 and a favorable volume variance of $50. Gore uses a two-way analysis of overhead variances.

REQUIRED:

1. Compute factory overhead absorbed (applied) in November.
2. How much actual factory overhead was incurred in November?

13–29
AICPA Adapted

Missing Information On May 1, 19X5, Bovar Company began the manufacture of a new mechanical device known as "Dandy." The company used a standard cost system to account for manufacturing costs. The standard costs for a unit of Dandy are as follows:

Raw materials (6 lb at $1 per lb)	$ 6.00
Direct labor (1 hour at $4 per hour)	4.00
Overhead (75% of direct labor costs)	3.00
	$13.00

The following data were obtained from Bovar's records for the month of May:

	Units
Actual production of Dandy	4,000
Units of Dandy sold	2,500

	Debit	Credit
Sales		$50,000
Purchases (26,000 lb)	$27,300	
Materials price variance	1,300	
Materials quantity variance	1,000	
Direct labor rate variance	760	
Direct labor efficiency variance		800
Manufacturing-overhead total variance	500	

The materials price variance shown above is applicable to raw materials purchased during May.

REQUIRED: Compute each of the following items for Bovar for the month of May. Show computations in good form.

1. standard quantity of raw materials allowed (in pounds)
2. actual quantity of raw materials used (in pounds)
3. standard hours allowed
4. actual hours worked

5. actual direct labor rate
6. actual total overhead

13–30
ICMA Adapted

Capacity Measures and Overhead Variances Nolton Products developed its overhead application rate from the current annual budget. The budget is based on an expected actual output of 720,000 units requiring 3,600,000 direct labor hours (DLH). The company is able to schedule production uniformly throughout the year.

A total of 66,000 units requiring 315,000 DLH was produced during May. Actual overhead costs for May amounted to $375,000. The actual cost as compared to the annual budget and one-twelfth of the annual budget are shown below.

	Annual Budget				
	Total Amount	Per Unit	Per Direct Labor Hour	Monthly Budget	Actual Costs for May 19X3
Variable					
Indirect labor	$ 900,000	$1.25	$ .25	$ 75,000	$ 75,000
Supplies	1,224,000	1.70	.34	102,000	111,000
Fixed					
Supervision	648,000	.90	.18	54,000	51,000
Utilities	540,000	.75	.15	45,000	54,000
Depreciation	1,008,000	1.40	.28	84,000	84,000
Total	$4,320,000	$6.00	$1.20	$360,000	$375,000

REQUIRED:

1. Define each of the following production facility capacity measures:
   a. theoretical capacity
   b. practical capacity
   c. normal capacity
   d. expected actual or master budget level of activity.
2. Calculate the following amounts for Nolton Products for May 19X3:
   a. absorbed (applied) overhead costs
   b. variable overhead spending variance
   c. fixed overhead budget (spending) variance
   d. variable overhead efficiency variance
   e. volume variance.
   Be sure to identify each variance as favorable (F) or unfavorable (U).

13–31
ICMA Adapted

Flexible Budgeting and Overhead Variances The Jason Plant of Cast Corporation has been in operation for 15 months. Jason employs a standard cost system for its manufacturing operations. The first six months' performance was affected by the usual problems associated with a new operation. Since that time the operations have been running smoothly. Unfortunately, however, the plant has not been able to produce profits on a consistent basis. As the production requirements to meet sales demand have increased, the profit performance has deteriorated.

The plant production manager commented at a staff meeting in which the plant general manager, the corporate controller, and the corporate budget director were in attendance that the changing production requirements make it more difficult to control manufacturing expenses. He further noted that the budget for the plant, included in the company's annual profit plan, was not useful for judging the plant's performance because of the changes in the operating levels. The meeting resulted in a decision to prepare a report that would compare the plant's actual manufacturing expense performance with a budget of manufacturing expense based on actual direct labor hours in the plant.

The plant production manager and the plant accountant studied the cost patterns for recent months, and volume and cost data from other Cast plants. Then they prepared the following flexible-budget schedule for a month with 200,000 planned production hours, which at standard would result in 50,000 units of output:

Manufacturing Expenses	Amount	Per Direct Labor Hour
Variable		
Indirect labor	$160,000	$ .80
Supplies	26,000	.13
Power	14,000	.07
		$1.00
Fixed		
Supervisory labor	64,000	
Heat and light	15,000	
Property taxes	5,000	
	$284,000	

The manufacturing expense reports prepared for the first three months after the flexible-budget program was approved were pleasing to the plant production manager. They showed that manufacturing expenses were in line with the flexible-budget allowance. This was also reflected by the report prepared for November, (at the top of page 503) when 50,500 units were manufactured. However, the plant was still not producing an adequate profit because the variances from standard costs were quite large.

REQUIRED:

1. Explain the advantages of flexible budgeting over fixed budgeting for cost control purposes.
2. Calculate the excess amount over standard spent on manufacturing expense items during November 19X9. Analyze this excess amount into those variances due to:

Jason Plant

Manufacturing Expenses

November 19X9

220,000 Actual Direct Labor Production Hours

	Actual Costs	Allowed Costs	(Over) Under Budget
Variable			
Indirect labor	$177,000	$176,000	$(1,000)
Supplies	27,400	28,600	1,200
Power	16,000	15,400	(600)
Fixed			
Supervisory labor	65,000	64,000	(1,000)
Heat and light	15,500	15,000	(500)
Property taxes	5,000	5,000	0
	$305,900	$304,000	$(1,900)

    a. variable overhead spending variance
    b. variable overhead efficiency variance
    c. fixed overhead budget (spending) variance
    d. fixed overhead volume variance.
3. Explain what the management of Jason Plant should do to reduce any unfavorable variances.
4. What should management do about any favorable variance?

13–32 **Comprehensive Missing Information—Variance Analysis** The Copeland Company has the following standard cost card for its only product:

Standard Cost per Unit of Product	
Materials (3 gallons at $3 per gallon)	$ 9.00
Direct labor (2 hours per unit at $8 per hour)	16.00
Variable factory overhead (2 hours at $ (a))	(b)
Fixed factory overhead (2 hours at $ (c))	(d)
Total unit cost	$35.00

    Due to a casualty, some of the unit standard cost information, designated (a) through (d), is missing. The following additional information is available, however:

(1) The company budgeted 80,000 direct labor hours for the month and estimated that variable factory overhead would be $160,000 and fixed factory overhead would be $240,000.
(2) During January, production was below budget and the following variances from standard were noted:

Materials price variance based on purchases	
($.05 per gallon)	$ 5,500 U
Materials quantity variance	6,000 U
Labor rate variance	7,200 U
Labor efficiency variance	16,000 U
Variable overhead spending variance	1,000 U
Variable overhead efficiency variance	4,000 U
Fixed overhead spending variance	2,000 F
Fixed overhead volume variance	30,000 U

REQUIRED:

1. Determine the following for the Copeland Company for January:
   a. number of units produced (*Hint:* Begin your work with the fixed overhead volume variance.)
   b. actual quantity of materials purchased
   c. actual labor hours worked and actual payroll cost
   d. actual variable and actual fixed overhead incurred
   e. fixed overhead applied to production
   f. number of excess gallons of materials (gallons above standard) and excess labor hours (hours above standard) used in January.
2. Prepare summary general journal entries for January. Copeland closes all variances to cost of goods sold. Assume no inventory in process at either the beginning or end of the period.

13–34
AICPA Adapted

Standard Cost Variances The Terry Company manufactures a commercial solvent that is used for industrial maintenance. This solvent is sold by the drum and generally has a stable selling price. Due to a decrease in demand for this product, Terry produced and sold 60,000 drums in December 19X6, which is 50% of normal capacity.

The following information is available regarding Terry's operations for the month of December 19X6:

(1) Standard costs per drum of product manufactured were as follows:

Materials	
10 gallons of raw material	$20
1 empty drum	1
Total	$21
Direct labor (1 hour)	$ 7
Factory overhead (variable) (per direct labor hour)	$ 6
Factory overhead (fixed) (per direct labor hour)	$ 4

(2) Costs incurred during December 19X6 were:

- Raw materials:
  600,000 gallons were purchased at a cost of $1,150,000.
  700,000 gallons were used.
- Empty drums:
  85,000 drums were purchased at a cost of $85,000.
  60,000 drums were used.

- Direct labor: 65,000 hours were worked at a cost of $470,000.
- Factory overhead:

Depreciation of building and machinery (fixed)	$230,000
Supervision and indirect labor (semivariable)	360,000
Other factory overhead (variable)	76,500
Total	$666,500

(3) The fixed overhead budget for the December level of production was $275,000.

(4) In November 19X6, at normal capacity of 120,000 drums, supervision and indirect labor costs were $680,000. All cost functions are linear.

REQUIRED: Prepare a schedule computing the following variances for the month of December 19X6:

1. materials price variance (computed at time of purchase)
2. materials usage (quantity) variance
3. labor rate variance
4. labor usage (efficiency) variance
5. factory overhead using a four-variance method. (Each of the four variances should be appropriately titled.)

Indicate whether each variance was favorable or unfavorable.

13–35 **THOUGHT STIMULATION CASE.** Refer to the Antaeus Manufacturing Company situation described in problem 12–31. After identifying its constraining factor (the assembly department) and scheduling production so that the 2-hour buffer inventory supplying the assembly department is fully stocked at all times to ensure this department operates continuously, without interruption, Antaeus observed the following results:

(1) Other than the buffer inventory required for the assembly department, work in process decreased by 98%.

(2) Because of detailed production scheduling, use of materials became more predictable, so the purchasing department could coordinate purchases more closely with uses of materials. Therefore, the inventory of raw materials decreased by 40%.

(3) Because production is scheduled to supply the bottleneck final assembly department with parts on an as-needed basis, smaller numbers of parts are constructed in each cost center before finished parts are transferred to the next cost center. Thus, parts can be transferred by hand rather than requiring a fork lift, resulting in a drastic reduction in materials handling costs.

(4) Overhead costs, since they now include costs formerly categorized as direct labor, have increased significantly. Applying overhead on the basis of materials costs (rather than on a direct labor basis, as was done in the past) seems to be working well—that is, no complaints have been received from marketing, production, or design personnel.

Antaeus's management is now analyzing the question of whether to broaden their product line to include paging devices. (The assembly department is to be expanded so it no longer constrains production.) The paging devices would be produced in the same departments as the radios, but will not require the same production activities. Management is convinced that the current single overhead application rate system will be inappropriate if more than one product (with vastly different costs of raw materials) is produced.

REQUIRED:

1. What condition(s) could have convinced management that a single overhead application rate is inappropriate if they broaden their line to include more than one product?
2. Why should Antaeus Manufacturing Company be concerned at all about an overhead application rate? That is, since finished-goods inventory is minimal or zero, why can't total overhead be allocated to cost of sales?
3. If Antaeus decides to modify their overhead application procedures, how might they design a new system? And what effect would the new system have on overhead variance analysis?

Part IV

Managerial Use of Cost Data

Chapter 14

Variable (Direct) Costing:
Gateway to Decision Making

Learning Objectives

When you have finished your study of this chapter, you should

1. Be aware of the shortcomings of absorption costing in matching costs with revenues on the basis of cause-and-effect relationships.
2. Know how to account for the accumulation and allocation of costs when using a variable- (direct-) costing system, and how to assemble those data in an income statement.
3. Understand how net operating income derived from a given set of data will differ when using variable costing versus absorption costing.
4. Recognize how to use contribution-margin data in making short-term operating decisions.
5. Be able to convert data from a variable-costing financial statement to data suitable for externally presented financial statements.

I f all accounting were separated into two categories—(1) accounting for external purposes (published financial statements and tax returns, for example), and (2) accounting for internal purposes (for example, planning and controlling)—two distinct cost accounting systems would emerge. An absorption-costing system would be used to fulfill the information requirements of external reporting, while a variable-costing system would most appropriately provide the information requirements for making internal decisions.

Chapters 4–13 presented the procedures followed in establishing and maintaining absorption (or traditional) cost accounting systems. Those systems are designed primarily to allocate all manufacturing costs (direct materials, direct labor, and manufacturing overhead) to the products being manufactured. Since absorption costing is the generally accepted accounting practice for allocating and accumulating manufacturing costs, that is the method that must be used to provide data for published financial statements. However, as we said in Chapter 2, for certain other purposes, **variable costing** (**direct costing**) is a desirable alternative to absorption costing.

Strictly from the point of view of cause-and-effect relationships, we can argue that only variable manufacturing costs should be allocated to the products being manufactured because they are incurred as goods are produced. Fixed manufacturing expenses, however, are incurred to position a firm to produce and are associated with the passage of time rather than with the level of production achieved. Therefore, variable costing, where fixed costs are expensed in the period in which they are incurred, seems to more realistically relate manufacturing costs to their causative factors. Such a system matches the variable manufacturing costs (direct materials, direct labor, and variable manufacturing overhead) against the revenues produced by the sale of products; at the same time, it matches fixed manufacturing costs against revenues realized during the periods in which the fixed costs are incurred.

Although variable costing is not a generally accepted accounting practice for external financial reporting, such a system may still be maintained for use by internal managers in making various operating decisions. It is truly the gateway to decision making. As we will explain later in this chapter, the data produced by direct costing are much more useful to management in making short-term decisions than are the data produced by absorption costing.

The accounting profession, in considering the objectives of cost accounting discussed in Chapter 1, has concluded that absorption (traditional) costing most appropriately assigns values to manufactured inventory. However, the data produced by a variable-costing system are more useful in meeting the other three objectives (controlling operations, planning future operations, and making day-to-day operating decisions). Therefore, as this chapter develops the procedures to follow in establishing and maintaining a variable-costing system, remember that the data produced by such a system will be used primarily by internal management in making short-term operating decisions and is *never* used in reporting to outsiders. It is unnecessary, however, to keep two sets of records—one based on direct costing and the other based on absorption costing—to meet both needs. The data produced by direct costing, as we will demonstrate, easily can be converted to an absorption-costing basis.

As we develop the procedures to be followed in maintaining a direct-costing system, we shall:

1. briefly discuss the problems associated with absorption costing when such a system is evaluated in terms of the extent to which it adheres to cause-and-effect relationships in the allocation of manufacturing costs
2. develop the procedures for establishing and maintaining a variable-costing system
3. examine the effect each system (variable costing and absorption costing) has on periodic net income from operations
4. examine the contribution-margin approach to managerial decisions
5. consider other ways in which variable-costing data may be used in decision making
6. explain how the data produced by variable costing can be converted to data that would meet the requirements of generally accepted accounting practices insofar as external financial reporting is concerned.

Manufacturing Costs: Cause-and-Effect Relationships

In Chapter 2, we observed that the variable costs of producing goods are considered product costs because they stem directly from identifiable production activities. We also noted that fixed manufacturing costs are incurred for the purpose of providing and maintaining facilities required to manufacture the product, but that they are associated with the passage of time rather than the volume of production, and within a relevant range of production levels, do not change as production changes. Many of them, such as the costs associated with providing buildings and equipment (depreciation, long-term rentals, insurance, and property taxes), cannot be changed in the short run because a firm has to commit itself to these costs for long periods of time. Therefore, proponents of variable costing contend that fixed manufacturing costs *logically* should be allowed to flow into the revenue–expense stream as they are incurred, by relating them on a cause-and-effect basis to the passage of time. Such reasoning leads us to conclude that only the variable manufacturing costs should be allocated to the product and be matched against revenues as those products are sold. Following the same logic, the fixed manufacturing costs should be matched against the revenues of the period associated with their incurrence. Therefore, if we adhere to that cause-and-effect logic, we can conclude that variable-costing procedures should be followed in allocating and accumulating manufacturing costs. Within such a system, only variable manufacturing costs would be included in the costs of products manufactured. All fixed manufacturing costs would be treated as period costs.

We also can observe that goods cannot be produced *without* the incurrence of fixed manufacturing costs generated by the acquisition of facilities and contractual commitments required to provide production capability. Following that line of reasoning, the accounting profession has concluded that fixed manufacturing costs, as well as variable manufacturing costs, should be allocated to products as they are manufactured. All manufacturing costs, variable and fixed, will then flow into cost of sales as the units are sold. Fixed manufacturing costs, along with variable manufacturing costs, associated with units still on hand will be included in end-of-period inventories. That system of allocating all manufacturing costs to units produced, known as absorption costing, is the system presented in Chapters 4–13.

The incurrence of variable manufacturing costs is caused by **short-term operating decisions** relating to the manufacture of the product. On the other hand, fixed manufacturing costs are incurred as a result of **long-term decisions** relating to the production capacity to be provided. Logically, therefore, short-term decisions should be based on short-term cause-and-effect relationships, and long-term decisions on long-term cause-and-effect relationships. Because most of the decisions management must make day to day are short-term ones, variable (direct) costing in which only the variable costs are allocated to the product should provide the most useful data. Be aware, however, that some of the decisions made on the basis of only the variable cost data are incorrect *in the long run* because they do not consider costs relating to long-term cause-and-effect relationships. For example, a firm may correctly decide to accept an order for goods at a price in excess of the variable cost but less than the total cost of producing them if it has excess capacity—a short-term decision. However, if that is the maximum price at which the product can be sold, no firm would construct a new plant to produce it—a long-term decision.

Variable-Costing Procedures

A variable- (direct-) costing system can operate within either a job-order or process-costing format; it can also use either historical (that is, actual) costs or standard costs. The only difference between this system and the absorption-costing system described in Chapters 4–13 is in the treatment of manufacturing-overhead costs. With variable costing, those costs are divided into variable and fixed elements. The variable portion of overhead, plus direct materials costs and direct labor costs, is accumulated and allocated to the units of product as they are produced. Fixed overhead costs relating to the period of time covered by the financial reports are allowed to flow into the income statement as part of the expenses of the reporting period.

Because the same cost-accumulation devices (job-order cost sheets or cost-of-production reports) are used for both variable costing and absorption costing, we shall, in this section, emphasize primarily the ways in which the unit cost of a finished product under variable costing will differ from the unit cost under absorption costing. Keep in mind that unit costs, when using an actual cost system, may have been *calculated* from costs accumulated in either job-order cost sheets or cost-of-production reports. If a standard cost system is used, the unit costs will have been carefully estimated and reflected on standard cost cards. However, when using variable-costing procedures, the unit-cost data will include *only* the projected variable manufacturing costs (direct materials, direct labor, and variable manufacturing overhead).

To illustrate the difference between variable and absorption costing systems, let's assume that Ace Manufacturing Company's accounting records reveal the aggregate cost and other data shown in the top part of Figure 14-1. As you can see, variable (direct) costing requires the determination of unit costs only for variable manufacturing costs (direct materials, direct labor, and variable overhead), with those costs then being assigned to the finished units as they are produced. The costs associated with the units sold would be reflected in the income statement as cost of sales (in this case, 8,000 @ $37 = $296,000); and the costs associated with units remaining on hand (in this case, 2,000 @ $37 = $74,000) would be reflected as part of the ending inventory of finished goods. With this cost-accumulation and -allocation system, all fixed (period) manufacturing expenses incurred during the reporting period ($100,000 here) would be shown as expenses for the period.

With a variable-costing system, we generally organize the income statement to show the **contribution margin** as a separate item. This is the difference between the revenue from sales and the total variable costs (manufacturing and selling) associated with those sales. It shows the part of the sales revenue *contributed* to the coverage of fixed (period) costs and the realization of net operating income. The bottom line in the operations part of the income statement is labeled *net operating income* and reflects the part of sales revenue that ultimately is available for use in paying taxes, paying dividends, or increasing owners' equity. Exhibit 14-1 uses the data in Figure 14-1, plus some additional assumptions, to illustrate an income statement showing a contribution margin. The sales price is assumed to be $60 per unit. Operating expenses are assumed to be $50,000, made up of $30,000 of fixed costs and $20,000 ($2.50 per unit sold) of variable costs.

Ace Manufacturing Company

Assumed Data

Fixed manufacturing overhead	$100,000
Variable manufacturing overhead	$ 20,000
Direct materials costs	$200,000
Direct labor costs	$150,000
Beginning inventory	0
Units produced	10,000
Units sold	8,000

Costs Assigned to Each Unit of Finished Goods

Variable Costing:

Variable manufacturing overhead ($20,000/10,000)	$ 2.00
Direct materials ($200,000/10,000)	20.00
Direct labor ($150,000/10,000)	15.00
Total variable manufacturing cost per unit	$37.00

Absorption Costing:

Variable cost per unit	$37
Fixed overhead per unit $100,000/10,000	10
Total cost	$47

FIGURE 14–1 Manufacturing Cost per Unit: Variable Costing Versus Absorption Costing

Had we been using absorption costing, our unit cost would have been $47 rather than the $37 shown for direct costing. Also, under absorption costing, the income statement would have been presented in the conventional format, seen earlier in the text, in which variable and fixed manufacturing costs associated with the units sold are combined to arrive at an amount for cost of sales, and all selling and administrative costs (variable and fixed) are subtracted from gross margin to arrive at net income from operations.

Detailed income statement formats for absorption costing and variable costing using the Ace Manufacturing Company data, assuming no beginning or ending work-in-process inventory and no beginning finished-goods inventory, are presented in Exhibit 14–2. Note that total costs on the absorption-costing statement in the exhibit are separated into fixed and variable components. This arrangement facilitates comparison with the variable-costing income statement format.

Although the schedule approach to calculating cost of sales is familiar, we will use the more efficient direct calculation (Units sold × Cost per unit) in most of our illustrations in this chapter.

EXHIBIT 14–1 ▬▬▬▬▬▬▬▬▬▬▬▬▬▬▬▬▬▬▬▬▬▬

Ace Manufacturing Company

Variable-Costing Income Statement

Sales (8,000 @ $60)	$480,000
Variable costs	
Manufacturing (8,000 @ $37)	296,000*
Selling and administrative (8,000 @ $2.50)	20,000
Total variable costs	$316,000
Contribution margin	$164,000
Fixed costs	
Manufacturing overhead	100,000
Selling and administrative	30,000
Total fixed costs	$130,000
Net operating income	$ 34,000

*Alternatively, variable manufacturing costs could be calculated from the following schedule:

Beginning inventory	0
Current variable manufacturing costs	$370,000
Less ending inventory (2,000 units @ $37)	(74,000)
Variable manufacturing cost of sales	$296,000

Variable Costing and Net Operating Income

Because absorption costing always allocates fixed manufacturing overhead to the units produced, net operating income will be different for the two systems anytime the inventory level changes. That portion of fixed manufacturing overhead that has been assigned to units in ending inventory will be deferred with absorption costing, while fixed manufacturing overhead is entirely expensed during the period for which it is incurred in a variable-costing system.

To help you understand the difference in net operating income, we now present three income statements for Ace Manufacturing Company, prepared from the cost data in Figure 14–1, using both absorption and variable costing. We assume the same level of production (10,000 units) but shall use three alternate assumptions regarding units sold. First we assume that the number of units sold is the same as the number produced. Then we assume that Ace sells fewer units than it produces. Finally, we assume that Ace sells more units than it produces. In each case, we assume that work-in-process inventory remains constant.

While the data are organized differently, total variable costs are the same on both types of statements. Differences result solely from the treatment of fixed costs.

EXHIBIT 14–2
Detailed Income Statement Formats

Ace Manufacturing Company
(Data in thousands of dollars)

Absorption Costing			Variable Costing		
Sales		$480	Sales		$480
Cost of sales			Variable Costs		
Beginning finished-goods inventory	0		Variable cost of sales:		
Cost of goods manufactured:			Beginning (variable) finished-goods inventory	0	
Beginning work-in-process inventory	(0)		Variable cost of goods manufactured		
Current manufacturing costs			Beginning (variable) work-in-process inventory	(0)	
Variable			Current (variable) manufacturing costs		
Direct materials ($200)			Direct materials ($200)		
Direct labor (150)			Direct labor (150)		
Variable overhead (20)	(370)		Variable overhead (20)	($370)	
Fixed manufacturing overhead	(100)		Beginning work-in-process + current manufacturing	($370)	
Beginning work-in-process + current manufacturing	($470)		Ending (variable) work-in-process inventory	0	
Ending work-in-process inventory	0		Variable cost of goods manufactured	($370)	
Cost of goods manufactured	(470)		Beginning finished goods + variable cost of goods manufactured	(370)	
Beginning finished-goods + cost of goods manufactured	(470)		Ending (variable) fin-ished-goods inventory	74	
Ending finished-goods inventory	94		Total variable cost of sales	($296)	
Total cost of sales		(376)	Selling and administra-tive costs	(20)	
Gross margin		$104	Total variable costs		(316)
			Contribution margin		$164
Selling and administrative costs:			Fixed costs		
Variable	($ 20)		Manufacturing overhead	($100)	
Fixed	(30)		Selling and administrative	(30)	
Total selling and administrative		(50)	Total fixed costs		(130)
Net income from operations		$ 54	Net income from operations		$ 34

EXHIBIT 14–3

Ace Manufacturing Company

Income Statement

For Current Reporting Period *(units sold = units produced)*

	Variable Costing		Absorption Costing	
Sales (10,000 units @ $60)		$600,000		$600,000
Variable costs				
Manufacturing costs (10,000 units @ $37)	$370,000			
Operating costs (10,000 units @ $2.50)	25,000	395,000		
Contribution margin		$205,000		
Cost of sales (10,000 units @ $47)				470,000
Gross margin				$130,000
Manufacturing overhead (fixed)	$100,000			
Operating costs (fixed)	30,000	130,000		
Operating costs (variable)			$25,000	
Operating costs (fixed)			30,000	55,000
Net operating income		$ 75,000		$ 75,000

When Sales Equals Production

So far, we have assumed that 10,000 units were produced and 8,000 units sold. To demonstrate how variable costing affects net operating income, we shall now assume that all 10,000 units produced were sold, meaning all variable costs will be based on 10,000 units. For example, the variable operating expenses will amount to 10,000 units × $2.50 per unit = $25,000, rather than the $20,000 shown in Exhibit 14–1. Comparative income statements will now be as shown in Exhibit 14–3. Observe that net operating income is the same regardless of whether variable- or absorption-costing procedures are used.

When Sales Is Less Than Production

To illustrate the effect on net operating income when production exceeds sales, Exhibit 14–4 assumes that 10,000 units are produced but only 8,000 units are sold. Observe that net operating income is $20,000 more with absorption costing than with variable costing. This difference can be explained by the difference in the amount of fixed manufacturing-overhead costs that are matched against sales. Variable costing shows total fixed manufacturing overhead of $100,000 on the income statement for the period. On the other hand, absorption costing includes only $80,000 of fixed overhead (8,000 units at $10 per unit). Here is another way of explaining that difference: since the

EXHIBIT 14–4

Ace Manufacturing Company

Income Statement

For Current Reporting Period *(units sold = units produced)*

	Variable Costing		Absorption Costing	
Sales (8,000 units @ $60)		$480,000		$480,000
Variable costs				
Manufacturing costs (8,000 units @ $37)	$296,000			
Operating costs (8,000 units @ $2.50)	20,000	316,000		
Contribution margin		$164,000		
Cost of sales (8,000 units @ $47)				376,000
Gross margin				$104,000
Manufacturing overhead (fixed)	$100,000			
Operating costs (fixed)	30,000	130,000		
Operating costs (variable)			$20,000	
Operating costs (fixed)			30,000	50,000
Net operating income (before income taxes)		$ 34,000		$ 54,000

2,000 units added to inventory are valued at $10 more per unit with absorption costing than with variable costing, absorption costing shows 2,000 units × $10/unit = $20,000 more costs allocated to inventory and a compensating $20,000 smaller amount as cost of sales matched against revenues for the reporting period. Thus, net operating income is $20,000 more with absorption costing.

When Sales Exceeds Production

To illustrate the effect that sales in excess of production would have on net operating income, we shall now assume that Ace had 5,000 units of inventory at the beginning of the period, valued at $37 per unit under variable costing and $47 per unit under absorption costing, and that 12,000 units were sold and 10,000 units produced during the period. The resultant comparative income statements for Ace Manufacturing Company are shown in Exhibit 14–5. Here again, the $20,000 difference between the two net operating incomes can be explained by the difference in the amount of fixed manufacturing overhead matched against sales. Variable costing shows total fixed manufacturing expense of $100,000 for the period. Absorption costing includes a total of 12,000 units × $10 per unit = $120,000 of fixed manufacturing expenses as

EXHIBIT 14–5

Ace Manufacturing Company

Income Statement

For Current Reporting Period *(units sold > units produced)*

	Variable Costing		Absorption Costing	
Sales (12,000 units @ $60)		$720,000		$720,000
Variable costs				
Manufacturing costs (12,000 units @ $37)	$444,000			
Operating costs (12,000 units @ $2.50)	30,000	474,000		
Contribution margin		$246,000		
Cost of sales (12,000 @ $47)				564,000
Gross margin				$156,000
Manufacturing overhead (fixed)	$100,000			
Operating costs (fixed)	30,000	130,000		
Operating costs (variable) @ $2.50			$30,000	
Operating costs (fixed)			30,000	60,000
Net operating income		$116,000		$ 96,000

part of cost of sales. The difference between net operating income with absorption costing and with variable costing also can be explained as the difference between fixed costs in beginning inventory and fixed costs in ending inventory when following absorption-costing procedures. In this example, these amounts are:

Fixed manufacturing costs in beginning inventory (ending inventory of previous period) (5,000 units × $10)	$50,000
Fixed manufacturing costs in ending inventory (3,000 units × $10)*	30,000
Decrease in fixed manufacturing costs in inventory during the period	$20,000

*$100,000 total fixed manufacturing costs
   10,000 units produced

Since the fixed manufacturing costs included in inventory *decreased* by $20,000 during the period (entirely due to the inventory decrease of 2,000 units), absorption-costing net operating income will be $20,000 less than variable-costing net operating income. This is true because absorption costing allocates all production costs between ending inventory and cost of sales. Therefore, if the ending inventory part of those costs has decreased by $20,000 during the period, cost of sales must be $20,000 larger. This can be illustrated as follows:

Absorption-Costing Detail Calculations

Beginning finished-goods inventory (production costs from previous period)		
Variable costs (5,000 units @ $37)	$185,000	
Fixed costs (5,000 units @ $10)	50,000	$235,000
Current production		
Variable costs (10,000 units @ $37)	$370,000	
Fixed costs (10,000 units @ $10)	100,000	470,000
Total available (to be separated into cost of sales and ending inventory)		$705,000
Ending finished-goods inventory		
Variable costs (3,000 units @ $37)	$111,000	
Fixed costs (3,000 units @ $10)	30,000	141,000
Cost of sales		
Variable costs (12,000 units @ $37)	$444,000	
Fixed costs (12,000 units @ $10)	120,000	$564,000

It is clear that whereas fixed costs of $100,000 were incurred during the period, $120,000 were charged to cost of sales. This $20,000 increase was "shifted" from fixed costs in inventory, which decreased by an identical $20,000 (from $50,000 in beginning inventory to $30,000 in ending inventory).

Note that variable costs are irrelevant in explaining the difference between net operating income under absorption costing versus direct costing. Even though they are shown in different parts of the income statement, total variable costs are identical for both systems.

In the special case where fixed cost per unit does not change from one period to the next (as assumed in this example), the difference between variable- and absorption-costing net operating income can be explained as the change in units of finished-goods inventory (5,000 beginning inventory + 10,000 units produced − 12,000 units sold = ending inventory of 3,000 units, a decrease of 2,000 units during the period) times the $10 fixed manufacturing cost per unit: $2,000 \times \$10 = \$20,000$ higher income with variable costing.

Our illustration assumed that work-in-process inventory remained constant. Changes in the volume of work-in-process would affect net operating income in the same ways as do changes in the number of finished units in inventory. That is, if work-in-process inventory *increased* during the period and other items remained the same, absorption-costing net income would be higher than variable-costing net income, by the increased amount of fixed manufacturing costs in the work-in-process inventory. If work-in-process inventory *decreased* during the period, absorption-costing net income would be less than variable-costing net income.

Contribution-Margin Approach to Operating Decisions

Given that *contribution margin* is the difference between the revenue from sales and the total variable costs associated with those sales, the contribution margin per unit then equals the difference between the sales price per unit and the total variable cost per unit. We also refer to the sales revenue from one additional unit or a specifically identifiable group of units as the **incremental revenue (marginal revenue)** attributed to the unit or group of units. We use the term **incremental manufacturing cost (marginal manufacturing cost)** to describe the additional cost required to produce the extra unit or group of units. The difference between marginal revenue and marginal manufacturing cost, reduced by the variable operating costs to sell the unit or group of units, is the **incremental contribution margin (marginal contribution margin)** for the unit or group of units.

We have already observed that the short-term cause-and-effect (effort and achievement) relationships, in general, can best be measured by matching variable costs against sales revenues to arrive at the contribution margin. Assuming fixed costs do not change, short-term operating decisions can best be made by basing them on the marginal relationships between variable costs incurred and the revenues produced by those costs. In effect, the variable costs are the *relevant costs* to be considered in such decisions. Relevant costs, then, are those costs that would be changed in the short run as a result of a management decision.

The contribution margin, representing the difference between sales revenues and variable costs, reflects the amount that sales revenues are "contributing" toward the coverage of fixed costs and net income. The graph in Figure 14–2, based on the cost data for Ace Manufacturing Company, should help you see how that occurs.

Line *A* in the graph represents aggregate variable costs at various levels of sales, amounting to $39.50 per unit ($37.00 manufacturing cost plus $2.50 operating costs). Line *B* shows aggregate total costs at various levels of sales and is equal to aggregate variable costs at each level plus fixed costs ($100,000 manufacturing cost plus $30,000 operating costs). Line *C* shows the aggregate sales revenues at various levels of sales (units sold multiplied by the $60 sales price per unit). The area between the sales line (*C*) and the total-variable-costs line (*A*) is the amount contributed first toward covering fixed costs (Area 1) and ultimately toward net income (Area 2) at various possible levels of sales. Remember, each point on the variable-costs line (*A*) equals the variable cost per unit multiplied by the number of units shown immediately below it on the sales line. Observe that total fixed cost remains the same ($130,000) regardless of the level of production achieved. This is ex-

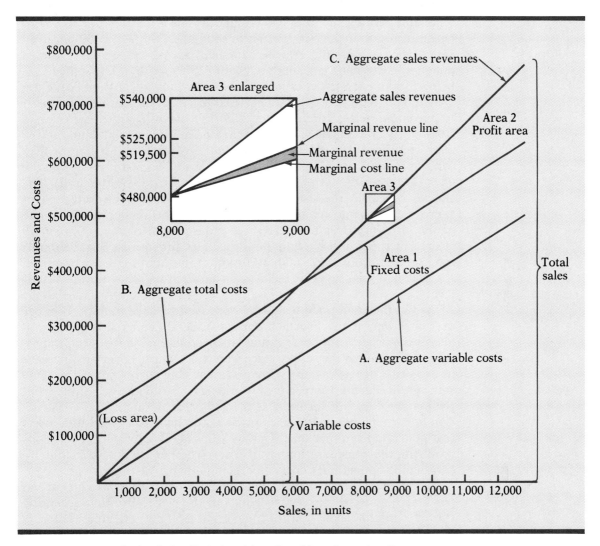

FIGURE 14–2 Cost–Sales Relationships, Ace Manufacturing Company

pected to be true as long as the firm operates within the limits of its present capacity to produce. Therefore, it follows that in any situation where a firm has **excess** (unused) **capacity**, it can improve its profitability by accepting a sales order at a price that is in excess of the variable cost per unit to produce and sell it ($39.50 per unit in our illustration), provided that regular sales are not affected.

To illustrate, let's assume that Ace Manufacturing Company, whose cost data are graphed in Figure 14–2, has the capacity to produce 12,000 units and is currently selling and producing only 8,000 units per reporting period. The data show that variable costs amount to $39.50 per unit and that the firm normally sells these units for $60 per unit. Fixed costs are assumed to be $130,000 per period. Suppose that a potential customer from another locality offers to buy 1,000 units of the firm's product at $45 per unit. If we consider only absorption-cost data, we will conclude that, since the offered price is less than the total cost to make and deliver the product ($55.75 if Ace allocates fixed costs to 8,000 units and $53.94 if Ace allocates fixed costs to 9,000 units), the offer would be rejected. However, variable-cost data show that the firm can improve its net income from operations by $5,500 if it accepts the offer (1,000 units × the contribution margin of $5.50 per unit). The effect of accepting the order appears in Figure 14–2 as the dotted extension of the sales line at a price of $45 per unit. The net operating income of the firm improves by $5,500 (see enlargement of Area 3), demonstrated in the graph by extending the sales line out to the 9,000-unit level of operations ($525,000) and ploting the marginal-cost line from the $480,000 sales level for 8,000 units out to $519,500 at the 9,000-unit level.

The net income of Ace would be improved by accepting the $45 per unit offer *only* if the firm has unused (excess) capacity. It would not accept the order if it had to expand its production facilities to produce those units, unless the selling price were sufficient to cover any increase in fixed cost as well as any increase in variable costs and still provide some profit. Furthermore, a firm would never build a new plant to meet the market demands for units at the $45 price. To justify the construction of the new plant, the sales price would have to exceed total costs (variable and fixed) per unit. These actions involve long-term decisions requiring the consideration of all costs, whether fixed or variable, including the opportunity cost of foregoing other investments.

Management, in considering the opportunity to sell its product at $45 per unit, also would be concerned about the possibility that accepting this offer might "spoil" part of the normal ($60 per unit) market for its goods. That could occur if regular customers became aware of the special sales price granted to the new customer and demanded the same. Before accepting the offer, the company also should determine whether it might be violating discriminatory-pricing laws.

Other Uses of Variable-Costing Data

We have just explained how contribution-margin data can be used in responding to a customer's offer to purchase units of product at a price below average total cost. In the chapters that follow, we shall explain how contribution-margin and other cost/volume data are used in making various short-term operating decisions. Here we consider three other operating decisions relating to actions that might be taken to increase income by increasing the volume of sales. More specifically, we look at the ways contribution-margin data can help make decisions regarding the income potential of:

- expanding a firm's sales efforts into a new market
- engaging in special promotional activities
- initiating a new product line.

Evaluating the Income Potential of a New Market

Net income often can be increased by expanding a company's sales efforts into new markets. A company considering such action should first evaluate the sales potential of the new market through a market survey directed toward estimating the number of units that could be sold at various possible prices.

Once the market potential has been determined, the company should estimate the pertinent costs per unit to produce and deliver the product, after first determining whether the additional units can be produced with existing facilities. If the firm has unused capacity, the *relevant cost* to be considered for producing the units expected to be sold in the new market will equal the total variable cost per unit multiplied by the number of units expected to be sold. The cost of selling and delivering the goods in the new market must be included as part of the projected total costs. When additional period or fixed costs have to be incurred to enter the new market, the firm should first match the anticipated sales revenue against the anticipated total variable costs *plus* any **traceable fixed costs**.

To illustrate how the income potential of a new market can be evaluated, let's assume a firm has unused capacity capable of producing 30,000 more units than at present, and that its variable manufacturing costs amount to $5.00 per unit. A market survey shows the potential of marketing 20,000 units of product per year in the new market if they can be sold at $9.00 per unit. The selling and delivery costs are expected to be $1.50 per unit plus the $25,000 annual salary of the new company representative responsible for coordinating sales activities in the new market. The following analysis shows that the company can expect to increase its net operating income by $25,000 if it enters the new market:

Sales (20,000 units @ $9.00)	$ 180,000
Relevant cost to manufacture 20,000 units @ $5.00	(100,000)
Relevant operating costs (20,000 units @ $1.50)	(30,000)
Company representative's salary	(25,000)
Increase to net operating income	$ 25,000

Evaluating the Income Potential of Special Promotional Activities

Sales volume also can be increased through special promotional activities, such as the issuance of credits or coupons with products sold that are redeemable in merchandise or services. For example, the various frequent-flyer credits offered by most airlines are part of a special promotional activity that is expected to increase regular ticket sales. In evaluating the desirability of such a program, the airline first must estimate the expected increase in regular ticket sales. Next, the cost of providing the free tickets must be calculated. Since persons using the free tickets will be occupying seats that would otherwise be vacant, the cost of providing a free ticket will equal the variable cost of having the seat occupied. In the airline industry, this is typically little more than the cost or providing meals enroute. However, the airline also must estimate the loss in regular ticket sales revenue that might otherwise be generated from passengers using the free tickets, sometimes referred to as a "second-degree" effect. In summary, the plan involves (1) estimating the increased regular ticket sales that will be realized from the special promotional activity; (2) considering only the variable cost of providing the free tickets as a direct cost of providing those tickets (assuming excess capacity); and (3) considering the extent to which the regular ticket sales market might be spoiled (that is, reduced) by providing the free tickets.

Evaluating the Income Potential of a New Product

Sometimes a firm can increase its net income by adding a new product to its sales line, generally a product the firm believes it will have a competitive advantage in producing and marketing. That competitive advantage can come from common know-how associated with the production of current products and the new product or the capability of using idle machine time on presently existing equipment. Dependence on the latter—the availability of excess capacity—would enable the firm to use the marginal cost of producing the new product as the relevant cost in evaluating the probable net operating income potential of the new product.

To illustrate, let's assume that a refrigerator manufacturer is considering expanding into the manufacture of kitchen stoves. A market survey shows that the firm could sell 5,000 stoves a year at $600 each. Although the firm has enough excess capacity in its metal stamping, welding, and finishing departments to absorb that type of work on the stove parts, special equipment costing $100,000 and having a 10-year life with no salvage value will have to be acquired to produce parts that are unique to stoves, such as burners. Metal stamping dies costing $30,000 and expected to have a 2-year life with no salvage value will have to be acquired in order for the metal stamping presses to produce parts for the stoves. The new equipment can be installed within the currently available floor space. The variable manufacturing cost of producing a stove amounts to $350.00. Variable operating (selling and general and administrative) expenses are expected to amount to $50 per stove. This firm then can project a $975,000-per-year increase in net income by entering the kitchen stove market, calculated as follows:

Projected sales of stoves (5,000 @ $600)	$3,000,000
Variable manufacturing costs (5,000 @ $350)	($1,750,000)
Variable operating costs (5,000 @ $50)	(250,000)
Other costs relating to stove production	
Depreciation of new equipment ($100,000 ÷ 10)	(10,000)
Depreciation of new dies ($30,000 ÷ 2)	(15,000)
Total marginal costs	($2,025,000)
Projected product margin per year	$ 975,000

Variable-Costing Data and the Financial Statements

Even though variable-costing data may be extremely useful in making short-term operating decisions, a firm using such a system must still provide unit-cost data on an absorption-costing basis for purposes of external financial reporting. One way of meeting this requirement is to maintain parallel systems, with the absorption-costing data being used in assigning values to inventory and cost of sales in the published financial statements. However, such an arrangement involves much duplication of effort and excessive clerical and computer costs. Therefore, if a firm uses a variable-costing system, it should consider converting inventory and cost-of-sales data based on variable costing to an absorption-costing basis at the end of each reporting period. In developing the necessary conversion procedures, we must recognize that the primary objective in the conversion process is to arrive at generally accepted bases for valuing inventory and cost of sales for external financial statements. Pricing and other operating decisions already will have been made on the basis of data provided by the variable-costing system.

Recall that in absorption costing we allocate underapplied or over-applied overhead and variances to inventories and cost of sales on the basis of the relationships of the cost elements included in each of those accounts to the totals included in all of them. We can use the same procedures to allocate fixed manufacturing-overhead cost to work in process, finished goods, and cost of sales when using a variable-costing system. In doing so, we must first decide which element or elements of direct cost should be used as the basis for allocation. We could, for example, conclude that the best cause-and-effect basis for allocating fixed manufacturing-overhead costs would be the amount of combined direct labor and variable overhead costs included in each of the inventories and cost of sales. Two other possibilities would be to allocate fixed overhead to inventory and cost-of-sales accounts on the basis of materials or direct labor dollars included in each of those items. The apparent cause-and-effect relationships existing between the various fixed overhead costs and the various variable manufacturing costs should be determined before deciding on the activity base (or bases) to be used in making the fixed overhead cost allocations.

Once the appropriate "activity" base has been chosen, the allocation can be made in exactly the same manner as was illustrated earlier for underapplied or overapplied overhead and standard cost variances. Also, just as with those allocation entries, the inventory parts of this entry should be *reversed* after the financial statements have been prepared, to allow inventories to be valued at the variable cost per unit required by the variable-costing system as operations continue into the next period.

For example, if fixed manufacturing overhead is to be allocated on the basis of direct labor dollars, the total direct labor dollars in work in process, finished goods, and cost of sales would be used to make the allocation. Assuming total fixed manufacturing costs of $100,000 and direct labor dollars of $50,000, $75,000, and $150,000 in work in process, finished goods, and cost of sales, respectively, the allocation would be accomplished as follows:

	Direct Labor	Allocated Fixed Overhead
Work-in-process inventory	$ 50,000	50/275 × $100,000 = $ 18,182
Finished-goods inventory	75,000	75/275 × $100,000 = 27,273
Cost of sales	150,000	150/275 × $100,000 = 54,545
	$275,000	$100,000

The following journal entry would be used to record this allocation:

Work-in-process inventory	18,182	
Finished-goods inventory	27,273	
Cost of sales	54,545	
Fixed manufacturing overhead		100,000

The required reversing entry, recorded after the financial statements have been prepared, would be as follows:

Fixed manufacturing overhead	45,455	
Work-in-process inventory		18,182
Finished-goods inventory		27,273

This reversing entry will return the inventory accounts to a variable-cost basis for the next period. The allocation to cost of sales is not reversed because cost of sales will be closed to retained earnings at the end of the period along with all other nominal accounts and will begin the next period with a zero balance. The fixed manufacturing overhead balance ($45,455) would then be closed to income summary to keep the internal accounting system operating on a variable costing basis. Another alternative is to use a worksheet rather than formal journal entries to convert the direct costing data to absorption costing.

SUMMARY

In this chapter, we explained how manufacturing costs should be allocated when following variable-costing procedures. First, we recognized some of the problems associated with the accumulation and allocation of fixed manufacturing costs required by an absorption-costing system when those allocations are evaluated against observed cause-and-effect relationships. Then we explained what should be done in allocating manufacturing costs to inventories and income statement accounts when following variable-costing procedures.

We examined the effects of variable-costing procedures on net operating income when compared with the net operating income produced by absorption costing. We also illustrated the differences between the format used for a variable-costing-oriented income statement and that used for an income statement prepared from absorption-costing data. Variable-costing statements emphasize the contribution margin, defined as the difference between the sales revenue and the variable costs required to produce and sell goods. We demonstrated the calculations required to reconcile net operating incomes derived from using the two systems.

Next, we examined the contribution-margin approach to managerial decisions and illustrated how variable costs and contribution-margin data can help managers make decisions relating to the acceptance of a special order for goods, entrance into new markets, production of new products, and engagement in special promotional activities.

Finally, we explained the procedures to follow in converting variable-costing data to an approximate absorption-costing basis, to facilitate the preparation of external financial statements, in accordance with generally accepted accounting practices.

GLOSSARY OF TERMS INTRODUCED IN THIS CHAPTER

contribution margin   An amount equal to the difference between sales revenue and variable costs.

direct costing   See *variable costing*.

excess capacity   A situation in which a firm has the capability of producing more goods than are currently being produced without expanding its manufacturing facilities.

incremental contribution margin   The additional contribution margin resulting from the sale of one additional unit or group of units; also called *marginal contribution margin.*

incremental manufacturing cost   The additional manufacturing cost required to produce one additional unit or group of units; also called *marginal manufacturing cost.*

incremental revenue   The additional revenue resulting from the sale of one additional unit or group of units; also called *marginal revenue.*

long-term decisions   Decisions relating to operations extending over a number of fiscal periods (beyond one year) and generally involving judgments about the acquisition of long-term assets and the amount of production capacity to be provided.

marginal contribution margin   See *incremental contribution margin.*

marginal manufacturing cost   See *incremental manufacturing cost.*

marginal revenue   See *incremental revenue.*

short-term operating decisions   Day-to-day operating decisions requiring no additional investment in long-term operating assets (operating decisions made within the constraint of the present investment base of the firm).

traceable fixed costs   Fixed costs that can be directly associated with a specific segment of a business's operations.

variable costing   A system for accumulating and allocating manufacturing costs that allocates only variable manufacturing costs to the units produced. All fixed manufacturing costs are allocated to the periods in which the costs were incurred. Also called *direct costing.*

QUESTIONS FOR CLASS DISCUSSION

14—1   What is the logic supporting the use of variable-costing procedures?

14—2   What arguments may be advanced for the use of absorption-costing procedures?

14—3   What is the primary difference between variable costing and absorption costing? Do both meet the requirements of generally accepted accounting practices? Explain.

14—4   How are cause-and-effect relationships used to support variable-costing procedures? How are they used to support absorption-costing procedures? Explain.

14—5 Will net operating income be the same with variable costing as with absorption costing? Explain.

14—6 What is the difference between an income statement prepared from variable-costing data and one prepared from absorption-costing data?

14—7 Assuming that a firm has excess capacity, can it profitably accept a customer's offer to buy the firm's product for less than the total cost to produce it? Explain.

14—8 What is meant by *contribution margin*? How is it calculated?

14—9 What is the relationship between sales price per unit, variable costs per unit, and contribution margin per unit?

14—10 What is the relationship between *contribution margin* and *marginal revenue*? Explain.

14—11 What procedures should the management of a firm follow in making a decision regarding expansion into a new market? Explain.

14—12 How should the probable profitability of engaging in special promotional activities be evaluated? Explain.

14—13 Why and under what conditions might a firm consider the manufacture of new products? How should their probable profitability be evaluated?

14—14 Does a firm using variable-costing also have to maintain an absorption-costing system to satisfy the accounting requirements for external financial reporting? Explain.

EXERCISES

14—15 **Variable Costing and Absorption Costing** The following information is available for Cone Corporation's new product line:

Selling price per unit	$30
Variable manufacturing costs per unit of production	$16
Total annual fixed manufacturing costs	$50,000
Variable selling and administrative costs	$60,000
Total annual fixed selling and administrative expenses	$30,000

There was no inventory at the beginning of the year. During the year, 12,500 units were produced and 10,000 units sold.

REQUIRED:

1. What value would be assigned to ending inventory if Cone uses variable (direct) costing?
2. What value would be assigned to ending inventory using absorption costing?
3. What amount of variable costs would be included in expenses for the year with absorption costing? with variable costing?

4. What amount of fixed costs would be included in expenses for the year with absorption costing? with variable costing?
5. Prepare statements showing the determination of operating income with absorption costing and with variable costing.

14–16   Inventory Valuation with Absorption Costing and with Variable Costing During January, Hall, Inc., produced 10,000 units of product A, with costs as follows:

Direct materials	$ 80,000
Direct labor	44,000
Variable manufacturing overhead	26,000
Fixed manufacturing overhead	20,000
	$170,000

REQUIRED:

1. Determine the cost per unit to be assigned to product A inventory on January 31 using variable costing.
2. What cost per unit would be assigned to product A inventory using absorption costing?

14–17   Inventory Valuation and Operating Income Realized with Absorption Costing and with Variable Costing Information from Cline Company's records for the year ended December 31, 19X1, is as follows:

Net sales	$2,800,000
Cost of goods manufactured:	
Variable	$1,260,000
Fixed	$630,000
Selling and administrative expenses:	
Variable	$196,000
Fixed	$280,000
Units manufactured	140,000
Units sold	120,000
Finished-goods inventory, January 1, 19X1	0

There was no work-in-process inventory at the beginning or end of 19X1.

REQUIRED:

1. What value would be assigned to end-of-year finished-goods inventory with variable costing? with absorption costing?
2. What amount would be shown as operating income with variable costing? with absorption costing?

14–18   **Multiple Choice—Variable (Direct) Costing** Select the *best* answer for each
AICPA Adapted   of the following items.

1. The basic assumption made in a direct-costing system with respect to fixed costs is that fixed costs are

    a. a sunk cost.
    b. a product cost.
    c. a fixed amount per unit.
    d. a period cost.
2. Net income reported under absorption costing will exceed net income reported under direct costing for a given period if
    a. production equals sales for that period.
    b. production exceeds sales for that period.
    c. sales exceed production for that period.
    d. the variable overhead exceeds the fixed overhead.
3. When using a direct-costing system, the contribution margin discloses the excess of
    a. revenues over fixed costs.
    b. projected revenues over the breakeven point.
    c. revenues over variable costs.
    d. variable costs over fixed costs.
4. Net earnings determined using full absorption costing can be reconciled to net earnings determined using direct costing by computing the difference between
    a. inventoried fixed costs in the beginning and ending inventories.
    b. inventoried discretionary costs in the beginning and ending inventories.
    c. gross margin (absorption-costing method) and contribution margin (direct-costing method).
    d. sales as recorded under the direct-costing method and sales as recorded under the absorption-costing method.
5. The absorption-costing method includes in inventory

	Fixed Factory Overhead	Variable Factory Overhead
a.	no	no
b	no	yes
c	yes	yes
d	yes	no

6. In an income statement prepared as an internal report using the direct (variable) costing-method, fixed selling and administrative expenses would
    a. not be used.
    b. be used in the computation of the contribution margin.
    c. be used in the computation of operating income but not in the computation of the contribution margin.
    d. be treated the same as variable selling and administrative expenses.
7. What will be the difference in net earnings computed using direct costing as opposed to absorption costing if the ending inventory increases with respect to the beginning inventory in terms of units?
    a. There will be *no* difference in net earnings.
    b. Net earnings computed using direct costing will be higher.
    c. The difference in net earnings *cannot* be determined from the information given.

    d. Net earnings computed using direct costing will be lower.

8. Fleet, Inc., manufactured 700 units of product A, a new product, in 19X5. Product A's variable and fixed manufacturing costs per unit were $6.00 and $2.00, respectively. The inventory of product A on December 31, 19X5, consisted of 100 units. There was *no* inventory of product A on January 1, 19X5. What would be the change in the dollar amount of inventory on December 31, 19X5, if the direct-costing method was used instead of the absorption-costing method?

    a. $800 decrease
    b. $200 decrease
    c. $0
    d. $200 increase

14–19 **Operating Income and Inventory Valuation** Haller Company began its operations on January 1, 19X2, and produces a single product that sells for $16 per unit. Gordon uses an actual (historical) cost system. In 19X2, 100,000 units were produced and 80,000 units were sold. There was no work-in-process inventory at December 31, 19X2.

Manufacturing costs and selling and administrative expenses for 19X2 were as follows:

	Fixed Costs	**Variable Costs**
Raw materials	—	$4.00 per unit produced
Direct labor	—	$2.50 per unit produced
Factory overhead	$240,000	$1.50 per unit produced
Selling and administrative	$140,000	$2.00 per unit sold

REQUIRED:

1. Determine Haller's operating income with use of (a) variable costing and (b) absorption costing.
2. Determine the value to be assigned to Haller's December 31 finished-goods inventory using (a) variable costing and (b) absorption costing.
3. Reconcile the difference between the amounts calculated in (a) above and (b) above.

14–20 **Net Operating Income with Beginning-of-Period Inventory Balances** Selected information concerning the operations of Cable Company for the year ended December 31, 19X1, is as follows:

Units produced	10,000
Units sold	9,000
Direct materials used	$80,000
Direct labor	$40,000
Fixed factory overhead	$50,000
Variable factory overhead	$24,000
Fixed selling and administrative expenses	$60,000
Variable selling and administrative expenses	$9,000

(Continues)

Finished-goods inventory, January 1, 19X1	500 units
Variable costing	$14.00 per unit
Absorption costing	$18.00 per unit
Selling price	$30.00 per unit

There were no work-in-process inventories at the beginning and end of 19X1. Cable uses the FIFO cost flow assumption.

REQUIRED:

1. Determine the value to be assigned to December 31, 19X1, finished-goods inventory using (a) variable costing and (b) absorption costing.
2. Determine the amount to be reported as operating income using (a) variable costing and (b) absorption costing.
3. Reconcile the difference in operating income using the two costing systems.

14–21 **Relevant Costs in a Sales Decision** Sliding Company has normal revenue, cost, and volume relationships, as follows:

Annual sales, 100,000 units at $4.00 per unit
Annual fixed costs, $150,000
Variable costs per unit of sales, $2.00
Average fixed cost per unit at 100,000-unit planned production level, $1.50
Annual production capacity, 140,000 units

The company received an offer from a Greek firm to purchase 20,000 units annually at a price of $2.50 per unit. All freight charges are to be paid by the Greek firm. The sale to the Greek firm has no impact on Sliding Company's regular market, and the sale is not illegal.

REQUIRED:

1. Should Sliding accept the offer of the Greek firm?
2. Prepare a report supporting your answer to requirement 1.

14–22 **Evaluation of Income Potential of a New Product** Venture Company, a manufacturer of bicycles, has excess plant capacity and is considering the possibility of also manufacturing mopeds. Management has investigated the market for this product and has developed the following data to be used in deciding whether to enter the moped market:

Projected sales of mopeds (6,000 @ $250)	$1,500,000
Variable costs of making and selling mopeds (6,000 @ $150)	900,000
Other costs relating to mopeds: Depreciation of new equipment ($1,500,000 ÷ 10 years)	150,000
Costs allocated from general overhead currently absorbed as part of bicycle manufacturing costs	600,000

REQUIRED:

1. Should Venture enter the moped market?
2. Prepare a report to management supporting your recommendation.

PROBLEMS

14–23 **Contribution Margin on Special Order** Fuller Company, which manufactures jeans, has enough idle capacity available to accept a special order for 15,000 pairs of jeans at $9 each. A predicted income statement for the year without this special order is as follows:

	Per Unit	Total
Sales	$12.50	$2,500,000
Manufacturing costs, variable	6.25	1,250,000
Manufacturing costs, fixed	1.75	350,000
Manufacturing costs, total	8.00	1,600,000
Gross profit	4.50	900,000
Selling expenses, variable	1.80	360,000
Selling expenses, fixed	1.45	290,000
Selling expenses, total	3.25	650,000
Operating income	$ 1.25	$ 250,000

REQUIRED:

1. How many pairs of jeans is Fuller currently selling?
2. What is the total average cost per pair of jeans currently being sold?
3. What would be the effect on operating income of accepting the special order?
4. Explain how such an order can be sold at less than total average cost and still increase the amount of operating income.

14–24 **Conversion of Variable- (Direct-) Costing-Based Income Statement to an**
ICMA Adapted **Absorption-Costing Basis** The vice president for sales of Huber Corporation has received its income statement for November 19X9. The statement, prepared on the direct-cost basis, follows. The firm has just adopted a direct-costing system for internal reporting purposes.

Huber Corporation

Income Statement

For the Month of November 19X9

($000 omitted)

Sales		$2,400
Less: Variable standard cost of goods sold		1,200
Manufacturing margin		$1,200
Less: Fixed manufacturing costs at budget	$600	
Fixed manufacturing cost spending variance	0	600
Gross margin		$ 600
Less: Fixed selling and administrative costs		400
Net income before taxes		$ 200

The controller attached the following notes to the statement:

(1) The unit sales price for November averaged $24.

(2) The standard unit manufacturing costs for the month were:

Variable cost	$12
Fixed cost	4
Total cost	$16

(3) The unit rate for fixed manufacturing costs is a predetermined rate based on a normal monthly production of 150,000 units.

(4) Production for November was 45,000 units in excess of sales.

(5) The inventory at November 30 consisted of 80,000 units.

REQUIRED:

1. The vice president for sales is not comfortable with the direct-cost basis and wonders what the net income would have been under the prior, absorption-cost basis.

   a. Present the November income statement on an absorption-cost basis.

   b. Reconcile (explain) the difference between the direct-costing and the absorption-costing net income figures.

2. Explain the features associated with direct-cost income measurement that should be attractive to the vice president for sales.

14–25

ICMA Adapted

Variable (Direct) Costing and Product-Discontinuance Decision CLK Company is a manufacturer of electrical components. The company maintains a significant inventory of a broad range of finished goods because it has built its business on prompt shipments of any stock item. Until recently, the company manufactured all items it sold. It has discontinued the manufacture of five items because the difference between the sales price per unit and the unit costs of manufacturing computed by the company's full-cost system did not provide a sufficient margin to cover shipping and selling costs. The five items are now purchased from other manufacturers at a price that enables CLK to make a very small profit after allowing for shipping and selling costs. CLK keeps these items in its product line in order to offer a complete line of electrical components.

The company president is disappointed at recent profitability performance. He had thought the switch from manufacture to purchase for the five items would improve profit performance. However, the reverse has occurred. All other factors affecting profits—sales volume, sales prices, and incurred selling and manufacturing costs—were as expected, so the profit problem can be traced to this decision. The president has asked the controller's department to reevaluate the financial effects of the decision.

The task was assigned to a recently hired assistant controller, who reviewed the data on which the decision to purchase rather than manufacture was based. Her conclusion is that the company should have continued to manufacture the items. In her opinion, the buy-versus-make decision was incorrect because full- (absorption-) cost data rather than direct- (variable-) cost data were used to make it.

REQUIRED:

1. Explain what features of direct (variable) costing, as compared to full (absorption) costing, make her conclusion possibly correct.
2. For internal measurement purposes, compare the income, return on investment, and inventory values under full (absorption) costing and direct (variable) costing for periods where:
   a. inventory quantities are rising.
   b. inventory quantities are declining.
   c. inventory quantities are stable.
3. What advantages are said to accrue to decision making if direct (variable) costing is used?

14–26 **Variable and Absorption Costing with a Volume Variance** BBG Corporation
ICMA Adapted is a manufacturer of a synthetic element. Gary Voss, president of the company, had been eager to get the operating results for the just-completed fiscal year. He was surprised when the income statement revealed that income before taxes had dropped to $885,000 from $900,000 even though sales volume had increased 100,000 kg. This drop in net income occurred even though Voss had implemented the following changes during the past 12 months to improve the profitability of the company:

(1) In response to a 10% increase in production costs, the sales price of the company's product was increased by 12%. This action was implemented on January 1, 19X2.
(2) The managements of the selling and administrative departments were given strict instructions to spend no more in fiscal 19X2 than in fiscal 19X1.

BBG's accounting department prepared and distributed to top management the following comparative income statements. The accounting staff also prepared related financial information, presented in the second schedule, to assist management in evaluating the company's performance. BBG uses the FIFO inventory method for finished goods.

BBG Corporation

Statements of Operating Income
For the Years Ended November 30, 19X1, and November 30, 19X2
($000 omitted)

	19X1	19X2
Sales revenue	$9,000	$11,200
Cost of goods sold	$7,200	$ 8,320
Manufacturing volume variance*	(600)	495
Adjusted cost of goods sold	$6,600	$8,815
Gross margin	$2,400	$ 2,385
Selling and administrative expenses	1,500	1,500
Income before taxes	$ 900	$ 885

*Recall that volume variance equals the difference between the number of units used to determine the fixed overhead cost per unit application rate and the number of units actually produced multiplied by the fixed application rate.

BBG Corporation

Selected Operating and Financial Data
For 19X1 and 19X2

	19X1	19X2
Sales price	$10/kg	$11.20/kg
Materials cost	$1.50/kg	$1.65/kg
Direct labor cost	$2.50/kg	$2.75/kg
Variable overhead cost	$1.00/kg	$1.10/kg
Fixed overhead cost	$3.00/kg	$3.30/kg
Total fixed overhead costs	$3,000,000	$3,300,000
Selling and administrative (all fixed)	$1,500,000	$1,500,000
Sales volume	900,000 kg	1,000,000 kg
Beginning inventory	300,000 kg	600,000 kg
Ending inventory	600,000 kg	450,000 kg

REQUIRED:

1. Explain to Gary Voss why BBG Corporation's net income decreased in the current fiscal year despite the sales price and sales volume increases.
2. A member of BBG's accounting department has suggested that the company adopt variable (direct) costing for internal reporting purposes.
   a. Prepare an operating income statement through income before taxes for the years ended November 30, 19X1, and November 30, 19X2, for BBG Corporation using variable (direct) costing.
   b. Present a numerical reconciliation for each year of the differences in income before taxes using absorption costing as currently employed by BBG and variable (direct) costing as proposed.
3. Identify and discuss the advantages and disadvantages of using variable (direct) costing for internal reporting purposes.

14–27 **Comparison of Variable and Absorption Costing Based Financial Statement Data** Crenshaw Company began operations on January 3, 19X3. Standard costs were established in early January assuming a normal production volume of 80,000 units. However, Crenshaw produced only 70,000 units of product and sold 50,000 units at a selling price of $180 per unit during 19X3. Variable costs totalled $3,500,000, of which 60% were manufacturing and 40% were selling. Fixed costs were projected at $6,600,000, of which 50% were manufacturing and 50% were selling. Crenshaw had no raw materials or work-in-process inventories at December 31, 19X3. Actual variable costs per unit of product and actual quantities per unit of product were equal to standard. Actual fixed costs were equal to amounts projected for them.

REQUIRED:

1. Determine the standard cost of Crenshaw's cost of goods sold for 19X3 using absorption costing.
2. Determine Crenshaw's operating income using absorption costing. Underapplied overhead is closed to cost of goods sold.

3. Determine the value assigned to the 12/31/X3 inventory using variable costing.
4. Determine Crenshaw's operating income using variable costing.
5. Reconcile the amounts calculated in requirements 2 and 4.

14–28
ICMA Adapted

Income Statements Based on Variable and Absorption Costing Data with Variable Cost Variance The S. T. Shire Company uses direct costing for internal management purposes and absorption costing for external reporting purposes. Thus, at the end of each year, financial information must be converted from direct costing to absorption costing in order to satisfy external reporting requirements.

At the end of 19X1, it was anticipated that sales would rise 20% the next year. Therefore, production was increased from 20,000 units to 24,000 units to meet this expected demand. However, economic conditions kept the sales level at 20,000 units for both years.

The following data pertain to 19X1 and 19X2:

	19X1	19X2
Selling price per unit	$30	$30
Sales (units)	20,000	20,000
Beginning inventory (units)	2,000	2,000
Production (units)	20,000	24,000
Ending inventory (units)	2,000	6,000
Unfavorable labor, materials, and variable overhead variances (total)	$5,000	$4,000

Standard variable costs per unit for 19X1 and 19X2:

Labor	$7.50
Materials	4.50
Variable overhead	3.00
	$15.00

Annual fixed costs for 19X1 and 19X2 (budgeted and actual):

Manufacturing	$ 90,000
Selling and administrative	100,000
	$190,000

The overhead rate under absorption costing is based on practical plant capacity, which is 30,000 units per year. All variances and under- or over-absorbed overhead are closed to cost of goods sold. Ignore all taxes.

REQUIRED:

1. Present the income statement for 19X2 based on direct costing.
2. Present the income statement for 19X2 based on absorption costing.

3. Explain the difference, if any, in the net income figures. Give the entry necessary to adjust the book figures to the externally presented financial statement figures, if one is necessary.

14–29 **Operating Income with Absorption and Variable Costing** Logan Company planned and actually manufactured 400,000 units of its single product in 19X5, the first year of operations. Variable manufacturing costs were $60 per unit of product. In 19X5, planned and actual fixed manufacturing costs were each $1,200,000, selling and administrative costs totaled $800,000 (30% variable), and 240,000 units of product were sold at $80 per unit.

REQUIRED:

1. Calculate Logan's operating income using absorption costing.
2. Calculate Logan's operating income using variable costing.
3. Reconcile the amounts calculated in requirements 1 and 2.

14–30 **Missing Items—Variable and Absorption Costing** Able Company uses a standard cost system that reflects the following unit cost data for Zeon, the only product it produces:

Direct materials	$ 2
Direct labor	4
Variable overhead	5
Fixed overhead	3
Total	$14

Fixed overhead is estimated at $60,000. The standard fixed overhead is based on an expected normal level of production.

During 19X1, Able produces 22,000 units. Sales amount to 21,000 units at $20 per unit. The company had 3,000 units on hand at the beginning of the year. Actual fixed overhead costs were $60,000. Actual variable costs per unit were the same as standard costs. Selling and administrative expenses are 40% variable.

The following partially completed income statements have been prepared using both variable and absorption costing:

	Absorption Costing	Variable Costing
Sales	$420,000	$420,000
Beginning inventory		
Cost of manufacturing at standard		
Ending inventory at standard		
Volume variance		XXXXX
Variable selling and administrative expense	XXXXX	
Fixed manufacturing expense*	XXXXX	
Selling and administrative expense		
Operating income	$ 52,000	$ 49,000

*Variable and fixed for absorption costing; fixed for variable costing.

REQUIRED:

1. Fill in the missing elements of each income statement.
2. What is Able Company's contribution margin?

14–31 **Variable (Direct) Costing and Standard Cost Variances for a Process Cost Accounting System** The Salter Division of Fleming Corp. specializes in the manufacture of a line of computer diskettes. The retail price of these disks ranges from $1 to $48 each, and they are normally sold in boxes of ten. The Salter Division has a single-department production process and employs a standard process cost system on a variable (direct) costing basis.

Model B, a 3.5-inch multipurpose microdiskette, is Salter's most popular product. Over one million units have been produced and sold in each of the past two years. Demand was expected to increase in 19X4, and 100,000 units were scheduled for production each month.

The quantity, time, and cost standards in effect for the model B diskette for 19X4 follow. The plastic raw material is added at the beginning of the process, conversion costs are incurred uniformly throughout the process, and the metal fittings are added at the end of processing.

Raw materials: 2 oz plastic per diskette @ $.80/lb	$.10
Metal fittings: 1 oz per diskette @ $.16/lb	.01
Direct labor: 0.5 hour per 100 diskettes @ $16/hour	.08
Variable overhead: 150 percent of direct labor cost	.12
Standard variable cost per diskette	$.31

The balance of Salter Division's work-in-process inventory account at the beginning of each month is the standard cost of the incomplete equivalent units still in production. The actual costs incurred during the month for raw materials, direct labor, and variable overhead are entered into the work-in-process inventory account. The completed units (finished goods) are transferred out at standard. The manufacturing variances are computed and removed from the work-in-process inventory account, leaving the account valued at standard for the start of the next month.

Data regarding the operations for November 19X4 follow. The variances have not yet been transferred out of the work-in-process inventory account.

Equivalent Units of Production	Total Units	Plastic Material	Conversion	Metal Material
Units completed				
From beginning inventory				
(40% complete on November 1)	14,500	—	8,700	14,500
Started and completed	91,800	91,800	91,800	91,800
Work-in-process, November 30 (70% complete)	11,200	11,200	7,840	—
Total	117,500	103,000	108,340	106,300

Summary of costs for November 19X4:

Work in process, November 1—at standard	$ 2,610
Raw materials plastics purchased and used—13,000 lb	10,140
Metal purchased and used—6,645 lb	1,050
Direct labor—550 hours	8,690
Variable overhead	$13,010
Total costs to account for	$35,500
Cost of units completed and transferred out—at standard (106,300 units)	32,953
Balance of work-in-process, November 30—before closeout of variances	$ 2,547

REQUIRED:

1. The manufacturing variances must be removed from Salter Division's work-in-process inventory account so the inventory account will be stated at standard variable manufacturing costs as of November 30, 19X4.
   a. Determine the standard cost of the work-in-process inventory account at November 30, 19X4.
   b. Identify and calculate the applicable raw materials, direct labor, and variable overhead variances for November 19X4.
2. What policy decision regarding recognition of materials price variances has Salter's management made? What problem(s) may arise because of this decision?
3. Assume model B variable selling and administrative expenses are $.01 per diskette, that each diskette sells for $1.00, and that both beginning and ending finished goods are zero. Construct a variable-costing income statement for model B diskettes through contribution margin.
4. Salter's fixed manufacturing costs (for the manufacture of all diskettes) total $80,000 per month. How do you suggest Salter reflect these costs in their divisional income statement?

14–32 **THOUGHT STIMULATION CASE—The Great Variable/Absorption Debate.** Western Electronics Company, Inc., manufactures three models of circuit boards in three parallel manufacturing cells. The pre-assembly department supercleans and dips all boards (purchased from an outside supplier) in a special solution. Boards are then transferred to one of the three manufacturing cells for assembly and finishing: Cell 1 assembles model C-152; cell 2 assembles H-180; cell three assembles D-40. Completed boards are packaged for shipping in a separate shipping department.

In the process of gathering data for a new management information system, Western, which does not have a standard cost system, has divided all costs for the last year into fixed and variable components. Work in process is negligible.

Costs incurred and production achieved for June 19X2 include the following:

	Product		
	C-152	**H-180**	**D-40**
Materials put into process (per unit)	$14.00	$48.00	$25.30
Overhead (including labor)			
Variable (per unit)	$20.10	$15.50	$32.25
Fixed (total)	$56,280	$44,400	$27,782
Production output (boards)	2,100	1,200	580

Comparable information for May (when beginning finished-goods inventories were zero), along with some additional information, is as follows:

	Product		
	C-152	**H-180**	**D-40**
Production output (boards)	2,600	1,515	600
Ending inventory (finished boards)	450	310	100
Variable cost per unit	$35.00	$63.00	$ 55.00
Fixed cost per unit	22.00	31.00	48.10
Total cost per unit	$57.00	$94.00	$103.10

During June, the marketing department reported the following information:

	C-152	H-180	D-40
Units sold	1,950	1,175	550

(*Note*: Western follows the policy of a FIFO physical flow and a FIFO cost flow.)

Top management is evaluating the internal accounting system, which will be computerized as part of a new management information system. Two polarized groups within the firm—one advocating traditional absorption costing and one pressing for variable costing—are campaigning to have their ideas incorporated into the system.

REQUIRED:

For a Class Debate: Two teams of three students each are to prepare a presentation to be made to a meeting of Western Electronics executives (the rest of the class). One group will present the case for traditional cost accounting; the other group will support a variable-costing system. The presentation format will consist of a 5- to 10-minute oral presentation from each group, followed by a 3-minute rebuttal of the other position by each group. Graphics incorporating Western Electronics data may be used. The *executives*, of course, may question the presenters at times agreed on by the class (that is, at any time during the debate, only during and after the rebuttal periods, or only after the rebuttal periods).

Individual Assignment: In anticipation of a debate in which you may be required to support either side, prepare one outline summarizing the strengths of traditional (absorption) cost accounting and the weaknesses of variable cost accounting and a second outline summarizing the strengths of variable cost accounting and the weaknesses of traditional (absorption) cost accounting.

Chapter 15

Development and Use of Budgets

Learning Objectives

When you have finished your study of this chapter, you should

1. Recognize the importance of budgeting in the effective management of a business.
2. Understand the relationships among the various elements of a master budget.
3. Know the responsibilities of management and the accountant in the preparation of the schedules included in the master budget.
4. Be able to prepare, from given data, the various budget schedules constituting a master budget, especially the cash budget.
5. Understand how the master budget may be used in coordinating and controlling business operations.

I nternal managers follow repetitive cycles of planning, executing, evaluating, and planning (PEEP) as they coordinate and control the operations of a business. Each of the three elements of a particular period's operating cycle (planning, executing, and evaluating) requires the appropriate use of accounting data and/or accounting procedures. Parts I and II of this text dealt with the accumulation, allocation, and use of accounting data primarily for the purpose of preparing financial statements. Chapter 14 introduced variable costing as the gateway to decision making and demonstrated how variable costs and contribution-margin data can be used in making selected short-term decisions. In this chapter, we turn to the use of accounting data in the planning phase of the PEEP cycle.

The planning phase of the operating cycle requires use of accounting data for the purpose of projecting management's plans in quantitative terms. We refer to these quantitative expressions of future plans as *budgets*. The **master budget** consists of a coordinated group of schedules that show, in financial terms, the projected results of all phases of operations, including projected financial statements for the period covered by the budget.

After operating plans have been expressed in quantitative budgetary terms, management will begin to execute (carry out) those plans. In this phase of the operating cycle, internal managers rely heavily on the firm's system of financial and administrative controls to ensure compliance with budgetary plans. Those controls require, among other things, the establishment of lines of authority and responsibility, plus appropriate accounting procedures, records, and reports that help make certain that management plans will be followed. This system, generally called the **internal control system**, is designed to synchronize management and employee actions and behavior patterns with the owners' operating objectives.

The evaluation of operations occurs as operations for the period unfold. Comparisons of actual achievements with budgeted and/or prior-period results help managers evaluate operations and provide clues as to how to improve future operations. Chapters 12 and 13 have shown how some of these evaluations are made through the analysis of standard cost variances. The development and use of cost data are required in preparing budgetary data and also in the executing and evaluating phases.

As the master budget is developed, the operating plan and the decisions relating to it become the responsibilities of company management. The accountant converts those plans into dollars. By quantifying management decisions, he or she tells management what the firm can expect to achieve in the way of net income and financial position as the result of a proposed course of action. A firm that foregoes the budgetary process commits its resources to courses of action without formally considering all the likely results of those actions or the relative merits of possible alternative courses of action.

A budget provides many other additional benefits: it forces management to do some precise thinking, to evaluate the firm's operating practices, to consider long-term goals, and to make conscious decisions regarding short-term goals. Furthermore, a budget communicates operating objectives to employees and can encourage a spirit of cooperation amongst supervisory personnel. Budgets also establish standards against which the operating results can be evaluated. Thus, while the master budget is primarily a planning device, it also helps in promoting coordination and control of a firm's operations, thereby becoming an effective tool in managing a firm and individual segments of a firm's operations.

A particular firm's system of budgeting may range from one that is quite minimal to one that includes a complete projection of the results of operations and end-of-period financial position. Indeed, it would be difficult to find a firm that makes no use of budgeting. Most decisions necessitate envisioning the probable results of those decisions, even without formal projection of them. The budgetary process developed in this chapter involves a master plan covering all phases of a business entity's operations for a future period, all the way through a projected income statement and statement of cash flows for the period and a balance sheet showing the anticipated financial position of the business at the end of the period.

A budget system, emphasizing profit planning and control, will not in and of itself answer all operating problems. However, it may bring some behavioral problems (human relations) into sharp focus. Without proper implementation by and participation of lower-level supervisors, there can be misconceptions, resentments, misinterpretations, speculations, and "game playing" by all levels of personnel operating under a budget umbrella. The budgetary process also may inhibit individual creativity, engender undesirable pressures if goals are unrealistically high, and weaken general morale if improperly implemented. These problems may be minimized, however, by: (1) involving all levels of personnel in the preparation of the budget, (2) developing a positive and enthusiastic attitude among management personnel toward the budget, (3) communicating the purposes and uses of the budget to all personnel, and (4) incorporating realistic and achievable goals into the budgetary plan.

In this chapter, we explain how a comprehensive budgetary system should operate so as to focus on the critical factors that enable a firm to accomplish its missions. We do this by describing briefly the procedures to be followed in:

- developing the budget
- using the budget for control purposes.

Then, as part of our continuing illustration of accounting for Ajax Chemical Company, we will show how parts of a master budget would be prepared for that company.

Development of the Budget

The budgetary plan must be the result of coordinated action amongst organization personnel. Typically, preparation of the budget begins with the establishment of a *budget committee* charged with developing an operating plan for one or more future periods. The accountant is then expected to convert the anticipated results of the operating plan into dollars. In this section, we identify management decision points and develop the accountant's part of the budgetary process for a manufacturing firm by:

- observing the relationships existing among the various elements of the master budget
- identifying decision points in the budget process
- describing formula relationships among the budgetary data
- discussing the considerations underlying the sales budget
- showing how the production budget is prepared
- explaining how the projected materials, direct labor, and overhead costs budgets are derived from the production budget
- discussing the considerations associated with the development of the operating-expenses budget
- identifying other elements of the budgetary plan
- relating the cash budget to the overall budgetary plan
- describing the summarization of budgetary data.

Budgets also are used by merchandising and service enterprises. The only difference between a master budget for a merchandising firm and one for a manufacturing firm is the substitution of a merchandise purchases budget for the production, direct materials purchases, direct labor, and manufacturing-overhead parts of the manufacturing firm's master budget (see Figure 15–1). A service enterprise will substitute a professional services payroll budget for those parts of the manufacturing firm's master budget. Figure 15–2 illustrates the general master budget process for a merchandising firm. Figure 15–3 shows the master budget process for a service firm. Because the budget process for a manufacturing firm includes all the budget elements of a merchandising firm or a service firm, plus additional considerations, we concentrate on the manufacturing firm. The procedures developed apply equally as well, though, to merchandising and service firms.

Relationships Among Elements of the Master Budget

The development of a master budget begins with a projection of the factor most critical to the success of the firm. In most cases, this **critical factor** is sales because that is generally the primary constraint on the overall level of operations. If a business could be sure of selling all the goods it could produce, production would be the most critical factor and the first step in the budgetary process would be the development of a production budget. However, because such situations are rare, we

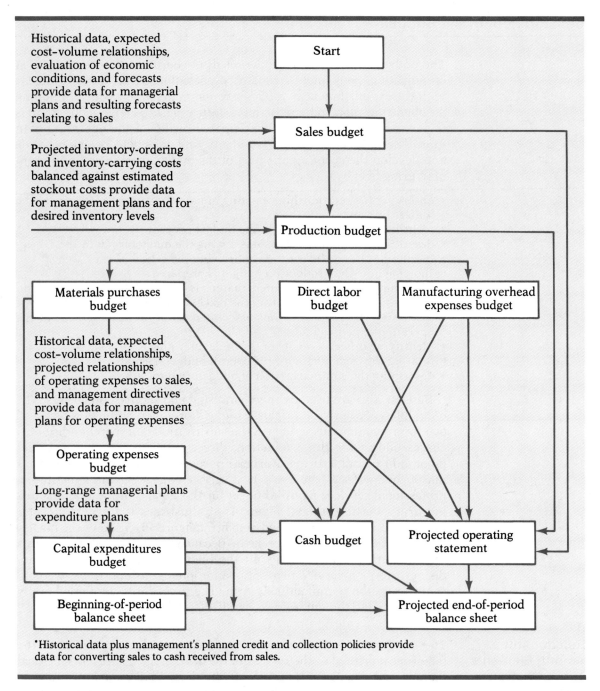

Historical data, expected cost–volume relationships, evaluation of economic conditions, and forecasts provide data for managerial plans and resulting forecasts relating to sales

Projected inventory-ordering and inventory-carrying costs balanced against estimated stockout costs provide data for management plans and for desired inventory levels

Historical data, expected cost–volume relationships, projected relationships of operating expenses to sales, and management directives provide data for management plans for operating expenses

Long-range managerial plans provide data for expenditure plans

Start

Sales budget

Production budget

Materials purchases budget

Direct labor budget

Manufacturing overhead expenses budget

Operating expenses budget

Capital expenditures budget

Cash budget

Projected operating statement

Beginning-of-period balance sheet

Projected end-of-period balance sheet

*Historical data plus management's planned credit and collection policies provide data for converting sales to cash received from sales.

FIGURE 15–1 Master Budget for a Manufacturing Firm

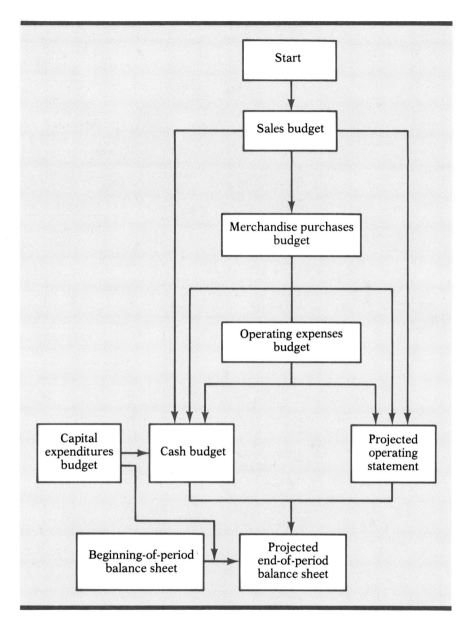

FIGURE 15–2 Master Budget for a Merchandising Firm

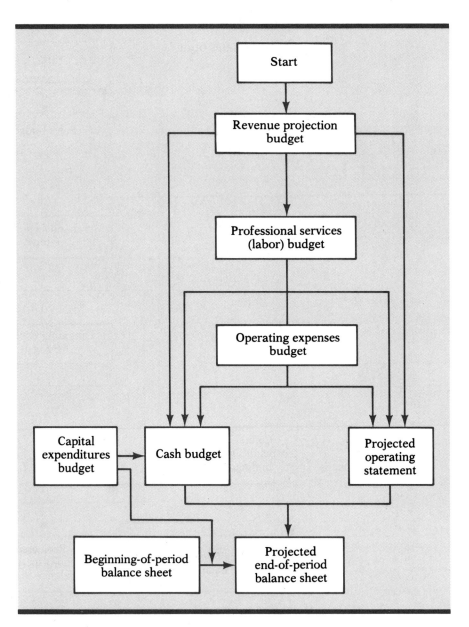

FIGURE 15–3 Master Budget for a Service Firm

begin by explaining how the sales budget is developed. The relationships of the sales budget to the other elements of a manufacturing firm's master budget are given in Figure 15–1. Observe that the budgetary process begins chronologically at the top of the figure. The data then flow toward the projected end-of-period balance sheet in the lower right corner. Refer to this figure as we discuss the master budget.

Decision Points in the Budgetary Process

All elements of the budgetary plan are derived from either managerial decisions about or formula relationships among the budgetary data. Certain elements of the budget, such as sales, production, and purchases, generally are expressed in terms of units of product before being converted to dollars by use of unit sales price and cost data provided by the cost accounting system. The final decisions concerning the projected volume of sales and planned inventory levels must be made by management. In most instances, the basic recommendations relating to those decisions will come from a budget committee.

The deliberations of the budget committee should begin with the **critical factor**, the operational element constituting the primary constraint on what the firm can do. Most firms operate under circumstances that, within the operating levels being considered, permit them to produce as much goods as they can sell. In those situations, the ability to sell is the primary constraining factor, and therefore the preparation of a master budget generally will begin with sales plans.

Once the level of operations, expressed in terms of projected sales, has been established, many other budgetary data will be developed by the use of what might be called **formula relationships** to sales. Other projected expenditures, such as those for advertising, research and development, and capital improvements, generally will be determined by the amounts that management decides to spend for them. We sometimes refer to those expenditures as **appropriation-controlled items**, because the amounts budgeted for them are based on management decisions. While such expenditures are expected to yield benefits to the company, the time lag between incurring the cost and the realization of benefits precludes the use of any type of simple, direct-formula relationship in budgeting them.

Observe on the left side of Figure 15–1 some of the budgetary decisions to be made by management. These budget **decision points**, which directly shape the quantitative data found in the various budget schedules, involve:

- the quantities of the various products management anticipates it can sell with the planned sales efforts and at the planned sales prices
- the planned sales price or prices to be used in converting units of sales into sales dollars
- the sales staff management proposes to use

- the quantities of various inventories management wishes to have on hand at the end of the budget period
- the planned credit policy for sales on account
- the amounts management proposes to spend for each of the various items subject to appropriation control, such as advertising, research and development, administration, and capital improvements
- the minimum cash balance management desires to have available
- plans for financing expenditures in excess of resources available to the firm from regular operations (that is, cash inflows required from borrowing and sale of equity securities).

After management has made these decisions, the accountant can use data provided by the cost system, plus knowledge of operating relationships, to project the complete set of budgets shown in Figure 15–1.

Formula Relationships Among Budgetary Data

Many elements of the master budget in Figure 15–1 are directly related to each other. The accountant has primary responsibility for recognizing such relationships and applying the formulas derived from them in developing the master budget. Stated another way, management is responsible for providing data about the decision points, after which the accountant must fit the data together by identifying relationships among them and applying the appropriate formulas to complete the master budget.

The most important formula used by the accountant is the four-element equation developed earlier in the text:

$$\text{Beginning balance} + \text{Additions} - \text{Removals} = \text{Ending balance}$$

We use this equation to develop the production budget, the raw materials purchases budget, and the cash budget.

When basic budget data—such as sales, production, and raw materials purchases—are initially expressed in units, those data will have to be converted to dollars by multiplying units by sales price per unit or cost per unit. Thus, we may think of the conversion of unit data to dollars as requiring a simple formula expressed as units multiplied by per-unit selling price or cost data. The cost data will be drawn from the particular cost system being used by the firm. While historical costs may be employed for this purpose, standard cost data are more directly useful to the budgetary process.

Some budgetary items will be formula-related to other budgetary items on a percentage or a time-lag basis. For example, budgeted expenditures for sales commissions should be projected as a percentage of budgeted sales. Also, projected cash receipts from sales should be calculated by identifying the expected time lag associated with the collection of accounts receivable. Budgeted cash disbursements for purchases will be calculated by giving consideration to expected credit terms on accounts payable.

Budgets may be developed for short or for long periods of time. Typically, budgetary data expected to apply to the next operating period will be projected in more detail than those for later operating periods. A firm with a comprehensive budgeting system may make general plans for as much as five years or more. With such a long-range system of budgeting, only the data for the next quarter are likely to be shown in complete detail. Data for the other three quarters of the next fiscal period generally will be assembled in condensed form to permit the accountant to project an operating statement for the period and a balance sheet for the end of the period. In recognition of the continuous need for budget data, some firms use a "rolling" approach, referred to as **continuous budgeting**, in which budgets for a new period are added each time an earlier period is dropped.

Development of the Sales Budget

The **sales budget**, represented in Figure 15–1 by the rectangle at the top of the flowchart, is developed by reference to historical sales data, managerial plans for pricing and selling, marketing department forecasts, and various forecasts regarding the general economy and the firm's industry or industries. The budget committee, in establishing its sales forecast, for example, might project an increase in the volume of sales if prices were to be reduced. Also, a stronger emphasis on advertising or a projected enlargement of sales staff should be expected to help the firm achieve a larger volume of sales. As the projected results of this analysis, often given first in terms of units, reach the accountant, he or she will convert them into the dollars of sales the firm is budgeted to achieve during the period.

In Figure 15–1, the sales data flow to the projected operating statement, cash budget, and production budget boxes. Sales becomes the first item in the projected income statement. Also, the sales data are formula-related to the production budget, and sales information is a major factor in arriving at the inflow of cash from sales. To properly relate the sales budget to the cash budget, and also to help establish the amount of receivables to show in the projected end-of-period balance sheet, the accountant needs to know about the company's credit policy and its actual collection experiences. The basic four-element formula for calculating projected cash inflows from sales on account may be stated as follows:

$$
\begin{array}{ll}
 & \text{Beginning balance of accounts receivable} \\
+ & \text{Projected credit sales} \\
- & \underline{\text{Projected end-of-period accounts receivable}} \\
= & \text{Projected cash inflows from credit sales}
\end{array}
$$

We demonstrate the application of this four-element formula as we discuss the cash budget and summarization of budget data.

The formal sales budget should give the quantities of various units of product projected to be sold multiplied by sales prices per unit. To illustrate, let's assume that management of Model Company, which sells a single product, decides that a total of 250 + 450 + 300 = 1,000 units can be sold at $1,000 per unit during the quarter ending June 30, with sales of 400 units monthly after that. The second-quarter sales budget would then be as follows:

	April	May	June	Total
Sales, in units	250	450	300	1,000
Selling price per unit	× $1,000	× $1,000	× $1,000	× $1,000
Total Sales	$250,000	$450,000	$300,000	$1,000,000

Development of the Production Budget

The sales budget contains management's best estimate of the number of units expected to be sold during the period. To avoid losing sales in the event that demand is greater than predicted, it is customary for management to set policy requiring that a certain number of finished units be on hand at the end of each period. After management has selected a desirable finished-goods inventory level, the accountant uses this information, along with the units of product projected to be sold and appropriate unit-cost data, to project the **production budget**. This budget shows the projected number(s) and cost(s) of finished units that must be produced to meet the requirements of the sales budget and the end-of-period inventory plans. The formula for the production budget, expressed in units, can be stated as follows:

	(1) Projected beginning inventory of finished units
+	(2) Units projected to be produced
−	(3) Units projected to be sold
=	(4) Projected ending inventory of finished units

This formula is a variation of the cost box first introduced in Chapter 1:

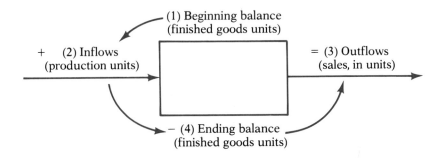

Element (1) is determined by estimating from current operating plans what the inventory will be at the end of the current period (the period immediately preceding the budget period). Element (3) comes from the sales budget. Element (4) is established by management directive. Element (2) then can be calculated from the three other elements. This standard "missing information" problem can be solved with the following formula:

> Units required to cover sales
> + Units required for desired ending inventory
> = Total units required
> − Units in beginning inventory
> = Units to be produced

Variations of this formula, involving only minor changes in descriptions of inflows and outflows, are used for projecting (1) materials purchases for a manufacturing firm and (2) merchandise purchases for a merchandising firm.

To illustrate how to calculate the unit data in the production budget, let's return to Model Company's sales budget, which projected the sale of 1,000 units of product A during the quarter ending June 30. If the beginning-of-period inventory shows 25 units of hand, and the budget committee has indicated it would like to have 10% of the following month's projected sales on hand at the end of each month, then the production budget would call for the firm to produce 1,015 units during the quarter ending June 30, calculated as follows:

Model Company
Quarterly Production Budget

	April	May	June	Quarterly Total
Units required for sales	250	450	300	1,000
+ Desired ending inventory	45	30	40	40
	295	480	340	1,040
− Projected beginning inventory	25		30	25
= Units to be produced	270	435	310	1,015

Alternatively, this schedule can be set up as follows:

Model Company

Alternative Quarterly Production Budget

	April	May	June	Quarterly Total
Units required for sales	25	45	30	25
+ Desired ending inventory	270	435	310	1,015
	295	480	340	1,040
− Projected beginning inventory	250	450	300	1,000
= Units to be produced	45	30	40	40

In this version, the units to be produced are treated as missing information and plugged in after considering the data already available.

If we assume that the standard cost card for the finished product shows a total cost of $700 per unit, the projected production data would be converted to dollars as follows:

	April	May	June	Total
Units to be produced	270	435	310	1,015
Standard cost per unit ×	$700	× $700	× $700	× $700
Total production cost	$189,000	$304,500	$217,000	$710,500

Materials Purchases, Labor, and Overhead Budgets

By using the quantitative information for raw materials from standard cost cards or similar information derived from a historical cost system, along with management's decisions regarding inventory levels of direct materials and work in process, we can plan the **materials purchases budget**—that is, the quantities of individual raw materials that should be purchased during the period.

Let's follow our production budget for Model Company a bit further by assuming that each of the 1,015 units of finished product budgeted to be produced during the quarter requires three units of material A, two units of material B, and one unit of material C. Let's further assume that the beginning inventories of these materials are 300 units for material A and 100 units each for materials B and C. Management wishes to maintain a raw materials ending inventory equal to 20% of production needs for the coming month. They feel that work-in-process inventory should be held at its beginning-of-period level. Using these data in the four-element formula, we can project the purchases needed to meet the firm's production requirements and inventory goals for the quarter as follows:

Model Company
Materials Purchases Budget (units)

Material A	April	May	June	Total
Units needed for production	810	1,305	930	3,045
+ Desired ending inventory	261	186	240* →	240
Total needed	1,071	1,491	1,170	3,285
− Beginning inventory	300	261	186	300
= Units of material A to be purchased	771	1,230	984	2,985

Material B	April	May	June	Total
Units needed for production	540	870	620	2,030
+ Desired ending inventory	174	124	160* →	160
Total needed	714	994	780	2,190
− Beginning inventory	100	174	124	100
= Units of material B to be purchased	614	820	656	2,090

Material C	April	May	June	Total
Units needed for production	270	435	310	1,015
+ Desired ending inventory	87	62	80* →	80
Total needed	357	497	390	1,095
− Beginning inventory	100	87	62	100
= Units of material C to be purchased	257	410	328	995

*Based on projected July production of 400 units (400 sales + 40 ending inventory − 40 beginning inventory).

After these quantities have been calculated, we can use cost data from standard cost cards or from recent purchase invoices to arrive at the number of dollars to be budgeted for purchases of raw materials. For example, if materials A, B, and C cost $100, $20, and $50, respectively, the materials purchases budgets, expressed in dollars, would be:

Model Company
Materials Purchases Budget (dollars)

Material A	April	May	June	Total
Units to be purchased	771	1,230	984	2,985
Cost per unit	× $100	× $100	× $100	× $100
Total cost	$77,100	$123,000	$98,400	$298,500

(*Continues*)

Material B		April		May		June		Total
Units to be purchased		614		820		656		2,090
Cost per unit	×	$20	×	$20	×	$20	×	$20
Total cost		$12,280		$16,400		$13,120		$41,800

Material C		April		May		June		Total
Units to be purchased		257		410		328		995
Cost per unit	×	$50	×	$50	×	$50	×	$50
Total needed		$12,850		$20,500		$16,400		$49,750

Of course, these two materials purchases schedules (units and dollars) may be combined into one schedule.

As Figure 15–1 shows, these purchase calculations are carried to the projected operating statement, where they will be used, along with direct labor, manufacturing overhead, and beginning and ending inventory data, to determine the *budgeted cost of sales*. Purchase data must be used, along with projections of the beginning and end-of-period accounts payable balances, to arrive at the amount of projected cash payments for purchases to be shown in the *cash budget*. The accountant uses past experience and past payment policies in projecting both the cash payments for purchases and the end-of-period accounts payable balance. The basic budget formula for determining the cash outflows for purchases is:

> Beginning balance for accounts payable
> + Projected cost of purchases
> − Projected end-of-period accounts payable balance
> = Projected cash outflows for purchases

We demonstrate the application of this formula as we discuss the preparation of the cash budget and summarization of budget data. Alternatively, purchase payments can be calculated directly and summed over the period to determine cash outflows.

Total direct labor hours can be calculated by multiplying the number of units budgeted to be produced (1,015 for Model Company) by the direct labor hours required to produce one unit. The **direct labor budget**, in dollars, then can be determined by multiplying total direct labor hours by the labor cost per hour as shown on the standard cost cards or in the historical cost data.

For example, if it requires 6 direct labor hours to manufacture each unit that Model Company produces and the average labor cost is $14 per hour, then for the quarter ending June 30 the direct labor budget for Model Company would be:

Model Company

Direct Labor Budget

	April	May	June	Total
Production (units)	270	435	310	1,015
Direct labor hours per unit	× 6	× 6	× 6	× 6
Total labor hours	1,620	2,610	1,860	6,090
Rate per hour	× $14	× $14	× $14	× $14
	$22,680	$36,540	$26,040	$85,260

The total amount shown in the direct labor budget of Figure 15–1 is carried to the projected operating statement as an element of cost of goods sold. The projected cost of direct labor also is one element of the projected cash outflows. Therefore, the data from the direct labor budget also must be carried to the cash budget as an element of projected cash outflows.

Manufacturing overhead constitutes the third element of cost associated with the production of goods. The **manufacturing-overhead budget** may be derived in either of two ways. By applying cost–volume analysis, described in Chapter 11, to individual manufacturing-overhead items, we can project the amounts to be incurred for individual items of manufacturing overhead at different levels of production. Such a projection, as we have observed earlier, is called a *flexible budget*. This method of estimating manufacturing overhead item-by-item is reasonably precise. The amounts shown for manufacturing-overhead items to be paid in cash also should be carried to the cash budget.

The total amount to be budgeted for manufacturing overhead also can be calculated by multiplying the projected manufacturing-overhead application rate or the standard cost of manufacturing overhead per unit (as described in Chapter 13) by the projected production, measured in hours or units. This also can be used as a check on the reasonableness of manufacturing-overhead items projected on an item-by-item basis. Put another way, the budgeted production multiplied by the manufacturing-overhead application rate associated with the anticipated level of production should give approximately the same projected total for manufacturing overhead as the sum of the items projected item-by-item. For example, if projected direct labor hours for the period total 8,000 and the overhead application rate is $1.50 per direct labor hour, overhead would be estimated at 8,000 × $1.50 = $12,000.

The Operating-Expenses Budget

The **operating-expenses budget** is divided into at least two subdivisions, one covering projected selling expenses and the other covering budgeted general and administrative expenses. A *budget for selling expenses* must be developed within the constraints of management plans and certain formula relationships. Some items, such as sales commissions, can be extended on a formula basis by referring to the sales budget. Other items, such as advertising expenses, must be projected on the basis of the amounts appropriated for that purpose by management. Therefore, the selling-expense budget must be worked out item-by-item, for which purpose the accountant must know the expected behavior of each item (whether a variable, a fixed, a mixed, or an appropriated cost). Cost estimation techniques (see Chapter 11) can be used to separate a mixed cost into its variable and fixed components. The *budget for administrative and general expenses* also must be projected item by item. Some items will be based strictly on historical data; others will be based on managerial plans.

The projected operating-expense items to be paid in cash also must be used in developing the cash budget. Because the time lag between incurring an operating expense and paying for it is generally short, there should be little difference between the accrual basis amounts shown on the income statement and the cash payments shown in the cash budget. Of course, depreciation and other noncash items must be eliminated from projected operating expenses in establishing the amount to be shown as disbursements in the cash budget. These data also become part of the projected operating statement (see Figure 15–1).

Other Elements of the Budgetary Plan

The amounts projected to be spent on such items as employee training and research and development will be determined almost entirely by managerial plans. Ultimately, of course, these expenditures are expected to produce results in the form of increased revenue, or to contribute to maintaining a desired competitive position in the industry. However, because of the time expected to pass between the incurrence of such expenditures and the times when the firm realizes benefits from them, it is impractical to derive them from formulas related to operational level. When, as a matter of policy, management chooses to spend a certain percentage of sales on a discretionary item such as research and development, this figure can be derived by multiplying the agreed-on percentage by the amount of projected sales. More often, however, these amounts are appropriated directly by management action, which becomes the basis for the amounts shown in, for example, the research and development budget. Cash outlays for these items will become a part of the cash budget.

The **capital expenditures budget** also is established primarily by managerial plans and directives. This budget forces management to think ahead in establishing its plans for acquiring fixed assets. For the most part, the amounts included in the capital expenditures budget will be those appropriated by management acting upon recommendations of the budget committee. The information developed in the capital expenditures budget, including financing arrangements, must be carried into the cash budget to determine total projected cash outflows. Balances expected to be owed on these acquisitions at the end of the period will be shown in the liability section of the projected balance sheet, and the resources to be acquired will be shown in the asset section of the projected balance sheet.

Cash Budget

The **cash budget** is an important part of any master budget because one of the reasons for developing a comprehensive budget is to determine how cash needs (outflows) can be expected to relate to cash inflows. It is important to have advance projections of anticipated cash shortages and overages so that appropriate loan and repayment arrangements can be worked out with the firm's bank. The cash budget is designed to relate all anticipated cash inflows and outflows to the times they are expected to be realized and disbursed. A primary source of cash inflows from operations is the amount expected to be realized from sales during the period (see Figure 15–1). Expected inflows from sales on account are determined by reference to the credit policies of the company and to historical collection experiences.

To illustrate how to calculate projected cash inflows from receivables, let's assume the following: a firm is selling its merchandise on terms calling for a cash discount of 2% for invoices paid within the first 10 days of the month following the date of sale. The net amounts of invoices must be paid no later than the end of the month following the month of sale. Past experience shows that 60% of the firm's customers pay their January accounts in February in time to realize the 2% discount. Cash receipts from those early-paying accounts can be projected as 98% of 60% of projected January sales on account. Experience further shows that an additional 35% of the firm's customers pay after the discount period but before the end of the month following the sale; so 35% of sales for January can be expected to be realized in the form of cash between the tenth day of February and the end of February. Past experience also will be used in determining what happens to the other 5% of the firm's sales on account. Some portion of these accounts quite likely will be collected in subsequent months; some will not be collected at all and must be recognized as bad debt losses. With budgeted January sales in the amount of $100,000, February collections from those sales would be calculated as follows:

January Sales Collected in February

Amounts collected by February 10 ($100,000 × 0.6 × 0.98)	$58,800
Amounts collected between February 10 and February 28 ($100,000 × 0.35)	35,000
Total projected cash collections of January sales in February	$93,800

Assuming the 5% of January sales not collected in February ($5,000) is projected to never be collected, this amount would never appear in the cash budget. Instead, a provision for bad debt losses would be included in the projected income statement for January.

As observed earlier, the primary outflows of cash are for payments of accounts payable, payroll, manufacturing overhead, various operating expenses, research and development expenditures, and capital expenditures. All of these must be included in the disbursements part of the cash budget for the periods during which they are expected to be paid. Accounts payable for materials purchases, for example, must be related to the average terms of payment in order to arrive at the timing of the outflows of cash required to cover them. Discounts available on accounts payable also will have an impact on both the time and the amount of cash projected to be required for payments of accounts payable. The formula for calculating the projected outflows for payments of accounts payable is similar to that used to project cash inflows from accounts receivable: beginning balance of accounts payable, plus current period purchases, less projected end-of-period accounts payable balance, equals gross projected cash outflows for accounts payable. Since a small cash discount for 10 or 15 days translates into a very high annual rate of interest (frequently over 38%), effective managers always pay their accounts payable in time to earn the discount, which will reduce gross outflows to expected actual disbursements.

Generally, projected expenditures for direct labor (see direct labor budget) can be carried directly from the direct labor budget to the cash budget because there will be only a short time lag between the incurrence of obligations for labor and the time they must be paid. Most manufacturing-overhead items requiring cash outlays must be related to the terms of payment in a manner similar to that used in projecting the cash outflows for purchases. Many operating expenses (see operating-expenses budget) must be paid at the time the obligations are incurred and, therefore, can be carried into the cash budget in much the same manner as are data from the direct labor budget.

As all of these data are drawn together, they are best organized via a four-element equation:

$$
\begin{array}{l}
\text{Beginning-of-period cash balance} \\
+ \text{ Projected cash receipts} \\
- \text{ Projected cash disbursements} \\
\hline
= \text{ Projected end-of-period cash balance}
\end{array}
$$

Because they serve as indicators of financial health and vigor, as well as provide operational flexibility, the periodic projected cash balances are very important to management, and the cash position of a firm must be monitored on a continuing basis. As a result, the cash budget equation typically will be developed in great detail for short intervals of time—generally for no longer than one month, and frequently for intervals as short as a week or even a day. Frequent readings of projected cash balances enable management to anticipate the need for short-term borrowing so advance arrangements can be made for such loans. Exhibit 15–1 presents the cash budget for Illustration Company, covering the first quarter of 19A. One supporting schedule (estimated collections on accounts receivable) is included, and parenthetical references are made to other supporting schedules used in preparing this budget but are not illustrated.

EXHIBIT 15–1

Illustration Company

Cash Budget

For First Quarter, 19A

	January	February	March	Quarter
Beginning cash balance	$5,000	$4,200	$3,500	$ 5,000
Cash receipts				
Cash sales (Schedule A, sales budget)	500	550	625	1,675
Collections on accounts receivable (Schedule B)	2,950	3,150	3,530	9,630
Total cash available	$8,450	$7,900	$7,655	$16,305
Cash disbursements				
Accounts payable (Schedule E, purchases budget)	$1,200	$1,400	$1,500	$ 4,100
Salaries (Schedule G, labor budget)	2,000	1,900	2,200	6,100
Factory overhead (Schedule H, factory-overhead budget)	500	490	520	1,510
Selling expenses (Schedule K, selling-expenses budget)	300	305	310	915
Administrative expenses (Schedule L, administrative expense budget)	200	200	200	600
Investment in U.S. treasury notes	50	—	—	50
Payment of dividends	—	105	—	105
Payment of income taxes	—	—	50	50
Total disbursements	$4,250	$4,400	$4,780	$13,430
Ending cash balance	$4,200	$3,500	$2,875	$ 2,875

Schedule B: Estimated Collections on Accounts Receivable, First Quarter, 19A

Collections per sales budget, Schedule A			
November sales	$ 300		
December sales	650	$ 250	
January sales	2,000	700	$ 280
February sales		2,200	750
March sales			2,500
Total	$2,950	$3,150	$3,530

For this time period, additional financing is assumed not to be required. If the projected cash balance as of any date is less than that required, we would have a lower section included in the cash budget to show the amount to be borrowed in order to maintain the required balance. As the projected loan is to be paid, we would also show the amounts of the expected payments in that section of the budget. To illustrate, let's assume that the management of Illustration Company wishes to maintain a cash balance of $3,500. The cash budget column for March and some subsequent month would then contain the following lower section:

	March	Subsequent Month
End-of-period cash balance (from Exhibit 15–1)	$2,875	$6,000
Projected borrowing	625	
Projected loan repayments		625 (plus interest on $625)
Final projected cash balance	$3,500	$5,375 (less interest on $625)

Earlier, we noted that the complete master budget would include a projected **statement of cash flows** for the budget period. The data in the cash budget can be reorganized to conform to the classification requirements of FASB 95 as the statement of cash flows is prepared. This reorganization is covered in intermediate accounting courses and is beyond the scope of this text.

Summarization of Budgetary Data

Figure 15–1 shows how data flows from the various budgets into the projected income statement, statement of cash flows (cash budget), and the projected end-of-period balance sheet. Data for these statements are drawn together in much the same way as are historical data associated with actual operations. There is, however, one important difference: the operating statement in the budget flowchart is a projected statement; if the results are not what management had hoped to see from its plan of operations, that plan can be completely reworked within a different framework of decision points to see what the results of alternate plans would be. This can best be accomplished if the budget schedules are prepared on a computer spreadsheet file. The ability to consider possible alternative courses of action is one of the real advantages of budgeting. Management is able to see the expected results of a given set of plans before it commits resources to implementation.

The projected balance sheet is prepared using the previous balance sheet (as a line-item pattern), previously prepared budget schedules, and general budget information. For example, end-of-period cash comes from the projected ending balance shown in the cash budget. Ending accounts receivable can be calculated via the following four-element account analysis:

Accounts Receivable

Beginning balance (from previous balance sheet) + Sales (from sales budget)	− Collections (from cash budget)
= Ending balance	

Or the ending balance can be logically deduced from the firm's projected collection policy. If, for example, 50% of a month's sales are projected to be collected in the month of sales and 48% the following month (2% being uncollectible), net accounts receivable at the end of any month equals 48% of that month's sales. Net property, plant, and equipment at the end of the period equals the balance shown on the previous balance sheet, plus additions to property, plant, and equipment shown on the capital expenditures budget, minus depreciation and planned disposals for the period:

Net Property, Plant, and Equipment

Beginning balance (from previous balance sheet) + Additions (from capital expenditures budget)	− Planned removals − Depreciation expense for period (from projected income statement)
= Ending balance	

Likewise, ending accounts payable can be calculated via account analysis:

Accounts Payable

− Payments (from cash budget)	Beginning balance (from previous balance sheet) + Purchases (from purchases budget)
	= Ending balance

Or it can be calculated directly from the expected payment plan. If, for example, 60% of a month's purchases are projected to be paid for in the month of purchase and 40% the following month, accounts payable at the end of any month will equal 40% of that month's purchases. Other items on the balance sheet may be calculated similarly.

The initial phases of developing a master budget require many thoughtfully planned decisions. Once these decisions have been made, the preparation of the supporting detailed schedules and the budget summaries involves a logical flow of data among the schedules.

Because of its calculating speed, the computer can be especially effective in projecting the effects that a change in managerial plans would have on the projected operating results and in considering a number of possible alternative plans of action. After all, a master budget may include hundreds of schedules. Once a budget plan is adopted, it becomes the basis for evaluating operations and for making operating decisions as the period progresses.

The Budget as a Control Device

Our discussion to this point has centered on the use of the budget as a *planning* device. Once adopted, a budget plan also can be used in controlling operations. Actual achievements for specified time periods can be compared with the budget projections for those periods, to identify deviations, help isolate their causes, and trigger the initiation of appropriate remedial action if required.

Many of the budgeted items, because of cost–volume relationships, are formula-related to the projected level of sales. For example, direct materials, direct labor, and manufacturing-overhead costs may have exceeded budgeted amounts because the firm has produced and sold more units than was anticipated in the production budget. The fundamental concern, particularly in analyzing unfavorable materials, labor, and manufacturing-overhead deviations, is to give special attention to the ones caused by *inefficient management*, which requires volume-adjusted budgetary data such as those discussed in Chapters 12 and 13.

The specific procedures followed in setting budgetary goals and in acting on deviations from those goals must consider the probable reactions of middle- and lower-level managers held accountable for attaining specific goals. A primary overall objective in implementing budgetary control is to improve the firm's long-term performance. This requires the cooperation of employees and managers at all levels. Upper-level managers may attempt to secure this in a number of ways, from the highly authoritative approach ("forcing" cooperation by relying on rank) to the participative approach (relying on synchronizing the goals of subordinates with those of the firm). The latter managers promote cooperation by involving lower-level managers and even non-managerial employees in the budgetary decision-making process. Participative managers also rely more on encouragement and rewards for achievement than on punitive actions.

These days, the participative-type manager generally will be more effective. However, sometimes authority must be asserted if managerial control is to be maintained. Such actions should be balanced with appropriate participation of lower-level managers and employees in establishing operating goals. The following guidelines are suggested for establishing budgetary goals and for evaluating the performances of managers charged with adherence to budgetary plans.

- Always involve lower-level managers in the establishment of *their* budgetary goals.
- Be sure budgetary goals are reasonably achievable but also that they demand "good" effort.
- Encourage two-way communication between upper-level managers and those charged with achieving specific budgetary goals.
- Provide frequent, timely, easily understood reports for managers showing how their achievements compare with budgetary plans. Such reports should reflect responsibility for only those costs controlled by the person receiving the report.
- Try to emphasize self-control of costs by lower-level managers rather than relying on policing actions.
- Give recognition to good performances, and work cooperatively with managers showing unfavorable budget deviations.

Budgets provide a standard against which the effectiveness of operations can be measured. An appropriate analysis of deviations from budget can help management identify and carry out appropriate corrective action.

Illustrative Budget Problem

To demonstrate how selected parts of a master budget may be developed, we will use previously assumed data for Ajax Chemical Company plus additional assumptions regarding management decisions. We will then use those data plus other assumptions to project an income statement for the year and a balance sheet at the end of the year.

Cost Data and Assumptions.

(1) Assumed inventories at beginning of budget period:

Finished goods (400 pounds @ $5.44)	$2,176
Material A (800 pounds @ $2.00)	$1,600
Material B (900 pounds @ $2.20)	$1,980
Material C (1,000 pounds @ $1.70)	$1,700

(2) Management decisions relating to operations during budget period:
  (a) Sales: 5,100 units @ $10 = $51,000
  (b) Finished-goods inventory is to be reduced to 50% of its beginning-of-period balance. Because of uncertainty regarding deliveries,

raw materials inventories are to be increased 150% during the budget period.

(3) Standard cost data from Chapter 11 (Figures 11–1 and 11–2):

Standard Cost Card

Part No. 101

Material A   Unit: Pound
   Standard cost per unit $2.00

Standard Cost Card

Part No. 102

Material B   Unit: Pound
   Standard cost per unit $2.20

Standard Cost Card

Part No. 103

Material C   Unit: Pound
   Standard cost per unit $1.70

Standard Cost Card

Finished Product No. 5001

	Quantity	Standard Cost per Pound	Total Cost
Direct materials			
Material A (part 101)	0.3 pound	$2.00	$ .60
Material B (part 102)	0.3 pound	$2.20	.66
Material C (part 103)	0.4 pound	$1.70	.68
Total standard cost of direct materials			$1.94

	Hours	Standard Rate per Hour	
Direct labor	0.2	$8.00	1.60
Manufacturing overhead	0.2	$9.50	1.90
Total standard cost per pound of finished product			$5.44

(4) Budgets and end-of-period balances not illustrated:

Operating expenses	$10,996
Cash budget (balance at end of period)	4,226
Accounts receivable (balance at end of period)	5,000
Accounts payable (balance at end of period)	4,932
Capital expenditures	4,000

(5) Assumed beginning-of-period balance sheet:

Assets	
Current Assets	
Cash	$ 2,500
Accounts receivable	4,000
Materials inventory	5,280
Work-in-process inventory	1,000
Finished-goods inventory	2,176
Total current assets	$14,956
Plant assets (net of depreciation)	50,000
Total assets	$64,956
Liabilities and Stockholders' Equity	
Current liabilities	
Accounts payable	$ 2,956
Stockholders' equity	
Common stock	50,000
Retained earnings	12,000
Total liabilities and stockholders' equity	$64,956

(6) Common stock of $5,000 is expected to be issued during the year, and dividends of $3,000 are expected to be declared and paid.

(7) Assumed tax rate is 30%.

REQUIRED:

1. Prepare sales, production, materials purchases, direct labor, and manufacturing-overhead budgets based on the assumptions, management decisions, and standard cost data [items (1), (2), and (3)]. Assume that work-in-process inventory remains constant.
2. Prepare a projected income statement and balance sheet using schedules prepared in requirement 1, along with the assumed budget and end-of-period data (item 4), beginning-of-period balance sheet (item 5), stockholders' equity information (item 6), and assumed tax rate (item 7).

Solution to Illustrative Budget Problem

1. **Preparation of Budgets.**

Sales Budget

5,100 units @ $10 = $51,000

Production Budget (units)

Beginning of Period Inventory of Finished Goods	+	Budgeted Production	−	Budgeted Sales	=	End-of-Period Inventory of Finished Goods
400		4,900 (2)		5,100		200 (1)

Production Budget (dollars)

4,900 units @ $5.44 = $26,656

Explanation:

(1) 50% of 400 units = 200 units
(2)   400 units + (?) − 5,100 units = 200 units
                400 units + 4,900 units − 5,100 units = 200 units

or

5,100 units + 200 units − 400 units = 4,900 units

Materials Purchases Budget (units)

Material	Beginning-of-Period Inventory	+	Budgeted Purchases	−	Budgeted to Be Used in Production	=	End-of-Period Inventory
A	800		2,670 (3)		1,470 (1)		2,000 (2)
B	900		2,820		1,470		2,250
C	1,000		3,460		1,960		2,500

Explanation:

(1) 4,900 units × 0.3 lb material A
(2) 800 + (1.5 × 800)
(3) 1,470 + 2,000 − 800 = 2,670

Materials Purchases Budget (dollars)

Material A (2,670 @ $2)	$ 5,340
Material B (2,820 @ $2.20)	6,204
Material C (3,460 @ $1.70)	5,882
	$17,426

Direct Labor Budget

4,900 units × 0.2 hr × $8/hr = $7,840

Manufacturing-Overhead Budget

4,900 units × 0.2 hr × $9.50/hr = $9,310

Summarization of Budgetary Data for Requirement 1

Sales		$51,000
Production (includes materials, labor, and overhead costs)		26,656
Finished goods, beginning of period (400 units @ $5.44)		2,176
Finished goods, end of period (200 units @ $5.44)		1,088
Materials purchases		17,426
Materials inventories, end of period		
Material A (2,000 @ $2.00)	$4,000	
Material B (2,250 @ $2.20)	4,950	
Material C (2,500 @ $1.70)	4,250	13,200
Direct labor		7,840
Overhead		9,310

2. Preparation of Income Statement and Balance Sheet.

Projected Income Statement

Sales		$51,000
Cost of sales		
Finished goods, beginning of period	$ 2,176	
Cost of goods manufactured	26,656	
Total	$28,832	
Finished goods, end of period	1,088	27,744
Gross margin		$23,256
Operating expenses		10,996
Operating income		$12,260
Tax expense (0.3 × $12,260)		3,678
Net income		$ 8,582

Projected Balance Sheet

Assets	
Current assets	
Cash	$ 4,226
Accounts receivable	5,000
Materials inventory	13,200
Work-in-process inventory	1,000
Finished-goods inventory	1,088
Total current assets	$24,514
Noncurrent assets	
Plant assets (net of depreciation)	52,000
Total assets	$76,514

(Continues)

Liabilities and Stockholders' Equity

Current liabilities	
Accounts payable	$ 4,932
Stockholders' equity	
Common stock	55,000
Retained earnings	16,582
Total liabilities and stockholders' equity	$76,514

Statement of Retained Earnings

Beginning-of-year balance	$11,000
Net income for period	8,582
	$19,582
Dividends paid	3,000
End-of-year balance	$16,582

SUMMARY

In this chapter, we explained budgeting and demonstrated how budgetary data are assembled and used. Because planning, coordinating, and controlling are vital functions in the management of any enterprise, the budgetary system is extremely important. Ideally, the system should be comprehensive enough to show where a given set of managerial plans is expected to lead the firm over a reasonable period of time, generally one year. Nevertheless, a great deal can be accomplished in the way of encouraging supervisory personnel to think through their problems and coordinate their efforts by developing projections for sales, production, capital expenditures, and selected other items. If the management of a firm is to think through a firm's operations to the point of formally planning these items, it will do a better job of operating the business than it would with no planning at all. When individual schedules are combined to provide projected financial statements, a master budget emerges.

While the budget is primarily a planning and coordinating device, it also can act as a control device by providing standards that can be used in evaluating actual achievements. Many deviations from budget may be caused by a difference between the level of operations budgeted and that actually achieved rather than by efficiencies and inefficiencies. Departmental supervisors and others responsible for managing specific segments of the operations should be consulted regarding the deviations. Inefficiencies should be discussed with the responsible managers to prevent their repetition and to decide what corrective actions should be taken. Efficiencies also should be recognized, and persons responsible for them should be rewarded.

GLOSSARY OF TERMS INTRODUCED IN THIS CHAPTER

appropriation-controlled items
In this chapter, those items for which the amount projected to be spent is decided by management action rather than by a relationship to other items in the master budget.

capital expenditures budget
A schedule included in a master budget that indicates the expected outlays for plant and equipment during the period covered by the budget.

cash budget
A schedule included in a master budget in which projected beginning and ending cash balances and inflows and outflows of cash are given; typically organized to show beginning cash balance plus projected receipts for the budget period minus projected disbursements for the budget period, to arrive at a projected end-of-period cash balance.

constraining factor
See *critical factor*.

continuous budgeting
A moving projection of financial operations for a series of periods immediately ahead. At the end of each period, the portion of the projection associated with that period is removed and a new projection for the next future period not previously budgeted is added to the series.

critical factor
In this chapter, the primary constraint on the overall level of operations of a firm, that determines the starting point for a master budget. In most instances, this is sales; therefore the sales budget is the starting point for the master budget of most firms. Also called *constraining factor*.

decision points
In this chapter, the points in the overall budgeting process at which management must make a decision regarding projected operations to allow the preparation of the master budget to proceed—for example, the decision as to the levels of inventory the firm should attempt to achieve by the end of the budget period.

direct labor budget
A schedule in which the amount of projected direct labor costs for the period(s) are summarized as part of the master budget.

formula relationships
In this chapter, the relationships expected to exist among various budgetary items programmed into the budgetary process. For example, with knowledge of beginning inventory, projected end-of-period inventory, and the amount of sales expected to be achieved, the number of units of finished goods to be produced can be calculated by use of the four-element equation showing beginning balance plus production minus sales equals ending balance.

internal control system	The system of documentation and mandated procedures within an organization that is designed to protect physical assets from misuse and to ensure the implementation of managerial directives.
manufacturing-overhead budget	A schedule included in a master budget in which the projected manufacturing overhead for the budget period is summarized.
master budget	A document that consolidates all budgets of an organization into an overall plan, including the projection of a cash flow statement and an operating statement for the budget period and a balance sheet for the end of the budget period.
materials purchases budget	A schedule included in a master budget in which projected materials purchases are shown.
operating-expenses budget	A schedule included in a master budget in which projected operating expenses (that is, selling expenses and general and administrative expenses) are shown.
production budget	A schedule included in a master budget in which production activities for the budgetary period are summarized.
sales budget	A schedule included in a master budget in which projected sales for the budgetary period are shown.
statement of cash flows	A statement showing cash inflows and outflows for a reporting period divided into operating, investing, and financing subsections.

QUESTIONS FOR CLASS DISCUSSION

15–1   Why is it important for a firm to develop and use budgets? Explain.

15–2   How does the budget relate to the plan–execute–evaluate–plan cycle in the operation of a business?

15–3   Why does the development of a master budget generally begin with the preparation of the sales budget? Explain.

15–4   How does the sales budget relate to the production budget?

15–5   What decision does management typically have to make before the accountant can prepare a production budget?

15–6   What is meant by the term *formula-related items* as used in the preparation of a master budget? Explain.

15–7   What are the responsibilities of management in the preparation of the budget? What are the accountant's responsibilities in the budgeting process?

15–8   What is meant by the term *appropriation-controlled items*?

15–9   How does the purchases budget relate to the production budget? Explain.

15—10 What are two approaches to the establishment of the manufacturing-overhead budget?

15—11 Are any of the expenses included in the operating-expenses budget formula related to other budgetary data? Explain.

15—12 How are the amounts budgeted for advertising and capital expenditures generally determined?

15—13 What is the four-element equation used in preparing the cash budget? How does that budget relate to the statement of cash flows?

15—14 How is the amount of projected cash receipts from sales for a period determined? How is the amount of cash disbursements for purchases for a period determined?

15—15 What adjustment must be made to projected operating expenses and manufacturing overhead in determining the amount of projected cash disbursements for those items?

15—16 What is the difference between authoritative management and participative management in the development and use of budgetary data? Explain.

EXERCISES

15—17 **Sales Budget** Beta Company manufactures and sells mopeds. During the previous year, moped sales amounted to $1,000,000 (4,000 mopeds at $250 each). Beta's management, in planning next year's operations, will direct its efforts toward increasing the company's share of the moped market. It proposes to do that by lowering the product's sales price by 10% and by extending its sales effort into a new territory. It is estimated that Beta's volume of sales can be increased by 20% as a result of the new pricing policy and that the new territory will provide sales of 500 units of product during the first year.

REQUIRED: Prepare a sales budget for next year based on management's plans and projections.

15—18 **Production Budget** The budget committee for Avery Company projects sales of 10,000 units of its only product, Bevco, for next year. The committee also decides that finished-goods inventory should be increased from the 1,500 units expected to be on hand at the end of the current year to 2,000 units at the end of next year. Each unit of Bevco requires 2 units of material M and 2 units of material O. Inventories of these products are expected to be 900 units and 1,200 units, respectively, at the end of the current year. The budget committee wishes to reduce each of those inventories by one-third during the year.

REQUIRED:

1. Calculate the number of units of Bevco budgeted to be produced during the coming year.
2. Determine the number of units of each of the direct materials required to produce Bevco that should be purchased during the next year.
3. Explain how the numbers calculated in requirements 1 and 2 would be converted to dollars in the production and purchases budgets.

15–19 Calculating Budgeted Cash Inflows Assume that the Gerry Company budgets sales on account for the next month in the amount of $100,000. The company also expects to sell $25,000 worth of merchandise for cash during that period. An analysis of the company's credit policies and collection experience indicates that $10,000 of the $100,000 worth of sales on account will remain uncollected at the end of the month. Beginning-of-the-month accounts receivable balance is $7,000. All except $500 of that amount, which is expected to be written off as uncollectible during the period, are projected to be collected during the month.

REQUIRED: Determine the amount of budgeted cash inflows for the month.

15–20 Raw Materials Purchases Budget Bear Corporation manufactures a product that requires three component raw materials. Each unit of finished product requires 2 units of material X, 4 units of material Y, and 1 unit of material Z. Sales for the next period have been projected at 5,000 units. The budget committee proposes to increase its finished-goods inventory by 100 units during the period. However, they also wish to reduce all raw materials inventories by 25% during the budget period. The beginning inventories of materials X, Y, and Z are 200 units, 400 units, and 100 units, respectively. The company expects to buy materials X, Y, and Z for $1, $2, and $3 per unit, respectively.

REQUIRED:

1. Calculate the amount to be budgeted for purchases of each of the raw materials.
2. Assume now that the balance of accounts payable associated with the purchase of the raw materials is expected to increase from $5,000 at the beginning of the period to $6,000 at the end of the period. Calculate the amount of cash required for raw materials purchased during the period.

15–21 Manufacturing-Overhead Budget Allen Company expects to incur fixed manufacturing-overhead costs of $10,000 during the next period. It also expects variable manufacturing-overhead costs to amount to $8 per unit of finished product.

REQUIRED:

1. Calculate the amount that should be budgeted for manufacturing overhead if the production budget calls for 15,000 units of finished product.

2. Calculate the amount that should be budgeted for manufacturing overhead if the budgeted production is 20,000 units of finished product.

3. Calculate the unit cost budgeted for manufacturing overhead under requirement 1 and under requirement 2.

4. Explain the difference between the projected unit-overhead cost at the two levels of production.

15–22 **Preparation of Cash Budget** Delmar Company expects to begin its fiscal year with a $5,000 cash balance. It projects cash in the amount of $800 from cash sales and $3,000 from collections of accounts receivable during the first month of the new year. Budgeted cash disbursements for the same period include estimated payments on accounts payable, $3,200; salaries and wages, $3,300; miscellaneous selling expenses, $500; and administrative expenses, $300.

REQUIRED:

1. Prepare a budget showing projected cash flows for the month and the projected end-of-the-month cash balance.

2. Assume now that the firm wishes to maintain a minimum cash balance of $5,000. What actions must be taken during the month to meet that budgetary goal?

15–23 **Projection of Cash Inflows from Sales** Ace Company projects sales of $20,000 for January. All sales are made on account under a credit arrangement normally resulting in 40% being collected during the period of sales, 50% in the month following the period of sales, and 10% in the second month following the period of sales. Sales for the preceding November and December were $10,000 and $40,000, respectively.

REQUIRED: Calculate the projected cash inflows from sales during January.

15–24 **Projecting Cash Outflows for Purchases** Ace Company (see exercise 15–23) also buys all of its merchandise on account. Purchases in the amount of $15,000 are projected for January. All merchandise is purchased under terms calling for 2% discount if invoices are paid within 10 days. Ace plans to pay all invoices during their discount periods. Accounts payable in the amount of $4,000 (before discount) are reflected in the December 31 balance sheet. All except $3,000 of January purchases must be paid during January to realize the discount on them.

REQUIRED: Calculate the projected cash outflow for January purchases.

15–25 **Multiple Choice Items—Budgeting** Select the *best* answer for each of the following items.

1. The starting point in preparing a comprehensive budget for a manufacturing company limited by its ability to produce and *not* by its ability to sell is

a. a sales forecast.

    b. an estimate of productive capacity.
    c. an estimate of cash receipts and disbursements.
    d. a projection of fixed asset acquisitions.
  2. The primary difference between a fixed budget and a flexible budget is that a fixed budget
    a. includes only fixed costs, while a flexible budget includes only variable costs.
    b. is a plan for a single level of sales, while a flexible budget can include several plans (one for each of several sales levels).
    c. is concerned only with future acquisitions of fixed assets, while a flexible budget is concerned with expenses that vary with sales.
    d. cannot be changed after the period begins, while a flexible budget can be changed after the period begins.
  3. Companies A and B begin 19X1 with identical cash account balances, and their revenues and expenses for the year are identical in amount except that company A has a higher ratio of cash to noncash expenses. If the cash balances of both companies increase as a result of operations (no financing or dividends), the ending cash balance of company A as compared to company B will be
    a. higher.
    b. the same.
    c. lower.
    d. indeterminate from the information given.

15–26 **Calculating Budgeted Fixed Costs** The following relationships pertain to a year's budgeted activity for Simpson Company:

Direct labor hours	300,000	400,000
Total costs	$129,000	$154,000

REQUIRED:

1. Calculate the budgeted fixed costs for the year.
2. Calculate the variable costs for each level of production.

15–27 **Calculating Estimated Cash Receipts from Sales** The following information is available concerning the accounts receivable for Dantley Company.

Estimated credit sales for May	$200,000
Actual credit sales for April	$150,000
Estimated collections in May for credit sales in May	20%
Estimated collections in May for credit sales in April	70%
Estimated collections in May for credit sales prior to April	$12,000
Estimated write-offs in May for uncollectible credit sales	$8,000
Estimated provision for bad debts in May for credit sales in May	$7,000

REQUIRED: Calculate the budgeted cash receipts from accounts receivable for the month of May.

15–28 **Production and Purchases Budgets** Walton Company is budgeting sales of 42,000 units of product Y for March 19X3. To make one unit of finished product, 3 pounds of raw material A are required. Actual beginning and desired ending inventories of raw material A and product Y are as follows:

	3/1/X3	3/31/X3
Raw material A	100,000 pounds	110,000 pounds
Product Y	22,000 units	24,000 units

There is no work-in-process inventory for product Y at the beginning or end of March.

REQUIRED:

1. Calculate the budgeted production (in units) for the month of March.
2. How many pounds of raw material A does the company plan to purchase?

15–29 **Budgeted Equivalent Units of Production** Barton Company produces canned vegetable soup and is budgeting sales of 250,000 units for the month of January. Actual inventory units at January 1 and budgeted inventory units at January 31 are as follows:

	Units
Actual inventory at January 1:	
Work in process (25% processed)	10,000
Finished goods	75,000
Budgeted inventory at January 31:	
Work in process (75% processed)	16,000
Finished goods	60,000

REQUIRED: Calculate the equivalent units of production budgeted for January.

15–30 **Cash Budget** Alex Company has budgeted its activity for the month of April. Selected data from estimated amounts are:

Net income	$120,000
Increase in gross amount of trade accounts receivable during month	35,000
Decrease in accounts payable during month	25,000
Depreciation expense	65,000
Provision for income taxes (none deferred)	80,000
Provision for doubtful accounts receivable	45,000
Cash balance on April 1	5,000

REQUIRED: Determine the estimated cash balance on April 30.

15–31   **Budgeted Maintenance Cost** Brooks Company uses the following flexible budget formula for the 19X2 annual maintenance cost in department T:

Total cost = $7,200 + $0.60 per machine-hour

The July 19X2 operating budget is based on 20,000 hours of planned machine time.

REQUIRED: Calculate the budgeted maintenance cost for July.

PROBLEMS

15–32   **Sales Budget, Purchases Budget, and Cash Budget** James Company marks up its merchandise at 25% of gross purchase price. All purchases are made on account, with terms of 1/10, net/60. Purchase discounts are always taken. Normally, 60% of each month's purchases are paid for in the month of purchase, while the other 40% are paid during the first 10 days of the first month after purchase. Inventories of merchandise at the end of each month are kept at 30% of the next month's projected cost of goods sold. Terms for sales on account are 2/10, net/30. Cash sales are not subject to discount. Fifty percent of each month's sales on account are collected during the month of sale, 45% are collected in the succeeding month, and the remainder are usually uncollectible. Seventy percent of the collections in the month of sale are subject to discount, and 10% of the collections in the succeeding month are subject to discount. Projected sales data for selected months are:

	Sales on Account, Gross	Cash Sales
December	$1,900,000	$400,000
January	1,500,000	250,000
February	1,700,000	350,000
March	1,600,000	300,000

REQUIRED: Calculate the projected:

1. inventory at the end of December
2. gross purchases for January and February
3. payments to suppliers during February
4. sales discounts for February
5. total cash received from customers during February.

15–33   TLK, Inc., has prepared the following data for its business plan for the first part of 19X7:

Budgeted Sales (in thousands)

January	40
February	50
March	45
April	40
May	50

BALANCE SHEET
December 31, 19X6
(in thousands)

Cash	$ 15	Accounts payable	$ 24
Accounts receivable (net)	30	Accrued commissions	4
Inventory	24	Common stock	200
Net fixed assets	220	Retained earnings	61
Total	$289	Total	$289

Additional information:

(1) All sales are credit sales; collection history:

In month of sales	30%
In month after sales	67%
Bad debts (written off immediately)	3%

(2) Cost of sales is 60% of sales.

(3) A 9% sales commission, the only variable cost besides cost of sales, is paid based on the previous month's sales.

(4) The firm keeps ending inventory units equal to the coming month's budgeted sales.

(5) The firm pays accounts payable in the month following purchases.

(6) Fixed operating costs are $12,000 per month, including $4,000 in depreciation.

REQUIRED:

1. Prepare a projected income statement for the quarter ended March 19X7.

2. Prepare a cash budget for the first three months of 19X7 with supporting schedules (collections of accounts receivable and purchases of inventory).

3. Prepare a pro forma balance sheet as of March 31, 19X7.

15–34 **Preparation of Selling Expense Budget** The Forthright Company has projected its sales for 19X1 at three levels: high—$600,000; medium—$450,000; low—$400,000. Selling expenses for the year have been projected as follows:

Sales manager's salary	$30,000
Advertising expense	$25,000
Miscellaneous	$10,000 (plus 2% of sales)

(Continues)

Salesperson's commissions	5% of sales
Shipping and delivery expense	6% of sales

REQUIRED:

1. Prepare a selling expense budget for 19X1 showing projected selling expenses at each level of sales.
2. What percentage of sales is expected to be spent for selling expenses at each level of operations?
3. Explain the differences between the percentages at the different levels of sales calculated in requirement 2.

15–35 **Missing Data in Cash Budget** A partially completed quarterly cash budget for Bluefish Company is as follows:

	January	February	March	Quarter
Beginning cash balance	(1)	(5)	(10)	(15)
Projected cash receipts	18,000	22,000	20,000	(16)
Projected cash disbursements	20,000	18,000	(11)	(17)
Ending cash balance	5,000	(6)	8,000	(18)
Bank borrowing	(2)	(7)	(12)	(19)
Bank repayments	(3)	(8)	(13)	(20)
Adjusted ending cash balance	(4)	(9)	(14)	(21)

The company has decided to maintain a minimum cash balance of $7,000.

REQUIRED: List the numbers 1 through 21 on separate lines of a sheet of paper. After each number, enter the corresponding missing amount in the budget.

15–36 **Projection of Income Statement Data** The Elite Company is planning its next year's net income based on the following estimated data:

Cost of goods sold	$2,000,000
Administrative expenses	160,000
Sales	2,800,000
Financial expenses	60,000

These data will result in a ratio of sales to invested capital of 2 to 1. The company has a goal of producing net income before income taxes equal to 20% of invested capital.

REQUIRED:

1. Determine the amount available for marketing expenses (the only expense not included in the preceding estimates) if the company is to achieve its goal for net income before income taxes.
2. Prepare a projected income statement.

15–37 **Projection of Income Statement Data** The Littlefield Manufacturing Company has developed the following budgetary data for 19X1:

(1) The sales budget shows expected revenue of $250,000.
(2) The production budget includes the following:
  (a) Direct materials necessary to meet the production budget requirement, $70,000
  (b) Direct labor costs, $60,000
  (c) Fixed factory overhead, $10,000
  (d) Variable factory overhead expected to amount to 100% of direct labor
(3) Selling and administrative expenses are estimated at 20% of the cost of goods sold.
(4) The company wishes to realize net income before income taxes equal to 10% of sales.
(5) Inventory data:

	Anticipated 1/1/19X1	Desired 12/31/19X1
Direct materials	$10,000	$12,000
Work in process	$12,000	$16,000
Finished goods	$12,000	$10,000

REQUIRED:

1. Prepare a projected income statement for the coming year with a schedule showing in detail the computation of cost of goods sold.
2. Will the budget plan allow the company to meet its net income goal? If not, what actions might be taken? Explain.
3. Determine the amount of direct materials the company expects to purchase.

15–38 **Projection of Cash Inflows from Sales** Lamarque Dress Shop has completed its sales budget for the third quarter of 19X1. It shows the following sales data: July—$50,000; August—$60,000; September—$70,000. All sales are made on credit terms of 2% discount if paid within 10 days, with the full price due within 30 days. The projected pattern of collections on accounts receivable is:

In month of sale:	
With 2% discount taken	50%
2% discount not taken	20%
In month following sale:	
With 2% discount taken	15%
2% discount not taken	10%
Uncollectible accounts, returns, and allowances	5%

REQUIRED: Prepare a schedule in proper form showing the expected cash inflow from the collections of accounts receivable for the month of September 19X1.

15–39   Projection of Purchase Budget from Sales Data The sales budget of Zeon Department Store projects net sales for July 19X1 to be $100,800. The store also projects the July 1 merchandise inventory to be $20,000 and plans for the July 31 merchandise inventory to be $16,000. The store's selling prices are determined by adding 80% gross profit to cost of sales.

REQUIRED: Prepare a schedule in good form showing the projected purchases of merchandise for July 19X1.

15–40   Comprehensive Sales and Manufacturing Budgets The Scarborough Corporation manufactures and sells two products, ThingOne and ThingTwo. In July 19X7, Scarborough's budget department gathered the following data in order to project sales and budget requirements for 19X8:

AICPA Adapted

19X8 Projected Sales

Product	Units	Price
ThingOne	60,000	$ 70
ThingTwo	40,000	$100

19X8 Inventories, in Units

Product	Expected January 1, 19X8	Desired December 31, 19X8
ThingOne	20,000	25,000
ThingTwo	8,000	9,000

In order to produce one unit of ThingOne and ThingTwo, the following raw materials are used:

		Amount Used per Unit	
Raw Material	Unit	ThingOne	ThingTwo
A	lb	4	5
B	lb	2	3
C	each		1

Projected data for 19X8 with respect to raw materials are:

Raw Material	Anticipated Purchase Price	Expected Inventories January 1, 19X8	Desired Inventories December 31, 19X8
A	$8	32,000 lb	36,000 lb
B	$5	29,000 lb	32,000 lb
C	$3	6,000 each	7,000 each

Projected direct labor requirements for 19X8 and rates are:

Product	Hours per Unit	Rate per Hour
ThingOne	2	$3
ThingTwo	3	$4

Overhead is applied at the rate of $2 per direct labor hour.

REQUIRED: Based upon these projections and budget requirements for 19X8 for ThingOne and ThingTwo, prepare the following budgets for 19X8:

1. sales budget (in dollars)
2. production budget (in units)
3. raw materials purchase budget (in quantities)
4. raw materials purchase budget (in dollars)
5. direct labor budget (in dollars)
6. budgeted finished-goods inventory at December 31, 19X8 (in dollars).

15–41
ICMA Adapted

Projection of End-of-Budget-Period Balance Sheet Einhard Enterprises has a comprehensive budgeting program. Pro forma statements of earnings and financial position are prepared as the final step in the budget program. Einhard's projected financial position as of June 30, 19X2, is presented below. Various 19X2–X3 master budget schedules based on the plans for the fiscal year ending June 30, 19X3, follow.

All sales are made on account. Raw materials, direct labor, factory overhead, and selling and administrative expenses are credited to vouchers payable. Federal income tax expense is credited to income taxes payable. The federal income tax rate is 40%.

Einhard Enterprises

Pro Forma Statement of Financial Position
As of June 30, 19X2
($000 omitted)

Assets

Cash	$ 800
Accounts receivable	750
Direct materials inventory	506
Finished-goods inventory	648
Total current assets	$ 2,704
Land	$ 1,500
Property, plant, and equipment	11,400
Less accumulated depreciation	(2,250)
Total long-term assets	$10,650
Total assets	$13,354

Liabilities and Equity

Vouchers payable	$ 1,230
Income taxes payable	135
Notes payable (due 12/30/X2)	1,000
Total liabilities	$ 2,365
Common stock	$10,200
Retained earnings	789
Total equity	$10,989
Total liabilities and equity	$13,354

Sales Schedule, in Units and Dollars

Unit Sales	Selling Price per Unit	Total Sales Revenue
2,100,000	$16	$33,600,000

Production Schedule, in Units and Dollars

Production, in Units	Cost per Unit	Total Manufacturing Cost
2,110,000	$12.00	$25,320,000

Raw Materials Purchases Schedule, in Units and Dollars

Purchases, in Pounds	Cost per Pound	Total Purchases Cost
4,320,000	$2.75	$11,880,000

Note: Two pounds of raw material are needed to make one unit of finished product.

Direct Labor Schedule, in Units and Dollars

Production, in Units	Direct Labor Cost per Hour	Total Direct Labor Cost
2,110,000	$8	$8,440,000

Note: Each unit requires one-half of direct labor time.

Manufacturing-Overhead Schedule, in Dollars (expected activity level—1,055,000 direct labor hours)

Variable expenses	$2,954,000*
Depreciation	600,000
Other fixed expenses	1,721,000*
Total manufacturing overhead	$5,275,000

*All require cash expenditures. The manufacturing-overhead rate is $5,275,000 ÷ 1,055,000 = $5.00 per direct labor hour.

Selling and Administrative Expense Schedule, in Dollars

Selling expenses	$2,525,000
Administrative expenses	2,615,000
Total	$5,140,000

Note: All selling and administrative expenses require the expenditure of cash.

Beginning Inventory Schedule, in Units and Dollars

	Quantity	Cost per Unit	Total Cost
Direct materials	184,000 pounds	$2.75 per lb	$506,000
Finished goods	54,000 units	$12.00 per unit	$648,000

Cash Receipts and Disbursements Schedule
($000 omitted)

Cash balance 7/1/X2 (estimated)	$ 800	
Cash receipts		
Collection of accounts receivable	33,450	
Total cash available		$34,250
Cash disbursements		
Payment of vouchers payable		
Direct materials	$11,900	
Direct labor	8,400	
Manufacturing overhead	4,650	
Selling and administrative expenses	5,200	
Total vouchers payable	$30,150	
Income taxes	1,100	
Purchase of equipment	400	
Cash dividends	820	
Total cash disbursements		$32,470
Excess cash		$ 1,780
Financing		
Repayment of note payable 12/30/X2	$ 1,000	
Interest expense	50	
Total financing cost		$ 1,050
Projected cash balance 6/30/X3		$ 730

REQUIRED: Construct a pro forma statement of financial position for Einhard Enterprises as of June 30, 19X3.

15–42 **Erwin Manufacturing Case** Erwin Manufacturing Company is a new firm organized to produce one product, a valve housing the firm calls E-1. E-1 sells for $107.00 a unit in a competitive market in which Erwin Manufacturing is a price-taker (that is, Erwin Manufacturing can't control the price).

The company was organized in 19X7, but operations will not begin until January 1, 19X9. The following balance sheet as of December 31, 19X8, has been prepared:

Erwin Manufacturing Company

BALANCE SHEET

As of December 31, 19X8

Cash	$ 9,200	Capital stock	$713,500
Equipment	321,700		
Building	382,600		
	$713,500		$713,500

A $100,000 line of credit (9.75% interest) has been set up at a local bank. Necessary loans will be initiated at the beginning of a month and repayments will be at the end of a month during which the cash necessary for repayment of both principal and interest is available. A minimum cash balance of $6,500 is desired at all times.

Merchandising Operations. The firm has estimated sales for each month for the year 19X9, but expects actual sales to fluctuate around those estimates. Therefore, management has decided to maintain an ending inventory of finished goods equal to 15% of the next month's sales so that stock-out costs can be minimized.

Sales are all made on credit. Management estimates that 55% of its customers will pay in the month of sale, 27% in the following month, and 14% in the month after that. Anticipated sales are:

19X9	Units
January	350
February	525
March	740
April	960
May	1120
June	1300
July	1160
August	1320
September	1250
October	1410
November	1450
December	1290

19Y0	Units
January	1110
February	1130

The selling price is expected to remain at $107 per unit for the foreseeable future.

Monthly selling and administrative expenses are expected to be:

Commissions	7% of sales
Advertising	6% of sales
Salaries	$3,100
Supplies	1.5% of sales
Miscellaneous	$300
Travel	$1,200

Manufacturing Operations. Engineers have drawn up a standard cost for E-1 that includes the following materials and direct labor:

5 lb steel @ $8.60 per lb
$1\frac{1}{2}$ hours labor @ $15.75 per hour

Overhead is to be applied on the basis of a predetermined overhead rate derived from total estimated overhead costs and direct labor hours for the year. Monthly underapplied or overapplied overhead should be deferred until the end of the year.

At anticipated volume levels, the following factor costs are expected to be incurred each month:

Depreciation	
Equipment	$1,875
Building	$1,320
Supplies	9% of raw materials cost (not units)
Indirect labor	13% of direct labor cost
Electricity	$500 plus $0.85 per unit of production
Maintenance	$140 plus $0.45 per unit of production

In addition, two other overhead items must be required:

(1) An insurance policy with an annual premium of $4,020 must be paid one-third in January, one-third in March, and one-third in May.
(2) Taxes totaling $2,600 must be paid one-half in June and one-half in December.

The firm desires to have an ending inventory of raw materials equal to 25% of the raw materials needed for the following month's production. All purchases of raw materials will be paid two-thirds in the month of purchase and one-third in the month following purchase.

REQUIRED: Prepare, on a monthly basis, an income statement and balance sheet and the following supporting schedules for the year 19X9:

1. sales budget
2. production budget, in units
3. raw materials purchases budget
4. direct labor budget
5. factory-overhead applied budget
6. actual factory-overhead incurred budget
7. cost of goods sold budget
8. selling and administrative expense budget
9. cash receipts and disbursements budget
10. a pro forma income statement for the year
11. a pro forma balance sheet at 12/31/X9.

A printed copy of the LOTUS®1-2-3® file setup, also referred to as a template master, appears on pages 591–596.

LOTUS®1-2-3® Hints (IBM PC or compatible):

(1) Sales units must be typed in for each month. This is the *only* time you must type in data for each month. Most schedules can be prepared (in formula form) for January and *copied* to the rest of the months. Use the tab keys, along with the arrow keys, to move the cursor back and forth rather than the arrow keys exclusively. (*Note:* The shift key and tab key, pressed simultaneously, move the cursor to the left.)

(2) The "/" key pulls up the menu at the top of the screen. You may select from the menu items by moving the arrow key to the command you want and pressing the "enter" (↵) key *or* by typing the first letter of the command you wish to initiate.

(3) Raw materials purchased is *not* the same as raw materials used. There is no schedule for raw materials used because it is merely raw materials needed for production (first line of Schedule 2) multiplied by the raw material cost per pound (next to last line of Schedule 3).

(4) To find the value of the ending finished-goods inventory (next to last line of Schedule 7), divide total manufacturing cost for the month by the number of units produced during the month (to get a cost per unit) and multiply this number by the number of units desired in ending finished-goods inventory (line 2 of Schedule 2).

(5) Format your file to display only whole numbers, except where decimals are shown on the template master. With this formatting, along with compressed print (015) the entire 12-month budget will print on five pages in the spacing indicated on the template master. Even though the worksheet may display rounded numbers, the actual numbers are used in all calculations.

Good luck!

ERWIN MANUFACTURING COMPANY

MASTER BUDGET
19X9

SCHEDULE 1
Sales Budget for Year ended 12/31/X9

	January	February	March	April	May	June	July	August	September	October	November	December	Total
Units													
Price/un	------	------	------	------	------	------	------	------	------	------	------	------	------
Total	======	======	======	======	======	======	======	======	======	======	======	======	======

SCHEDULE 2
Production Budget (in units) for Year ended 12/31/X9

	January	February	March	April	May	June	July	August	September	October	November	December	January
Planned Sales													
Desired End. Inv.	------	------	------	------	------	------	------	------	------	------	------	------	------
Total needed													
Beg. Inven.	------	------	------	------	------	------	------	------	------	------	------	------	------
Production	======	======	======	======	======	======	======	======	======	======	======	======	======

SCHEDULE 3
Raw Material Purchases Budget for Year ended 12/31/X9
(In RM Units)

	January	February	March	April	May	June	July	August	September	October	November	December	
Planned Produc-tion (RM Used)													
Desired End. Inv.	------	------	------	------	------	------	------	------	------	------	------	------	
Total needed													
Beg. Inven.	------	------	------	------	------	------	------	------	------	------	------	------	
Purchases in Units													
X Cost per lb.	------	------	------	------	------	------	------	------	------	------	------	------	
Cost-RM Purc. ($)	======	======	======	======	======	======	======	======	======	======	======	======	

SCHEDULE 4
Direct Labor Budget for Year ended 12/31/X9

	January	February	March	April	May	June	July	August	September	October	November	December
Production (Units)												
Labor Hrs./Unit	------	------	------	------	------	------	------	------	------	------	------	------
Total Hours												
Labor Cost/Hour	------	------	------	------	------	------	------	------	------	------	------	------
Total Labor Cost	======	======	======	======	======	======	======	======	======	======	======	======

SCHEDULE 5
Factory Overhead Applied Budget for Year ended 12/31/X9

	January	February	March	April	May	June	July	August	September	October	November	December
Dir. Labor Hours												
Predeter. OH Rate per DL Hour	------	------	------	------	------	------	------	------	------	------	------	------
OH Applied	======	======	======	======	======	======	======	======	======	======	======	======

SCHEDULE 6
Actual Factory Overhead Incurred for Year ended 12/31/X9

	January	February	March	April	May	June	July	August	September	October	November	December
Variable Costs:												
Supplies												
Indirect Labor												
Electricity												
Maintenance	------	------	------	------	------	------	------	------	------	------	------	------
Total Variable	------	------	------	------	------	------	------	------	------	------	------	------
Fixed Costs:												
Depreciation												
Equip.												
Building												
Insurance												
Taxes												
Electricity												
Maintenance	------	------	------	------	------	------	------	------	------	------	------	------
Total Fixed	------	------	------	------	------	------	------	------	------	------	------	------
Total Overhead	======	======	======	======	======	======	======	======	======	======	======	======

SCHEDULE 7
Cost of Goods Sold Budget for Year ended 12/31/X9

	January	February	March	April	May	June	July	August	September	October	November	December
Beg. Fin. Gds. Inv.												
RM Used in Prod.												
Direct Labor												
Factory OH Applied												
Total Mfg. Cost*												
Goods Available												
End. Fin. Gds. Inv.												
Cost of Gds. Sold												

*Same as Cost of Goods Manufactured since there is no beg. or end. Work in Process

SCHEDULE 8
Selling and Administrative Budget for Year ended 12/31/X9

	January	February	March	April	May	June	July	August	September	October	November	December
Variable Expenses												
Commissions												
Advertising												
Supplies												
Bad Debt Expense												
Total Var. Exp.												
Fixed Expenses												
Salaries												
Miscellaneous												
Travel												
Total Fixed Exp.												
Total Sell. & Ad.												

593

SCHEDULE 9
Cash Receipts and Disbursements Budget for Year ended 12/31/X9

	January	February	March	April	May	June	July	August	September	October	November	December
Beg. Cash Bal.												
Cash Receipts:												
Coll. of A/Rec.	------	------	------	------	------	------	------	------	------	------	------	------
Cash Available	------	------	------	------	------	------	------	------	------	------	------	------
Cash Disburse-												
ments:												
Raw Materials												
Direct Labor												
Indirect Labor												
Electricity												
Insurance												
Taxes												
Maintenance												
Commissions												
Advertising												
Salaries												
Supplies												
Travel												
Miscellaneous	------	------	------	------	------	------	------	------	------	------	------	------
Total Disburse.	------	------	------	------	------	------	------	------	------	------	------	------
Min. Cash Balance												
Total Cash Needed												
Excess (defi-												
ciency) of Cash	======	======	======	======	======	======	======	======	======	======	======	======
Financing:												
Borrowings												
Repayments												
Interest	------	------	------	------	------	------	------	------	------	------	------	------
Total Effects-												
Fin.	------	------	------	------	------	------	------	------	------	------	------	------
End. Cash Balance	======	======	======	======	======	======	======	======	======	======	======	======

Erwin Manufacturing Company
Budgeted Income Statement
For Year Ended 12/31/X9

	January	February	March	April	May	June	July	August	September	October	November	December	SOURCE
Sales													
Cost of Goods Sold	------	------	------	------	------	------	------	------	------	------	------	------	Sch. 1
													Sch. 7
Gross Margin													
Sell. & Ad. Exp.	------	------	------	------	------	------	------	------	------	------	------	------	Sch. 8
Operating Income													
Interest Expense	------	------	------	------	------	------	------	------	------	------	------	------	
Inc. Before Inc. Tax	======	======	======	======	======	======	======	======	======	======	======	======	

Erwin Manufacturing Company
Budgeted Balance Sheet
As of 12/31/X9

	January	February	March	April	May	June	July	August	September	October	November	December	SOURCE
Assets:													
Cash													Sch. 9
Accts. Rec. (net)													
Inventories													
Raw Mate-rials													
Finished Goods													Sch. 7
Under- (Over-) Applied OH													
Prepaid Insurance													
Equipment													B. S.
Accu. Depre.-Equip													B. S.
Building													
Accu. Depre.-Bldg.													
Total Assets													
Equities:													
Accts. Payable													
Taxes Payable													
Interest Payable													
Notes Payable													
Capital Stock													B. S.
Retained Earnings													
Total Equities													

15—43 THOUGHT STIMULATION CASE—Multiple-Product Firm Budget. Budget illustrations in this chapter involve firms that produce only one product. Most firms produce multiple products and have a great deal of control over their product mix. (That is, joint product situations, where the firm has little control over product mix, are not the norm.)

Obviously, the master budget process, for most multiple-product firms, will begin with a projection of sales mix. The most desirable sales mix is one that will optimize a firm's total contribution margin. A firm will not necessarily maximize its total contribution margin by producing the product(s) with the highest contribution margin per unit. Constraining factors (machine-hours, materials, or some other factor of production) and product production requirements must be considered. The product-mix decision is considered further in Chapter 21, where we also introduce constraint theory.

REQUIRED: Assuming that the appropriate starting point in the preparation of a master budget for a multiple-product firm is sales and that the sales mix has been determined, what effect will the production of more than one product have on the budget process?

Chapter 16

Cost–Volume–Profit Analysis

Learning Objectives

When you have finished your study of this chapter, you should

1. Know the meanings of *contribution-margin ratio* and *variable cost ratio* and be able to calculate them.
2. Be able to calculate the break-even point, in units and in dollars, for both single-product and multiproduct firms.
3. Know how to extend break-even calculations to cost–volume–profit analysis relating to targeted net operating income, changing sales mix, and changes resulting from the acquisition of new equipment.
4. Understand how to incorporate the effects of taxes into cost–volume–profit analysis involving a projected after-tax net income.

An understanding of **cost–volume–profit (CVP)** analysis is one of the most vital tools for management decision making. CVP analysis begins with break-even calculations and extends through projections of the results that can be expected from various operating plans. While many of the concepts coming out of CVP analysis are intuitive and eventually could be arrived at by using common sense, mastery of the materials in this chapter will enable you immediately to recognize and use those concepts. They should benefit you throughout your business career.

Chapter 14 introduced *variable costing,* which, as an alternative to the generally accepted practice of absorption costing, provides data that are more useful in making many decisions. A key element in variable costing is the determination of the contribution margin. We have already explained how those data can be used in making four types of short-term decisions.

Chapter 15 developed procedures for building a master budget that expresses in quantitative terms the expected results of a firm's operating plans for a future period, and showed how a number of management decisions made in establishing an operating plan are used by the accountant in building the budgetary schedules. One of the most important things management needs to know in making such decisions is the way costs can be expected to behave in relation to changes in the level of operations, knowledge that enables management to see the effect a deliberate change in planned costs or planned operating procedures would have on the business's cost structure and net income.

In this chapter, we describe some of the accounting tools useful in making budgetary and other decisions that require an understanding of how costs and profits should behave in relation to changes in the volume of operations. Normally, analysis begins with **break-even analysis** and extends through various possible alterations in operating procedures and cost-incurrence plans to an understanding of the effects those changes are expected to have on net income. We call the extension of break-even techniques to a variety of potential situations **sensitivity analysis**. Our discussion includes:

1. a review of the behavior patterns of fixed and variable costs
2. an explanation of break-even analysis for a single-product firm
3. an extension of break-even analysis to multiproduct operations
4. projections of expected results of alternative projected goals and operating plans *(sensitivity analysis)*
5. an illustration of the tax considerations associated with projecting different targeted net income goals
6. a brief consideration of cash break-even analysis.

Expected Behaviors of Fixed and Variable Costs

To master CVP analysis, you must thoroughly understand fixed costs and variable costs and their behavioral characteristics (see Chapter 2). Recall that because fixed costs, in the aggregate, remain constant regardless of changes in the volume of operations within the relevant range of operating levels being considered, per-unit fixed costs vary *inversely* with changes in those operating levels. That is, as the number of units produced and sold increases, the fixed cost per unit decreases. Thus, we can graphically portray aggregate fixed costs as having a linear relationship to changes in the volume of production, as in line *A* of Figure 16–1.

Recall also that total variable costs are expected to vary directly with changes in the level of operations: as the number of units produced and sold increases, total variable costs increase. Therefore, assuming a lin-

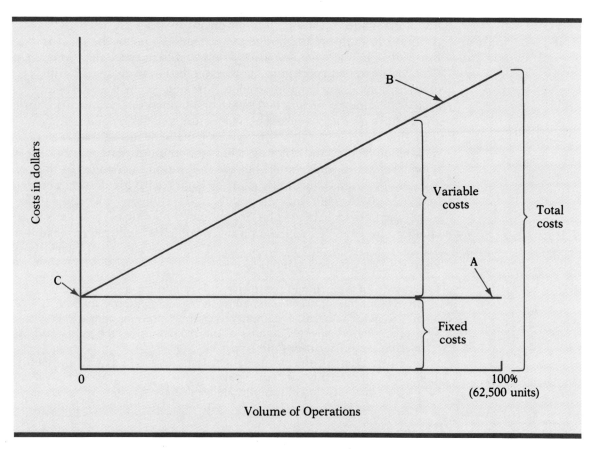

FIGURE 16–1 Relation Between Costs and Volume of Operations

ear relationship, variable costs per unit will remain constant over the relevant range of different volumes of operations being considered. As a result, variable costs can be graphed as a line sloping upward to the right (see line B of Figure 16–1). Because the variable-cost line has its zero amount equal to aggregate fixed cost in this graph (see point C), line B also can be read as expected total aggregate costs at the various levels of operations.

In Figure 16–1 the total costs of operations is the area between line B and the volume of operations shown on the horizontal axis. The amounts between those two reference points also can be expressed in the form of a linear algebraic equation:

$$TC = a + bx$$

where TC = total cost, a = aggregate fixed costs, b = variable cost per unit, and x = number of units (volume of operations).

Basic Break-Even Analysis: Single-Product Firm

In considering any business venture, a businessperson will almost certainly first want to know the level of operations required for the venture to break even. That *break-even point* is defined as the volume of sales required for revenues to exactly equal the total cost incurred in producing those revenues. At the break-even point, the firm will realize neither a net profit nor a net loss; that is,

Revenue = Total costs of producing that revenue

For a merchandising or manufacturing firm, that relationship can also be stated as follows:

Sales revenue at break-even point = Fixed costs + Variable costs

If we let S equal total sales dollars at the break-even point, the break-even relationship can be stated in terms of the linear equation just presented:

$$S = a + bx$$

S here equals the sales price per unit multiplied by the number of units (x).

If we wish to calculate the break-even point in terms of units, we can express S as px, where p is the sales price per unit. In both versions of the equation, b represents the variable cost per unit and x the number of units to be sold:

$$px = a + bx$$

where p = sales price per unit, x = number of units, a = aggregate fixed cost, and b = variable cost per unit. We then solve the equation for x, to arrive at the number of units that must be sold to break even.

To illustrate how to calculate the break-even point in units, let's assume that Blanco Company has total fixed costs (fixed manufacturing costs and fixed selling and administrative costs) amounting to $150,000, that the total variable cost per unit (including both manufacturing and selling and administrative costs) amounts to $9 per unit, and that the product sells for $15 per unit. The break-even point in units is calculated as follows:

$$\$15x = \$150,000 + \$9x$$
$$\$6x = \$150,000$$
$$x = 25,000 \text{ units}$$

Observe that $6x$ is the contribution margin per unit ($15 selling price − $9 variable costs) multiplied by the number of units required to be sold to break even. Thus, we also can express the equation for calculating the number of units required to break even as:

$$\text{Units of sales at break-even point} = \frac{\text{Fixed costs}}{\text{Contribution margin per unit}}$$

In our illustration that is

$$x = \frac{\$150,000}{\$6} = 25,000 \text{ units}$$

If sales at the break-even point are to be expressed in dollars, b in the break-even equation becomes the **variable cost percentage** (percentage relationship between variable costs and sales), sometimes called the *variable cost ratio*. The variable cost percentage can be calculated from either aggregate costs or per-unit costs by dividing variable costs by sales. The break-even equation then becomes:

$$\text{Sales in dollars} = a + (\text{Variable cost percentage}) \times (\text{Sales in dollars})$$

Or,

$$S = a + bS$$

where S = sales, in dollars, at break-even point (unknown until the equation is solved), a = aggregate fixed costs, and b = variable cost percentage. In our illustration, variable costs are 60% of the sales price:

	Per Unit	Percent
Sales	$15	100
Variable costs	9	60
Contribution margin	$ 6	40

Therefore, we can write the break-even equation as:

$$S = \$150,000 + 0.60S$$
$$0.40S = \$150,000$$
$$S = \$375,000$$

Observe that the $375,000 (break-even sales) equals the 25,000 units calculated earlier multiplied by the sales price of $15 per unit: 25,000 × $15 = $375,000. Notice also that 0.40 is the contribution margin expressed as the decimal equivalent of a percentage of sales, commonly referred to as the **contribution-margin ratio**. Thus, we also may state this break-even formula as:

$$\text{Sales, in dollars, at break-even point} = \frac{\text{Fixed costs}}{\text{Contribution-margin ratio}}$$

Or,

$$S = \frac{\$150,000}{0.4} = \$375,000$$

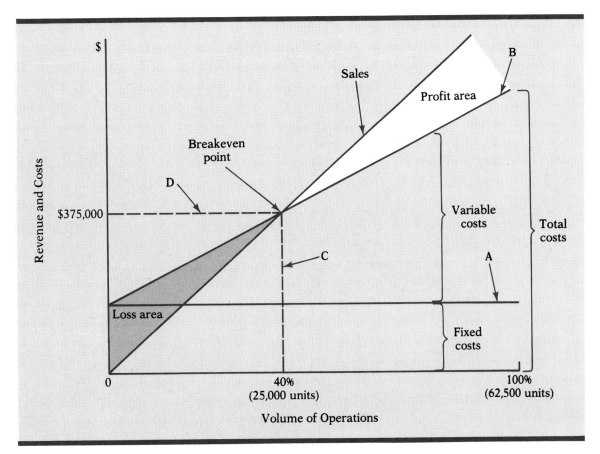

FIGURE 16–2 Break-Even Analysis Graph

The break-even analysis just presented can be shown graphically by plotting a line representing projected sales dollars at different levels of operations, as in Figure 16–2. The break-even point appears on the graph where the sales line crosses the total cost line (*B*). The units of sales required to break even can be found by drawing a vertical line (dashed line *C*) from the point where the sales and total costs lines intersect to the line representing volume of operations. The break-even point can be read as approximately 40% of capacity (25,000 units). Dollars of sales (and total expenses) at the break-even point ($375,000) also can be read directly, by drawing a horizontal line (dashed line *D*) to the vertical axis.

Because the first part of sales revenues is generally associated with the recovery of variable costs, with excess "contributions" related to the coverage of fixed costs and the generation of net income, it may be beneficial to present the data from Figure 16–2 in the form shown in Figure 16–3. Observe that the variable-costs line (line *A*) originates at the zero point and that fixed costs (area between line *A* and line *B*) are shown as additions to the variable costs.

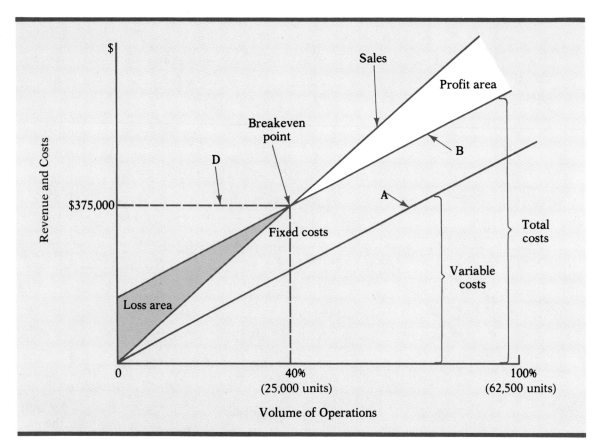

FIGURE 16–3   Alternate Break-Even Analysis Graph

Break-Even Analysis: Multiproduct Firm

For a multiproduct firm with no shared fixed costs (that is, each product has its own fixed costs), the break-even point for each product would be calculated just as for a single-product firm. However, situations where products are completely independent are rare.

In most situations, fixed costs are attributed jointly to the products being produced and sold. The individual products also typically will have different contribution margins. In these situations, we must begin our break-even analysis by determining the volume relationships (sales mix) among the products so we can develop either a weighted-average contribution margin for the projected mix of products or the contribution margin for a "sales package" that reflects the projected volume relationships. The break-even point then can be calculated via the standard equation.

One approach to the contribution-margin problem is to use the historical relationship between the aggregate variable costs of producing and selling the prior period's mix of products and the sales revenue realized from those products (variable cost percentage). That automatically provides a weighted-average variable cost ratio. The **weighted-average contribution-margin percentage** for the historical mix of products then can be determined by subtracting that percentage from 100%. To illustrate, let's assume that a firm's direct-costing-based income statement for a previous period was as follows:

	Product 1	Product 2	Product 3	Total	Percentage
Revenues	$400,000	$600,000	$500,000	$1,500,000	100%
Variable costs	300,000	390,000	360,000	1,050,000	70
Contribution margin	$100,000	$210,000	$140,000	$ 450,000	30%

and that the fixed costs for the next period are expected to be $300,000. Then the break-even point for the next period amounts to $300,000 ÷ 0.30 = $1,000,000 of sales. Such an approach implicitly assumes that the mix of the various products produced and sold will be the same during the next period as it was in the period from which the cost and sales data were drawn.

Since, as we shall see later, break-even analysis is most useful to management when the individual elements in the break-even equation can be changed to determine the anticipated results of such changes, it is generally desirable to work from the contribution-margin data for each of the individual products. This necessitates that we calculate a weighted-average amount (in dollars) of contribution margin per unit, or a *weighted-average percentage contribution margin* for each of the projected possible mix combinations of products to determine what the break-even point will be under each of the various assumptions. To illustrate, let's assume that Cinco Company is producing and selling three products—A, B, and C; that the projected sales mix (in units) for the three products is 30%, 50%, and 20%, respectively; that the contribution margins for the products amount to $5, $3, and $2 per unit, respectively; that fixed costs amount to $680,000; and that unit sales prices are $10, $8, and $5, respectively. We can calculate the break-even point in both units and dollars by using a weighted-average contribution-margin as illustrated below:

(1) Compute the weighted-average contribution margin per unit:

Product A (0.30 × $5)	$1.50
Product B (0.50 × $3)	$1.50
Product C (0.20 × $2)	.40
Total	$3.40

(2) Calculate the break-even point in units of sales:

$$\frac{\$680,000}{\$3.40} = 200,000 \text{ units}$$

(3) Separate the total units into individual quantities of A, B, and C:

Product A (0.30 × 200,000)	60,000
Product B (0.50 × 200,000)	100,000
Product C (0.20 × 200,000)	40,000
Total	200,000 units

(4) Calculate the total dollars of sales required to break even by multiplying the number of units of each product at the break-even level by its respective sales price:

Product A (60,000 × $10)	$ 600,000
Product B (100,000 × $8)	800,000
Product C (40,000 × $5)	200,000
Total	$1,600,000

The calculated break-even point can be proven as follows:

Sales		$1,600,000
Variable costs		
60,000 @ $5	300,000	
100,000 @ $5	500,000	
40,000 @ $3	120,000	920,000
Contribution margin		$ 680,000
Fixed costs		680,000
Net income		0

We can also use **sales-package contribution margin** to determine the number of units of each product that must be sold to break even. A "sales package," using the assumed percentages, would be made up of 3 units of A, 5 units of B, and 2 units of C. That projects out to a contribution margin of $34 for the "package":

Product	Package Contribution Margin
A	3 × $5 per unit = $15
B	5 × $3 per unit = $15
C	2 × $2 per unit = $ 4
	$34

With this "package" contribution margin of $34 and fixed costs of $680,000, the firm would have to sell 20,000 packages to break even:

$$\frac{\$680,000}{\$34} = 20,000 \text{ packages of products A, B, and C}$$

That total packages can then be converted to units of products A, B, and C:

Product	Units
A (20,000 × 3)	60,000
B (20,000 × 5)	100,000
C (20,000 × 2)	40,000

Another approach to calculating the break-even point for a multi-product operation involves weighing the contribution-margin percentage for each of the products by the *percentage of sales dollars* realized from each of the individual products. For our example, the contribution-margin percentages for products A, B, and C are:

	Product A		Product B		Product C	
Sales price	$10	100%	$8	100%	$5	100%
Variable costs	5	50%	5	$62\frac{1}{2}$%	3	60%
Contribution margin	$ 5	50%	$3	$37\frac{1}{2}$%	$2	40%

In most instances, the sales mix projected in dollars would be drawn from budgetary data. In our illustration, we shall assume that percentages of total sales attributed to each product are as follows:

	Product Sales	÷ Total Sales	= Percentage
Product A	$600,000	$1,600,000	37.5%
Product B	$800,000	$1,600,000	50.0%
Product C	$200,000	$1,600,000	12.5%

We then can calculate the weighted-average contribution margin:

	Sales Mix	×	Product Contribution Margin	=	Weighted-Average Contribution Margin
Product A	0.375		0.50		0.1875 (18.75%)
Product B	0.50		0.375		0.1875 (18.75%)
Product C	0.125		0.40		0.0500 (5.0%)
Total					0.425 (42.5%)

Finally, the sales dollars at the break-even point can be calculated:

$$\frac{\$680,000}{0.425} = \$1,600,000$$

This is the same amount as was projected by the units-of-sales solution illustrated earlier.

Basic Cost–Volume–Profit Assumptions

We also use the term "cost–volume–profit (CPV) analysis" to describe analyses of cost–volume relationships that deviate from specific break-even determination. The following assumptions always underlie those analyses. They should be viewed as "baggage" that must be handled rather than as "constraints" that cannot be violated. Review this list *each* time you use cost–volume–profit analysis.

• All costs can be classified as either fixed or variable.
• All costs behave in a linear manner.
• Selling prices remain constant.
• Each analysis involves only one product or a predetermined mix of products.
• Inventories do not change.
• Changes in volume are the only factors affecting costs.
• No consideration is given to the time value of money.
• All relationships occur within a relevant range of operations.

Projecting the Results of Alternate Goals and Operating Plans (Sensitivity Analysis)

The budgetary process, as explained in Chapter 15, typically requires a projection of the expected results of operations with different assumptions regarding operating plans. We now illustrate how CVP analysis is used in doing that when:

1. projected sales mix is changed
2. targeted net operating income is projected
3. effects of acquiring new equipment on the break-even point are desired.

The term *sensitivity analysis* often is used to describe these projections because they show how sensitive operating results are to changes in projected operating plans.

Changing the Sales Mix

As we have already observed, the amount of sales required to break even when producing two or more products depends on the sales mix. With the mix assumed earlier for Cinco Company (30% product A, 50% product B, and 20% product C), the firm had to sell a total of 200,000 units or $1,600,000 of sales to break even. Product A had the largest contribution-margin percentage (50%) but accounted for only 30% of total unit sales. Let's suppose the firm devises a sales plan that will increase the units of product A to 40% of total sales. They expect the sales of products B and C to be 50% and 10% of total units of sales, respectively. If this operating plan can be implemented, with no changes in other cost–volume relationships, the break-even point could be reduced to $1,562,166:

(1) Weighted-average contribution margin:

Product A (0.40 × $5)	$2.00
Product B (0.50 × $3)	1.50
Product C (0.10 × $2)	.20
Total	$3.70

(2) Break-even point in total units:

$$\$680,000 \div \$3.70 = 183,784 \text{ units (rounded)}$$

(3) Units of sales:

Product A (0.40 × 183,784)	73,514 units (rounded)
Product B (0.50 × 183,784)	91,892 units (rounded)
Product C (0.10 × 183,784)	18,378 units (rounded)
Total units	183,784

(4) Sales at break-even point:

Product A (73,514 × $10)	$ 735,140
Product B (91,892 × $8)	735,136
Product C (18,378 × $5)	91,890
Total	$1,562,166

The projected break-even point would be lowered by $1,600,000 − $1,562,166 = $37,834 as a result of this change in mix of products expected to be sold. This can be proven as follows:

Sales		$1,562,166
Variable costs		
Product A (73,514 @ $5)	$367,570	
Product B (91,892 @ $5)	459,460	
Product C (18,378 @ $3)	55,134	882,164
Contribution margin		$ 680,002
Fixed costs		680,000
Rounding error		$ 2

Projecting a Targeted Net Operating Income

Let's go back to two of our earlier illustrations and calculate the amounts of sales that would be required to realize a **targeted net operating income**. Assume that we are preparing budgetary data for Blanco Company, which produces one product selling for $15 and having variable costs of $9 per unit. Fixed costs are $150,000. We wish to determine the amount of sales that would have to be generated to produce net operating income (before taxes) of $60,000. Using the units-of-sales approach, we would calculate the sales required to meet that goal by adding the projected net income to the fixed costs that must be covered by the contribution margin in a break-even type equation:

$$\$15x = \$150,000 + \$60,000 + \$9x$$
$$\$6x = \$210,000$$
$$x = 35,000 \text{ units}$$

$$35,000 \text{ units @ } \$15 \text{ per unit} = \$525,000$$

Using sales dollars, the sales required to produce that before-tax net operating income could be calculated directly:

$$S = \$150,000 + \$60,000 + 0.60S$$
$$0.40S = \$210,000$$
$$S = \$525,000$$

We can use similar techniques to project the required sales for a multiproduct operation such as that of the Cinco Company. Let's assume management wishes to determine the amount of sales required to produce $85,000 of net operating income (before taxes). With the present mix of products (30%, 50%, and 20% for products A, B, and C, respectively), the projected sales required to meet that goal, using the units-of-product approach, can be calculated as follows:

$$\frac{\text{Units required to produce}}{\$85,000 \text{ net operating income}} = \frac{\$680,000 + \$85,000}{\$3.40}$$
$$= \underline{225,000} \text{ units}$$

0.30 × 225,000	67,500 units of A
0.50 × 225,000	112,500 units of B
0.20 × 225,000	45,000 units of C
Total	225,000

67,500 units of A @ $10	$ 675,000
112,500 units of B @ $8	900,000
45,000 units of C @ $5	225,000
Total sales	$1,800,000

We can also calculate the projected sales dollars directly by using the contribution-margin percentage:

$$\text{Sales required to produce \$85,000 net operating income} = \frac{\$680,000 + \$85,000}{0.425}$$
$$= \$1,800,000$$

If desired net operating income is stated as a percentage of sales and the sales price per unit is known, the operating income can be converted into an amount per unit and added to the variable cost per unit in the CVP equation. For Blanco Company, assume that management desires a target net operating income before taxes equal to 20% of sales. Since sales price is $15 a unit, Blanco's contribution margin of $15 sales price − $9 variable costs = $6 must cover $15 × 0.2 = $3 per unit of net operating income as well as fixed costs. Therefore, the units that must be sold to realize net operating income equal to 20% of sales can be calculated as follows:

$$\$15x = \$150,000 + \$9x + \$3x$$
$$\$3x = \$150,000$$
$$x = \$150,000 \div \$3 = 50,000 \text{ units}$$

If the sales price per unit is not known, the targeted net operating income can be factored into the direct sales-dollar approach using percentage relationships:

$$S = \$150,000 + 0.60S + 0.20S$$
$$0.2S = \$150,000$$
$$S = \$150,000 \div 0.2 = \$750,000$$

The correctness of this calculation can be proven by projecting the sales and expense elements of the income statement:

Sales (50,000 units × $15)	$750,000
Variable costs (50,000 units × $9)	450,000
Contribution margin	$300,000
Fixed costs	150,000
Net operating income	$150,000

$$\$150,000 \div \$750,000 = 20\%$$

Caution: Under *no* circumstances can a desired net operating income percentage be multiplied by some total sales dollar amount (such as break-even sales calculated without regard to operating income), and then added to fixed costs to determine the total sales needed. This is incorrect because it *assumes* a solution (the sales number used to multiply by the target income percentage) before the calculation has been performed.

Projecting the Effect of Equipment Acquisitions on the Break-Even Point

Let's assume Blanco Company is considering expanding its operations by acquiring additional sophisticated equipment that will increase fixed costs to $182,000. The equipment would provide the possibility of much larger net operating income, but managment is concerned about what the additional fixed costs would do to the company's break-even level. It is estimated that the variable costs could be reduced to $8.50 per unit if the new equipment were acquired. The new contribution margin then would be $15 − $8.50 = $6.50. The new break-even point would be:

$$\text{Units required to break even} = \frac{\$182,000}{\$6.50} = 28,000 \text{ units}$$

Thus the accountant can show management that the contemplated action would increase the break-even point from 25,000 to 28,000 units. Management will then have to decide, from that increase and information about the increase in potential net operating income, whether the firm should acquire the equipment.

The preceding illustrations only sample the alternative operating procedures that can be evaluated by use of CVP analysis. Other alternatives can be evaluated by the use of similar sensitivity analysis techniques.

Tax Considerations Associated with Targeted Net Income Goals

Up to now, we have been careful to label the targeted income as net operating income before income taxes. At break-even point, of course, there are no tax considerations involved because revenue equals expenses. At points where revenues exceed expenses, however, the tax effect must be considered in projecting the net income available to owners.

In our Blanco Company illustration, we projected a targeted net operating income before taxes of $60,000 from the sale of 35,000 units. If we assume a 40% tax rate, the "bottom line" net income projected from the sale of the 35,000 units would be $60,000 operating income before taxes − (0.4 × $60,000) in taxes = $36,000. That is, we would have projected the same number of sales in units to realize after-tax net income of $36,000. However, given a targeted net income after taxes of $60,000, we must work the tax considerations into the CVP equation to calculate the required sales. We must convert the after-tax income to a before-tax amount by dividing it by the difference between 1 and the tax rate, and then use that figure in the before-tax equation. In our illustration, that would be $60,000/(1 − 0.4) = $100,000 before taxes.

We can also incorporate the tax consideration directly into the CVP equation. Let's assume that management has targeted $60,000 as the desired net income after taxes. The number of units required to produce that can be calculated as follows:

$$\$15x = \$150,000 + 9x + \frac{\$60,000}{1 - 0.4}$$
$$\$6x = \$150,000 + \$100,000$$
$$x = \frac{\$250,000}{\$6} = 41,666\tfrac{2}{3} \text{ units}$$

$$41,666\tfrac{2}{3} \text{ units @ \$15 per unit} = \$625,000$$

The correctness of that figure can be confirmed from parts of the income statement:

Sales (41,666⅔ units @ $15)	$625,000
Variable costs (41,666⅔ units @ $9)	375,000
Contribution margin	$250,000
Fixed costs	150,000
Net operating income	$100,000
Income tax expense [0.4($100,000)]	40,000
Net income (1 − 0.4)($100,000)	$ 60,000

Sales dollars, using percentage relationships, can be calculated directly:

$$S = \$150,000 + 0.6S + \frac{\$60,000}{1 - 0.4}$$
$$0.4S = \$150,000 + \$100,000$$
$$S = \frac{\$250,000}{0.4} = \$625,000$$

We must *always* specify whether we are talking about net income *before* taxes or bottom line net income *after* taxes. If we are targeting bottom line net income (after taxes), we must use the adjustment procedures just illustrated. On the other hand, if the targeted amount is net operating income (before taxes), we can ignore the tax effect and use the formula presented earlier (see page 610) and add only the desired the formula presented earlier (see page 610) and add only the desired net operating income before taxes to fixed costs.

Cash Flow Break-Even Analysis

Sometimes management needs to know the volume of sales that would be required for cash inflows from operations to equal the cash outflows. To calculate this **cash-flow break-even point**, we begin by removing depreciation and other noncash expenses (such as amortization of patents, amortization of goodwill, and amortization of bond discount) from the expense elements of the break-even equation. In our illustration, we assume these are included as part of fixed costs.

Can we now proceed to calculate the break-even point, as described earlier, by dividing the remaining fixed costs by the contribution margin? No, for such a calculation does not consider that the noncash items removed from total fixed costs carry a tax benefit with them. To illustrate, let's return to the Blanco Company and assume that the $150,000 of fixed costs includes $30,000 of noncash items. A simplified (but incorrect) cash-flow break-even point (ignoring taxes) would then be calculated as follows:

Incorrect Cash Break-Even Point

$$\frac{\$150,000 - 30,000}{\$6} = 20,000 \text{ units}$$

This does not recognize the tax benefits associated with the $30,000 noncash costs eliminated.

A more sophisticated (and correct) cash-flow break-even point, based on an assumed tax rate of 40%, is calculated as follows:

Correct Cash Break-Even Point

$$\frac{(1 - 0.4)(\$150,000) - \$30,000}{(1 - 0.4)(\$6)}$$

$$\text{or,} \quad \frac{(1 - 0.4)(\$150,000 - \$30,000) - (0.4)(\$30,000)}{(1 - 0.4)(\$6)} = \frac{\$60,000}{\$3.60}$$

$$= 16,667 \text{ units (rounded)}$$

The numerator is a conversion of total fixed costs to after-tax outflow reduced by the tax savings generated by the $30,000 noncash items. The denominator is the after-tax contribution margin. The correctness of the calculated cash break-even figure can be proven as follows:

Sales (16,667 @ $15)		$250,005
Expenses		
Variable (16,667 @ $9)	$150,003	
Fixed costs	150,000	300,003
Loss		$ (49,998)
Tax benefit ($49,998 × 0.40)		19,999
Net loss after tax benefit		$ (29,999)
Noncash expenses		30,000
Change in cash		$ 1 (rounding error)

This assumes, of course, that the tax refund would be available immediately.

SUMMARY

In this chapter, we explained how management can use cost–volume–profit (CVP) analysis to project the effects of changes in the operating plans of a company as it develops budgetary and other data to be used in decision making. We began by reviewing behaviors of fixed and variable costs and relating those behaviors to the calculation of the break-even point for a firm producing and selling only one product.

We then covered the calculation of the break-even point for firms producing more than one product (multiproduct operations); explaining that because different products have different contribution margins, we need to determine a weighted-average contribution margin per unit or contribution-margin percentage to use in determining the break-even point stated in terms of units of product or sales dollars, respectively.

Then we explained how to use CVP analysis to project the sales required to meet targeted (before-tax) net operating income goals and new break-even points for alternative operating plans. After that, we described targeting of after-tax net income goals, with special attention given to the procedures required because of the taxes associated with that calculation. Finally, we explained how to calculate the cash-flow break-even point.

GLOSSARY OF TERMS INTRODUCED IN THIS CHAPTER

break-even analysis   Analysis of projected cost and volume data designed to show the level of operations, in terms of either dollars or units, at which a firm's total costs for a reporting period will exactly equal total revenues for the period.

cash-flow break-even point	The level of operations at which projected cash outflows will equal projected cash inflows.
contribution-margin ratio	The percentage relationship between contribution margin and sales, found by dividing contribution margin by sales.
cost–volume–profit (CVP) analysis	Analysis of the relationships between either historical or projected costs and the volume of operations; includes break-even analysis, but also extends to analysis of the level of operations required to achieve certain targeted levels of income, the effect that projected changes in operations are expected to have on the break-even level, and similar sensitivity issues.
sales mix	The relative composition of various products sold by a firm. *Product mix* (often used as a synonym) is a broader term, for it can relate to the relative composition of products manufactured and/or sold by a firm.
sales-package contribution margin	The contribution margin of a combination of products based on the expected relative volumes of the individual products to be sold. For example, if a firm manufactures and sells products A, B, and C, in the proportion 3 to 2 to 1, respectively, a sales package would be 3 units of A, 2 units of B, and 1 unit of C, and one weighted-average contribution margin can be associated with the "package."
sensitivity analysis	The process of identifying variations that might occur in projected data in relation to changes in other (key) data.
targeted net operating income	The amount of net operating income a firm wants to achieve during an operating period; typically used to project the amount of sales, in either dollars or units, that will be required to produce the desired operating income.
variable cost percentage	The percentage relationship between variable costs and sales, calculated by dividing variable costs by sales; also called *variable cost ratio*.
weighted-average contribution-margin percentage	The contribution-margin percentage expected to be achieved with a projected sales mix; calculated by weighting the dollar unit contribution margins of the products in accordance with the ratios of the numbers of units of each product expected to be sold relative to total units expected to be sold during the reporting period, *or* by weighting the contribution-margin percentages of the products by the ratios of the total sales dollars of each product expected to be sold relative to the total expected sales dollars of all products during the reporting period.

QUESTIONS FOR CLASS DISCUSSION

16–1 What is the relationship between variable costing, described in Chapter 14, and cost–volume–profit analysis? Explain.

16–2 What is the relationship between the development of a master budget, as discussed in Chapter 15, and the cost–volume relationships developed in this chapter? Explain.

16–3   How does cost–volume–profit (CVP) analysis relate to break-even analysis?

16–4   Why is it necessary to divide all costs into fixed and variable categories in projecting expected total costs at different levels of operations?

16–5   Are all costs either fixed or variable? Discuss.

16–6   What is the equation used to calculate the break-even point? Define its terms.

16–7   Should we include a provision for income tax expense in calculating the break-even point? Explain.

16–8   How can we determine the amount of variable costs expected to be incurred at the break-even point? Explain.

16–9   How is the calculation of the break-even point complicated by the production and sale of more than one product? How is that difficulty overcome? Explain.

16–10   How is a weighted-average contribution margin calculated for a firm producing and selling more than one product? Explain.

16–11   How may cost–volume–profit (CPV) analysis be used in projecting the effect of changes in sales mix? How may such data be used in the budgeting process? Explain.

16–12   What procedures are followed in projecting the required sales for a targeted net operating income? Explain.

16–13   How may the acquisition of special-purpose equipment affect the cost–volume–profit relationships for a firm? Explain.

16–14   What equation is used in projecting the sales required to produce a targeted net income after taxes? How is this projection different from the projection of sales required to produce a before-tax targeted net operating income?

16–15   How may the cash inflows required to match cash outflows be calculated?

EXERCISES

16–16   **Variable Cost and Contribution Margin** The following data apply to the Fall Corporation for the current operating period:

Total variable cost per unit	$1.75
Contribution-margin percentage	30%

REQUIRED:

1. Calculate the sales price per unit.
2. Calculate the variable cost percentage.
3. What is the contribution margin per unit?

16–17   **Contribution Margin and Break-Even Point** Hall Corporation expects to incur variable costs in the amount of $3 per unit. Sales price is $5 per unit. Assume that Hall also expects to incur $100,000 of fixed costs.

REQUIRED:

1. Determine the number of units required to break even.
2. Determine the dollar amount of sales required to break even.

16–18   **Fixed Costs at Break-Even Point** Glen Company expects to incur variable costs of $9 per unit. It expects to realize a contribution margin of 40%. Sales at break-even point have been determined to be $750,000.

REQUIRED:

1. Calculate the amount of fixed costs expected to be incurred.
2. Determine the anticipated sales price per unit.
3. Determine the number of units that must be sold to break even.

16–19   **Variable Costs and Fixed Costs** Total sales and production costs for May, Inc., are budgeted at $200,000 for 50,000 units of output. The company has a contribution margin of 40% and is contemplating increasing its sales to 60,000 units. Such a change would require a 25% increase in fixed costs and would result in total production costs of $232,000.

REQUIRED:

1. Calculate the variable cost per unit.
2. Calculate the total fixed cost at the 50,000-unit level.
3. Calculate the total fixed cost at the 60,000-unit level.
4. Calculate the amount of sales required to break even now and with the expansion of operations.

16–20   **Break-Even Analysis and Expansion of Operations** A company manufactures a product that it sells for $6 per unit. That sales price produces a 40% contribution margin. Fixed costs amount to $60,000 per year. The company is contemplating expanding its operations in a manner that would increase its fixed costs to $90,000 per year and at the same time increase its contribution margin from 40% to 45% with no change in sales price.

REQUIRED:

1. Calculate the amount of sales required to break even under the company's present operating arrangement.
2. Calculate the amount of sales required to break even if the proposed changes in operations are implemented.
3. What is the variable cost per unit with the company's present operating arrangement?
4. What is the expected variable cost per unit if the proposed changes are implemented?
5. Assume now that the maximum sales that can be realized with the present operating arrangement is $270,000. This can be increased to

$360,000 with the proposed change in operating plans. Explain, with calculations, some of the advantages and disadvantages associated with the proposed expansion project.

16–21 **Sales Required to Realize a Targeted Net Income** Tice Company is a medium-sized manufacturer of lamps. During the year a new line called "Horolin" was made available to Tice's customers. The break-even point for sales of Horolin is $200,000, with a contribution margin of 25%. Assume that net income before taxes for the Horolin line during the current year amounted to $120,000.

REQUIRED:

1. Calculate the amount of sales for the current year.
2. Calculate the fixed costs expected to be incurred by Tice.
3. Assume that Tice is subject to an income tax rate of 40%. Calculate the amount of sales required to produce a net income after taxes of $120,000.

16–22 **Selling Price Required to Yield a Targeted Net Income** Seahawk Company is planning to sell 200,000 units of product B. The fixed costs are $400,000, and the variable costs are 60% of the selling price. The company wishes to realize net income before taxes of $90,000. The tax rate is 40%.

REQUIRED:

1. Calculate the sales price required to realize the targeted before-tax net income.
2. What sales price would be required to realize net income after taxes of $90,000?

16–23 **Break-Even Point with Multiple Products** Taylor, Inc., produces only two products, A and B. These account for 60% and 40% of the total sales dollars of Taylor, respectively. Variable costs (as a percentage of sales dollars) are 60% for A and 85% for B. Total fixed costs are $210,000. There are no other costs.

REQUIRED:

1. Calculate the break-even point, in sales dollars.
2. Assume that Taylor's fixed costs increase by 30%. What amount of sales would be required to generate net income before taxes of 10% of sales.
3. Return to the original data. Assume that Taylor is able to change its sales mix to 80% A and 20% B. Calculate the new break-even point. Compare this figure with the amount calculated in requirement 1. Explain the difference.

16–24 **Elements of Break-Even Graph** The following break-even graph shows various relationships among costs, volume, and net income before taxes. Numbers are used to identify various elements of the graph.

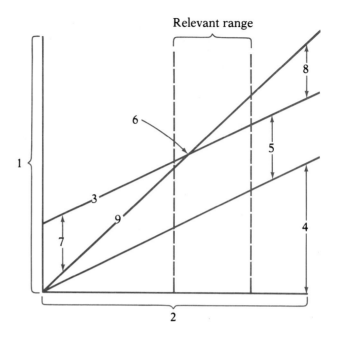

Relevant range

REQUIRED:

1. Place the numbers 1 through 9 on separate lines of a sheet of paper. Write beside each number the term used to describe the element of the graph identified by the number.
2. Discuss the significance of the term *relevant range* shown on the graph.

16–25 **Break-Even Analysis Based on Historical Income Statement Data** Buster Company presented the following summarized income statement for 19X1:

Sales (20,000 units at $40.00)		$800,000
Less expenses:		
Fixed	$400,000	
Variable (at $15.00 per unit)	300,000	700,000
Net income before income taxes		$100,000
Less income taxes at 35% effective rate		35,000
		$ 65,000

Buster Company considers the income statement results "normal."

REQUIRED:

1. Calculate the number of units and sales dollars required to break even.
2. Calculate the number of units that must be sold to produce $78,000 net income after taxes.
3. Calculate the sales dollars required to earn net income after taxes equal to 13% of sales.

16–26 **Graphic Reflection of Cost–Volume Relationships** Each of the graphs shown below reflects the behavior of a particular cost in relation to the volume of operations. Dollar amounts are shown on the vertical axis, and different levels of operations (volumes) are shown on the horizontal axis.

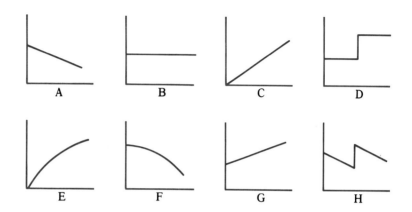

A   B   C   D

E   F   G   H

REQUIRED:

For each of the following independent cost-related terms, list the letter(s) that best reflect its relationship to volume of operations.

_____ **1.** Aggregate total costs
_____ **2.** Aggregate variable costs
_____ **3.** Aggregate fixed costs
_____ **4.** Aggregate step-variable costs
_____ **5.** Aggregate mixed (semivariable) costs
_____ **6.** Variable cost per unit
_____ **7.** Fixed cost per unit
_____ **8.** Mixed (semivariable) cost per unit
_____ **9.** Total cost per unit
_____ **10.** Step-variable cost per unit

PROBLEMS

16–27 **Contribution Margin and Fixed Costs** Runzit Equipment Company showed the following per-unit contribution margin for the year 19X1:

Selling price	$12.00
Less variable cost	5.00
Contribution margin	$ 7.00

REQUIRED: During 19X1, the company suffered a net loss of $21,000 (before recognition of tax benefit) while selling 10,000 units.

1. What was the amount of the company's total annual fixed costs for 19X1?
2. How many units would the company have had to sell during 19X1 to break even?
3. Assume now that Runzit is subject to a tax rate of 40%. How many units would have to be sold to realize net income after taxes of $21,000?

16–28
ICMA Adapted

CVP and Sales Sensitivity Analysis All-Day Candy Company is a wholesale distributor of candy. The company services grocery, convenience, and drug stores in a large metropolitan area.

Small but steady growth in sales has been achieved by the All-Day Candy Company over the past few years, while candy prices have been increasing. The company is formulating plans for the coming fiscal year. The following data were used to project the current year's after-tax net income of $110,400.

Average selling price	$4.00 per box
Average variable costs	
Cost of candy	$2.00 per box
Selling expenses	.40 per box
Total	$2.40 per box
Annual fixed costs	
Selling	$160,000
Administrative	280,000
Total	$440,000
Expected annual sales volume (390,000 boxes)	$1,560,000
Tax rate	40%

Manufacturers of candy have announced they will increase prices of their products an average of 15% in the coming year due to increases in raw materials (sugar, cocoa, peanuts, and so forth) and labor costs. All-Day Candy Company expects all other costs to remain at the same rates or levels as the current year.

REQUIRED:

1. What is All-Day Candy Company's break-even point, in boxes of candy, for the current year?
2. What selling price per box must All-Day Candy Company charge to cover the 15% increase in the cost of candy and still maintain the current contribution-margin ratio?
3. What volume of sales in dollars must the All-Day Candy Company achieve in the coming year to maintain the same net income after taxes as projected for the current year if the selling price of candy remains at $4.00 per box and the cost of candy increases 15%?

16–29   **Step-Variable Costs and CVP Analysis** Waco Corporation wishes to market a new product for $1.50 a unit. Fixed costs to manufacture this product are $90,000 for less than 500,000 units and $150,000 for 500,000 or more units. Variable costs are expected to be 80% of sales.

REQUIRED:

1. How many units must be sold to break even?
2. How many units must be sold to realize $30,000 net income before taxes?
3. How many units must be sold to realize $120,000 net income before taxes?
4. Express both requirements 2 and 3 in dollars.

16–30   **CVP Analysis with Multiple Products** Jerry Co. has fixed costs of $200,000. It sells two products, A and B, at a ratio of 2 units of A to 1 unit of B. The contribution margin is $1 per unit for A and $2 per unit for B.

REQUIRED:

1. Calculate the number of units of A and B that must be sold to break even.
2. How many units of each product would have to be sold to realize $100,000 net income before taxes?
3. Assume now that the ratio of products sold can be reversed (2 units of B to 1 unit of A). How many units must now be sold to break even?

16–31   **CVP Analysis Based on Historical Data** Bada Company had the following income statement for 19X1:

Sales (100 units at $100 a unit)		$10,000
Manufacturing cost of goods sold:		
Direct labor	$1,500	
Direct materials used	1,400	
Variable factory overhead	1,000	
Fixed factory overhead	500	
Total manufacturing cost of goods sold		4,400
Gross profit		$ 5,600
Selling expenses:		
Variable	$ 600	
Fixed	1,000	
Administrative expenses		
Variable	500	
Fixed	1,000	
Total selling and administrative expenses		3,100
Operating income		$2,500

REQUIRED: Calculate the:

1. number of units that must be sold to break even.
2. operating income if sales were to increase by 25% in 19X2.
3. break-even point if fixed factory overhead increases by $1,700 in 19X2.

16–32   **Multiple Choice CVP Analysis The Following Data Apply to Items 1–4.**
ICMA Adapted   Pawnee Company operated at normal capacity during the current year, producing 50,000 units of its single product. Sales totaled 40,000 units at an average price of $20 per unit. Variable manufacturing costs were $8 per unit, and variable marketing costs were $4 per unit sold. Fixed costs were incurred uniformly throughout the year and amounted to $188,000 for manufacturing and $64,000 for marketing. There was no year-end work-in-process inventory.

Select the *best* answer for each item.

1. Pawnee's break-even point, in sales dollars, for the current year is
   a. $732,000.
   b. $420,000.
   c. $470,000.
   d. $630,000.
2. If Pawnee is subject to an income tax rate of 30%, the number of units required to be sold in the current year to earn an after-tax net income of $126,000 is
   a. 47,250.
   b. 54,000.
   c. 57,500.
   d. 84,000.
3. Pawnee's variable manufacturing costs are expected to increase 10% in the coming year. Pawnee's break-even point, in sales dollars, for the coming year will be
   a. $700,000.
   b. $741,177.
   c. $702,000.
   d. $522,223.
4. If Pawnee's variable manufacturing costs do increase 10%, the selling price that would yield Pawnee the same contribution-margin rate in the coming year is
   a. $20.80.
   b. $20.67.
   c. $22.00.
   d. $21.33.

The Following Data Apply to Items 5–7.   Moorehead Manufacturing Company produces two products, for which the following data have been tabulated. Fixed manufacturing cost is applied at a rate of $1.00 per machine-hour.

Per Unit	XY-7	BD-4
Selling price	$4.00	$3.00
Variable manufacturing cost	2.00	1.50
Fixed manufacturing cost	.75	.20
Variable selling cost	1.00	1.00

The sales manager has had a $160,000 increase in her budget allotment for advertising and wants to apply the money on the most profitable product. The products are not substitutes for one another in the eyes of the company's customers.

Select the *best* answer for each item.

5. Suppose the sales manager chose to devote the entire $160,000 to increased advertising for XY-7. The minimum increase in *sales units* of XY-7 required to offset the increased advertising would be
   a. 640,000 units.
   b. 160,000 units.
   c. 80,000 units.
   d. 128,000 units.

6. Suppose the sales manager chose to devote the entire $160,000 to increased advertising for BD-4. The minimum increase in *sales dollars* of BD-4 required to offset the increased advertising would be
   a. $160,000.
   b. $320,000.
   c. $960,000.
   d. $1,600,000.

7. Suppose Moorehead has only 100,000 machine-hours that can be made available to produce XY-7 and BD-4. If the potential increase in sales units for either product resulting from advertising is far in excess of these production capabilities, which product should be advertised and produced, and what is the estimated increase in contribution margin earned?
   a. Product XY-7 should be produced, yielding a contribution margin of $75,000.
   b. Product XY-7 should be produced, yielding a contribution margin of $133,333.
   c. Product BD-4 should be produced, yielding a contribution margin of $250,000.
   d. Product BD-4 should be produced, yielding a contribution margin of $187,500.

16–33   **CVP and Expense Sensitivity Analysis** R. A. Ro and Company, maker of
ICMA Adapted   quality hand-made pipes, has experienced a steady growth in sales for the past 5 years. However, increased competition has led Mr. Ro, the president, to believe that an aggressive advertising campaign will be necessary next year to maintain the company's present growth.

To prepare for next year's advertising campaign, the company's accountant presented Mr. Ro with the following data for the current year, 19X2:

Cost Schedule

Variable costs:	
Direct labor	$ 8.00/pipe
Direct materials	3.25/pipe
Variable overhead	2.50/pipe
Total variable costs	$13.75/pipe

(Continues)

Fixed costs:	
Manufacturing	$ 25,000
Selling	40,000
Administrative	70,000
Total fixed costs	$135,000
Selling price, per pipe	$ 25.00
Expected sales, 19X2 (20,000 units)	$500,000
Tax rate	40%

Mr. Ro has set the sales target for 19X3 at a level of $550,000 (or 22,000 pipes).

REQUIRED:

1. What is the projected after-tax net income for 19X2?
2. What is the break-even point, in units, for 19X2?
3. Mr. Ro believes an additional selling expense of $11,250 for advertising in 19X3, with all other costs remaining constant, will be necessary to attain the sales target. What will be the after-tax net income for 19X3 if the additional $11,250 is spent?
4. What will be the break-even point, in dollar sales, for 19X3 if the additional $11,250 is spent for advertising?
5. If the additional $11,250 is spent for advertising in 19X3, what is the required sales level, in dollar sales, to equal 19X2's after-tax net income?
6. At a sales level of 22,000 units, what is the maximum amount that can be spent on advertising if an after-tax net income of $60,000 is desired?

16–34
ICMA Adapted

CVP and Cash Flows Mr. Calderone started a pizza restaurant in 19X0. For this purpose a building was rented for $400 per month. Two women were hired to work full-time at the restaurant, and six college students were hired to work 30 hours per week delivering pizza. An outside accountant was hired for tax and bookkeeping purposes. For this service, Mr. Calderone pays $300 per month. The necessary restaurant equipment and delivery cars were purchased with cash. Expenses for utilities and supplies have been rather constant. Mr. Calderone increased his business between 19X0 and 19X3, and profits have more than doubled since 19X0, but Mr. Calderone does not understand why his profits have increased faster than his volume.

A projected income statement for 19X4 has been prepared by the accountant and is shown at the top of page 627.

Note: The average pizza sells for $4.00. Assume that Mr. Calderone pays out 30% of his income in income taxes.

REQUIRED:

1. What is the break-even point, in number of pizzas that must be sold?
2. What is the cash-flow break-even point, in number of pizzas that must be sold?
3. If Mr. Calderone withdraws $4,800 for personal use, how much cash will be left from the 19X4 income-producing activities?

Calderone Company

Projected Income Statement

For the year ended December 31, 19X4

Sales		$95,000
Cost of food sold	$28,500	
Wages and fringe benefits of restaurant help	8,150	
Wages and fringe benefits of delivery people	17,300	
Rent	4,800	
Accounting services	3,600	
Depreciation of delivery equipment	5,000	
Depreciation of restaurant equipment	3,000	
Utilities	2,325	
Supplies (soap, floor wax, etc.)	1,200	73,875
Net income before taxes		$21,125
Income taxes		6,338
Net income		$14,787

4. Mr. Calderone would like an after-tax net income of $30,000. What volume must be reached, in number of pizzas, in order to obtain the desired income?

5. Briefly explain to Mr. Calderone why his profits have increased at a faster rate than his sales.

6. Briefly explain to Mr. Calderone why his cash flow for 19X4 will exceed his profits.

16–35

ICMA Adapted

THOUGHT-STIMULATION PROBLEM Candice Company has decided to introduce a new product. The new product can be manufactured by either a capital-intensive method or labor-intensive method. The manufacturing method will not affect the quality of the product. The estimated manufacturing costs by the two methods are as follows:

	Capital Intensive	Labor Intensive
Raw materials	$5.00	$5.60
Direct labor	0.5 direct labor hour @ $12: $6.00	0.8 direct labor hour @ $9: $7.20
Variable overhead	0.5 direct labor hour @ $6: $3.00	0.8 direct labor hour @ $6: $4.80
Directly traceable incremental fixed manufacturing costs	$2,440,000	$1,320,000

Candice's market research department has recommended an introductory unit sales price of $30. The incremental selling expenses are estimated to be $500,000 annually, plus $2 for each unit sold (regardless of manufacturing method).

The estimated break-even point, in annual unit sales of the new product, using each method is:

Capital-Intensive Manufacturing Method:

$$\frac{\$2,440,000 + \$500,000}{\$14} = 210,000 \text{ units}$$

Labor-Intensive Manufacturing Method:

$$\frac{\$1,320,000 + \$500,000}{\$10.40} = 175,000 \text{ units}$$

REQUIRED:

1. How would Candice Company determine the annual unit sales volume at which the firm would be indifferent between the two manufacturing methods?
2. Suppose the capital-intensive manufacturing method involved the elimination of all direct labor. How would break-even analysis be affected?
3. Identify the business factors that Candice must consider before selecting the capital-intensive versus labor-intensive manufacturing method.

Chapter 17

Controlling Operations

Learning Objectives

When you have finished your study of this chapter, you should

1. Understand responsibility accounting and the procedures followed in implementing it.
2. Understand how goals are established for managers and how those goals are used in evaluating managerial performance.
3. Know how to control costs for merchandising operations, service enterprises, and manufacturing operations.
4. Be able to perform gross-margin analysis for single-product and multiproduct firms.
5. Be able to prepare a schedule relating elements of manufacturing-overhead variance to specific overhead items.
6. Be aware of the ways in which employees may be motivated to meet their operational responsibilities.

C hapter 16 explained how cost–volume–profit (CVP) analysis can be used to determine the expected break-even point for a business and the projected results of alternative operating plans as its master budget is developed. In this chapter, we discuss the use of information about a business's costs and revenues as the "execute" and "evaluate" phases of its plan–execute–evaluate–plan cycle unfold.

One of the principal overall long-term objectives of a business is to maximize the return to owners in the form of net income. Sales prices basically are controlled by forces of the marketplace. Management's pricing options primarily involve being either aggressive (that is, taking the lead in changing prices) or passive (that is, following the pricing lead of other companies). The costs associated with the operations of a business, however, can, within certain limits, be controlled by management. Therefore, the primary emphasis in this chapter will be on increasing income by controlling costs.

In identifying the data needed by managers at various levels to control costs, we begin by recognizing that top-level managers will be interested in the *overall* relationships between costs and revenues. Lower-level managers, on the other hand, are responsible for controlling the operations of *segments* of the business, and, therefore, are concerned with **segment revenue and cost data**. The accountant must provide data useful to *both* of these groups in controlling those parts of a company's operations for which they are responsible.

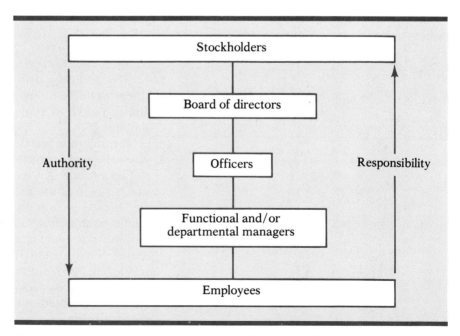

FIGURE 17–1   A Business's Authority–Responsibility Relationships

A fundamental requirement in controlling a firm's costs is to make specific employees responsible for managing identifiable elements of the firm's operations. This means the business's organization must clearly spell out authority–responsibility relationships. Figure 17–1 shows how responsibility is delegated by the stockholders (owners of a business) to the officers and ultimately to lower-level managers: Authority runs from the top of the organization downward, while responsibility runs in the other direction.

Typically, a company will have a formal organization chart, such as the one shown in Figure 17–2, with detailed job descriptions for each of the positions listed. Notice that the plant superintendent, often designated as vice-president in charge of production, delegates authority

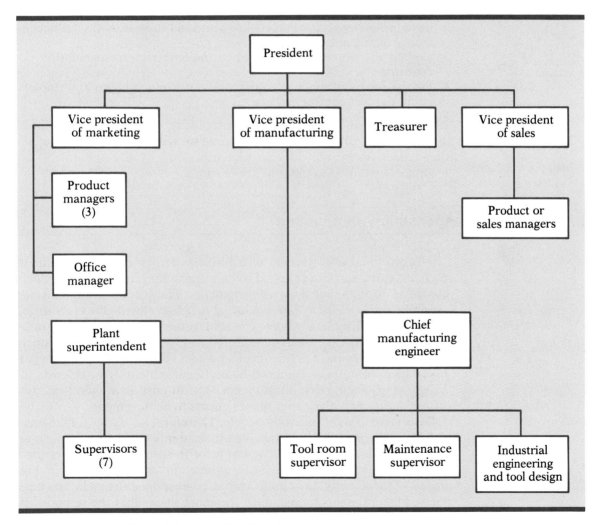

FIGURE 17–2 A Formal Organization Chart

to the various departmental supervisors, meaning that the operating responsibilities extend upward from the departmental supervisors to the plant superintendent and ultimately to the president of the company. The president, of course, is accountable to the board of directors, which represents the stockholders, for the overall results of operations.

Within such an operating framework, the accountant should develop a system of data accumulation and allocation that will show the extent to which each person responsible for a segment of the firm's operations has measured up to the challenge of the authority granted in carrying out his or her activities. As we consider the subsystem to be used in allocating and accumulating the data designed to facilitate the control of operations, we shall:

1. develop an overview of the elements of a responsibility accounting system
2. explain how goals are established and used in evaluating the performance of managers at all levels
3. explain the procedures followed in implementing responsibility accounting
4. discuss the importance of proper motivation of managers and employees in the cost-control process.

Division or segment managers are responsible for generating revenues as well as controlling costs. Therefore, as we will explain in Chapter 18, their effectiveness typically will be measured by the amount of net income contributed to the firm's operations.

Introduction to Responsibility Accounting

The operational effectiveness of a business entity, or any segment of such an entity, can be evaluated by relating achievements to the efforts expended in realizing those achievements. The income statement, for example, provides information relating to achievement/effort factors for the business entity as a whole. The achievements are reflected as revenues. The efforts expended are reflected as expenses. We evaluate operational effectiveness of segments of a business entity by relating output, in the form of units or standard hours (achievements), to the costs incurred in producing that output (efforts). Unit-cost data, therefore, constitute another measure that relates efforts to achievements.

Costs must be controlled by people. Therefore, as top-level managers delegate responsibilities to specified individuals within the firm, those individuals should be held accountable for the proper execution of their responsibilities. We can use an organization chart like that in Figure 17–2 to formally show those authority–responsibility relationships. Viewed from the top, for example, the chart shows that the responsibility for overall manufacturing activities has been delegated to the vice-president of manufacturing, who in turn delegates the responsibility for the production of goods to the plant superintendent, who then delegates the responsibilities for controlling individual departments to the departmental supervisors. Viewed from the bottom up, the organization chart shows that departmental supervisors are responsible to the plant superintendent, who in turn is responsible to the vice-president in charge of manufacturing, who is responsible to the president of the organization for all manufacturing activities.

In another part of the organization chart, we see a vice-president being held responsible for carrying out the sales (marketing) efforts of the company. Product sales managers, in turn, are responsible to that vice-president for amounts of sales of each product. In other situations, these authority–responsibility relationships may be delegated on a territorial basis rather than by product. Achievements for sales employees, no matter how the marketing department is structured, will be measured in terms of sales generated; their efforts will be reflected in the costs they incur in generating those sales. Thus, effort–achievement relationships can be measured in terms of the relationship between sales expenses and the sales revenue generated.

We refer to the technique of systematically allocating costs to the cost centers responsible for incurring them as **responsibility accounting.** In effect, the accountant organizes the firm's record-keeping system so that performance reports may be prepared for each cost-accumulation center and for each product or territory, depending on the firm's organizational structure. In that way, a specific identifiable person (manager) will be held responsible for each specific segment of operations. Such reports provide feedback to managers that will be helpful in controlling (that is, improving) future operations. None of us can change what has already occurred, but we can use historical data to identify problems that should be solved and opportunities that should be explored prior to carrying out future operations.

The underlying concept of responsibility accounting may best be understood by recognizing in the organization chart of Figure 17–2 that costs are allocated to the different operating centers managed by *designated* individuals; the firm's president is charged by the stockholders with the responsibility of earning an appropriate return on their invested capital. Either directly or indirectly, the chief executive officer's success will be measured by the extent to which that goal has been achieved. At the same time, the stockholders provide the president with the authority to use the firm's resources as he or she sees fit in carrying out company operations. How the president has discharged that responsibility to the stockholders is then evaluated by measuring the rate of return earned on the firm's resources, most directly in terms of earnings per share, which can be related to the market price of the stock, along with the change in market price since the investment was acquired, to arrive at the rate of return on their investments.

Just as the stockholders have delegated authority and responsibility for general operational effectiveness to the president, that person in turn delegates authority and responsibility to the managers under his or her supervision. Those managers are given authority to incur costs in operating their segments of the business and at the same time are held responsible for properly controlling those costs or generating revenues so that overall operations will be appropriately profitable.

It is important that the performance reports developed via responsibility accounting be organized so they highlight the things important in controlling costs or in realizing revenues at the level of responsibility assigned to each individual manager. Generally, the higher the level of management to which the report is being addressed, the more comprehensive the scope and the more condensed the details of the report must be. (See Figure 17–3.) No report should be made more complex than is necessary to carry the message it is intended to convey.

Thus, the president of a company is primarily interested in the income statement for the company as a whole. The vice-president of sales is held accountable for sales revenues generated and the expenses incurred in generating those sales. The vice-president of manufacturing is concerned with controlling setup, tooling, maintenance, and production costs. The vice-president in charge of production or the plant superintendent is concerned with the overall costs of production, and the chief manufacturing engineer is responsible for managing tooling, maintenance, and designs. The various departmental supervisors are primarily concerned with the aggregate costs incurred in operating their departments over specified periods of time and the costs per unit of output (units or standard hours) produced during the period.

Also, as a general rule, reports to higher-level managers can cover longer periods of time than those made to departmental supervisors

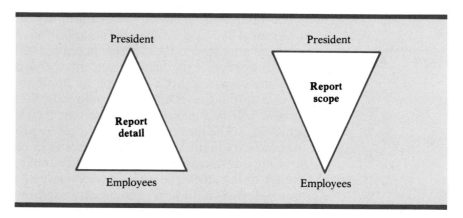

FIGURE 17–3 Report Detail and Scope Vary According to Where on the Organizational Structure the Report Is Aimed

and other lower-level managers. Thus, while it is generally important that a departmental supervisor be advised each day of certain cost–output relationships for the preceding day (so adjustments may be made on a timely basis), the company president may need financial statements no more than once a month.

The designer of a responsibility accounting system should clearly recognize the problem of emphasizing local performance to the detriment of overall firm performance, however, and continuously evaluate the appropriateness of selected measures. (See Chapter 24.)

Establishment and Use of Cost-Incurrence Goals

Parts II and III of this text show how cost accounting systems accumulate and allocate costs to the various segments and products of a business. Performance reports, which in some way relate efforts to achievements, are prepared for each of those segments. Managers then must have something to measure those performance results against as they evaluate operations. We generally refer to these measuring sticks or benchmarks as *operating goals*. Only with this type of comparison can cost-incurrence decisions be appropriately evaluated. At the point of sale, for example, a top management official can compare total costs with selling prices to judge the adequacy of the margin realized. However, lower-level managers, who are charged with controlling costs in the various stages of production, will need other guidelines for evaluating the efficiencies of their activities—for example, relating cost data for the current period to that from other periods, in which case, the historical cost data are being used as standards or goals in measuring the effectiveness of the current cost-incurrence decisions. More frequently, however, we relate departmental cost data to the goals established during the development of the budget, preferably based on standard costs.

Perhaps the most common and most effective goals are developed from standard costs. Most firms today use standard costs in developing budget data that are used to evaluate the effectiveness of segments of operations. When cost goals have been established, managers are then concerned with determining whether or not the costs incurred are within the established guidelines. If there are significant deviations, the causes of the deviations should be determined so that operating procedures may be modified in future periods to more nearly achieve the projected results.

Regardless of the standard used (historical cost, standard cost, competitor's cost, or whatever), the subordinate manager and his or her supervisor *must* have something to measure actual achievements against to determine whether or not the costs incurred are appropriate for the results achieved. Furthermore, by making this comparison, along with an analysis showing reasons for the differences between actual and expected costs, decisions can be made as to what should be done to improve cost-incurrence procedures in the future.

As observed in Chapters 11–13, a standard cost system emphasizes variances from standard costs. Some of the employees within a firm typically held responsible for explaining those variances are:

- materials price variance: purchasing agent
- materials quantity or usage variance: departmental supervisors in charge of departments that process the materials
- direct labor rate variance: departmental supervisors or, possibly, personnel department manager
- direct labor efficiency variance: departmental supervisors under whose supervision the employees causing the variance worked
- controllable or budget overhead variance: departmental supervisors
- overhead volume variance: sales manager.

Thus, the variance reports developed within a standard costing system constitute one part of a responsibility accounting system designed to control manufacturing costs. The goals (or standards) against which actual costs are measured in that part of the system are the quantities and dollar amounts shown on the standard cost cards.

Implementing Responsibility Accounting Procedures

As just stated, variances from operating goals are used in controlling cost. For example, variances from the standards included in standard cost data are used in controlling direct materials costs, direct labor costs, and manufacturing-overhead costs. We will now extend our discussion of responsibility accounting to the data that can be used in controlling the costs of merchandising operations and service enterprises, as well as manufacturing operations.

Controlling Costs of Merchandising Operations

As observed earlier, the relationship between achievements (revenues) and efforts (expenses incurred to earn those revenues) is important in evaluating the overall effectiveness of a firm's operations. In a merchandising firm, or the merchandising operations of a manufacturing firm, this evaluation involves the analysis and management of changes in gross margin and the management of operating expenses.

Analysis of Changes in Gross Margin. Since the relationship between the cost of goods and the price those goods can command in the market is an important indicator of the operational effectiveness of merchandising operations, a firm's manager must carefully monitor both the dollar amount of gross margin and its percentage relationship to sales over sequential operating periods. As those data are evaluated, the manager seeks to understand what has caused the gross margin to change, so that appropriate actions may be taken. Obviously, the manager wants to eliminate or change any actions that reduce the margin amount and to continue or possibly expand any actions that increase gross margin. Effective analysis of those data begins with the recognition that any difference in the dollar amount of gross margin from one period to another or between actual and projected results can be caused either by a change in the relationship between cost and sales price—**gross-margin (profit) variance**—or by a change in the volume of goods sold—**(sales volume variance)**.

An unfavorable change in the relationship between cost and sales price may be the responsibility of the buyer if the goods have not been purchased at the best available cost. Or the change may have been caused by deliberate reductions in sales prices in an attempt to increase the volume of sales. A third cause could be greater competition or a weaker economy that has forced down the sales price. Once an unfavorable gross-margin variance has been identified, management should try to trace it to one or more of these three causes. If the variance has been caused by higher-than-expected purchase prices, the buyers should be consulted. If sales prices have been reduced in an attempt to increase sales volume, it should be determined whether the expected increase in volume variance (see next paragraph) has occurred. If the variance is attributed to greater competition or a weaker economy, management should consider appropriate actions (diversification, for example). In any event, a sales price variance is calculated by multiplying the actual number of units sold by the *change* (from previous year or from budget) in sales price per unit.

A decline in volume of goods sold is an unfavorable change, and generally would be considered the responsibility of the sales department. (If the sales department obtained orders that could not be filled because they could not be produced, however, the production department would be responsible for the unfilled-order portion of the sales volume variance.) In controlling changes in gross margin, a dollar amount should be assigned to the portion of the change caused by the change in volume. Supply-and-demand factors, though, can cause trade-offs between the gross-margin variance and the sales volume variance that are beyond the control of the sales department. Management may deliberately initiate a sales pricing policy that causes one of these variances to be unfavorable, with the intention of more than compensating for that variance through a favorable performance in the other variance. This can occur, for example, when the sales price is reduced—thus creating an expected unfavorable gross-margin variance—with the objective of realizing a favorable sales volume variance in excess of the unfavorable margin variance. The dollar amount assigned to the portion of the change caused by the change in volume is calculated by multiplying the difference between the actual and expected volumes, expressed in units, by the expected margin per unit.

To illustrate, let's assume a firm sells 10,000 units of product X at $10 per unit in year 1, thereby producing sales in the amount of $100,000, and that the cost of goods sold during that period amounts to $6 per unit, thus allowing the firm to earn a gross margin of $40,000, or $4 per unit. In year 2, management attempts to secure a larger share of the market by lowering the sales price to $9 per unit, in the hope that a sales volume increase will more than compensate for the effect of the price decrease. And volume increase also may allow unit costs to be reduced through better purchasing arrangements. The primary objective is to increase total gross margin by selling more units. During year 2, the firm is able to increase its sales to 13,000 units, and the increased volume enables it to reduce cost per unit to $5.50. The results may be summarized as follows:

	Year 1	Year 2
Sales		
10,000 units @ $10	$100,000	
13,000 units @ $ 9		$117,000
Cost of sales		
10,000 units @ $ 6	60,000	
13,000 units @ $ 5.50		71,500
Gross margin	$ 40,000 ($4/unit)	$ 45,500 ($3.50/unit)

Sales for year 2 amounted to $117,000, with cost of sales at $71,500, thus producing a gross margin of $45,500, an increase over year 1 of $45,500 − $40,000 = $5,500.

We can analyze the change caused by this action by treating the data from year 1 as the standards against which year 2 results are evaluated. First, the sales and costs of sales may be separately analyzed:

Sales price variance [13,000 units × ($9 − $10)]	$13,000 (U)
Sales volume variance [(13,000 units − 10,000 units) × $10]	30,000 (F)
Sales variance	$17,000 (F)

Cost of sales cost variance [13,000 units × ($5.50 − $6)]	$ 6,500 (F)
Cost-of-sales-volume variance [(13,000 units − 10,000 units) × $6]	18,000 (U)
Cost-of-sales variance	$11,500 (U)

Gross-margin variance: $17,000 (F) − $11,500 (U) = $5,500 (F)

The gross margin variance also can be analyzed as follows:

Margin (price−cost) variance [13,000 units × ($4 − $3.50)]	$ 6,500 (U)
Volume variance [(13,000 units − 10,000 units) × $4]	12,000 (F)
Total gross-margin variance	$ 5,500 (F)

These analyses are summarized in Figure 17–4. If cost of sales is composed entirely of variable costs (as generally would be the case for a merchandising firm), gross margin and contribution margin from sales would be identical. In this example, the $5,500 (F) gross-margin variance also would be the contribution-margin variance.

If actual sales prices are less than expected, the sales price variance will be unfavorable. If actual costs are less than expected, however, the cost−price variance will be favorable. With volume variances, it should be obvious that a decrease in units sold from those expected to be sold results in an unfavorable sales volume variance and a favorable cost-of-

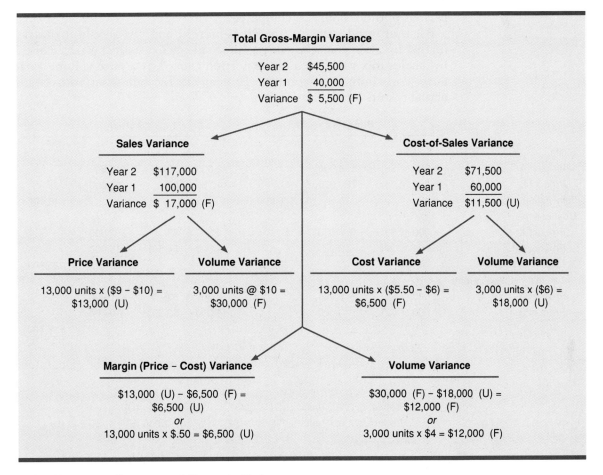

FIGURE 17–4 Summary of Example Variances

sales-volume variance. (Think about a firm's attitude toward sales versus its attitude toward costs to determine the "sign" of the variance.)

In our illustration, management should not interpret the increase in margin resulting from its pricing policy necessarily to justify further price reductions. When the loss of margin caused by decreasing the sales price finally exceeds the increase in margin attributed to a larger sales volume, management may perhaps improve the margin only by increasing sales price. If the product's demand curve were known, this point could be calculated. Unfortunately, this information is almost never available in advance of action.

The purchasing department can be very important to the firm in the situation just described by favorably controlling the cost of goods acquired for resale, that is, by securing (a) the best possible prices for the goods, (b) favorable cash discount terms, and (c) lower transportation costs per unit as goods are purchased. As part of this effort, costs for similar items from various vendors and costs for identical items over periods of time should be compared.

For multiproduct firms, the gross-margin analysis should include a further breakdown of the sales volume variance into the portion caused by a **sales mix variance** and the portion caused by a **pure volume variance**. For example, assume the JP firm has the following budget and actual results for the current year:

	Budgeted			Actual		
Sales						
Product A	(1,000 @ $8)	$ 8,000		(2,600 @ $6)	$15,600	
Product B	(5,000 @ $6)	30,000		(4,000 @ $7)	28,000	
Total sales			$38,000			$43,600
Cost of sales						
Product A	(1,000 @ $3)	$ 3,000		(2,600 @ $3)	$ 7,800	
Product B	(5,000 @ $4)	20,000		(4,000 @ $4.50)	18,000	
Total cost of sales			23,000			25,800
Gross margin (gross profit)						
Product A	(1,000 @ $5)	$ 5,000		(2,600 @ $3)	$ 7,800	
Product B	(5,000 @ $2)	10,000		(4,000 @ $2.50)	10,000	
			$15,000			$17,800

The margin (cost–price) and volume variances may then be calculated:

Margin (price–cost) variance		
Product A: 2,600 units × ($3 − $5)	$5,200 (U)	
Product B: 4,000 units × ($2.50 − $2)	2,000 (F)	$3,200 (U)
Volume variance		
Product A: (2,600 − 1,000)($5)	8,000 (F)	
Product B: (4,000 − 5,000)($2)	2,000 (U)	6,000 (F)
Net variance in gross margin		$2,800 (F)

Furthermore, when more than one product is involved, we can apportion the volume variance into the part caused by the change in mix of products sold and the part attributed only to the change in volume. In this example, the JP firm expected to sell 1,000 units of product A and 5,000 units of product B. If the product mix proportions remain the same for any total number of units sold, the firm would expect 1/6 of them to be product A and 5/6 of them to be product B (based on the original 1 : 5 relationship). Therefore, out of *total actual sales* of 2,600 units of product A + 4,000 units of product B = 6,600 units, about 1/6, or 1,100, were expected to be product A and 5/6, or 5,500, were expected to be product B:

	Budgeted Units	Expected Units
Product A	1,000	1/6 × 6,600 = 1,100
Product B	5,000	5/6 × 6,600 = 5,500
Total	6,000	6,600

We can now show that the firm had a $4,500 favorable sales mix variance:

Product A: (2,600 − 1,100) × ($8 − $3)	$7,500 (F)
Product B: (4,000 − 5,500) × ($6 − $4)	3,000 (U)
Total sales mix variance	$4,500 (F)

The pure volume variance can be calculated as follows:

Product A: (1,100 − 1,000) × ($8 − $3)	$ 500 (F)
Product B: (5,500 − 5,000) × ($6 − $4)	1,000 (F)
Total pure volume variance	$1,500 (F)

The sum of the sales mix variance and the pure volume variance equals the volume variance for the JP firm:

Sales mix variance	$4,500 favorable
Pure volume variance	1,500 favorable
Total (sales volume variance)	$6,000 favorable

These relationships are summarized in Figure 17–5.

The appendix to this chapter illustrates a triangle approach to gross-margin analysis that is similar to the triangle analysis of standard cost variances introduced in the appendixes to Chapters 12 and 13.

Managing Operating Expenses. Operating expenses include the costs incurred in carrying out the selling and administrative functions of a

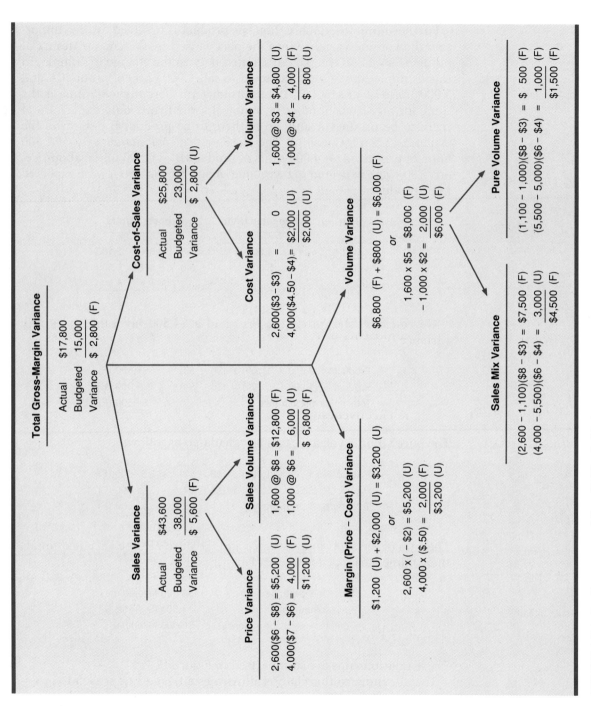

FIGURE 17–5 Summary of the JP Firm's Variances

business. Selling expenses constitute an important element of costs for most businesses. For analytical and control purposes, it is desirable to divide those expenses into three categories: advertising expenses, direct selling expenses, and shipping expenses. The last two should then be subdivided into fixed and variable elements.

As we observed in Chapter 15, the amount a firm spends on advertising depends largely on what management appropriates or sets aside for that purpose. Therefore, this expense can be treated as discretionary (determined by management policy). Obviously, the decision to spend any specified amount for advertising has to be based on the assumption that the advertising will produce future benefits in the form of increased sales. However, the benefits realized from most advertising programs typically lag significantly behind the time of cost incurrence and, for that reason, cannot be controlled by expecting them to be formula-related to current-period sales.

Ideally, the accountant would like to recognize advertising costs as expenses in the period(s) benefiting from those expenditures so as to better relate efforts to achievements (match costs against revenues). However, because there often is no objective way to determine the time when the benefits of advertising expenditures will be realized in the form of increased sales, the accountant takes a conservative position and requires these outlays to flow into the income statement as expenses during the periods in which the advertising services are rendered. Nevertheless, management must make some general judgments as to the effectiveness of advertising outlays by relating them to increases in future-period sales. Largely on the basis of such analyses, even though very general and imprecise, management will judge whether specific advertising programs should be continued, enlarged, or curtailed.

Direct selling expenses include both fixed and variable costs. For example, sales employees' salaries established at a specified amount per week or per month and depreciation on sales office space and equipment, within a relevant range of sales, are fixed expenses, whereas sales employees' commissions based on the amount of sales generated by the employees are variable expenses. The typical analysis calls for us to relate direct selling expenses to sales, often by calculating a percentage relationship between the variable selling expenses and sales or by determining the number of cents out of every sales dollar that has been used to cover variable selling expenses. Actual fixed selling expenses may be compared with budgeted amounts to determine favorable and unfavorable variances.

To illustrate, let's assume a firm budgets $50,000 and $100,000 of fixed and variable selling expenses, respectively, with the expectation of realizing sales in the amount of $1,000,000, that actual sales amount to $1,200,000, and that actual fixed and variable selling expenses are $52,000 and $110,000, respectively. The following schedule can be prepared to help management evaluate the performance of the sales department:

	Budgeted	Budgeted Costs Adjusted to Actual Level of Operations	Actual	Variance
Sales	$1,000,000		$1,200,000	$200,000 (F)
Fixed selling expenses	$ 50,000	$ 50,000	$ 52,000	$ 2,000 (U)
Variable selling expenses	$ 100,000	$120,000	$ 110,000	$ 10,000 (F)

Management must then judge whether the variances in direct selling expenses are material enough to require further attention. If so, decisions will be made regarding the ways in which sales practices will be changed in future periods. (The sales variance would be analyzed further as described previously (see pages 636–641).

Shipping expenses for deliveries to customers, frequently entitled *freight out*, also include both fixed and variable elements. They include all costs associated with the delivery of goods to customers. For analytical purposes, the variable items again should be related, on a percentage basis, to sales. However, if shipping costs are to be appropriately controlled, management also must be able to relate them to the order size and delivery distance. That is the reason, for example, that firms often establish maximum delivery distance and minimum orders that will be delivered without charge.

Since administrative costs generally are fixed within the relevant range of anticipated operating levels, they should be compared with budget or prior-period data to determine if there have been significant variances. If general administrative costs become too large in relation to sales, management often will be forced to take action, such as the elimination of certain administrative costs. Because most of such costs are fixed, the administrative cost per unit also can be reduced by increasing the volume of sales. However, if sales cannot be increased, the firm may have to resort to reducing administrative personnel as a means of controlling the amount of administrative expenses per unit of sales.

Managing the Costs of Service Enterprises

A service enterprise sells services rather than goods. Therefore, the basic concepts of cost control must center around the relationships between the cost of performing services and the revenues realized from those services. Specific cost-management procedures will vary significantly among such organizations because of the differences in the types of services performed. In this section, we discuss the management of the costs of providing professional services and the costs of providing repetitive standardized services.

Managing the Costs of Professional Services. In a professional office, such as that of a lawyer or an accountant, costs generally are controlled by relating them to the amounts budgeted for each job or case handled. This is a form of job-order costing, with budgeted amounts established for each job before it is performed. When particular jobs do not produce what is considered to be an appropriate difference between fees earned and professional costs incurred, the firm will review its operations, with the thought of either improving the efficiency with which the service is performed or increasing the billing price on subsequent jobs of a similar nature. Fees for such services may be charged on a per diem basis, on the basis of a quoted price for a job, or on a contingent fee basis. It is important to develop realistic estimates of probable costs for the services to be performed under either the job or contingent fee arrangement before accepting a job. With contingent fees, it is also important to realistically estimate, before the firm commits itself to performing the service, the probable revenues to be realized from an engagement.

Managing the Costs of Repetitive Standardized Services. Service enterprises that perform repetitive standardized functions—such as barbershops, banks, and hotels—should project an estimated cost per unit of service performed that serves as the basis for deciding whether the fee structure established by the market for such services is adequate to justify entering that market. The prices to be charged for most of the services performed by these entities will be determined by economic forces in the marketplace (supply and demand). However, prices in some instances can be improved by enlarging the amount or quality of service provided. Cost control must be directed primarily toward improving the efficiency with which the services are performed. Also, because many of the costs of such enterprises are fixed, unit costs often can be reduced only by enlarging the volume of services sold without increasing aggregate fixed costs. In a very real sense, *any* effort to enlarge the volume of services sold is a cost-control measure for such enterprises.

Managing Manufacturing Costs

We will now consider the ways in which cost data may be used to improve the efficiency of manufacturing activities. We shall examine the procedures to be followed in managing each of the following: direct materials costs, direct labor costs, and manufacturing-overhead costs.

Managing Direct Materials Costs. Since the direct materials cost per finished unit equals the prices paid for the materials or parts multiplied by the quantities of those materials or parts required to produce the unit, measures designed to control this cost element must look to the firm's buying practices and the system designed to control the usage of materials. Properly trained purchasing personnel and appropriate buying policies are fundamental in controlling the prices paid for direct materials. It is, of course, important for the purchasing department to carefully consider both the price and the quality of materials as they are purchased, with the goal of minimizing the ultimate direct materials cost per unit of finished product within the qualitative standards established for each unit produced. Development of economic order quantities (EOQs) (see Chapter 21) are used by some firms in controlling the acquisition and carrying costs of inventory items. As observed in Chapter 12, management monitors the price element of materials cost by the periodic determination of materials price variance data. Any delay in the delivery of materials may interrupt production (causing a loss of income), so the purchasing department may, in some instances, need to incur unfavorable materials price variances to assure timely deliveries of materials.

Excessive usage of direct materials may result from using inferior materials, improper care in handling and storing materials, or careless operating practices that result in excessive inventory shrinkage, scrap, and spoilage. Inventory shrinkage can be minimized through proper storage and appropriate inventory control. An effective inventory control system for materials requires perpetual-inventory records, appropriate materials-receiving procedures and records, and a requisition system to account for materials as they are issued. Those procedures should call management's attention to shrinkages and will place the responsibility for those shrinkages on the shoulders of specific persons within the firm. That, in turn, opens the way for remedial action by the persons responsible for controlling direct materials costs.

Periodically determined materials usage variance data relating to the costs of spoiled units should be used to control this element of materials usage. Increases in production costs caused by excessive amounts of scrap and spoilage should be related to the causes of the scrap and spoilage. *Scrap and spoilage reports*, such as the one shown in Figure 17–6, that disclose the reasons for the excess usage of materials (e.g., careless operating practices, malfunctioning equipment, inferior quality of materials, and improper operating procedures) should be prepared.

Once the causes have been identified, the manager can take appropriate corrective action for future periods. The collection and disposal of scrap and spoiled units should be monitored in a manner similar to that used in accounting for finished goods, to prevent the proceeds from their sales from being misappropriated.

Managing Direct Labor Costs.   Since the direct labor cost per unit of finished product equals the number of hours worked to produce the unit multiplied by the rate of pay per hour, excessive direct labor cost per finished unit may be caused by too many hours of labor in relation to units produced (*labor efficiency variance*) or by a higher-than-expected

Description	Department	Cause of Spoilage
20 units product A	Finishing	Defective painting
40 units product B	Press	Improper die installation
15 units product C	Press	Machine malfunction
25 units product D	Welding	Inferior materials

FIGURE 17–6 Spoilage Report

pay rate per hour (*labor rate variance*). When, as in many situations, the labor rate per hour is established by union contract, most of management's efforts to control labor costs must be directed toward improving the efficiency of labor and avoiding the use of higher-priced labor for production activities expected to be performed by less skilled employees. Care must be exercised in training employees for the tasks they are to perform, to help minimize unfavorable labor efficiency variances. Other improvements in labor efficiency may come from technological advances that make the equipment used more productive per man hour. A periodic review of plant layout, sequencing of operations, worker motivation, and work schedules also are important to effectively manage this element of cost and to minimize unplanned idle time of direct labor employees.

Managing Manufacturing Overhead Costs. As observed earlier, each departmental supervisor is held accountable for departmental controllable (budget) overhead variance. Such expenses must be controlled item-by-item at the departmental level. Probably the most effective device available to management in judging whether the amounts of costs incurred for individual manufacturing-overhead items exceed what they should be is the *flexible budget* (see Chapters 11 and 13), which shows the amount of each individual element of manufacturing overhead that a department should incur at different levels of production.

Exhibit 17–1 is an example of a flexible budget for the milling department of Model Company. It shows the amounts expected to be incurred for each of the various manufacturing-overhead items at different levels of production, ranging from 80% to 100% of capacity. The flexible budget shows the same amount for each of the fixed manufacturing-overhead items for all levels of activity. An underlying assumption here is that 80% to 100% of capacity is the relevant range of activity for the Model Company over which fixed costs, in the aggregate, should remain unchanged. Also, the total amounts shown for each of the variable manufacturing-overhead items will vary directly with changes in the level of operations. The three "mixed" cost items have

EXHIBIT 17–1 ▐▬▬▬▬▬▬▬▬▬▬▬

Model Company Milling Department

Flexible Manufacturing-Overhead Budget
For One Month

Item	Type*	Percentage of Capacity/Standard Labor Hours 80%/8,000	90%/9,000	100%/10,000
Superintendence	(F)	$ 7,000	$ 7,000	$ 7,000
Inspection	(F)	5,000	5,000	5,000
Indirect labor	(F)	2,000	2,000	2,000
	(V)	8,000	9,000	10,000
Indirect materials	(F)	400	400	400
	(V)	2,000	2,250	2,500
Payroll taxes	(V)	2,400	2,700	3,000
Electricity	(F)	600	600	600
	(V)	1,600	1,800	2,000
Depreciation	(F)	2,000	2,000	2,000
Insurance	(F)	1,000	1,000	1,000
Totals		$32,000	$33,750	$35,500
Indirect manufacturing:				
Fixed cost rate		$2.25	$2.00	$1.80
Variable cost rate		$1.75	$1.75	$1.75
Overhead rate per direct labor hour		$4.00	$3.75	$3.55

*variable (V); flexible (F)

been separated into fixed (F) and variable (V) elements. Chapter 11 explained the techniques used to separate a mixed cost into its fixed and variable components (see pages 374–379).

To illustrate, let's assume that Model Company decides that the 90% (9,000 direct labor hours) level of production would be the probable level of activity for the next period. It would then apply manufacturing overhead to production at a rate of $3.75 per direct labor hour, calculated as follows:

Total estimated manufacturing overhead at expected level of operations (90%)	$33,750
Expected direct labor hours at expected level of operations (90%)	9,000
Manufacturing-overhead application rate per direct labor hour ($33,750 ÷ 9,000)	$3.75

The fixed and variable portions of this overhead application rate, calculated in the same way as the total manufacturing-overhead rate, are $2.00 and $1.75, respectively.

Now assume that, during a month of 19A, the milling department of Model Company actually spent $33,650 (see Exhibit 17–2, "Actual" expense column) for manufacturing overhead while achieving an output equal to 8,500 standard hours of production. The Model Company's cost records would show:

Actual manufacturing overhead for period	$33,650
Applied manufacturing overhead during period	
(8,500 standard hours of production × $3.75)	31,875
Underapplied manufacturing overhead	$ 1,775

The underapplied manufacturing overhead in the amount of $1,775 constitutes an unfavorable variance. As explained in Chapter 13, it can be divided into two variances:

1. *Volume Variance:* $1,000 Unfavorable. This is caused by the fact that 9,000 − 8,500 = 500 fewer standard direct labor hours of production were experienced than were anticipated when the overhead application rate was established. Therefore, the applied fixed manufacturing overhead is (9,000 − 8,500) × $2 fixed overhead application rate per hour = $1,000 less than would have been applied if the firm had turned out 9,000 standard hours of production.
2. *Controllable (Budget) Variance:* $775 Unfavorable. The controllable (budget) variance reflects the amount spent by the department in excess of what should have been spent for the production achieved. It is calculated by comparing actual overhead ($33,650) with the flexible budget amount allowed for the 8,500-hour level of production ($32,875) (see Exhibit 17–2). This variance is caused by the department's having to be kept in operation longer than was expected for the production achieved or its simply spending more than should have been spent for individual overhead items. Exhibit 17–2 shows how this variance can be associated with each of the individual items of overhead.

The unfavorable volume variance results from production facilities having actually turned out fewer units of product (requiring fewer standard direct labor hours) than was anticipated when the overhead application rate was established. A volume variance should be identified with its cause or causes and associated with the person or persons responsible. Possible causes include lack of orders, machinery breakdowns, unplanned employee vacations, shortages of materials, and employee absenteeism. The controllable variance in Exhibit 17–2 is associated only with variable overhead items. However, fixed items also can contribute to the total controllable variance if they have been over-

EXHIBIT 17–2

Model Company Milling Department

Manufacturing Overhead: Actual Compared with Budget
Month X, 19A
8,500 Direct Labor Hours

Item	Type*	Actual	Flexible-Budget Allowance**	Actual − Flexible Budget = Controllable Variance	
Superintendence	(F)	$ 7,000	$ 7,000		
Inspection	(F)	5,000	5,000		
Indirect labor	(F)	2,000	2,000		
	(V)	8,900	8,500	$400	unfavorable
Indirect materials	(F)	400	400		
	(V)	2,100	2,125	(25)	favorable
Payroll taxes	(V)	2,900	2,550	350	unfavorable
Electricity	(F)	600	600		
	(V)	1,750	1,700	50	unfavorable
Depreciation	(F)	2,000	2,000		
Insurance	(F)	1,000	1,000		
Total		$33,650	$32,875	$775	unfavorable

*variable (V); flexible (F)

**Variable items in this column represent 85% of the amounts shown in the 100%-capacity column in Exhibit 17–1. By definition, fixed items are the same amount within all levels of the relevant range of activity.

spent or underspent. The individual items included in the total controllable variance should be associated with the person or persons responsible for incurring them. Probable causes of these variances include labor inefficiencies that force the department to be kept in operation longer than was expected for the production achieved and simply spending more than should have been spent for individual expense items. Exhibit 17–2 shows how this variance can be traced to individual items of overhead. Chapter 13 explained how the total controllable (budget) variance can be divided into the amounts attributed to efficiency of operations (efficiency variance) and to spending more than was expected for individual items (spending variance). It also showed (through four-way analysis of overhead) how the total spending variance can be divided into variable spending variance and fixed spending (budget) variance.

Motivation and Cost Control

The placement of responsibility for the control of specific costs and the development of standards for the measurement of effort–achievement relationships will accomplish little unless the individuals charged with controlling costs are motivated to control them. Thus, another condition that must be present for effective control of costs is an environment that motivates individuals to exercise those controls. Fundamentally, the problem of motivating people to control the costs they are responsible for incurring begins by recognizing that individual goals may be different from or even in conflict with the goals of the company. A prudent supervisor, therefore, will make every effort to provide an environment in which the self-interest goals of subordinates can be synchronized with the operating goals of the company.

The first requirement for promoting the congruence of individual and company goals is to involve the participants in the establishment of their goals. A departmental manager who has had a voice in setting departmental cost–output standards will have a greater motivation to meet those standards than if the standards had been established arbitrarily by his or her supervisor.

One of the most direct and obvious ways of bringing about a reconciliation of individual and company goals is to develop a system of compensation that rewards each person in relation to his or her contribution to the overall profitability of the company. The basis for determining remuneration incentives must be one over which the person being compensated has control and which is directly related to that person's contribution to overall company profitability. If a company relates compensation to an *improper* measure of individual performance, this unintentionally creates a type of motivation that fails to contribute to profitability.

For example, let's assume a firm pays its salespeople commissions based on gross sales. This arrangement implicitly assumes that a greater sales volume will produce a larger profit for the company. It naturally leads the salespeople to push those goods that can be sold most easily, even if they have a small profit margin. Such an arrangement also can encourage salespeople to spend lavishly in promoting sales and perhaps even make promises regarding delivery or product performance that will create future ill will or possibly cause the firm to pay excessive delivery or warranty costs. Thus, when a salesperson is paid a commission based solely on the amount of his or her gross sales, the impression is created that the only important thing is the total amount of sales generated by that person. With such a system, a salesperson will be motivated to strive toward maximum total sales regardless of the costs involved in securing sales and regardless of the fact that management ultimately desires to maximize total *contribution margin* rather than total sales. A more appropriate incentive plan would base a salesperson's commission on the contribution margins generated.

Another practice that can severely reduce motivation to properly control costs is a faulty system of cost allocation. Individuals charged with controlling costs must be held responsible only for those costs over which they exercise control as they carry out their responsibilities. Responsibility should always be consistent with assigned authority. If a firm attempts to hold a manager responsible for costs arbitrarily allocated to his or her department or area of responsibility on the basis of some activity over which that person lacks total control, the manager can correctly conclude that he or she is being expected to assume a responsibility for something outside his or her control. Recognizing that efforts to control those costs will be futile, the manager also may give minimal attention to those costs that he or she *can* control.

An environment designed to motivate managers to control their costs also should include an arrangement whereby each person charged with controlling costs will receive promptly, in readily understood language, pertinent cost-comparison data. The data included in such reports may be given in dollars and cents, but the actual/expected comparison also may be conveyed through reports such as those relating direct labor hours to production or showing percentages of output goals achieved. Regardless of the specific form used, it is extremely important that those data be presented promptly, that they place strong emphasis on items or functions that are out of line, and that they be easily understood by the person charged with controlling the included items. Large, prominently displayed graphs or posters charting progress also may be helpful.

Another way of promoting employee and company goal congruence is to encourage employees to acquire ownership interest in the company. Plans that give employees special stock purchase privileges can build an environment that will be especially effective in motivating employees to act in the best interests of the company as they carry out their work responsibilities.

Illustrative Problem

Nelson Industries installs commercial lighting units on a job-order basis. The master budget prepared in 19X2 for the year 19X3, based on 5,000 units, used the following standard costs for one commercial lighting unit:

Materials (400 lb @ $1.90)	$ 760
Labor (2 hr @ $11)	22
Variable overhead (2 hr @ $6)	12
Fixed overhead (2 hr @ $120)	240
Total	$1,034

Nelson Industries

Budgeted Income Statement
For the Year 19X3

Sales (5,000 @ $1,400)		$7,000,000
Cost of goods sold		
Materials (5,000 lb @ $760)	$3,800,000	
Labor (5,000 @ $22)	110,000	
Variable overhead (5,000 @ $12)	60,000	
Fixed overhead (5,000 @ $240)	1,200,000	5,170,000
Gross margin		$1,830,000
Variable selling and administrative expenses		270,000
Fixed selling and administrative expenses		120,000
Net operating income		$1,440,000

During 19X3, the sales department generated orders for 4,870 lighting units, but the firm was able to produce and sell only 4,770 units at an actual average selling price of $1,360. Nelson Industries had no inventories at either the beginning or the end of 19X3 and prepared the following traditional income statement at the end of 19X3:

Nelson Industries

Income Statement
For the Year 19X3

Sales (4,770 @ $1,360)		$6,487,200
Cost of goods sold		
Standard cost (4,770 @ $1,034)	$4,932,180	
Volume variance (230 @ $240)	55,200	
Other variances (net)	28,050	5,015,430
Gross margin		$1,471,770
Variable selling and administrative expenses		270,460
Fixed selling and administrative expenses		120,940
Net operating income		$1,080,370

Manufacturing activity reports during 19X3 revealed the following:

(1) 1,927,000 pounds of materials were purchased at an average cost of $1.89 and used in the installation of units.

(2) 9,500 labor hours were worked at an average cost of $11.20 per hour.
(3) Actual variable overhead incurred was $57,000.
(4) Actual fixed overhead incurred was $1,210,000.

REQUIRED:

1. Prepare an analysis of gross margin that explains the difference between the budgeted and actual gross margins. Show details for sales and cost of sales.
2. Prepare a detailed analysis of all manufacturing costs (materials, labor, variable overhead, and fixed overhead).
3. Prepare a schedule of variable and fixed selling and administrative expense variances.
4. Reconcile the actual and master budget net operating income using detailed variance information.

Solution to Illustrative Problem

1. Analysis of Gross Margin.

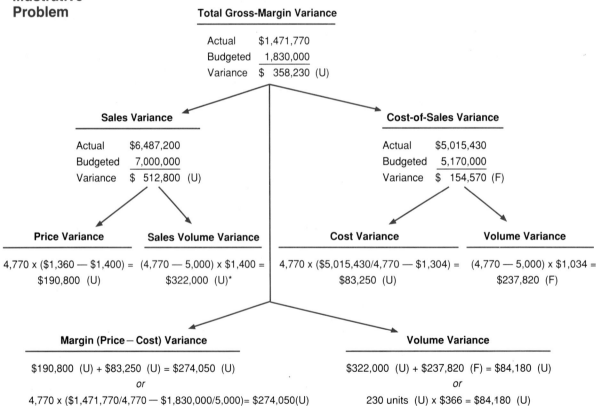

Total Gross-Margin Variance

Actual	$1,471,770
Budgeted	1,830,000
Variance	$ 358,230 (U)

Sales Variance

Actual	$6,487,200
Budgeted	7,000,000
Variance	$ 512,800 (U)

Cost-of-Sales Variance

Actual	$5,015,430
Budgeted	5,170,000
Variance	$ 154,570 (F)

Price Variance

4,770 x ($1,360 — $1,400) =
$190,800 (U)

Sales Volume Variance

(4,770 — 5,000) x $1,400 =
$322,000 (U)*

Cost Variance

4,770 x ($5,015,430/4,770 — $1,304) =
$83,250 (U)

Volume Variance

(4,770 — 5,000) x $1,034 =
$237,820 (F)

Margin (Price — Cost) Variance

$190,800 (U) + $83,250 (U) = $274,050 (U)

or

4,770 x ($1,471,770/4,770 — $1,830,000/5,000)= $274,050(U)

Volume Variance

$322,000 (U) + $237,820 (F) = $84,180 (U)

or

230 units (U) x $366 = $84,180 (U)

*130 × $1,400 = $182,000 is the responsibility of the sales department, and 100 × $1,400 = $140,000 is the responsibility of the production department.

2. Analysis of Manufacturing Costs. Since there was no change in inventory, manufacturing costs of the period equal cost of goods sold.

Actual cost of goods sold	$5,015,430
Budgeted cost of goods sold	5,170,000
Variance	$ 154,570 (F)

Manufacturing Cost Variances

Materials price (1,927,000 lb × $.01)	$19,270 (F)	
Materials quantity [(1,927,000 − 1,908,000), × $1.90]	36,100 (U)	$ 16,830 (U)
Labor rate [9,500 × ($11.20 − $11)]	$ 1,900 (U)	
Labor efficiency [(9,500 − 9,540) × $11]	440 (F)	$ 1,460 (U)
Variable overhead spending [$57,000 − (9,500 × $6)]	0	
Variable overhead efficiency [(9,500 − 9,540) × $6]	$ 240 (F)	240 (F)
Fixed overhead spending ($1,210,000 − $1,200,000)	$10,000 (U)	
Fixed overhead volume [(4,770 − 5,000) × $240]	55,200 (U)*	65,200 (U)
		$ 83,250 (U)
Cost savings from not producing budgeted number of units, (volume variance) [(5,000 − 4,770) × $1,034]		237,820 (F)
Total cost-of-goods-sold variance		$154,570 (F)

*The total fixed overhead variance for 19X3 is $10,000, unfavorable (actual fixed overhead of $1,210,000 less budgeted fixed overhead of $1,200,000). The $55,200 unfavorable fixed-overhead volume variance results from fixed overhead being underapplied to work in process. [For example, if there were no fixed-overhead spending variance, actual overhead would have been $1,200,000, whereas applied fixed overhead was only $1,144,800 (4,770 × $240).] This unfavorable volume variance is offset by an identical amount of cost savings imbedded in the cost-of-goods-sold favorable volume variance from not producing 5,000 − 4,770 = 230 units. This apparent anomoly is caused by the treatment of fixed overhead as a variable cost in the cost-of-goods-sold volume variance.

3. Schedule of Selling and Administrative Expenses.

	Master Budget (5,000 units)	Flexible Budget (4,770 units)	Actual	Variances
Variable selling expense	$270,000	$257,580	$270,460	$12,880 (U)
Fixed selling expense	$120,000	$120,000	$120,940	940 (U)
Variances requiring investigation (if material)				$13,820 (U)
Master budget cost savings from not delivering all planned units [(5,000 − 4,770) × $54]				12,420 (F)
Total selling and administrative variance [Actual selling and administrative costs − Budgeted selling and administrative costs = ($270,460 + $120,940) − ($270,000 + $120,000)]				$ 1,400 (U)

4. Reconciliation of Net Operating Income.

Budgeted net operating income				$1,440,000
Gross-margin variances				
Sales price	$190,800 (U)			
Sales volume	322,000 (U)		$512,800 (U)	
Cost-of-goods-sold cost variances				
Materials price	$ 19,270 (F)			
Materials quantity	36,100 (U)			
Labor rate	1,900 (U)			
Labor efficiency	440 (F)			
Variable overhead spending	0			
Variable overhead efficiency	240 (F)			
Fixed overhead spending	10,000 (U)			
Fixed overhead volume	55,200 (U)	$ 83,250 (U)		
Cost-of-goods-sold volume variances		237,820 (F)	154,570 (F)	358,230 (U)
Selling and administrative expense variances				
Variable		$ 12,880 (U)		
Fixed		940 (U)		
Cost savings from units not sold		12,420 (F)		1,400 (U)
Actual net operating income				$1,080,370

SUMMARY

In this chapter, we explored the procedures a firm follows in controlling costs. We began by observing that these controls are achieved, basically, by holding individuals within the firm responsible for effort–achievement relationships within the segments of operations that they have been given the authority to manage, that is, by relating expenses (expired costs) to revenues, or by developing cost data that are compared with achieved output. The accounting practices used to accomplish this responsibility accounting were described.

Next, we dealt with the establishment of operating goals for segments of operations. These can be derived from prior-period operating data, standard cost data, or budgetary projections. In most instances, standard costs will underlie the data against which the effort–achievement relationships of segments of operations are evaluated. We demonstrated how such goals can be used to manage and control the costs of merchandising operations, service enterprises, and manufacturing operations. We illustrated some of the performance report data that can be used to evaluate the efforts of departmental managers in controlling the costs associated with their spheres of responsibilities.

Finally, we examined ways to motivate individuals within a firm to most effectively control the costs for which they are responsible: participation of those persons in establishing the goals for their segments of operations; synchronizing rewards with the achievement of those goals; and holding persons responsible only for those costs over which they have control authority.

APPENDIX: Alternative "Triangle" Analysis of Gross-Margin Variances

Gross-margin variance analysis also may be visualized using the triangles introduced in the appendixes to Chapters 12 and 13. The basic structure of the triangle is identical: actual amounts are placed on the lower left corner of the triangle, standard (that is, benchmark) amounts are placed on the lower right corner, and some combination of actual/ standard amounts is placed at the peak of the triangle.

Variances are calculated as the difference between clockwise pairs of amounts on each point of the triangle. For example, the sales price variance [(4) on the Figure 17–7 sales triangle] can be calculated as the difference between total actual sales (1) minus total actual/standard sales (2). Whereas cost variances are unfavorable if the "actual" amount is greater than the "standard," with sales variances, it is just the opposite. In the following sales variance analysis, for example, if total actual sales (1) is greater than total actual/standard sales (2), the sales price variance is favorable. Also, if the total actual/standard sales (2) is greater than the total standard sales (3), the sales volume variance (5) is favorable.

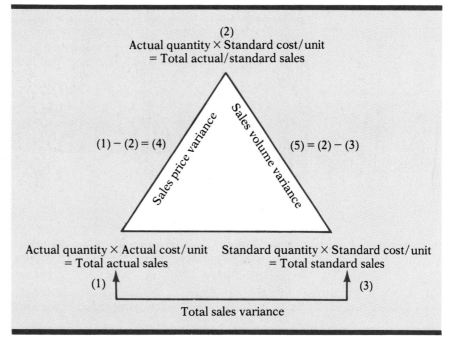

FIGURE 17–7 Sales Variance Analysis

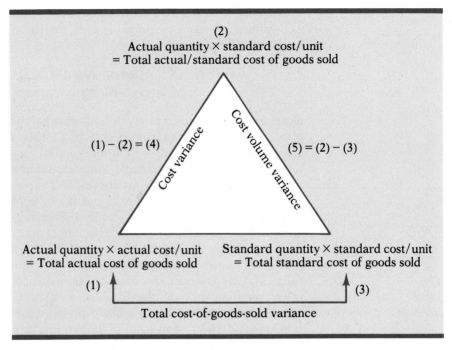

FIGURE 17—8   Cost-of-Goods-Sold Variance Analysis

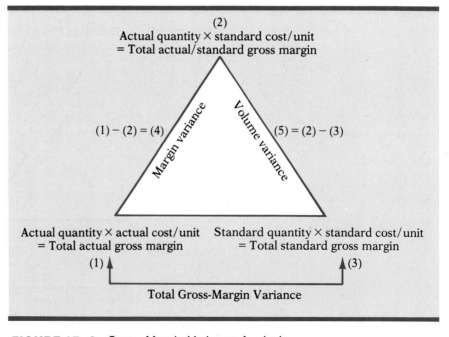

FIGURE 17—9   Gross-Margin Variance Analysis

Cost-of-goods-sold variances calculated by triangle analysis follow the same pattern. (See Figure 17–8.) This summary cost measure obeys the favorable/unfavorable "rules" for all costs: if "actual" costs are greater than "standard" costs, the variance is unfavorable. Thus, if total actual cost of goods sold (1) is greater than total actual/standard cost of goods sold (2), the cost variance (4) is unfavorable.

When sales and cost of sales are combined into gross-margin analysis, the variances are favorable if "actual" amounts exceed the "standard" amounts. (See Figure 17–9.)

For multiproduct firms, the gross-margin volume variance should be separated into a mix variance and a pure volume variance. The actual/standard amount at the top of the triangle, however, represents the expected mix for the actual total quantity of units sold. Note that the "actual" amount on the lower left of the volume variance triangle in Figure 17–10 is the same as appears at the top of the gross-margin triangle (Figure 17–9).

To illustrate the complete triangle approach, data about the JP multiproduct firm (see page 640) for current year is repeated here and followed by a complete gross-margin analysis in Figure 17–11.

	Budgeted			Actual		
Sales						
Product A	(1,000 @ $8)	$ 8,000		(2,600 @ $6)	$15,600	
Product B	(5,000 @ $6)	30,000		(4,000 @ $7)	28,000	
Total sales			$38,000			$43,600
Cost of sales						
Product A	(1,000 @ $3)	$ 3,000		(2,600 @ $3)	$ 7,800	
Product B	(5,000 @ $4)	20,000		(4,000 @ $4.50)	18,000	
Total cost of sales			23,000			25,800
Gross margin (gross profit)						
Product A	(1,000 @ $5)	$ 5,000		(2,600 @ $3)	$ 7,800	
Product B	(5,000 @ $2)	10,000		(4,000 @ $2.50)	10,000	
			$15,000			$17,800

GLOSSARY OF TERMS INTRODUCED IN THIS CHAPTER

gross-margin (profit) variance   The difference between actual gross margins of succeeding periods, or the difference between the projected gross margin and actual gross margin of a reporting period; can be divided into price and volume components.

pure volume variance   The difference in the expected and actual gross margin of a multiproduct firm that is attributed entirely to the difference in the volume of products being sold. The amount attributable to each product equals the sum of the differences between the quantities of each product expected to be sold (based on projected sales mix and total quantity of products actually

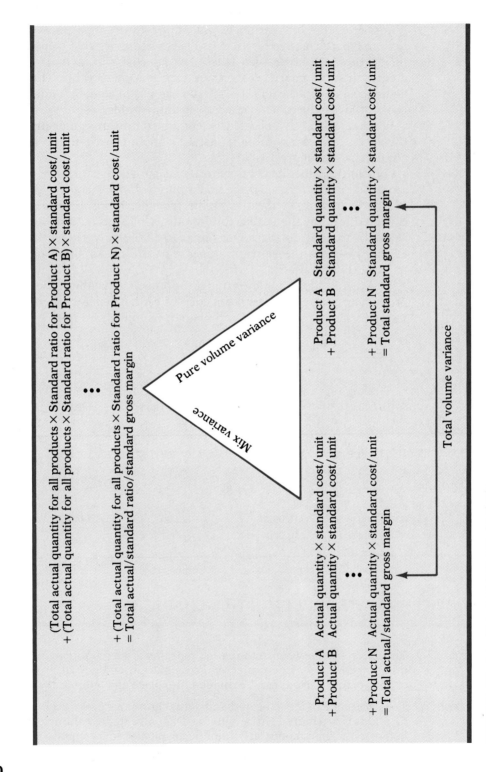

FIGURE 17–10 Volume Variance Analysis

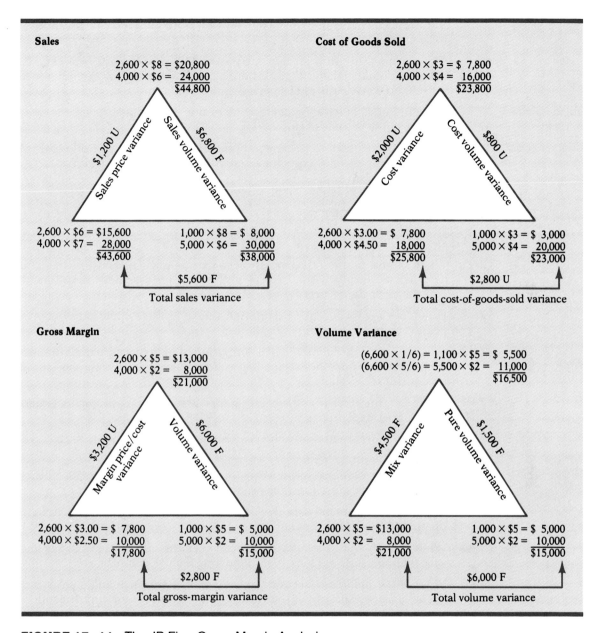

Sales

2,600 × $8 = $20,800
4,000 × $6 = 24,000
$44,800

$1,200 U Sales price variance

Sales volume variance $6,800 F

2,600 × $6 = $15,600
4,000 × $7 = 28,000
$43,600

1,000 × $8 = $ 8,000
5,000 × $6 = 30,000
$38,000

$5,600 F
Total sales variance

Cost of Goods Sold

2,600 × $3 = $ 7,800
4,000 × $4 = 16,000
$23,800

$2,000 U Cost variance

Cost volume variance $800 U

2,600 × $3.00 = $ 7,800
4,000 × $4.50 = 18,000
$25,800

1,000 × $3 = $ 3,000
5,000 × $4 = 20,000
$23,000

$2,800 U
Total cost-of-goods-sold variance

Gross Margin

2,600 × $5 = $13,000
4,000 × $2 = 8,000
$21,000

$3,200 U Margin price/cost variance

Volume variance $6,000 F

2,600 × $3.00 = $ 7,800
4,000 × $2.50 = 10,000
$17,800

1,000 × $5 = $ 5,000
5,000 × $2 = 10,000
$15,000

$2,800 F
Total gross-margin variance

Volume Variance

(6,600 × 1/6) = 1,100 × $5 = $ 5,500
(6,600 × 5/6) = 5,500 × $2 = 11,000
$16,500

$4,500 F Mix variance

Pure volume variance $1,500 F

2,600 × $5 = $13,000
4,000 × $2 = 8,000
$21,000

1,000 × $5 = $ 5,000
5,000 × $2 = 10,000
$15,000

$6,000 F
Total volume variance

FIGURE 17–11 The JP Firm Gross-Margin Analysis

sold) and the quantity of each product budgeted to be sold multiplied by the budgeted gross margin per unit for each product.

responsibility accounting

A method of internal reporting that assigns costs to organizational subunits of a firm based on controllability. Each subunit report contains the

	items they have the ability to control. Therefore, they have responsibility for controlling them.
sales mix variance	The variance in gross margin attributed to the difference between the sales mix budgeted and the sales mix actually realized, or the difference between the sales mix of one period and the sales mix of another period.
sales volume variance	The difference between expected and actual sales that is caused by the change in the volume of sales.
segment cost data	The costs attributed to a segment of business, including variable costs of the segment plus fixed costs incurred by or on behalf of the segment.

QUESTIONS FOR CLASS DISCUSSION

17–1 What should be the relationship between assigned responsibilities and assigned authority within a firm if the firm is to achieve appropriate controls over the incurrence of costs?

17–2 How does a cost-per-unit calculation relate to the evaluation of effort–achievement relationships? Explain.

17–3 What devices other than the determination of unit costs are used in measuring relationships between efforts and achievements in the operation of a business? Explain.

17–4 What are the efforts and achievements associated with earnings-per-share data? Explain.

17–5 How are efforts related to achievements when using a standard cost system?

17–6 What is the relationship between the implementation of responsibility accounting procedures and the organization chart of a business?

17–7 How may we best analyze a deviation in the gross margin for a merchandising firm for the purpose of determining the causes of that deviation?

17–8 What is likely to be the relationship between the sales price variance and sales volume variance for a merchandising firm? Explain.

17–9 What is the difference between a pure volume variance and a sales mix variance in the analysis of the variance in gross profit for a multiproduct merchandising firm?

17–10 How do we manage operating expenses? Explain.

17–11 How do we manage the cost of professional services in a service enterprise?

17–12 How do we manage direct materials and direct labor costs in a manufacturing firm?

17–13 How do we manage manufacturing-overhead costs in a manufacturing firm? Explain.

17—14 How does managerial motivation enter into the control of costs? Explain.

17—15 What is the basic difference between authoritative management and participative management? Which is the more effective? Explain.

EXERCISES

17—16 **Analysis of Change in Gross Margin** A merchandising firm selling only one product realized a $75,000 gross margin in selling 15,000 units during 19X1. In 19X2, the company sells 20,000 units and realizes $80,000 of gross margin.

REQUIRED:

1. Explain in a meaningful manner what has caused the $5,000 increase in gross margin between 19X1 and 19X2.
2. Assume now that the sales price per unit was reduced by $.75 from $12.50 to $11.75 between 19X1 and 19X2. Why might management have taken such action? Has the action been successful? Show calculations to support your answer.

17—17 **Professional Services Costs** A public accounting firm has budgeted $10,000 for professional services on an auditing job to be billed on a per diem basis.

REQUIRED:

1. Under such a billing arrangement, what problems may the firm encounter in the event that time spent on the job exceeds the budgeted amount?
2. Assume now that the code of ethical conduct for accountants permits the firm to enter into a contract to perform the services for $12,000. This price is intended to include a margin of $2,000 for the public accounting firm. Assume further that the time required of professional personnel costs the firm $1,000 more than the amount budgeted for the job. How does this affect the operating result of the public accounting firm?
3. Refer to requirement 2. Assume now that the thoroughness with which the audit services must be performed is subject to the judgment of the public accounting firm. What is likely to happen as the firm begins to see that its actual cost of professional services will probably exceed the amount budgeted for them?
4. What are the implications of the situation cited in requirement 3 for the use of competitive bidding by public accounting firms?

17—18 **Materials Price Variance** A manufacturing firm uses material A, which has a standard cost of $1 per unit, in the production of its finished good. The purchasing department acquires 10,000 units of the material at an invoice cost of $10,500.

REQUIRED:

1. Calculate the materials price variance to be recognized as the goods are purchased.
2. Which person within the firm will be held primarily responsible for the variance? Explain.

17–19 **Materials Usage Variance** A manufacturing firm uses material A, with a standard cost of $1 per unit, in the production of its finished good. The standard cost card for the finished product calls for eight units of material A to be used in each unit of finished product. These are the only materials used in the manufacture of the finished product. The firm produces 1,000 units of finished product during the period. You also ascertain that 9,000 units of material A were used in the manufacturing process during the period.

REQUIRED:

1. Calculate the standard cost of material for each unit of finished product.
2. Calculate the materials usage variance for material A during the period.
3. What could have caused the materials usage variance calculated in requirement 2?
4. Which person(s) within the firm will be expected to explain what caused the variance? Explain.

17–20 **Direct Labor Variance** The direct labor costs of a manufacturing firm amounted to $20,000 during an operating period in which 8,000 units of product were produced. The standard cost card for the finished product calls for the use of one hour of direct labor at a cost of $2.25 per hour for each unit of product. The payroll records show that direct laborers actually worked 10,000 hours during the period.

REQUIRED:

1. Calculate the direct labor price variance for the period.
2. Calculate the direct labor efficiency variance for the period.
3. What implications can be attached to the analysis of variances calculated in requirements 1 and 2?
4. Which person(s) within the firm will be expected to explain what caused the variances?

17–21 **Manufacturing-Overhead Application Rate** The Mode Company uses a flexible budget in projecting and controlling its manufacturing-overhead costs. The amount of manufacturing overhead budgeted for a period at the 80%, 90%, and 100% levels of production are as follows:

Percentage of capacity	80%	90%	100%
Direct labor hours	8,000	9,000	10,000
Total manufacturing costs	$64,000	$67,500	$71,000

REQUIRED:

1. Calculate the manufacturing-overhead application rate per direct labor hour at each of the three possible levels of production.
2. Calculate the variable manufacturing-overhead rate per direct labor hour at each level of production.
3. Calculate the amount of fixed manufacturing overhead at each level of production.
4. Calculate the fixed manufacturing-overhead rate per direct labor hour at each level of production.

17–22 **Analysis of Variance in Selling Expenses** Downtown Department Store pays a commission equal to 10% of the sales value of merchandise sold by each salesperson. The firm's operating expense budget shows sales commissions in the amount of $50,000. Other variable selling expenses are budgeted at $25,000. Fixed selling expenses are budgeted at $100,000. Actual sales amounted to $750,000 for the budget period. Actual selling expenses for the period amounted to $214,000, of which $105,000 were fixed.

REQUIRED:

1. What amount of sales did the firm hope to achieve during the budget period?
2. At the end of the period, actual sales commissions amounted to $75,000; the sales manager is concerned about the fact that actual selling expenses have exceeded the amounts budgeted for them by $39,000 ($214,000 − $175,000). Analyze and explain in a meaningful manner the $39,000 difference between the actual and budgeted amounts for selling expenses.

17–23 **Calculation of Overhead Variance** A manufacturing firm estimates its total manufacturing overhead at normal capacity of 18,000 direct labor hours to be $67,500 for the period. The amount actually spent for manufacturing overhead during the period was $67,300. The company produced 8,500 units and expected that two standard hours of direct labor would be required for each unit.

REQUIRED:

1. Calculate the manufacturing-overhead application rate per direct labor hour.
2. Calculate the standard cost of manufacturing overhead for each unit of finished product.
3. Calculate the underapplied or overapplied manufacturing overhead for the period.

17–24 **Analysis of Underapplied Overhead** A manufacturing firm, using a standard cost system, shows underapplied manufacturing overhead for a period in the amount of $7,000. Further analysis shows this variance has been caused by the firm's working 2,000 fewer standard direct labor hours than had been budgeted (36,000 − 34,000). The manufacturing overhead application rate is $3.50 per direct labor hour, including $2.00 fixed manufacturing overhead.

REQUIRED:

1. What was the amount of actual overhead?
2. What portion of the underapplied overhead can be characterized as a volume variance? What may have caused this part of the variance? Explain.
3. Calculate the amount of the "controllable" portion of the under-applied manufacturing overhead. What are possible causes of that part of the variance from the budgeted amount?
4. Which person(s) within the firm should be expected to explain these variances?

17–25 **Controllable and Volume Variances** Actual manufacturing overhead for the Zee Company amounts to $134,600 for the period. Applied manufacturing overhead for the period is $120,000. The manufacturing-overhead application rate is $7.50 per direct labor hour ($4.50 fixed and $3.00 variable). This rate has been calculated based on a budgeted level of 18,000 direct labor hours.

REQUIRED:

1. Calculate the number of finished units produced, assuming that each finished unit requires 4 standard hours of direct labor.
2. Calculate the controllable (budget) variance for the period.
3. Calculate the volume variance for the period.
4. Reconcile the amounts calculated in requirements 2 and 3 with the amount of overapplied or underapplied manufacturing overhead for the period.

PROBLEMS

17–26 **Analysis of Changes in Sales, Cost of Sales, and Gross Margin** Winston Company, which sells a single product, provided the following data from its income statements for the calendar years 19X1 and 19X0:

	19X1	19X0 (base year)
Sales	$750,000 (150,000 units)	$720,000 (180,000 units)
Cost of sales	525,000	575,000
Gross profit	$225,000	$145,000

REQUIRED:

1. Analyze the change in gross margin to show the amount caused by the change in sales and the amount caused by the change in cost of sales.
2. Analyze the change in sales to show the amount caused by the change in sales price and the amount caused by the change in volume of sales.

3. Analyze the change in cost of sales to show the amount caused by the change in cost per unit and the amount caused by the change in volume of sales.
4. Analyze the change in gross margin to show the amount caused by the change in margin per unit and the amount caused by the change in volume of sales.

17–27
ICMA Adapted

Analysis of Variances from Budget Handler Company distributes two home-use power tools to hardware stores—a heavy-duty ½-inch hand drill and a table saw. The tools are purchased from a manufacturer that attaches the Handler private label to the tools. The wholesale selling prices to the hardware stores are $60 each for the drill and $120 each for the table saw.

The 19X2 budget and actual results follow. The budget, adopted in late 19X1, was based on Handler's estimated share of the market for the two tools.

During the first quarter of 19X2, Handler's management estimated that the total market for these tools would actually be 10% below its original estimates. In an attempt to prevent Handler's unit sales from declining as much as industry projections, management developed and implemented a marketing program. Included in the program were dealer discounts and increased direct advertising. The table saw line was emphasized in this program.

Handler Company

Income Statement
For the Year Ended December 31, 19X2
(000s omitted)

	Hand Drill		Table Saw		Total		
	Budgeted	**Actual**	**Budgeted**	**Actual**	**Budgeted**	**Actual**	**Variance**
Sales in units	120	86	80	74	200	160	(40)
Revenue	$7,200	$5,074	$9,600	$8,510	$16,800	$13,584	$(3,216)
Cost of sales	6,000	4,300	6,400	6,068	12,400	10,368	2,032
Gross margin	$1,200	$ 774	$3,200	$2,442	$ 4,400	$ 3,216	$(1,184)
Unallocated costs							
Selling					$ 1,000	$ 1,000	$ —
Advertising					1,000	1,060	(60)
Administration					400	406	(6)
Income taxes (35%)					700	263	437
Total unallocated costs					$ 3,100	$ 2,729	$ 371
Net income					$ 1,300	$ 487	$ (813)

REQUIRED:

1. Analyze the gross-margin variance to show the amount caused by
   a. margin (price–cost) variance and volume, by product
   b. sales variance, by product
   c. cost-of-sales variance, by product
   d. sales price variance, by product
   e. sales volume variance, by product
   f. cost-of-sales price variance, by product
   g. cost-of-sales-volume variance, by product.
2. Discuss the apparent relationship between Handler's special marketing program and these variances.

17–28 Marketing Department Performance Responsibility Dana Corporation has a practical production capacity of 1 million units. The current year's master budget was based on projected production and sales of 900,000 units. Actual production for the current year was 920,000 units, while actual sales amounted to only 800,000 units. The units are sold for $20 each, and the variable cost percentage is 70%. Budgeted and actual fixed costs are $1,350,000.

REQUIRED:

1. Calculate the manufacturing volume variance. Who would most likely be held responsible for this variance? Why?
2. Calculate the amount of operating income variance most appropriately attributable to the marketing department.
3. Assuming that production was curtailed to the level required for sales (800,000 units), calculate the volume variance.
4. Under the assumption given in requirement 3, who should be accountable for the volume variance?
5. Discuss the implications of the preceding information for absorption costing and variable costing.

17–29 *ICMA Adapted* **Sales Mix Variance and Evaluation of Salespeople** Caprice Company manufactures and sells two products—a small portable office file cabinet it has made for over 15 years, and a home-travel file introduced in 19X1. The files are made in Caprice's only manufacturing plant. Budgeted variable production costs per unit of product are:

	Office File	Home-Travel File
Sheet metal	$ 3.50	—
Plastic	—	$3.75
Direct labor (@ $8 per direct labor hour)	4.00	2.00
Variable manufacturing overhead (@ $9 per direct labor hour)	4.50	2.25
	$12.00	$8.00

Variable manufacturing-overhead costs vary with direct labor hours. The annual fixed manufacturing-overhead costs are budgeted at $120,000. A total of 50% of these costs are directly traceable to the office file department, and 22% are traceable to the home-travel file department. The remaining 28% are not traceable to either department.

Caprice employs two full-time salespersons—Pam Price and Robert Flint. Each salesperson receives an annual salary of $14,000 plus a sales commission of 10% of her or his total gross sales. Travel and entertainment expense is budgeted at $22,000 annually for each salesperson. Price is expected to sell 60% of the budgeted unit sales for each file, and Flint the remaining 40%. Caprice's remaining selling and administrative expenses include fixed administrative costs of $80,000 that cannot be traced to either file, plus the following traceable selling expenses:

	Office File	Home-Travel File
Packaging expenses per unit	$2.00	$1.50
Promotion per unit	2.55	3.05

Data regarding Caprice's budgeted and actual sales for the fiscal year ended May 31, 19X4, are presented in the following schedule. There were no changes in the beginning and ending balances of either finished-goods inventory or work-in-process inventory.

	Office File	Home-Travel File
Budgeted sales volume, in units	15,000	15,000
Budgeted and actual unit sales price	$29.50	$19.50
Actual unit sales		
Pam Price	10,000	9,000
Robert Flint	5,000	11,000
Total units	15,000	20,000

Data regarding Caprice's operating expenses for the year ended May 31, 19X4, follow.

(1) There were no increases or decreases in raw materials inventory for either sheet metal or plastic, and there were no usage variances. However, sheet metal prices were 6% above budget, and plastic prices were 4% below budget.

(2) The actual direct labor costs incurred per unit were the same as the budgeted amounts.

(3) Fixed manufacturing overhead costs were incurred at the same amounts as budgeted, and all variable manufacturing overhead costs were incurred at the budgeted hourly rates.

(4) All selling and administrative expenses were incurred at budgeted rates or amounts except the following travel and entertainment items:

Pam Price	$24,000
Robert Flint	28,000
	$52,000

REQUIRED:

1. Calculate the budgeted contribution margin per unit, excluding traceable fixed costs, for each product.
2. Calculate the actual contribution margin per unit, excluding traceable fixed costs, for each product.
3. Calculate the total product-segment-margin variance, including traceable fixed costs, for each product.
4. What part of the total contribution-margin variance for each product can be attributed to the difference between the budgeted and actual volumes of sales?
5. What part of the total volume variance calculated in requirement 4 can be attributed to deviation in sales mix?
6. Evaluate the sales performance of Price and Flint. Comment on the firm's sales commission policy as it relates to your findings.

17–30
ICMA Adapted

Flexible Budget and Analysis of Variances in Manufacturing-Overhead Items Berwin, Inc., is a manufacturer of small industrial tools with an annual sales volume of approximately $3.5 million. Sales growth has been steady during the year, and there is no evidence of cyclical demand. Production has increased gradually during the year and has been distributed evenly throughout each month. The company employs a process-costing system. The four manufacturing departments—casting, machining, finishing, and packaging—are all located in the same building. Fixed manufacturing overhead is assigned using a plant-wide rate.

Berwin has always been able to compete with other manufacturers of small industrial tools. However, its market has expanded only in response to product innovation. Thus, research and development is very important and has helped Berwin to expand as well as maintain demand.

Carl Viller, controller, has designed and implemented a new budget system in response to concerns voiced by George Berwin, president. An annual budget that has been divided into 12 equal segments has been prepared to assist in the timely evaluation of monthly performance. Berwin was visibly upset on receiving the May performance report for the machining department. Berwin exclaimed, "How can they be efficient enough to produce nine extra units every working day and still miss the budget by $300 a day?" Gene Jordan, machining department supervisor, could not understand "all the red ink" when he knew the department had operated more efficiently in May than it had in months. Jordan stated, "I was expecting a pat on the back and instead the boss tore me apart. What's more, I don't even know why!" The performance report for the machining department follows. Similar performance reports are prepared for the other three departments.

Berwin, Inc.

Machining Department Performance Report
For the Month Ended May 31, 19X4

	Budget	Actual	(Over) Under Budget
Volume in units	3,000	3,185	(185)
Variable manufacturing costs			
Direct material	$24,000	$24,843	$ (843)
Direct labor	27,750	29,302	(1,552)
Variable factory overhead	33,300	35,035	(1,735)
Total variable manufacturing costs	$85,050	$89,180	$(4,130)
Fixed manufacturing overhead			
Indirect labor	$ 3,300	$ 3,334	$ (34)
Depreciation	1,500	1,500	
Taxes	300	300	
Insurance	240	240	
Other	930	1,027	(97)
Total fixed overhead costs	$ 6,270	$ 6,401	$ (131)

REQUIRED:

1. Based on the information presented in the May performance report for the machining department of Berwin, Inc.,
   a. discuss the strengths of the new budget system in general.
   b. identify the weaknesses in the way the performance report was presented, and explain how the report should be revised to eliminate each weakness.
2. Prepare a revised performance report for the machining department.

17–31
ICMA Adapted

Analysis of Variances from Budgeting Data JK Enterprises produced and sold 550,000 units during the first quarter ended March 31, 19X1. These sales represented a 10% increase over the number of units budgeted for the quarter. In spite of the sales increase, profits were below budget, as shown in the following condensed income statement:

JK Enterprises

Income Statement

For the First Quarter Ended March 31, 19X1

($000 omitted)

	Budget	Actual
Sales	$2,500	$2,530
Variable expenses		
Cost of goods sold	$1,475	$1,540
Selling	400	440
Total variable expenses	$1,875	$1,980
Contribution margin	$ 625	$ 550
Fixed expenses		
Selling	$ 125	$ 150
Administration	275	300
Total fixed expenses	$ 400	$ 450
Income before taxes	$ 225	$ 100
Income taxes (30%)	68	30
Net income	$ 157	$ 70

The accounting department always prepares a brief analysis that explains the difference between budgeted net income and actual net income. This analysis, which has not yet been completed for the first quarter, is to be submitted to top management with the income statement.

REQUIRED:

1. Prepare an explanation of the $125,000 unfavorable variance between the first quarter budgeted and actual before-tax income for JK Enterprises by calculating a single amount for each of the following variations:
   a. sales price variance
   b. sales volume variance
   c. variable unit-cost and total variable cost variance
   d. volume variance related to variable costs
   e. fixed cost variance.
2. Reconcile the variances calculated in requirement 1 to the total variance of $125,000.

17–32 Analysis of Manufacturing-Overhead Variance The Futility Production Company uses a normal-cost system (historical costs for direct materials and direct labor, along with applied overhead) for its accounting reports. The company developed its manufacturing-overhead application rate by use of the following formula:

$$\frac{\text{Estimated manufacturing overhead for year, \$900,000}}{\text{Estimated direct labor hours for year, 300,000}} = \$3.00 \text{ per direct labor hour}$$

Further analysis of the manufacturing-overhead application rate indicates it was composed of a fixed element of $2.00 and a variable element of $1.00. During the year, direct laborers worked 310,000 hours. The company incurred overhead costs of $925,000 (including $610,000 of fixed overhead).

REQUIRED:

1. What is the amount of underapplied or overapplied manufacturing overhead for the year?
2. Calculate the total dollars of fixed manufacturing overhead included in the numerator as the overhead application rate was calculated.
3. What is the manufacturing-overhead controllable or budget variance?
4. How would these variances be used in a responsibility accounting system?

17–33 **Analysis of Direct Materials and Direct Labor Variances** Black Company, which inspects units at the end of processing, has developed the following standard cost card for one unit of an item it produces:

3 lb of material at $1.00 per lb	$ 3.00
1 hr of direct labor at $6.00 per hr	6.00
2 hrs of manufacturing overhead at $4.00 per labor hour	8.00
	$17.00

The following data are applicable to the month of March:

(1) Beginning work-in-process inventory, 4,000 units (one-half complete as to all elements of cost).
(2) Ending work-in-process inventory, 3,000 units (one-third complete as to all elements of cost).
(3) Units started into production during March, 20,000.
(4) Actual labor hours worked, 21,000.
(5) Actual labor cost, $128,100.
(6) Actual materials used, 56,500 pounds.
(7) Normal loss, all from units started during March, 500 units.
(8) Transferred to finished goods, 20,500 units.

REQUIRED:

1. Calculate the equivalent units of production (same for all elements of cost), assuming a first-in, first-out flow of costs.
2. Calculate the dollar amount of materials quantity variance.
3. Calculate the labor rate and labor efficiency variances.
4. How would the figures calculated in requirements 2 and 3 be used in a responsibility accounting system?

17–34 Analysis of Manufacturing-Overhead Variance Coots Manufacturing Company uses standard costing. In analyzing manufacturing-overhead costs for September, the following data were available:

Equivalent units of production achieved	22,000 units
Standard fixed cost per unit	$2.00
Standard variable cost per unit	$4.00
Budgeted fixed cost	$40,000
Actual fixed cost	$42,000
Actual variable costs	$91,000

REQUIRED:

1. Determine the manufacturing-overhead controllable variance for September.
2. Determine the manufacturing-overhead volume variance for September.
3. How would these variances be used in a responsibility accounting system?

17–35 Analysis of Manufacturing-Overhead Variance Refer to the data in problem 17–34, assuming the $6.00 standard cost per unit also is expressed as $3.00 per direct labor hour ($1.00 fixed and $2.00 variable), and that 45,000 direct labor hours actually were worked during September.

REQUIRED:

1. Determine the manufacturing-overhead spending variance for the month (in total and broken down into variable and fixed spending variances).
2. Determine the manufacturing-overhead efficiency variance for the month.
3. Explain how these variances would be used in a responsibility accounting system.

17–36 THOUGHT STIMULATION CASE—The Sales Game. During a consultation engagement with Taylor Company, you are given the following information about two of the company's salespersons.

	Salespersons	
	McKinney	**Sims**
Gross sales	$247,000	$142,000
Sales returns	17,000	2,000
Cost of goods sold	180,000	85,000
Reimbursed expenses (e.g., entertainment)	5,500	2,100
Other direct charges (e.g., samples distributed)	4,000	450
Commission rate on gross sales dollars	5%	5%

You learn that McKinney has been with the company for 10 years. Sims was hired last year.

REQUIRED:

1. Prepare a schedule of each salesperson's contribution to operating income before taxes. What significant behavioral characteristics do you find implicit in these data?
2. What would you suggest the company do to synchronize sales generation behavior with company goals? Discuss.

17–37
ICMA Adapted

THOUGHT STIMULATION CASE—Responsibility Accounting System Design. Kelly Petroleum Company has a large oil and natural gas project in Oklahoma. The project has been organized into two production centers (petroleum production and natural gas production) and one service center (maintenance).

Maintenance Center Activities and Scheduling. Don Pepper, maintenance center manager, has organized his maintenance workers into work crews that serve the two production centers. The maintenance crews perform preventive maintenance and repair equipment, both in the field and in the central maintenance shop.

Pepper is responsible for scheduling all maintenance work in the field and at the central shop. Preventive maintenance is performed according to a set schedule established by Pepper and approved by the production center managers. Breakdowns are given immediate priority in scheduling so that downtime is minimized. Thus, preventive maintenance occasionally must be postponed, but every attempt is made to reschedule it within 3 weeks. Preventive maintenance work is the responsibility of Pepper. However, if a significant problem is discovered during preventive maintenance, the appropriate production center supervisor authorizes and supervises the repair after checking with Pepper.

When a breakdown in the field occurs, the production centers contact Pepper to initiate the repairs. The repair work is supervised by the production center supervisor. Machinery and equipment sometimes need to be replaced while the original equipment is repaired in the central shop. This procedure is followed only when the time to make the repair in the field would result in an extended interruption of operations. Replacement of equipment is recommended by the maintenance work crew supervisor and approved by a production center supervisor.

Routine preventive maintenance and breakdowns of automotive and mobile equipment used in the field are completed in the central shop. All repairs and maintenance activities taking place in the central shop are under the direction of Pepper.

Maintenance Center Accounting Activities. Pepper has records identifying the work crews assigned to each job in the field, the number of hours spent on the job, and parts and supplies used on the job. In addition, records for the central shop (jobs, labor hours, parts, and supplies) have been maintained. However, this detailed maintenance information is not incorporated into Kelly's accounting system.

Pepper develops the annual budget for the maintenance center by planning the preventive maintenance that will be needed during the year, estimating the number and seriousness of breakdowns, and estimating the shop activities. He then bases the labor, parts, and supply costs on his plans and estimates and develops the budget amounts by line item. Because the timing of the breakdowns is impossible to plan, Pepper divides the annual budget by 12 to derive the monthly budget.

All costs incurred by the work crews in the field and in the central shop are accumulated monthly and then allocated in the two production cost centers based on the field hours worked in each production center. This method of cost allocation has been used on Pepper's recommendation because he believed it was easy to implement and understand. Furthermore, he believed a better allocation system was impossible to incorporate into the monthly report due to the wide range of salaries paid to maintenance workers and the fast turnover of materials and parts. The November cost report for the maintenance center that is provided by the accounting department is shown below.

Oklahoma Project

Maintenance Center Cost Report

For the Month of November 19X2

(in thousands of dollars)

	Budget	Actual	Petroleum Production	Natural Gas Production
Shop hours	2,000	1,800	—	—
Field hours	8,000	10,000	6,000	4,000
Labor				
Electrical	$ 25.0	$ 24.0	$ 14.4	$ 9.6
Mechanical	30.0	35.0	21.0	14.0
Instrumentation	18.0	22.5	13.5	9.0
Automotive	3.5	2.8	1.7	1.1
Heavy equipment	9.6	12.3	7.4	4.9
Equipment operation	28.8	35.4	21.2	14.2
General	15.4	15.9	9.6	6.3
Parts	60.0	86.2	51.7	34.5
Supplies	15.3	12.2	7.3	4.9
Lubricants and fuels	3.4	3.0	1.8	1.2
Tools	2.5	3.2	1.9	1.3
Accounting and data processing	1.5	1.5	.9	.6
Total	$213.0	$254.0	$152.4	$101.6

Production Center Managers' Concerns. Both production center managers have been upset with the method of cost allocation. Furthermore, they believe the report is virtually useless as a cost-control device. Actual costs always seem to deviate from the monthly budget, and the proportion charged to each production center varies significantly from month to month. Maintenance costs have increased substantially since 19X0, and the production managers believe they have no way to judge whether such an increase is reasonable. The two production managers, Pepper, and representatives of corporate accounting have met to discuss these concerns. They concluded that a responsibility accounting system could be developed to replace the current system. In their opinion, a responsibility accounting system would alleviate the production managers' concerns and accurately reflect the activity of the maintenance center.

REQUIRED:

1. Explain the purposes of a responsibility accounting system, and discuss how such a system could resolve the concerns of the production center managers of Kelly Petroleum Company.
2. Describe the behavioral advantages generally attributed to responsibility accounting systems that the management of Kelly Petroleum Company should expect if the system were effectively introduced for the maintenance center.
3. Describe a report format for the maintenance center that would be based on an effective responsibility accounting system, and explain which, if any, of the maintenance center's costs should be charged to the two production centers.

Chapter 18

Segmental Control and Transfer Pricing

Learning Objectives

When you have finished your study of this chapter, you should

1. Recognize the difference between a revenue center and a profit center.
2. Understand the operating characteristics of an autonomous segment or division of a corporation.
3. Be able to develop return-on-investment (ROI) data for use in evaluating the effectiveness of divisional operations.
4. Know how to calculate residual income, and understand the advantages of using it to evaluate division operations.
5. Be able to identify the problems associated with transfer pricing when the selling division has excess capacity as well as when it has no unused capacity.

C hapter 17 explained how a firm's internal operating costs are controlled through the use of cost-accumulation centers and the preparation of performance reports that compare actual costs to budgetary standards or historical costs, that disclose deviations (variations) from operating plans or past-period operations, and that relate achievements (usually output) to the effort (usually cost) exerted in realizing those achievements. In this chapter, we study the evaluation of effort–achievement relationships based on the use of resources to generate net income from a company's **autonomous operating entities.** This type of control is used when firms are decentralized to the point where divisional managers are given operational autonomy. Resources (the investment base) committed to each division are controlled by corporate management. In such decentralized situations, the operational efficiency of each division is evaluated primarily on the basis of the net operating income it earns in relation to its investment base. A segment's pricing policy for intracompany sales—**transfer pricing**, or the pricing of goods transferred from one company segment to another—is an important element in shaping its net operating income.

Transfer pricing can be intercompany as well as intracompany. Since legally separate companies can be related through common stock ownership—for example, two distinct corporations (subsidiaries) may be wholly owned by another corporation (the parent)—transfer pricing also can occur *between* companies. Rather than being governed by legal form, we rely on economic reality. Thus, our discussion of interdivisional sales also applies to intercompany sales between related companies.

As we develop the basic criteria underlying segmental control and transfer pricing, we shall

1. explain the difference between a revenue center and a profit center
2. develop procedures for evaluating the operations of investment centers
3. discuss the problems associated with pricing interdivisional sales.

Revenue Centers and Profit Centers

Because the generation of revenue is the primary or only responsibility of the marketing department of a corporation, we refer to such a department as a **revenue center.** When the marketing department in turn delegates the responsibility for generating sales revenues to regional sales offices or, in some instances, to specific product sales offices, each of those subdivisions constitutes a separate revenue center responsible to the corporate marketing department. In such situations, the regional or the product sales managers need performance reports comparing actual with budgeted sales for their specific regions or products. The difference between actual and budgeted sales revenue for each revenue center can be considered a **sales revenue variance**, which can be broken down into a *sales price variance* and a *sales volume variance* (as illustrated in Chapter 17, pages 638–639) for use in evaluating a center's operating efficiency.

One problem associated with this approach to evaluating revenue center managers is the failure to recognize the importance of controlling costs incurred in generating revenues. If managers are evaluated solely on the basis of sales revenues generated, they may incur excessive costs in promoting sales that do not provide an appropriate contribution margin for the company. The regional or product sales managers conceivably might even reduce selling prices (if they have authority to do so) to the point where sales would produce a negative contribution margin.

To avoid such problems, the individual revenue centers can be evaluated by using a contribution-margin or gross-profit approach, as suggested in Chapter 17 (see pages 639–642). This can be carried one step further by granting the revenue centers operational autonomy, thereby making them **profit centers**. When costs incurred in generating revenues are formally matched against the revenues generated in evaluating the performance of such centers, the effectiveness of center managers is measured by the profits realized over a period of time in relation to the resources invested in the center. Such profit centers are often characterized as **segments** (or divisions) **of a business. Common costs** incurred for the benefit of all segments generally should not be allocated to the segments because segment managers have no control over such costs. Segments managers, though, should be kept informed of common costs.

We now turn our attention to the problems associated with evaluating segments of a business on the basis of the profits earned by those segments. Because the net incomes earned by such segments or divisions are expected to be related to the net assets committed to them, we can think of them as **investment centers**.

Investment Centers

The organization chart in Figure 18–1 demonstrates how a corporation may be divided into separate, autonomous divisions. An officer such as a corporate vice-president will be charged with controlling the operations of each of those divisions. For example, General Motors Corporation operates with separate divisions for Buick, Cadillac, Chevrolet, Oldsmobile, and Pontiac automobile companies. The operational effectiveness of the managers of each division typically would be evaluated on the basis of some measure of the divisional earnings. Each of the

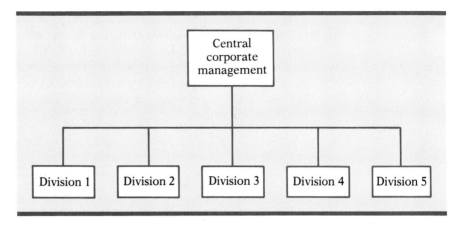

FIGURE 18–1 Organization of a Corporation into Separate Divisions

divisional managers (a vice-president, for example) would then be granted the authority to "run" that segment of the business without direct operational supervision from corporate management.

Since divisions typically have differing amounts of resources available to them, it would be inappropriate to evaluate the effectiveness of any specific divisional manager's operations by simply looking at the amount on the bottom line of the divisional income statement. To be meaningful, a division's operational effectiveness should be evaluated by relating its net operating income to the resources available to it, measured in terms of the division's net assets (assets minus liabilities). If we think of the net assets as being the efforts committed to the division by the corporation, then the primary measure for evaluating operational effectiveness is *return on investment (ROI)*, which can be calculated by dividing division net income by the net assets available to the division. Ideally, net assets should be stated at current values rather than in accordance with generally accepted accounting principles, to provide the most meaningful return-on-investment data. The divisor in the calculation should be *average* net assets available during the reporting period. Assuming net assets are acquired evenly though the year, average net assets can be calculated by adding beginning-of-period net assets to end-of-period net assets and dividing the total by 2. If net assets aren't acquired (or disposed of) evenly through the year, a monthly weighted average can be found by adding together net assets at the end of each month and dividing by 12. We can state the ROI calculation as follows:

$$\text{ROI} = \frac{\text{Net income}}{\text{Average net assets}}$$

To obtain additional information, the ROI percentage can be divided into two subsets, investment turnover and return on sales. *Investment turnover* is calculated by dividing sales by the average net assets available during the period over which the sales were realized. *Return on sales* is calculated by dividing net income by net sales. The relationship between ROI, investment turnover, and return on sales is given in the following equation:

$$\text{ROI} = \text{Investment turnover} \times \text{Return on sales}$$

$$= \frac{\text{Sales}}{\text{Average net assets}} \times \frac{\text{Net income}}{\text{Sales}}$$

Managers of a corporation's autonomous segments (holding other factors constant) can increase the ROI percentage by increasing the investment turnover or by increasing the return on sales. Investment turnover can be increased by increasing sales or decreasing net assets if the other factor, in turn, is held constant. Likewise, the return on sales can be increased either by increasing net income or decreasing sales while the other factor is held constant. These relationships motivate managers to strive for an optimum combination of sales volume, net income, and resource base. We can illustrate the necessary calculations with the following assumed data for a division being evaluated:

Net assets at beginning of period	$ 200,000
Net assets at end of period	$ 300,000
Net income for period	$ 50,000
Sales for period	$1,000,000

The three elements of evaluation data then would be calculated as follows:

$$\text{ROI} = \frac{\$50,000}{(\$200,000 + \$300,000)/2} = 20\%$$

$$\text{Investment turnover} = \frac{\$1,000,000}{\$250,000} = 4$$

$$\text{Return on sales} = \frac{\$50,000}{\$1,000,000} = 0.05$$

ROI also can be calculated from investment turnover and return on sales:

$$\text{ROI} = 4 \times 0.05 = 0.20, \text{ or } 20\%$$

While individual ROI numbers are interesting, they should be compared with some benchmark to achieve an appropriate evaluation of performance. Although those comparison figures could be the comparable data for other divisions, they are more often the division's prior-period data or the division's budgetary data.

Evaluation on the basis of ROI can lead to interdivisional investment that is optimal at the division level but suboptimal for the overall firm. To illustrate, let's assume there are three divisions in a firm contributing the following returns on investment:

	ROI
Division 1	$\dfrac{\$50,000}{\$250,000} = 20\%$
Division 2	$\dfrac{\$25,000}{\$100,000} = 25\%$
Division 3	$\dfrac{\$75,000}{\$500,000} = 15\%$
Firm ROI	$\dfrac{\$150,000}{\$850,000} = 17.65\%$

Any project that could earn a return greater than the firm's overall return of 17.65% would improve the overall ROI. However, no division would want to invest in a project earning less than its average return on investment because it would *decrease* that division's ROI. Thus, in their own self-interests, Division 1 would not invest in a project returning less than 20% and Division 2 would not invest for a yield of less than 25%. There is no incentive for a division to approve projects that would improve the firm's overall ROI if that would lower the division's ROI.

To minimize this short-sighted, local perspective, a division's operations also may be evaluated on the basis of the amount of **residual income** earned, that is, the income left after providing a designated amount for the cost of capital. For example, if we assume in the previous illustration that the imputed cost of providing the net assets for each division is 12%, residual income for Division 1 would be:

$$\text{Residual income} = \$50,000 - 0.12(\$250,000) = \$20,000$$

This evaluation would encourage divisions to accept all orders producing net income greater than the 12% cost of obtaining resources. It also is more appropriate in situations where divisional investment decisions are made by corporate rather than divisional managers.

If desired, a residual rate of return on investment can be calculated by relating residual income to average investment in net assets (that is, residual income divided by average net assets). The residual incomes, residual rates of return, and standard ROIs for Divisions 1, 2, and 3 and the entire firm are:

	ROI	Residual Income	Residual ROI
Division 1	20%	$20,000	8%
Division 2	25%	$13,000	13%
Division 3	15%	$15,000	3%
Firm	17.25%	$48,000	5.65%

There are two additional problems in using ROI for evaluation purposes. One relates to the potential inflation problem and the other is the short-term orientation usually associated with ROI. Generally accepted accounting principles require that net assets be valued at the depreciated historical cost of total assets less liabilities. In a period during which there has been a significant amount of inflation, the ROI based on historical cost data may be misleading when making interdivisional comparisons.

To illustrate, let's assume that Division 1 average net assets of $250,000 includes $100,000 of **monetary assets** (cash and items not affected by price-level changes) and $150,000 worth of **nonmonetary assets**, and that the price index, reflecting changes in the purchasing power of the dollar, has increased from 100 to 150 since the nonmonetary assets were acquired. Current price-level-adjusted average net assets then would be calculated as follows:

Average monetary net assets	$100,000
Average nonmonetary assets [$150,000 × (150/100)]	225,000
Total	$325,000

Observe that with use of the price-level-adjusted data for the average investment, the return on investment is slightly more than 15% ($50,000/$325,000 = 0.1538), rather than the 20% calculated earlier. Also, because the depreciation deducted in arriving at net income will have been based on historical costs rather than price-level-adjusted costs, the net income of $50,000 also will be overstated. For example, if the depreciation based on the price-level-adjusted values for nonmonetary net assets were $5,000 more than the depreciation based on historical costs, a more realistic ROI would be slightly less than 14% ($45,000/325,000 = 0.1385).

Also, these calculations have been made as if the investment and the return on investment occurred in the same reporting or evaluation period. Typically, the investment must be made in one period and the return from that investment captured in a future period or periods. A myopic, short-term attitude on ROI can encourage mobile managers to ignore profitable long-term ventures in favor of "acceptable" short-term projects. This short-sighted attitude could eventually compromise the continuity of the firm. If a firm desires to use ROI to evaluate managers, it should consider using a longer time period (such as 3 to 5 years).

Unfortunately, many managers do not stay in the same position long enough to make the use of such a long-term analysis feasible.

Thus, ROI evaluations of divisional operations should be used with the understanding that it has certain inherent weaknesses as a device to motivate divisional managers to make decisions that advance the interests of the corporate entity. At best, it should be employed with care and should be supplemented by other measures, such as the residual income generated by each division or physical measures of productivity that are critical to the division's success.

Problems Associated with Pricing Interdivisional Sales

Up to this point, we have assumed that the autonomous division being evaluated sold all its goods or services in a market that would allow the prices charged to be determined by the economic forces of supply and demand. However, in many instances, the divisional units of a corporation will buy from and sell to each other in a noncompetitive market, thereby creating problems about the prices charged in related-company transactions, that is, **transfer prices.** We will now:

1. explore the economics of transfer pricing
2. identify policies that might minimize transfer-pricing problems
3. evaluate possible solutions to transfer-pricing problems.

Economics of Transfer Pricing

Since in a decentralized firm divisional managers typically are given operational autonomy and then are held accountable for overall division operations, each divisional manager wants to sell goods at a price that will maximize the division's profits. In a competitive environment, divisional pricing policy will be (or should be) based on supply and demand.

Pricing problems can occur, however, in connection with interdivisional sales any time the competitive environment is modified through corporate management's imposition of transfer-pricing rules. Transfer-pricing problems intensify as the size of the product market decreases, and they are most acute where there is no competitive market, as the following table illustrates:

Sellers (producers)	Purchasers	Pricing Problems
Multiple	Multiple	Minimal
Multiple	Few	
Few	Multiple	
Few	Few	
One	Multiple	
One	Few	
One	One	Severe

In any environment, the price demanded by the selling division, and therefore presumed to be the price at which its profits will be maximized, may not necessarily be the price that would provide maximum earnings for the corporation. In such a situation, corporate management faces the dilemma of either taking away some of the divisional manager's autonomy or accepting a divisionally determined selling price that may not maximize total corporate profit. Thus, the benefits derived from decentralization are not without costs. The minimum transfer price that should be accepted by the selling division to maximize corporate profits equals the relevant cost to produce the product. When the selling division has excess productive capacity, the transfer price generally would be the variable cost per unit—more specifically, the marginal cost of producing that lot of units. The maximum selling price at which the buying division should be indifferent between purchasing the goods from the selling division or buying from an outside firm would be the price on the open market.

Thus, when selling divisions have excess capacity and seek interdivisional prices in excess of those quoted by an outside firm, corporate management may feel obligated to establish transfer prices that will maximize corporate profits. However, an overriding problem with such interference in divisional operations is that it tends to destroy the divisional autonomy on which management depends to encourage the division to operate aggressively and efficiently. Therefore, corporate management often will be faced with deciding whether to let divisional managers settle their pricing problems among themselves, with minimal intervention, or ceasing to treat the divisions as autonomous units.

Without excess capacity, the relevant cost to produce the units generally would be made up of the variable costs to produce and ship the units plus any opportunity costs associated with using the facilities to produce those units. Thus, for the corporation, the decision whether or not to use goods produced by one division in another division's operations is nothing more than a conventional *make-or-buy decision* that requires comparison of the relevant costs to make the product with the price quoted by an outside supplier.

The sales of products from one division to another at an amount equal to relevant costs of production would preclude the selling division's realizing a profit on the sale. Since division managers are being evaluated (and probably rewarded) on the basis of the profits earned by their divisions, this would not be a satisfactory arrangement for the selling division as an autonomous unit. We show, by illustration, the pricing–net-income relationships on pages 688–692.

Transfer-Pricing Policy

Because of the problems just described, corporate management must establish a policy regarding the prices to be charged on sales between divisions. There are three general approaches for establishing transfer prices:

1. *Prices based on the market prices* that could be realized from the goods if they were sold to outside firms. The same prices are charged to both external and internal customers.
2. *Prices negotiated* between the selling and buying divisions.
3. *Prices based on costs* (either absorption or variable) expected to be incurred in producing and delivering the goods. This can include the full costs or full costs adjusted for costs not incurred on interdivisional sales.

No matter which method is used, the transfer prices may lead to operating practices that will *not* maximize total corporate net income.

In adopting a transfer-pricing policy, corporate management must recognize that a selling division having an *outside market* for its product can provide the largest contribution toward corporate net income by pricing its sales to another division at an amount at least equal to the relevant costs of producing and delivering the goods or services, including opportunity costs, but no higher than would cause the buying division to acquire the product(s) from an outside supplier and leave the selling division with excess capacity.

If a selling division has *excess capacity*, the minimum transfer price generally would equal the variable costs of producing and delivering the goods, since the opportunity cost would be zero. Stated another way, with excess capacity any transfer price producing a positive contribution margin for the selling division and still allowing the goods or services to be acquired within the company would tend to maximize total corporate net income. For the selling division, however, the benefit associated with selling goods at a price designed to recover only relevant costs would accrue entirely to the other division(s) and the corporation as a whole; there would be no increase in the selling division's net income as a result of a sale at cost. However, if the buying division purchases some of the goods going into its production from outside firms that could have been purchased from another division with idle capacity because the outside firm will provide them at a lower price that is still in excess of the selling division's variable costs, then the corporation as a whole will not be maximizing its net income.

If a selling division with an outside market has *no excess capacity*, then sales within the company, from the corporation's point of view, should be priced to at least equal the variable costs of producing the units plus the opportunity cost of using the facilities to produce those goods.[1] This opportunity cost generally equals the contribution margin on the units that must be withdrawn from the outside market by the

---

[1] Aside from the transfer-pricing problem, if a selling division has no excess capacity, prices being charged to outside customers may need to be reviewed to determine whether they could be increased to the point where the outside demand for its product will decrease to equal its capacity to produce that product. Alternatively, the division may need to increase its productive capacity to meet the demand for its product at present prices.

selling division in order to fill an interdivisional order. Because of selling and delivery efficiencies, though, the interdivisional price could be lower than the price charged to outside customers. If a division is operating at full capacity, it would appear to be equitable to price interdivisional sales at the prices charged to outside customers reduced by any costs of selling outside that would not be incurred on sales between divisions. For example, there would be no sales commission expenses and probably little or no delivery expenses incurred on sales to other divisions.

If the selling division has *no outside market* for its product, there is little justification for its being treated as an autonomous operating entity, regardless of whether it has excess capacity. In this situation, the division should be treated as a cost center, and corporate management should exercise control over the division by evaluating production and operating costs through performance reports that relate performance to established goals, as explained in Chapter 17. If a cost center division has excess capacity, the firm should look for ways to use that capacity in the production of other products.

To illustrate how these various pricing arrangements affect divisional and corporate net income, let's assume that a selling division has a capacity to produce 10,000 units, with variable costs of $5 per unit, including sales commissions of $.50 a unit that do not have to be paid on intercompany sales, and a normal selling price of $8.00. However, the division is currently selling only 7,000 units to outsiders. If a buying division purchases 1,000 units from an outsider at $7.00 per unit rather than buying them from the selling division at $8 per unit, the firm, as a whole, will be worse off by $2,500. The buying firm will be better off, but the selling firm will be worse off, as illustrated here:

Buying firm cost savings/unit [($8 − $7) × 1,000 units]	$1,000 better off
Selling firm lost profit/unit [($8 − $4.50) × 1,000 units]	3,500 worse off
Corporation as a whole	$2,500 worse off

Therefore, a multidivisional firm may want to adopt the following basic transfer-pricing policies:

1. If a market price exists, use it (perhaps adjusted for selling and delivery costs not incurred on intracompany sales).
2. If a buying division has obtained a cheaper price from an outside firm and the selling division will not match the outside price, the buying division is free to buy outside.
3. If a selling division matches a buying division's outside price quotation, the buying division must buy from the selling division.
4. If conflicts arise, formal negotiation procedures may be followed.

Although these policies provide possible ways of resolving transfer-pricing disputes, current thinking has moved away from forcing prices on divisional managers. The corporate net income lost by a failure of divisional buyers and sellers to agree on a price is instead recognized as a cost of decentralization.

To further illustrate, let's assume that a corporation has two divisions, 1 and 2, that manufacture products A, B, and C. Both A and B are manufactured by Division 1. Product A is used in Division 2 to manufacture product C. Each unit of product C requires one unit of product A. The firm expects to have the following costs and sales prices during the next operating period:

	Division 1		Division 2
	Product A	**Product B**	**Product C**
Variable cost to produce and sell	$6.00	$5.00	$4.00 plus cost of product A
Sales price	$11.00	$8.00	$18.00
Projected sales	30,000 units*	10,000 units	10,000 units
Fixed costs	$90,000		$20,000

*20,000 units sold outside the firm

With Division 1 supplying product A for Division 2, corporation net income can be summarized as follows:

	Division 1	Division 2	Total
Sales			
Product A (30,000 @ $11)	$330,000		$330,000
Product B (10,000 @ $8)	80,000		80,000
Product C (10,000 @ $18)		$180,000	180,000
Total sales	$410,000	$180,000	$590,000
Variable costs			
Product A (30,000 @ $6)	180,000		180,000
Product B (10,000 @ $5)	50,000		50,000
Product C (10,000 @ $15)		$150,000	150,000
Total variable costs	$230,000	$150,000	$380,000
Contribution margin	$180,000	$ 30,000	$210,000
Fixed costs	90,000	20,000	110,000
Net operating income	$ 90,000	$ 10,000	$100,000

An outside firm offers to sell Division 2 as many units of product A as required for production of product C at a price of $8.00 per unit. Because their production requirements are similar, Division 1 fixed costs are allocated to products A and B at an equal amount of $2.25 per unit. This results in projected total costs of products A and B of $8.25 and $7.25, respectively. Division 1 refuses to match the $8 outside purchase price for product A because that amount is less than the $8.25 total production cost. Observe that Division 1 has sufficient capacity to produce all of the 40,000 units required for projected sales of products A and B. The net operating income, by divisions and in total, if (1) a transfer price of $8.00 is negotiated between Divisions 1 and 2, or (2) Division 2 buys product A from an outside firm would be as follows:

(1) Negotiated Price for Product A (excess capacity available)

	Division 1	Division 2	Total
Sales			
Product A			
20,000 @ $11	$220,000		$220,000
10,000 @ $8	80,000		80,000
Product B (10,000 @ $8)	80,000		80,000
Product C (10,000 @ $18)		$180,000	180,000
Total sales	$380,000	$180,000	$560,000
Variable costs			
Product A (30,000 @ $6)	$180,000		$180,000
Product B (10,000 @ $5)	50,000		50,000
Product C (10,000 @ $12)		$120,000	$120,000
Total variable costs	$230,000	$120,000	$350,000
Contribution margin	$150,000	$ 60,000	$210,000
Fixed costs	90,000	20,000	110,000
Net operating income	$ 60,000	$ 40,000	$100,000

In this situation, Division 1 is worse off by $30,000, Division 2 is better off by $30,000, and the corporation as a whole is in exactly the same position as before the transfer-pricing question arose. If Division 1 refuses to accept the $8 sales price on the 10,000 units required by Division 2, those units will be purchased from the outside firm and the following results will occur:

(2) Product A Acquired from Outside Firm (excess capacity available)

	Division 1	Division 2	Total
Sales			
Product A (20,000 @ $11)	$220,000		$220,000
Product B (10,000 @ $8)	80,000		80,000
Product C (10,000 @ $18)		$180,000	180,000
Total sales	$300,000	$180,000	$480,000
Variable costs			
Product A (20,000 @ $6)	$120,000		$120,000
Product B (10,000 @ $5)	50,000		50,000
Product C (10,000 @ $12)		$120,000	$120,000
Totals	$170,000	$120,000	$290,000
Contribution margin	$130,000	$ 60,000	$190,000
Fixed costs	90,000	20,000	110,000
Net operating income	$ 40,000	$ 40,000	$ 80,000

Total net operating income will be $20,000 less if product A is purchased from an outside firm. This can be proven as follows:

$$\text{Foregone contribution margin on product A} =$$
$$10,000 \times (\$8.00 - \$6.00) = \$20,000$$

Division 1, by refusing to negotiate a price of $8, will show $20,000 less net income than it could have earned. It is true that the $60,000 net operating income with the $8 negotiated price is $30,000 less than Division 1's previous net operating income of $90,000, but the realization of an $11 price for sales to Division 2 is no longer possible.

Now let's assume that Division 1 has a capacity to produce only 30,000 units and therefore must forego sales of 10,000 units to outsiders to provide Department 2 with 10,000 units of product A. Since the contribution margin on product A is $5 while the contribution margin on product B is only $3, production of B should be eliminated—provided its elimination will not adversely affect sales of product A. The minimum negotiated price between Divisions 1 and 2 in this situation would be $9, computed as follows:

Variable cost of product A	$6
Opportunity cost of foregoing production of product B—projected contribution margin for product B	3
Total	$9

We now project the expected net income to be realized if (1) a transfer price of $9.00 is negotiated between Divisions 1 and 2, or (2) Division 2 buys product A from an outside firm for $8 per unit.

(1) Negotiated Price for Product A (no excess capacity available)

	Division 1	Division 2	Total
Sales			
Product A			
20,000 @ $11	$220,000		$220,000
10,000 @ $9	90,000		90,000
Product C (10,000 @ $18)		$180,000	180,000
Total sales	$310,000	$180,000	$490,000
Variable costs			
Product A (30,000 @ $6)	$180,000		$180,000
Product C (10,000 @ 13)		$130,000	$130,000
Total variable costs	$180,000	$130,000	$310,000
Contribution margin	$130,000	$ 50,000	$180,000
Fixed costs	90,000	20,000	110,000
Net operating income	$ 40,000	$ 30,000	$ 70,000

(2) Product A Acquired from Outside Firm (no excess capacity available)

	Division 1	Division 2	Total
Sales			
Product A (20,000 @ $11)	$220,000		$220,000
Product B (10,000 @ $8)	80,000		80,000
Product C (10,000 @ $18)		$180,000	180,000
Total sales	$300,000	$180,000	$480,000
Variable costs			
Product A (20,000 @ $6)	$120,000		$120,000
Product B (10,000 @ $5)	50,000		50,000
Product C (10,000 @ $12)		$120,000	120,000
Totals	$170,000	$120,000	$290,000
Contribution margin	$130,000	$ 60,000	$190,000
Fixed costs	90,000	20,000	110,000
Net operating income	$ 40,000	$ 40,000	$ 80,000

When Division 1 has no excess capacity, total net operating income is expected to be $10,000 larger if product A is purchased from an outside firm. This can be explained as follows:

Division 1 is indifferent between the $9 transfer price on product A with no sales of product B and no transfer of A with sales of 10,000 units of product B because the contribution margin is the same $3 per unit ($9 − $6 versus $8 − $5).

Division 2, however, saves ($9 transfer price − $8 outside price) × 10,000 units = $10,000 on the cost of components going into product C by buying outside.

SUMMARY

In this chapter, we examined some of the techniques used to control the operations of autonomous segments (divisions) of a corporation. In such a decentralized situation, a corporation delegates operational responsibility to the division managers, who are then held accountable for their actions through the net income earned by their divisions. We evaluate the effectiveness of their efforts and achievements by comparing current period divisional net income to budgetary projections or previous period net income. Those income data also are considered in relation to net assets committed to the division, by determining the rate of return that has been earned on the company's investment in the division.

Return-on-investment (ROI) evaluation can be useful but also has some weaknesses. A special problem in holding the autonomous segments of a decentralized corporation profit-accountable to corporate management occurs when goods are purchased and sold between related entities (divisions, or related companies, for example), because the pricing policy that may provide the greatest benefit to the autonomous unit may not be the one that maximizes total corporate or consolidated net income. At the same time, corporate management generally should refrain from dictating transfer prices to division managers or chief executive officers (CEOs) of subsidiary companies because that would detract from the autonomous nature of the segments and therefore make the profit-accountability evaluation less valid.

In view of the difficulties associated with transfer pricing, we suggested that corporate managers first determine whether the firm's operational characteristics are such that it can function most effectively as a decentralized company. If they find characteristics favoring decentralization, division managers or CEOs should be given full operational responsibility and be held accountable for profits generated by their operations. If those characteristics are not present, that segment should be controlled by monitoring the cost and production relationships as described in Chapter 17. We concluded that unless a division has a significant amount of sales outside the company, or is producing a product or service so widely available that a market price is readily determinable, it is probably preferable not to provide it with autonomous status. However, if a corporation decides to operate as a decentralized entity, with operating autonomy being given to division managers or subsidiary CEOs, corporate managers generally should not interfere in divisional pricing practices other than to set up some general policy guidelines.

GLOSSARY OF TERMS INTRODUCED IN THIS CHAPTER

autonomous operating entity A corporate subsidiary of a parent corporation or a segment of a corporation for which managers are given operational autonomy, meaning their operational effectiveness will be evaluated by relating operating results to the segment's investment base.

common costs Costs of facilities or services associated with the output of two or more operations, products, or services; also known as *joint costs*.

investment center A segment of a corporation whose performance is measured in terms of the relationship of operating results to the resources committed to the segment (investment base).

monetary assets Cash, or claims to cash, that are fixed in dollar amounts regardless of changes in the level of prices.

net assets	Assets minus liabilities; also *owners' equity*.
nonmonetary assets	Assets other than monetary assets, including assets whose values can increase or decrease due to changes in the purchasing power of the monetary unit (dollars in the United States).
profit center	A business's responsibility center that has authority to affect both the revenues earned and the costs incurred by the center. Operational effectiveness is evaluated in terms of the amount of profit generated.
residual income	The income left after deducting a designated amount for the cost of the capital provided to earn that income from net income before this deduction.
return on investment	Net income divided by average net assets; also defined as the ratio of net sales to investment used to produce those sales multiplied by the ratio of net income to net sales.
revenue center	A corporation's responsibility center that is primarily responsible for generating corporate revenues and whose effectiveness is measured chiefly by the amount of revenues generated.
sales revenue variance	The difference between the actual and budgeted sales revenues for a revenue center, or the difference between the sales revenues of one period and those of another (previous) period; can be divided into two parts— *sales price variance* (change in price times the actual units sold) and *sales volume variance* (change in volume times the budgeted or previous sales price per unit).
segment of a business	A component of a business whose activities constitute a separately identifiable line of business or class of customer or territory.
transfer pricing	The pricing of goods or services transferred from one segment of a business to another.

QUESTIONS FOR CLASS DISCUSSION

18–1 How does a decentralized firm control the operations of its divisions? How do such controls relate to the responsibility accounting procedures discussed in Chapter 17? Explain.

18–2 What is the difference between a revenue center and a profit center? Explain.

18–3 What is the relationship between a profit center and an investment center? Explain.

18–4 What effort–achievement relations are typically used to control the operations of the autonomous segments of a large corporation? Explain.

18–5 Why is it important to use average net assets rather than end-of-period net assets as the denominator in calculating return on investment?

18–6   What interdivisional pricing problems may result from using complete profit accountability control for the divisions of a corporation? Explain.

18–7   What is meant by the term *residual income*? Why may residual income be a better device for evaluating the effectiveness of divisional managers than net income? Explain.

18–8   What special complications do price-level changes bring into the profit-accountability evaluation of divisional managers? Explain.

18–9   How may complete autonomy in the pricing of a division's sales work to the disadvantage of overall corporate operations? Explain.

18–10   What effect should the existence of excess capacity within a division have on its interdivisional pricing policies? Explain.

18–11   What are three general policies that might be followed in establishing interdivisional transfer prices? Which of these should be followed in the effective management of a corporation? Explain.

EXERCISES

18–12   **Calculation of Performance Indicators** The following selected data pertain to Bird Co.'s Celtic Division for the past year:

Sales	$1,000,000
Variable costs	$600,000
Traceable fixed costs	$250,000
Average invested capital	$400,000
Imputed interest rate	15%

REQUIRED:

1. Calculate the residual income for the Celtic Division.
2. Calculate the rate of return on Bird's investment in Celtic.
3. Calculate the investment turnover for Celtic.
4. Calculate the rate of return on sales.
5. Explain the relationship of the answer for requirement 2 to the answers for 3 and 4.

18–13   **Relationship Among Performance Measurement Data** Assume that the amounts of sales, net income, and average invested capital remain the same as in exercise 18–12.

REQUIRED:

1. What would happen to the rate of return on investment if investment turnover decreases?
2. What would happen to the rate of return on investment if average invested capital increases?
3. Discuss the implications of your answers to requirements 1 and 2.

18—14 **Relationship Among Performance Measurement Data** Assume that the rate of investment turnover remains constant.

REQUIRED:

1. What would happen to the rate of return on average invested capital if the rate of return on sales increases?
2. What would happen to that rate of return on average investment if net income increases? Explain.

18—15 **Transfer Pricing** Conglom, Inc., operates Alex Division, which produces a chemical used in the manufacture of a product produced by another division of the company. Historically, approximately two-thirds of Alex's potential output has been sold to the other division. Alex has sold the remainder of its potential output to outsiders. Last year's operating data for Alex are as follow:

	To Other Division	To Outsiders
Sales	$350,000 (10,000 gal @ $35)	$250,000 (5,000 gal @ $50)
Variable costs	250,000	125,000
Fixed costs	75,000	37,500
Total costs	$325,000	$162,500
Operating income	$ 25,000	$ 87,500

The other division has an opportunity to purchase 3,000 gallons of the chemical from an outside supplier at a price of $30 per gallon.

REQUIRED:

1. Assume that Alex is unable to increase its sales to outsiders to compensate for the lost sales to the other division. Should the offer be accepted? Discuss the decision from the point of view of both Conglom, Inc., and the other division. Develop a report in support of your answer. Discuss possibilities for resolving the matter.
2. Assume that Alex is able to increase its sales to outsiders to compensate for the 3,000 gallons that can be purchased from the outside supplier. Explain the effects of accepting the offer on the operations of both divisions and Conglom.

18—16 **Transfer Pricing** Buller, Incorporated, is a decentralized company that manufactures various types of lawn maintenance equipment. Managers of its divisions are held net-income accountable. Division A produces a motor that can be sold to outside firms as well as to other divisions within the company. The competitively determined sales price of the motor is $200 each. Division B buys the motors for a mower that it sells for $350. Variable costs are $150 and $250 per unit for Divisions A and B, respectively. The manager of Division B seeks a lower transfer price from Division A because at the current price the division is unable to realize a profit from the sale of its mowers.

REQUIRED:

1. Compute Division B's contribution margin per mower.
2. Assuming Division A can sell all of its motors in the open market, should it consider reducing the price of its motors to Division B? Discuss.
3. Assume now that Division A can sell only 1,000 of the 2,000 motors it can produce on the open market at $200 each. The remainder can be sold at $160 each to a foreign firm. Should a price concession be made to Division B? If so, at what price and for how many units? Develop a report in support of your answer.

18–17 **Transfer Pricing and Profit Accountability** Beatrice Company operates a mine and an ore smelting division. The ore can be sold to other smelters for $200 per ton. If the ore is smelted, the ingots from 1 ton of ore can be sold for $275. Variable costs of operating the mine total $100 per ton of ore. The variable costs of smelting 1 ton of ore amount to $80 per ton. Although the smelting division can process 10,000 tons of ore each year, the mine can produce only 9,000 tons a year. Management wishes to evaluate each division on the basis of the operating income it earns.

REQUIRED:

1. Prepare a report showing the contribution margin for each division and for the company, under the assumption that the mine sells its production at the market price to the smelting firm, which then operates at 90% of its capacity. Discuss the implications of the data in your report.
2. Assume now that the management of Beatrice establishes a transfer-pricing policy requiring the ore to be transferred to the smelting division at 110% of variable costs. Calculate the contribution margins of both divisions and the company under this arrangement. Discuss the implications of these data in relation to those included in your report from requirement 1.
3. What suggestions would you make to Beatrice management regarding future operations?

18–18 **Transfer Pricing** Albert Company manufactures farm equipment. It carries out its operations through five divisions, which we shall call A, B, C, D, and E. Each division operates as an autonomous unit and is evaluated on the basis of the operating income earned. Division B has always purchased a frame component from A at $135 per unit. When informed that A was raising its price to $150 per unit because of the recent installation of new equipment and a resulting increase in depreciation, B's management decided to purchase frames from an outside firm at $135 per unit. Division A's management asks Albert's management to require Division B to continue to buy the frames internally. You gather the following information relating to the past year's operations:

B's purchases of frames from A	2,000 units
A's variable cost per frame	$120
A's fixed cost per frame	$20

REQUIRED:

1. Assuming that the 2,000 frames A has been selling to B cannot be sold on the open market and that no alternate use is possible for each division's facilities, determine whether Albert will benefit from B's purchase of the frames from an outside firm. Support your answer.
2. Assume now that if A does not produce the 2,000 frames for B, A's equipment can be used in other operations to produce cash savings of $36,000. Should B purchase the frames from an outside firm? Support your answer.

PROBLEMS

18–19 **Return on Investment** Alpha Division of Albert Company produces photo prints that are sold for $2.00 each. During the past year, Alpha produced and sold 300,000 prints. It incurred the following costs during the year:

	Variable	Fixed
Direct materials	$200,000	
Direct labor	150,000	
Factory overhead	70,000	$42,000
General, selling, and administrative	30,000	48,000
Totals	$450,000	$90,000

Albert's investments in Alpha at the beginning and end of the year were $500,000 and $700,000, respectively.

REQUIRED:

1. Calculate Alpha's return on investment for the year.
2. Assume that Albert acquires Fair Advertising Agency, which it will operate as a separate division. Fair's manager offers to purchase all of its advertising photo prints from Alpha at a price of $1.50 each. Alpha can produce these photos without increasing its fixed costs. Fair estimates that it will need 100,000 photo prints per year. No additional selling or advertising expenses would be incurred by Alpha. Should Alpha accept the offer? Prepare a report in support of your answer.
3. Calculate Alpha's projected rate of return on investment for next year, assuming outside sales of 300,000 prints, a cost structure like that of last year, and acceptance of Fair's offer. Albert's investment in Alpha is expected to remain at $700,000 during the next year.

18–20 **Rate of Return on Investment and Management Decisions** Venture Corporation invested $100,000 in new equipment for one of its divisions at the beginning of the current year. The analysis made at that time indicated the equipment would save $36,400 in operating expenses per year. At the end of the year, the division manager asked the accounting section to "break out" the figures related to this investment over the past year for the purpose of determining the return on the investment. The equipment has an estimated life of 5 years, with no salvage value. Depreciation is recognized on a straight-line basis. The accounting section was able to identify the equipment and its contribution to the department's operations. The information presented to the department manager at the end of the first year was:

Reduced out-of-pocket operating expenses due to new equipment $36,400

REQUIRED:
1. Calculate the rate of return on the investment for the past year.
2. Assume that the same cost savings are expected to be realized during the second year the equipment is used. What would be the projected rate of return on the investment for that year?
3. What weakness is implicit in using the data from requirements 1 and 2 to evaluate the efficiency of division management for each of those years? Discuss.
4. Relate your discussion in requirement 3 to the effects of inflation.

18–21 **Analysis of Returns on Investments for Three Divisions** The rate of return on investment in a division is sometimes expressed as follows:

$$\text{Return on investment} = \text{Investment turnover} \times \text{Rate of return on sales}$$

Selected data for three divisions of Conglom Corporation are as follows:

	Alpha	Beta	Gamma
Sales	$1,000,000	$500,000	_____
Income	$ 100,000	$ 50,000	_____
Average invested capital	$ 500,000	_____	$5,000,000
Income as a percentage of sales	_____	_____	0.5%
Turnover of invested capital	_____	_____	2
Return on invested capital	_____	1%	_____

REQUIRED:
1. Fill in the blanks in the data summary.
2. Comment on the performance of each division.

18–22 **Return on Investment and Residual Income** Acme Corporation has two divisions (Alpha and Beta). The following information relates to the past year's performance and the financial position of each division at the beginning and end of the year.

	Alpha Division	Beta Division
Investment at beginning of year	$1,800,000	$9,500,000
Investment at end of year	$2,000,000	$10,500,000
Net income	$400,000	$1,500,000
Imputed rate for cost of capital	20%	15%

REQUIRED:

1. Calculate the rate of return on investment for each division.
2. Calculate the residual income for each division.
3. Calculate the residual rate of return on investment for each division.
4. What justification might there be for use of different imputed rates for the cost of capital for the two divisions?
5. Which division has operated more successfully? Discuss.

18–23 Different Measures of Profitability Compton Corporation operates through three autonomous divisions. Managers of the divisions have been promised bonuses based on profitability, measured either in terms of the percentage return on investment or in terms of residual income. Invested capital is defined as gross book value at the beginning of the year. The following data are available for the past year:

Division	Gross Book Value at Beginning of Year	Conventional Net Income
A	$800,000	$95,000
B	760,000	92,000
C	500,000	61,600

Compton imputes a rate of return on invested capital of 10% for all divisions.

REQUIRED:

1. Calculate the rates of return on gross book value at the beginning of the year using conventional net income.
2. Calculate the amounts of residual income earned by each division for the year.
3. Discuss the implications of the answers to requirements 1 and 2 in determining the bonuses to be awarded each manager for the past year's operations.

18–24 Performance Measures Based on Historical Costs Versus Price-Level-Adjusted Costs Monte Del Corporation carries out its operations through three autonomous plants, which we shall label Old, Middle, and Youth Divisions. The following data are provided by each division's accounting records:

	Old	Middle	Youth
Operating income before depreciation	$400,000	$ 640,000	$1,000,000
Depreciation	140,000	200,000	240,000
Operating income	$260,000	$ 440,000	$ 760,000
Fixed assets (book value)	$280,000	$1,800,000	$2,640,000

All fixed assets have an estimated useful life of 12 years, with no salvage value. The ages of the respective plants are:

Old	10 years
Middle	3 years
Youth	1 year

The general price-level index for selected years is:

10 years ago	100
3 years ago	136
1 year ago	160
Current year	170

REQUIRED:

1. Compute the rates of return on investment (defined as total assets) for each division, based on historical cost data.
2. Adjust the appropriate elements of the preceding data to compensate for price-level changes, and calculate the rate of return for each division, based on the price-level-adjusted data.
3. Comment on the implications of the rates calculated in requirements 1 and 2.

18–25

ICMA Adapted

Transfer Prices and Divisional Performance National Industries is a diversified corporation with separate and distinct operating divisions. Each division's performance is evaluated on the basis of net income before taxes and the percentage return on division investment.

The WindAir Division manufactures and sells air conditioning units. The coming year's budgeted income statement for the division, based on a sales volume of 15,000 units, appears at the top of page 702.

WindAir's manager believes sales can be increased if the unit selling price of the air conditioners is reduced. A market research study conducted by an independent firm indicates that a 5% reduction in the selling price ($20) would increase sales volume 16%, or 2,400 units. WindAir has sufficient production capacity to manage this increased volume with no increase in fixed costs.

At the present time, WindAir uses a compressor in its units that it purchases from an outside supplier for $70 each. The division manager of WindAir has approached the manager of National's Compressor Division regarding the possible purchase of compressor units. Compressor Division currently manufactures and sells a unit exclusively to outside firms that is similar to the unit used by WindAir. The specifications of the

WindAir Division

Budgeted Income Statement

For the 19X3–X4 Fiscal Year

	Per Unit	Total (000 omitted)
Sales revenue	$400	$6,000
Manufacturing costs		
Compressor	$ 70	$1,050
Other raw materials	37	555
Direct labor	30	450
Variable overhead	45	675
Fixed overhead	32	480
Total manufacturing costs	$214	$3,210
Gross margin	$186	$2,790
Operating expenses		
Variable selling	$ 18	$ 270
Fixed selling	19	285
Fixed administrative	38	570
Total operating expenses	$ 75	$1,125
Net income before taxes	$111	$1,665

WindAir compressor are slightly different, which would reduce raw materials cost by $1.50 per unit. Compressor Division would not incur any variable selling costs for the units sold to WindAir. The manager of WindAir wants all of the compressors it uses to come from one supplier and has offered to pay $50 each for the total number of units needed.

The Compressor Division has the capacity to produce 75,000 units. The coming year's budgeted income statement for the division, shown at the top of page 703, is based on a projected sales volume of 64,000 units without considering WindAir's proposal.

REQUIRED:

1. Should WindAir Division institute the 5% price reduction on its air conditioner units even if it cannot acquire the compressors internally for $50 each? Support your conclusion with appropriate calculations.
2. Without prejudice to your answer to requirement 1, assume WindAir needs 17,400 units. Should the Compressor Division be willing to supply the compressor units for $50 each? Support your conclusions with appropriate calculations.
3. Without prejudice to your answer to requirement 1, assume WindAir needs 17,400 units. Would it be in the best interest of National Indus-

Compressor Division

Budgeted Income Statement
For the 19X3–X4 Fiscal Year

	Per Unit	Total (000 omitted)
Sales revenue	$100	$6,400
Manufacturing costs		
Raw materials	$ 12	$ 768
Direct labor	8	512
Variable overhead	10	640
Fixed overhead	11	704
Total manufacturing costs	$ 41	$2,624
Gross margin	$ 59	$3,776
Operating expenses		
Variable selling	$ 6	$ 384
Fixed selling	4	256
Fixed administrative	7	448
Total operating expenses	$17	$1,088
Net income before taxes	$ 42	$2,688

tries for the Compressor Division to supply the compressor units at $50 each to the WindAir Division? Support your conclusions with appropriate calculations.

18–26 **Transfer Prices and Divisional Performance** Able Division of Doyle Corporation produces electric motors, 20% of which are sold to Gray Division of Doyle and the remainder to outside customers. Doyle treats its divisions as profit centers and allows division managers to choose their sources of materials. Corporate policy requires that all interdivisional sales and purchases be made at variable cost. Able Division's estimated sales and standard cost data for the year ending December 31, 19X2, based on a full capacity of 200,000 units, are as follows:

	Gray	Outsiders
Sales	$1,800,000	$16,000,000
Variable costs	(1,800,000)	(7,200,000)
Fixed costs	(600,000)	(2,400,000)
Gross margin	$ (600,000)	$ 6,400,000
Unit sales	40,000	160,000

Able has an opportunity to sell the 40,000 units projected to be sold to Gray to an outside customer on a continuing basis at a price of $75 per unit. Gray can purchase its requirements from an outside supplier at a price of $85 per unit.

REQUIRED:

1. Can Able improve its gross margin by selling the 40,000 units to the outside customers? Prepare a report in support of your answer.
2. Would your answer to requirement 1 also maximize Doyle's gross margin? Prepare a report in support of your answer.
3. Assume now that Doyle management permits its divisions to negotiate their transfer prices and that they agree on a price of $75 per unit. How would such an arrangement affect the gross margins of Able, Gray, and Doyle?

18–27 **Profit Centers and Transfer Pricing** A.R. Oma, Inc., manufactures a line of

ICMA Adapted men's perfumes and after-shaving lotions. The manufacturing process is basically a series of mixing operations involving the addition of certain aromatic and coloring ingredients; the finished product is packaged in a company-produced glass bottle and packed in cases containing six bottles.

A.R. Oma believes the sale of its product is heavily influenced by the appearance and appeal of the bottle and has, therefore, devoted considerable managerial effort to bottle production. This has resulted in the development of certain unique bottle-production processes in which management takes considerable pride.

The two areas (perfume production and bottle manufacture) have evolved over the years in an almost independent manner; in fact, a rivalry has developed between management personnel as to "which division is more important" to A.R. Oma. This attitude is probably intensified by the fact that the bottle manufacturing plant was purchased intact 10 years ago and no real interchange of management personnel or ideas (except at the top corporate level) has taken place.

Since the acquisition, all bottle production has been absorbed by the perfume manufacturing plant. Each area is considered a separate profit center and evaluated as such. As the new corporate controller, you are responsible for the definition of a proper transfer value to use in crediting the bottle-production profit center and in debiting the packaging profit center.

At your request, the bottle division general manager has asked certain other bottle manufacturers to quote a price for the quantity and sizes demanded by the perfume division. These competitive prices are:

Volume	Total Price	Price per Case
2,000,000 equivalent cases*	$ 4,000,000	$2.00
4,000,000	7,000,000	1.75
6,000,000	10,000,000	1.67

*An "equivalent case" represents six bottles each.

A cost analysis of the internal bottle plant indicates they can produce bottles at the following costs:

Volume	Total Price	Price per Case
2,000,000 equivalent cases	$3,200,000	$1.60
4,000,000	5,200,000	1.30
6,000,000	7,200,000	1.20

(Your cost analysis reveals that these costs represent fixed costs of $1,200,000 and variable costs of $1.00 per equivalent case.)

These figures have given rise to considerable corporate discussion as to the proper value to use in the transfer of bottles to the perfume division. This interest is heightened by the fact that a significant portion of a division manager's income is an incentive bonus based on profit center results.

The perfume production division has the following costs in addition to the bottle costs:

Volume	Total Cost	Cost per Case
2,000,000 cases	$16,400,000	$8.20
4,000,000	32,400,000	8.10
6,000,000	48,400,000	8.07

After considerable analysis, the marketing research department has furnished you with the following price–demand relationship for the finished product:

Sales Volume	Total Sales Revenue	Sales Price per Case
2,000,000 cases	$25,000,000	$12.50
4,000,000	45,600,000	11.40
6,000,000	63,900,000	10.65

REQUIRED:

1. A.R. Oma has used market-price transfer prices in the past. Using the current market prices and costs, and assuming a volume of 6,000,000 cases, calculate the income for:
   a. the bottle division
   b. the perfume division
   c. the corporation.
2. Indicate whether this production and sales level is the most profitable volume for each of the following. Explain your answers.
   a. the bottle division
   b. the perfume division
   c. the corporation

3. A.R. Oma uses the profit-center approach for divisional operation.
  a. Define a "profit center."
  b. What conditions should exist for a profit center to be established?
  c. Should the two divisions of A.R. Oma be organized as profit centers?

18—28
ICMA Adapted

Opportunity Costs and Transfer-Pricing Policy PortCo Products is a divisionalized furniture manufacturer. The divisions are autonomous segments, with each division being responsible for its own sales, costs of operations, working capital management, and equipment acquisition. Each division serves a different market in the furniture industry. Because the markets and products of the divisions are so different, there have never been any transfers between divisions.

The Commercial Division manufactures equipment and furniture that is purchased by the restaurant industry. The division plans to introduce a new line of counter-and-chair units that feature a cushioned seat for the counter chairs. John Kline, the division manager, has discussed the manufacturing of the cushioned seat with Russ Fiegel of the office division. They both believe a cushioned seat currently made by the office division for use on its deluxe office stool could be modified for use on the new counter chair. Consequently, Kline has asked Russ Fiegel for a price for 100-unit lots of the cushioned seat. The following conversation took place about the price to be charged for the cushioned seats:

Fiegel: John, we can make necessary modifications to the cushioned seat easily. The raw materials used in your seat are slightly different and should cost about 10% more than those used in our deluxe office stool. However, the labor time should be the same because the seat-fabrication operation basically is the same. I would price the seat at our regular rate—full cost plus 30% markup.

Kline: That's higher than I expected, Russ. I was thinking that a good price would be your variable manufacturing costs. After all, your capacity costs will be incurred regardless of this job.

Fiegel: John, I'm at capacity. By making the cushioned seats for you, I'll have to cut my production of deluxe office stools. Of course, I can increase my production of economy office stools. The labor time freed by not having to fabricate the frame or assemble the deluxe stool can be shifted to the frame fabrication and assembly of the economy office stool. Fortunately, I can switch my labor force between these two models of stools without any loss of efficiency. As you know, overtime is not a feasible alternative in our community. I'd like to sell it to you at variable cost, but I have excess demand for both products. I don't mind changing my product mix to the economy model if I get a good return on the seats I make for you. Here are my standard costs for the two stools and a schedule of my manufacturing overhead. [See schedules on page 707.]

Kline: I guess I see your point, Russ, but I don't want to price myself out of the market. Maybe we should talk to corporate to see if they can give us any guidance.

Office Division
Standard Costs and Prices

	Deluxe Office Stool		Economy Office Stool
Raw materials			
Framing	$ 8.15		$ 9.76
Cushioned seat:			
Padding	2.40		—
Vinyl	4.00		—
Molded seat (purchased)	—		6.00
Direct labor			
Frame fabrication (0.5 × $7.50/direct labor hour)	3.75	(0.5 × $7.50/direct labor hour)	3.75
Cushion fabrication (0.5 × $7.50/direct labor hour)	3.75		—
Assembly* (0.5 × $7.50/direct labor hour)	3.75	(0.3 × $7.50/direct labor hour)	2.25
Manufacturing overhead (1.5 direct labor hours × $12.80/direct labor hour	19.20	(0.8 direct labor hour × $12.80/direct labor hour)	10.24
Total standard cost	$45.00		$32.00
Selling price (30% markup)	$58.50		$41.60

*Attaching seats to frames and attaching rubber feet

Office Division
Manufacturing-Overhead Budget

Overhead Item	Nature	Amount
Supplies	Variable—at current market prices	$ 420,000
Indirect labor	Variable	375,000
Supervision	Nonvariable	250,000
Power	Use varies with activity; rates are fixed	180,000
Heat and light	Nonvariable—light is fixed regardless of production while heat/air conditioning varies with fuel charges	140,000
Property taxes and insurance taxes	Nonvariable—any change in amounts/rates is independent of production	200,000
Depreciation	Fixed dollar total	1,700,000
Employee benefits	20% of supervision, direct and indirect labor	575,000
Total overhead		$3,840,000
Capacity in direct labor hours		300,000
Overhead rate per direct labor hour		$12.80

REQUIRED:

1. John Kline and Russ Fiegel did ask PortCo corporate management for guidance on an appropriate transfer price. Corporate management suggested they consider using a transfer price based on variable manufacturing cost plus opportunity cost. Calculate a transfer price for the cushioned seat based on variable manufacturing cost plus opportunity cost.
2. Which alternative transfer price system—full cost, variable manufacturing cost, or variable manufacturing cost plus opportunity cost—would be better as the basis for an intracorporate transfer-price policy? Explain your answer.

18–29
ICMA Adapted

Transfer Pricing and Performance Evaluation DePaolo Industries manufactures carpets, furniture, and foam in three separate divisions. DePaolo's operating statement for 19X3 is reproduced on page 709. Additional information regarding DePaolo's operations is:

(1) Included in the foam division's sales revenue is $500,000 in sales made to the furniture division that were transferred at manufacturing cost.

(2) The cost of goods sold is comprised of the following costs:

	Carpet	Furniture	Foam
Direct materials	$ 500,000	$1,000,000	$1,000,000
Direct labor	500,000	200,000	1,000,000
Variable overhead	750,000	50,000	1,000,000
Fixed overhead	250,000	50,000	0
Total cost of goods sold	$2,000,000	$1,300,000	$3,000,000

(3) Administrative expenses include the following:

	Carpet	Furniture	Foam
Segment expenses			
Variable	$ 85,000	$140,000	$ 40,000
Fixed	85,000	210,000	120,000
Home office expenses (all fixed)			
Directly traceable	100,000	120,000	200,000
General (allocated on sales dollars)	30,000	30,000	40,000
Total	$300,000	$500,000	$400,000

(4) Selling expense is all incurred at the segment level and is 80% variable for all segments.

John Sprint, manager of the foam division, is not pleased with DePaolo's presentation of operating performance. Sprint claimed, "The foam division makes a greater contribution to the company's profits than what is shown. I sell foam to the furniture division at cost and it gets our share of the profit. I can sell that foam on the outside at my regular markup, but I sell to furniture for the well-being of the company. I think my division should get credit for those internal sales at market. I think we should also revise our operating statements for internal purposes. Why don't we consider preparing these internal statements in a contribution-approach reporting format, showing internal transfers at market?"

DePaolo Industries

Operating Statement

For the Year Ended December 31, 19X3

	Carpet Division	Furniture Division	Foam Division	Total
Sales revenue	$3,000,000	$3,000,000	$4,000,000	$10,000,000
Cost of goods sold	2,000,000	1,300,000	3,000,000	6,300,000
Gross profit	$1,000,000	$1,700,000	$1,000,000	$ 3,700,000
Operating expenses				
Administrative	$ 300,000	$ 500,000	$ 400,000	$ 1,200,000
Selling	600,000	600,000	500,000	1,700,000
Total operating expenses	$ 900,000	$1,100,000	$ 900,000	$ 2,900,000
Income from operations before taxes	$ 100,000	$ 600,000	$ 100,000	$ 800,000

REQUIRED:

1. John Sprint believes the intracompany transfers from the foam division to the furniture division should be at market price rather than manufacturing cost for measuring divisional performance.
   a. Explain why Sprint is correct.
   b. Identify and describe two approaches used for setting transfer prices, other than manufacturing cost used by DePaolo Industries and market price as recommended by Sprint.
2. Using the contribution approach and market-based transfer prices, prepare a revised operating statement, by division, for DePaolo Industries for 19X3 that will promote the evaluation of divisional performance.
3. Discuss the advantages of the contribution approach for internal reporting purposes.

18–30 THOUGHT STIMULATION PROBLEM—Segmental Performance Evaluation. Appropriate performance evaluation of top managers is one of the most difficult tasks facing corporations today. Return-on-investment measures discussed in this chapter (including the residual income and inflation modifications), because they concentrate on income performance for a rather short, discrete period of time (usually one year), do not measure the complete performance of a manager. Also, because top management job descriptions are usually broad and sometimes rather vague, a manager can appear successful, due to certain environmental conditions, *in spite* of his performance.

Background descriptions of the business situation and brief summaries of annual reports from three division managers for Sunshine Industries, a decentralized corporation, follow.

PC-Power Division.   This division was organized 5 years ago, when a small software company was purchased, to develop and market personal computer software. Most of its sales for the last 2 years were generated by one package, which was developed over the preceding 2½ years and is distributed through computer stores. Several other products are in various stages of development, ranging from experimental design in progress technologically feasible through to products approved for production. One product that reached technologically feasible status 2 years ago and one that was similarly designated last year are expected to generate more sales than the previous top-seller. Management has estimated that one of the products should be approved for production in 6 months and the others in 18 months. Sales last year increased by 80% over the preceding year, and operating income increased by 63%. Return on investment, though, has been less than 7%.

Home-Free Division.   This well-established division produces and markets a line of about 200 home products and usually reports a return on investment of 15–17%. Operating income has been fairly constant over the last several years. Most of its products have been on the market for 3–5 years. During the past 2 years, about 10 new products per year have been introduced. The current management has extended the sales territory from five states to nine states. The business plan for the next 5 years calls for steady growth in sales by expanding into additional markets. Even though it is not especially challenging, management of this division is considered to be a "plum" assignment.

Wonder Chemical Division.   To ensure the Home-Free division a stable supply of chemicals for its products, Stephen Wonder Chemical Company was purchased 7 years ago and organized as a separate division of Sunshine Industries and named Wonder Chemical Division. Wonder Chemical has maintained the reputation for quality products developed by Stephen Wonder, the founder of Stephen Wonder Chemical Company. Approximately 30% of Wonder Chemical's output is sold to Home-Free at variable cost of production plus 10%. The plant operates at full capacity. It hasn't had to turn down any outside sales to provide deliveries to Home-Free, but its sales department is small and is considered ineffective by the present division manager. This manager wants to reorganize the sales department under a new, youthful sales manager and solicit new customers.

Division managers have been evaluated in the past based primarily on a variation of the standard return-on-investment (ROI) calculation. Sunshine Industries is dissatisfied with using ROI to evaluate division managers because it feels that ROI encourages a short-term perspective that doesn't appropriately consider future performance.

REQUIRED:

1. Discuss the shortcomings or possible inconsistencies of using return on investment as the sole criterion to evaluate the performance of Sunshine's division managers.
2. For each division, make a list of the criteria you believe should be used in evaluating the division manager. (The list might be the same for all three divisions and might include criteria such as profitability, market position, productivity, lead time, product leadership, quality, personnel development, employee attitudes, public responsibility, and balance between short-range and long-range goals.)
3. Discuss the advantages and disadvantages of using multiple criteria versus a single criterion to evaluate divisional management performance.
4. What transfer-pricing problem might occur in the future, and how would you recommend that Sunshine Industries deal with it?

Chapter 19

Using Cost Data in Making Short-Term Operating Decisions

Learning Objectives

When you have finished your study of this chapter, you should

1. Know the four general guidelines for gathering and using cost and revenue data to make short-term and long-term decisions.
2. Know the steps followed in making decisions.
3. Recognize pertinent (relevant) revenues and costs.
4. Be able to apply appropriate analytical techniques to solve make-or-buy decisions, pricing decisions, process-or-sell decisions, and decisions regarding discontinuance of a segment.
5. Recognize the items to be considered in establishing inventory and purchasing policies.
6. Be aware of the potential behavioral problems that may be created by following a compensation policy for salespeople that includes commissions based on gross sales.
7. Know how to identify production constraints and select an optimal production (sales) mix.

I n several chapters, we have already discussed utilizing costs for decision-making purposes. In this chapter, we deal with a group of specific short-term operating decisions that require the use of selected cost data and analysis techniques. We will help you identify and appropriately use the costs that are pertinent to these short-term operating decisions, that is, decisions requiring no additional investment in long-term operating assets (no increase in the firm's investment base). We will deal with long-term decisions involving the commitment of additional resources to a firm's operations in Chapter 20.

The performance of a business can be greatly enhanced by taking advantage of opportunities as they arise. There is always a danger, however, in viewing operating decisions as totally short-term in nature. Short-term decisions also must blend into long-term operating plans. Therefore, consideration must be given to the long-term implications of short-term operating decisions as those decisions are made.

Here are four general guidelines for drawing together and using the data essential in making short-term and long-term decisions:

1. *Use modified historical costs* to indicate the effects of expected changes. Historical costs, per se, are irrelevant.
2. *Use only pertinent cost and revenue data.* This means ignoring certain costs incurred in the past that cannot be recovered *(sunk costs).* **Pertinent costs (relevant costs)** for a particular decision are those costs that will be changed as a result of the decision.
3. *Impute the costs of any foregone opportunities.* Because accounting records do not include such costs, they must be separately identified and calculated. For example, since funds committed to a project cannot be otherwise invested, the investment income that could have been earned is an *opportunity cost* of embarking on the project that should be included in the analysis. The opportunity cost of accepting one alternative is the income (or reduced costs) of the next best unaccepted alternative.
4. *Consider the tax consequences* when they are pertinent to the decision. In effect, our tax laws allow the government to share in our gains (through taxes on them) and to bear a portion of our losses (by allowing them to be deducted in calculating taxable income). After-tax cost equals cost multiplied by the difference between 1 and the tax rate, and after-tax revenue equals revenue multiplied by the difference between 1 and the tax rate. We use the term **tax shield** to describe the amount of tax benefit associated with a noncash expense (such as depreciation or a loss on disposal of an asset) when we develop cash-flow projections.

We begin our discussion of decision making by presenting a decision model framework. Then we show how to apply that framework to decisions regarding

• making or buying parts
• pricing merchandise for sale

- further processing or sale of semifinished goods
- purchasing and inventory levels
- possible discontinuance of a segment of a business
- performance of salespeople
- optimizing production or sales mix based on one constraining factor.

Decision Model Framework

All decisions involve the same basic sequence of steps:

1. Recognize a problem or opportunity.
2. Identify alternative possible courses of action.
3. Gather information relating to each alternative.
4. Organize the information.
5. Evaluate each alternative and select the optimal one.
6. Implement the decision.
7. Evaluate the outcome.

Step 1, though obvious, actually is one of the most difficult. It takes a special talent to analyze a situation, sift through mounds of information, and recognize a problem that needs to be solved or an opportunity that can be seized. This talent must be cultivated over time by thoroughly understanding the goals and objectives you are trying to achieve, by being alert to current operations, and by continually looking for ways to simplify and improve your product or service. In this chapter and Chapter 20, we present the analytical techniques for organizing information that helps one make appropriate decisions as well as recognize problems and opportunities as they arise.

Once a problem or opportunity has been recognized, we are ready for *Step 2*: plot out feasible alternative courses of action. This is a creative activity that may be approached in a number of ways. (A group of people *brainstorming* is quite common.) There are always at least two alternatives: (1) do something and (2) do nothing.

Step 3 involves gathering relevant information about each alternative identified in Step 2. Relevant information may come from many sources, such as historical accounting records, forecasts, economic projections, articles in periodicals and newspapers, price lists, government documents and reports, and personal experience.

Step 4 involves organizing the information to facilitate the decision-making process. The more complicated the decision and the more alternatives being considered, the more important it is to properly organize the information. Relevant information from Step 3 for *each* alternative being considered should be organized for the evaluation and decision-making steps. This may take the following form:

Alternative X

	Cash Inflows (Outflows)	Necessary Adjustments (e.g., tax effects, present value factors)	Net Cash Inflows (Outflows)
Relevant item 1	x	x	x
Relevant item 2	x	x	x
⋮	⋮	⋮	⋮
Relevant item n	x	x	x̲
Total			x

Total net amounts for each alternative can then be compared. With only two alternatives, the relevant information may then be arranged as follows:

Asset Investment Analysis

Cost of asset with 10-year life and no salvage value: $100,000

	Alternative 1: With Investment	Alternative 2: Without Investment	Difference: Incremental Income
Annual net income	$70,000	$58,000	$12,000

$$\text{Accounting rate of return} = \frac{\$12,000}{\$100,000} = \underline{\underline{12\%}}$$

Step 5: Once the relevant information has been assembled, each alternative should be evaluated. If a decision is to be made based solely on the objectively determinable dollar data (or some decision rule, such as a ratio or index, based on dollars), complete information for the decision will be available from Step 4. More frequently, however, subjective, nonquantifiable data must be combined with the "objective" data before a decision can be made.[1] For example, judgments regarding an alternative's environmental impact, increased governmental regulation, or increased competition may have to be combined with the quantitative data before a decision is made. The optimal decision may be determined by the rules of the specific model being used. Each of the four methods of evaluating a long-term investment opportunity developed in Chapter 20, for example, has its own decision rule that states the criterion to be used in making the investment decision. Other things

---

[1]"Objective" data for decision making is *not* the same as objective accounting data. Projections, educated guesses, and similar "soft" data can be treated as "objective" in this sense.

being equal, the alternative that provides the most favorable projected result will be selected.

Step 6: After the decision has been made, it must be implemented. This requires the same meticulous processing as the decision itself. In addition, controls must be established to ensure that the approved plan is being followed.

Step 7: The final step, evaluating the outcome, occurs after the decision has been implemented and some time has passed. Actual results will be compared with those anticipated at the time the project was accepted.

This chapter and Chapter 20 focus on Steps 4 and 5 of the decision model framework (organizing the decision information and evaluating alternatives). However, all 7 steps should be kept in mind as these steps are explained.

Make-or-Buy Decisions

Managers often must make a **make-or-buy decision**—that is, decide whether their firms should make particular parts or buy them from an outside vendor. Such a question may arise when an outside vendor offers to provide the part for less than it historically has cost the firm to make it. Using only the immediately available recorded data can lead a manager to make an improper decision. Such readily available cost data, based on full absorption costing, generally will include some costs that would be incurred even if the firm elected to buy the part. These *continuing costs* are irrelevant to the make-or-buy decision because they will be incurred regardless of whether the part is manufactured or purchased. Since they will not affect the outcome of the decision, they should be eliminated from the data when selecting the costs pertinent to the decision.

To illustrate, let's assume that a firm presently produces 10,000 units at a cost of $1 per unit, of a part that is later used in its production process. An outside vendor offers to provide the part at $.90 per unit. If the firm buys the part, it will discontinue operations in the department that is presently producing it. In making the part, the firm typically incurs $7,500 of variable labor and materials costs that it will avoid if the part is purchased and $2,500 of depreciation and other fixed costs that will continue even if the part is purchased. Assuming that the equipment and space presently used in making the product would have no alternate use and cannot be sold, we must eliminate the $2,500 of fixed costs from the cost of producing the part to arrive at the pertinent cost to make the part that then should be compared with the proposed purchase price. The pertinent cost of producing 10,000 units is $7,500, or $.75 per unit rather than $1 per unit. The avoidable $.75 per unit is the appropriate cost to compare with the proposed purchase price in deciding whether to make or buy the part. Observe that the use of pertinent cost data leads to a different decision than would have been reached by using *total* cost: The firm should continue to produce the part rather than buy it from the outside vendor because it is ($.90 − $.75) × 10,000 = $1,500 better off making the part.

Let's now evaluate the tax considerations. If the firm disposes of the equipment used to manufacture the product and receives no salvage value, it would realize a tax benefit equal to the tax rate multiplied by the equipment's book value. However, since the same total deduction can be recovered through depreciation over the remaining useful life of the equipment if it is used to manufacture the part, then, except for time-value considerations, it is appropriate to ignore taxes in making this decision.

This make-or-buy decision also would be influenced by possible alternative use of the space used to manufacture the part. If, for example, the space could be used to manufacture another product that would yield a profit of $3,000, it would be advantageous to purchase the part because we would then need to impute that profit as an opportunity cost of making the part:

Make:

Pertinent cost to make 10,000 units	$ 7,500
Opportunity cost	3,000
Total	$10,500

Buy:

Purchase cost (10,000 @ $.90)	$9,000

Several nonquantitative considerations also can enter into the make-or-buy decision. Management, for example, will be concerned about the possibility of the purchased parts being of inferior quality and thus causing warranty or customer-dissatisfaction problems. It also may be concerned about possible interruptions in production if the vendor fails to meet delivery schedules. Furthermore, some time after the firm discontinues producing the part, the vendor might raise the part's price. All of these nonquantifiable factors must be considered along with the pertinent cost data in making the final make-or-buy decision.

Pricing Decisions

Decisions relating to pricing a firm's product are among the most important of all actions taken by management. Although prices ultimately are determined by the forces of supply and demand, conventional pricing procedures seek the recovery of total cost plus a reasonable margin. This generally takes the form of **gross-margin pricing**. Sales prices are set to provide a specified amount of markup above cost of product acquisition, stated either as a percentage of sales price or as a percentage of cost.

To illustrate, let's assume that a product costing $6 per unit is to be priced to yield a 40% markup on sales price. The product price would be: $6 (the cost) ÷ (100% − 40%) = $10 per unit. If the product is to be priced to yield a 40% markup on cost, however, it would be priced at $6.00 + 0.4($6) = $8.40. These relations can be summarized as follows:

Markup Based on Sales			Markup Based on Cost of Sales		
Sales	$10	100%	Sales	$8.40	140%
Cost of sales	6	60%	Cost of sales	6.00	100%
Gross margin	$ 4	40%	Gross margin	$2.40	40%

To achieve a gross margin of $4, the markup based on cost of sales would have to be 66⅔% and sales would be 166⅔% of cost of sales.

Markup Based on Cost of Sales		
Sales	$10	166⅔%
Cost of sales	6	100 %
Gross margin	$ 4	66⅔%

Note that operating costs are not included in the cost on which the margin is based. In gross-margin pricing, the margin must cover expected selling and administrative (operating costs) as well as provide operating income.

In other instances, a firm may attempt to price its products to provide a targeted percentage return (that is, net income from operations) on assets employed to produce the product or a targeted percentage return above total product acquisition and operating costs. Such pricing policies require the specific identification of assets used to produce the product and the allocation of operating expenses to the products being produced.

While such conventional pricing policies may define a desired selling price, supply and demand also must be considered. Since pricing decisions directly influence the volume of operations, a firm must be concerned not only with the recovery of costs plus an appropriate margin but also with realizing enough sales to use its facilities effectively. The ultimate objective, then, is to realize a price that will maximize a firm's total profit. Because variances in gross margin are related to the change in margin per unit (a price variance) and change in volume of units sold (a volume variance; see Chapter 17), each pricing decision must be considered in relation to the effect it is expected to have on volume.

We will now explore the procedures to follow in deciding whether to accept a potential purchaser's offer to buy a portion of a firm's output at a price that is less than the total unit cost of product acquisition (production costs for a manufacturing firm and purchase costs for a merchandising firm). We shall assume that the sale can be made without violating price discrimination regulations and without affecting the normal market for the product. If a firm has excess capacity, the *marginal cost per unit* (variable cost per unit plus any incremental fixed cost per unit) is the pertinent cost to be compared with the prospective purchaser's offer. In effect, when a firm has excess capacity, its opportunity cost of manufacturing and selling additional units beyond those it is currently selling (up to capacity) is zero and it can improve its net income by selling additional units at any price above the marginal cost to produce and sell them. Such sales will yield a positive incremental margin that will increase operating income.

To illustrate, let's assume a company has the capacity to produce 30,000 units but currently is producing only 20,000 units selling for $10 per unit, with $150,000 in costs of producing and selling made up of $100,000 of variable costs and $50,000 of fixed costs. A quick calculation shows it costs the firm $7.50 to produce each unit at its present level of production. Now a prospective purchaser from a completely differentiated market offers to buy 5,000 units at $7 per unit. Figure 19–1 shows that by selling the extra 5,000 units at $7 per unit, the company can improve its net operating income by $10,000. This is equal to 5,000

Plant capacity		30,000 units
Presently producing and selling		20,000 units
Regular sales price		$10 per unit

	Total	Per Unit
Variable costs	$100,000	$5.00
Fixed costs	50,000	2.50
Total	$150,000	$7.50

	Regular Sales Only	Including Extra Order
Sales	$200,000	$235,000
Costs	150,000	175,000
Net income	$ 50,000	$ 60,000

FIGURE 19–1 Analysis of Special-Order Pricing Decision

units multiplied by the $2 difference between the $7 sales price per unit and the $5 total variable costs per unit (or the contribution margin per unit).

When such purchase offers require the incurrence of *special* costs, those costs also must be considered in deciding whether to accept the potential buyer's offer. For example, extra delivery costs or the cost of employing another production supervisor to complete the order are pertinent and should be added to the total variable cost to arrive at the total pertinent cost. If, on the other hand, a firm is able to eliminate some variable costs—such as sales commissions—those costs should be eliminated from the variable cost in arriving at the pertinent cost.

As stated earlier, a firm always should be concerned with the possibility of "spoiling" the market for its regular sales, as, for example, when regular customers become aware of the special price and demand the same terms. A firm in that situation would reject such a sale even though it would yield a temporary positive contribution margin.

Process-or-Sell Decisions

When a market exists for semifinished units, a firm faces a **process-or-sell decision**—that is, it must decide whether to finish the product or sell it in a semifinished state. The primary consideration here centers around determining the pertinent amounts of further processing costs (relevant costs of additional processing). That figure then is compared to the difference between selling prices for finished and semifinished units, in order to decide whether to sell or process further. To illustrate, assume it costs $6 to produce a semifinished unit and an additional $2 in pertinent costs to finish the unit, and that the sales prices are $12 for the semifinished unit and $15 for the finished unit. With those assumptions, it is advantageous to process the unit beyond the semifinished state, as shown here:

	Semifinished Unit	Finished Unit
Sales prices	$12	$15
Pertinent costs		2
Margin	$12	$13

Net income will be increased by $1 per unit if the units are finished. This difference also can be calculated by comparing the $3 addition to the sales price per unit with the relevant $2 additional cost to finish each unit. The $6 cost to produce a semifinished unit is not pertinent (relevant) because it will be incurred regardless of whether units are sold in a semifinished or a completely finished state.

We assumed here that the finishing department had sufficient capacity to finish all units. If the final processing department has less capacity, than is required to process all units coming from the prior processing department, it will be advantageous, with present capacity, to sell the units in excess of finishing department capacity as semifinished goods. When the semifinished units cannot be sold for a price that yields a positive contribution margin, the firm will be faced with the choice of either curtailing semiprocessing production or expanding finishing capacity. The first option would eliminate the negative contribution margin to be realized from the sale of semifinished products at an unfavorable price. The second option also would avoid the unfavorable sale of semifinished products but it might increase relevant (pertinent) costs to the point where they exceed the difference in selling prices and thus produce a negative contribution margin. Expansion of facilities is a long-term decision and is considered further in Chapter 20.

When the final processing department *has* adequate capacity, it may be advantageous to finish the product even though the difference between finished and semifinished selling prices is less than the total additional processing cost per unit. Figure 19–2 demonstrates such a situation. We assume a difference between the semifinished and finished sales price per unit to be $13.25 − $12.00 = $1.25. The total cost of finishing the product is $10.00 − $8.50 = $1.50 per unit, suggesting a negative effect on gross margin of $.25 per unit for the finishing process. However, as the figure shows, it still would be profitable to finish the units before they are sold because fixed costs in the amount of $6,000 ($.60 per unit at the present level of production) would be incurred regardless of whether the units are finished before being sold. This $6,000 is an irrelevant (sunk) cost that must be ignored in making the process-or-sell decision. Eliminating the $.60 per unit for fixed costs leaves $.90 per unit (variable cost) as the relevant (pertinent) cost to be compared with the $1.25 increase in sales price per unit for purposes of making the process-or-sell decision. Observe that the $32,500 − $29,000 = $3,500 difference in gross margin is equal to 10,000 units × ($1.25 − $.90).

Note: a firm would *not* install a finishing process operating with the conditions shown in Figure 19–2. This is a long-term decision and is considered further in Chapter 20. In this situation, we are trying to minimize the damage from a past investment decision. However, the fixed costs of the final processing department should be examined. It is possible that the $1.50 cost per unit associated with the finishing process is more than it should be because the firm is using obsolete equipment. It is logical to assume that the sales price data result from the market forces of supply and demand and that a modernized depart-

Semifinished cost per unit	$ 8.50
Semifinished sale price per unit	$12.00
Finished cost per unit	$10.00
Finished sale price per unit	$13.25

Finishing department is capable of processing 10,000 units.

Finishing Department Costs	Total Costs	Costs per Unit (10,000 units)
Variable costs	$ 9,000	$ .90
Fixed costs	6,000	.60
Total	$15,000	$1.50

	Assumed Sale of Units in Finished State		Assumed Sale of Units in Semifinished State
Sales (10,000 units @ $13.25)	$132,500		
Cost of sales			
10,000 @ $8.50	(85,000)	10,000 @ $12.00	$120,000
10,000 @ $ .90	(9,000)	10,000 @ $ 8.50 (85,000)	
Fixed costs	(6,000)	Fixed costs (6,000)	(91,000)
Gross margin	$ 32,500		$ 29,000

FIGURE 19–2 Analysis of Costs for Process-or-Sell Decision

ment should be able to complete the finishing process at a total cost of less than $1.25 per unit when operating at a normal level of production. Nevertheless, in our assumed short-term situation, the units should be finished before selling them because the additional pertinent costs are less than the $1.25 per unit increase in selling price.

Purchasing and Inventory Decisions

All merchandising and manufacturing firms must make decisions regarding the amount of inventory to carry and the amount of goods to order each time an item of inventory is replenished. In making such inventory-control decisions, management seeks to minimize the total costs of providing goods for sale, including inventory-carrying costs and inventory-acquisition costs plus the opportunity cost of being out of stock.

The costs associated with carrying inventory items include the cost of providing storage space for them, the cost of insuring them, losses from obsolesence and spoilage while stored, and the foregone opportunity of investing in some other income-producing asset the money invested in inventory. On the other hand, the costs of failing to carry enough inventory include losses caused by production interruptions, idle time, and possibly even lost sales due to customer dissatisfaction. Acquisition costs include the prices paid for goods plus the costs of ordering them. The level of inventory to carry is the one that minimizes the *total* of acquisition and carrying costs, assuming throughput is not affected.

Efforts to minimize total inventory costs, in the absence of perfect information, typically lead to the establishment of a **minimum inventory level** (safety stock) that the company will strive to maintain for each item of inventory. However, this must take into account that a firm can seldom afford to carry enough inventory to completely avoid work interruptions or some loss of sales caused by inadequate amounts of stock on hand. At the same time, the firm must always seek to hold these interruptions and losses of sales to a reasonable level. The minimum inventory level for any specific item must also take into consideration the proximity and the dependability of the item's suppliers.

Having established a targeted minimum inventory level, the next step in controlling total inventory acquisition and carrying costs traditionally has been to determine the **economic order quantity (EOQ)**, that is, the quantity of an inventory item that should be purchased each time it is ordered so as to minimize total ordering and carrying costs. Calculation of the EOQ requires an estimate of the cost of placing an order and the cost (including all materials handling) of carrying an inventory item. These procedures are dealt with in Chapter 21. After deciding the quantity to be included in each purchase, we can target the **maximum inventory level** as the minimum level plus the calculated order size.

To carry out such analysis, most costs connected with the inventory and purchasing decisions must be derived from the accounting data. And opportunity costs such as those associated with interruptions of operations or losses of sales must be imputed into the analysis if management is to make the right judgments.

The cost elements to use in making inventory and purchasing decisions (especially opportunity costs) may be difficult to establish with precision. We can, however, make some generalizations about the factors to consider. For example, the cost of carrying small, low-unit-cost materials and parts will be relatively low in relation to the costs associated with having an inadequate stock of such units on hand because many of the carrying costs are directly related to inventory size and value, whereas the "stockout" costs for a small, inexpensive item can be just as large as those for a large, expensive item. Therefore, a firm generally will establish larger minimum balances for small, inexpensive items. Ordering and carrying costs for more expensive, difficult-to-however, should be more closely monitored. Other things being the same, a lower minimum quantity in relation to projected needs and smaller order sizes should be established for large, expensive items.

The justification for such a policy is clear when we realize that a production department can be shut down by its failure to have in stock a special bolt-and-nut assembly, even though it costs less than, say, 10¢ a unit and requires very little storage space. It would be foolish not to have an adequate stock of such items on hand to prevent a possible costly interruption of operations. The same interruption also might result from the shortage of a large, more expensive, perishable part. Nevertheless, management normally would be willing to assume some risk of running out of that type of part because of the higher cost of carrying a large inventory of it.

Purchasing and inventory decisions are rapidly becoming part of more global optimization schemes, however, and the importance of EOQ is being reduced by practical realities and greater information processing capabilities. With computerized systems, for example, the cost of placing an order is approaching zero, which has been shown[2] to cause the economic inventory level to approach zero. This is consistent with the zero-inventory concept of just-in-time (JIT) inventories first popularized by the Japanese and discussed in Chapter 3. One American response to JIT is a computer software package called *optimized production technology* (OPT), which is designed to spot and control production bottlenecks, eliminate excess inventory, and increase profit. This approach questions the use, in the EOQ formula, of the fixed average demand for units. For example, assume a simple situation with two interdependent machines in which output of the first machine must be processed through the second before a completed unit emerges. Output of the first unit averages 4 units per hour, and output of the second averages 4 units per hour. Assuming a 40-hour week and a 50-week year, annual demand for raw materials entering the first machine would then be:

4 units per hour × 40 hours per week × 50 weeks = <u>8,000</u> units

However, the actual output of the machines is a function of a statistical process. If we assume a very simple uniform distribution with equal probability of two outcomes, output is greatly affected. For example, given the following additional information:

	Probability		
	.5	.5	Average
Machine 1 output per hour	2	6	4
Machine 2 output per hour	2	6	4

[2]D. G. Sauers, "Analyzing Inventory Systems," *Management Accounting* (May 1986), pp. 30–36.

actual output combinations will be:

Hour	Machine 1	Machine 2	Finished Units
1	2	2	2
2	2	6	2
3	6	2	2
4	6	6	6
			12

Thus, even with this simple situation, demand for raw materials entering the first machine, based on probable units completed by both machines, would be 12/4 = 3 units per hour, not 4, and average demand would be

$$3 \text{ units per hour} \times 40 \text{ hours per week} \times 50 \text{ weeks} = \underline{6,000} \text{ units}$$

A **buffer stock** for machine 2 of units completed by machine 1 can alleviate, but not eliminate, this interdependency. More complex interdependencies and more sophisticated probability distributions would have an even greater impact on average demand.

Theoretically, EOQ is sound if all costs are known, properly included, and the formula is applied to each separate resource. But purchasing and inventory decisions can no longer be treated in isolation from other operating decisions and from firmwide interdependencies.

Discontinuance of a Division or Segment of Operations

Chapter 18 discussed the procedures for controlling the operations of segments or divisions of a business by holding them accountable for their operating results. As those operating results are analyzed, we may encounter situations in which a particular department or segment of operations shows losses over several consecutive periods. Management's first inclination in such cases may be to consider eliminating the department or segment in order to improve the firm's overall profitability.

Before taking action, however, it is important to analyze the situation more thoroughly using the contribution-margin approach. The gross revenue that the department or segment has been generating should be matched against the variable expenses plus the **direct** (traceable, not allocated) **fixed costs** associated with earning that revenue. If the segment then shows a positive margin, it should be continued unless the space and facilities can be used profitably in another way, in which case the potential net revenue from that use should be imputed into the analysis as an opportunity cost (additional relevant cost) of continuing present operations. Only if the analysis then shows a negative net margin (revenues − all relevant costs) should segment operations be discontinued. If the segment has a negative margin and there is an imputed opportunity cost, it should be discontinued and the facilities converted to the alternate use.

Again, only the relevant (pertinent) costs are matched against segment revenue in determining the segment's contribution margin. Irretrievable or sunk costs must be eliminated from the analysis, and opportunity costs associated with continuing operations should be imputed (added) as a pertinent cost if the appropriate decision is to be made regarding possible discontinuance of the segment.

As an illustration of a continue-or-discontinue decision, let's assume that the Zunker Company, a retailing firm, has been conducting its operations in three divisions. Divisional income statements show that Divisions 1 and 2 are profitable while Division 3 is generating a net loss. Zunker management, as a result of a proposed discontinuance of Division 3, is analyzing the division's operating revenues and expenses. The results of the firm's operations for the past year are summarized in the first three columns of Exhibit 19–1. We assume these operating results are typical of those reported over several years. Management also has

EXHIBIT 19–1

Zunker Company

Proposed Discontinuance of Division 3

	Present Operations			
	Division 3	Other Divisions	Total with Division 3	Total without Division 3
Sales	$200,000	$900,000	$1,100,000	$900,000
Cost of goods sold (all variable)	(150,000)	(500,000)	(650,000)	(500,000)
Contribution margin	$ 50,000	$400,000	$ 450,000	$400,000
Direct departmental expenses	(30,000)	(200,000)	(230,000)	(200,000)
Segment margin	$ 20,000	$200,000	$ 220,000	$200,000
Allocated indirect expenses	(25,000)	(100,000)	(125,000)	(120,000)*
Net income (loss) before income taxes	$ (5,000)	$100,000	$ 95,000	$ 80,000

*$25,000 + $100,000 − $5,000 that could be eliminated.

developed the following conclusions regarding the possible discontinuance of Division 3:

(1) The area vacated by Division 3 could not be put to alternative use by the company, and it is not feasible to rent the space to another party.
(2) Only $5,000 of Division 3's allocated indirect expenses would be eliminated if its operation were discontinued.
(3) Discontinuance of Division 3 operations would cause no appreciable change in the contribution margins of the remaining two departments.

These data were used to prepare the last column of Exhibit 19–1, which shows that the annual net income before income taxes would be $15,000 less if Division 3 were discontinued, a decrease that can be attributed to Division 3's segment margin reduced by the allocated indirect costs that would be eliminated:

Division 3 segment margin	$20,000
Less eliminated indirect costs	(5,000)
Advantage to retaining Division 3	$15,000

Observe that in this marginal or incremental approach, as opposed to the total dollar approach of Exhibit 19–1, the allocated indirect costs that would not be eliminated are excluded from the analysis because they are not relevant to the decision.

This example assumed that the elimination of Division 3 would cause no appreciable change in the contribution margins of the other divisions. Often, this is not a realistic assumption. If the discontinuance of a division is expected to reduce the contribution margins of other divisions, that anticipated reduction should be included in the analysis as an opportunity cost of discontinuance. In such a situation, it could be advantageous to continue to operate a division having a negative segment margin from its own operations to preserve the contribution margins of the other divisions. This would be true if the total expected reductions in the contribution margins of the other divisions exceeded the negative net segment margin for the division being considered for discontinuance.

If there is a profitable alternate use for a segment's facilities, the foregone net income from such use should be included as an opportunity cost of continuing the current operation of the segment. For example, if the space occupied by Zunker Company's Division 3 can be subleased for $12,000 a year, this information should be included in the analysis, as shown in Exhibit 19–2. (The opportunity cost of continuance is shown as revenue under the discontinuance option. Alternatively, it could have been shown as an expense of present operations. This choice will not affect the net difference between the two choices.)

EXHIBIT 19–2

Zunker Company Division

Proposed Discontinuance of Division 3 with Alternate Use

	With Proposed Discontinuance	Present Operations
Sales	$900,000	$1,100,000
Cost of goods sold (all variable)	(500,000)	(650,000)
Gross margin (contribution margin)	$400,000	$ 450,000
Direct departmental expenses	(200,000)	(230,000)
Contribution margin	$200,000	$ 220,000
Allocated indirect expenses	(120,000)	(125,000)
Rental of Department 3 space	12,000	
Net income (loss) before income taxes	$ 92,000	$ 95,000

Rather than using a "total operations" (total dollar) analysis, as in Exhibit 19–2, we can use a marginal net income approach, as in Exhibit 19–3, which shows that the alternate use does not generate sufficient revenue ($12,000) to offset the loss caused by the discontinuance of Division 3 ($15,000, as calculated earlier). Therefore, Division 3 should continue to operate.

This decision is the one that would be made if the resource base for Division 3 already is in place (see Chapter 18). The indirect (long-term) costs that cannot be eliminated ($20,000 in this case) would not be considered in such a situation, because, as sunk costs (costs that, in the short-term, cannot be avoided), they are irrelevant to the decision. However, the firm would never make a long-term decision to invest in

EXHIBIT 19–3

Zunker Company

Proposed Discontinuance of Division 3 with Alternate Use

Marginal Approach

Marginal segment margin with present operations		$20,000
Less:		
Difference in allocated indirect costs	$ 5,000	
Opportunity cost of continuance	12,000	(17,000)
Advantage to retaining Division 3		$ 3,000

facilities to initiate the operation of Division 3 unless it could be operated more efficiently than it is with its present resource base.

Decisions Regarding the Performance of Sales Personnel

The sale of goods is a crucial event in the operations of most business enterprises. Put another way, unless a firm can sell its product, there is no reason to engage in buying or manufacturing it. As a result, sales personnel often are paid a commission based on gross sales, to motivate them toward greater sales efforts. When compensation is based on gross sales, sales personnel can be motivated to increase sales without regard for the effect those sales have on net income. It can also cause them to be unnecessarily lavish in entertaining potential customers and in their product claims.

Because the firm's goal is to maximize net income rather than simply maximize sales, it is desirable to evaluate the productivity of sales personnel by calculating the amount each person contributes to net income. That calculation requires determining the contribution margins of each of the various products being sold and relating those to the units sold by each salesperson. Records must be maintained showing other traceable costs incurred by each salesperson so that entertainment expenses, returns and allowances, and perhaps warranty costs can be matched against each salesperson's total contribution margin. Figure 19–3 shows how salesperson Mary Brown contributed more to the

	Mary Brown	John Doe	Total
Sales	$100,000	$150,000	$250,000
Variable cost of goods sold	60,000	110,000	170,000
Contribution margin of goods sold	$ 40,000	$ 40,000	$ 80,000
Entertainment expenses	$ 3,000	$ 5,000	$ 8,000
Travel expenses	8,000	9,000	17,000
Total expenses	$ 11,000	$ 14,000	$ 25,000
Contribution to net income before commissions	$ 29,000	$ 26,000	$ 55,000
Commissions (5% of sales)	5,000	7,500	12,500
Contribution to net income	$ 24,000	$ 18,500	$ 42,500

FIGURE 19–3 Analysis of Income Contribution of Sales Personnel

	Mary Brown	John Doe	Total
Contributions to net income before commissions (see Figure 19–3)	$29,000	$26,000	$55,000
Commissions (22.726% of contribution to net income before commissions)	6,591	5,909	12,500
	$22,409	$20,091	$42,500

FIGURE 19–4   Sales Commissions Based on Income Contribution

firm's net income than did John Doe, even though Doe received a higher sales commission (because commissions were based on gross sales).

As the figure shows, a more equitable arrangement would be based on the amounts contributed to net income *before* commissions. For example, a 22.726% commission on each salesperson's contribution to net income before commissions results in approximately the same total commissions cost but would pay $6,591 to Brown and $5,909 to Doe. These commissions, shown in Figure 19–4, appear to be more equitable than those generated by the current system and should motivate sales personnel to work more directly toward the company's income goal. This type of performance evaluation also is consistent with responsibility accounting (see pages 632–650) as applied to a merchandising firm.

Optimal Production or Sales Mix with One Constraining Factor

The importance of sales mix for a multiproduct firm was emphasized in Chapter 16 when we discussed cost–volume–profit analysis. There we assumed a constant sales mix and allowed total sales to vary. However, if sales are constrained to a certain amount and sales mix is allowed to vary, income is maximized by selling the products with the highest contribution margin *ratio*, not the highest absolute contribution margin per unit. This may seem counterintuitive. For example, suppose product 1 sells for $20 and has variable costs of $10 and a contribution margin of $10 whereas product 2 sells for $10, and has variable costs of $4 and a contribution margin of $6. Which product would you prefer to sell in meeting a certain budgeted sales amount? You might pick product 1 because its contribution margin is $4 higher than product 2's. But we should prefer always to sell product 2 if total sales are held constant. Thus, assuming total sales of $100, total contribution margins if each product were sold exclusively would be:

	Product 1	**Product 2**
Sales	$20 × 5 units = $100	$10 × 10 units = $100
Variable costs	$10 × 5 units = 50	$4 × 10 units = 40
Contribution margin	$ 50	$ 60

The contribution margin per sales dollar (the constraining factor) is $50/$100 = $10/$20 = $.50 for product 1 and $60/$100 = $6/$10 = $.60 for product 2. With one constraining factor, then, the optimal decision is to select the option (the action) that maximizes the contribution margin per unit of scarce resource.

The same idea applies if the constraint is in production, as when a firm has sales backorders and some element of production presents the constraint. Suppose a firm has only 20,000 machine-hours (current capacity) to produce two products requiring machine processing. If product 2 requires 2 hours of machine time and provides a contribution margin of $10 per unit whereas product 1 requires 1 hour of machine time and provides a contribution margin of $6 per unit, and the firm produces only one product, the following contribution margins will result:

Maximum Contribution Margin	**Only Product 1 Produced**	**Only Product 2 Produced**
$6 × (20,000/1)	$120,000	
$10 × (20,000/2)		$100,000

Under these conditions, the firm obviously should produce all of product 1 it can sell before it produces any units of product 2 because the contribution margin per machine-hour (the scarce resource) for product 1 is $6/(1 hour) = $6, while the contribution margin per machine-hour for product 2 is only $10/(2 hours) = $5.

When a firm faces multiple constraints, such as limited time on several machines, limited raw materials, and maximum sales volume, the analysis is more complex and **linear programming**, a simultaneous mathematical solution we discuss in Chapter 21, should be used in deciding on optimal production. Alternatively, the Theory of Constraints discussed below and in Chapter 24 may be used.

Theory of Constraints

The basic idea of maximizing the contribution margin per unit of scarce resource is the foundation of the **Theory of Constraints**, developed by the Avraham Y. Goldratt Institute and taught in their management seminars. The theory is a type of step-wise optimization consisting of attacking one constraint at a time through the following steps:

1. Identify the system constraints (scarce resources).
2. Decide how to exploit the system's most binding constraint. That is, given the constraint, maximize productivity or throughput. (*Through-*

put as defined by the Goldratt Institute is sales price minus raw materials cost, which is the only cost they identify as variable. Therefore, throughput, in effect, is equivalent to contribution margin.)

3. Subordinate all other activities to maximize production through the constraint identified in Step 1, to ensure that the constraining factor is used at 100% of capacity.
4. Relax (elevate) the constraint by obtaining more of it.
5. As soon as this constraint has been relaxed, go back to Step 1, find the next most binding constraint, and repeat Steps 2 through 5.

This approach implicitly recognizes *inertia* (the failure to constantly look for the next constraint) as a constraint. We discuss this theory more thoroughly in Chapter 24.

The illustrative problem that follows has been provided courtesy of the Avraham Y. Goldratt Institute.

Illustrative Problem

A firm produces two products, P and Q, that are sold for $90 and $100, respectively. The market potential (demand) for P is 100 units per week; the market potential for Q is 50 units per week. The firm can manufacture any combination of products P and Q.

The production process for P and for Q is diagrammed in Figure 19–5. Raw materials unit costs are shown where they enter the production process. Total production time required for P is 55 minutes (15 minutes in Department A, 15 minutes in Department B, 15 minutes in Depart-

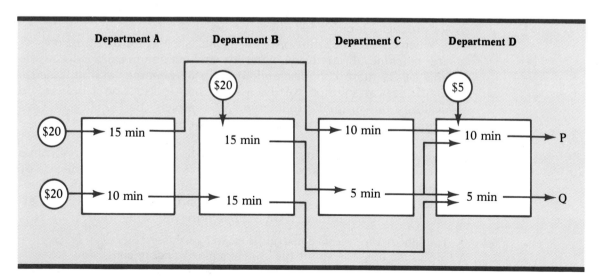

FIGURE 19–5 Departmental Production Process for Illustrative Problem

ment C (total time for two parts), and 10 minutes in Department D). Total production time for Q is 50 minutes (10 minutes in Department A, 30 minutes in Department B (15 minutes on each of two parts), 5 minutes in Department C, and 5 minutes in Department D.

The firm has four production workers: one in each of the departments. Each employee works an 8-hour shift each day, 5 days a week, meaning each worker is available 2,400 minutes a week. In each department, the worker can be assigned to work on the units going into product P or those going into product Q (any combination, as long as the maximum of 2,400 minutes is not exceeded). All labor and overhead, amounting to $6,000, are considered fixed costs. Materials are the only variable costs of production.

REQUIRED:

1. What should be the firm's optimal product mix, and what operating income will result from this mix?
2. Suppose the firm now hires another Department B worker for $400 per week and has the opportunity to sell 100 units of product P and 50 units of product Q in a foreign market for $72 and $80, respectively. The products to be sold in the foreign market (denoted P' and Q') are the same products (that is, they require the same production procedures and the same costs) as those sold in the domestic market. What should be the firm's optimal product mix now (that is, what combination of products P, Q, P', and Q' should be produced and sold), and what operating income will result from this mix?

Solution to Illustrative Problem

1. Situation Analysis.

	Worker Availability		Production Time (in minutes)			Time Required to Meet All Demand (in minutes)		
Dept.	Time (min)		P	Q	Total	100 P	50 Q	Total
A	2,400		15	10	25	1,500	500	2,000
B	2,400		15	30	45	1,500	1,500	3,000
C	2,400		15	5	20	1,500	250	1,750
D	2,400		10	5	15	1,000	250	1,250

Department B production time is the obvious constraining factor.

Throughput (Contribution Margin) for Each Product

	Product P	Product Q
Sales price per unit	$90	$100
Materials cost	$45	$ 40
Throughput (contribution margin)	$45	$ 60
Constraining factor (minutes of Dept. B)	÷ 15	÷ 30
Throughput (contribution margin) per minute $\left(\frac{\text{Throughput}}{\text{Dept. B minutes}}\right)$	= $ 3	= $ 2

The firm should fill all the demand for P, then produce Q with the remaining time available.

Department B time available	2,400 minutes
Time required for 100 units of P	1,500 minutes
Remaining time for Q	900 minutes
Minutes required per unit of Q	÷ 30
Production of Q $\left(\frac{900}{30}\right)$	= 30 units

Operating Income per Week

	Product P	Product Q	Total
Throughput (contribution margin) per unit	$45	$60	
Optimal production (units)	× 100	× 30	
Total throughput (contribution margin)	$4,500	$1,800	$6,300
Fixed costs			6,000
Operating income per week			$ 300

2. Situation Analysis.

Worker Availability		Production Time (in minutes)			Time Required to Meet All Demand (in minutes)		
Dept.	Time (min)	P	Q	Total	P + P'	Q + Q'	Total
A	2,400	15	10	25	3,000	1,000	4,000
B	4,800	15	30	45	3,000	3,000	6,000
C	2,400	15	5	20	3,000	500	3,500
D	2,400	10	5	15	2,000	500	2,500

Four departments now cannot fill demand, and it is not obvious which department is the most binding constraint. Using worker availability time and total required production time, however, it is clear that Department A production time is the most binding constraint.

Worker Availability		Total P + Q Production	Ratio of Time Available
Dept.	Time (min) ÷	Time Required =	to Time Required*
A	2,400	4,000	.600
B	4,800	6,000	.800
C	2,400	3,500	.685
D	2,400	2,500	.960

*The smaller this number, the more binding is the constraint.

Throughput (Contribution Margin) for Each Product

	Product P	Product Q	Product P′	Product Q′
Sales price per unit	$90	$100	$ 72	$80
Materials cost	$45	$ 40	$ 45	$40
Throughput (contribution margin)	$45	$ 60	$ 27	$40
Constraining factor (minutes of Dept. A)	÷ 15	÷ 10	÷ 15	÷ 10
Throughput (contribution margin) per minute $\left[\dfrac{\text{Throughput}}{\text{Dept. A minutes}}\right]$	= $ 3	= $ 6	= $1.80	= $ 4

The firm should fill all the demand for product Q, then fill the demand for product Q′ and product P (in that order), and only then consider filling the demand for product P′.

Department A time available	2,400 minutes
Time required for 50 units of Q	500 minutes
Remaining time for other products	1,900 minutes
Time required for 50 units of Q′	500 minutes
Remaining time for other products	1,400 minutes
Minutes required per unit of P	÷ 15
Production of P	= 93 units

Since all of the demand for product P cannot be met, no product P′ (product P in the foreign market) should be sold.

Operating Income per Week

	Product Q	Product Q′	Product P	Total
Throughput (contribution margin) per unit	$ 60	$ 40	$ 45	
Optimal production (units)	× 50	× 50	× 93	
Total throughput (contribution margin)	$3,000	$2,000	$4,185	$9,185
Fixed costs				6,400
Operating income per week				$2,785

SUMMARY

In this chapter, we demonstrated how selected cost data should be used in making various types of short-term decisions regarding the day-to-day operations of a business:

1. whether a part should be purchased or manufactured
2. what pricing policies should be followed in special sales of goods
3. whether a product should be sold in a semifinished or finished state

4. what a firm's inventory and purchase policies should be
5. whether a department or segment that is showing a loss should be retained or discontinued
6. how the performance of sales personnel should be measured and rewarded
7. how an optimal production and/or sales mix should be selected when there is one constraining factor or scarce resource.

Attention has been directed to recognizing and using relevant cost and revenue data in decision making. The relevant cost data can be considerably different from those recorded in the accounting records.

GLOSSARY OF TERMS INTRODUCED IN THIS CHAPTER

buffer stock	The stock of goods held to provide a cushion (or buffer) to keep operations from being interrupted because of lack of units to process.
direct fixed costs	The fixed costs that can be directly associated with the implementation of an operating decision.
economic order quantity (EOQ)	The number of units (order quantity) of a raw material that should be purchased each time an order is placed in order to minimize the total ordering and carrying costs.
gross-margin pricing	A pricing procedure that endeavors to realize a price for merchandise that will provide for recovery of the cost of the goods plus a specified margin, in dollars or a percentage, calculated on the basis of sales price or on the basis of cost.
linear programming	A mathematical model used in making operating decisions involving the allocation of scarce resources when the achievement of the operating objective (the objective function) is subject to multiple constraints; requires a quantitative statement of the objective function (maximization of contribution margin or minimization of costs) and of each of the constraints associated with carrying out operations.
make-or-buy decision	Narrowly, a decision as to whether a particular part or subassembly should be manufactured or should be purchased from an outside vendor. More generally, any decision concerning internal versus external construction.
maximum inventory level	The largest number of units of an inventory item that should ever be held in stock; equal to the minimum inventory level plus the economic order quantity.
minimum inventory level	The smallest number of units of an inventory item that a company should ever have in stock, to protect against interruptions of production or loss of sales due to delays in delivery of the item.
pertinent costs	Costs that will be incurred in the future that are different for alternative courses of action; also called *relevant costs*.

process-or-sell decision	A decision management may be required to make when a market exists for its product in a semifinished state—that is, whether to finish the product or sell it in its semifinished state.
relevant costs	See *pertinent costs.*
short-term operating decisions	Day-to-day operating decisions requiring no additional investment in long-term operating assets (operating decisions made within the constraint of the present investment base of the firm).
tax shield	The amount of tax benefit associated with a noncash expense, such as depreciation or loss on the disposal of an asset when cash-flow projections are developed.
Theory of Constraints	A theory that postulates that there are identifiable constraints associated with the operations of any business and that management should exercise control over firm operations by identifying those constraints and managing them so as to use the firm's resources most effectively. Also applied to the determination of sales mix."

QUESTIONS FOR CLASS DISCUSSION

19–1 How are short-term operating decisions defined in this chapter?

19–2 How may historical costs be used in projecting the anticipated results of alternative courses of action? Explain.

19–3 What is meant by *pertinent (relevant) costs?* How do they relate to sunk costs? Explain.

19–4 What are imputed costs? Are they recorded in the accounting records? Explain.

19–5 What two items should be matched against each other in deciding whether to make or to buy a part? Explain.

19–6 What effect does the existence of excess capacity have on the make-or-buy decision? Explain.

19–7 Will a firm ever be willing to sell its product at a price that is lower than total cost per unit allocated to it? Explain.

19–8 What effect does the existence of excess capacity have on a firm's pricing policies? Explain.

19–9 What items are matched against each other in making a process-or-sell decision?

19–10 What effect does the existence of excess capacity in the additional processing department of a business have on the process-or-sell decision? Explain.

19–11 What costs are considered in making purchase and inventory decisions? Are all those costs recorded in the accounting records? Explain.

19–12 Why does a firm normally maintain a certain minimum inventory level for each of its materials?

19—13   What is likely to be the difference between the targeted minimum inventory level for a large, expensive-to-store raw material and a low-cost, easy-to-store item? Explain.

19—14   Why may it not always be appropriate to discontinue a department or segment of a business that has been consistently showing an operating loss over a number of periods? Explain.

19—15   How does the contribution margin of a department or division relate to the decision to discontinue or continue its operations? Explain.

19—16   How may the use of sales commissions based on gross sales conflict with the achievement of a firm's overall profit objective? Explain.

19—17   On what basic concept is the *Theory of Constraints* built?

EXERCISES

19—18   **Make-or-Buy Decision** Alex Company manufactures a part at a cost of $2.00 per unit, including $.75 of allocated fixed costs. The fixed-cost allocation is based on expected production of 40,000 units. The purchasing department has discovered a source that sells this part for $1.75 per unit.

REQUIRED:

1. Assuming the firm has no alternate use for the facilities currently being used to manufacture the part, should the part be purchased or manufactured? Show calculations in support of your answer.
2. Assume now that the facilities can be used profitably in the manufacture of other parts. Should the part be purchased? Show calculations to support your conclusion.

19—19   **Pricing Decision** Barrett Company manufactures and sells a product at $10 per unit. The cost based on normal production of 30,000 units is $7 per unit, including $5 of variable costs. Plant capacity for production of this part is 40,000 units. The firm has just received an offer to purchase 8,000 units at $6 per unit.

REQUIRED:

1. Basing your answer only on the quantitative data just given, should the firm agree to manufacture and sell the additional units?
2. Show calculations in support of your answer to requirement 1.
3. What other factors may need to be considered in deciding whether or not to accept the offer?

19—20   **Process-or-Sell Decision** A firm manufactures a product that can be sold in a semifinished state at a price of $2.00 per unit. If the firm finishes the unit, it can be sold for $3.00 per unit. Costs associated with the production of the unit are:

	Semifinished	Finished
Variable costs	$.90	$1.80
Fixed costs	.50	.90

REQUIRED:

1. Assuming that the production facilities used to finish the units cannot be used for other purposes in the event the units are sold in a semifinished state, should the firm process the units through the finishing process, or should it sell them in a semifinished state? Support your answer with calculations.
2. Assume now that the production facilities used to complete the processing of the units can be put to profitable use manufacturing another product that can be sold at a price that will cover the fixed costs and $.20 per unit in excess of variable costs. Should the firm sell the units it is presently producing in a semifinished or a finished state? Develop a report in support of your answer.

19–21 **Discontinuance-of-Department Decision** Vargle Department Store operates a lunch counter that has consistently shown an operating loss. Based on the past 5 years of operating data, the management of the company expects to lose approximately $5,000 annually from lunch counter operation, as shown in the following projected income statement:

Sales	$80,000
Cost of sales	60,000
Gross margin	$20,000
Operating costs	
Directly chargeable for salaries, wages, supplies, etc.	16,000
Allocated costs for heat, light, and space	9,000
Total operating cost	$25,000
Net loss from operations	$ 5,000

The company has received an offer from a local vending company to lease the space for $1,500 per year and operate the lunch counter.

REQUIRED:

1. Should the firm accept the lease proposal?
2. Support your answer in requirement 1 by preparing a schedule showing the benefit accruing to the company if it follows your proposed course of action.

19–22 **Pricing Decision** Cole Company, the manufacturer of a single product, operated at 80% of normal capacity of 100,000 units in 19X1. Since Cole bases its overhead rate on normal capacity, the company had a significant amount of underapplied overhead for the year. Early in 19X2, Cole receives an order for 10,000 units at 30% off the regular sales price of $14.00. The controller wants to accept the order because $1.60 of the total manufacturing cost of $10.00 per unit is fixed overhead and because the additional units can be produced with the company's present facilities.

REQUIRED:

1. Should the order be accepted?
2. Prepare a report showing the effect on operating profit of accepting the offer.

19–23 Purchasing and Inventory Decisions Kelly Corporation manufactures a product requiring two units of raw material A for each unit of finished product. It expects to produce 40 units of finished product per day during the next year. The normal delivery time for raw material A is 20 days from the time the order is placed. On some occasions this may extend to as many as 25 days. Kelly has determined its economic order size to be 2,000 units.

REQUIRED:

1. What should Kelly establish as a minimum inventory level for the critical raw material A to prevent delays in production due to running out of the material?
2. What should be the maximum inventory level for raw material A?
3. Assume now that Kelly wishes to implement a JIT inventory policy. How would that change the company's purchasing procedure and inventory balances? Discuss.

19–24 Consideration of Special Sales Order Mod Threads Company presently is manufacturing suits to fill orders already on hand for next season. Orders from regular customers for 60,000 suits have been received. The company has basic facilities to produce 100,000 suits for the season.

The regular selling price of Mod suits is $80.00 each. Total fixed costs budgeted for the current season are $960,000. Variable production costs are $40.00 per suit. Direct selling costs are $5.00 per suit.

An offer has been received from Bob Hull, Inc., a nationwide chain of low-overhead clothing stores, for 20,000 suits at a price of $48.00 per suit. The suits would carry the brand name of Hull, Inc. Mod Threads believes the Hull order could be produced in time to meet Hull's needs. In order to produce the additional 20,000 suits, an additional $40,000 of fixed overhead would be incurred. Variable production costs would remain the same. Direct selling costs would be only $.50 per suit (rather than the regular $5.00). A Hull order for the forthcoming year is not anticipated.

REQUIRED:

1. Should Mod accept the Hull order?
2. Prepare an analysis in good form to support your answer.

19–25 Consideration of Special Order A company regularly produces and sells 100,000 units of a product a year at a sales price of $10.00 per unit. The average total cost of producing each unit is $6.00. The company has an opportunity to sell 40,000 additional units to a chain discount store for $4.50 per unit.

REQUIRED:

1. What additional information would you need to prepare a recommendation for management regarding acceptance of the order?
2. Determine the conditions for requirement 1 that would cause management to be indifferent as to acceptance of the order.

PROBLEMS

19–26 **Make-or-Buy Decision** Cole Company manufactures part no. 1923 for use in the production of a product it manufactures. The costs per unit for 10,000 units are:

Direct matrials	$ 4
Direct labor	24
Variable overhead	10
Fixed overhead applied	14
	$52

Globe Company has offered to sell Cole 10,000 units of part no. 1923 for $54 per unit. If Cole accepts the offer, some of the facilities presently used to manufacture part no. 1923 could be used in producing part no. 2011. Such use of the facilities would save $50,000 in relevant costs in the manufacture of that part. Six dollars per unit of the fixed overhead applied to part no. 1923 would be totally eliminated if the part were purchased.

REQUIRED: Prepare a report showing the amount by which operating income would be increased or decreased by acceptance of Globe's offer.

19–27 **Consideration of Special Order with Capacity Limitation** The manufacturing capacity of Cassell Company's facilities is 60,000 units of product a year. A summary of operating results for the year ended December 31, 19X2, follows:

Sales (36,000 units @ $100)	$3,600,000
Variable manufacturing and selling costs	1,980,000
Contribution margin	$1,620,000
Fixed costs	990,000
Operating income	$ 630,000

A foreign distributor has offered to buy 30,000 units at $90 per unit during 19X3. Assume that all of Cassell's costs would be at the same levels and rates in 19X3 as in 19X2.

REQUIRED:

1. If Cassell accepts the foreign distributor's order, it will have to forego some sales to regular customers or expand its facilities. Prepare a report indicating the effect that acceptance of the order would have on operating income if the company continues to operate within its present capacity limits.
2. Assume now that Cassell decides to expand its production facilities so it can accept the foreign order and still service all of its regular customers. The proposed expansion would increase Cassell's productive capacity by 25%. The expansion would increase fixed costs by $250,000. Prepare a report showing the effect of accepting the order under these conditions.
3. What other factors should be considered before the expansion option is accepted or rejected?

19–28 **Elimination of a Department** Wheat Corporation currently operates two departments, which had operating results for the year ended December 31, 19X2, as follows:

	Department A	Department B
Sales	$1,200,000	$600,000
Variable costs	620,000	400,000
Contribution margin	$ 580,000	$200,000
Fixed costs	220,000	140,000
Margin over direct costs	$ 360,000	$ 60,000
Allocated corporate costs	180,000	90,000
Operating income (loss)	$ 180,000	$ (30,000)

Since Department B also sustained an operating loss during 19X1, Wheat's president is considering the elimination of this division. Assume that departmental fixed costs and 20% of allocated corporate costs would be eliminated if the department were eliminated.

REQUIRED:

1. Prepare a report showing the effect that elimination of the department would have on corporate operating income.
2. Explain why the result given in your report is correct.

19–29 **Decision to Sell or Rework Obsolete Inventory Items** A company has 10,000 obsolete lamps that are carried in inventory at a cost of $10 each. In its effort to reduce inventory, the company finds that the lamps can be sold as they are for $2 each. However, they can also be reworked at a cost of $40,000, after which, it is believed, they can be sold for $7 each.

REQUIRED:

1. What is the sunk cost in this situation?
2. Prepare a report showing which of the two options should be followed and the benefit that would be associated with following that option.

19—30 **Alternate Sales Policies** The Coulter Company produces a single product, which currently sells for $10 per unit. Fixed costs are expanded to amount to $120,000 for the year, and variable manufacturing and administrative costs are expected to be incurred at a rate of $6 per unit. Coulter has two salespeople, paid strictly on a commission basis (10% of the sales dollars each generates).

REQUIRED:

1. Coulter's management considers spending $10,000 on an advertising plan emphasizing the uniqueness of its product. It believes that by doing so, the selling price of the product can be increased to $12 per unit without an excessive decrease in the volume of sales. Prepare a report projecting the company's net income before taxes if 60,000 units can be sold at that price.
2. Compare the result shown in requirement 1 with the presently projected net income before taxes based on estimated sales of 65,000 units at $10 per unit.
3. Assume, as an alternate possibility, that Coulter is approached by a potential one-time customer desiring to purchase 10,000 units. Coulter has the capacity to produce these units without enlarging its facilities. Furthermore, there would be no sales commission on this sale. What price would Coulter have to charge for these units to earn additional profit of $20,000 before taxes?

19—31 **Purchases and Inventory Levels** The following information pertains to widgets, a critical part used by Gray Company in the manufacture of gadgets:

Annual usage	36,500 units
Normal lead time on purchases	20 days
Maximum lead time on purchases	30 days

Gray operates every day of the year. Management also has determined that widgets should be purchased in 5,000-unit lots.

REQUIRED:

1. Determine the minimum or safety stock level required to be sure that production is not stopped because of a shortage of widgets.
2. Determine the maximum number of widgets that should be on hand at any time.
3. Using the data in requirements 1 and 2, calculate the average inventory level.
4. Assume that Gray is able to work out a just-in-time (JIT) inventory arrangement with a supplier of widgets to provide each day's production requirements as needed. Assume also that it costs $2 per widget per year to carry a unit of inventory. How much would be saved in inventory carrying costs each year by the JIT inventory arrangement?

19—32 **Make-or-Buy Decision** The management of Gale Company asks you to help it decide whether to continue to make a component part of its finished product or buy it from an outside firm. You are given the following information:

(1) Gale expects to need 5,000 units of the component. The firm has a quotation of $35 per unit from an outside supplier.

(2) If the component part is purchased, the equipment used to manufacture the component would be sold at its book value.

(3) The following manufacturing costs applying to the component were incurred by Kelly during the past year in producing 5,000 of the component parts:

Materials	$67,500
Direct labor	50,000
Indirect labor	20,000
Light and heat (allocated)	5,500
Power	3,000
Depreciation	10,000
Property taxes and insurance	8,000
Payroll taxes and other benefits	9,800
Allocated fixed costs	5,000

REQUIRED: Prepare a report summarizing the costs associated with the two possible courses of action, and make a recommendation to Gale.

19–33
ICMA Adapted

Discontinuance of a Market The Justa Corporation produces and sells three products, A, B, and C, which are sold in a local market and in a regional market. At the end of the first quarter of the current year, the following income statement was prepared:

	Total	Local	Regional
Sales	$1,300,000	$1,000,000	$300,000
Cost of goods sold	1,010,000	775,000	235,000
Gross margin	$ 290,000	$ 225,000	$ 65,000
Selling expenses	$ 105,000	$ 60,000	$ 45,000
Administrative expenses	52,000	40,000	12,000
Total expenses	$ 157,000	$ 100,000	$ 57,000
Net income	$ 133,000	$ 125,000	$ 8,000

Management is concerned about the regional market because of the extremely poor return on sales. This market was entered a year ago because of excess capacity. It was originally believed that the return on sales would improve with time, but after a year no noticeable improvement can be seen from the results as reported in the preceding quarterly statement.

In attempting to decide whether to eliminate the regional market, the following information has been gathered:

	Product		
	A	**B**	**C**
Sales	$500,000	$400,000	$400,000
Variable manufacturing expenses as a percentage of sales	60%	70%	60%
Variable selling expenses as a percentage of sales	3%	2%	2%

Sales, by Markets

	Local	Regional
A	$400,000	$100,000
B	300,000	100,000
C	300,000	100,000

All administrative expenses and fixed manufacturing expenses are common to the three products and the two markets and are fixed for the period. Remaining selling expenses are fixed for the period and separable by market. All fixed expenses are based on a prorated yearly amount.

REQUIRED:

1. Prepare the quarterly income statement, showing contribution margins by markets.
2. Assuming there are no alternative uses for the Justa Corporation's present capacity, would you recommend dropping the regional market? Prepare a report supporting your conclusion.
3. Prepare the quarterly income statement showing contribution margins by products.
4. It is believed that a new product can be ready for sale next year if the Justa Corporation decides to go ahead with continued research. The new product can be produced by simply converting equipment presently used in producing product C. This conversion will increase fixed costs by $10,000 per quarter. What must be the minimum contribution margin per quarter for the new product to make the changeover financially feasible?

19–34
ICMA Adapted

Contribution Margin and Pricing E. Berg and Sons builds custom-made pleasure boats that range in price from $10,000 to $250,000. For the past 30 years, Mr. Berg, Sr., has determined the selling price of each boat by estimating the costs of materials, labor, and a prorated portion of overhead and adding 20% to those estimated costs.

For example, a recent price quotation was determined as follows:

Direct materials	$ 5,000
Direct labor	8,000
Overhead	2,000
	$15,000
Plus 20%	3,000
Selling price	$18,000

The overhead figure was determined by estimating total overhead costs for the year and allocating them to orders at 25% of direct labor.

If a customer rejected the price and business was slack, Mr. Berg, Sr., often would be willing to reduce markup to as little as 5% over estimated costs. Thus, average markup for the year is estimated at 15%.

Mr. Ed Berg, Jr., has just completed a course on pricing and believes the firm could use some of the techniques discussed in the course. The course emphasized the contribution-margin approach to pricing, and Mr. Berg, Jr., feels such as approach would be helpful in determining the selling prices of their custom-made pleasure boats.

Total overhead, which includes selling and administrative expenses for the year, has been estimated at $150,000, of which $90,000 is fixed and the remainder variable in direct proportion to direct labor costs.

REQUIRED:

1. Assume the customer in the example rejected the $18,000 quotation and also rejected a $15,750 quotation (5% markup) during a slack period. The customer countered with a $15,000 offer.
   a. What would be the difference in net income for the year between accepting or rejecting the customer's offer?
   b. What is the minimum selling price Mr. Berg, Jr., could have quoted without reducing net income?
2. What advantages does the contribution-margin approach to pricing have over the approach used by Mr. Berg, Sr.?
3. What pitfalls are there, if any, to contribution-margin pricing?

19–35
ICMA Adapted

Pricing Procedures The Fiore Company manufactures office equipment for sale to retail stores. Tim Lucas, vice-president of marketing, has proposed that Fiore introduce two new products to its line—an electric stapler and an electric pencil sharpener.

Lucas has requested that Fiore's profit planning department develop preliminary selling prices for the two new products for his review. Profit planning is to follow the company's standard policy for developing the projected selling prices using as much data as available for each product. Data accumulated by profit planning regarding these two new products are:

	Electric Stapler	Electric Pencil Sharpener
Estimated annual demand in units	$12,000	10,000
Estimated unit manufacturing costs	$10.00	$12.00
Estimated unit selling and administrative expenses	$4.00	Not available
Assets employed in manufacturing	$180,000	Not available

Fiore plans to employ an average of $2,400,000 of assets to support its operations in the current year. The following condensed pro forma operating statement represents Fiore's planned goals with respect to cost relationships and return on assets employed for the entire company for all of its products:

Fiore Company

Pro Forma Operating Income Statement

For the Year Ending May 31, 19X5

($000 omitted)

Revenue	$4,800
Cost of goods sold (manufacturing costs)	2,880
Gross profit	$1,920
Selling and administrative expenses	1,440
Operating profit	$ 480

REQUIRED:

1. Calculate a potential selling price for the:
   a. Electric stapler using return-on-assets pricing.
   b. Electric pencil sharpener using gross-margin pricing.
2. Could a selling price for the electric pencil sharpener be calculated using return-on-assets pricing? Explain your answer.
3. Which of the two pricing methods—return-on-asset pricing or gross-margin pricing—is more appropriate for decision analysis? Explain your answer.
4. Discuss the additional steps Tim Lucas is likely to take after he receives the potential selling prices for the two new products (as calculated in requirement 1) to set an actual selling price for each of the two products.

19–36
ICMA Adapted

Sell or Process Further The Cum-Clean Corporation produces a variety of cleaning compounds and solutions for both industrial and household use. While most of its products are processed independently, a few are related.

"Grit 337" is a coarse cleaning powder with many industrial uses. It costs $1.60 a pound to make and has a selling price of $2.00 a pound. Variable selling costs amount to $.10 per pound.

A small portion of the annual production of this product is retained for further processing in the mixing department, where it is combined with several other ingredients to form a paste marketed as a silver polish selling for $4.00 per jar. This further processing required one-quarter pound of Grit 337 per jar. Other ingredients, labor, and variable overhead associated with this further processing cost $2.50 per jar. Variable selling costs amount to $.30 per jar. If the decision were made to cease production of the silver polish, $5,600 of fixed mixing department costs could be avoided.

REQUIRED:

1. Prepare a report showing the contribution margin per pound of Grit 337 associated with further processing it into silver polish.

2. What is the minimum number of jars of silver polish that must be produced to justify continuing production of silver polish.
3. Assume the company is currently producing and selling 8,000 jars of silver polish. Prepare a report showing the effect on operating income of an increase in sales of 4,000 jars.

19–37   **Alternative Sales Options**   Auer Company had received an order for a piece
ICMA Adapted   of special machinery from Jay Company. Just as Auer Company completed the machine, Jay Company declared bankruptcy, defaulted on the order, and forefeited the 10% deposit paid on the selling price of $72,500.

Auer's manufacturing manager identified the costs already incurred in the production of the special machinery for Jay as follows:

Direct materials used		$16,600
Direct labor incurred		21,400
Overhead applied:		
Manufacturing		
Variable	$10,700	
Fixed	5,350	16,050
Fixed selling and		
administrative		5,405
Total cost		$59,455

Another company, Kaytell Corp., would be interested in buying the special machinery if it is reworked to Kaytell's specifications. Auer offered to sell the reworked special machinery to Kaytell, as a special order, for a net price of $68,400. Kaytell has agreed to pay the net price when it takes delivery in 2 months. The additional identifiable costs to rework the machinery to the specifications of Kaytell are:

Direct materials	$ 6,200
Direct labor	4,200
	$10,400

A second alternative available to Auer is to convert the special machinery to the standard model. The standard model lists for $62,500. The additional identifiable costs to convert the special machinery to the standard model are:

Direct materials	$2,850
Direct labor	3,300
	$6,150

A third alternative for the Auer Company is to sell, as a special order, the machine as is (that is, without modification) for a net price of $52,000.

REQUIRED:

1. Determine the dollar contribution each of the three alternatives will add to the Auer Company's before-tax profits.
2. Which offer should be accepted? Prepare a report supporting your answer.
3. If Kaytell makes Auer a counteroffer, what is the lowest price Auer should accept for the reworked machinery? Explain your answer.

19–38
ICMA Adapted

Pricing a Custom Order George Jackson operates a small machine shop. He manufactures one standard product available from many other similar businesses and he also manufactures products to customer order. His accountant prepared the following annual income statement:

	Custom Sales	Standard Sales	Total
Sales	$50,000	$25,000	$75,000
Materials	$10,000	$ 8,000	$18,000
Labor	20,000	9,000	29,000
Depreciation	6,300	3,600	9,900
Power	700	400	1,100
Rent	6,000	1,000	7,000
Heat and light	600	100	700
Other	400	900	1,300
Total costs	$44,000	$23,000	$67,000
Operating income	$ 6,000	$ 2,000	$ 8,000

The depreciation charges are for machines used in the respective product lines. The power charge is apportioned on the basis of estimated power consumed. The rent is for the building space, which has been leased for 10 years at $7,000 per year. The rent, and heat and light are apportioned to the product lines based on amount of floor space occupied. All other costs are current expenses identified with the product line causing them.

A valued custom parts customer has asked Mr. Jackson if he would manufacture 5,000 special units for him. Mr. Jackson is working at capacity and would have to give up some other business in order to take this business. He can't renege on custom orders already agreed to, but he could reduce the output of his standard product by about one-half for 1 year while producing the specially requested custom part. The customer is willing to pay $7.00 for each part. The materials cost will be about $2.00 per unit, and the labor will be $3.60 per unit. Mr. Jackson will have to spend $2,000 for a special device that will be discarded when the job is done.

REQUIRED:

1. Calculate and present the following costs related to the 5,000-unit customer order:

      a. the incremental cost of the order
      b. the full cost of the order
      c. the opportunity cost of taking the order
      d. the sunk costs related to the order.
   2. Should Mr. Jackson take the order? Explain your answer.

Chapter 20

Long-Term Investment Decisions

Learning Objectives

When you have finished your study of this chapter, you should

1. Be able to identify the pertinent (relevant) costs to use in deciding whether to replace an existing asset, and recognize the limitations of a simplistic analysis.
2. Know how to apply cost–volume–profit analysis in determining a firm's optimum capacity.
3. Understand how to evaluate the attractiveness of an investment opportunity by using the accounting rate-of-return method, the payback method, the net-present-value method, and the time-adjusted rate-of-return method.

T hroughout the text, we have emphasized the importance of fixed costs in the operations of a business. Since a firm becomes committed to fixed costs—such as depreciation of long-term assets—at the time it invests liquid resources in those assets, the decision to invest or to not invest in a long-term asset or project is one of the most important and far-reaching that management must make. In this chapter, we deal with the analytical procedures normally associated with such decisions.

Long-term decisions, like the short-term decisions discussed in Chapter 19, require the appropriate use of accounting information. Historical-cost and revenue data, adjusted for expected changes, are used, when available; when not available, the probable costs and revenues expected to be associated with a venture must be estimated for use in decision making. The uncertainties associated with long-term projections must be recognized as such decisions are made. Uncertainties about cash flow and cost of capital are some of the risks associated with entering into business ventures.

The four basic guidelines for using cost data in making short-term decisions (listed in Chapter 19) also apply to long-term decisions:

1. Use historical costs only to predict future costs.
2. Use only pertinent (relevant) costs.
3. Consider any opportunity-cost consequences.
4. Consider the tax consequences, when appropriate.

The decisions discussed in this chapter require the commitment of additional liquid resources, with the expectation of increasing net income either by reducing costs or by increasing revenues. Long-term decisions typically involve:

- examining the investment opportunity
- evaluating the projected results of the project being considered.

Examining Investment Opportunities

Opportunities to invest additional liquid resources in long-term assets can be divided into two categories: (1) replacement of existing fixed assets and (2) acquisition of assets to increase capacity.

Equipment Replacement

We are experiencing today what some have called a **technological revolution**. Indeed, ours is a period in which technological developments are making most equipment obsolete before it has lost its physical productive capability. Frequently, management must decide whether to replace physically sound equipment with new equipment that would be more efficient. In doing so, it is easy to fall into the trap of comparing the historical recorded cost of producing goods using the present equipment to the estimated cost of producing them with the new equipment. Because the new equipment is more efficient, use of those data alone would always lead to a decision to acquire the new equipment. However, because of the sunk costs associated with using the existing equipment and the need for imputing the opportunity cost associated with the additional investment required for the new equipment, that decision might be incorrect.

When determining whether it will be beneficial to the company to replace an existing piece of equipment, only those costs expected to be changed by the decision should be considered. We must isolate the *relevant costs*—that is, those that affect future cash flows and that are different for the alternatives being considered. *Sunk costs*—those already incurred and that cannot be recovered—always are irrelevant to the replacement decision. Therefore, we should begin by identifying and eliminating the sunk costs from the available cost data. For example, in preparing an analysis of costs associated with two options, the depreciation expense associated with the difference between the book value and the salvage value of existing assets should be eliminated from the costs of using the existing assets because it is sunk (cannot be recovered).

In addition to eliminating the sunk costs from the normally recognized costs of using the existing equipment, it is important to impute an opportunity cost equal to the revenue that could be earned from investing the additional funds required to purchase the new equipment as an addition to the other costs of using the new equipment.[1] It is also important in projecting probable unit costs of production with the new equipment to use the level of operations the firm is likely to achieve rather than the capacity of the new equipment, if that is greater than the projected level of operation.

To illustrate, let's assume that a firm currently is using a machine acquired 5 years ago for $100,000. Its original estimated life was 20 years, at the end of which time it was expected to have no salvage value. It is capable of producing 20,000 units per year, with total out-of-pocket operating costs of $40,000 per year. **Out-of-pocket costs** are the amount of **net working capital** that must be given up to operate the machine. Management has concluded that, because of likely technological improvements, the currently estimated remaining useful life of the machine is only 4 years. Depreciation expense based on the unrecovered original cost would be $100,000 − $25,000 ÷ 4 = $18,750 per year for the next 4 years. A new machine, capable of producing 30,000 units per year, is now available. It will produce 20,000 units with out-of-pocket operating costs of $30,000 per year. The cash purchase price of the new machine is $125,000, and it has an estimated physical life of 20 years.

[1]Present-value techniques, discussed on pages 763–770, automatically include this type of opportunity cost.

However, the firm believes that it, too, will be obsolete in 4 years, when it is expected to have a disposal value of $30,000. The firm has been earning 10% interest from investing its surplus funds and can borrow funds at that rate. The firm selling the new machine is willing to allow $25,000 for the present machine against the cash purchase price of the new equipment. Production data from previous periods show that the firm has been operating at a level that calls for the production of 20,000 units per year. It anticipates no increase in sales in the near future. What savings, if any, might be realized from investing in the new machine?

Our first inclination might be to divide the adjusted historical costs of operating the old equipment ($40,000 plus $18,750 depreciation) by 20,000 units to arrive at a cost of $2.9375 per unit if the firm continues to use the present machine. Then we might turn to the projected data for the new machine and divide the total operating cost [$30,000 plus depreciation of ($125,000 − $30,000) ÷ 4 = $23,750] by 20,000 units to arrive at a cost of $2.6875 per unit if the firm uses the new machine. On the basis of these data, the firm clearly would realize a cost benefit by acquiring the new machine.

The use of *appropriate* cost data (ignoring taxes), however, shows this to be the wrong decision. As Figure 20–1 indicates, the relevant cost per unit using the old equipment is $2.3125 rather than $2.9375. Other costs

	Present Equipment	New Equipment
Annual out-of-pocket operating costs	$40,000	$30,000
Annual pertinent depreciation, old machine ($25,000* ÷ 4)	6,250	
Annual depreciation, new equipment [($125,000 − $30,000) ÷ 4]	—	23,750
Annual interest on added investment, average over 4 years ($50,000** @ 10%)	—	5,000
Total annual pertinent costs	$46,250	$58,750
Pertinent cost per unit (20,000 units)	$2.3125	$2.9375

*Current trade-in value
**Average added annual investment calculated as follows:

$$\frac{\$100,000 \text{ (initial investment)} + 0 \text{ (ending invetment)}}{2} = \$50,000$$

FIGURE 20–1 Analysis of Pertinent Costs for Making Replacement Decision (ignoring taxes) are irrelevant because they are sunk costs. After imputing interest at 10% on the *average additional funds* required to finance the purchase of the new equipment, and dividing the total pertinent annual costs of operating that machine by 20,000 units (expected level of sales), we find the projected cost per unit with the new equipment is $2.9375. (It is a coincidence that this per-unit figure is the same as the "first pass" cost per unit of the old equipment.) Thus, the company should *not* acquire the new equipment.

So far, we have ignored any tax effects that might be associated with acquisition of the new machine. The tax consequences depend on whether the new equipment is considered "similar" to the old equipment. If it is, a loss (but never a gain) would be recognized for accounting purposes, though neither a gain nor a loss is recognized for tax purposes. Instead, the adjusted book value to be depreciated, for tax purposes, would be the $75,000 book value of the old equipment plus the $125,000 − $25,000 = $100,000 cash given up for the new equipment, a total of $175,000. Depreciation for tax purposes with the present equipment would be $18,750. With the new equipment it would be ($175,000 − $30,000) ÷ 4 years = $36,250. Assuming a 40% tax rate, the tax benefit associated with depreciation would be $7,500 with the present equipment and $14,500 with the new equipment, amounting to $.375 and $.725 per unit, respectively. The projections after giving effect to taxes are shown in Figure 20–2. Thus, even with the largest tax benefits expected to be associated with acquiring the new equipment, the appropriate decision still is to continue to use the present equipment.

A weakness in the preceding analysis is that it ignores the **time value of money.** We can overcome that by accumulating all cash flows on an after-tax present-value basis, as shown in Figure 20–3. Observe, however, that the decision again favors retaining the present equipment.

Our original assumption was that the volume of sales would remain at 20,000 units. If the firm expected to increase sales to 30,000 units (the capacity of the new machine) without reducing the sales price per unit,

	Present Equipment	New Equipment
Pertinent cost per unit (from Figure 20–1)	$2.3125	$2.9375
Tax benefit from depreciation	.3750	.7250
Pertinent unit costs	$1.9375	$2.2125

FIGURE 20–2 Cash-Flow Analysis of Replacement Decision

Present Equipment	After-Tax Cash Flows	Present-Value Factor*	Present Value of 4 years of Cash Flows*
Annual out-of-pocket operating costs ($40,000 × 0.6)	$(24,000)	3.170	$ (76,080)
Depreciation ($18,750 × 0.4)	7,500	3.170	23,775
			$ (52,305)
New Equipment			
Purchase cost (differential) ($125,000 − $25,000)	$(100,000)	1	$(100,000)
Annual out-of-pocket operating costs ($30,000 × 0.6)	(18,000)	3.170	(57,060)
Depreciation ($36,250 × 0.4)	14,500	3.170	45,965
			$(111,095)

*See discussion of present value and present-value factors, pages 763–769. Assumed discount rate used here = 10%.

FIGURE 20–3 Analysis of Pertinent Costs for Making Replacement Decision

the new machine probably should be acquired, to allow the firm to realize the contribution margin from selling the additional 10,000 units. Also, if the new equipment provides quality improvements or significantly reduces **cycle processing time** (time required to produce a completed unit), these benefits also should be incorporated into the analysis as the replacement decision is being made.

This example shows that an equipment replacement decision is not simple, and that even with the isolation of relevant costs it is possible to "slant" the analysis to support either retaining the present equipment or replacing it. We recommend that you identify pertinent costs, construct an analysis, and then try to imagine all the implications and ramifications of the decision.

Equipment to Increase Capacity

As firms are organized and operate, they must decide the maximum amount of production they wish to handle. Initially, as the firm organizes, its capital requirements will be directly related to the capacity the founders anticipate will be needed. Buildings and equipment must be acquired in anticipation of operating within a certain range of output. This is the point at which a firm commits itself to many of its fixed costs, so decisions relating to initial anticipated capacity and subsequent changes in that capacity are especially important.

Some of the key considerations in determining the desirable capacity are the anticipated market for the product, the probable compositions of fixed and variable costs at the various possible levels of operations, and the capital available. Judgments regarding the potential market for a product can be based on market analysis and economic projections. Cost–volume–profit (CVP) models based on several alternative assumptions regarding sales volume and different possible combinations of variable and fixed costs can be used to project alternative operating budgets, to help target a specific operating capacity. The amount of capital available to the firm is always a factor limiting targeted capacity.

The accountant is primarily responsible for projecting the **profit potential** and break-even points associated with the various capacities being considered. Management then analyzes the projections and selects the desired capacity. Since most mass production firms can produce effectively only if willing to commit to a large initial investment in highly specialized equipment, they generally must be prepared to accept a significant amount of fixed costs and a relatively high break-even point for reasonable profit potential.

High fixed costs, coupled with large production capacity, generally provide a firm with maximum profit potential. At the same time, however, a firm gearing up for a large capacity is raising its break-even point each time it increases the proportionate part of its total costs that are fixed. Stated another way, other things being the same, a firm with fixed costs that are a smaller part of total costs will have a lower break-even point than one that has a larger part of its costs fixed. However, as demonstrated in Chapter 16, other things being the same, such a low-fixed-cost firm will never have as large a profit potential as the high-fixed-cost, large-capacity firm. Even with focused, flexible management philosophies, the low-fixed-cost firm ultimately may be unable to compete with the high-volume firms that make extensive use of expensive, automated equipment.

Any firm anticipating increasing its capacity should consider the effect that increased capacity will have on both its break-even point and its profit potential, before committing to the expansion. Because of inherent tradeoffs in any manufacturing process (such as the substitution of computer-controlled equipment for labor), increased fixed costs often will result in a decreased variable cost ratio. That type change is illustrated in Figure 20–4.

All of these factors should be considered when deciding whether liquid resources should be committed to enlarging the capacity of a business or to other projects designed to increase the business's net income. These are long-term investment decisions that commit a firm to a particular operating format over a long period of time.

	Present Facilities		**Expanded Facilities**	
Sales at capacity		$1,500,000		$3,500,000
Variable expenses	$600,000		$1,050,000	
Fixed expenses	400,000	1,000,000	1,000,000	$2,050,000
Net income (at capacity)		$ 500,000		$1,450,000
Sales at break-even point		$ 666,667[a]		$1,428,571[b]

[a]Variable costs   = 40% of sales
Break-even sales = Variable costs + Fixed costs
$$S = 0.40S + \$400,000$$
$$0.60S = \$400,000$$
$$S = \$666,667$$

[b]Variable costs = 30% of sales
$$S = 0.30S + \$1,000,000$$
$$0.70S = \$1,000,000$$
$$S = \$1,428,571$$

FIGURE 20–4   Comparative Break-Even Analysis

Evaluating Long-Term Investment Opportunities

After projecting the probable increase in net income to be realized from additional investments in fixed assets, either through decreased costs or increased revenues, we must consider the relationship between the expected return and the investment required to implement it. One or more of four methods typically are used to evaluate this effort–achievement relationship:

1. accounting rate-of-return method
2. pay-back method
3. net-present-value method
4. time-adjusted rate-of-return method.

Accounting Rate-of-Return Method

The **accounting rate-of-return method** (often called the *accountant's method*) relates the projected increase in net income from an investment to the required investment:

$$\text{Accounting rate of return} = \frac{\text{Incremental income}}{\text{Incremental investment}}$$

It, like other such devices, relates efforts (added investment) to achievements (**incremental income** expected to be realized from the investment). The increment to net income may be determined by subtracting the net income currently being earned, based on historical data adjusted for anticipated changes, from the amount of net income the firm anticipates earning if the investment is made. **Incremental investment** may be calculated in several ways. In one approach, the incremental investment is the additional investment by the firm's owners, which may be given or may be calculated by subtracting the amount of net assets (assets less liabilities) before the investment from the expected net assets if the project is accepted. Since net assets, by definition, is equivalent to owners' equity, this investment–revenue relationship emphasizes return on owners' equity. Therefore, this version of the accounting rate-of-return method can include an element of **trading on the equity**[2] if the project is financed by an increase in debt.

Another approach calls for determining the initial investment figure by direct reference to the total required outlay, without considering whether it was acquired through debt or equity financing. This separates the investment decision from its financing. If the total outlay is used as the investment base, any interest to be paid on loans incurred in acquiring the asset should be added back to the expected amount of incremental net income, to arrive at the income figure used in calculating the accounting rate of return on the investment. This emphasizes the **rate of return on assets** rather than the **rate of return on equity capital** and focuses only on project operations rather than on the combined results of operating and financing the project. Obviously, the rates of return from these two calculations may be quite different for a project when debt financing is used. The analyst should clearly indicate which method is being used and address the issue of the additional risk involved in highly **leveraged projects (investments)** if the net-asset approach is used.

After having determined the expected periodic incremental net income and the investment base to be used, we can calculate the rate of return on the new investment by dividing net income by the investment. At this point, management would compare the calculated rate of return with the minimum rate of return the firm desires to realize on either its equity capital or its assets, depending on the investment base that has been used. If the rate of return exceeds the minimum acceptable rate set by the firm, the project normally would warrant further consideration. If not, it would be rejected. For reasons cited later in this section, the accountant's rate-of-return method has weaknesses when used as a basis for investment decisions, and so should not be used as the only evaluation device. The value of the accounting rate of return primarily lies in establishing a benchmark return that can be compared to actual results of projects that have been accepted.

---

[2]**Trading on the equity** refers to financing investment with debt on which the rate of interest is less than the rate of return expected to be earned by the investment. This allows owners to "trade" on the debt equity provided by nonowners and thereby increase the return to owners. However, a disadvantage of such a highly **leveraged project** (that is, a project financed primarily through debt) is that if the project does not generate a return at least equal to the interest on the debt, the owners will be penalized with a lower return.

To demonstrate how the accountant's method is used, let's assume a firm is considering investing $100,000 in an asset having a useful life of 10 years and no salvage value. The probable annual net income after taxes is expected to be $70,000 if the firm invests in the new project. The present level of net income after taxes is $58,000 pcr year. To simplify, let's assume the acquisition will be financed entirely with equity capital, meaning both the equity-capital and total-asset measurements associated with the investment will be the same. The projected incremental net income of $70,000 − $58,000 = $12,000 then will be divided by the $100,000 increase in assets and owners' equity to get a rate of return of 12% based on the initial investment, as shown in the following summary.

Asset Investment Analysis

Cost of asset with 10-year life and no salvage value = $100,000

	With Investment	Without Investment	Incremental Income
Annual net income	$70,000	$58,000	$12,000

Accounting rate of return: $\dfrac{\$12,000}{\$100,000} = 12\%$

Management must then judge whether the 12% probable return is satisfactory before deciding whether to accept or reject the investment opportunity based, in part, on the cost of equity capital. If the capital can be secured for less than 12% (that is, if the opportunity cost of the owners' increasing their investment is not greater than 12%), the firm can benefit from the venture.

This example assumed the life of the asset to be acquired was 10 years. Because the firm would be realizing periodic investable resource inflows[3] $10,000 per year greater than the incremental net income, by virtue of depreciation charges against operations, we can logically question whether use of the $100,000 initial incremental investment presents the most realistic rate of return. We can argue, with considerable justification, that instead of dividing the $12,000 incremental net income by $100,000 (the amount of the initial investment), we should divide it by the **average investment** of $100,000 ÷ 2 = $50,000, which would show an incremental rate of return of 24% rather than 12%. If the firm is in position to profitably reinvest resources recovered in excess of the projected net income, it seems reasonable to use the average incremental investment as the basis for calculating the rate of return.

[3]Other things held constant, investable resource inflows are equivalent to cash inflows.

Regardless of which investment base is used, the accountant's method clearly has major weaknesses. The components of the rate-of-return formula (for example, the investment base) have been shown to be arbitrary, and the length of the investment and the time value of money are ignored. Using only this method could cause a superior alternative to be rejected in favor of a less profitable one. It is difficult to rank alternatives that have different net incomes (across years and across alternatives) and different lengths of useful life. This method is more involved than the *pay-back method* (which is discussed next). On the other hand, it has one distinct advantage. The investment-return data tie into the accounting data and can be related directly to the return (on equity capital or on assets) that the firm has been realizing in prior periods. In our illustration, if the return on equity capital has been 10% per year, the firm would probably look with favor on an opportunity to sell additional shares of stock that would produce a return of 12%, which would tend to increase the earnings per share for present stockholders. If we accept the 24% rate of return as more realistic, the opportunity should be even more attractive to the company.

Pay-Back Method

A potential investor should always be concerned with the period of time required to recover the investment from operating inflows. This is particularly true during a period of accelerated technological development. In such instances, assets associated with a project frequently become obsolete before the ends of their useful lives based on expected physical deterioration. The simplest way of evaluating this aspect of an investment is to use the **pay-back method**, which relates the projected annual **net liquid resource inflows** (also called *cash flows*) to the required investment to determine how long it will take to completely recover the initial capital outlay. If a project is expected to produce equal periodic cash inflows, the number of periods (generally years) can be determined by dividing the investment by the anticipated periodic inflow:

$$\text{Payback period} = \frac{\text{Required investment}}{\text{Periodic resource (cash) inflow}}$$

Effort in this formula is in the form of the investment. Net liquid resource inflows indicate the achievements. If projected periodic inflows vary, the pay-back period can be calculated by chronologically listing and accumulating the inflows until they equal the initial investment. The number of periods required to do that is the pay-back period.

Periodic net liquid resource inflows can be projected by adding depreciation expense and other noncash expenses back to the project's anticipated net income. In our preceding illustration, the amount of projected annual cash inflow would be $22,000, which includes $12,000 of incremental net income and the $10,000 annual depreciation charge.

The $100,000 investment is then divided by $22,000 to get a pay-back period of approximately 4.55 years:

$$\text{Pay-back period: } \frac{\$100,000}{\$22,000} = 4.55 \text{ years}$$

How does the net income figure relate to net liquid resource inflows (henceforth referred to as *cash inflows*)? If in our illustration we assume a tax rate of 40%, we can reconstruct the pertinent data as follows:

(1) Net income before depreciation and taxes	$30,000
(2) Less depreciation	10,000
(3) Net income before taxes	$20,000
(4) Less taxes	8,000
(5) Equals net income	$12,000

Item (1) often is called **cash inflow before taxes.** It equals Item (5) + Item (2) ($22,000). You should be familiar enough with the relationships among these items to be able to derive Item (5) from Item (1) or Item (1) from Item (5) if you are given the tax rate and amount of depreciation. You should also be able to determine the after-tax cash inflow ($22,000 in this case) from the same data. After-tax cash flow also can be derived by calculating the after-tax amount for each income statement item. For example:

	Income Statement Amount	Tax Effect (40% rate)	After-Tax Amount
Net income before depreciation and taxes	$30,000	1 − 0.4	$18,000
Depreciation (tax shield)	10,000	0.4	4,000
After-tax cash inflow			$22,000

   Having determined the number of periods (years) over which the investment is expected to be recovered, the next step is to compare that figure with the number of periods anticipated to be benefited by the investment. In the present example, we have estimated that to be 10 years, the anticipated life of the asset. If management, on the basis of established goals, decides the difference between the number of years required to recover the investment and the anticipated useful life of the asset is adequate, it will look with favor on this investment. Otherwise, the project will be rejected.

   As you can see, the pay-back calculation is simple, and the comparison between the pay-back period and the estimated life of the asset can provide the basis for a simple and direct evaluation of the investment opportunity. Nevertheless, it has the disadvantage of producing no result that is directly comparable to anything normally included in the recorded accounting data. Furthermore, it ignores the time value of money.

Net-Present-Value Method

A dollar in-hand today is worth more than a dollar to be received in the future, because interest can be earned from money on hand. Since, assuming a 10% interest rate, a dollar loaned out today would be worth $1.10 in a year, then the value today of $1 to be received a year from today would be the amount that could be loaned today at 10% interest that would accumulate to $1 one year from today, that is, $.909. We refer to this as the *present value* of $1 to be received one year from now. (Similarly, $1 is the future value, one year from now, of $.909 invested at 10% interest.) The *discounted cash-flow method* of evaluating investment opportunities takes the timing of cash flows and appropriate interest rate(s) into consideration; that is, it recognizes the time value of money.

To illustrate more fully the discounting of future cash flows, let's assume that 10% per year is an acceptable discount (interest) rate, so $1.00 to be received 1 year from now should be worth approximately $.909 at this time (calculated by dividing $1.00 by 1.10). We can divide the $.909 by 1.10 to get the present value of $1.00 to be received 2 years from now as approximately $.826. These values and others associated with different interest rates and different periods of time are given in a "present value of one" table such as that shown in Figure 20–5.

If we are to receive $1.00 at the end of 1 year and another $1.00 at the end of 2 years, the present value of those dollars at an assumed discount rate of 10% would be $.909 + $.826 = $1.735. These values quite frequently are brought together in a "present value of an annuity of one" table, such as is shown in Figure 20–6. This table can then be used to calculate the present value of equal periodic cash inflows over a number of periods, by multiplying the amount of the periodic inflow by the discount factor shown in the table for the discount rate and number of periods over which the amounts will be received. For example, the present value of $1,000 to be received at the end of each year for 5 years, assuming an interest rate of 10%, is $1,000 × 3.791 = $3,791, which, except for $.001 rounding difference, is also the sum of the first five figures in the 10% column of Figure 20–5:

$$0.909 + 0.826 + 0.751 + 0.683 + 0.621 = 3.790$$

In using the **net-present-value method**, we begin by calculating the present value of the periodic after-tax cash inflows expected to be realized from an investment. That, in effect, converts future-period dollars to what they are worth at the time the investment is to be made. We can then compare the present value of the investment with its expected return in evaluating the investment opportunity. Effort, for this method, is measured by the amount of the investment (which also is the present value of the investment, since the discount factor for the current time

No. of Periods	4%	6%	8%	10%	12%	14%	16%	18%	20%	22%	24%	26%	28%	30%	40%
1	0.962	0.943	0.926	0.909	0.893	0.877	0.862	0.847	0.833	0.820	0.806	0.794	0.781	0.769	0.714
2	0.925	0.890	0.857	0.826	0.797	0.769	0.743	0.718	0.694	0.672	0.650	0.630	0.610	0.592	0.510
3	0.889	0.840	0.794	0.751	0.712	0.675	0.641	0.609	0.579	0.551	0.524	0.500	0.477	0.455	0.364
4	0.855	0.792	0.735	0.683	0.636	0.592	0.552	0.516	0.482	0.451	0.423	0.397	0.373	0.350	0.260
5	0.822	0.747	0.681	0.621	0.567	0.519	0.476	0.437	0.402	0.370	0.341	0.315	0.291	0.269	0.186
6	0.790	0.705	0.630	0.564	0.507	0.456	0.410	0.370	0.335	0.303	0.275	0.250	0.227	0.207	0.133
7	0.760	0.665	0.583	0.513	0.452	0.400	0.354	0.314	0.279	0.249	0.222	0.198	0.178	0.159	0.095
8	0.731	0.627	0.540	0.467	0.404	0.351	0.305	0.266	0.233	0.204	0.179	0.157	0.139	0.123	0.068
9	0.703	0.592	0.500	0.424	0.361	0.308	0.263	0.225	0.194	0.167	0.144	0.125	0.108	0.094	0.048
10	0.676	0.558	0.463	0.386	0.322	0.270	0.227	0.191	0.162	0.137	0.116	0.099	0.085	0.073	0.035
11	0.650	0.527	0.429	0.350	0.287	0.237	0.195	0.162	0.135	0.112	0.094	0.079	0.066	0.056	0.025
12	0.625	0.497	0.397	0.319	0.257	0.208	0.168	0.137	0.112	0.092	0.076	0.062	0.052	0.043	0.018
13	0.601	0.469	0.368	0.290	0.229	0.182	0.145	0.116	0.093	0.075	0.061	0.050	0.040	0.033	0.013
14	0.577	0.442	0.340	0.263	0.205	0.160	0.125	0.099	0.078	0.062	0.049	0.039	0.032	0.025	0.009
15	0.555	0.417	0.315	0.239	0.183	0.140	0.108	0.084	0.065	0.051	0.040	0.031	0.025	0.020	0.006
16	0.534	0.394	0.292	0.218	0.163	0.123	0.093	0.071	0.054	0.042	0.032	0.025	0.019	0.015	0.005
17	0.513	0.371	0.270	0.198	0.146	0.108	0.080	0.060	0.045	0.034	0.026	0.020	0.015	0.012	0.003
18	0.494	0.350	0.250	0.180	0.130	0.095	0.069	0.051	0.038	0.028	0.021	0.016	0.012	0.009	0.002
19	0.475	0.331	0.232	0.164	0.116	0.083	0.060	0.043	0.031	0.023	0.017	0.012	0.009	0.007	0.002
20	0.456	0.312	0.215	0.149	0.104	0.073	0.051	0.037	0.026	0.019	0.014	0.010	0.007	0.005	0.001
21	0.439	0.294	0.199	0.135	0.093	0.064	0.044	0.031	0.022	0.015	0.011	0.008	0.006	0.004	0.001
22	0.422	0.278	0.184	0.123	0.083	0.056	0.038	0.026	0.018	0.013	0.009	0.006	0.004	0.003	0.001
23	0.406	0.262	0.170	0.112	0.074	0.049	0.033	0.022	0.015	0.010	0.007	0.005	0.003	0.002	
24	0.390	0.247	0.158	0.102	0.066	0.043	0.028	0.019	0.013	0.008	0.006	0.004	0.003	0.002	
25	0.375	0.233	0.146	0.092	0.059	0.038	0.024	0.016	0.010	0.007	0.005	0.003	0.002	0.001	
26	0.361	0.220	0.135	0.084	0.053	0.033	0.021	0.014	0.009	0.006	0.004	0.002	0.002	0.001	
27	0.347	0.207	0.125	0.076	0.047	0.029	0.018	0.011	0.007	0.005	0.003	0.002	0.001	0.001	
28	0.333	0.196	0.116	0.069	0.042	0.026	0.016	0.010	0.006	0.004	0.002	0.002	0.001	0.001	
29	0.321	0.185	0.107	0.063	0.037	0.022	0.014	0.008	0.005	0.003	0.002	0.001	0.001	0.001	
30	0.308	0.174	0.099	0.057	0.033	0.020	0.012	0.007	0.004	0.003	0.002	0.001	0.001		
40	0.208	0.097	0.046	0.022	0.011	0.005	0.003	0.001	0.001						

FIGURE 20–5   Present Value of One: $PV = \dfrac{S}{(1 + i)^n}$

period, 0, is 1), and achievement is represented by the present value of projected cash inflows. In effect, this method converts the anticipated future cash inflows and outflows to the acquisition-date dollars used to measure the investment required to initiate the project.

No. of Periods	4%	6%	8%	10%	12%	14%	16%	18%	20%	22%	24%	25%	26%	28%	30%	40%
1	0.962	0.943	0.926	0.909	0.893	0.877	0.862	0.847	0.833	0.820	0.806	0.800	0.794	0.781	0.769	0.714
2	1.886	1.833	1.783	1.736	1.690	1.647	1.605	1.566	1.528	1.492	1.457	1.440	1.424	1.392	1.361	1.224
3	2.775	2.673	2.577	2.487	2.402	2.322	2.246	2.174	2.106	2.042	1.981	1.952	1.923	1.868	1.816	1.589
4	3.630	3.465	3.312	3.170	3.037	2.914	2.798	2.690	2.589	2.494	2.404	2.362	2.320	2.241	2.166	1.849
5	4.452	4.212	3.993	3.791	3.605	3.433	3.274	3.127	2.991	2.864	2.745	2.689	2.635	2.532	2.436	2.035
6	5.242	4.917	4.623	4.355	4.111	3.889	3.685	3.498	3.326	3.167	3.020	2.951	2.885	2.759	2.643	2.168
7	6.002	5.582	5.206	4.868	4.564	4.288	4.039	3.812	3.605	3.416	3.242	3.161	3.083	2.937	2.802	2.263
8	6.733	6.210	5.747	5.335	4.968	4.639	4.344	4.078	3.837	3.619	3.421	3.329	3.241	3.076	2.925	2.331
9	7.435	6.802	6.247	5.759	5.328	4.946	4.607	4.303	4.031	3.786	3.566	3.463	3.366	3.184	3.019	2.379
10	8.111	7.360	6.710	6.145	5.650	5.216	4.833	4.494	4.192	3.923	3.682	3.571	3.465	3.269	3.092	2.414
11	8.760	7.887	7.139	6.495	5.988	5.453	5.029	4.656	4.327	4.035	3.776	3.656	3.544	3.335	3.147	2.438
12	9.385	8.384	7.536	6.814	6.194	5.660	5.197	4.793	4.439	4.127	3.851	3.725	3.606	3.387	3.190	2.456
13	9.986	8.853	7.904	7.103	6.424	5.842	5.342	4.910	4.533	4.203	3.912	3.780	3.656	3.427	3.223	2.468
14	10.563	9.295	8.244	7.367	6.628	6.002	5.468	5.008	4.611	4.265	3.962	3.824	3.695	3.459	3.249	2.477
15	11.118	9.712	8.559	7.606	6.811	6.142	5.575	5.092	4.675	4.315	4.001	3.859	3.726	3.483	3.268	2.484
16	11.652	10.106	8.851	7.824	6.974	6.265	5.669	5.162	4.730	4.357	4.033	3.887	3.751	3.503	3.283	2.489
17	12.166	10.477	9.122	8.022	7.120	6.373	5.749	5.222	4.775	4.391	4.059	3.910	3.771	3.518	3.295	2.492
18	12.659	10.828	9.372	8.201	7.250	6.467	5.818	5.273	4.812	4.419	4.080	3.928	3.786	3.529	3.304	2.494
19	13.134	11.158	9.604	8.365	7.366	6.550	5.877	5.316	4.844	4.442	4.097	3.942	3.799	3.539	3.311	2.496
20	13.590	11.470	9.818	8.514	7.469	6.623	5.929	5.353	4.870	4.460	4.110	3.954	3.808	3.546	3.316	2.497
21	14.029	11.764	10.017	8.649	7.562	6.687	5.973	5.384	4.891	4.476	4.121	3.963	3.816	3.551	3.320	2.498
22	14.451	12.042	10.201	8.772	7.645	6.743	6.001	5.410	4.909	4.488	4.130	3.970	3.822	3.556	3.323	2.498
23	14.857	12.303	10.371	8.883	7.718	6.792	6.044	5.432	4.925	4.499	4.137	3.976	3.827	3.559	3.325	2.499
24	15.247	12.550	10.529	8.985	7.784	6.835	6.073	5.451	4.937	4.507	4.143	3.981	3.831	3.562	3.327	2.499
25	15.622	12.783	10.675	9.077	7.843	6.873	6.097	5.467	4.948	4.514	4.147	3.985	3.834	3.564	3.329	2.499
26	15.983	13.003	10.810	9.161	7.896	6.906	6.118	5.480	4.956	4.520	4.151	3.988	3.837	3.566	3.330	2.500
27	16.330	13.211	10.935	9.237	7.943	6.935	6.136	5.492	4.964	4.524	4.154	3.990	3.839	3.567	3.331	2.500
28	16.663	13.406	11.051	9.307	7.984	6.961	6.152	5.502	4.970	4.528	4.157	3.992	3.840	3.568	3.331	2.500
29	16.984	13.591	11.158	9.370	8.022	6.983	6.166	5.510	4.975	4.531	4.159	3.994	3.841	3.569	3.332	2.500
30	17.292	13.765	11.258	9.427	8.055	7.003	6.177	5.517	4.979	4.534	4.160	3.995	3.842	3.569	3.332	2.500

FIGURE 20–6 Present Value of an Annuity of One: $PV_A = \dfrac{1}{i}\left[1 - \dfrac{1}{(1 + i)^n}\right]$

The discounted cash-flow method requires management to decide on an acceptable discount (interest) rate before the present value of the anticipated cash inflows can be calculated. Using our previous data, and assuming a discount rate of 12%, we find that the present value of the anticipated cash inflows over 10 years is $124,300, calculated by multiplying 5.65, the present value of an annuity of $1 at 12% for 10 years, by the $22,000 anticipated annual cash inflow.

To decide whether to undertake the investment, we compare the $124,300 present value of cash inflows with the $100,000 of outlay required. Because the present value of the anticipated cash inflows exceeds the investment, the investment is worthy of further consideration (assuming that the 12% discount rate is acceptable to the firm). Because the present value of cash inflows is greater than the $100,000 investment, the firm will realize more than a 12% return. A detailed calculation is given in Figure 20–7.

Total after-tax cash inflows of $18,000 + $4,000 = $22,000 per year are used in Figure 20–7. The after-tax cash outflow is the full $100,000 initial investment, with no adjustment for taxes because its tax effect appears as depreciation and is deducted over the life of the asset. Regular revenue and expense items can be converted to after-tax flows by multiplying them by 1 minus the tax rate (1 − 0.4, in this example). Depreciation is a noncash expense and serves to "shield" that amount of cash inflow from taxation. Having a $10,000 depreciation deduction, therefore, reduces total income taxes by $10,000 × 0.4 = $4,000. This can be treated, in isolation (assuming income taxes of at least $4,000 would otherwise have to be paid), as equivalent to a $4,000 cash inflow. This separation or isolation is desirable when evaluating multiple alternatives so that we consider only relevant data (future data that is *different* for the various alternatives).

The difference between the present values of the outflows and the inflows is the **net present value (NPV)** of the venture. If, as in our illustration, the inflows exceed the outflows, it is a **positive net present value.** It indicates a return in excess of 12%. If the net present value had been zero, the return would have been exactly 12%. Alternatively, if we

	After-Tax Cash Flow	Present-Value Factor (12%)	Present Value
Purchase of asset	($100,000)	1.00	$(100,000)
Net income before depreciation ($30,000 × (1 − 0.4)	18,000	5.65	101,700
Depreciation tax shield ($10,000 × 0.4)	4,000	5.65	22,600
Net present value			$ 24,300

FIGURE 20–7 Net Present Value of Asset Acquisition

had used a discount rate of 18%, the net present value of expected inflows would have been a **negative net present value** of $1,132:

Net Present Value Using an 18% Discount Rate

After-tax cash inflow ($22,000 × 4.494)	$ 98,868
Cash outflow investment	(100,000)
Negative net present value	$ (1,132)

The effect that depreciation has as a "tax shield" in determining the present value of discounted cash flows is important. Our illustration has assumed straight-line depreciation in projecting the incremental after-tax net income of $12,000 per year. Figure 20–8 shows the calculation of after-tax net income, assuming a tax rate of 40%, and the adjustment required to obtain the after-tax cash flow from operations. The tax benefit provided by depreciation is 40% of $10,000 = $4,000 per year with straight-line depreciation, meaning that the cash outlay for taxes would be $12,000 (instead of $8,000) per year if the company were not allowed to deduct depreciation in calculating its tax obligation. We say that the cash outlay for taxes has been shielded by the amount of $4,000 because of depreciation.

If the firm chooses to use accelerated depreciation in calculating its tax obligation, it will pay smaller amounts of taxes during the early years of the life of the project and compensatingly larger amounts in later years. That, in turn, will produce a larger total present value for anticipated cash inflows because of the smaller amounts of taxes that would be paid during the earlier years (due to larger depreciation charges during those years), resulting in larger tax shields in the earlier

	Period of 1 Year
Net income before depreciation and taxes	$30,000
Depreciation expense	10,000
Net income before taxes	$20,000
Tax expense (based on 40% tax rate)	8,000
Net income after taxes	$12,000
Add back noncash expense of depreciation	10,000
After-tax cash flow from operations	$22,000

FIGURE 20–8 Straight-Line Depreciation in Projecting Incremental After-Tax Net Income

	After-Tax Cash Flow	Present-Value Factor (12%)	Present Value
Year of Purchase			
$[0.4(\$100,000 \times 28.57\% \times \frac{1}{2})]$	$5,714	0.893	$ 5,103
Year 2			
$\{0.4[(\$100,000 - \$14,286) \times 28.57\%]\}$	9,796	0.797	7,807
Year 3			
$\{0.4[(\$85,714 - \$24,490) \times 28.57\%]\}$	6,997	0.712	4,982
Year 4			
$\{0.4[(\$61,224 - \$17,493) \times 28.57\%]\}$	4,998	0.636	3,179
Year 5			
$\{0.4[(\$43,731 - \$12,495) \times 28.57\%]\}$	3,570	0.567	2,024
Year 6 $\{0.4[(\$31,236 - \$8,925) \div 2.5]\}$	3,570	0.507	1,810
Year 7	3,570	0.452	1,614
Year 8	1,785	0.404	721
Present value of tax shield			$27,240

Note: The ACRS method illustrated here uses the 200% double-declining balance depreciation until it is advantageous to switch to the straight-line basis in Year 6. ACRS also requires the "half-year" convention, whereby one-half year's depreciation is taken in the year of acquisition and one-half in the year of disposal. The present value of the tax shield when using accelerated depreciation is $27,240 rather than $22,600 (see Figure 20–7) when using straight-line depreciation. Therefore, the use of accelerated depreciation causes the net present value for the venture to be −$100,000 + $101,700 + $27,240 = $28,940 rather than $24,300 from the straight-line method.

FIGURE 20–9 Present Value of Depreciation Tax Shield Using Internal Revenue Service Accelerated Cost Recovery System (ACRS), Life of 7 Years

years, when the present-value factors are the largest. There is a present-value advantage in using accelerated depreciation for tax purposes because it produces a greater tax shield in earlier years—when dollars have a greater present value—than in later years.

If accelerated depreciation is used, the after-tax cash inflows will vary from period to period, in which case the net present values of inflows will have to be determined separately for each year by using data from a "present value of one" table. The sum of all of the individual present values will then be the present value of cash inflows. For example, using our $100,000 asset with a 10-year useful life and **Accelerated Cost Recovery System (ACRS)**[4] depreciation required by the Internal Revenue Service and an assumed ACRS life of 7 years yields a depreciation tax shield of $27,240, as shown in Figure 20–9.

Because the discounted cash-flow method and the time-adjusted rate-of-return method (to be discussed next) explicitly consider the time

[4]Modified ACRS does not substantially change this example.

value of money, they are more precise and therefore provide a more realistic evaluation of an investment opportunity than do either the accounting rate-of-return method or the pay-back method. However, the assumed discount rate used with either of the present-value methods relates cash flows to total investment in the project rather than the accounting-oriented return-on-investment figure. So, in deciding whether or not to undertake a project, management will be utilizing figures not specifically related to any amount in the recorded accounting data. Thus, for evaluation purposes, once an alternative has been accepted, the accounting rate of return also should be projected for each year so it can be used as a benchmark for evaluating the project's subsequent performance.

Time-Adjusted Rate-of-Return Method

With the discounted cash-flow method, management must decide on an acceptable discount (interest) rate before the analysis can be carried through. It often is desirable to know, based on the projected investment and cash-flow data, a project's exact discount rate. The analyst can then relate that figure to returns anticipated from similar business ventures in deciding whether a particular project should be undertaken. Fundamentally, the **time-adjusted rate-of-return method** is a device for determining the discount rate that will make the present value of projected cash inflows equal to the investment, in other words, the discount rate that yields a zero net present value. When determined in this manner, the discount rate is called the *time-adjusted rate of return*, or **internal rate of return.**

If projected periodic cash inflows are uniform, we can write the formula for determining the time-adjusted rate of return as follows:

Initial investment
= Present value of an annuity of one for the life of the venture
× Projected periodic cash inflows

Because we know the amount of the initial investment and the projected periodic cash inflows, we can rewrite this equation as:

Present value of annuity of one for the life of the venture
$$= \frac{\text{Initial investment}}{\text{Projected periodic cash inflows}}$$

The figure we get from this calculation is the same one we got when we calculated the pay-back period. In that case, however, it represented the number of years required to recover the original investment. In this equation it should be interpreted as the present value of an annuity of one for the life of the venture at a presently undetermined rate of discount. Using the data from our previous illustration, we find the present value of the annuity of one is $100,000 ÷ $22,000 = $4.55. If we look for that (or the nearest) figure in the 10-periods row in Figure 20–6, we find the time-adjusted rate of return to be somewhere between the 16% and 18% columns. Interpolating, we find the time-adjusted rate of return to be approximately 17.67%. The exact rate of return is actually 17.68%.

If management judges that the 17.67% (or 17.68%) rate of return is adequate to justify investing in the project, then, by our analysis, the investment should be given further consideration.

Where annual cash flows are not identical, or where an exact rate of return for the project is desired, the calculations require the following three-step procedure:

1. Prepare a schedule showing after-tax cash flows for each year.
2. Use a personal computer or programmable calculator to calculate the rate of return for the full life of the project.
3. Make the decision based on the rate of return result(s).

Consideration of Alternatives

Up to this point, we have assumed that the decision management was required to make involved either accepting or rejecting a specific investment opportunity. Decisions in the business world seldom are quite so simple. Often, there will be other alternatives, sometimes an infinite number, and there may be certain limitations on risk and financing that can further complicate the decision. If management feels it can develop only, say, $100,000 of financing, it may have to consider a number of alternative investments: for example, two $50,000 projects, or any one of several projects requiring $100,000.

With competing investment opportunities, management must establish an order of priorities so that the best opportunities available will be accepted first. Even with more than one alternative, it still is possible to use the types of analyses presented in this chapter to establish an order of priorities for the various opportunities being considered in order to choose that opportunity or combination of opportunities that will maximize the return to the firm.

In spite of the theoretical superiority of the net-present-value and time-adjusted rate-of-return methods, investment decisions continue to be made on the basis of the pay-back period and, less commonly, on the basis of the accounting rate-of-return method. One reason may be the extreme difficulty in predicting the cash-flow implications of all aspects of an investment decision. For example, what are all the cash-flow effects of a higher-quality product that a new machine (or factory) could produce? Or what is the cash-flow advantage of constructing a "flexible" factory that can be refitted in a very short period of time to produce a new product or products? Another reason may be that **product life cycles** have grown so short that the time value of money is less important.

SUMMARY

In this chapter, we discussed various aspects of capital expenditure decisions, noting that they are some of the most important decisions that business managers must make because of the long-term effect they have on fixed costs and future operations. We reviewed the procedures commonly followed in considering whether to replace equipment, pointing out the arbitrary nature of some elements of the analysis. Then we examined some of the considerations involved in investing in new equipment, with particular emphasis on deciding the capacity a firm should achieve to optimize its return to shareholders.

In deciding whether or not to commit resources to a long-term project, managers should relate the probable return from the project to the investment required to implement it. We discussed four analytical techniques management may use to make such investment decisions: the accounting rate-of-return method, the pay-back method, the net-present-value method, and the time-adjusted rate-of-return method.

GLOSSARY OF TERMS INTRODUCED IN THIS CHAPTER

Accelerated Cost Recovery System (ACRS)	A method of depreciation of tangible property prescribed in the Economic Recovery Tax Act of 1981; classifies depreciable assets into one of several property class-life categories, each of which has a designated pattern of allowable depreciation for tax purposes.
accounting rate-of-return method	A method of evaluating investment profitability by relating the anticipated accounting net income per year from the investment to the amount of the investment (either initial investment or average investment).
average investment	The average amount invested in a project over a period of time, calculated (in a simple way) by dividing by 2 the sum of beginning investment and ending investment.
cash inflow after taxes	The inflow of spendable resources after paying taxes on the income generated; calculated by adding depreciation and other long-term asset amortization and noncash expenses to net income after taxes.
cash inflow before taxes	The inflow of spendable resources before deducting income taxes; calculated by adding depreciation and other long-term amortization and noncash expenses to net income before taxes.
cycle time	The time required to produce a completed unit.
incremental income	The change in income (revenue) attributed to (a) the addition of one unit

of sales, or (b) the addition of one item to the firm's resource base; also called *incremental revenue*.

incremental investment	The additional investment required to embark on a proposed project such as the addition of equipment or enlargement of facilities.
internal rate of return	The rate of interest at which the present value of expected cash inflows from a project equals the present value of expected cash outflows. This is the interest rate earned by the project, and it is compared with the cost of capital, stated as a percentage, to determine whether the project should be given further consideration; also called *time-adjusted rate of return*.
leveraged project (investment)	A project financed with borrowed funds.
negative net present value	An amount equal to the excess of the present value of the investment in a project plus the projected present value of cash outflows from the project over the projected present value of cash inflows from the project, all based on a predetermined discount rate. Projects with negative net present values would not be accepted.
net liquid resource inflows	More correctly describes what is generally called *cash inflows*. Calls attention to the fact that part of the so-called cash flows may be in the form of increases in short-term receivables, decreases in short-term payables, or increases in other noncash current assets.
net present value (NPV)	The difference between the projected present value of net cash inflows from operating an investment project, discounted at a specified rate, and the present value of the cost of investment in the project.
net-present-value method	A method of evaluating an investment opportunity that compares the present value of the required investment with the present value of projected net cash inflows, based on a specified rate of discount.
net working capital	The difference between current assets and current liabilities at a particular instant in time; often called *working capital*.
out-of-pocket costs	Incurred costs that are paid for in cash, by giving up other current assets or by the incurrence of current liabilities; also can be thought of as variable costs (that is, costs other than the fixed costs or sunk costs associated with a product or operations).
pay-back method	A method of evaluating an investment opportunity that provides a measure of the time required to recover the initial amount invested in a project.
positive net present value	An excess of the projected present value of liquid resource inflows from a project over the present value of resource outflows from the project plus the present value of the investment required to implement the project, all based on a specified rate of discount. Projects with positive net present values would be considered for acceptance.
product life cycle	The period of time during which a product can be produced and marketed profitably.

profit potential	The profit that should be realized from a project or product during an operating period.
rate of return on assets	A measure of asset profitability, calculated by dividing net income by total assets.
rate of return on equity capital	A measure of investment performance for owners, calculated by dividing net income by equity capital.
technological revolution	A period when technological developments occur so rapidly that most equipment becomes obsolete before it has lost its physically productive capability.
time-adjusted rate-of-return method	See *internal rate of return*.
time value of money	The value associated with the use of money over a period of time that causes cash currently held to be worth more than a future claim to cash.
trading on the equity	Financing an investment through debt with the intention that the investment will produce a return in excess of the interest to be paid on the debt. See *leveraged project*.

QUESTIONS FOR CLASS DISCUSSION

20–1 What is the difference between the type of decisions discussed in this chapter and the ones discussed in Chapter 19?

20–2 How do the costs used in determining whether to replace an existing fixed asset differ from recorded costs? Explain.

20–3 Should the cost of existing equipment be used in deciding whether to replace equipment? Explain.

20–4 Are there opportunity costs to be considered in an equipment-replacement decision? Explain.

20–5 What are the factors to consider in making a decision regarding increasing the capacity of plant assets?

20–6 What are the tradeoffs generally involved as management considers expanding its facilities? Explain.

20–7 How is the accounting rate of return calculated when it is used in evaluating a long-term investment opportunity?

20–8 What are the different possible investment figures that may be used in calculating the accounting rate of return? Discuss.

20–9 How is the pay-back period calculated? What is the meaning of that figure? Explain.

20–10 What is the achievement element when using the net-present-value method? Explain.

20–11 Why is a dollar a person presently holds worth more than the right to receive a dollar in the future? Explain.

20–12 What is the relationship between the "present value of one" table and the "present value of an annuity of one" table?

20–13 How does the use of accelerated depreciation for tax purposes, rather than straight-line depreciation, affect the total projected present value of cash inflows used in applying the net-present-value method? Explain.

20–14 How is the time-adjusted rate-of-return method related to the net-present-value method? Discuss.

20–15 How is the formula used to calculate the present value of an annuity of one when using the time-adjusted rate-of-return method with identical cash flows related to the formula used in applying the pay-back method?

20–16 Briefly describe how alternative investment opportunities may be considered in the decision-making process.

EXERCISES

20–17 **Replacement of Machine** Grove Company has an opportunity to acquire a new machine to replace one of its present machines. The new machine would cost $180,000 and have a 10-year life and no estimated salvage value. Variable operating costs would be $200,000 per year. Grove can earn a 10% return on its investments.

The present machine has a book value of $100,000 and a remaining life of 10 years. Its disposal value now is $10,000, but it would be zero after 10 years. Variable operating costs are $215,000 per year.

Each machine is capable of producing 10,000 units per year. Ignore income taxes.

REQUIRED:

1. Calculate the expected total *recorded* manufacturing cost per unit with the use of each machine.
2. Calculate the pertinent cost per unit with use of the present machine.
3. Is there a cost benefit associated with acquisition of the new machine? Explain.
4. Relate the terms *sunk cost* and *opportunity cost* to the appropriate elements of the preceding data.

20–18 **Replacement of Machine** Bynum Company is considering replacement of a machine. Data relating to the two machines are:

	New Machine	Present Machine
Cost	$90,000	—
Book value	—	$50,000
Estimated life	5 years	5 years
Variable operating expenses	$100,000	$125,000
Current disposal value	—	5,000

Each machine yields the same output. Neither is expected to have any salvage value at the end of 5 years.

REQUIRED:

1. Prepare an analysis to show whether costs would be reduced by acquisition of the new machine. Ignore tax and present-value considerations.
2. If you find a cost saving would result from the acquisition, calculate the amount that would be saved each year.
3. What is the next step in the process of determining whether to invest in the new machine?

20–19 **Investment in Project** Lowe, Inc., is considering expanding its operations by investing $240,000 in an asset having a 10-year life. Lowe estimates that the annual cash inflow, net of income taxes, from this project will be $40,000. Scott's desired rate of return on investments of this type is 10%. The asset is expected to have no salvage value at the end of 10 years. Information on present-value factors is:

	At 10%	At 12%
Present value of $1 for 10 periods	0.386	0.322
Present value of an annuity of $1 for 10 periods	6.145	5.650

REQUIRED:

1. What is the approximate discount rate implicit in this investment?
2. Calculate the incremental net income after taxes that this project should yield.
3. Calculate the incremental rate of return (accountant's method) (a) based on the initial investment; (b) based on the average investment.

20–20 **Net Cash Inflow; Pay-Back Period** Cathey, Inc., a calendar-year company, purchased a new machine for $56,000 on January 1, 19X0. The machine has an estimated useful life of 8 years, with no salvage value, and is being depreciated on the straight-line basis. The accounting (book value) rate of return is expected to be 15% on the initial increase in required investment. The tax rate is expected to be 40%.

REQUIRED:

1. Calculate the amount of taxes expected to be paid on the income from this machine.

2. Calculate the expected annual cash inflows before taxes and net of taxes.

3. Calculate the pay-back period.

20–21   Net-Present-Value Method Malone, Inc., is considering investing in a machine with a useful life of 5 years and no salvage value. The machine will be depreciated using the straight-line method. The annual cash inflow from operations, net of income taxes, is expected to be $10,000. The present value of an ordinary annuity of $1 in arrears for 5 periods at 12% is 3.605. The present value of $1 for 5 periods at 12% is 0.567.

REQUIRED:

1. Assuming Malone is willing to accept a 12% discount rate, what is the maximum amount the company will be willing to pay for the machine?

2. Assuming the asset can be purchased for $35,000, what is the projected net present value?

20–22   Pay-Back Method; Net Present Value Caper Company is considering investing in a 4-year project. The company considers a discount rate of 10% to be satisfactory. Additional information about the project is as follows:

Year	Cash Inflow from Operations, Net of Income Taxes	Present Value of $1 at 10%
1	$4,000	0.909
2	4,400	0.826
3	4,800	0.751
4	5,200	0.683

REQUIRED:

1. An analysis of the project shows the project should produce a positive net present value of $2,027. Calculate the amount of the original investment.

2. What is the pay-back period?

3. Assuming straight-line depreciation with no salvage value, calculate the incremental net income expected from the average investment each year.

20–23   Multiple Choice Allo Foundation, a tax-exempt organization, invested
AICPA Adapted $200,000 in a 5-year project at the beginning of 19X5. Allo estimates that the annual cash savings from this project will amount to $65,000. The $200,000 of assets will be depreciated over their 5-year life on a straight-line basis. On investments of this type, Allo's desired rate of return is 12%. Information on present-value factors is as follows:

	At 12%	At 14%	At 16%
Present value of 1 for 5 periods	0.57	0.52	0.48
Present value of an annuity of 1 for 5 periods	3.6	3.4	3.3

1. The net present value of the project is
   a. $34,000.
   b. $36,400.
   c. $90,000.
   d. $125,000.
2. Allo's internal rate of return on return on this project is
   a. less than 12%.
   b. less than 14%, but more than 12%.
   c. less than 16%, but more than 14%.
   d. more than 16%.
3. For the project's first year, Allo's accounting rate of return, based on the project's average book value for 19X5, would be
   a. 14.4%.
   b. 13.9%.
   c. 12.5%.
   d. 12.0%.
4. The pay-back period for the project is
   a. 5 years.
   b. 3.07 years.
   c. 1.90 years.
   d. not determinable from the data given.

PROBLEMS

20–24   **Replacement of Equipment** A firm is considering replacing a piece of equipment originally costing $100,000 that has an anticipated remaining service life of 10 years, with no salvage value. The accounting records show accumulated depreciation in the amount of $40,000. A new, more efficient piece of equipment costing $150,000 and having the same production capability, an expected service life of 10 years, and no salvage value is being considered as a replacement for the old machine. The chief advantage cited for the new equipment is the fact that out-of-pocket cost can be reduced by approximately $10,000 per year. The estimated current salvage value of the old equipment is $20,000.

REQUIRED:

1. Based only on the information provided, should the firm purchase the new equipment?
2. Show calculations in support of your answer to requirement 1.
3. Assume now that the company normally pays 8% interest on borrowed funds. What amount should be imputed for annual interest costs based on the average additional investment required to purchase the new equipment?
4. Does the imputation of interest in the decision-making process change your decision regarding the acquisition of the new equipment? Show supporting calculations.
5. What other aspects of this equipment-replacement decision should be investigated?

20–25   **Investment in Office Building Concession Center** Major Realty, Inc., which manages the activities of an office building, is considering putting in certain concessions in the main lobby. An accounting study produces the following estimates, on an average annual basis:

Salaries		$14,000
Licenses and payroll taxes		400
Cost of merchandise sold:		
Beginning inventory	$ 4,000	
Purchase	80,000	
Available	84,000	
Ending inventory	4,000	80,000
Share of heat, light, etc.		1,000
Pro rata building depreciation		2,000
Concession advertising		200
Share of company administrative expense		800
Sales of merchandise		98,000

The investment in equipment, which would last 10 years, would be $4,000.

As an alternative, a catering company has offered to lease the space for $1,500 per year, for 10 years, and to put in and operate the same concessions at no cost to Major Realty. Heat and light are to be furnished by the office building at no additional charge.

REQUIRED:

1. Prepare a report analyzing the concessions proposals.
2. Which course of action should Major Realty follow? Explain.

20–26   **Purchase of New Machine** Bell Company is considering purchasing production machinery costing $200,000. The machinery's expected useful life is 5 years, with no residual value. Depreciation is recognized on a straight-line basis. Bell requires a rate of return of 20% and has calculated the following data pertaining to the projected purchase and operation of this machinery:

Year	Estimated Annual Cash Inflow	Present Value of 1, at 20%
1	$120,000	0.91
2	60,000	0.76
3	40,000	0.63
4	40,000	0.53
5	40,000	0.44
Totals	$300,000	3.27

REQUIRED:

1. Calculate the projected average annual incremental (accounting) rate of return from the new machinery based on the average investment.
2. Calculate the pay-back period.
3. Determine the projected net present value of the venture.

20–27 **Purchase of New Machine** Garrett, Inc., is considering the purchase of a new machine for $60,000. The pay-back period is expected to be 5 years. The new machine is expected to have a life of 6 years, with no salvage value. It is expected to produce a cash flow from operations, net of income taxes, of $14,000 a year in each of the next 3 years and $11,000 in the fourth year. Depreciation of $10,000 a year will be charged to income for each of the 5 years of the pay-back period.

REQUIRED:

1. What amount of cash flow, net of taxes, is expected to be received during the fifth year of the pay-back period?
2. What is the accountant's rate of return on the original investment during each of the first 3 years?

20–28 **Investment in New Machine—Comprehensive Problem** Osage company is considering the purchase of a new machine for $1,000,000. The new machine is expected to produce cash flows from operations, before income taxes, of $320,000 a year in each of the next 5 years. Depreciation of $200,000 a year will be charged to income for each of the next 5 years. Assume that the income tax rate is 40%.

REQUIRED:

1. What is the projected annual net income before depreciation and taxes?
2. Calculate the projected annual net income from use of the new machine?
3. Determine the projected annual incremental (accountant's) rate of return based on the average investment in the machine.
4. Calculate the projected annual cash flow net of taxes.
5. What is the pay-back period?
6. Assume that the company is willing to invest in this project at a discount rate of 10%. Using the appropriate data from the tables in this chapter, calculate the net present value of the investment.
7. What is the discount rate (time adjusted rate of return) implicit in the projected data for the investment.

20–29 **Purchase of Equipment and Cost of Capital** Hilltop Hospital, a nonprofit institution not subject to income taxes, is considering the purchase of new equipment costing $40,000, in order to achieve cash savings of $10,000 per year in operating costs. The equipment's estimated useful life is 10 years, with no salvage value. Hilltop cost of capital is 14%.

REQUIRED:

1. Using the appropriate data from the tables in this chapter, determine the present-value factor to use in evaluating the proposed acquisition of equipment.
2. Calculate the net present value of the proposed acquisition.
3. Calculate the pay-back period.
4. What is the accounting rate of return based on Hilltop's average investment?
5. What is the discount rate (time-adjusted rate of return) implicit in the data relating to the purchase?

20–30

ICMA Adapted

Expansion of Operations The management of Bay Company is considering a proposal to install a third production department within its existing factory building. With the company's present production setup, raw materials are passed through Department 1 to produce materials A and B in equal proportions. Material A is then passed through Department 2 to yield product C. Material B is presently being sold "as is" at a price of $20.25 per pound. Product C has a selling price of $100.00 per pound.

The per-pound standard costs currently being used by the Bay Company are:

	Department 1 (materials A and B)	Department 2 (product C)	Department 3 (material B)
Prior department costs	—	$53.03	$13.47
Direct materials	$20.00	—	—
Direct labor	7.00	12.00	—
Variable overhead	3.00	5.00	—
Fixed overhead:			
Attributable	2.25	2.25	—
Allocated (⅔, ⅓)	1.00	1.00	—
	$33.25	$73.28	$13.47

These standard costs were developed by using an estimated production volume of 200,000 pounds of raw materials as the standard volume. The company assigns Department 1 costs to materials A and B in proportion to their net sales values at the point of separation, computed by deducting subsequent standard production costs from sales values. The $300,000 of common fixed overhead costs are allocated to the two producing departments on the basis of the space used by the departments.

The proposed Department 3 would be used to process material B into product D. An investment of $200,000 would be required to install Department 3. It is expected that any quantity of product D can be sold for $30.00 per pound. Standard costs per pound under this proposal were developed by using 200,000 pounds of raw materials as the standard volume and are as follows:

	Department 1 (materials A and B)	Department 2 (product C)	Department 3 (material B)
Prior department costs	—	$53.03	$13.20
Direct materials	$20.00	—	—
Direct labor	7.00	12.00	4.60
Variable overhead	3.00	5.00	1.00
Fixed overhead:			
Attributable	2.25	2.25	1.75
Allocated (½, ¼, ¼)	.75	.75	.75
	$33.00	$73.03	$21.30

REQUIRED: Assume (a) sales and production levels are expected to remain constant in the foreseeable future, and (b) there are no foreseeable alternative uses for the available factory space.

1. Based on the foregoing unit-cost data, should Bay Company install Department 3? Prepare a report supporting your answer.
2. Assume that Bay Company can earn 10% interest on its investments. What other consideration should be injected into the decision?

20–31

ICMA Adapted

New Product Helene's, a high-fashion women's dress manufacturer, is planning to market a new cocktail dress for the coming season. Helene's supplies retailers in the eastern and mid-Atlantic states.

Four yards of material are required to lay out the dress pattern. Some material remains after cutting, which can be sold as remnants. The leftover material could also be used to manufacture a matching cape and handbag. Equal amounts of the remnant material would be required for each item. However, if the leftover material is to be used for the cape and handbag, more care will be required in the cutting, which will increase the cutting costs.

The company expected to sell 1,250 dresses if no matching cape or handbag were available. Helene's market research reveals that dress sales will be 20% higher if a matching cape and handbag are available. The market research indicates that the cape and/or handbag will be sold individually but only as accessories with the dress. The various combinations of dresses, capes, and handbags expected to be sold by retailers are as follows:

	Percentage of Total
Complete set of dress, cape, and handbag	70%
Dress and cape	6
Dress and handbag	15
Dress only	9
Total	100%

The material used in the dress costs $12.50 a yard, or $50.00 for each dress. The cost of cutting the dress if the cape and handbag are not manufactured is estimated at $20.00 a dress, and the resulting remnants can be sold for $5.00 for each dress cut out. If the cape and handbag are to be manufactured, the cutting costs will be increased by $9.00 per dress. There will be no salable remnants if the capes and handbags are manufactured in the quantities estimated.

The selling prices and the costs to complete the three items once they are cut are:

	Selling Price per Unit	Unit Cost to Complete (Excludes Cost of Material and Cutting Operation)
Dress	$200.00	$80.00
Cape	27.50	19.50
Handbag	9.50	6.50

REQUIRED:

1. Calculate the unit cost of producing the dress under both arrangements.
2. Calculate the unit costs of producing the cape and the handbag.
3. Prepare a report comparing the results of following each possible course of action.

20–32
ICMA Adapted

Acquisition of New Machine The WRL Company makes cookies for its chain of snack food stores. On January 2, 19X1, WRL Company purchased a special cookie-cutting machine; this machine has been utilized for three years. WRL Company is considering the purchase of a newer, more efficient machine. If purchased, the new machine would be acquired on January 2, 19X4. WRL Company expects to sell 300,000 dozen cookies in each of the next 4 years. The selling price of the cookies is expected to average $.50 per dozen.

WRL Company has two options: (1) continue to operate the old machine or (2) sell the old machine and purchase the new machine. No trade-in was offered by the seller of the new machine. The following information has been assembled to help decide which option is more desirable:

	Old Machine	New Machine
Original cost of machine at acquisition	$80,000	$120,000
Salvage value at the end of useful life for depreciation purposes	$10,000	$20,000
Useful life from date of acquisition	7 years	4 years
Expected annual cash operation expenses:		
Variable cost per dozen	$.20	$.14
Total fixed costs	$15,000	$14,000
Estimated cash value of machines:		
January 2, 19X4	$40,000	$120,000
December 31, 19X7	$7,000	$20,000

WRL Company is subject to an overall income tax rate of 40%. Depreciation is calculated on a straight-line basis.

REQUIRED:

1. Use the net-present-value method to determine whether WRL Company should retain the old machine or acquire the new machine. WRL requires an after-tax return of 16%. Use data from the tables provided in the chapter.
2. Prepare an analysis of projected operations with the new machine using relevant cost data to arrive at the accounting rate of return projected to be associated with the investment on both initial investment and average investment bases.

20–33
ICMA Adapted

Replacement of Equipment Hazman Company plans to replace an old piece of equipment that is obsolete and is expected to be unreliable under the stress of daily operations. The equipment is fully depreciated, and no salvage value can be realized on its disposal.

One piece of equipment being considered would provide annual cash savings of $7,000 before income taxes. The equipment would cost $18,000 and have an estimated useful life of 5 years. No salvage value would be used for depreciation purposes because the equipment is expected to have no value at the end of 5 years.

Hazman uses the straight-line depreciation method on all equipment for both book and tax purposes. The company is subject to a 40% tax rate. Hazman has an after-tax cost of capital of 14%.

REQUIRED:

1. Calculate for Hazman Company's proposed investment in new equipment the after-tax:
   a. pay-back period
   b. accounting rate of return
   c. net present value
   d. internal rate of return.
   Assume all operating revenues and expenses occur at the end of the year. Use the appropriate discount tables provided in the chapter.
2. Identify and discuss the issues Hazman Company should consider when deciding which of the four decision models identified in requirement 1 it should employ to compare and evaluate alternative capital investment projects.

20–34

THOUGHT STIMULATION PROBLEM—Capital Budgeting and Global Competition. Capital budgeting techniques discussed in this chapter have been criticized because they don't appropriately incorporate data essential for U.S. firms to compete in an international market. This essential information relates to speed [that is, *lead time* (time required to obtain materials from suppliers and adapt equipment and/or factory layout for a particular product or project) and *cycle time* (actual time required to complete a product or project)]; *quality* (such as zero defects); and *competitive position* (that is, flexibility to respond to changing conditions; introduction of new products as a result of research and development).

Because of preceived deficiencies in all extant capital budgeting techniques being taught in business schools today, some firms are resorting to ad hoc investment rules to maintain an international competitive edge. As an experiment, one large corporation put its entire new investment budget at the disposal of an executive committee that was instructed to invest in the *best* projects submitted to them without regard to any of the traditional cost analyses.

Assume you are working (as an employee or a consultant) for a consumer products firm that has experienced a decline in the average life of its average product from 5 years to less than 1 year.

REQUIRED:

1. What data would you want to accumulate for long-term investment decisions?
2. How would you organize the data?
3. What decision rule would you suggest to evaluate opportunities? (Indicate how investment proposals might be ranked.)

Chapter 21

Accounting Data and Quantitative Analysis

Learning Objectives

When you have finished your study of this chapter, you should

1. Understand what is meant by simulation and model building and how these techniques can be used by management.
2. Be able to apply probability analysis to bidding on a contract and to determining the quantities of a perishable product to be purchased each period (day) to maximize profits from the sales of the products.
3. Know how to formulate and use an objective function and constraint equations associated with linear programming problems.
4. Be able to apply linear programming to decisions regarding resource allocation and production optimization.
5. Know how to use the economical order quantity (EOQ) formula in determining how many units to purchase, know how the result relates to targeted minimum and maximum inventory levels, and understand EOQ limitations.

For many years, it has been accountants who were primarily responsible for handling quantitative data for business and nonprofit enterprises. In the past, processing limitations prevented them from providing much more than a historical record of transactions for preparation of financial statements. However, the flexibility and high-speed calculating and processing capabilities of the computer have now made it practical to draw together historical and projected data that permit managers to use various quantitative analytical techniques in decision making that previously were primarily theoretical, including simulations and model building. We can, for example, apply statistical probability data to business decisions, use linear programming techniques to allocate resources, and develop sophisticated inventory planning and control systems. All of these techniques often are grouped under the heading **operations research** (OR), which is basically an analysis of business operating data directed toward improving the effectiveness of a firm's operations. These techniques can help management decide what level of inventory to maintain, how to use manufacturing facilities, where bottlenecks will occur, how many salespeople to employ, how to allocate advertising expenditures among the various media, and help answer other similar questions that continually arise in the operation of a business.

Operations research is not a substitute for good management, but it can add precision and supporting justification to decision making. OR techniques also enable us to consider more alternatives in making a specific decision. As OR techniques have become more widely used, we have found methods used to answer one question often can be applied to the solution of others.

The quantitative emphasis currently placed on decision making perhaps should carry with it a caveat: OR techniques often lead to a greater reliance on numerical estimates, which could be interpreted as more precise than they really are. Persons using such quantitative techniques must always consider the quality of the estimates and underlying assumptions as final decisions are made.

Because cost accountants are concerned with various quantitative data and inevitably work with these models, it is critical that they know about various quantitative analysis techniques. The real challenge is in actively seeking out creative applications of older techniques and being alert to the development of new ones. In this chapter, we

1. examine simulation and model building
2. demonstrate how to apply probability analysis to decision making
3. discuss applications of linear programming
4. describe techniques for determining economic order quantities for purchases and for maintaining optimum levels of inventory.
5. survey other quantitative analytical techniques frequently used in making operating decisions.

Simulation and Model Building

The terms *simulation* and *model building* are closely related and are often used interchangeably. We further explore this topic by defining more specifically the terms associated with these techniques and illustrating how to apply them.

Definition of Terms

The term **simulation** suggests pretending that something that is not actually happening is occurring. In the decision-making process, we pretend certain things are happening in order to project possible results. If we like the projection, we can then introduce those hypothetical actions into actual business operations.

In **model building**, we construct a device that depicts interrelationships among factors that can exist in a real situation. It does not duplicate reality. It relates to reality by including the key factors relevant to the situation; and the data used must be subject to reasonably accurate measurement. To be more precise, we simulate a model possessing the characteristics we are trying to evaluate. For such a model to be effective in decision making, the proper data must be selected and the relevant factors, along with their interrelationships, must be clearly identified. Insofar as decision making is concerned, the model is used in a simulated environment to replace, or in some instances to supplement, the hunches or guesses management previously may have used.

Simulation and Model Building Illustrated

When we project several budget plans (see Chapter 15), in order to help management decide which operating plan to follow during the next period, we have engaged in simulation or model building. In effect, we construct a model that shows what operating results can be expected if certain decisions are introduced into the operating plan. When the expected results of those decisions have been projected, management can decide whether the proposed operating plans should be implemented or revised. This allows probable results of alternate decisions to be evaluated *before* resources are committed to carrying them out.

A more sophisticated application of simulation involves estimating the probability distributions of certain events (for example, the individual revenues and costs used in constructing a budget) and then using a computer to simulate the results of a large number (say 20,000) repetitions using random numbers generated from each distribution, to observe the interactive effects on some net result (such as net income).

Using probabilities in this way, simulation can describe the results of a model for any system or process. **Queuing (waiting line) theory**, for example, involves the use of specialized simulations that help determine what facilities to provide to meet uneven demands on those facilities.

The term **PERT (program evaluation and review technique)** describes a diagrammatic report presentation showing the sequencing of interrelated activities (that is, the order in which the activities must be completed), along with the times expected to be required to perform the sequence, in order to complete a project. A PERT network model is designed to identify potential bottlenecks in a particular production process, before the process is actually initiated. It can also be used to evaluate progress once the project is under way. A PERT/cost network is illustrated in Figure 21–1. The numbered nodes represent activities, and the lines represent the necessary connections between the activities. The least-cost time required between activities is shown beside each line, along with, in parentheses, the minimum time required to accomplish the task. The dollar amounts represent the costs that must be incurred to secure the faster times. Solving this type of problem involves recognizing the critical path and determining whether reduced time(s), on a cost–benefit basis, is desireable. This is an extremely time-

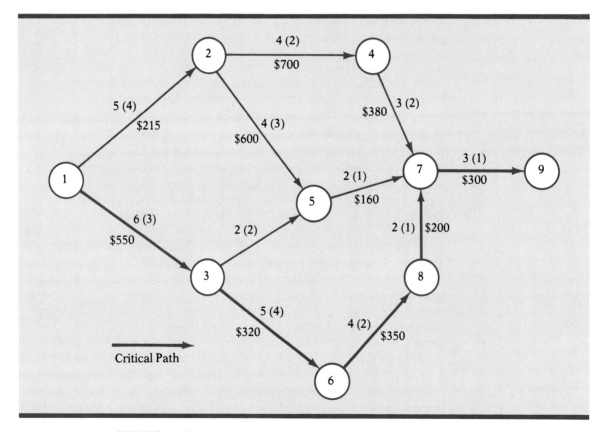

FIGURE 21–1 PERT/Cost Network

consuming iterative process to do by hand. However, computers speed up the work. PERT software programs, such as **Microsoft® PROJECT** (available in both IBM® and Apple® formats for personal computers) can be learned in a matter of hours.

Many of the new "manufacturing excellence" programs basically involve repeated applications of PERT-type *thoughtware*[1] analyses to the entire manufacturing process (design, construction, marketing, and so forth) to find problems, eliminate them, and decrease lead time.

The simulation/model-building technique frequently requires coordinating the skills of mathematicians, statisticians, engineers, and accountants in order to collect and process the data associated with the simulation. In some instances, businesses employ operations research specialists whose primary responsibility is coordinating the efforts of the various technicians involved in operations research projects.

Statistical Probability Analysis

Uncertainty is ever-present in business operations. In making their decisions, business managers always have had to judge the likelihood of particular events occurring or not occurring. With the computer, they have found it practical to consider some uncertainties associated with business decisions by assigning probabilities to possible outcomes associated with a particular action or decision. In using **probability analysis**, one must assign probabilities to the various alternatives so they total 100%. In effect, this requires the decision maker to quantify estimates of the likelihood of each of the possible results, and to then simulate the results expected from each of the possible alternatives. The action to be taken is then based on those data rather than on intuition.

We now explain how **statistical probability analysis** can be used in:

- bidding on a contract
- deciding the amounts of goods to purchase to meet merchandise needs for different possible levels of sales
- establishing the amounts of goods to purchase in order to maintain a given level of customer satisfaction
- projecting the value of perfect knowledge relating to the market for goods or services.

Bidding on a Contract

A contractor, in deciding how much to bid on a particular project, may find it advantageous to estimate the probabilities of receiving the contract at different bids. Those data can then be used to determine more precisely the bid to tender. If the contractor has had sufficient experi-

---

[1]*Thoughtware* means using the human brain as opposed to a computer program (software).

(1)	(2)	(3)	(4)	(3) × (4)
Bid	Cost	Contract Margin	Probability of Being Awarded Contract	Expected Margin
$100,000	$80,000	$20,000	20%	$4,000
95,000	80,000	15,000	50	7,500
90,000	80,000	10,000	70	7,000
85,000	80,000	5,000	80	4,000
80,000 or less	80,000	0	100	0

FIGURE 21–2   Probability Analysis for Bidding on Contract

ence in contracting for that type of project, the probabilities of receiving the contract at different bid prices can be projected from past experience. A probability analysis can be used to decide the bid to tender, by preparing a schedule like the one in Figure 21–2, which shows the amount of *contract margin*[2] that can be expected to be realized at various bid prices ranging from $100,000 through $80,000. Each of the expected contract margins should be multiplied by the probability of receiving the contract to arrive at a *probability-weighted contract margin*. If the contractor is not fully committed to other projects or is operating with idle capacity, then the price bid should be the one at which the probability-weighted contract margin is expected to be greatest, which is $95,000 in Figure 21–2.

A contractor that has all available equipment and other resources committed to other jobs, and who therefore might not be especially anxious to receive the job, might well bid $100,000, reasoning that, if the contract is won, it will produce an excellent contract margin. On the other hand, with idle equipment and resources, the contractor might choose to bid $85,000 because that would provide a greater probability of getting the contract and would still produce a positive contract margin.

Purchases Required to Meet Probable Sales

Businesses purchase or manufacture merchandise to meet anticipated sales. The amounts of sales during specified periods, determined by customer desires, are subject to considerable uncertainty. With perishable goods or goods likely to become obsolete quickly, the purchasing decision is particularly critical. Probability analysis often can help optimize losses from spoilage or obsolescence and, therefore, improve overall profits.

---

[2]*Contract margin* equals contribution margin if all costs are variable, or equals "segment" margin if costs include variable costs and direct (traceable) fixed costs.

To illustrate, let's assume a firm is purchasing and selling a highly perishable fruit that must be sold on the date of purchase or completely lose its value. For its last hundred days of sales, the firm had unit sales as follows:

Units of Products Sold per Day	Number of Days
5,000	10
10,000	20
15,000	40
20,000	30

Each unit of product sells for $1 and costs $.40. Any unsold units at the end of each day have to be scrapped or given away.

We can use probability analysis to decide how many units of product to purchase each day, by preparing a *payoff table* similar to the one in Figure 21–3. This model, which projects the expected long-term payoff at each of the four possible levels of operations, suggests that the firm purchase 15,000 units every day to realize the greatest long-term profit from the sale of its product.

A model like that in Figure 21–3 also can help determine the changes that might occur as a result of altering some of the variables. The two basic assumptions in our example are the $.60 contribution margin per

Probabilities	.1	.2	.4	.3	Expected
Purchase \ Sales (units)	5,000	10,000	15,000	20,000	Value
5,000 units Profit or loss	$3,000	$3,000	$3,000	$ 3,000	$3,000
10,000 units Profit or loss	$1,000	$6,000	$6,000	$ 6,000	$5,500[b]
15,000 units Profit or loss	−$1,000	$4,000	$9,000	$ 9,000	$7,000
20,000 units Profit or loss	−$3,000[a]	$2,000	$7,000	$12,000	$6,500

[a]Sample calculation of profit or loss:

Sales (5,000 units @ margin of $.60 each)	$3,000
Loss by spoilage (15,000 units @ $.40 each)	6,000
Loss	−$3,000

[b]Sample calculation of expected value:
.1($1,000) + .2($6,000) + .4($6,000) + .3($6,000) = $5,500

FIGURE 21–3 Payoff Table for Different Possible Purchase/Sales Levels (selling price $1; cost $.40) unit and the probabilities of selling different specified quantities of the product. Changing the cost of the product to $.80 per unit, with the same table of probabilities, would produce the payoff table in Figure 21–4, which shows that the firm should now purchase only 10,000 units per day. The smaller daily purchases are caused by the increased costs associated with unsold units.

Let's now change the probabilities for the four possible levels of sales, as follows:

5,000 units	.3
10,000 units	.4
15,000 units	.2
20,000 units	.1

Combined with the earlier selling price–cost assumptions, these probabilities yield the payoff table in Figure 21–5, which indicates that 10,000 rather than 15,000 units of product should be purchased each day to maximize profitability. This difference is caused by the increased probability of selling fewer than 15,000 units.

The models in Figures 21–3, 21–4, and 21–5 help us arrive at two general observations that should assist a firm in developing its general operating policy for maximizing long-term profit:

1. From Figure 21–4 we can conclude that as the potential contribution margin of products becomes smaller, other things being equal, a more conservative buying policy should be followed.
2. Figure 21–5 shows that if the probabilities of achieving high levels of sales are reduced, other things being equal, a more conservative buying policy should be followed.

Probabilities	.1	.2	.4	.3	Expected Value
Purchase \ Sales (units)	5,000	10,000	15,000	20,000	
5,000 units					
Profit or loss	$ 1,000	$1,000	$1,000	$1,000	$1,000
10,000 units					
Profit or loss	−$ 3,000	$2,000	$2,000	$2,000	$1,500
15,000 units					
Profit or loss	−$ 7,000	−$2,000	$3,000	$3,000	$1,000
20,000 units					
Profit or loss	−$11,000	−$6,000	−$1,000	$4,000	−$1,500

FIGURE 21–4 Payoff Table for Different Possible Purchase/Sales Levels (selling price $1; cost $.80)

Probabilities	.3	.4	.2	.1	Expected
Purchase \ Sales (units)	5,000	10,000	15,000	20,000	Value
5,000 units					
Profit or loss	$3,000	$3,000	$3,000	$ 3,000	$3,000
10,000 units					
Profit or loss	$1,000	$6,000	$6,000	$ 6,000	$4,500
15,000 units					
Profit or loss	−$1,000	$4,000	$9,000	$ 9,000	$4,000
20,000 units					
Profit or loss	−$3,000	$2,000	$7,000	$12,000	$2,500

FIGURE 21–5 Payoff Table for Different Possible Purchase/Sales Levels (selling price $1; cost $.40)

These observations are intuitively appealing. The opposite actions would be suggested if each of the variables moved in the opposite direction. Because both the projected contribution margin on the product and the probabilities projected for different levels of sales are subject to change and uncertainty, multiple payoff tables can help a manager develop a general purchasing policy. This can be accomplished easily on a personal computer with a spreadsheet program.

Purchases Required to Maintain Customer Satisfaction

We have just dealt with the problem of identifying the amounts of goods to purchase to maximize long-term profits when the levels of customers' demand for the goods are uncertain but it is possible to assign probability levels to them. In some instances, it may be desirable, in the long run, to determine the amount of goods to purchase to maintain a specified level of customer satisfaction. The reasoning here is that if a firm is out of goods too often, customers will go to another firm to satisfy their needs. The model in Figure 21–5, shows that long-term profit will be maximized by buying 10,000 units each day. However, if the manager wants to be prepared to meet the needs of at least 90% of the customers every day to preserve satisfactory customer relations, 15,000 units would be purchased each day. That would mean that only on the days when 20,000 units were demanded would the firm be short of stock and thus be unable to satisfy the demands of all customers. The probable cost of preserving this level of customer satisfaction is $4,500 − $4,000 = $500.

Value of Perfect Knowledge

If managers were clairvoyant and could know the days on which each volume of sales would be realized, they could vary the firm's purchasing pattern to match expected demand and realize a greater profit than by resorting to probability analysis. In Figure 21–3, we see that the expected contribution margin yielded by purchasing 15,000 units per day is $7,000. If the manager could know precisely the days on which to buy 5,000, 10,000, 15,000, or 20,000 units so as to exactly meet customer demand each day, an average daily contribution margin of $8,700 could be realized, calculated as follows:

$$.1(\$3,000) + .2(\$6,000) + .4(\$9,000) + .3(\$12,000) = \$8,700$$

Thus, the value of **perfect knowledge** to the manager would be $1,700— the difference between $8,700 and the $7,000 optimum purchase level with imperfect knowledge in Figure 21–3. That is, the manager would be willing to pay up to $1,700 for information that revealed, with certainty, the customer demand each day.

Linear Programming

Most businesses involve a finite number of interacting variables (such as direct labor and equipment use), whose uses ultimately must be resolved within overall constraints on their availability or the number of units of one or more of the finished products that can be produced. *Linear programming* is a quantitative analysis technique for solving such optimal-resource-allocation problems. It involves three basic steps:

1. Formulate an *objective function*, that is, an equation reflecting the operating objective to be met, such as the maximization of contribution margin or minimization of costs.
2. Formulate equations that express the basic constraints associated with the operations to be carried out in meeting that objective.
3. Manipulate these equations to arrive at a mathematically optimal solution.

Ideally, the accountant or manager should not only understand all three steps but be able to accomplish them. Because of the widespread availability of computer programs for calculating optimal solutions, however, the formal solution in step 3 is almost trivial. We will present a simple graphical solution, primarily to illustrate how steps 1 and 2 are combined to provide a solution. As a cost accountant, you should be able to recognize situations where linear programming is appropriate and be able to write the required objective function and constraint equations. We will also demonstrate a linear programming computer solution to a joint cost-allocation problem.

Step 1: Identifying the Operating Objective

The first step in solving a resource-allocation problem is to develop an equation that reflects the firm's primary operating objective in the use of those resources. For example, this might be the maximization of contribution margin. In other instances, such as deciding the mixture of ingredients to use in a feedlot operation, the objective might be to minimize the cost of ingredients required to produce a targeted amount of nutritional value. In still other situations, such as with a railway or bus company, the objective might be to minimize idle miles (miles traveled without being loaded). In any case, the first step is to identify, and express quantitatively, the objective to be achieved. To illustrate, for a firm that manufactures products X and Y, with contribution margins of $14 and $4, respectively, the objective of maximizing total contribution margin realized from those products would be stated as follows:

$$\text{Maximize } (14X + 4Y)$$

Step 2: Defining the Constraints

Most of the resources entering into the production of an item inevitably must be subject to limitations that can be expressed in algebraic form. The simultaneous solution of such equations will then tell us how the resources should be used so as to maximize the total contribution margin of all products manufactured. Thus, the second step in a linear programming model involves formulating the equations reflecting the constraints associated with the production of the company's services or products.

Regardless of the specific objective function, constraint equations are formulated in the same way for all linear programming applications. Since constraints must be stated as inequalities ($\leq$ or $\geq$), those that are equalities (for example, product X must equal 1,000 units) must be stated as two inequalities, illustrated as follows:

Situation	Constraint
X = 1,000	X ≤ 1,000
	X ≥ 1,000

Most linear programming computer programs make this and similar adjustments internally and therefore permit a constraint to be entered as an equality.

Step 3: Solving the Problem

It is relatively easy to solve an equation with one unknown. But with more unknowns and the necessary additional equations, the solution becomes increasingly more involved and more difficult. Whereas standard mathematical procedures will not accommodate a simultaneous system in which the number of variables is greater than the number of equations, linear programming will. Since linear programming problems typically involve many interacting variables requiring many equations to be solved simultaneously using tedious matrix iterations, this technique for resolving resource-allocation problems was impractical until the computer came into existence. Linear programming techniques now are used extensively to solve many such problems, including the joint cost-allocation application presented later.

With linear programming, as with other quantitative techniques, the accountant provides some of the information. Often, however, particularly with complicated problems, the accountant must be prepared to work with other technicians, such as mathematicians and computer personnel. Generally, the accountant provides most of the quantitative elements associated with the objective function and the constraints present in the operating situation. A mathematician may then express the objectives and constraints in the form of a normalized set of equations. Later, computer personnel may be called on to locate or develop a program for processing the equations so the appropriate course of action may be identified. Of course, one person using a personal computer could perform all these tasks.

Even though the computer ordinarily would be used to solve linear programming problems, we can demonstrate the technique graphically in the simplified case of only two products and a limited number of constraint equations. Continuing our earlier illustration, let's assume the firm manufacturing products X and Y operates with the following constraints on its production process:

(1) Each unit of product X requires twice as much manufacturing time as is required for each unit of Y.

(2) The firm is limited by machining capacity to the manufacture of a combined total of 2,000 units of X and Y per day.

(3) The material used to make both products X and Y is limited. The firm can acquire enough material to make no more than 1,600 units (X and Y combined) per day.

(4) Each unit of X requires an attachment, of which only 800 per day are available.

(5) Each unit of Y requires a special attachment, of which only 1,400 units per day are available.

(6) The firm can sell all of the products (X or Y) that it can produce.

The following equations show these constraints are:

$$2X + Y \leq 2,000 \quad \text{(constraints 1 and 2)}$$
$$X + Y \leq 1,600 \quad \text{(constraint 3)}$$
$$X \leq 800 \quad \text{(constraint 4)}$$
$$Y \leq 1,400 \quad \text{(constraint 5)}$$
$$X \geq 0; \quad Y \geq 0 \quad \text{(to eliminate the mathematical possibility of "negative" production)}$$

Determining the Optimum Solution Graphically

These equations can now be solved simultaneously to arrive at the optimum production level for each product by graphing the constraint equations as in Figure 21–6. (Note: More than four constraining factors or more than two products would make a graphic solution highly impractical. Since that is the typical situation, we usually need a computer to solve real-life linear programming problems.) The area from (0, 0) on the graph out to the nearest constraining lines contains all of the combinations of production levels that are feasible within the con-

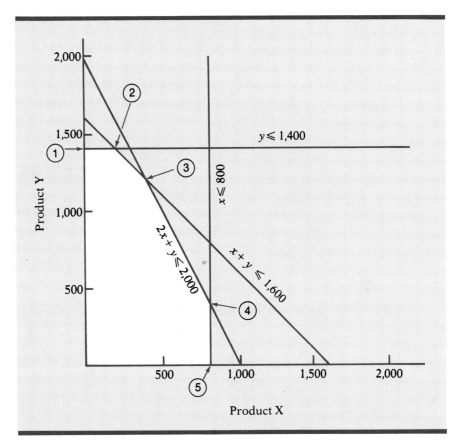

FIGURE 21–6 Graph of Product Mix Constraints and Feasible Solution Area

straints; that is, it is the area in which all constraints are met. The optimal combination of products X and Y always will be at one of the points at which the constraining lines intersect—a "corner" solution. We can therefore determine which of the intersections (corners) indicates the numbers of units of X and Y that would maximize the contribution margin by substituting in the objective equation the quantities shown for X and Y at each intersection. For our illustration, we have numbered the corners 1 through 5. The total contribution margin to be realized from producing the quantities of X and Y shown at each of the corners can then be calculated as follows:

(1) 1,400 units of Y at $4 = $5,600
(2) 200 units of X at $14 + 1,400 units of Y at $4 = $8,400
(3) 400 units of X at $14 + 1,200 units of Y at $4 = $10,400
(4) 800 units of X at $14 + 400 units of Y at $4 = $12,800
(5) 800 units of X at $14 = $11,200

The fourth option (800 units of X and 400 units of Y) is the level of operations that would maximize the firm's contribution margin and thus maximize its net income.

An alternate method of finding the optimal corner of the feasible solution area involves overlaying lines that represent the objective function equation on the constraint equation lines. This can be accompanied by arbitrarily setting the objective function equal to some number and graphing the slope of the equation. Figure 21–7 shows the objective function 14X + 4Y arbitrarily set equal to $7,000 and graphed as a dashed line. The slope of the line is determined by finding the number of units of products X and Y that independently will produce a contribution margin of $7,000 (500 units of X or 1,750 units of Y) and drawing a dashed line between those two points. This same slope is then used to draw parallel lines until the furthest point from the (0, 0) origin in the feasible solution area is reached. That will always be the maximum contribution (corner 4). In a minimization problem, the objective func-

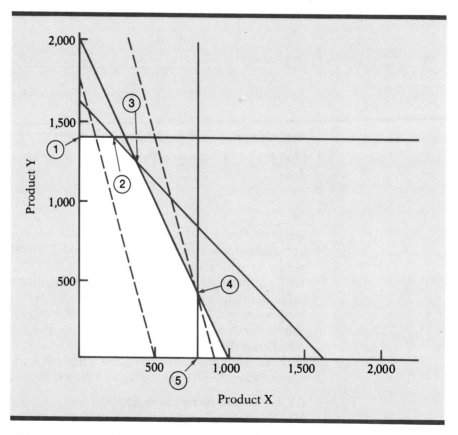

FIGURE 21–7 Determining Optimum Product Mix Graphically

tion slope (representing the cost of the products) is extended in [toward (0, 0)] to the lowest innermost point in the feasible solution area, to find the minimum-cost corner solution.

A Linear Programming (LP) Application to Joint Cost Allocation

Because there is no cause-and-effect relationship between joint costs incurred in a joint process and any one resultant joint product, several (arbitrary) methods of allocating joint costs were illustrated in Chapter 9. Linear programming can be used to allocate joint costs on the basis of marginal revenues, rather than relative sales values or some other method, at the same time an optimal-production decision is being made.

A recent paper by Manes and Cheng[3] develops a marginal approach to the allocation of joint costs that is rational, useful, and feasible. An added benefit is that the optimal resources to be entered into the joint process are included in the LP solution. Manes and Cheng demonstrate how the economic values of a firm's joint product inventories can be determined from the data used in production planning. The only additional information required for this procedure beyond that required for other allocation methods is an estimate of the demand for each joint product.

We will illustrate this marginal approach using the data, with a few modifications, from the illustrative problem at the end of Chapter 9 (page 303). To simplify the analysis, we will assume that beginning and ending work-in-process inventories in the additional processing departments are zero, the same as in the joint-processing department. Figure 21–8 reviews the data given for Multi-Prod Refining Company, adds the estimated market demand of 400 units of product A, 4,000 units of product B, and 7,500 units of product C and quantifies the material input (12,500 units of material X) into the joint process. In this illustration, products A, B, and C are produced in the ratios 500/12,500 (or 0.04), 4,000/12,500 (or 0.32), and 8,000/12,500 (or 0.64), respectively.

The following schedule can then be prepared:

Product	Estimated Demand	Estimated Demand in Terms of X	Contribution Margin per Unit	Normalized Contribution Margin*
A	400 units	10,000.00 units**	$ 1.20***	$1.20 × 0.04 = $ .048
B	4,000 units	12,500.00 units	10.00	$10 × 0.32 = 3.200
C	7,500 units	11,718.75 units	6.15	$6.15 × 0.64 = 3.936

*Contribution margin or marginal revenue of each product occurring as a result of joint process production of one unit of input X.

**400/0.04 = 10,000. That is, to produce 400 units of A, 10,000 units of X would have to be put into the joint process.

***$3 selling price less additional processing costs of $1.80.

[3]Rene P. Manes and Agnes C. S. Cheng, "The Marginal Approach to Joint Cost Allocation," American Accounting Association Annual Meeting, August 1988.

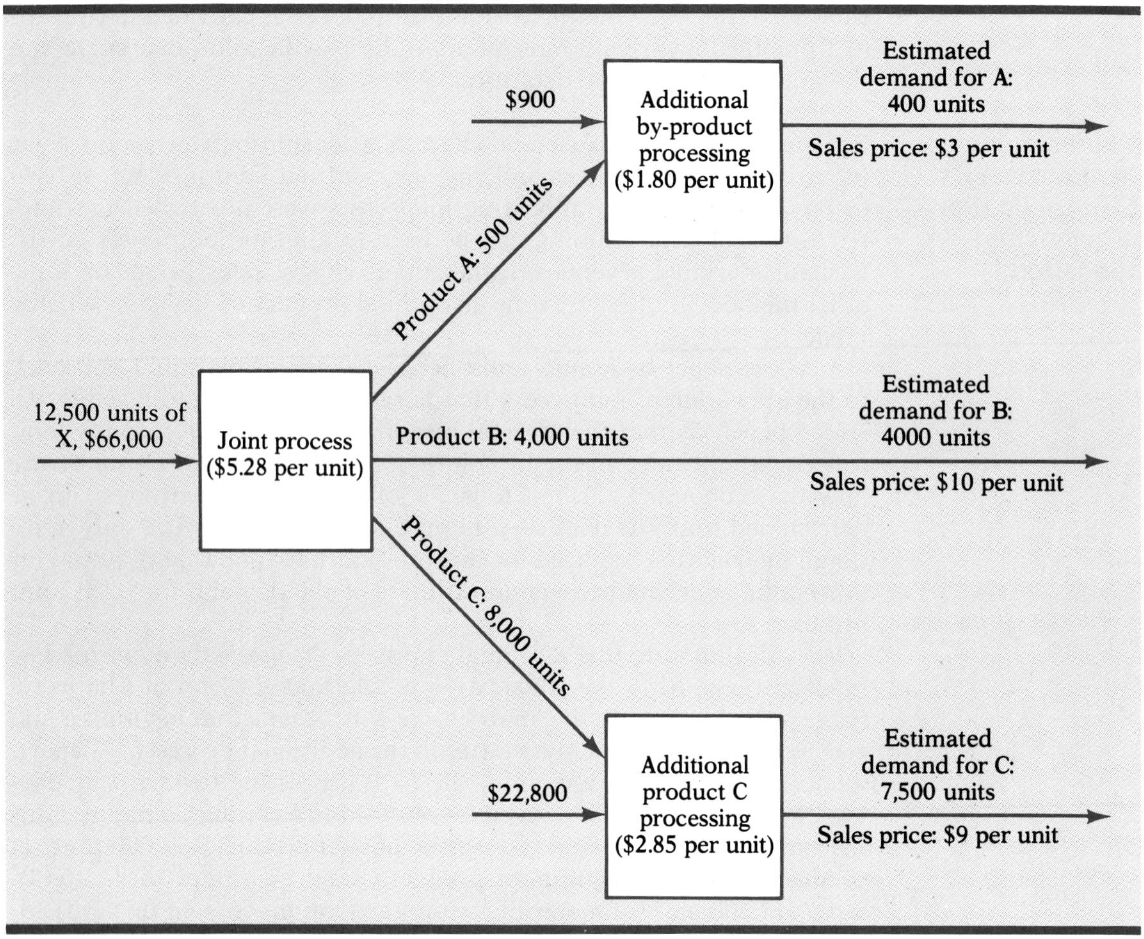

FIGURE 21—8   Multi-Prod Refining Company Data

This information is displayed graphically in Figure 21–9. The horizontal axis represents the demand for joint products in terms of the raw material X. The vertical axis measures the dollar cost per unit of X and the marginal revenues of each of the joint products. The marginal revenue (that is, the normalized contribution margin) of each of the joint products is entered on the graph, beginning with the product with the highest demand in terms of X (product B), then that with the next highest demand (product C), and so on, in cumulative fashion. The first "step" is represented by the $3.20 marginal revenue and 12,500 estimated demand (both in terms of material X) of product B. The next step consists of product C's $3.936 marginal revenue, which, when added to B's marginal revenue of $3.20, equals $7.14, at 11,718.75 units of X. The

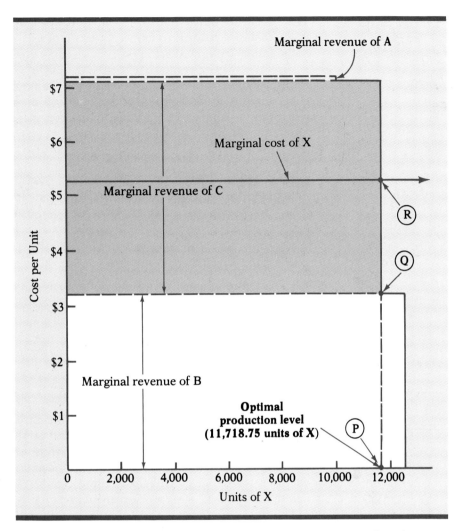

FIGURE 21–9 Graphic Demonstration of Optimal Production Level Determination and Joint Cost Allocation

marginal revenue of product A ($.048) is so small that it barely appears as a step at 10,000 X units. Finally, the marginal cost of X is drawn in at $5.28 ($66,000/12,500). The optimal production level is where marginal cost intersects marginal revenue, at 11,718.75 units of X. Thus, the optimal input of material X into the joint process is 11,718.75 units (not 12,500 units), which would result in the following output:

Product A: 11,718.75 × 0.04 = 468.75
Product B: 11,718.75 × 0.32 = 3,750.00
Product C: 11,718.75 × 0.64 = 7,500.00

The allocation of the $5.28-per-unit joint-processing cost to product B is the distance from P to Q ($3.20) in Figure 21–9, and to product C is the distance from Q to R ($2.08).

Just as with the standard graphical solution to any linear programming problem, more complex problems cannot be solved graphically. However, any situation can be solved with a computer LP algorithm when relationships are expressed in appropriate equations. For our example the objective function would be

$$\text{MAX}(\$1.2AS + \$10BS + \$6.15CS - \$5.28X)$$

where AS, BS, and CS represent sales (quantity) of products A, B, and C, respectively, and X is the quantity of material X. AP, BP, and CP used in the constraints represent quantities produced of products A, B, and C, respectively.

There are nine constraints:

- 3 setting up the separate output relations
- 3 constraining sales to production (since we have no beginning finished-goods inventory)
- 3 constraining sales not to exceed demand.

The first set of three constraints would be

$$-X + 25AP = 0$$
$$-X + 3.125BP = 0$$
$$-X + 1.5625CP = 0$$

These constraints can be explained by concentrating on one product at a time. If all (that is, 100%) of X's output could be channeled to one product, the coefficients of AP, BP, and CP represent the quantities of A, B, and C, respectively, that could be produced from one unit of X. Thus, each joint product coefficient is the reciprocal of its output ratio. For example, $1/(500/12{,}500) = 25$ units of product A.

The next three constraints, which prohibit the "short sale" of units that aren't available, are

$$AS - AP \le 0$$
$$BS - BP \le 0$$
$$CS - CP \le 0$$

The final three demand constraints, explicitly recognizing the maximum number of units that can be sold, are

$$AS \le 400$$
$$BS \le 4{,}000$$
$$CS \le 7{,}500$$

Figure 21–10 summarizes the objective function of all nine constraints and shows a computer solution to this LP problem. The solution indicates the following optimal values:

$$\text{MAX}\ (1.20\text{AS} + 10.00\text{BS} + 6.15\text{CS} - 5.28\text{X})$$

Subject to:

$$
\begin{aligned}
-1.00\text{X} + 25.00\text{AP} &= 0 && (1)\\
-1.00\text{X} + 3.125\text{BP} &= 0 && (2)\\
-1.00\text{X} + 1.5625\text{CP} &= 0 && (3)\\
+1.00\text{AS} - 1.00\text{AP} &\le 0 && (4)\\
+1.00\text{BS} - 1.00\text{BP} &\le 0 && (5)\\
+1.00\text{CP} - 1.00\text{CP} &\le 0 && (6)\\
+1.00\text{AS} &\le 400 && (7)\\
+1.00\text{BS} &\le 4000 && (8)\\
+1.00\text{CS} &\le 7500 && (9)
\end{aligned}
$$

```
SOLUTION

THE OPTIMAL VALUE OF THE OBJECTIVE      22230
          VARIABLES              VALUE
          AP                     468.75
          BP                     3750
          CP                     7500
          SLK 4                  68.75
          BS                     3750
          CS                     7500
          AS                     400
          SLK 8                  250
          X                      11718.75

SENSITIVITY ANALYSIS
CONSTRAINT    SHADOW      LOWER BOUND   CURRENT    UPPER BOUND
        1    0.00E+00    -1.72E+03     0.00E+00   1.70E+38
        2    3.20E+00    -1.17E+04     0.00E+00   7.81E+02
        3    2.08E+00    -7.81E+02     0.00E+00   1.72E+03
        4    0.00E+00    -6.88E+01     0.00E+00   1.70E+38
        5    1.00E+01    -3.75E+03     0.00E+00   2.50E+02
        6    3.25E+00    -5.00E+02     0.00E+00   1.10E+03
        7    1.20E+00     0.00E+00     4.00E+02   4.69E+02
        8    0.00E+00     3.75E+03     4.00E+03   1.70E+38
        9    2.90E+00     6.40E+03     7.50E+03   8.00E+03

VARIABLE COST COEFFICIENTS
  AS                      0.00E+00     1.20E+00   1.70E+38
  BS                      4.20E+00     1.00E+01   1.65E+01
  CS                      3.25E+00     6.15E+00   1.70E+38
  X                      -7.14E+00    -5.28E+00  -3.20E+00
  AP                     -4.64E+01     0.00E+00   5.20E+01
  BP                     -5.80E+00     0.00E+00   6.50E+00
  CP                     -2.90E+00     0.00E+00   3.25E+00
```

FIGURE 21–10 LP Marginal Approach to Joint Cost Allocation

(1) Total contribution margin will be $22,230.
(2) Production of A, B, and C should be
  Product A   468.75 units
  Product B   3,750.00 units
  Product C   7,500.00 units
(3) Sales of A, B, and C should be
  Product A   400.00 units
  Product B   3,750.00 units
  Product C   7,500.00 units
(4) Amount of material X that should be used is 11,718.75 units. The shadow prices shown under "Sensitivity Analysis" in Figure 21–10 reveal the joint cost allocations. The shadow prices of the first three constraints indicate how X's unit cost of $5.28 should be allocated to products A, B, and C (zero to A, $3.20 to B, and $2.08 to C); the shadow prices of the next three constraints (4, 5, and 6) reveal the allocation of joint costs to each *unit* of products A, B, and C—zero to each unit of product A, $10 to each unit of product B, and $3.25 to each unit of product C. These last values are the amounts we should use to value any units in inventory. For example, the $10 amount for product B represents the economic value of having one unit of inventory on hand that could immediately be sold for $10, and the $3.25 amount for product C can be thought of as a "plug" number. Since the only units left in inventory are 68.75 units of product A (production of 468.75 units less sales of 400 units) that have no economic value because they are "surplus" units, ending inventory has a zero value.

Using this approach, the partial income statement for Multi-Prod Refining Company would be:

Revenue		
400 units of A @ $3	$ 1,200	
3,750 units of B @ $10	37,500	
7,500 units of C @ $9	67,500	
Total revenue		$106,200
Cost of Sales		
Processing costs		
Additional processing:		
400* units of A @ $1.80	$ 720	
7,500 units of C @ $2.85	21,375	
Joint processing: 11,718.75 units @ $5.28	61,875	
Total processing costs	$83,970	
Less ending inventory		
Product C (68.75 units @ $0)	0	83,970
Gross profit (same as contribution margin)		$ 22,230

*Assumes additional processing was not performed on the 68.75 units that couldn't be sold. If this additional processing had been completed, the processing cost of 68.75 × $1.80 = $123.75 would be included in ending inventory, so the net cost of sales would be the same as indicated above.

For comparative purposes, we reproduce here the joint cost per unit allocated to the products in Chapter 9 using the relative-sales-value method, along with the Manes-Cheng Marginal LP allocation:

	Relative-Sales-Value Allocation	Marginal Allocation
Product A	0 (by management policy)	0
Product B	$7.50	$10.00
Product C	$4.50	$ 3.25

Thus, while the marginal approach illustrated here and the relative-sales-value method from Chapter 9 are both based, theoretically, on revenues, they result in different allocations. The marginal approach has stronger theoretical support, and it is directly tied to the optimal-production decision.

Economic Order Quantity and Inventory Levels

As we observed in Chapter 19, both merchandising and manufacturing firms, in the past, have established purchasing and inventory policies that sought to minimize the combined cost of purchasing goods and maintaining an appropriate level of inventory. In considering this problem, management was concerned about the trade-offs between the costs associated with buying frequently enough to permit the maintenance of a low level of inventory and the carrying costs associated with holding a large inventory. We now deal more specifically with the theoretical solution of this problem by

- reviewing and discussing further the considerations involved in establishing minimum and maximum inventory levels
- identifying some of the nonproduct costs associated with purchasing goods
- relating these factors to the establishment of quantities to be purchased on each order and the level of inventory to be maintained.

Establishing Inventory Levels

Although the accounting records typically show no items labeled as costs of carrying inventory, there are costs associated with that activity. They include the costs of providing storage space for the inventory, the cost of insuring the inventory, losses from obsolescence and spoilage while stored, the cost of warehouse employees (including security personnel), and the foregone opportunity of investing money committed to inventories in some other income-producing assets. Typically, the cost of providing storage space for inventory will be shown in such accounts as depreciation of buildings, warehouse rentals, and interest expense associated with mortgages on warehouse facilities. The cost of insuring inventory is included in insurance expense. Also, losses from obsolescence and spoilage generally will show up as part of costs of goods sold.

Warehouse employees' salaries generally are classified as salaries and wages expense in the operating expense section of the income statement. The opportunity cost of investing a firm's resources in inventory does not appear in the accounting records but is nevertheless a pertinent cost associated with carrying inventory.

There are also costs associated with the failure to carry an inventory that is large enough to meet the firm's needs, including losses due to the interruption of production (thereby causing idle time) and lost sales. The first of these will be included in manufacturing overhead. The other, lost sales, is an unrecorded cost and typically shows up in the form of loss of customer goodwill and eventually a decline in sales and net income.

Some costs of carrying inventory items will vary directly with the cost of the item or the storage problems associated with it. Large or perishable items, for example, are more expensive to store. Because the unrecorded costs of inadequate inventory are likely to be about the same for all items regardless of cost or storage problems, the minimum inventory levels (safety stock) for high-cost or difficult-to-store items normally should be lower in relation to demands for them (usage) than for low-cost or easy-to-store items.

The decision regarding the targeted minimum quantity of an item to be held in inventory requires consideration of the costs of carrying the inventory item in relation to the costs associated with having none of it when it is needed for production or to make a sale. Management must then consider how much of each of these costs can be traded off for the other, for each inventory item. Having made that decision, the anticipated requirements for the goods should be used to establish the normal and maximum lead times required to replenish the item.

To illustrate, let's assume a firm expects to use 50 units of an item per day, and that the time normally required for delivery by the vendor is 20 days, though, in some cases, that may extend to 45 days. If the firm wishes always to have the item on hand when needed, it would establish a minimum inventory level of 45 days − 20 days × 50 units = 1,250 units per day. However, if the firm is willing to accept some "stock out" costs as a trade-off for some inventory carrying costs, it might establish a targeted minimum inventory level of, for example, 1,000 units. As a general rule, the minimum inventory balance should be large enough to avoid undue losses from the interruption of production and lost sales caused by delayed deliveries from suppliers, and small enough to avoid excessive inventory carrying costs.

Costs of Processing Purchases

The targeted minimum inventory level, coupled with the economic order size, as explained next, has been used to determine the targeted maximum inventory level for each item of inventory. The cost of placing an individual purchase order is one of the things that has been considered in arriving at the quantity of goods to acquire with each purchase order. The cost of placing such an order includes all of the clerical expenses associated with handling the order as well as the cost of analyzing vendor quotations and so forth that should precede order placement.

Inventory-Purchasing Policy

Because the level of inventory to carry and the purchase order size are directly related, they have been considered together in implementing traditional inventory-control and -purchasing practices. One way to do this has been to use an economic order quantity (EOQ) formula that takes into consideration both the costs of ordering goods and inventory carrying costs. The economic order quantity has been calculated with the following equation:

$$\frac{\text{Economic}}{\text{order quantity}} = \sqrt{\frac{2(\text{Annual requirements})(\text{Cost of placing order})}{(\text{Annual carrying cost per unit})^4}}$$

This determined the number of units of an item that should be purchased each time a purchase order is originated. The maximum level of inventory would then be set at the minimum (safety stock) level plus the economic order size. Theoretically, the targeted minimum level for an inventory item would be missed only when deliveries from vendors were delayed. The targeted maximum level would be exceeded only when orders were delivered ahead of schedule.

To illustrate how to calculate the economic order size, let's assume a company sells product X at $40 per unit. After a number of years of operations, it has determined that demand for this item is 4,000 units per month. The units cost $20 each. The cost of placing an order is $2.40, and the annual carrying cost of inventory is 10% of the purchase price per unit. The economic order quantity then would be calculated as follows:

$$\begin{aligned} \text{EOQ} &= \sqrt{\frac{2(48{,}000)(\$2.40)}{(\$20)(0.10)}} \\ &= \sqrt{115{,}200} \\ &= 339+, \text{ or } 340 \text{ units} \end{aligned}$$

With an EOQ of 340 units and an assumed safety stock (minimum inventory level) of 200 units, the inventory would be projected to fluctuate between a minimum of 200 units and a maximum of 540 units, as shown in Figure 21–11. If we assume a lead time of 2 days, the reorder point (467 units) would be calculated as follows:

[4]To determine EOQ in terms of units, the annual carrying cost per unit can be defined as materials cost per unit times carrying cost expressed as a percentage of unit inventory value.

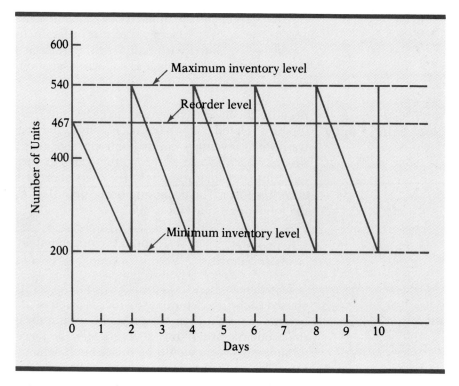

FIGURE 21–11 Inventory-Level for EOQ of 340 Units and Lead Time of 2 Days

Projected requirements	4,000 units every 30 days
Requirement per day	$133\frac{1}{3}$ units
Requirement during 2-day lead time $(2 \times 133\frac{1}{3})$	267 units

$$267 \text{ units} + \text{Minimum inventory level of } 200 \text{ units} = 467 \text{ units}$$

Thus, we see that establishing an EOQ inventory-purchasing policy has related directly to two interrelated elements of quantitative data, namely, a targeted minimum inventory level and an economic order size. Individual item minimum inventory levels have been established by ascertaining the delay that could occur in delivery of the goods and considering the trade-offs between the costs of carrying the item in inventory and the costs of running out of it. After that, the targeted maximum inventory level for the item was determined by adding the economic order quantity to the targeted minimum level.

EOQ and JIT Production

The EOQ formula can be used to establish the *optimum production run*—that is, the quantity of a unique product that should be produced during one setup of equipment. The cost of setup here is analogous to the cost of placing an order, and the cost of carrying the finished-goods inventory is identical to the EOQ purchase-decision inventory carrying cost. Unfortunately, this approach may maximize the use of production facilities but be suboptimal for the firm as a whole.

As explained in Chapter 3, just-in-time (JIT) production basically views all labor as indirect. Therefore, rather than spreading setup cost amongst the largest possible number of units, modern production techniques concentrate on reducing setup times and setup cost in order to increase throughput. The JIT concept rejects localized optimum production and requires each process to produce parts only when they are needed and only in the quantity needed to optimize the overall operation. When properly executed, JIT can shorten production time and decrease work-in-process and finished-goods inventories. This operating policy focuses on filling orders, not on efficient localized production. To facilitate JIT, suppliers must be kept fully informed of exact delivery requirements, meaning they, too, must be operating on the JIT basis, to avoid having the inventory carrying costs transferred up the line to them. Successful applications of JIT usually involve computer linkages to a small number of suppliers.

Where the costs of placing an order (or the costs of setup for a production process) decrease and approach zero, as is possible in a computer environment (with equipment designed to minimize setup costs), the total cost of carrying inventory is targeted to be minimized by forcing inventory toward a zero level. Thus, the EOQ formulation is not inconsistent with JIT. However, EOQ loses much of its usefulness in a JIT environment.

Management rarely knows, with certainty, the elements of the EOQ formula, and some implicit assumptions (such as annual requirements are spread equally throughout the year) frequently are violated. The caution here is that any quantitative technique must be thoroughly understood and properly used. Many companies have abandoned the use of EOQ.

Other Quantitative Analysis Techniques

In addition to using probability analysis, linear programming, and inventory-purchase practices in deciding what courses of action to follow, managers also employ a number of other quantitative techniques to assist them in making decisions.

PERT (program evaluation and review techniques), described earlier, is used to formally diagram the times required for the completion of several interrelated activities that are needed to complete a project. It is meant to improve the management of time and costs in completing a project requiring the coordination of a number of interrelated activities, by assisting management in scheduling and coordinating the activities involved.

Correlation analysis aids in discovering and evaluating possible cause-and-effect relationships among two or more variables. The primary objective of correlation analysis is to improve the predictability of the future behavior of one or more variables included in a model based on the way it is expected to behave in relation to another variable.

Regression analysis helps to make predictions or estimates of the values of a dependent variable from given values of an independent variable or variables. The predictive benefit coming from this analytical technique depends on an expected consistent relationship between variables over a period of time. Earlier in the text (see page 378), we explained how regression analysis can be used to divide a mixed cost into fixed and variable elements.

SUMMARY

In this chapter, we showed how selected quantitative analytical techniques, depending at least partially on the use of data generated by the accounting records, can be used in decision making. These techniques are a part of what is often called operations research (OR) activities.

First we explained the general meaning of simulation and modeling techniques, which are used to project what is likely to happen in an assumed operating situation and with identifiable projected relationships among the variables included in the model. Budgeting is basically an exercise in model building, since projections of probable operating results are based on certain assumed operating conditions, formula relations among selected variables, and specified decisions on the part of management.

We then demonstrated how probability analysis can help managers make decisions regarding the bidding of contracts and determining the quantities of goods to be purchased to maximize long-run profits. Next we illustrated the use of linear programming (LP), a technique used to determine how resources should be allocated so as to allow a firm to meet a quantitative objective such as maximizing profits or minimizing costs. We demonstrated the various steps involved in applying this technique to an assumed operating situation involving the objective of maximizing profits from the manufacture of two products subject to specified constraints on resources and on the quantities of each unit that could be manufactured. We then demonstrated an application of

LP with a specialized graphical and computer solution to a problem of optimizing joint cost allocation and joint process production.

Finally, we demonstrated how a model has been developed to identify an inventory-purchase policy that seeks to minimize the total of inventory carrying costs, the costs of purchasing goods, and the costs of insufficient inventory. We also described other selected quantitative techniques sometimes used in decision making.

GLOSSARY OF TERMS INTRODUCED IN THIS CHAPTER

correlation analysis	A technique used to discover and evaluate possible relationships amongst two or more variables, with the objective of predicting future behavior of one or more of the variables. CAUTION: Correlation does not necessarily imply causation.
Microsoft® PROJECT	A computer software program designed to solve network-type problems. Critical paths and slack times are identified, and budget capability links costs with activities.
model building	The construction of some device (for example, an equation, flowchart, or diagram) that depicts interrelationships among factors that can exist in a real situation.
operations research (OR)	Work done in solving management problems, particularly those of a complex nature that can benefit from mathematical or statistical modeling; also called *management science*.
perfect knowledge	An ideal state connected with the use of probability analysis in which the decision maker would know the appropriate action to take and the payoff(s) associated with that action and thus be able to calculate the value (or cost) of perfect information.
PERT (program evaluation and review technique)	A network-based technique for planning and controlling projects or production that shows precedence relationships among tasks or activities to be completed. Allows the decision maker to focus on critical paths that, if shortened, would hasten completion of the project or decrease production time.
probability analysis	A technique used to assist decision making that assigns probabilities to the outcomes of various possible courses of action.
queuing theory	A branch of probability theory, involving waiting lines (often referred to as *queues*), by which the cost of time lost (by personnel or by products) and the cost of additional facilities can be determined accurately.
simulation	A method of studying operational decisions in which a model of the system or process is subjected to a series of manipulations under varying assumptions related to the decisions; can range from simple cost–

volume–profit relationships for a single period to the use of complex computer-based models to examine problems involving uncertainty.

statistical probability analysis The implementation of probability analysis within the constraints of statistical rules.

waiting line theory See *queuing theory*.

QUESTIONS FOR CLASS DISCUSSION

21–1 What is meant by the terms *simulation* and *model building*? Explain.

21–2 How can the use of a simulation model help the management of a firm? Explain how such a model is used.

21–3 How can probability analysis be used by a contractor bidding on a contract? Explain.

21–4 How can probability analysis be used by a firm in determining the amount of perishable goods to be purchased each day? In making such an analysis, what effect does a change in the contribution margin of the product have on the targeted amount to be purchased?

21–5 In what kind of situations might a firm use linear programming?

21–6 What is meant by the objective function in linear programming analysis?

21–7 What is meant by the constraint factors in the application of the linear programming technique?

21–8 What three types of constraint equations are required for a linear programming problem designed to determine joint process production and joint cost allocation?

21–9 What can shadow prices tell us about joint cost allocation?

21–10 What are the costs associated with carrying inventories? Are all of those costs reflected in the accounting records? Explain.

21–11 What are the costs associated with minimizing inventory levels? Are all of those costs recorded in the accounting records? Explain.

21–12 How does the economic order quantity (EOQ) formula give consideration to the costs of acquiring inventory and the costs of holding inventory? Explain.

21–13 Is the EOQ formula consistent with the concept of just-in-time inventory? Explain.

21–14 How are program evaluation and review techniques (PERT) used by management?

21–15 What is correlation analysis?

21–16 What is regression analysis?

EXERCISES

21–17 **Probability Analysis—Bidding on Contract** James Jones is bidding on a contract with an estimated cost of $40,000. He has bid on a large number of similar contracts in the past and as a result of that experience has developed the following table of probabilities of receiving a contract at various possible bid prices:

Probability of Obtaining Contract	Bid Prices
100%	$40,000
90	42,500
75	45,000
55	47,500
20	50,000

He believes there is no possibility of being awarded the contract if the bid exceeds $50,000.

REQUIRED:

1. What bid should Jones submit if he wishes to maximize his long-term profits from contracts of this type?
2. Would your answer to requirement 1 be different if the contractor's equipment and employees were already heavily committed to other contracts? Explain.

21–18 **Probability Analysis—Use of Payoff Table to Determine Purchases** Joan Allen operates a newsstand at a busy corner in a large city. Each day she has the option of purchasing as many copies of the *Daily Tribune* as she feels she can sell. Unsold copies of the newspaper have no value and therefore are destroyed at the end of the day. Allen is required to purchase newspapers in 100-unit lots. She purchases them for $.18 each and sells them for $.25 each. Allen has carefully observed her sales over a period of time and from those observations has developed the following table showing probabilities of achieving various levels of sales:

Sales (units)	Probabilities
5,000	.4
6,000	.3
7,000	.3

REQUIRED:

1. How many newspapers should Allen buy each day?
2. Assume now that the cost of newspapers is $.08 each and that they can be sold for $.25 each. How many newspapers should be purchased each day?

3. Assume now that Allen feels she must be able to satisfy at least 70% of her customers' demands each day to operate successfully. How many newspapers should be purchased each day?
4. Calculate the value of perfect knowledge regarding the number of newspapers that could be sold each day.

21–19   **Linear Programming—Optimal Production of Two Products** Jones Company manufactures products A and B. The contribution margins of the two products are $7 and $1, respectively. Each unit of A requires 4 hours of manufacturing time; each unit of B requires 2 hours of manufacturing time. The firm has a total of 1,000 hours of manufacturing time available to it during each period. Product A requires a special type of material. The firm can acquire only enough of this material to manufacture 200 units per period. Only 800 units of product B can be sold each period.

REQUIRED:

1. Write the objective function and constraint equations required to incorporate the given information into a linear programming model designed to help the company decide how many units of product A and product B should be manufactured each period.
2. Draw lines representing the constraint equations on a graph.
3. Read from the graph the possible combinations of units A and B that could be produced within the constraint limitations.
4. Test the various possibilities identified in requirement 3 to determine the optimum production mix.

21–20   **Economic Order Size** Zee Company wishes to calculate the economic order size for an inventory item used in producing its finished product. You are given the following information relating to the cost of acquiring and carrying this item of inventory. Zee expects to purchase the item at $10 per unit. The cost of originating a purchase requisition is $2, and the annual carrying cost of inventory is 15% of the cost per unit. Annual requirements of this item are estimated to be 24,000 units.

REQUIRED: Using the formula presented in the chapter, calculate the economic order quantity for this unit of raw material.

21–21   **Maximum and Minimum Inventory Levels** A firm has calculated its economic order size of a purchased part to be 800 units. Management anticipates that the firm will use 200 units per week and that the time normally required for delivery after an order is placed will be 3 weeks. Management has decided that, due to uncertainties in projecting uses and delivery time, a minimum inventory of 400 units should be maintained.

REQUIRED:

1. Calculate the maximum inventory level.
2. At what inventory level should new orders be placed?

21—22 **Multiple Choice Questions**
AICPA Adapted
1. A production department in a manufacturing company does machining on two categories of parts, each of which requires work from three machines. If the time and capacity restrictions on the machines are stringent, a relevant quantitative technique that permits machine usage on the most profitable basis is
   a. linear programming.
   b. queuing analysis.
   c. sensitivity analysis.
   d. statistical quality control.
2. A firm wishes to predict the demand for some of its consumer products. In the past, the sales volume of these products has increased or decreased (with a lag) with increases and decreases in disposable income (as reported in the Federal Reserve Bulletin). The firm does not know how closely sales and disposable income are related or how much of the sales demand is caused by extraneous (nonincome) factors. The relevant quantitative technique that should be applied to measure the degree of these relationships is
   a. correlation analysis.
   b. cost–volume–profit analysis.
   c. game theory analysis.
   d. linear programming.
3. A company is controlling a complex project by determining the activities that must take place and the relationships between these activities. Attention then is focused on those activities that have the greatest influence on the project's estimated completion date. The quantitative technique most relevant to this situation is
   a. cost–volume–profit analysis.
   b. parametric programming.
   c. program evaluation review techniques (PERT).
   d. queuing analysis.

PROBLEMS

21—23 **Linear Program** Stangren Corp., your client, wants your opinion of a technique suggested by a young accounting graduate employed as a cost analyst. The following information was furnished you for the corporation's two products, trinkets and gadgets:

AICPA Adapted

	Cutting Department	Finishing Department	Sales Price per Unit	Variable Cost per Unit
Trinkets	400	240	$50	$30
Gadgets	200	320	$70	$40

(1) The daily capacities of each department represent the maximum production for *either* trinkets *or* gadgets. However, any combination of trinkets and gadgets can be produced as long as the maximum capacity of the department is not exceeded. For example, 2 gadgets can be produced in the cutting department for each trinket not produced and 3 gadgets can be produced in the finishing department for every 4 trinkets not produced.

(2) Material shortages prohibit the production of more than 180 gadgets per day.

Equations derived from the preceding constraint information are plotted on the following graph:

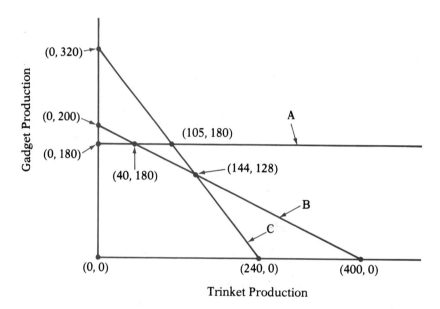

REQUIRED:

1. Identify by letter (A, B, or C) the graphic coordinates representing the
   a. cutting department's capacity
   b. production limitation for gadgets because of the materials shortage
   c. finishing department's capacity.
2. Compute the contribution margin per unit for trinkets and gadgets.
3. Compute the total contribution margin of each of the points of intersections of lines bounding the feasible (possible) area.
4. Identify the best production alternative.

21–24 **Probability Analysis Applied to Sales** Gerald Corporation requested your assistance in determining the potential loss on a binding purchase contract that will be in effect at the end of the corporation's fiscal year. The corporation produces a medical product that deteriorates and must be discarded if not sold by the end of the month during which it is produced.

The total variable cost of the manufactured compound is $50 per unit. It is sold for $80 per unit. The product can be acquired from a vertically integrated competitor at $80 per unit plus $10 freight per unit. It is estimated that failure to fill orders would result in the complete loss of 8 out of 10 customers placing orders for the product.

The corporation has sold the product for the past 30 months. Demand has been irregular, and there is no predictable sales trend. During this period sales per month have been:

Units Sold per Month	Number of Months
8,000	6
10,000	15
12,000	9

REQUIRED: For each of the following, prepare a schedule (with supporting computations in good form):

1. Probability of sales of 8,000, 10,000, or 12,000 units in any month.
2. Marginal income if sales of 8,000, 10,000 or 12,000 units are made in one month and 8,000, 10,000, or 12,000 units are manufactured for sale in the same month. Assume all sales orders are filled. (Such a schedule is sometimes called a *payoff table*.)
3. Average monthly marginal income the corporation should expect over the long run if 10,000 units are manufactured every month and all sales orders are filled.

21–25 **Linear Programming** Nelson Corporation manufactures and sells three grades of wood product: A, B, and C. Each grade must be processed through three phases—cutting, fitting, and finishing—before it is sold. Only 5,000 board-feet per week can be obtained. The cutting department has 180 hours of labor available each week. The fitting and finishing department each have 120 hours of labor available each week. No overtime is allowed.

Contract commitments require the company to make 50 units of A per week. In addition, company policy is to produce at least 50 additional units of A and 50 units of B and 50 units of C each week to actively remain in each of the three markets. Because of competition, only 130 units of C can be sold each week. Data relating to a unit of each product follow:

	A	B	C
Selling price	$20.00	$30.00	$40.00
Direct labor	$10.00	$12.00	$18.00
Direct materials	$1.40	$1.40	$2.00
Variable overhead	$2.00	$2.40	$3.60
Fixed overhead	$1.20	$1.44	$2.16
Materials requirements, in board-feet	7	7	10
Labor requirements, in hours			
Cutting	3/6	3/6	4/6
Fitting	1/6	1/6	2/6
Finishing	1/6	2/6	3/6

REQUIRED: Formulate and label the objective function and constraint equations that would be used in a linear programming model to determine the amount of each product that should be produced to maximize the firm's contribution margin.

21–26   Economic Order Quantity Blake Company uses 3,600 units of material X evenly over each year. The cost per unit is $100, and it costs $200 to place each order. The annual inventory carrying cost is estimated at 25% of unit cost.

REQUIRED:

1. Calculate the EOQ amount that should be ordered each time an order is placed.
2. Assume that Blake has a policy of carrying a safety stock of 160 units of X to provide for possible delays in delivery. What would be the projected maximum inventory level?
3. Based on a 360-day year, how many units does Blake expect to use each day?
4. Assume that 12 days are normally required after placing an order for material X before it is received. At what inventory level should each order be placed?

21–27   Use of EOQ Procedures to Determine Production Runs Tracy, Inc., manufactures a toy. The company expects to make and sell 6,000 of the toys evenly over the year. Each production run requires a machine setup costing $200. The cost of carrying a toy in inventory for a year is $.60.

REQUIRED:

1. Using the EOQ technique, determine the number of toys that should be produced during each run.
2. Assume that setup costs increase to $500 per setup and all other data remain the same. How many toys should be produced during each run?
3. Assume that it costs $1 to carry a toy in inventory for a year. All other data remain the same as originally stated. How many toys should be produced during each run?
4. Discuss the implications of your answers to requirements 1, 2, and 3 as they relate to the elements of the EOQ equation.

Part V

Cost Accounting in an Automated or Synchronized Manufacturing Environment

Introduction   Cost accounting currently is in a state of evolution (some have called it *revolution*). In the final three chapters of this book, we address the important new questions that must be answered and some proposed solutions. At the time this text is being written, we are at (or beyond) the frontier of accepted managerial accounting practices, in an area where consensus has not been achieved. Nevertheless, we feel obligated to expose you to the changes that are occurring and to the positions leading accountants are taking on these changes. We do this in Chapters 22 and 23. In Chapter 24, we present what we believe will become the dominant management philosophy, the *Theory of Constraints*, and introduce accounting reports that are consistent with that philosophy. Following Chapter 24, we have also included a bibliography of articles and books relating to Part V.

Undoubtedly, later editions of this text will incorporate the material from these final three chapters into the earlier chapters. We hope that our desire to cover new uncharted territory will earn us your forgiveness for the inevitable errors that time and further developments may expose.

Chapter 22

Management Accounting Practices Reevaluated[1]

Learning Objectives

When you have finished your study of this chapter, you should

1. Be aware of the historical background of the present-day movement toward automated manufacturing.
2. Recognize the important considerations and unique problems involved in making decisions about factory automation.
3. Be able to identify some changes in management accounting practices that should be made in response to increased factory automation and new manufacturing techniques.

[1]Much of the material included in this chapter has been drawn from papers presented at a seminar sponsored by the National Association of Accountants, entitled "Cost Accounting for the 90s—The Challenge of Technological Change," in April 1986. Used with permission.

Chapter 3 briefly described the likely effects of increased factory automation and an operating policy calling for minimizing inventories on cost accounting practices. Since those changes probably will involve modifications of current practices rather than the development of a completely new system, an understanding of current practices is essential. Parts II, III, and IV of this book therefore have explained current management accounting practices (accounting for resource-conversion activities). Because managers and forward-thinking accountants are raising legitimate questions regarding the appropriateness of presently accepted management accounting practices in the competitive international economic environment, we now critically evaluate the systems discussed in the earlier parts of the book.

Critics maintain that present-day management accounting systems fail to provide the appropriate, timely, and detailed information about processing activities that managers need to most effectively control costs and improve productivity. For example, they criticize present-day systems for distributing large amounts of overhead costs to products or services via simplistic volume-related bases such as direct labor and machine-hours, which, they maintain, do not appropriately recognize cause-and-effect relationships. Many overhead costs, they say, are related to number of transactions (such as work orders or purchase orders), rather than to volume. This, they maintain, generates improper product costs, thereby creating an opportunity for misguided decisions about engineering improvements, product pricing, product mix, and response to competition.

Critics further maintain that present-day systems lead managers to focus their actions on short-term results rather than on the firm's long-term profitability because company evaluation measures emphasize short-term profit goals such as those presented in interim and annual financial reports. This, undoubtedly, has caused management to avoid incurring expenditures that, in the long run, would be beneficial but, in the short-run, would decrease earnings per share. For example, since presently accepted accounting principles require research and development (R&D) expenditures to be expensed as they are incurred, a manager under pressure to maintain or improve current period earnings per share is likely to reject or materially reduce current R&D expenditures, even though the firm might realize significant long-term benefits from them. Such things as plant modernization expenditures also may be rejected because of current financial statement pressures.

Japanese manufacturers, over the past ten to twenty years, have captured much of the world market for automobiles, appliances, and so forth. One reason for their success is their strong emphasis on long-term objectives rather than short-term profits. They have been willing to commit considerable sums of resources to research and development activities to obtain a larger market share over a longer period of time, for example.

The development of international trade following World War II and the more recent acceleration of global competition have revealed that many U.S. firms engaged in the manufacture of steel, automobiles, and other products are not competitive internationally in price or quality. Part of this stems from the significantly higher labor costs in the United States. However, some managers and accountants believe that the problem also may be traced to the use of improper product costing as a basis for determining whether a firm is making money or losing money on the sale of individual products. Other causes probably include a reluctance on the part of U.S. firms to commit adequate resources to the improvement of long-term competitiveness, particularly when generally accepted accounting procedures would cause those expenditures to temporarily reduce short-term earnings per share. Thus, management accounting systems that are designed primarily to accumulate and allocate costs according to generally accepted accounting practices so external financial statements can be prepared from the accounting data must accept part of the responsibility for management decisions that adversely affect long-term profitability.

Manufacturing practices have changed significantly over the last 60 or more years and the *rate* of change appears to be continually increasing. Global competition and government deregulation are causing some of these changes: increasingly, U.S. manufacturing firms are being forced to update their technology, emigrate to other countries, or cease operations. Some have suggested that the United States should now become a producer of services rather than a manufacturing nation. However, if citizens of the United States are to continue to enjoy their present standard of living, we must attempt to retain our position in the production of goods *as well as* services.[2] The production of tangible products (resource conversion) is the wealth-producing sector of the economic system, whereas service industries feed on wealth—they do not create wealth. We cannot forfeit our basic productive industries, such as agriculture, manufacturing, and mining with the idea of expanding service industries to fill the void if we are to continue as a leading nation. Just as service departments in a manufacturing firm would not exist if the production departments ceased operating, service industries cannot exist without an industrial base to service.

Manufacturing accountants must meet the challenge of appropriately accounting for and reporting on the results of manufacturing operations in a period of technological change. This requires, among other things, a critical reevaluation of current management accounting practices

---

[2]Every town and city that has lost manufacturing plants can bear witness to the fact that service firms disappeared shortly thereafter.

plus the utilization of the latest developments in information systems technology to provide management appropriate, timely information.

Some U.S. firms have recognized the need for changing their manufacturing and accounting procedures to meet global competition. For example, Borg-Warner made the following statement in its 1985 annual report: "To be competitive worldwide on a cost and quality basis, [the automotive division's] traditions and strategies had to be radically changed." Borg-Warner changed its manufacturing procedures by phasing in automation, and, as a result, modified its management accounting system along the lines suggested in Chapters 23 and 24.[3]

Any accounting system must adapt itself to the environment in which it operates. A reevaluation of present-day resource-conversion practices and the associated accounting procedures may lead to dramatic changes in the ways we collect, accumulate, and allocate costs. We now have computing capability that enables us to organize our accounting and information systems to provide detailed information that could not be provided by manually maintained systems. Next, we shall:

1. examine the historical background underlying existing manufacturing accounting practices
2. identify some of the changes that have occurred in our resource-conversion environment over the period during which present-day management accounting practices have evolved
3. discuss some of the changes management accountants should consider making if they are to successfully cope with current and anticipated changes in the resource-conversion segment of our economy.

Historical Background

The accounting profession generally traces its roots to Fra Pacioli, who first developed the double-entry system of accounting some 500 years ago. Because of the business environment in which Pacioli worked, he was primarily interested in accounting for merchandising ventures involving the shipments of goods to foreign countries in exchange for goods from those countries returned by the same ships or caravans. He made no attempt to account for the results of a venture until the ship or caravan had returned and all of the merchandise acquired abroad had been sold, at which time he could establish the profitability of the venture by matching cash outflows against cash inflows.

Later, authors developed various accounting refinements. Charles Babbage, for example, in his book *On the Economy of Machinery and*

---

[3]Dennis P. Fishlias and Peter Chalos, "High-Tech Production's Impact on Cost Accounting: A Case Study," *Journal of Accountancy*, November 1986, pp. 158–167.

Manufacturing, published in 1832, rationalized the machine as part of the management process. Alexander Hamilton Church, in 1917, introduced the idea of the production center, which we take for granted in management accounting today. He also developed the **machine-hour labor rate** concept which, in effect, treats the machine as a laborer. He also urged getting rid of overhead as an element of cost. In 1927, D. R. Scott, professor of accounting at the University of Missouri, emphasized, in his book *The Cultural Significance of Accounts*, that accountants should be concerned not solely with debits and credits but also with information. A still later influence was J. Brooks Heckert's book entitled *The Analysis and Control of Distribution Costs for Sales Executives and Accountants* (1940).

Other important names in the development of management accounting include Stanley B. Henrica who wrote *Standard Costs for Manufacturing*. David Solomons, in his 1965 book *Divisional Performance: Measurement and Control*, called attention to the fact that a division of a firm may make decisions that are rational from the point of view of the division but that reduce overall firm profitability. This bit of genius, which often has not been fully appreciated, was counterbalanced by his encouragement of the use of the capital budgeting technique in considering the possible use of robots without insisting that opportunity costs be formally inserted in the analysis.

Perhaps the latest milestone is a recently published book entitled *Relevance Lost: The Rise and Fall of Management Accounting*, by H. Thomas Johnson and Robert S. Kaplan (Cambridge, Mass.: Harvard Business School Press, 1987), which traces the historical evolution of management accounting as it relates to the development of our economic system. The authors believe that managerial accounting had its roots in the industrial revolution, when business owners were required to commit significant sums of capital to their firms' production processes in order to take advantage of economies of scale. The emergence of large centrally managed hierarchical organizations created demands for information relating to the performance of individual managers and segments. In the mid-nineteenth century, accounting procedures were developed to help top-level managers oversee these diverse and widely dispersed operations. For example, measures such as *cost per ton-mile* were created and reported for various segments of railroad operations. Later, retail chains such as Marshall Fields, Sears, and Woolworth developed their own measures of internal performance to support their managerial planning and control activities. Further advances in management accounting came in connection with the scientific management movement, as engineers such as Frederick Taylor attempted to improve efficiency in the utilization of labor and materials. The return-on-investment (ROI) concept for providing an overall measure of efficiency of an operating unit is traced to the DuPont Company, whose top managers used ROI to help direct allocations of capital and evaluate the performance of operating divisions. According to Johnson and Kaplan, most of our contemporary management accounting practices had been developed by 1925, and during the period since 1925, many companies have been dominated by executives who prided themselves on running their firms by the numbers produced by the accounting systems. They suggest that the failure of systems to change in response to changes in production and information technology, coupled with greater reliance on the data produced by those systems, probably have exaggerated the decision errors made by businesses in recent years.

So, why have management accounting practices remained virtually unchanged over the last 60 years, even though the product and process technologies of manufacturing firms have changed significantly? Many believe that this stagnation can be attributed, to some extent, to the increasing importance of published (externally reported) financial statements during the twentieth century. Certainly, generally accepted accounting principles (GAAP) have proliferated during this time—especially during the last decade. Accountants have been hard pressed to stay abreast of procedures required for external financial reporting and have not had the leisure to concentrate on internal reporting. Auditors, mindful of the potential liability to users of financial statements, have insisted on conservative accounting practices based on objective and verifiable evidence. Even though they realize the information they provide to management is flawed, management accountants, because of the need to make their external reporting practices conform to GAAP, have given little attention to the development of innovative practices that mirror production realities.

While problems in current management accounting reporting have been recognized, solutions are just beginning to be formulated. Johnson and Kaplan feel that management accounting practices will not change significantly until firms develop *separate systems* designed specifically to provide data that engineers and management accountants believe are relevant to the internal decision-making process in today's economic environment. It is not clear exactly how these systems should be designed. Perhaps one step in that direction would be more widespread use of direct or variable costing systems (discussed in Chapter 14) even though generally accepted accounting principles require full absorption costing for external reporting purposes.

If we are to have rapid and significant changes in management accounting systems, the managerial accounting academic community, in its research and education roles, will have to emerge from its recent near-dormancy and begin to examine the procedures and practices needed to produce the information managers find most useful in properly coordinating and controlling a resource-conversion firm's operations. However, as current problems belatedly are being addressed, we must identify the likely future changes (and problems) as firms move toward more completely automated factories, more intense international competition, and ever-shorter product life cycles.

Changes in the Resource Conversion Environment

Manufacturing firms historically have carried out their activities by using either a **manual manufacturing system**, a **fixed automated manufacturing system**, or a combination of these systems. In the first system, employees are the primary work initiators. Work is delivered to them at their work stations, and they perform the operations on the products for which they are responsible, after which the products are moved to another work station or to a storage area. Fixed automated systems involve expensive limited-purpose equipment within an assembly line layout. A piece of specialized equipment performs perhaps only one specific task. An automobile assembly line of the 1960s is a good example. Most present-day managerial accounting systems are meant to account for the accumulation and allocation of costs in these older types of operating environments, which emphasized economies of scale with a limited range of products and long production runs designed to minimize departmental unit costs. However, some accountants maintain that the presently used system of absorption costing, which allocates large amounts of overhead on the basis of some measure of prime cost, such as direct labor or materials cost, fails to provide the information most useful in making operating decisions when multiple products are produced.

In recent years, most U.S. manufacturing firms, because of international competition, have been forced to choose among (1) further automating their operations in the United States, (2) emigrating to some other country where labor costs are lower, or (3) going out of business. Some firms have already emigrated and established manufacturing divisions in other countries. Others have started developing more completely automated plants in the United States or have ceased to operate. Unfortunately, some firms have delayed making any choice, unrealistically hoping the environment will improve.

As U.S. citizens, we have to be concerned when firms move their operations to other countries or are forced out of business. Increased automation would seem to have a greater relative advantage for firms in the United States: because of the relatively high wage scale maintained here, the advantage of substituting robots for production-line employees should be greater for us. In the remainder of this chapter and much of Chapter 23, we will be identifying possible changes in management accounting that might adapt it to an environment in which all or a significant portion of a firm's manufacturing activities are automated. We shall

1. examine some of the changes in the activities on which to report
2. identify some of the characteristics of the automated factory
3. note some of the changes in resource-conversion activities associated with global competition and a deregulated trade environment.

Activities to Be Reported

Conventional managerial accounting, as we have observed a number of times, strongly emphasizes determining the full cost of manufacturing each product. This cost-allocation objective has often led accountants to allocate a large amount of overhead without examining the cause-and-effect relationships between those costs and the allocation base. Total manufacturing cost is divided into materials, labor, and manufacturing-overhead elements, and we typically accumulate and allocate those costs in such a way that the costs incurred by individual processes or departments also can be identified. When a firm is decentralized into profit-accountable divisions, we also determine the return on investment (ROI) associated with divisional operations, using similar cost-allocation procedures.

Those critical of current managerial accounting practices maintain that, as automation increases, the present systems fail to allocate some overhead costs on appropriately determined cause-and-effect bases. In some instances, this is done because the costs of tracing cause-and-effect relationships have been judged to be greater than the benefits expected to be realized from the more precise allocation procedures. Increased automation could create a further need for dramatic changes in the activities management accountants should be reporting on if the system is to be appropriately adapted to that environment.

Some innovative ideas for planning and controlling manufacturing operations have been developed. For example, **material requirements planning (MRP)**—a computer system using bills of materials, inventory data, and a master production schedule to calculate materials requirements—and **manufacturing resource planning II (MRP II)**—a systems planning and control program that integrates production and inventory plans into the financial accounting system—were developed to automate production information. These systems, however, merely automated current procedures (along with their inefficiencies).

Some managers and accountants have suggested that, in an automated manufacturing setting, more emphasis should be placed on maintaining **total quality control (TQC) with zero defects** by making workers (instead of inspectors) responsible for quality. Others emphasize the need to minimize inventory balances. If these are accepted as operating objectives, management accountants will have to develop reporting procedures that measure the extent to which those goals have been achieved. The introduction of **computer-integrated manufactur-**

ing (CIM)—in which not only machine operations are controlled by computer programs but design, purchasing, routing, and deliveries are computerized and totally integrated—certainly will change the fundamental technology of processing and the management accounting procedures required to report on such operations.

In an automated factory, for example, it is important to exercise oversight over the materials put into process, the processing activities performed by the robotic equipment, and the scheduling of processing activities. This requires close inspection (preferably by the supplier) of materials acquired, to be sure they meet established quality standards before they are used. Because processing is automatic, there is no need to relate the quantity of output to elapsed time (as when calculating direct labor efficiencies); instead we are concerned with the proper functioning of the equipment so that only good products are turned out. Scheduling is important because that allows smooth production, with no unnecessary delays, and permits inventories to be minimized in relation to the demand for the product. These changes probably will lead to shifts in the organization of production processes. The typical cost centers or departments tend to disappear with the use of robots. Instead, we will have what has been called *manufacturing cells*, each of which may include a number of processes and, in effect, operate as a minifactory.

Goods produced in such an environment should go through very short *manufacturing cycles*. Many of the manufacturing processes will require large investments in engineering design before the first commercial unit can be produced. As a result, accounting systems based on the distinction between fixed and variable costs and concerned with the distribution of fixed costs to all products may be unrealistic. The traditional periodic profit measurement may be difficult to achieve if the management accounting system is geared to produce useful information about a highly automated factory producing products with extremely short manufacturing cycles. We deal more specifically with the ways in which management accounting may have to be changed later in the chapter.

Characteristics of the Automated Factory

A factory operates by using labor and manufacturing overhead to convert raw materials into finished products. The conventional cost system typically allocates direct materials to units of product as those materials are put into process. Labor and overhead (conversion costs) are accumulated and allocated to various cost centers or departments within the factory to aid management in evaluating departmental performance and in assigning costs to products on a job-order, process, or other basis. In a labor-driven plant, where most of the output can be attributed to the physical labor of human workers, manufacturing overhead primarily consists of the cost of supporting direct laborers on the production line; overhead typically is allocated to the units of product on the basis of the direct labor charged to the product.

In an automated factory, we are likely to find very few direct laborers (production line employees). Robots will do more of the work previously carried out by production line employees, and, instead of *direct labor*, we will have well-paid, professionally trained *indirect* employees who oversee the processing activities. Such an environment requires a reassessment of the causes of various overhead costs and reconsideration of the ways in which those costs should be allocated to the goods being produced. Instead of the factory being kept in operation for the purpose of providing places for production line employees to work and in that way providing a justification for allocating overhead on the basis of direct labor costs, factory facilities are maintained primarily to house automated equipment that performs various manufacturing activities on a wide range of products. Therefore, the cause-and-effect relationships associated with overhead costs have to be completely reevaluated in developing a cost system for a computer-integrated (completely automated) factory.

Global Competition and a Deregulated Trade Environment

In an attempt to become competitive in world markets by increasing productivity, U.S. factories have substituted machines for direct laborers. However, because greater productivity was not achieved in time, much of the manufacturing segment of our economy has already been lost. The movement toward increased productivity certainly will have to be accelerated for U.S. manufacturing firms that hope to continue operations in the United States in the face of global competition.

Service industries also have been impacted by major changes. Certain service industries within our economy historically have been subject to governmental regulations designed to force what was believed to be a more equitable allocation of resources and better protection for consumers than might occur in a free marketplace economy. In recent years, however, an evolution in political thinking has led to the opinion that consumers might be better served by deregulating those industries and letting competition direct the allocation of resources. The airline, communications, and banking industries are examples of firms that have had to revise their operations drastically to cope with deregulation.

The movement toward deregulation, placing increased dependence on the marketplace to determine how resources should be allocated, has unleashed an enormous demand for improved cost accounting practices in many service industries. Until about 1978, the cost in such industries as utility, telephone, airline, and banking were passed on to customers with little regard for cause-and-effect relationships as prices were set. Instead, arbitrary decisions based on "fairness" or "ability to pay" sometimes were made. With deregulation, these industries are being forced to determine how they should manage and price their diverse products and services to realize a profit from each of them. More sophisticated cost-accumulation and -allocation systems are required in this type environment so that each of the products or services being sold can be priced individually to recover costs and realize a profit. Fortunately, the computing power to handle the detail required for this is readily available. The end result should be the production of more goods or services for the dollars expended by consumers because of a more efficient allocation of resources. It seems safe to conclude that deregulation, like global competition, could well motivate firms in many industries toward increased productivity through automation. That, in turn, should lead to substantial modifications in their management accounting systems.

Coping with Changes in Today's Resource Conversion Environment

With a computer, a firm can now maintain, without much additional clerical effort, a separate management accounting system designed solely to provide information for decision making regardless of whether that information meets the requirements of generally accepted accounting practices. The computer can generate much more detailed data than can a manually maintained system. In fact, care often must be exercised to avoid generating too many reports with too much detail.

In examining some of the actions the management accountant might take in coping with today's operating environment, we shall relate the extent of automation and production realities to the need for changes in the firm's management accounting system and discuss ways to measure achievements against the goal of long-term profitability.

Extent of Automation

Though management accounting must keep pace with technological change, the extent of the change required for a specific firm depends on how far the firm goes toward automating its operations or changing its procedures to increase productivity. However, before a program of automation can be adopted, the management accountant will be expected to assemble the appropriate data for management to use in deciding whether the firm should automate and, if so, how far it should go toward the ultimate level of automation commonly referred to as computer-integrated manufacturing (CIM). Traditionally, we have looked at a factory modernization decision as involving two major options or a combination of them: (1) adopt a manual manufacturing system or (2) go to a fixed automation (assembly line) operation.

Now manufacturers have a third option: introduce robots into the production line, thereby eliminating many direct laborers. Some have called the typical use of programmable robots that can be adapted to perform a range of activities a **flexible automated manufacturing system**. However, these systems have widely varying degrees of automation and flexibility. Today, the ultimate automated system, a computer-integrated manufacturing (CIM) system, is computer controlled all the way from the design of the product to the handling of shipments to customers.

Management accounting's concern in such a plant is the accumulation and allocation of the costs of activities starting with the design of the product and continuing through the point at which the product is sold. For example, a firm using computer-aided design (CAD) techniques can increase its designers' efficiency by having them design and test a three-dimensional product on a computer. The management accountant must decide how the design costs should be handled. There probably are organizations today that can take a computer design terminal to a customer's office, design the part there, and press a button that begins the part's manufacture in a distant plant. Such an arrangement would seem to call for the accumulation of all costs associated with the design, production, and delivery of such a product on a job-order basis, where the "job" is the product and indirect product costs are to be recovered over the life of the product.

One of the big elements of computer-integrated manufacturing is, of course, robots, often designed in the form of articulated arms. Basically, the robot replaces a worker. Today, we already have in general use programmable robots that handle spray painting and spot welding, and that carry out pick-and-place movements (in which the robot simply picks up a part from one place and puts it down in another). If a firm can extend the use of programmable robots to materials handling systems, along with the ability to design those systems, we have what may be characterized as a completely automated flexible manufacturing system.

Some have suggested that, in such a flexible manufacturing system, management should be concerned primarily with scheduling the machines so as to maximize throughput. **Throughput** is defined as the extent to which the system generates profit through sales. Throughput commonly is calculated as sales price less materials cost, which, when all other manufacturing costs are fixed, is equivalent to contribution margin. With emphasis on maximizing throughput, production that accumulates as inventory—no matter how "efficiently" produced—or output that is returned because of poor quality, does not contribute to profit. In managing an operation so as to maximize throughput, inventory and poor quality are to be avoided. In an automated plant, errors in operations can quickly lead to large losses from defective products. Therefore, the operations must be monitored carefully so as to minimize such errors. Technical experts in this area are now experimenting with systems that will self-correct. That amounts to building **artificial intelligence** into the systems.

Coupling flexible automation with the idea of minimizing inventory, manufacturers have implemented just-in-time production systems (see Chapter 3). This means that the planning and control of production must be organized so that perfect-quality materials will reach input points at exactly the times they are needed. That, in theory, leads to the idea of zero level of materials inventory. Overall, such a system would be targeted toward having no wasted resources and minimal materials, work-in-process, and finished-goods inventories. Wasted resources do not include idle machine time. Machines (or workers) should be active only when their output is needed. In contrast, resources are considered wasted if unneeded units are produced.

The initial step for firms choosing to automate must center on selecting the *type* (degree) of automation. Many firms have become quite comfortable operating a fixed automation (assembly line) system. The new choices then range from that type system (using a significant number of production line employees) to a completely automated factory (with few employees). A completely automated factory theoretically calls for operations to be carried out by turning on a switch and letting the robots produce goods while being monitored by one or two employees watching banks of video screens. Deciding how much automation is appropriate for a particular firm involves considerations similar to those discussed in Chapter 20 (replacement of equipment and capital budgeting). Because most firms moving to automation lack experience with automated operations, many elements of the capital budgeting analysis will, at best, have to be based on rather tentative estimates. We can, however, cite some of the items that should be given special consideration.

1. A long-term perspective, emphasizing rather than ignoring the *strategic benefits* that can be realized by acquiring the new equipment, is vital. This will require examining a number of factors previously ignored. Traditionally, the justification of new automation has been based on labor savings, including documentation of the number of workers that would be replaced. In today's environment, however, particular attention must be given to *the opportunity cost of not automating* that may include the firm being forced out of business. Other costs include charges for long **lead times** and cycle times, lack of flexibility, and poor quality (anything less than perfection).

2. Robots are not infallible. They can fail to do what they are built to do and create a real problem on an assembly line.

3. There are a number of different types of flexibility that can be built into an automated plant, including flexibility in product mix, the number of parts that can be made, routing, design, and volume of production. While all types of flexibility can be put into two

categories—*product characteristics* and *process characteristics*—both categories must be thoroughly evaluated when making automation decisions.

Measuring Progress Toward Long-Term Profitability

All of these possible changes are likely to require dramatic changes in the management accounting system if it is to provide data appropriate for making operating decisions. The extent of the change will depend largely on the creativity of the firm's management accountants and the extent to which factory automation is implemented by the firm. A firm could easily reach the point where, in the interests of controlling inventory level and minimizing losses from obsolescence, it might not produce a product until it had an order for the product. In that case, the management accounting system would be directed toward accumulating by individual customer orders all costs, both direct and indirect, from design through delivery of goods as required.

Without doubt, accountants have so far failed to develop management accounting procedures to fully meet the requirements of the new manufacturing environment. In fact, they often have been perceived as rigidly blocking changes in procedures rather than facilitating them. Now it seems we have limited time and limited management resources for catching up. However, here are some suggestions for synchronizing accounting information systems with the changed operating environment in which businesses now operate:

1. Consider the purposes or goals of the company. Logically, the only one that makes sense for a manufacturing business is to make money, both today and tomorrow (long-term profitability). In evaluating progress toward that goal, we almost certainly will still need some measure of profit and return on investment. Because bankruptcy can occur even when assets are greater than liabilities if obligations cannot be met in a timely manner, we need to provide a measure of cash flow as well. Long-term profit considerations also must incorporate social responsibility considerations.
2. In a manufacturing business, determine what actions to take to move the business toward the goals of the firm. Certainly, the emphasis has to be on efficiency, which customarily has been measured with unit-cost data. Within the new environment, the emphasis should be on productivity and the minimization of inventory carrying costs. Certainly, a firm must avoid manufacturing goods simply to keep the factory in operation and thus spread fixed costs over a larger number of units. Therefore, some measures of throughput, inventory, and fixed operating expenses will be required.
3. Develop appropriate measures of processing performance. Firms within the new environment must try to cut **total product lead times** in order to be competitive. Attention, therefore, must be given to developing information regarding the time required to manufacture each product (**manufacturing lead time**).

4. Furnish timely data to managers. Appropriate cost information must be available instantaneously (in real time) so the entire production/ sales cycle is not delayed.

Current management accounting systems seek to measure a firm's achievement of its long-term profit goals through periodically determined profits (generally measured as earnings per share) to facilitate the determination of return on investment (ROI). Short-term measurements of profit and ROI, along with management's inclination to maximize those figures, could be counterproductive in achieving long-term profitability.

Focus on short-term profit has caused managers, for a number of years, to concentrate on output instead of quality. As a result, domestic quality, relative to foreign quality, became unacceptable to many consumers. Ultimately, inferior quality (quality below the minimum quality expectations of users or consumers) adversely affected profitability. For example, consider the effect on customer purchase decisions of an automobile purchaser's perception of the quality of domestic automobiles as compared with that of Japanese imports. Because many potential purchasers seem to believe that domestic automobiles are inferior, the domestic automobile industry has suffered severe declines in demand for its products, which has led to significant decreases in the net incomes of auto firms. Thus, we see there is a need for information about the *quality* of a firm's product and *market expectations* of minimum quality so that aspect of operations can be controlled.

High product quality has become necessary for a firm to remain competitive in the world market. For example, if Ford Motor Company's slogan "Quality is job one" is an important operating objective, its management accounting system should have been designed to highlight the status of quality. If this had been done, the firm might not have lost so many customers by selling lower quality automobiles.

How do we assign an opportunity cost to poor quality? That cost, in the form of contribution margin previously realized from lost customers, is significantly more than the typically recognized costs of spoiled units and warranties. True, money can be saved by cutting spoilage and scrap costs. However, the cost in lost orders resulting from customer dissatisfaction with poor product quality also must be explicitly considered, no matter how "soft" such data are. The ideal situation would be perfect quality control with zero defects achieved at no additional cost.

Inspection cannot locate all defective units. Responsibility for quality, therefore, must fall on the builder of the product at the point where defects originate so the problem can be corrected immediately. Internal reports that monitor physical measures of quality should be incorporated into management accounting systems.

As we suggested earlier, greater emphasis could be placed on controlling inventory levels to reduce inventory carrying costs, including losses due to obsolescence. Robert E. Fox, current president of the Avraham Y. Goldratt Institute, suggests three measures to help managers control operations: throughput, inventory, and operating expense. As Fox points out, production is not throughput if the product isn't sold, and it isn't automatically sold simply because it is produced. His definition of *inventory*, which differs from the conventional one, is that it is all the money invested in things that the system expects to resell, including, for a manufacturing firm, only raw materials and purchased components. No value added (that is, direct labor or overhead) would be included in work in process or finished goods held by the company. *Operating expense* he defines as the amount the company spends in order to turn inventory (raw materials and purchased components) into throughput, and includes both labor and overhead. Thus, operating expense can be equivalent to the fixed costs (manufacturing plus selling) discussed earlier in the book (see especially Chapter 2).

Fox justifies his definition of inventory as follows: A plant manager evaluated on the basis of conventionally determined operating income can increase work-in-process and finished-goods inventories and thus absorb overhead and labor so those outlays will be allocated to inventories (on the balance sheet) and thereby create an increase in net operating income (by the amount of costs deferred in inventories) even though the goods have not been sold. (This effect was illustrated as we discussed direct costing in Chapter 14.) He then explains how these new measures relate to our conventional bottom line measure (net income): other things being equal, a firm is better off if throughput is increased or if inventory and operating expenses are decreased. If a firm were able to increase its throughput without increasing inventory or operating expenses, it would show improvements in net income and return on investment. Furthermore, if the firm could reduce operating expense without affecting inventory or throughput, it would again improve income and ROI. And if inventory, as defined above, is reduced, the firm also will reduce some operating expenses—for example, interest, storage, materials handling, and scrap (inventory deterioration), as well as some other factors normally buried in operating expenses. Thus, the three measures (throughput, inventory, and operating expense) can have both a direct and indirect impact on income and ROI.

To further support the Goldratt position on inventory, Fox cites the attitude of the Japanese, who have been so successful as manufacturers, and who see inventory as an evil and something to be totally rooted out and eliminated. The Japanese maintain they have to reduce inventory to have a competitive edge in the marketplace. Further, Fox cites the following example to show how inventory affects quality, margins, and lead time. A plant has an order for 1,000 units of a product that requires materials to be processed sequentially through five operations. The plant, operating in a high-inventory environment, processes this order in a single batch through each operation. It releases material for all pieces at the first operation, takes a certain amount of time to process it, moves it to the second operation, takes an additional amount of time to process it, and so on for each process, all the way through the plant. Even if the plant is run at maximum capacity, it may take perhaps four months to finish the order.

Now contrast these operating practices with what we would do in a low-inventory environment by making two small changes. First, instead of moving the material through the plant from one operation to another in batches of 1,000, move it in smaller batches, say 200. When 200 pieces complete the first operation, we immediately move those units to the second operation. In that way, we split and overlap the work so that several machines in different operations can be working on the order simultaneously. The other change involves avoiding releasing materials for processing simply to keep the first operation busy. Since there is always some constraining element of operations that takes more time than the rest to complete materials processing, we release material so as to keep that *critical (constraining) element* busy. The constraint determines the pace for the rest of the factory. This way, the firm has less inventory and can also produce the order in a shorter period of time. This repetitive, synchronized manufacturing application is similar to a single application of PERT (program evaluation and review technique) described in Chapter 21, except one operation does not have to be entirely finished before the next operation is begun and the complete process is continually modified and repeated.

Fox also stresses the importance of quality. Many firms conventionally use statistical quality control to identify spoilage and scrap. In the new environment, a firm uses quality control not just to separate good parts from bad but also to locate the cause of the bad parts and eliminate the problems creating them. Thus, a firm uses quality control to check each *process* rather than the *product*, for, after all, the firm can never inspect the product as well as the customer can.

Unfortunately, our present operating practices typically call for the discovery of defective products at the conclusion of operations rather than at the point in the process at which the defect is introduced. In a low-inventory environment, because a portion of the "batch" is transferred to the next process while the rest is still being processed, we should find the defect while we still are running the products in the first operation. Firms with the highest-quality products typically also have by far the lowest inventory.

Optimized production technology (OPT) is a computer software program which was developed by Creative Output, a predecessor of the Goldratt Institute, to simulate the production process so that bottlenecks can be spotted before they occur.[4] Its objective is to balance the flow of goods, not plant capacity. Because users of the software did not fully understand the concepts on which the software was based and how operating policies had to be consistent with the software, most implementations were not successful for a long period of time. The ideas prompting the development of OPT have been incorporated into a manufacturing control system, **synchronous manufacturing**, which is promoted by the Goldratt Institute as part of its theory of constraints management philosophy (see Chapter 24).

Fox emphasizes the importance of a firm's cutting lead times in the manufacture of its product in order to increase sales. Shortened manufacturing lead times are made possible by reducing what is conventionally called work-in-process inventory. If it takes a shorter time to manufacture a product (because queues are decreased), the firm will need to maintain a smaller number of units on hand. However, it is important to decrease inventory without decreasing throughput or increasing operating expense. Fox suggests doing that by using the just-in-time (JIT) and optimal production technology (OPT) approaches (now combined in the concept of synchronous manufacturing). Such a system, where processing is strictly controlled to meet 100% of the constraint (internal or external) requirements, obviously is at odds with EOQs, efficiencies, and variances, as those things are measured in current management accounting systems. This suggests that our current cost measures often may lead us in the wrong direction, for they lead us to build inventory "profits" (work in process and finished goods) that are not real profits.

As a new measure of inventory performance, Fox suggests **dollar-days**, which quantifies deviations of inventory from amounts scheduled to meet production requirements. This approach begins by defining inventory cost as raw materials and purchased components and then treats excess inventory as if it were a loan from the bank (a "cost"), not as an asset. The dollar "cost" of inventory is then measured not by looking back toward the original purchase date, as is traditionally done but by looking forward to when those materials will be sold or will leave the plant. This allows us to break total inventory into planned and unplanned elements. Since inventory that deviates from scheduled production requirements results in loss of throughput, the "cost" of excess inventory can be calculated with this measure.[5] For example, material

---

[4]For a description of OPT, see R. E. Fox, "Main Bottleneck on the Factory Floor," *Management Review* (November 1984), pp. 55–61.

[5]Loss of throughput can occur because there is too much (unplanned) inventory, resulting in a longer manufacturing cycle or lead time that delays shipments, or because there is too little inventory—that is, planned inventory buffers are not maintained and vital work stations are starved for parts, resulting in idle time and unmet deliveries.

with a cost of $1,000 that was expected to be completed and sold, say, 10 days ago for $1,800 has a (negative) value of ($1,800 − $1,000) × 10 = 8,000 throughput dollar-days. If the material is still in process 2 days later, it has a (negative) value of $800 × 12 = 9,600 throughput dollar-days. The department or process responsible for holding up the inventory required for the late order would be charged with imputed interest on the throughput dollar-days. Such an approach requires a schedule detailing the amount of materials a firm has, the location of those materials as they move through the plant, plus the time needed for delivery to a customer (or another process or buffer).

In using dollar-days to measure performance relating to inventory, we charge the dollar-days "penalty" to the person responsible for getting the inventory through to the point at which it is needed (ultimately, the shipping point), when it is needed. *Valid* (planned) inventory then becomes the inventory needed to protect the production schedule. *Excess* (unplanned) inventory is any amount above that and is converted to dollar-days. To illustrate, suppose a firm decides it has to keep a buffer of $500 of raw materials inventory to protect against late delivery. However, it actually has $800 of raw materials on hand, and the $300 excess will not be needed by the factory for 10 days. We would then charge the purchasing department for imputed interest on $300 × 10 = 3,000 dollar-days for bringing the material in early. Thus, individuals within the firm are made responsible for specific amounts of dollar-days. The objective, of course, is to minimize dollar-days by holding only the planned inventory at all times. Such an arrangement motivates individuals within the firm to adhere to planned inventory levels and thus it helps minimize total inventory.

SUMMARY

In this chapter, we discussed certain aspects of currently accepted cost accounting practices, acknowledging that management accounting must respond to the needs of the environment in which firms operate, and must keep pace with technological change. We presented the historical background of present-day management accounting practices, recognizing that innovations in management accounting have lagged behind the technological changes in resource-conversion activities, and we concluded that adequate attention has not been given to the information likely to be needed in an automated manufacturing economy.

Next, we considered some of the changes that have occurred and are likely to occur as manufacturing firms move toward increased automation. The systems at the two extreme automation possibilities are a manual, employee-oriented system and a computer-integrated manufacturing system complete with robotics and a very limited number of plant employees.

After discussing the characteristics likely to be associated with future manufacturing environments, we considered some of the changes that might be made in the data required to meet the information needs of managers of automated factories, especially data relating to minimizing inventory, improving product quality, and minimizing lead times. All of these actions are designed to improve long-term profitability in new manufacturing environments. Finally, we explored some of the possibilities for measuring the extent to which those goals have been achieved.

GLOSSARY OF TERMS INTRODUCED IN THIS CHAPTER

artificial intelligence In manufacturing, machines (robots) that can sense an unaligned state or an improper setting and automatically correct it.

computer-integrated manufacturing (CIM) Completely automated manufacturing, in which the computerized elements of factory automation, such as computer-aided design (CAD) and computer-aided manufacturing (CAM), have been integrated. More recently, CIM has been extended to include people, policies, procedures, information, and business strategy along with technology.

dollar-days A measure of inventory control performance compared to planned inventory; calculated by multiplying the number of days inventory is late (early) by the throughput (cost) that will be realized (incurred early).

fixed automation manufacturing system A conventional assembly line manufacturing system that includes elements of automation—automated equipment that is single-purpose and not adaptable to new (different) uses.

flexible automated manufacturing system A manufacturing system that is completely automated but has flexibility built into it through the medium of alternate computer programs that permit the manufacture of differentiated items in small batches for specific customers or markets.

lead time See *manufacturing lead time* and *total product lead time*.

machine-hour labor rate A concept developed by Alexander Hamilton Church that, in effect, treats the machine as a laborer, with the cost of operating the machine converted to an hourly rate.

manual manufacturing system A manufacturing system in which the line employees are the primary work initiators: work is delivered to production employees at their work stations, where they perform the operations for which they are responsible, after which the products are moved to another work station or to a storage area.

manufacturing lead time The time required to completely produce a product (from the time materials are added until the finished unit is ready for shipment).

manufacturing resource planning (MRP-II)	A planning and control computer program that integrates production and inventory plans into the financial accounting system and permits "What if?" questions of its considerable database.
material requirements planning (MRP)	An automated information system that uses bills of materials, inventory data, and the master production schedule to calculate materials requirements and to generate necessary paperwork.
optimal productior technology (OPT)	Computer software that simulate's the production process so bottlenecks can be spotted before they occur. Its objective is to balance the flow of goods through manufacturing operations.
real time	A computer term; refers to the ability to change data and access new information instantaneously without waiting for batch processing.
synchronous manufacturing	A manufacturing control system that focuses on the key constraints and control points in the plant in order to optimize total system performance (rather than individual subsystem efficiency).
throughput	The extent to which a manufacturing system has generated profit through sales of goods; usually calculated as total sales less materials costs. Where materials represent the only variable cost of production, and sales throughput is equivalent to contribution margin.
total product lead time	The time required to design a product, modify or design equipment, conduct market research, and obtain all necessary materials. *Lead time* begins when a decision has been made to accept an order or produce a new product and ends when production commences.
total quality contro (TQC)	A manufacturing approach whose ultimate goal is zero defects. To achieve this goal, responsibility for quality is placed on the worker (builder of the product) rather than on an inspector.

QUESTIONS FOR CLASS DISCUSSION

22–1 If the present-day cost accounting practices described earlier in this text are likely to change as a result of manufacturing automation, what is the justification for giving so much attention to them? Explain.

22–2 How can improper management accounting practices cause management to make inappropriate operating decisions?

22–3 What is the relationship between global competition and manufacturing automation in the United States?

22–4 What contributions did the following people make to management accounting as we know it today? (a) Charles Babbage, (b) Alexander Hamilton Church, (c) J. Brooks Heckert, (d) David Solomons.

22–5 What special contributions have been made to the development of managerial accounting by H. Thomas Johnson and Robert S. Kaplan?

22–6 What is the difference between a manual manufacturing system and a fixed automated manufacturing system? Explain.

22–7 What is the difference between a fixed automated manufacturing system and a flexible automated manufacturing system? Explain.

22–8 What special problem is associated with the allocation of overhead costs on the basis of some measure of direct labor in an automated manufacturing environment? Discuss.

22–9 What is the cost to the firm of producing a product of inferior quality? Discuss.

22–10 How has the deregulation of service enterprises affected the resource-conversion processes for firms in industries that were previously regulated? Discuss.

22–11 How does the introduction of robotic equipment into the manufacturing process affect the composition of the costs of manufacturing a product?

22–12 Why is the careful monitoring of processing quality especially important in an automated factory?

22–13 What are some of the problems that the management accountant faces in applying capital budgeting techniques to decisions relating to the acquisition of robotic equipment? Explain.

22–14 What is *throughput*?

22–15 What is meant by the term *dollar-days*? How may dollar-days be used in evaluating how well the inventory of a manufacturing firm has been controlled?

PROBLEMS

22–16 **Throughput, Inventory, and Operating Expenses** Foxx Company produces fasteners for the garment industry. Their conventional cost accounting system has accumulated the following information for the past period's activity:

	Beginning-of-Period Inventory (28,000 units)
Raw materials	$2,200
Direct labor	5,600
Overhead	8,960

	Cost of 330,000 Units Produced
Raw materials	$ 26,400
Direct labor	69,300
Overhead	110,900

	Other Costs
Executive office	$25,000
Marketing fees	5,000

	Revenues
Sales (320,000 units)	$345,600
Sales returns (15,000 units)*	(16,200)

*From current production.

Overhead has been estimated as approximately 30% variable and 70% fixed. Foxx uses first-in, first-out to value inventory. The company has been operating at about 75% of capacity, but Foxx has resisted laying off any workers because of the cost of recruiting and training new workers.

REQUIRED:

1. Using the terms as defined in this chapter, calculate (a) throughput, (b) ending inventory, and (c) operating expenses.
2. Calculate operating income for the period (before income taxes).
3. Assuming that assets other than inventory total $457,060, compute Foxx's return on investment. (Ignore taxes.)
4. Treadle Corporation has contacted Foxx with the offer to buy 100,000 fasteners for $35,000 for a special one-time contract order they have received. Should Foxx accept the offer? What would be the effect on net income if they do accept the special order? Discuss.

22–17 **THOUGHT STIMULATION PROBLEM.** This chapter has stressed primarily the rapid changes affecting the manufacturing environment and the critical need for management accounting to keep pace with those changes.

Among other duties, assume that you are responsible for the internal accounting for Snyder Company, a manufacturing firm with three divisions and total sales for the last fiscal year of $70 million. You spend most of your time in your office but check with the users of your reports at least once a year to see if they have any comments or questions.

REQUIRED: Make a list of indicators that your reporting system may be out of date and has not kept pace with users' needs.

Chapter 23

Management Accounting in an Automated or Synchronized Manufacturing Environment[1]

Learning Objectives

When you have finished your study of this chapter, you should

1. Be familiar with the considerations underlying changes to an automated and synchronized manufacturing environments.
2. Be able to relate some of the ideas for adapting management accounting to an automated or synchronized manufacturing environment to the modification of conventional management accounting practices.
3. Be aware of the nature and possible uses of a new cost accounting system.
4. Know what activity-based cost (ABC) accounting is and be familiar with its advantages and disadvantages.

[1]Much of the material in this chapter is drawn from papers presented at an April 1986 seminar sponsored by the National Association of Accountants entitled "Cost Accounting for the '90s—The Challenge of Technological Change." Used with permission.

C hapter 22 discussed the historical background of present-day management accounting practices. Since those practices have not kept pace with technological change in resource-conversion enterprises, management accountants must now critically evaluate conventional cost-accumulation and -allocation procedures and the reports derived therefrom to determine how current practices might be modified to give managers the most useful information for making both strategic and operating decisions.

Forward-thinking managers and management accountants maintain that much of the data provided by existing systems could lead to improper decisions. This would be particularly damaging in today's highly competitive global environment, the result of free foreign trade and the deregulation of many service enterprises. An increasingly competitive environment has prompted many manufacturing firms to automate, to consider automating their production lines, or to otherwise change their manufacturing procedures to improve efficiency. The extent of automation ranges from fixed automation through varying levels of flexible sophistication, including completely flexible computer-integrated manufacturing (CIM) systems. Where automation is not practiced, some firms have redesigned their manufacturing process to emulate an automated environment by synchronizing production to create a smooth flow of goods, via step-wise optimization (for example, see Chapter 19, pages 730–732) and use of the Theory of Constraints (see Chapter 24). In this chapter, we further examine some of the effects automation and synchronization could have on management accounting practices and discuss ideas advanced by progressive management accountants seeking to develop sharper tools for making strategic and operating decisions. In reality, management accountants will be working with firms operating with varying degrees of automation and synchronization. However, to simplify our presentation, we will first discuss some of the changes that may be required for the totally automated or synchronized factory. We shall

1. expand our discussions of the key considerations underlying automation and synchronization introduced in Chapter 22
2. relate some of those ideas to establishing a cost accounting system for an automated or synchronized manufacturing firm
3. consider the development of a new cost accounting system
4. examine activity-based cost (ABC) accounting.

Automation and Synchronization Considerations Expanded

As manufacturing firms in the United States and elsewhere have realized the need for automation, management accountants frequently have been criticized for failing to provide data needed in deciding whether or not to automate, and where automation has occurred, for failing to provide data appropriate for operating decisions. The first criticism pits engineers and managers against management accountants. That is, managers and engineers see an imperative need for extensive investment in automated equipment that the data provided by management accountants often fail to support. The second criticism concerns the usefulness of information, in terms of both relevance and timeliness, for decision making. It raises questions discussed earlier as to whether management accounting has kept pace with changes in the operating environments of manufacturing firms. The lack of relevant cost accounting information also has been noted by firms not yet totally automated (or even significantly automated) but that have redesigned their production processes to emphasize throughput—the synchronous manufacturing firm.[2] The cost accounting problems faced by automated and synchronized manufacturing firms are almost identical. In this section of the chapter, we

- summarize the effects that changes in the operating environment associated with automation or synchronization can bring about
- examine changes in performance measures that incorporate factory automation or synchronization into management accounting systems
- summarize the problems and weaknesses associated with present-day management accounting as observed by H. Thomas Johnson, Robert S. Kaplan, and others in some recent publications.

Effects of Changes in the Operating Environment

Ignoring, for the moment, the shortcomings of present cost accounting systems for manual or fixed automated production systems, let's examine some of the changes that occur as a firm moves toward the flexible automated system described in Chapter 22 (see Borg-Warner example in Chapter 22, page 823). In this environment, computer operated equipment, including robotic workers, process materials. Since the old manufacturing systems were *labor paced* rather than *machine paced* as in an automated factory, much attention historically has been given to direct labor costs and the measurement of efficiency variances. In a machine-paced, completely automated factory, these become unimportant because there is little or no direct labor, as conventionally defined, and the pace of production is determined by the speeds programmed into the robotic equipment.

Another major change involves the nature of plant employees. In a conventional manufacturing plant, operations are divided into departments, with direct laborers working under departmental supervisors. In an automated plant, there are few, if any, such direct laborers. In-

---

[2]This term is frequently attributed to Dr. Eliyahu M. Goldratt, who explains its derivation in a foreword to M. Michael Umble and M. L. Srikauth, *Synchronous Manufacturing: Principles for World Class Excellence* (Cincinnati, Ohio: South Western, 1989).

stead, there is a limited number of highly paid, skilled professionals overseeing the robotic operations. For example, when something goes wrong, industrial engineers concerned with setting up equipment, setting up runs, and monitoring the processes will go into the factory and correct the problem. Obviously, management controls over such employees will have to be considerably different from those historically used in supervising direct laborers.

Plants where production has been synchronized, with the emphasis on throughput, may have departments (or manufacturing cells) with direct laborers, but the laborers will have more responsibilities (for proper use of their time and for monitoring quality, for example). Theoretically, there should be little difference between the work they perform—and the associated reporting—and the work and required reporting for automated equipment.

In Chapter 22, we referred to the problems in allocating overhead costs to provide information useful to management in making pricing and operating decisions. Conventional procedures fail to allocate overhead costs on the basis of the cause of their incurrence. Automated or synchronized plants have significantly different problems associated with the application of overhead. Within such an environment, we can still trace the cost of direct materials to the finished product; however, all other operating costs, based on conventional definitions, would fall into the category of overhead. Since management may want unit direct-cost data, we need to take another look at the procedures for allocating traceable overhead costs to the product in an automated or synchronized manufacturing environment.

Measures of Performance

Measures of performance should be designed to relate performance to the attainment of a firm's goals. Traditionally, we have assumed it was best first to allocate costs to the various departments within a firm and then to reallocate them to the goods produced. Those data were then used to make decisions on departmental performances and sales prices.

Robert Kaplan[3] suggests that these conventional procedures for accumulating and allocating costs may have contributed to manufacturing inefficiencies by causing management to

- misdirect its marketing efforts
- fail to appropriately manage overhead costs
- misplace its emphasis on cost-cutting programs as a way to increase productivity
- use modern, flexible machining systems to produce standard parts in high volume rather than custom parts in small lots
- fail to initiate investments in computer-aided production systems.

[3]See "Yesterday's Accounting Undermines Production," *Harvard Business Review* (March–April 1986), pp. 38–47, and "Must CIM Be Justified by Faith Alone?" *Harvard Business Review* (March–April 1986), pp. 87–95.

Kaplan maintains that today's management cost systems do a miserable job of tracing the actual consumption of indirect or overhead resources to products by using direct labor as a basis for allocating those costs when the costs are not "caused" by direct labor. He further points out that large categories of costs, such as marketing, distribution, and engineering support, may not even be attributed to products or product lines. He believes these allocation weaknesses cause the system to provide misleading targets for management's day-to-day operating decisions. Furthermore, because of those weaknesses, many firms have made inappropriate strategic decisions relating to their operations.

As we seek to identify more useful new measurements, we shall divide management decisions into two categories (1) strategic decisions and (2) operating decisions.

Strategic Decisions. Though management makes **strategic decisions** infrequently, they have great impact on a company's future operations. For example, decisions based on capital budgeting procedures are strategic planning decisions. Since capital budgeting information inevitably works its way into the data on which strategic decisions are based, we need to recall how these data are prepared. As discussed earlier, conventional management accounting uses one or more of the following four techniques in determining whether or not a firm should enter into a proposed investment project:

1. *Accountant's (simple rate of return) method:* We project the anticipated rate of return on the investment by dividing the projected annual net income from the investment by the amount of the required investment.
2. *Pay-back method:* We subtract from the required investment the anticipated periodic cash inflows from the investment to determine how long it will take for the firm to recover its investment. (If the cash flows are constant each year, we simply divide the investment by one annual cash inflow to determine the pay-back period in years.)
3. *Net-present-value method:* The present value of the required investment and other cash outflows is matched against the projected present value of expected cash inflows from the investment to determine whether the investment can be expected to produce a positive net present value (signifying a rate of return greater than the discount rate used to calculate the present values).
4. *Time-adjusted rate-of-return (internal rate-of-return) method:* We determine (by trial and error or by use of a computer program) the *implicit discount rate* based on the investment and the projected cash inflows from the investment, that will yield a projected net present value of exactly zero.

Most forward-thinking managers and management accountants favor use of the net-present-value or time-adjusted rate-of-return method. The problem with these methods, however, centers around quantifying the cash flows associated with benefits, such as customer satisfaction (or demands) or competitive position expected to be realized from the investment, particularly when a firm is considering major investments in automated equipment. Typically, engineers see great advantages from such investments; however, management accountants, considering the investments' readily discernible, quantifiable benefits, often develop analytical data showing that it is unwise to enter into such a venture, at which point, the engineers become frustrated, believing that management accounting fails to provide the appropriate data needed for such decisions.

Accountants have been accused of focusing on costs and ignoring benefits—especially increased revenues that can be generated by a more competitive market position. There are a number of potential benefits of an investment that are not considered in the typical net-present-value analysis. For example, by investing in the equipment required to implement a computer-integrated manufacturing system, the firm should certainly realize a competitive advantage through improved product quality and enhanced customer service. Also, if a competitor invests in automated equipment while we pass up the investment, does the competitor force us out of business? Or, what happens if both of us invest in the equipment? If our net-present-value analysis is to include all considerations associated with such an investment, these and certain other opportunity costs and benefits must be quantified. But how can this be done?

Another problem frequently encountered in making such a strategic decision is the inclination to overlook the so-called *indirect cost reductions*, resulting from such things as inventory reduction made possible by a shortened manufacturing cycle. Again, the problem centers around assigning quantitative values to those indirect benefits. However, if the net-present-value model is to provide management with the information needed to make the appropriate decision, such items should be included in the analysis.

Besides the failure to include difficult-to-quantify items in the analysis, some critics maintain that the accountant's conservative attitude also can lead to the use of excessive discount rates in calculating net present value.[4] The selection of an appropriate discount rate, of course, is a judgmental element of the net-present-value analysis. Traditionally, this rate has been adjusted upward with higher levels of risk, almost assuring a negative result for a highly innovative proposal.

Although we do not have all the answers regarding appropriate data for strategic decisions, there are a few observations we can make:

---

[4]The higher the discount rate, the lower the present value. To illustrate, assume an investment will earn $1,000 a year forever (infinity). If 10% is used, the present value is $1,000 ÷ .1 = $10,000. A 50% increase in the discount rate to 15% lowers the present value to $1,000 ÷ .15 = $6,666.67.

- Management accountants must be able to perceive *all* of the possible advantages of an investment and be willing to work on techniques for quantifying them. Quantification based on estimated data (even if the data must be estimated from conversations with "experts") is better than giving no consideration at all to these difficult, sometimes intangible, items.
- Management accountants must review the justification for discount rates used in the net-present-value model, particularly when they seem to be excessive, and make every effort to arrive at a realistic rate. It might be beneficial to prepare a series of analyses with different discount rates. For example, three reports might be prepared: one using an "optimistic" (low) discount rate, one using a "normal" (average) discount rate, and one using a "pessimistic" (high) discount rate. Alternatively, the opportunity cost of doing nothing should be factored into the analysis.
- Management accountants must recognize that it is not their responsibility to rationalize engineers' wishes for automation. Accountants have a responsibility to objectively evaluate such proposals to avoid encouraging a clearly unjustified investment. Situations in which management has opted for computing equipment with capabilities completely beyond those required reveal the need for independent evaluations for such decisions. Often, the latest such equipment, like the robotic manufacturing equipment now available, is desired by some managers and engineers as "toys" to be experimented with, rather than as verifiably beneficial additions to the firm's assets.

Operating Decisions.   Operating decisions are management decisions relating to the day-to-day operations of a firm, such as coordinating and controlling operations. In conventional manufacturing, such decisions typically are made by the vice-president of production or the production superintendent, with some delegation of decision making to departmental supervisors; for example, the assignment of direct labor employees to specific tasks within the various departments, or the acquisitions of materials and routing of materials through the plant. In the marketing area, corporate managers are required to make pricing decisions. Although prices are determined by supply and demand, managers must still decide how competitive the firm's prices will be. They may, for example, take an aggressive position by pricing below the market in an attempt to secure a larger volume of sales. Closely associated with the pricing decision is the decision regarding which products to emphasize or "push" in the market—presumably, the products the firm believes yield larger contribution margins. This appears to require the determination of the costs of individual products—which brings accountants and managers right back to the cost-allocation issue.[5]

---

[5]Most ardent critics of cost accounting, who claim that physical measures are sufficient and dollar values are not needed at all, fall back to comparative cost-per-unit data to make decisions on product mix. Chapter 24 offers an alternative approach.

Pricing decisions are particularly critical for the firm that manufactures many products. A single-product firm can determine per-unit cost by dividing total manufacturing costs by the number of units produced. For the multiproduct firm, however, the way indirect costs are allocated significantly influences the individual product cost. Therefore, many

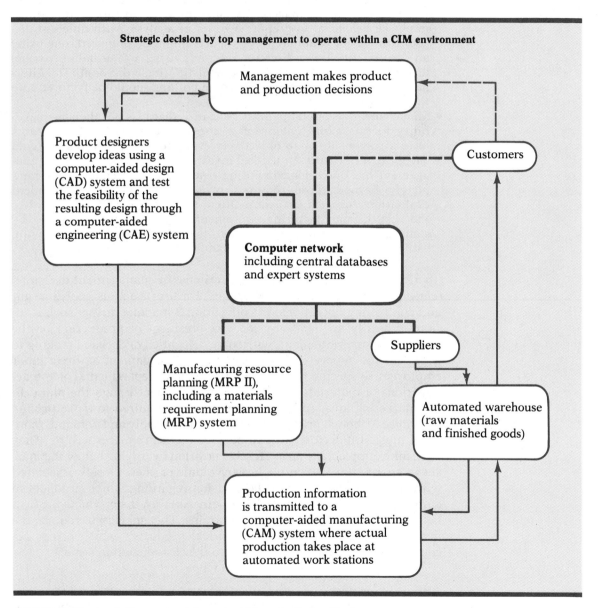

FIGURE 23–1 A Computer-Integrated Manufacturing System

accountants believe management accounting must provide data on full direct cost per unit by allocating costs on the basis of the causes (or drivers) of those costs. This approach has been called activity-based cost (ABC) accounting. We discuss this development further in the final section of this chapter.

Other management decisions that are critical in a computer-integrated manufacturing (CIM) environment include scheduling, appropriateness of various day-to-day costs, utilization of available resources, use of professionally trained engineers within the plant, whether to make or buy parts, and adequacy of performance of divisions. These are in addition to the typical decisions that are required to be made within a conventional manufacturing format. Figure 23–1 depicts a CIM environment.

A synchronous manufacturing firm would be organized exactly as a computer-integrated manufacturing firm, but some portion of design and production would be conducted manually by humans instead of by use of computer software and automated equipment. A large synchronous manufacturing firm would need a computer database and computer programs (MRP II or something similar) to obtain timely information to coordinate production and make appropriate decisions.

The management accounting system of the future should provide different costs for different types of decisions. To produce the most useful information for different decisions, it is clear that a management accounting system *should not be* bound by the requirements of generally accepted accounting practices (GAAP). Johnson and Kaplan and others maintain that we need some determination of full cost per unit of product in order to direct the firm's marketing efforts, and those costs must include expenditures for research and development, engineering, and marketing. We need differential costs in making make-or-buy decisions. We need responsibility related costs to determine whether costs incurred by various segments of the business are appropriate in relation to the work performed. These cost reports can be generated from a centralized computer database such as the one shown in Figure 23–1. The techniques for preparing these reports have been given earlier in this text (see Chapter 17), the only modification being the addition of some nontraditional, logically derived, but difficult-to-quantify data.

Performance Measure for the Factory of the Future

Robert A. Howell talks about four areas of measurement that are important for an automated factory: (1) resource acquisitions, (2) resource utilization, (3) processing performance, and (4) output.

Measurements Relating to Resource Acquisitions. **Resource acquisitions measures** are among the most useful for management accountants in automated factories. Measuring the cost of materials used in the manufacturing process, of course, is important. However, so is measurement of quality, achieved through the monitoring of defective parts acquired from specific vendors. Outlays for the acquisitions of raw materials will be the primary (and sometimes the only) variable cost of finished units in an automated factory. Since robots can handle and process the materials automatically once they are placed in production, it is vital that flaws in direct materials be detected early to eliminate defective manufactured parts. Without question, the cost system of the future must provide good measurements of quality as well as of the costs of incoming materials.

Materials quality controls are vital, even in a less than totally computer-integrated manufacturing environment if manufacturing operations are to be synchronized. In such a low-inventory manufacturing environment, where goods are being "pulled" through the factory (rather than "pushed" by efficient departments or processes), poor-quality materials can stop the entire production line.

Measures of Resource Utilization.   **Resource utilization** is another critical area of measurement in an automated environment. Though just-in-time inventory procedures—where raw materials, work-in-process, and finished-goods inventories effectively are close to zero—may be idealistic, today's manufacturing firms still must do a better job of managing inventories. Inventory can be a cash trap. Carrying excessive inventories is expensive and increases the probability of losses due to obsolescence. The management accounting system of the future, therefore, must measure the amount of inventory held in relation to inventory needs. Raw materials inventories can be reduced by more efficient coordination of deliveries from dependable suppliers. Work-in-process inventories can be reduced by decreasing total processing time (manufacturing or cycle lead time) through reduction of lot (batch) size.[6] Finished-goods inventories can be minimized by decreasing processing time so items may be produced to order. If it is necessary to produce to forecast, finished goods can be minimized with improved forecasts from the marketing division, if possible, or by holding partially completed inventory that can be completed to customer specification in a short period of time. Since the objective is to minimize *excess* inventory, special attention must be given to measuring the extent to which the production schedule has been maintained, including the maintenance of appropriate buffers of inventory at strategic locations, and the extent to which the production of finished units deviates from planned output.

Resource utilization, of course, includes the utilization of equipment (and labor) as well as the appropriate management of materials. Unlike conventional evaluations, where effective utilization means a piece of

---

[6]It is not necessary that the processing batch (the number of units produced from one setup) be reduced as long as the transfer batch (the number of completed units that must accumulate before the units are transferred to the next process) is reduced.

equipment (or laborer) should be constantly producing, equipment in an automated or synchronized plant is considered effectively utilized if it can perform the work required *when* it is demanded. It also includes appropriate management of the professionally trained plant employees needed to monitor and maintain an automated system. The efficient utilization of these employees is particularly important because of the salaries they command. One of the best ways to manage such personnel may be the way professional service organizations, such as public accounting firms, manage their professional personnel: by establishing a hierarchy of relationships, from partners through managers and seniors down to lower staff. That way the more capable people (like the partners) can be assigned the responsibilities most critical to the firm. Evaluations are then made from the partners down. These professionally trained plant employees are in reality "executives" of a totally new genre. Performance evaluation by each supervisor then should be based on the employee's contribution to overall plant performance.

Some measure of the relationship between employee costs and the equipment being monitored also is needed to help judge the effectiveness with which employees have been utilized. For example, if 1 employee is required to monitor 20 machines, that employee's salary should be considered part of the cost of operating the machines. This type of information should also be considered in making equipment replacement decisions.

In factories where laborers work on a product in a synchronous manufacturing environment, what we previously have called *direct* labor generally will be considered indirect and will be evaluated based on whether the workers followed production scheduling orders (including not producing when the schedule calls for them to be idle) and on the operating improvements they have recommended or implemented.

Measures of Processing Performance. In an automated plant, **processing performance measures** include measures of start-up costs, changeover costs, inventory, throughput (output that has been sold), and operating expenses. **Start-up costs** are costs associated with getting a new product on the production line; for example, product design and manufacturing feasibility testing. **Change-over costs**, sometimes called set-up costs, are those costs associated with converting the equipment from the production of one product to the production of another. Since all processing costs in a totally automated manufacturing environment or a synchronous manufacturing environment, including change-over costs, may be considered indirect costs, inventory may consist of the cost of purchased materials only. *Throughput* has come to refer to a "net retail" value rather than a cost measurement. As observed earlier, *throughput* is the amount of sales generated over a period of time less the costs of direct materials included in goods sold. When direct labor and directly variable overhead costs are minimal, as is generally the case in automated factories, this is roughly equivalent to the contribution margin in a conventional direct costing system. *Operating expenses*, including other manufacturing and nonmanufacturing costs, are then matched against throughput to arrive at net operating income. Observe that throughput is *not* measured in terms of production. It reflects the *sales* realized from production. These measures emphasize a global approach to measuring processing performance rather than a local, piecemeal approach.

Measures of Output Performance. Because scheduling is so important in an automated or synchronous plant, management accountants need to develop **output measures** indicating the extent to which a company has met its delivery schedules. At the final stage of production, this can be expressed in terms of the percentage of jobs that go out on time, along with information about the quantity of back orders. At earlier stages in production, output should be measured in terms of compliance with production schedules. There should also be measures showing the relationship between the actual and targeted amounts of output. Output also can be measured in terms of the throughput measure discussed earlier.

Measures of departmental output should be included in overall performance evaluation reports. Each department or division should be evaluated on how well its production schedules have been met. It should be expected to turn out the production scheduled for it. However, if a department is scheduled to be idle for a period of time, production during that period should be considered a deviation from schedule and treated as unfavorable performance.

The Cost Accounting System of the Future

Current accounting literature usually recommends one of two ways for management accounting systems to accommodate the new operating environment: (1) a new system or (2) a modification of a present system.

New System

Robert A. Howell is one of the advocates of a totally new system for management accounting. He suggests, for example, that such things as standard costing should be discarded, that overhead absorption (allocation) will become more obviously irrelevant, and that *full cost* as conventionally defined will be meaningless. He believes that product costs—that is, manufacturing cost or inventory cost—won't be important. According to him, virtually everything the cost accountant currently relies on and is paid for doing should be eliminated. Instead of being concerned with developing traditional cost accounting data, the new system should focus on business strategy and policy. It should measure data regarding resources the firm acquires, how those resources are utilized, processing performance, and output.

In measuring the resources a firm uses, he maintains, it will be especially important to include vendor-monitoring systems that tell who one's vendors are, what they are delivering, whether delivered materials meet specifications, and whether they are being delivered on time. In an automated manufacturing environment, he stresses it is especially important for the firm to be certain that the right quality materials are being fed into processing. As we noted earlier, this emphasis on materials quality is vital for synchronous manufacturing firms, too.

For dealing with resource utilization, Howell would have the management accounting system indicate the efficiency with which the firm is managing its inventories, with the objective of keeping them as close to zero as possible. Basically, this would require a very good system of forecasting market demand for products whose production time is greater than the time customers are willing to wait for delivery, coupled with very precise scheduling of production. He suggests that the system will need to provide management with knowledge of inventory levels on virtually a real-time (instantaneous) basis. Also because it is important to closely monitor scrap and defective parts in managing inventory, the system should provide timely disclosures of such information so corrections can be implemented before the associated losses become significant.

Professionally trained employees responsible for setting up equipment, setting up runs, monitoring processing, and so forth will have to be properly managed if they are to be utilized effectively. Because such people become much more valuable as they gain experience working with the firm, some measure of personnel turnover is needed. To assist the managing of these people, Howell suggests, a manufacturing firm should create a hierarchy of personnel, such as that typically found in a professional accounting firm, so the best people get assigned to the most critical positions. It is also valuable to keep records of what these professional people are working on so the firm can put their time to the most effective use.

As for equipment utilization, Howell suggests we think of the factory as a big box, with the firm's capability represented by the configuration of pieces of equipment available to it. It can take raw materials into one end of the box and produce finished goods out the other end. The extent of that capability must be determined and then used for decision purposes, such as helping management decide whether particular marketing demands can be met. (Today, a great many firms do not even know the exact capacity of their plants.) He maintains that the performance of individual pieces of equipment must be measured and made available to management. He calls these **equipment performance records**.

With expensive equipment, a preventive maintenance program must be followed and the extent to which this is being done should be indicated in a *repair and maintenance record*.

For measuring processing performance, Howell places particular emphasis on maintaining records of start-ups and changeovers to improve the efficiencies with which they are carried out. He also recommends measuring **throughput speed** (how long it takes a product to get through the manufacturing process and be sold).

Output measures are Howell's final measures to help management monitor and control business strategy and policy in an automated firm. These reports would evaluate how well the company has been meeting its delivery schedules, including the percentage of the jobs that go out on time. They should show the extent to which the firm has met the production targets set at the beginning of each period.

Howell's basic philosophy in proposing such a radical new system is expressed in his own words as follows:

> I don't believe that you make money by concentrating on money in the first place. The right combination of customers, productive capability, and products will maximize your cash flows as well as the return on your invested capital. Your job as a management accountant is to help your managers find the combination. I don't think you do it exclusively through the cost accounting system. I think you do it to a much greater extent by getting out into the factories, understanding what's going on operationally, and contributing to the operational management of your business.

In essence, Howell is advocating that management accountants focus on the processes and the reporting required to monitor those processes rather than on conventional cost determination.

The authors of this text agree with Howell that cost accounting must be viewed from the user's perspective. His comments are only theoretical, however, and we will need specific procedures to be able to implement a new system. However, we believe that Eliyahu Goldratt, of the Goldratt Institute, has developed the framework for a management philosophy that will ultimately identify the internal information requirements of all firms. In Chapter 24, we discuss that new management philosophy, the *Theory of Constraints*, and suggest the accounting procedures that might be followed in providing the information required by management.

Modification of Present System

Some forward-thinking managers and management accountants suggest that appropriate modifications to the present system would eliminate the observed weaknesses and meet the needs of an automated or synchronous manufacturing environment. As Allen H. Seed, III, has stated, "I do think that the solutions to the problems that we have to face can be done within the framework of the system, rather than throwing the baby out with the bath." Accountants taking this position try to develop solutions to the problems we have already discussed, primarily the weaknesses associated with present methods of allocating costs.

Steven M. Hronec suggests that one of the underlying difficulties is an excessive use of cost allocation when we should be attributing costs to products *directly*, if at all possible. This means we should look for cause-and-effect relationships between specific items of cost and the products or services being produced so that, as far as possible, costs will be attributed directly to products rather than be allocated to them. Recently, the term "cost driver" has been used to refer to what has caused a cost to be increased. The products that cause or "drive" the incurrence of specific costs should be identified so that those costs can be attributed directly to the products.

Since automated firms have little in the way of direct labor, as conventionally defined, and firms following synchronous manufacturing procedures may well categorize their direct laborers as indirect laborers, we can divide the total costs of operating an automated or synchronized factory into two categories, *direct materials* and *conversion costs*, rather than the three categories (direct materials, direct labor, and overhead) conventionally used in present-day cost accounting. Direct materials costs easily can be attributed to the products being produced. We can then subdivide conversion costs into *directly attributable (traceable) costs* and *indirect costs* that must be allocated to products, as diagrammed in Figure 23–2.

Since there is no problem attributing direct materials costs to individual products, we need to distinguish between those conversion costs driven by (attributed to) specific products and those we are forced to allocate to products on the best basis available, in order to arrive at a total cost per unit. Allen Seed, in a paper entitled "Cost Accounting in the Age of Robotics," has suggested we use the term *direct* to designate attributable costs and characterize costs that cannot be attributed to products as 'indirect." He then compares various types of costs based on that distinction for a man-paced environment versus a machine-paced (or synchronous) environment (see Figure 23–3). Robert Kaplan further suggests that set-up costs (not shown in Figure 23–3) also can be attributed to individual products. Obviously, the objective in accounting for costs in this way is to attribute as many conversion costs as possible to the individual products on the basis of the activity performed and then look for the most appropriate basis to use in allocating the indirect (nonattributable) costs to the product.

If indirect (nonattributable) costs are machine driven rather than labor driven, it seems appropriate to allocate them on the basis of machine costs, size, or use. Seed suggests that computer-integrated manufacturing should reduce total conversion costs (primarily because of reduced labor costs) and presents what he considers a typical situation

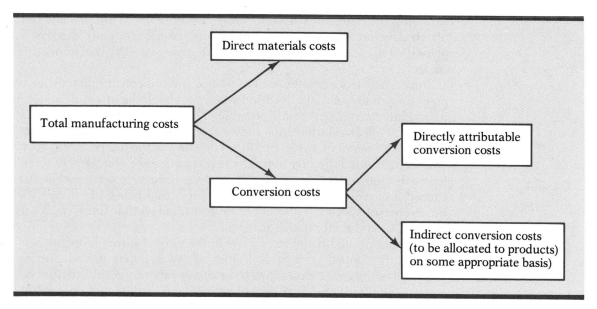

FIGURE 23–2 Categories of Manufacturing Costs

	Man-Paced Environment	Machine-Paced or Synchronous Environment
Direct labor	Direct	Direct
Material-handling labor	Direct	Eliminated
Quality-control labor	Direct	Direct
Direct repairs and maintenance	Direct	Direct
Overtime premium	Direct	Direct
Payroll taxes and benefits	Direct	Direct
Energy	Direct	Direct
Operating supplies	Direct	Direct
Supervision	Indirect	Indirect
Production support services	Indirect	Largely indirect
Building occupancy	Indirect	Indirect
Insurance and taxes	Indirect	Direct
Depreciation	Indirect	Direct

FIGURE 23–3 Direct and Indirect Conversion Costs

(see Figure 23–4). Since machine-hours may be used as the basis for allocating indirect conversion costs in a machine-paced or synchronous environment, we could remove from total conversion costs those costs directly attributable to (driven by) the product and attach them directly to products. We would then have to allocate, on the basis of a cost per machine-hour (or some other activity), only those conversion costs not directly attributable to products. However, even here we may refine our allocation to the use of more than one basis. For example, space occupancy costs may be allocated to individual machines on the basis of space occupied by each machine (and this cost can be passed on to products based on individual machine times used in producing them). Also, set-up costs may be allocated on a "transaction" basis, whereby the number of set-ups and the hours required to perform them can be used as a basis for allocating set-up costs to machines and thence to products (based on the number of units processed by the machines). If these procedures are followed, we could value both work-in-process and finished-goods inventories on the basis of either generally acceptable full cost or only directly attributable costs.

Another approach to inventory valuation for decision purposes would be to distinguish between those costs that clearly add value to the product and those judged to add no value. The former costs would be allocated to the product, while the latter costs would be expensed as period costs. Hronec demonstrates that distinction by listing materials-handling cost as an example of a non-value-added cost. For example, the movements of inventory in and out of stores add nothing directly to the value of the product and therefore would not be allocated to the

	Man-Paced Environment	Machine-Paced or Synchronous Environment
Labor	$ 5,000	$ 500
Overhead	9,000	11,100
Total conversion cost	$14,000	$11,600
Standard man-hours	1,000	
Cost per standard man-hour	$14.00	
Engineered machine-center-hours		100
Cost per machine-center-hour		$116.00

FIGURE 23–4 Conversion Costs (CIM reduces conversion costs and changes basis of calculation)

product. At the same time, management periodically should be aware of the amounts of such costs. If the system reports costs that way, attention will be drawn to the non-value-added costs, which in turn should stimulate management to try to decrease such costs to help eliminate manufacturing inefficiencies.

If we add to the modifications already discussed Howell's measure of resources used, resource utilization, processing performance, and output, we might achieve a more useful cost accounting system for an automated resource-conversion environment. Then, all that management accountants would need to do is indentify and quantify some of the opportunity costs associated with automation decisions and critically evaluate the imputed discount rates used in net-present-value models prepared to help make those decisions. These are not trivial tasks, however, and may be extremely difficult to achieve.

A frequently suggested modification to present cost systems is some variation of an activity-based cost (ABC) accounting system. While many firms are implementing such systems, it has not yet been established that such systems can deliver desired results.

Activity-Based Cost Accounting

Some leading accounting researchers (including Robert Kaplan, H. T. Johnson, Robin Cooper, Peter Turney, and George Foster, among others) have proposed a solution to the problem of the lack of relevant cost data for internal management use that involves the complete revision of the way overhead is allocated to products, but that also preserves most of the elements of current cost procedures. That is, total manufacturing costs (raw materials, direct labor, and overhead) are assigned to products, and the resulting cost per unit then can be used for financial statement purposes or for internal decision making.

The two major objectives of an activity-based cost system are (1) to provide detailed information that describes the range, cost, and consumption of operating activities in the entire manufacturing organization and (2) to provide accurate cost information to managers to improve their decisions.

The simple one- and two-product systems illustrated earlier in this text are not representative of many manufacturing firms today. Because product life cycles are continually decreasing, and most firms face an increasing need to differentiate products for segmented markets, it is not unusual now for firms to produce hundreds (or thousands) of products. Traditional cost systems use fairly simplistic procedures to allocate overhead to those products based on labor, machine-hours, or some other volume measure (such as raw material content) that permeates all parts of the factory. Even though multiple allocations may be made (for example, one overhead rate for each department), little effort has been made to logically trace the incurrence of specific overhead dollars to their cause(s). The result is that huge amounts of various overhead dollars are allocated rather arbitrarily to different products. Resulting product costs universally are recognized as *inaccurate* and are not useful in encouraging appropriate improvements in design, process, or quality and do not provide information that encourages the best (from the standpoint of the company as a whole) short-term and long-term investment and marketing decisions.

 Activity-based costing, which attempts to treat costs as *direct* rather than *indirect*, has been designed for multiple-product firms that desire *accurate* unit product costs. This method tries to trace the cost of each activity (such as purchasing, receiving, disbursing, set-ups, production reorganizations, engineering product and process improvements, inspections, and so forth) to the product on whose behalf the activity was incurred. It is designed to eliminate cross-subsidies between products. For example, if one product is produced in small batches while another is produced in large batches, activity-based costing might use this lot size information (activity) to determine the allocation of set-up costs.

To demonstrate, assume a company has only two products, X and Y, and has accumulated the following information relating to set-up costs:

	Product X	Product Y	Total
Total units produced	100	10,000	
Batch size	10	500	
Number of set-ups	10	20	
Cost per set-up*	$1,000	$1,000	
Total set-up cost	$10,000	$20,000	$30,000

*Set-up crew expense ÷ 50 (average set-ups per period)

A traditional cost system normally would allocate the total set-up cost, along with all other *overhead* items, on the basis of direct labor hours. If we assume that each unit of product X or Y requires 2 hours of direct labor, we would calculate this part of the traditional overhead application rate based on labor as shown below:

	Product X	Product Y	Total
Direct labor hours per unit	2	2	
Total units produced	100	10,000	
Total direct labor (DL) hours	200	20,000	20,200

Traditional overhead rate $\dfrac{\$30,000}{20,200} = \$1.4851485$ per DL hour

Therefore, overhead cost per unit for set-up costs under each method would be

	Product X	Product Y
Activity-based overhead per unit:		
$\left(\dfrac{\$10,000}{100}\right)$	$100.00	
$\left(\dfrac{\$20,000}{10,000}\right)$		$2.00
Traditional overhead per unit		
($1.4851485 × 2 DL hours)	$ 2.9703	$2.9703

It is obvious that the total cost of product X would be changed significantly if activity-based instead of traditional overhead allocation procedures are used. Because overhead frequently is such a large percentage of total product cost ($\geq$ 40% in some industries), the approximate $1.00 change in product Y's overhead cost also might be significant relative to the total product cost. If this firm uses total product cost to make decisions on pricing or accepting special orders, or a host of other actions, a traditional cost system could give them totally misleading information.

Thus, the activity-based cost system aims to provide a more detailed *tracking* of costs incurred. Each *activity* of a company, administrative as well as manufacturing, would be allocated on some rational basis to the product that caused the activity to occur. For example, the cost of purchasing activities might be allocated on the basis of the number of unique part numbers ordered, resulting in a larger allocation to complex products with a large number of parts. This allocation would encourage design engineers to use standardized parts and simplified product designs, both of which would ease product manufacture and reduce lead time. Therefore, the first objective of activity-based cost accounting (to provide detailed information about operating activities throughout the manufacturing organization) could be achieved.

Implementing an activity-based cost accounting system would require product *routings* through administrative and service areas and perhaps *bills of materials* as well. This information, which generally has been available for manufacturing activities for a long time, is needed to analyze the requirements of products over their entire life cycle. For most companies, this is not a minor task, but it can be accomplished.

Because activity-based cost accounting retains a full absorption *cost* orientation, though, we do not believe it will provide the most useful information to managers for operating decisions. For example, suppose product X in the earlier example has raw materials costs of $400, labor costs of $100, and total activity-based overhead of $300, and normally sells for $1,200. A new customer offers to buy 20 units for $650; this sale won't affect regular sales. Should the offer be accepted? The more accurate total cost of $800 ($400 + $100 + $300) will not be useful in making this decision. The manager would need information on capacity (labor capacity[7] as well as overhead capacity), any changes in requirements for critical resources caused by this order, and out-of-pocket costs for the additional 20 units to make an appropriate decision.

If an operating decision concerning batch size were to be made—for example, decreasing the batch size of product Y from 500 to 250— would the more accurate set-up cost and total product cost be helpful? The total set-up cost under the old batch size was $20,000. Under the new batch size, the total set-up cost will be $40,000 (10,000 ÷ 250 = 40; 40 × $1,000 = $40,000, or, since the batch size has been cut in half, twice the original set-up cost), and the unit set-up cost will increase by $2 (from $2 to $4). This more *accurate* information, however, would not assist the manager in making this decision. The manager would need information on the capacity of this machine, the capacity of the set-up crew (there probably would be excess capacity since the cost of the set-up crew is based on 50 set-ups and only 30 are being used), the impact on inventory (the work-in-process inventory of product Y might be expected to decrease by 50%), and the effect on manufacturing lead time and the total throughput of the firm.

For strategic decisions, such as whether to enter a foreign market, detailed full absorption cost information also can be misleading. The illustrative problem in Chapter 19 shows this. The data for that problem are repeated below.

A firm produces two products, P and Q, which are sold for $90 and $100, respectively. The market potential (demand) for P is 100 units per week, and the market potential for Q is 50 units per week. The firm can manufacture any combination of products P and Q.

The production process of both products P and Q is illustrated in Figure 23–5. Raw material unit costs are shown where they enter the production process.

Total production time required for P is 55 minutes (15 minutes in Department A, 15 minutes in Department B, 15 minutes in Department C, and 10 minutes in Department D). Total production time for Q is 50 minutes (10 minutes in Department A, 30 minutes in Department B, 5 minutes in Department C, and 5 minutes in Department D).

The firm has 4 production workers: 1 each in Departments A, B, C, and D. Each employee works an 8-hour shift each day, 5 days a week. Therefore, each worker is available 2,400 minutes per week. In each department, the worker can be assigned to work on the units going into product P or the units going into product Q (any combination as long as the maximum of 2,400 minutes is not exceeded). All labor and over-

---

[7]The current work force, for example, may be able to process the additional order without the necessity of hiring new workers.

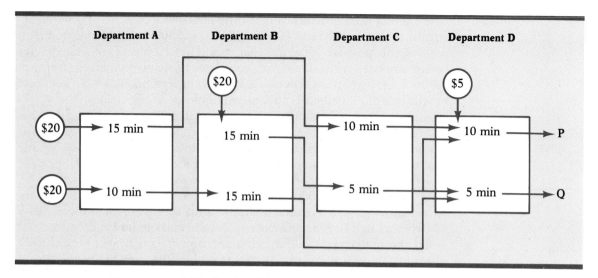

FIGURE 23–5 Departmental Production Process for Illustrative Problem (Chapter 19)

head are considered fixed costs. Materials are the only variable costs of production.

The process flow of products P and Q (the way engineers typically interpret the system) is depicted in Figure 23–6. It shows the same situation as the original diagram but instead is organized by parts, as they logically flow into the final product, rather than by departments.

The most common way to approach strategic decisions, in this situation, is to calculate the total cost and total profit for each product. Assuming the company has an activity-based accounting system, the biggest problem of arbitrary overhead allocation will be alleviated. For example, traditional cost systems would result in the following analysis:

Traditional Cost Accounting Analysis

	Product P	Product Q
Selling price	$90.00	$100.00
Costs		
Raw material	45.00	40.00
Labor (@$8/hr.*)	7.33	6.67
Overhead (@250% of labor*)	18.33	$16.67
Net profit	$19.34	$ 36.66

*assumed

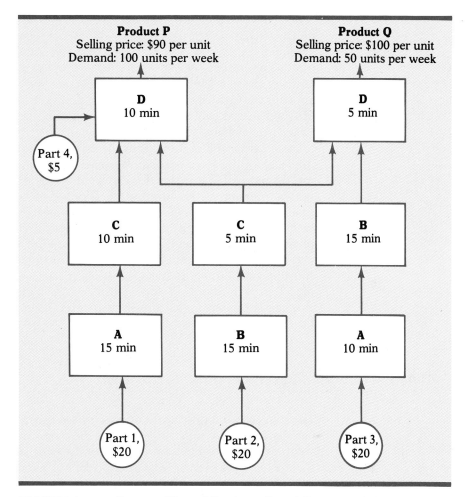

FIGURE 23–6 Process Flow of Products P and Q

Thus, product Q appears to be the more profitable. However, from the solution in Chapter 19, we know that, given current capacity, product P is the better product to emphasize. But, with the addition of one worker in Department B and additional demand in a foreign market, the most desirable product then becomes Q. If we were to trace each overhead cost, rather than allocating it on the basis of labor, we undoubtedly would have more *accurate* costs (in terms of tracing each cost to the product for which it was incurred) and would come up with some net profit for each product. This information, however, would not help us make strategic decisions relating to product mix and markets unless the overhead costs (and labor) were totally variable (in the *possibly unknown* time frame of the decision) and could be eliminated immediately if so required by our new decisions.

Activity-based costing allows us to trace the incurrence of costs to products that *caused* those costs to be incurred. Most decisions, though, are made in the context of an established resource base. It does not matter precisely why we acquired the resources, but rather how we can best use those resources. In all fairness, activity-based cost accounting appears to work beautifully if used before any resources are acquired. After an initial acquisition, though, resource interactions must be inserted into the analysis.

Thus, while the first objective of activity-based cost accounting definitely is fulfilled, the second objective is questionable. We do not need more precise information for external financial statements; we need better information for internal decisions. Since the decision to implement an activity-based cost system costs money, its usefulness should be carefully evaluated before it is installed. Perhaps the first objective of providing more detailed information could be fulfilled better, on a nondollar basis, by engineers, who are accustomed to documenting routings and bills of materials, rather than accountants. Furthermore, direct costing data that appear to be more useful for decision making can easily be converted to full absorption costs for external reporting purposes (see Chapter 14).

Automated Accounting/Data Information System

The suggested modifications of present cost accounting systems depend heavily on the availability and use of computers. Since the pace of technological development assures that the demand for most products will be heaviest in their introduction and growth stages, with few products maintaining a high demand in their mature stages, the revision of traditional cost accounting should give appropriate recognition of those stages. Relevant data must be developed early in the life of a product and must be available without delay when needed. This requires close cooperation between engineers and accountants.

An **automated accounting/data information system** could be developed that would make use of an extensive database, including projected data for such things as the cost per unit for various direct materials, time required for processing a unit through each of the various possible operations that the factory is capable of performing, elements of start-up costs for a product, and elements of changeover costs. These data could then be called up on a computer screen, along with some measures of current capacity utilization,[8] in the format and frequency de-

---

[8]At a minimum, physical measures of practical capacity, planned capacity, and actual work center loadings, along with estimated operating expenses at various levels of capacity, would be required to evaluate capacity utilization and estimate the impact of a proposed change.

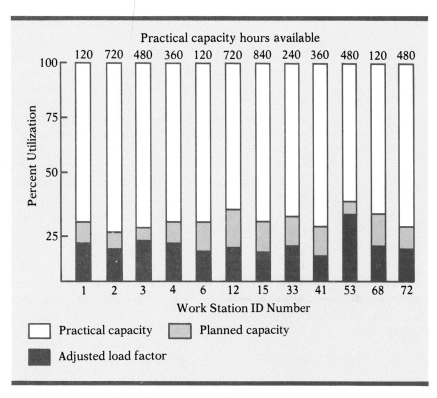

FIGURE 23–7 Work-Station Labor Capacities

sired for use in planning and controlling operations, and in making short-term and long-term decisions. An example of an on-line capacity utilization report is shown in Figure 23–7.

SUMMARY

In this chapter, we have presented some of the current thinking about changes in management accounting practices that might adapt them to an automated resource-conversion environment or a synchronous manufacturing environment. We began by reviewing some of the key considerations involved in automating manufacturing operations. We discussed changes in the ways things are done and some possible performance measures for reporting on the operations of an automated plant. We then noted some of the weaknesses that forward-thinking managers and accountants believe exist in present-day management accounting systems.

Next, we summarized some of the ideas for creating a management accounting system more appropriate for an automated or synchronous manufacturing environment, dividing them into those that involve the development of a completely new system designed primarily to help management make strategic and policy decisions and those that accommodate the new technology by modifying the present system.

Activity-based cost accounting, as currently developed, was examined and evaluated. While we feel that the more detailed information will be useful, we believe that activity-based cost accounting will not provide the information that would be most useful for decision-making purposes.

Finally, we proposed use of an automated cost accounting system that would work from an extensive database of predetermined costs and other manufacturing data. The organization of information in this manner would permit flexibility in designing either unique or repetitive reports as needed.

GLOSSARY OF TERMS INTRODUCED IN THIS CHAPTER

activity-based costing	A cost accumulation and allocation system that traces costs to products according to the activities performed on them; intended to provide cost information for strategic, design, and operational control decisions.
automated cost accounting system	A cost accounting system with an extensive database, including projected cost data for various direct materials, processing operations, start-up costs, and elements of change-over costs that can be called up to project the costs to be incurred in the production of various products.
change-over costs	The costs associated with changing from the production of one product to the production of another. Such costs are found both in an automated manufacturing environment and in a nonautomated environment.
cost driver	The item or activity that causes the incurrence of a specific cost.
equipment performance records	Records evaluating the performance of individual pieces of equipment within an automated manufacturing environment.
output measures	The extent to which a company has met its delivery schedules; should disclose the relationships between actual and targeted amounts, to call attention both to a failure to produce goods as needed and to the failure of equipment (and labor) to be idle when it is scheduled to be idle.
processing performance	Measures of start-up costs, change-over costs, inventory, and throughput in an automated manufacturing environment.
resource acquisitions measurements	Measures of the cost and quality of resources, primarily materials acquired for the production process.
resource utilization measure	Measure of the amount of inventory held in relation to the needs for inventory; the extent to which the production of finished units deviates

from sales or production forecasts within an automated or synchronous manufacturing environment.

start-up costs   The costs associated with getting a new product on the production line, including the costs of designing the product and testing its manufacturing feasibility. All costs incurred during the total product lead time (see Chapter 22 glossary).

strategic decisions   Policy-setting decisions management makes infrequently but that have a great impact on the future operations of a company—for example, the decision to implement a total quality control (TQC) system or the decision to operate in a JIT manufacturing environment.

throughput speed   The length of time it takes a product to move through the manufacturing process and be sold; equal to manufacturing lead time (see Chapter 22 glossary) plus the time to sell and deliver (ship) the product.

QUESTIONS FOR CLASS DISCUSSION

23—1   What has been the relationship between our free foreign trade policy and manufacturing automation?

23—2   What has been the relationship between the deregulation of certain service industries and automation of the functions carried out by enterprises in those industries?

23—3   What is a computer-integrated manufacturing (CIM) system?

23—4   How can the attitudes of production engineers influence management accounting practices? Is such influence appropriate? Discuss.

23—5   How does the nature of plant employees change with the installation of robotic equipment?

23—6   How does the nature of plant employees change with the decision to operate a synchronous plant that "pulls" products through the factory?

23—7   What special problem is encountered in allocating overhead costs in an automated manufacturing environment? Discuss.

23—8   What are some of the measures of performance that may be especially important in a computer-integrated manufacturing environment? Explain.

23—9   What are some of the special problems encountered in applying capital budgeting techniques to decisions regarding the installation of robotic equipment? Discuss.

23—10   What elements of capital budgeting require special attention when developing data for the strategic decisions associated with manufacturing automation?

23–11   Are generally accepted accounting practices helpful in determining the appropriate management accounting practices for automated resource-conversion activities? Discuss.

23–12   Why is it particularly important to monitor the quality of incoming materials that are to be used in an automated or synchronous factory? Discuss.

23–13   What are some valuable measures of processing performance in a cost accounting system for an automated factory?

23–14   What are some measures of output that may be useful in the management of an automated or synchronous factory?

23–15   What two general positions have been taken regarding the establishment of appropriate management accounting practices for automated or synchronous factories? Discuss.

23–16   Will automated factories be likely to have direct laborers such as those found in today's more conventional factories? What effect is this likely to have on the allocation of overhead costs to products?

23–17   Compare accounting for the direct labor performed in a synchronous factory with the accounting treatment of direct labor in a conventional factory.

23–18   What is the difference between attributed costs and allocated costs? Explain.

23–19   What are some of the characteristics that might be incorporated into an automated cost accounting system? Discuss.

EXERCISES

23–20   **Activity-Based Cost Drivers** Listed below are several activities that are considered indirect (overhead) items under traditional cost systems but which would be traced to products under new activity-based systems.
  a. purchase of raw materials
  b. hiring new personnel
  c. engineering time spent on design changes
  d. precision testing required for certain high-performance products

REQUIRED:

For each activity,

  1. Describe the *driver* of the activity (the reason or reasons the activity is being performed).
  2. Propose how the cost of the activity ultimately might be allocated to products produced.

23–21   **Activity-Based Cost System** A basic assumption of activity-based costing is that activities consume resources and products consume activities.

Listed below are several activities that are considered indirect (overhead) items under traditional cost systems.

a. special maintenance required for a new NCX machine
b. set-ups
c. engineering time spent on process changes
d. depreciation on special-purpose equipment

REQUIRED: Assuming that more than one product is consuming the activities listed above, how might these costs of the activities be allocated to products?

23–22 Activity-Based Cost Procedures Given the following information on set-ups, compute (a) traditional set-up overhead per unit and (b) activity-based set-up overhead per unit.

	Product A	Product B
Total units produced	1,000	9,000
Batch size	100	100
Cost per set-up	$750	$500
Direct labor hours per unit	3	3

22–23 Activity-Based Cost Procedures Given the following information on engineering changes, compute (a) traditional engineering change overhead per unit and (b) activity-based engineering change overhead per unit.

	Product C	Product D
Total units produced	10,000	5,000
Cost per engineering change	$800	$800
Number of engineering changes	5	25
Direct labor hours per unit	3	2

PROBLEM

23–24 Activity-Based Cost Procedures Action Industries produces instruments used to measure various pressures in enclosed systems. These instruments are used in a variety of applications ranging from pipeline systems to nuclear reactors. The instruments intended for nuclear reactors must undergo several unique procedures and are subjected to much more rigorous and expensive testing than the instruments designed to be sold for other industrial uses. The nuclear testing area is manned by one skilled engineer, who monitors the testing equipment, and two workers who actually perform the tests. Normal testing is performed mechanically with random samples of the machine-inspected units personally inspected by a trained engineer.

All instrument testing has been considered an overhead item under Action Industries traditional cost system. Inasmuch as the instruments intended for nuclear reactors must undergo the special testing as well as the regular inspections given to units intended for other markets, Action has decided to separate the inspection activity into two divisions, normal and nuclear.

An administrative assistant has gathered the following annual information concerning the inspection activity:

	Inspection Costs			
	Common Mechanical Inspection	**Nuclear Instrument Inspection**	**Other Instrument Inspection**	**Other Overhead Costs**
Depreciation of equipment	$12,000	$ 19,500	—	
Maintenance of equipment	$ 5,000	$ 4,800	—	
Wages	—	$115,000*	$32,000	
Space (% of total area of 25,000 sq ft)	1%	2%	—	
Depreciation and maintenance of building				$140,000
Personnel department**				$ 80,000

*The engineer spends 75% of his total employment time performing other activities and the two workers spend 75% of their time doing other things. All these other activities are classified as indirect.

**There are approximately 90 workers total. Each area has about the same employee turnover rate.

Other than inspection, the labor required to produce a nuclear reactor instrument averages 15 hours while the labor required to make a regular instrument averages 5 hours. During the past two years, 20% of Action Industries's total foreign and domestic sales have been to nuclear reactor operators and 80% have been to all other industrial users. In the coming year, Action expects to achieve a total sales volume of 24,000 units.

REQUIRED:

1. Compute the total labor hours that Action Industries will budget for the coming year.
2. Assuming Action uses a traditional cost system, calculate (a) the overhead rate (based on labor) they would use and (b) the total overhead cost per unit.
3. Assuming Action Industries desires to use activity-based cost procedures, calculate (a) the total overhead associated with the inspection of each type of instrument (nuclear and normal) and (b) the total overhead cost per unit.
4. Action Industries is preparing to respond to a request for bids on the complete instrumentation for 2 nuclear reactors for the government of France. Assuming Action has implemented a complete activity-based cost system throughout the company, will they need any additional internal information to prepare a competitive bid?

Chapter 24

Management Accounting and the Theory of Constraints[1]

Learning Objectives

When you have finished your study of this chapter, you should

1. Understand the logic underlying the Theory of Constraints.
2. Know how to relate the decision-making process to the management of constraints.
3. Be familiar with some of the accounting measures that can be helpful to managers embracing the Theory of Constraints.
4. Understand how operating practices can affect externally imposed constraints.
5. Know the basic procedures for accumulating and allocating costs in a constraint-management environment.

[1]Much of the material in this chapter has been adapted from a seminar developed by Dr. Eliyahu M. Goldratt and presented by the Avraham Y. Goldratt Institute of New Haven, Connecticut, entitled "Executive Decision Making." Used with permission.

Once managers realized that their old management and accounting procedures were contributing to a poor international competitive position, they began a frantic search for new methods. Three new dominant management philosophies have emerged from this search: (1) *total quality management* (TQM), (2) *just in time* (JIT), and (3) *Theory of Constraints* (TOC). While their specific techniques differ, all three offer improvements on conventional management practices. *Total quality management* focuses on quality but uses it to create improvements throughout the entire firm. In reality, TQM is a management philosophy. *Just in time*, while it focuses on inventory, is not just an inventory reduction method (even though many imperfect copies of techniques developed by the Japanese have assumed this); it is a way to create ongoing improvements. JIT is also a management philosophy. Similarly, the *Theory of Constraints* offers a way to deal with production bottlenecks, but it is far more than a program to synchronize production. TOC is a management philosophy that focuses attention on ongoing improvement in all operations.

Management and management (cost) accounting are in a state of dramatic change with competing programs and philosophies. The benefits of TQM and JIT, however, can be realized while applying the Theory of Constraints. In addition, TOC offers global measures that can be tracked at the local level and lends itself to the development of new measurements in a firm's management accounting system. Because we feel that TQM and JIT, while they admittedly can result in ongoing improvements, can be encompassed within the Theory of Constraints, we have decided to concentrate our attention in this chapter on TOC.

Chapters 3, 22, and 23 described the changes in our manufacturing environment resulting from global competition and the use of robotic equipment. This altered environment has led management to try to maximize throughput while minimizing inventory and controlling operating expenses (rather than controlling unit costs), as a means of maximizing long-term net income and return on investment. These changes in management objectives have been instrumental in creating a new management philosophy that has shifted its emphasis from controlling departmental costs per unit to *identifying and managing operating constraints*. This new philosophy is based on what is known as the **Theory of Constraints** (TOC). This theory postulates that there are identifiable constraints associated with the operation of any business and that management should exercise control over operations by identifying these constraints and managing them so as to use most effectively the resources associated with them. We mentioned the Theory of Constraints in Chapter 19 when we illustrated its use in decision making, but did not stress its power.

In this chapter, we analyze and illustrate this new approach to management and suggest accounting measures that managers adopting the new philosophy will need. We shall

1. examine the logic underlying the Theory of Constraints
2. describe the decision-making process followed in managing constraints
3. suggest accounting measures helpful to managers embracing this new management philosophy
4. explore new measures for evaluating local performance
5. consider how some operational practices might affect externally imposed constraints
6. illustrate the procedures for accumulating and allocating cost and revenue data in this operating environment.

The Logic Underlying the Theory of Constraints (TOC)

Because businesses are financed by owners (stockholders in the case of corporations) primarily to realize returns (dividends or increased value of investment), a major goal of each company should be the maximization of return on investment by earning the highest possible net income over the long term with a given set of resources. Logically, then, management should try to achieve that goal.

Historically, management actions to achieve desired objectives have been carried out through a pyramid of control. Companies organized themselves similar to the model diagrammed in Figure 24–1, with orders being passed down from one level to the next. On the assumption that net income could be maximized by carrying out an aggressive sales effort plus effectively controlling departmental unit costs, cost-control responsibilities were placed on the shoulders of various departmental

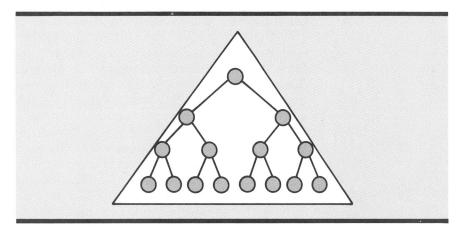

FIGURE 24–1 Pyramidal Organization

managers. Since it was believed that total unit costs would be minimized if each local area effectively controlled costs, the managers of local areas were evaluated on the basis of cost incurrence reflecting the efficiency with which they had used the resources (labor and equipment, primarily) available to them. However, with increased automation, the effectiveness of this concentration on optimizing production and costs at the local level has been questioned. As an alternative to local (departmental) production and cost controls, the Theory of Constraints focuses on global measures of throughput (precisely defined later, but basically a preliminary measure of income), investment, and total expenses for achieving continuous improvement.

We now present the logic supporting the TOC philosophy of managing a business to achieve progress toward the global objective of long-term maximization of return on investment by: (1) exposing fallacies associated with historical cost control practices; (2) identifying operating goals to replace the goal of unit-cost containment historically sought by management; and (3) demonstrating how these operating goals relate to the major goal of maximizing return on investment.

Problems Associated with Departmental Cost Control Procedures

A basic justification for departmental cost control is the assumption that, by controlling individual departmental costs per unit, management could maximize the difference between company revenues and company expenses and thus maximize return on investment. Chapter 18, however, demonstrated how some actions, obviously beneficial to some segments of a business, were not the most beneficial actions for the company as a whole. Unfavorable impact on the company as a whole also can occur as a result of actions taken to minimize departmental costs per unit.

For example, an individual department can reduce costs per unit through long production runs that spread set-up and other fixed costs over a large number of units but that also can create situations not beneficial to the firm as a whole—such as excess inventories to be moved and stored and the resultant increased handling costs and inventory carrying costs and increased losses due to obsolescence. Long production runs often create resource capacity constraints (bottlenecks) that seem to move around the factory. Also, manufacturing cycle (lead) time is lengthened. The excess inventory at each work station can delay a new order or new product that needs to be produced, forcing it to wait its turn behind the backlog of previous work awaiting completion. This makes the time required from start of production of an order to its completion (manufacturing cycle or lead time) much longer than necessary. In addition, assuming the department has some discretionary control over the sequencing of production orders, there is little incentive, in the absence of direct management orders, to produce low-volume parts necessary to complete an order, especially if a set-up must be broken to produce the required part. In this environment, it is com-

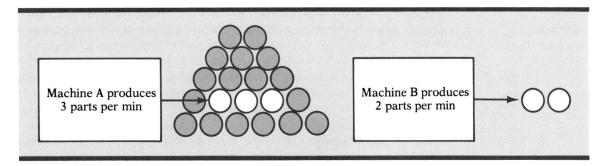

FIGURE 24–2 Unsynchronized Machine Rates Result in Excess Inventory

mon to have excess inventory almost everywhere and yet have expeditors working furiously to locate parts needed to complete overdue orders. These results are detrimental to the company as a whole, even though the actions producing them may allow the individual departments to show a high level of efficiency (low unit-processing costs).

The focus on direct labor efficiency at the departmental or workstation level contributes to difficulty in achieving a smooth flow of production through the plant. When direct labor is virtually removed from the manufacturing environment, as it is in a fully automated plant, the fallacy of trying to maximize the utilization of each resource is easy to see. For example, in a completely automated plant, it is clearly irrational to allow one piece of equipment to produce at a rate that, though optimal for that equipment, exceeds the capacity of the equipment to which it is feeding parts. As illustrated in Figure 24–2, the effect, if carried to ridiculous limits, would be the accumulation of a vast quantity of inventory between two machines with different production capabilities. Moreover, if the two machines were in different departments, the cost per unit in the first department—because of fixed costs being spread over a large number of units—would be minimized by producing at the maximum capacity if there is no "penalty" for excess inventory. A penalty, though, merely treats the symptom (excess inventory) rather than the cause (unsynchronized production).

This simple example illustrates a basic principle: *The sum of local optimums does not equal a global optimum.* Likewise, the sum of local cost optimums (where the lowest cost is the optimum) does not equal a global cost optimum.

More Appropriate Operating Goals

Chapter 14 explained how data provided by direct costing could be more useful in internal decision making than those provided by absorption costing. Chapter 18 showed that by using direct costing data, autonomous divisions of a firm can be led into decisions on transfer prices beneficial to the division but not to the entire firm. Because the investors in a business want to maximize the net income of the business as a whole, we need measures that help synchronize departmental operating objectives with the ROI objective of the company as a whole.

Forward-thinking managers believe that one of the best goals associated with plant operations in the new manufacturing environment is the increase of *throughput*, calculated as sales less the direct cost of those sales. In an automated plant, or in a semiautomated or labor-intensive plant, where the labor force is fairly constant in number regardless of production (within some range of expected levels of operations), throughput, for practical purposes, can be calculated as sales less the cost of raw materials included in goods sold. In most cases, the only other direct costs would be things such as power, which constitute a relatively minor part of total cost. This adaptation of direct costing suggests that increasing the amount of sales less the cost of raw materials included in goods sold should be one of the subordinate goals sought in order to maximize ROI. Following the terminology developed by the Avraham Y. Goldratt Institute, we call this difference between revenue and out-of-pocket costs (primarily raw materials) throughput.[2]

Since **operating expenses** (that is, all costs other than out-of-pocket costs incurred in producing and selling goods during a reporting period) will be subtracted from throughput to arrive at operating income, a second desirable goal is to *decrease operating costs* in relation to throughput.

The just-in-time (JIT) policy (see Chapters 3 and 22) focuses on the need for minimizing inventory. Since the various costs associated with excess inventory must be carefully controlled, the third goal to be achieved in maximizing ROI is to *decrease inventory (investment) in relation to throughput*. That is, we seek to minimize inventory, but not at the expense of throughput. Some inventory is required to avoid production interruptions. Also, over a longer time period, "inventory" can refer to any asset held to ensure uninterrupted production. Thus, "inventory" can be broadly interpreted as "investment."

Based on the measures just suggested, management should make internal decisions with the objective of increasing throughput, decreasing operating expenses, and minimizing inventory.

While not a measure, cash also must be considered. It is a necessary condition: If a firm has enough cash, then cash is not important; if it doesn't have enough cash, nothing else is important. Businesses require cash to operate, and they must have an adequate cash balance if they

---

[2]In the terminology of this text, throughput is referred to as contribution margin or segment margin. (Given the Goldratt definition of throughput, we probably would call it *net* throughput if the terminology were still being developed.) Decisions on special orders, as demonstrated in Chapter 19, can be made on the basis of throughput. For a given set of resources, throughput, plus information on the utilization of resources (see Figure 23–7 on page 867 for an example of how this information might be portrayed), provides the data required to make product mix decisions.

are to survive. To most effectively use a plant's resources, attention must be given to the availability of cash in relation to operations, and resource acquisition and use must be carefully scheduled to allow the firm to maximize the use of its constrained resources.

Relating Operating Goals to ROI

We can think of maximizing long-term return on investment as "making money." We can also think of it as making the most money in relation to the resources available to the firm.

Return on investment can be calculated as

$$ROI = \frac{T - OE}{I}$$

where T = throughput, OE = operating expenses, and I = investment (inventory plus other assets required to operate). Of course, these measures can be combined in various ways to show performance. For example,

$$T - OE = \text{Operating income}$$

and a measure of productivity might be T/OE.

To illustrate how throughput, inventory, and operating expenses are related to effective management decisions, assume that we were considering the purchase of a money-making machine—literally, a machine that physically produces money—with several models from which to choose. In making the purchase decision, we would need answers to the following questions:

1. How much money do we need to acquire the machine ("inventory" or investment)?
2. How much money will the machine produce per unit of time (throughput)?
3. How much money does it take to operate the machine per unit of time (operating expenses)?

Question 1 relates to the assets (the "inventory" or investment) that owners must hold in order to produce money. Question 2 refers to the throughput of the money machine. Question 3 asks about the operating expenses associated with making the money. The life of a money machine, which determines how much total money can be made, can be imbedded in question 1 and/or question 2. For example, ignoring the time value of money, if 1 machine, which costs $1 million, will produce 1,000 $20 bills per day and lasts for 2 years, while another machine costs $500,000 and will produce the same 1,000 $20 bills per day but only lasts 1 year, the 2 machines are equivalent as far as purchase cost and rate of output are concerned. With these particulars concerning throughput, inventory/investment, and operating expenses, we could decide whether to acquire the money-making machine. The same three measures can be used to decide the appropriate batch size or whether to accept special orders at a lower-than-normal price. The manager of the Valmont/ALS plant[3] in Brenham, Texas, smilingly admits that his firm has even extended this type analysis to making a decision as to whether to replace an office copying machine.

No matter what the particular circumstances, we know that even if we have an ideal manufacturing set-up, we cannot produce an infinite amount of net operating income. In our money-making example, if we have an unlimited supply of paper (raw material), some resource (for example, the portion of the machine that cuts the paper used in making the money, or the element used to print the money) will be in short supply in relation to the capacity of the rest of the machine. This internal (capacity) constraint limits the total net operating income the firm can earn. Whichever element constrains throughput is the *constraining resource*. The output of that constrained resource will limit the amount of money produced. Any firm that does not face an external market constraint and that requires more than one resource will have among its resources one that is in short supply in relation to the need for it, resulting in a constraint that limits achieving higher performance.

Analogously, any manufacturing operation that can sell everything it can produce will have some resource that constrains its throughput. Greater throughput, however, can be achieved by effective and efficient use of the constrained resource. Therefore, to maximize the return on investment from a manufacturing operation, management first must concentrate on achieving the optimal use of the constrained resource and must subordinate all other activities to the requirements of the constraint.

The New Decision-Making Process

The new operating goals just described significantly change the management decision-making process. We now discuss the steps to follow in this new decision-making process and illustrate how they are carried out.

Steps in the Decision-Making Process

The five-step TOC procedure for decision making was introduced but not explained in Chapter 19 (see pages 731–732). We now review the steps and relate them to the constraint management philosophy applied to a manufacturing plant

Step 1. The first step in managing a plant on the basis of the Theory of Constraints is to identify the most binding constraint associated with

[3]Valmont was one of the first companies to adopt the Theory of Constraints philosophies. Their initial successes are documented in David S. Koziol (then controller for Valmont), "A Job-Shop Operation," *Management Accounting* (June 1987), pp. 44–49.

plant operations. Such constraints can be divided into two categories: **externally imposed constraints**, such as the volumes of each of the products that can be sold or the quantity of raw materials available from suppliers, and **internal constraints**, such as a resource that limits production to less than market demand.

An externally imposed constraint, such as the volumes of individual products that can be sold, can be handled by finding new markets, increasing demand in current markets, or developing new products. If the constraint involves the availability of raw materials and new supplies can't be located, the price offered to suppliers for materials may be increased to obtain more of the needed materials. External constraints may be a more serious problem than internal constraints. Their solution requires creative thinking and each situation is unique. Internal constraints, which are more general, can be managed in a way that increases throughput to the maximum extent possible without unacceptable increases in inventory and operating expenses. After all constraints have been located (true constraints should be few in number), the most binding constraint should be identified.

Step 2.   Once the most binding internal constraint on operations has been identified management should do whatever is necessary to maximize the flow of goods through that constraint. This requires production activities organized so the constraint is kept in operation 100% of the time. Thus, the constraint should never be idle, waiting for a set-up crew, for employees to take breaks, or for changes in worker shifts. Also, if some part of the production cycle can be shifted from the constrained resource to another internal resource without jeopardizing throughput or quality of production, management should do that.

Step 3.   After the internal constraint on operations has been identified and operations have been organized to keep that resource operating at its maximum capacity, the other resources required to complete the manufacturing process should be synchronized with the use of the constraint; that is, their output should be paced to the constraint requirements. The acquisitions and uses of raw materials must be subordinated to the requirements of the constrained resource. The inputs of materials must be timed so that partially processed goods will be available for further processing when the constraint is available for use. Management often can increase the productivity of the constrained resource by stockpiling materials ahead of the constraint, thereby assuring the availability of input materials as needed. Whatever action is required to maximize the output of the constrained resource, without unacceptable increases in inventory or operating expenses, should be taken. Each minute of lost production on a constraint results in an irretrievable loss of throughput. Allowing the constraint to set the production pace requires management to subordinate all other activities in order to maximize the utilization of the constraint. Given current resources, this subordination will maximize the throughput of the plant.

Step 4. If there is unfilled market demand, management also must do all it can to increase the capacity of the constrained resource. The most obvious action is to acquire an additional resource unit to supplement the capacity of the constraint. However, this requires cash, which may not be available, and generally involves some waiting period before the new resource unit can be put into operation. Therefore, this step should not be taken until the steps discussed above have been accomplished.

Step 5. If the capacity of the constrained resource is increased sufficiently so it ceases to be a constraint, and the firm still is unable to produce all of the goods that can be absorbed by the market, that means the constraint has shifted to another resource. To keep improving throughput, it will then be necessary to identify the new constraint and adapt operations to maximize the output from the new resource constraint. A plant will *always* have some constraint—market demand, materials furnished by suppliers, or production resources. Management decides, by conscious choice or by inertia, where its constraint will be.

To summarize, the five steps in the decision-making process are:

1. Identify the most binding constraint in the system. This is the constraint that limits throughput.
2. Exploit the constraint. That is, given the constraint, do everything possible to maximize its output.
3. Subordinate all other activities to the operations of the identified constraint. Let the constraint set the pace for all the other activities.
4. Relax (raise or elevate) the constraint by obtaining more of it.
5. Go back to step 1, find the new constraint, and repeat steps 2 through 5. If this step is ignored, management inertia becomes the most binding constraint.

The introduction of uncertainty about machine breakdowns and possible delays in the delivery of raw materials, as well as in work-station output, complicates the situation. However, for simplicity in demonstrating how the internal scheduling of production would be carried out so as to maximize the productivity from a constrained resource, we assume that all such uncertainties have been eliminated.

The Decision Process Illustrated

Figure 24–3 presents a flowchart for a simulated factory producing three products called Aaton, Daton, and Faton. The flowchart is organized by manufacturing operation, not by the usual departmental/work-station orientation. Though the machines are in fixed locations, they can accomplish multiple operations by changing their set-up. For example, the two cutting machines are required to do four separate operations. Changing from one operation (say, cutting ARM at oper-

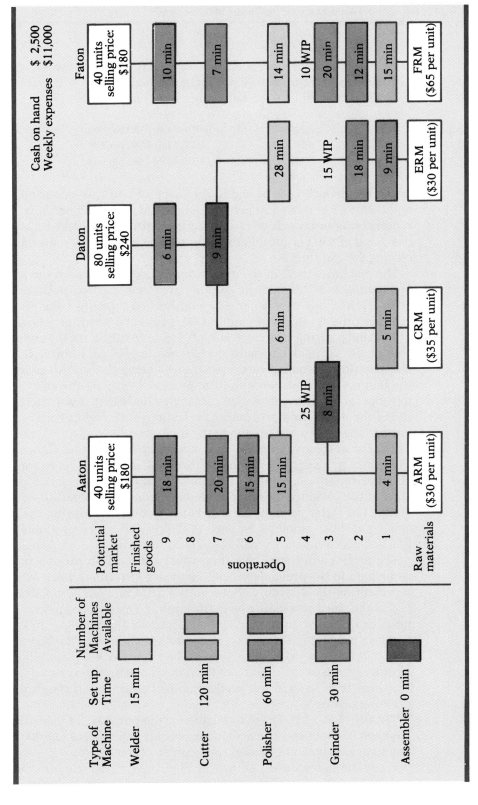

FIGURE 24–3 Flowchart for Simulated Plant *Adapted from a seminar entitled "Executive Decision Making," presented by the Avraham Y. Goldratt Institute, New Haven, Connecticut. Used with permission.*

ation 1) to another operation (cutting FRM at operation 1) requires 120 minutes of set-up before production can begin.

The flowchart shows the following market potential:

Aaton	40 units @ $180 per unit
Daton	80 units @ $240 per unit
Faton	40 units @ $180 per unit

Aaton requires the use of one unit of each of two raw materials, ARM and CRM. ARM costs $30 per unit, and CRM costs $35 per unit. Daton requires one unit each of raw materials ARM, CRM, and ERM. ERM has a cost of $30 per unit. Faton requires one unit of raw material FRM, costing $65 per unit.

The machines used in the production process (shown on the left side of Figure 24–3) include one welder, two cutters, two polishers, two grinders, and one assembler. The numbers to the left of the machines represent the set-up time required each time the machine is activated. The manufacturing processes are labeled in numbers on the right-hand side of the vertical bar, with operations numbered 1 through 9. The numbers in the shaded rectangles representing the machines indicate the number of minutes required to process each part through the various operations. The unshaded rectangles represent raw materials entering the production process (at the bottom of the figure) or the sale of units to the market (at the top of the figure).

If there were any finished goods inventory, it would be shown above the ninth processing level (after the final polishing operation). Our simulated plant does not have finished goods inventory on hand at the start of the period. Since market demand consists of 40 units of Aaton, 80 units of Daton, and 40 units of Faton, production during the period can equal those amounts for each of the three finished products before finished-goods inventory will begin accumulating.

The production lines show three stocks of work in process partially completed in the previous period. There are 25 units of work in process representing the assembly of one unit of ARM and one unit CRM at the end of the third processing level (through the assembly process). These units can be used to produce either Aaton or Daton. Also, 15 units of ERM for producing Daton have been processed through the second level (through the first grinding process). The third stock of beginning work in process consists of 10 units of FRM that have been processed through the third level toward the production of Faton (also through the first grinding process).

The firm has $2,500 cash available for the purchase of materials and payment of expenses. The firm incurs weekly expenses of $11,000. These amounts are shown in the top right corner of the figure.

From the calculations shown in Figure 24–4, we can see that the internal constraint is the welding machine. It is clear that the plant

	Welder		Cutter		Polisher		Grinder		Assembler	
Aaton (40 units)		0	40(4 + 5 + 15)	960	40(15 + 18)	1,320	40(20)	800	40(8)	320
Daton (80 units)	80(6 + 28)	2,720	80(9)	720	80(9 + 6)	1,200	80(18)	1,440	80(8 + 9)	1,360
Faton (40 units)	40(14)	560	40(15)	600	40(12 + 10)	880	40(12 + 7)	760		0
Total time required for 1 week of sales		3,280		2,280		3,400		3,000		1,680
Time available for 40-hour week		2,400*		4,800**		4,800**		4,800**		2,400*

*60 min. × 8 hr × 5 days × 1 machine = 2,400 min
**2,400 min × 2 machines

FIGURE 24—4 Machine Production Times (in minutes) Needed to Meet Market Requirements for 1 Week does not have enough welding capacity to complete all units demanded by the marketplace. To meet the potential market demand, the firm would need 3,280 minutes of welding machine time. However, only 2,400 minutes (including set-up time) are available during a 40-hour work week. All of the other machines have excess capacity—that is, there is more time available for production than is required.

With this analysis, we have completed the first step in the decision-making process: we have identified the welding machine as the production constraint (the internal constraint) and (because it doesn't require the welding machine) the market demand for Aaton as an external constraint. At this point, the total market demand for Daton and Faton is not limiting throughput because there isn't enough time available on the welding machine to produce enough of those units to meet the market demand.

For the second step in the decision-making process (maximize throughput through the welding machine constraint), we must decide how many of each of the products should be produced. To do that, we must first determine the amount of throughput that can be realized from each product per minute of welding processing time, calculated as follows:

Product	Selling Price	− Materials Cost	÷ Minutes of Welding Time Required	= Throughput (CM) per Minute
Aaton	$180	$65	0	∞
Daton	$240	$95	34	$4.26
Faton	$180	$65	14	$8.21

This shows that our first priority should be production of the 40 units of Aaton the market is capable of absorbing because that requires no use of the constraint. Our next priority should be production of the 40 units of Faton the market demands (another external constraint) because, with the limited time available on the welding machine, we will realize almost twice as much throughput per minute than we would from producing and selling Daton. The remaining welding machine time available should be directed toward producing Daton. If we (arbitrarily) allow 90 minutes for 6 set-ups, we could then produce 51 units of Daton as shown below:

Total machine time available (5 days × 8 hr per day × 60 min per hr)	2,400 minutes
Time used for set-ups	(90) minutes
Time used for Faton (40 units × 14 min)	(560) minutes
Time available to produce Daton	1,750 minutes

Time required for each unit of Daton = 34 minutes
Then, 1,750 ÷ 34 = 51.5 units

Thus, we can maximize our throughput by manufacturing 40 units of Aaton, 40 units of Faton, and 51 units of Daton. Note that we have just found the product that provides the most throughput per unit of constraining factor (minutes of welding machine time available), as described in Chapter 19 (page 735).

The next step in the decision process involves scheduling all other production activities so the welding machine will be used as close as possible to 100% of the time. However, since purchases of raw materials require cash (a necessary condition, not a constraint), we first should complete the units in process so that cash on hand can be increased through sales of those units. At the same time, we must schedule our input of raw materials into the first processing level so there are the appropriate number of ARM and CRM subassemblies through the third processing level, an equal number of units of ERM through the second processing level, and some number of FRM units through the third processing level in time to keep the welding machine in continuous operation. That is, we need a buffer of partially completed units awaiting processing by the welding machine so it is never idled because of lack of parts to work on. Again, in scheduling materials issuances and the initiation of level-one processing for all products, all activities should be subordinated to the needs of the welding machine to avoid losing throughput. Each minute the welding machine is idle, the firm loses (forever!) $8.21 or $4.26, depending on whether all 40 units of Faton have been produced.

Once we have squeezed the maximum productivity out of the welding machine, the next step could involve either obtaining another welding machine or subcontracting some of the welding work, to eliminate the constraint associated with the welding operation. At that point, the new constraint must be identified and a new decision cycle implemented.

Following this decision process will improve the throughput of a firm and all measures of its effectiveness—throughput will increase, overall inventory will decrease (in spite of maintaining certain necessary stocks of partially completed units), and operating expenses will decrease (because of a decrease in expediting activities and elimination of overtime). Although we may have achieved dramatic results, the entire procedure must be repeated to avoid stagnation. If we stop here, we will lose the continuous improvement desired. The decision process is very simple, but its real power is in leading us toward higher and higher productivity and profitability through continuous improvement of all activities of a firm.

The Goldratt Institute has developed a computer simulation program that automatically schedules the acquisitions and releases of materials and automatically activates the machines so as to maximize the output of the welding machine. If this were an automated factory, we also could develop a similar computer program to schedule materials acquisitions and releases and to schedule machine activations on the factory floor. The Goldratt Institute is in the process of developing scheduling software that can be manually implemented. The next step—complete computer control of operations—may not be far away.

Measuring Management Effectiveness

Reports summarizing operating data within a format similar to the one shown in Figure 24–5 can be used to evaluate management's weekly performance. The financial statement portion gives net profit for the week, cash at the end of the week, return on investment, throughput, sales, inventory value, inventory dollar-days, and operating expenses. Larger balances are desirable for net profit, cash, return on investment, throughput, and sales; smaller values are desirable for inventory, inventory dollar-days (inventory times number of days until inventory is needed—see examples on pages 837–838 and 890), and operating expenses. These data can be presented on a comparative basis from week to week to help evaluate management action in terms of financial results. Trend data are extremely important for tracking continuous improvement and each element of financial statement data easily can be shown in a graph that plots performance over time.

Figure 24–5 also tabulates the percentage of machine time utilized for production and for set-up. Here, we want a high percentage of the

Financial Statement Data		Utilization of Machines			
			% of Time Spent in Activity		
		Machine	Breakdowns	Production	Set-Ups
Net profit: _____					
Cash at end of week: _____					
Return on investment: _____		Welder			
Throughput (*sales minus raw material*): _____					
Sales: _____		Cutter			
Inventory—Raw materials value: _____					
Inventory dollar-days: _____		Polisher			
Operating expenses: _____					
		Grinder			
		Assembler			

Products Demanded: Aaton ____40____   Daton ____80____   Faton ____40____

Products Sold: Aaton _____   Daton _____   Faton _____

FIGURE 24–5 Firm Weekly Performance Report *Adapted from a seminar entitled "Executive Decision l by the Avraham Y. Goldratt Institute of New Haven, Connecticut. Used with permission.*

constrained resource (welding machine) time devoted to production. However, we are also concerned, in a minor way, with the percentages of other machine times that have been devoted to production and set-up as an indication of potential further constraints.

New Measures for Evaluating Local Performance

Measures of throughput, inventory, and operating expenses are useful in evaluating not only the performance of segments of operations but that of the entire firm, as well. Local areas (for example, work stations) previously evaluated primarily by "efficiency" measures, however, need new benchmarks in a TOC environment. Just as the firm is evaluated on the basis of deviations from planned (optimum) performance and improvements in performance, local areas can be evaluated on the basis of deviations from planned performance and contribution to improvement. Deviations from planned performance may be classified as either (1) actions that should have been taken but were not taken or (2) actions that should not have been taken but were taken.

Actions That Should Have Been Taken

Because adherence to plans is vital in a TOC environment, if a local area fails to complete a production assignment, the performance of the firm may be diminished. Therefore, a measure of local failure to perform should be maintained. One such measure is throughput dollar-days. Each local area can be viewed as the supplier for the next production center, with internal delivery dates. Then, each day a local area is overdue in completing an order, the final throughput represented by that order is "charged" to the late area.

Assume, for example, that work station no. 30 is 20 days late completing an order for parts that ultimately will combine with other materials for a total materials cost of $20,000 and a selling price of $30,000. The throughput, therefore, is $10,000. Since work station no. 30 is preventing the realization of the $10,000 throughput, it would be charged with $10,000 throughput $\times$ 20 days = 200,000 throughput dollar-days. The ideal performance for the work station would be a charge of zero total throughput dollar-days.

Actions That Should Not Have Been Taken

Just as actions that should have been taken and were not can result in poor performance, actions that should not have been taken but were can contribute to suboptimal performance. If a local area produces a different item from the one scheduled, for example, then the firm will be penalized in two ways—(1) for not having the correct item when it is needed (because another item was incorrectly produced) and (2) for having excess inventory before it is needed.

To illustrate, assume that work station no. 39, which is responsible for feeding parts to work station no. 40, a constraint resource, fails to switch over from producing part 89A to producing part 54C, as scheduled. Because of this error, 500 excess units of 89A exist that will not be needed until the following times (from now):

Units of 89A	Days in the Future When Needed
100	5
250	10
150	20

There is no storage cost associated with these extra units and the raw materials cost for each unit is $.90. Besides having excess inventory of 89A, 400 units of part 54C are not available when needed by work station no. 40, resulting in 64 minutes of idle time for that vital (constrained) resource. The throughput for work station no. 40 is $6 per minute; that is, for each minute work station no. 40 is idle, the firm irretrievably loses $6 in throughput. The "cost" of the error of work station no. 39, in terms of "penalty" dollars (throughput dollar-days plus inventory dollar-days), can be calculated as follows:

"Cost" (in throughput dollar-days) of Shortage of Unit 54C

Forced (unfavorable) idle time of critical resource	64 minutes
× Throughput resulting from each minute of operation of this resource	$ 6
Lost throughput dollar days	$384

"Cost" of Excess Units of 89A

Units of 89A	Days in the Future When Needed	Inventory (raw materials) Cost per Unit	Total
100	5	$.90	$ 450
250	10	.90	2,250
150	20	.90	2,700
Excess inventory dollar days			$5,400

Thus, the total "cost" of production error is

$384 + $5,400 = $5,784 (in throughput and inventory dollar-days)

Improvements in Performance

Local area evaluation can be undertaken in a positive as well as negative mode. To encourage local improvements, contributions to increased throughput, reduced unplanned inventory, or reduced operating expenses also should be recognized. If a worker suggests a process change that increases throughput, the positive impact of the change should be credited to that worker. For example, if a worker devises a way to complete in 8 minutes processing that previously required 10 minutes on work station no. 40 (a capacity-constrained resource), the increased throughput on an annual basis, assuming a 40-hour week and a 50-week year, would be

Previous Production

$$(60 \text{ min} \times 8 \text{ hr} \times 5 \text{ days} \times 50 \text{ weeks})/(10 \text{ min}) = 12{,}000 \text{ units}$$

New Production

$$(60 \text{ min} \times 8 \text{ hr} \times 5 \text{ days} \times 50 \text{ weeks})/(8 \text{ min}) = 15{,}000 \text{ units}$$

The throughput of \$6 per min $\times$ 10 min = \$60 per unit $\times$ 3,000 additional units = \$180,000 (throughput dollars) would be "credited" to the worker. In this way, positive as well as negative measures can be used to evaluate local performance.

Note that all the local measures will involve some variation of throughput, inventory, or operating expenses.

Possible Operational Effects on External Constraints

In our illustration, we referred to the market demand for products Aaton and Faton as externally imposed constraints on the realization of unlimited throughput.[4] Ordinarily, we would expect the sales department to be responsible for easing these market constraints through its sales and promotional efforts. However, a consistent delivery of high-quality goods in accordance with customer needs also can help overcome the market constraint. Firms that deliver high-quality units in small batches as customers need them are more likely to be considered as sources of additional purchases than are those that deliver poor-quality goods or complete orders behind schedule. Therefore, attention must be given to effectively meeting the needs of customers as one way to enlarge the limits of the market constraint. Reports indicating the extent to which this objective has been achieved, such as various

[4]Demand for Daton is not a constraint because all the current demand cannot be met.

quality-related reports and due date delivery and late delivery reports, during each operating period should be useful to management.

Cost-Accumulation and Cost-Allocation Procedures

The accounting system used in accumulating and allocating costs in a Theory of Constraints management environment should be consistent with the objectives of that environment. To demonstrate, let's assume the following regarding the operations of Simulated Plant (see Figure 24–3) and show how events might be recorded and results summarized for managerial use.

Assumptions:

(1) Sales:

Aaton	38 units @ $180 per unit
Daton	48 units @ $240 per unit
Faton	35 units @ $180 per unit

(2) Beginning materials inventory, including those in process (see Figure 24–3):

30 units of material ARM @ $30 per unit ⎫ (25 of ARM and CRM assembled together,
30 units of material CRM @ $35 per unit ⎭ are in process at processing level 4)
25 units of material ERM @ $30 per unit (15 are in process at processing level 3)
15 units of material FRM @ $65 per unit (10 are in process at processing level 4)

(3) Purchases during the period:

93 units of material ARM @ $32 per unit
93 units of material CRM @ $37 per unit
53 units of material ERM @ $30 per unit
40 units of material FRM @ $68 per unit

(4) Ending materials inventory, including those in process (see Figure 24–3):

34 units of material ARM, including 20 units in process at processing level 4
35 units of material CRM, including 20 units in process at processing level 4
28 units of material ERM, including 10 units in process at processing level 3
18 units of material FRM, including 12 units in process at processing level 4

(5) Operating expenses for the period: $11,500

(6) With perfect synchronization of operations, Simulated Plant can produce and sell:

> 40 units of Aaton @ $180 per unit
> 51 units of Daton @ $240 per unit
> 40 units of Faton @ $180 per unit

(7) Materials are expected to be purchased at the following costs:

> Material ARM: $30 per unit
> Material CRM: $35 per unit
> Material ERM: $30 per unit
> Material FRM: $65 per unit

(8) Expected operating expenses for period: $11,000

If Simulated Plant were to achieve all of these goals, its operating statement would show net operating income of $5,595, as follows:

Simulated Plant

Operating Statement

Sales		
40 units of Aaton @ $180	$ 7,200	
51 units of Daton @ $240	12,240	
40 units of Faton @ $180	7,200	
Total sales		$26,640
Materials		
40 units of material ARM @ $30	$ 1,200	
40 units of material CRM @ $35	1,400	
51 units of material ARM @ $30	1,530	
51 units of material CRM @ $35	1,785	
51 units of material ERM @ $30	1,530	
40 units of material FRM @ $65	2,600	
Total cost of materials		10,045
Throughput (contribution margin)		$16,595
Operating expense		11,000
Net operating income		$ 5,595

The financial data for the assumed operating period could be recorded at actual cost, as shown in the following T accounts (FIFO cost flow assumed). The beginning inventory of materials was purchased at projected cost per unit. Following the T accounts, journal entries for the numbered transactions also are shown.

Materials Inventory				Sales		Operating Expenses	
Beginning balance	3,675 A	(3)	9,955 E		(1) 24,660 B	(4) 11,500	
Purchases (2)	10,727 C						
	4,447 D						

Cost of Materials Used			Cash or Receivables		Cash or Payables, etc.	
(3)	9,955		(1) 24,660		(2) 10,727	
					(4) 11,500	

Explanation:

A. Beginning inventory of materials:

30 units of material ARM @ $30	$ 900
30 units of material CRM @ $35	1,050
25 units of material ERM @ $30	750
15 units of material FRM @ $65	975
Total	$3,675

B. Sales for the period:

38 units of Aaton @ $180	$ 6,840
48 units of Daton @ $240	11,520
35 units of Faton @ $180	6,300
Total	$24,660

C. Invoice cost of materials purchased:

93 units of material ARM @ $32	$ 2,976
93 units of material CRM @ $37	3,441
53 units of material ERM @ $30	1,590
40 units of material FRM @ $68	2,720
Total	$10,727

D. Ending inventory of materials at FIFO cost:

34 units of material ARM @ $32	$1,088
35 units of material CRM @ $37	1,295
28 units of material ERM @ $30	840
18 units of material FRM @ $68	1,224
Total	$4,447

E. Cost of materials used $3,675 + $10,727 − $4,447 = \underline{\$\ 9,955}$

General journal entries:

(1) Cash or receivables   24,660

       Sales   24,660

      To record sales.

(2) Materials inventory   10,727

       Cash or payables, etc.   10,727

      To record purchases.

(3) Cost of materials used   9,955

       Materials inventory   9,955

      To record materials used.

(4) Operating expenses   11,500

       Cash or payables, etc.   11,500

      To record operating expenses.

The preceding data are summarized in the following operating statement:

Sales	$24,660
Cost of materials used	9,955
Throughput (contribution margin)	$14,705
Operating expenses	11,500
Net operating income	$ 3,205

These data reflect actual costs based on a FIFO cost flow assumption. However, if we accept the data in the operating statement projected for perfectly synchronized operations (see page 893) as standard data, we can provide more useful information for management by recording the assumed operating data as in the following entries:

(1) Cash or receivables   24,660

      Sales variance   1,980

        Sales   26,640

      To record sales.

(2) Materials inventory   10,235 (a)

      Material price variance   492

        Cash or payables   10,727

      To record purchases of materials.

Explanation:

(a)		
93 units of material ARM @ $30	$2,790	
93 units of material CRM @ $35	3,255	
53 units of material ERM @ $30	1,590	
40 units of material FRM @ $65	2,600	
Total	$10,235	

(3) Cost of materials   10,045 (b)
Material quantity variance   350 (e)
    Materials cost variance   740 (d)
    Materials inventory   9,655 (c)

To record materials costs associated with sales.

Explanation:

(b) Materials cost from standard statement (see operating statement, page 893).

(c) Actual quantities of materials used at standard cost per unit.

Material ARM: (30 + 93 − 34) @ $30	$2,670
Material CRM: (30 + 93 − 35) @ $35	3,080
Material ERM: (25 + 53 − 28) @ $30	1,500
Material FRM: (15 + 40 − 18) @ $65	2,405
Total	$9,655

(d) Difference between standard and actual sales at standard cost per unit.

Aaton: (40 − 38) @ $65	$130
Daton: (51 − 48) @ $95	285
Faton: (40 − 35) @ $65	325
Total	$740

(e) Amount proven as follows:

Material	Actual Number of Units Used	Standard Allowed	Unit Variance*	Standard Cost/Unit	Cost Variance*
ARM	89	86	3 U	$30	$ 90 U
CRM	88	86	2 U	35	70 U
ERM	50	48	2 U	30	60 U
FRM	37	35	2 U	65	130 U
					$350 U

*U = unfavorable

(4) Operating expenses   11,000
Operating expense variance   500
    Cash, payables, etc.   11,500

To record operating expenses.

By recording the operating data as in the preceding entries, we can show management what has caused net operating income to deviate from what was expected to be achieved in a perfectly synchronized environment. Those data can be summarized as shown at the top of page 897.

This $3,013 net operating income can be reconciled with the $3,205 net operating income using actual costs (page 895) by removing the materials price variance included in the ending inventory of materials at actual costs from the net operating income determined by using actual costs.

Net operating income projected with perfectly synchronized operations (see page 893)		$5,595
Decrease due to reduced throughput		
Unfavorable sales variance	$(1,980)	
Favorable materials cost variance	740	(1,240)
Decrease due to other variances		
Unfavorable materials price variance		(492)
Unfavorable materials quantity variance		(350)
Unfavorable operating expense variance		(500)
Total variances		(2,582)
Net operating income for period		$3,013

Material Price Variance Included in End-of-Period Materials Inventory Carried at Actual Cost

34 units of material ARM @ $2	$ 68
35 units of material CRM @ $2	70
18 units of material FRM @ $3	54
Total	$192

Subtracting this $192 materials price variance from the $3,205 net income calculated using actual costs with no recognition of materials price variances results in the same actual net operating income for the period as shown earlier.

Reconciliation of Two Actual Net Income Amounts

Income with no variance recognition	$3,205
Material price variance in ending inventory	− 192
Net operating income for period (including variance recognition)	$3,013

In our analysis of deviations from the projected operating result, based on maximum usage of the constrained resource, we have identified six variances. Each of these variances can be subdivided into component elements to provide more useful information for management. Sales and cost variances can be subdivided into amounts caused by each of the products sold. The total sales variance can be divided into price and volume (product mix and pure volume) variances. Both materials price and quantity variances can be subdivided into amounts associated with each of the materials used in production. The operating expense variance can be subdivided to show the amounts caused by each of the individual operating expenses. Procedures for calculating these variances were shown in earlier portions of this text.

SUMMARY

In this chapter, we explained how the Theory of Constraints leads to a new philosophy of management that gives primary attention to identifying and exploiting constraints as a means of maximizing return on investment. With this management philosophy, all actions are meant to promote the maximum utilization of the constraint. That concentration on the constraint is expected to be achieved within an environment that also carefully synchronizes (subordinates) other activities with maximization of (to) constraint utilization and monitors inventory levels and operating expenses. We demonstrated how management decisions are made in a Theory of Constraints environment and compared them with the decisions typically made within a conventionally managed firm.

We then illustrated Theory of Constraints management techniques. In that illustration, all decisions relating to raw materials acquisitions and use, and to set-ups and machine activations, were made with the objective of keeping the constrained resource operating at as close to 100% of the time available as was possible. This maximized throughput, one of the primary overall objectives of plant operations.

Next, we suggested some accounting measures for showing the extent to which the operating objectives have been achieved, including throughput, inventory, operating expenses, and resource utilization. We also illustrated some new measures that might be used to evaluate local performance.

Finally, we developed the framework for a manufacturing accounting system that can be used to accumulate and allocate cost and revenue data in a constraint-managed operating environment. This system includes the determination of throughput, materials price, materials quantity, and operating cost variances from standards based on the "best possible" operating plan. We demonstrated how management decisions are made as that optimum objective is being pursued so that this approach can be compared with the typical decisions made in a conventionally managed firm.

GLOSSARY OF TERMS INTRODUCED IN THIS CHAPTER

constraint Anything that limits the system from achieving higher performances in terms of its goal.

externally imposed constraint A constraint on the level of operations imposed by the environment in which a firm operates, such as the maximum volume of the firm's product that can be sold at a specified price.

internal constraint	A constraint on the level of operations caused by the limited availability of a resource such as machine time that makes it impossible for the firm to produce as many units as the market will absorb at a specified price.
operating expenses	The total of all manufacturing expenses (except materials used) plus selling and administrative expenses incurred during an operating period. Note: This special definition is used *only* in this chapter.
perfectly synchronized operations	The operations of a plant in which the internally constrained resource is being used at as near 100% of its available time as is practically feasible and all other resources are subordinated to the needs of the constrained resource.
Theory of Constraints	The theory that there are identifiable constraints associated with the operations of any business and that management should exercise control over firm operations by identifying those constraints and managing them so as to use the firm's resources most effectively.
throughput variance	The difference between the amount of throughput actually realized and the throughput that could have been realized with perfectly exploited and synchronized operations.

QUESTIONS FOR CLASS DISCUSSION

24–1 What should logically be the major goal of a company? Discuss.

24–2 What operating goals are associated with management through use of the Theory of Constraints?

24–3 How can a strong emphasis on controlling departmental unit costs conflict with the goal of long-term maximization of return on investment? Explain.

24–4 What is the relationship between increased automation and the conventional practice of measuring departmental performance efficiencies?

24–5 What are some of the unfavorable operating practices that can be encouraged by emphasizing departmental unit costs as measures of efficiency of performance.

24–6 Why should automated or synchronized manufacturing plants try to operate with a minimum amount of inventory? How does this operating objective relate to JIT?

24–7 What is meant by *throughput* as used in this chapter?

24–8 What is the relationship between throughput and the contribution margin calculated by use of direct or variable costing in Chapter 14?

24–9 What is the difference between an externally imposed constraint and an internal constraint? Discuss.

24—10   What relationship should exist among the various operating decisions in a constraint-management environment?

24—11   What steps should be followed in making decisions in a constraint-managed operating environment?

24—12   What are some of the things management can do in managing an internal constraint so as to maximize throughput?

24—13   Assume that a constrained resource is used to produce more than one product. How does management determine which product should be given first priority in scheduling production?

24—14   How can the operating practices of a firm contribute toward the management of an externally imposed constraint such as the maximum volume of units that can be sold?

24—15   What are the implications of an unfavorable throughput variance? Discuss.

24—16   What are the implications of an unfavorable materials price variance? Is such a variance always undesirable? Explain.

24—17   What are the implications of an unfavorable materials usage variance? Discuss.

24—18   What are the implications of an unfavorable operating expense variance? Discuss.

PROBLEMS

24—19   **Managing Operations Using the Theory of Constraints** Exotic Products, Inc., produces three products (Good, Excellent, and Special) from four raw materials, which we shall call RM1, RM2, RM3, and RM4, expected to be purchased at the following prices:

RM1: $15 per unit
RM2: $17.50 per unit
RM3: $15 per unit
RM4: $32.50 per unit

Production is carried out through various combinations of heat treatment, grinding, polishing, special treatment, and assembly operations. The plant (including each operating center) operates for 40 hours (2,400 minutes) per week.

Good is produced through the following steps:

(1) RM1 is heat treated for 6 minutes. RM2 is heat treated for 4 minutes.
(2) One unit of each (RM1 and RM2) is put together in an assembly operation requiring 8 minutes per assembled unit.

(3) Each assembled unit is heat treated for 7.5 minutes.
(4) Each assembled unit is polished for 7.5 minutes.
(5) Each unit is ground to specifications. This requires 10 minutes per unit.
(6) After grinding, each unit is polished again for 9 minutes to make it ready for sale.

Excellent is produced through the following steps.

(1) Each unit of RM3 is polished for 4.5 minutes.
(2) Each unit is ground to specifications. This requires 9 minutes per unit.
(3) Each subassembly of RM1 and RM2 to be used in producing Excellent is specially treated for 6 minutes.
(4) Each ground unit of RM3 is specially treated for 28 minutes.
(5) One specially treated subassembly of RM1 and RM2 is assembled with one specially treated RM3. This requires 9 minutes per assembled unit.
(6) Each assembled unit is polished for 3 minutes to make it ready for sale.

Special is produced through the following steps:

(1) Each unit of RM4 is heat treated for 11 minutes.
(2) Each heat treated unit is polished for 6 minutes.
(3) Polished units are ground to specifications. This operation requires 10 minutes per unit.
(4) Each unit is specially treated for 14 minutes.
(5) Each unit is again ground for 3.5 minutes
(6) The units are polished for sale. This requires 5 minutes per unit.

The equipment for each operation must be cleaned and adjusted each time the material being processed is changed. The times required for the changes are as follows:

Heat treatment	120 minutes
Grinding	30 minutes
Polishing	60 minutes
Special treatment	15 minutes
Assembly	0 minutes

One piece of equipment for each type of operation is available for 40 hours (2,400 minutes) per week. Exotic begins the week with 25 subassemblies of RM1 and RM2 (assembled), 15 units of RM3 processed through grinding, and 10 units of RM4 processed through its first grinding operation.

The sales department projects the following sales for the week:

40 units of Good @ $90 per unit
80 units of Excellent @ $120 per unit
40 units of Special @ $90 per unit

Operating expenses are projected to be $6,000 per week.

REQUIRED:

1. Prepare a production flowchart for Good, Excellent, and Special like the one in Figure 24–3.
2. Determine the internal constraint in the production of Good, Excellent, and Special.
3. Determine the targeted production (sales mix) of each product for the week.
4. Calculate the net income that should be realized during the week with perfectly synchronized operations. (Ignore income taxes.)

24–20 **Recording and Reporting Financial Data** Assume that Exotic (see problem 24–19) achieved the following operating results during the past week:

(1) Beginning inventories were as stated in problem 24–19.
(2) Purchases of materials:

> 94 units of RM1 @ $16 per unit
> 94 units of RM2 @ $18.50 per unit
> 54 units of RM3 @ $16 per unit
> 40 units of RM4 @ $34 per unit

(3) Operating expenses: $6,200
(4) Sales for the week:

> 37 units of Good @ $90 per unit
> 46 units of Excellent @ $120 per unit
> 36 units of Special @ $90 per unit

(5) Materials inventory, including units in process:

> 14 units of RM1 unprocessed
> 15 units of RM2 unprocessed
> 10 units of RM3 unprocessed
> 1 unit of RM4 unprocessed
> 20 units of RM1 and RM2 assembled
> 10 units of RM3 processed through grinding
> 12 units of RM4 processed through the first grinding operation

REQUIRED: For the following, assume a FIFO cost flow.

1. Record the financial data relating to operations in T accounts, as illustrated in the chapter on page 894.
2. Prepare an operating statement for the week.
3. Record the financial data relating to operations in T accounts using the perfect synchronization data from problem 24–19 as standard data, with appropriate recognition of variances. (Ignore taxes.)
4. Prepare an operating statement deviation report for the week from the data accumulated in requirement 3.
5. Reconcile the net operating income figures shown in parts requirements 2 and 4.

Bibliography of Articles and Books Relating to Part V

Chalos, Peter, and Allan H. Bader, "High-Tech Production: The Impact on Cost Reporting Systems," *Journal of Accountancy* (March 1986).

Cooper, R., "Cost Management Concepts and Principles: The Rise of Activity-Based Costing—Part One: What Is an Activity-Based Cost System?" *Journal of Cost Management* (Summer 1988).

Cooper, R., "Cost Management Concepts and Principles: The Rise of Activity-Based Costing—Part Two: When Do I Need an Activity-Based Cost System?" *Journal of Cost Management* (Fall 1988).

Cooper, R., "Cost Management Concepts and Principles: The Rise of Activity-Based Costing—Part Three: Determining the Number and Nature of Cost Drivers," *Journal of Cost Management* (Winter 1989).

Cooper, R., "Cost Management Concepts and Principles: The Rise of Activity-Based Costing—Part Four: What Do Activity-Based Costing Systems Look Like?" *Journal of Cost Management* (Spring 1990).

Cooper, R., "Does Your Company Need a New Cost System?" *Harvard Business Review* (Spring 1987).

Cooper, R., and R. S. Kaplan, "How Cost Accounting Systematically Distorts Product Costs," *Field Studies in Management and Control* (Boston, Mass.: Harvard Business School Press, 1987).

Deakin, Edward B., "Cost Accounting in a Capital Intensive Economy," *Today's CPA* (April/May 1987).

Dilts, David M., and Grant W. Russell, "Accounting for the Factory of the Future," *Management Accounting* (April 1985).

Edwards, James B., and Julie A. Heard, "Is Cost Accounting the No. 1 Enemy of Productivity?" *Management Accounting* (June 1984).

Engwall, Richard L., "Investment Justification–CIM/JIT Investment Justification," *Journal of Cost Management* (Fall 1989).

Engwall, Richard L., "Investment Justification—Need for Change," *Journal of Cost Management* (Summer 1989).

Fox, Robert E., "The Constraint Theory" (New Haven, Conn.: Avraham Y. Goldratt Institute, 1989).

Goldratt, Eliyahu M., and Jeff Cox, *The Goal: A Process of Ongoing Improvement* (Croton-on-Hudson, N.Y.: North River Press, 1986).

Goldratt, Eliyahu M., and Robert E. Fox, *The Race* (Croton-on-Hudson, N.Y.: North River Press, 1986).

Hodder, James E., "Evaluation of Manufacturing Investments: A Comparison of U.S. and Japanese Practices," *Financial Management* (Spring 1986).

Hohner, Gregory, "The Factory in Transition—Managing the Flow of Quality Information in Manufacturing: Distributed Processing and Manufacturing Cells," *Journal of Cost Management* (Fall 1989).

Howell, Robert A., and Stephen R. Soucy, "Capital Investment in the New Manufacturing Environment," *Management Accounting* (November 1987).

Howell, Robert A., and Stephen R. Soucy, "Cost Accounting in the New Manufacturing Environment," *Management Accounting* (August 1987).

Jaouen, Pauline R., and Bruce R. Neumann, "Variance Analysis, Kanban, and JIT: A Further Study," *Journal of Accountancy* (June 1987).

Jason, Susan, "Goldratt and Fox: Revolutionizing the Factory Floor," *Management Accounting* (May 1987).

Johnson, H. T., "Activity-Based Information: Accounting for Competitive Excellence," *Target* (Spring 1989).

Johnson, H. T., and R. S. Kaplan, *Relevance Lost: The Rise and Fall of Management Accounting* (Boston, Mass.: Harvard Business School Press, 1987).

Kaplan, Robert S., "Yesterday's Accounting in Today's Economy," *Harvard Business Review* (July–August 1984).

Kaplan, Robert S., "Yesterday's Accounting Undermines Production," *Harvard Business Review* (July–August 1984).

King, Alfred M., "Cost Accounting in the 1990s: Can Production Executives and Financial Executives Learn to Keep in Touch?" *Financial Executive* (November 1986).

Koziol, David S., "How the Constraint Theory Improved a Job-Shop Operation," *Management Accounting* (May 1988).

Lee, John Y., *Managerial Accounting Changes for the 1990s* (Reading, Mass.: Addison-Wesley, 1987).

Lessner, John, "Performance Measurement in a Just-in-Time Environment: Can Traditional Performance Measurements Still Be Used?" *Journal of Cost Management* (Fall 1989).

Longmire, Robert J., "Cost Accounting in a CIM Environment," *Production and Inventory Management Review* (February 1987).

McIlhatten, Robert D., "How Management Systems Can Support the JIT Philosophy," *Management Accounting* (September 1987).

MacKay, James T., "11 Key Issues in Manufacturing Accounting," *Management Accounting* (January 1987).

McNair, Carol J., "Timely Information for High Tech," *New Accounting* (November 1988).

Miller, J. G., and T. E. Vollmann, "The Hidden Factory," *Harvard Business Review* (September–October 1985).

Nanni, Alfred J., Jeffrey G. Miller, and Thomas E. Vollmann, "What Shall We Account For?" *Management Accounting* (January 1988).

National Association of Accountants Conference, *Cost Accounting for the 90s: The Challenge of Technological Change* (1986). Papers presented include:

   Fox, Robert E., "Coping with Today's Technology: Is Cost Accounting Keeping Up?"

   Goodman, Jeffrey S., "User Productivity—Software Solutions for Business Management."

   Greenberg, David, "Robotics: One Small Company's Experience."

   Howell, Robert A., "Changing Measurements in the Factory of the Future."

   Hronec, Steven M., "The Effects of Manufacturing Productivity on Cost Accounting and Management Reporting."

   Johansson, Henry J., Thomas E. Vollmann, and Vivian Wright, "The Effect of Zero Inventories on Cost (Just-in-Time)."

   Kaplan, Robert S., "Strategic Cost Analysis."

   Russell, Grant W., and David M. Dilts, "Are Accountants Delaying the Automation of America?"

   Seed, Allen H., III, "Cost Accounting in the Age of Robotics."

   Slinkard, John D., Richard G. Mulligan, and Mark S. Coran, "How Government Contractors Approach Factory Automation: The Accounting Implications."

   Vangermeersch, Richard, "Milestones in the History of Management Accounting."

Parker, Christopher, "Taming Technology for the 90s," *New Accounting* (November 1988).

Pryor, Tom E., "Executive Briefing—In Search of a Strategy," *Journal of Cost Management* (Fall 1989).

Sandretto, Michael J., "What Kind of Cost System Do You Need?" *Harvard Business Review* (January–February 1985).

Schwarzbach, Henry R., "The Impact of Automation on Accounting for Indirect Costs," *Management Accounting* (December 1985).

Stokes, Carolyn R., and Kay W. Lawrimore, "Selling a New Cost Accounting System," *Journal of Cost Management* (Fall 1989).

Stromberg, Dan, and Brian H. Kleiner, "Implementing a Participation Cost Management Program," *Journal of Cost Management* (Fall 1989).

Tishlias, Dennis P., and Peter Chalos, "High-Tech Production's Impact on Cost Accounting: A Case Study," *Journal of Accountancy* (November 1986).

Turney, Peter B. B., "Using Activity-Based Costing to Achieve Manufacturing Excellence," *Journal of Cost Management* (Summer 1989).

Turney, Peter B. B., and Bruce Anderson, "Accounting for Continuous Improvement," *Sloan Management Review* (Winter 1989).

Umble, M. Michael, and M. L. Srikauth, *Synchronous Manufacturing: Principles for World Class Excellence* (Cincinnati, Ohio: South Western, 1990).

Master Glossary

The chapters in which each term or concept is introduced and defined are shown in parentheses at the end of the definition.

abnormal-spoilage costs
Costs associated with units lost in excess of those a firm normally expects to lose in its manufacturing operations on a regularly recurring basis. Such costs, which are considered avoidable, are expensed in the period incurred and are *not* allocated to good units. (8)

abnormal-spoilage loss
Loss through shrinkage or spoilage in excess of that expected to occur under normally cost-efficient operating conditions (normal spoilage). (5)

absorption costing
A system of accumulating and allocating costs in which all manufacturing costs, both fixed and variable, are allocated to the units of product being produced. Also known as *full costing* or *traditional costing*. (2)

Accelerated Cost Recovery System (ACRS)
A method of depreciation of tangible property prescribed in the Economic Recovery Tax Act of 1981; classifies depreciable assets into one of several property class-life categories, each of which has a designated pattern of allowable depreciation for tax purposes. (20)

accounting costs
Recorded values of resources and services given up in acquiring other resources and services. (1)

accounting rate-of-return method
A method of evaluating investment profitability by relating the anticipated accounting net income per year from the investment to the amount of the investment (either initial investment or average investment). (20)

activity base
Measure of output or performance that is highly correlated with the amount of cost incurred; used as a basis for allocating manufacturing-overhead costs. (13)

activity-based costing
A cost accumulation and allocation system that traces costs to products according to the activities performed on them; intended to provide cost information for strategic, design, and operational control decisions. (23)

actual costs
The actual dollar values of resources given up to acquire goods and services; also known as *historical costs*. In Chapter 11, the term describes the dollar amounts of resources given up for direct materials, direct labor, and manufacturing overhead; in other chapters, refers to any cost actually incurred. (11)

actual-cost system	A cost system that accumulates and allocates actual manufacturing costs (direct materials, direct labor, and manufacturing overhead) to the units of goods produced. (Unit costs can't be determined until the end of a period, when total costs and production are known.) (4)
aggregate costs	The accumulated total amount of a particular item of cost over a period of time. (2)
applied overhead	See *total applied (standard) overhead costs.*
appropriation-controlled items	Those items for which the amount projected to be spent is decided by management action rather than by a relationship to other items in the master budget. (15)
artificial intelligence	In manufacturing, machines (robots) that can sense an unaligned state or an improper setting and automatically correct it. (22)
automated cost accounting system	A cost accounting system with an extensive database, including projected cost data for various direct materials, processing operations, start-up costs, and elements of change-over costs that can be called up to project the costs to be incurred in the production of various products. (23)
autonomous operating entity	A corporate subsidiary of a parent corporation or a segment of a corporation for which managers are given operational autonomy, meaning that their operational effectiveness will be evaluated by relating operating results to the segment's investment base. (18)
average investment	The average amount invested in a project over a period of time, calculated (in a simple way) by dividing by 2 the sum of the beginning investment and ending investment. (20)
backflush costing system	A system used in accounting for cost flows in which the allocation of costs is delayed until the point when goods are manufactured or sold. Costs are allocated by *backflushing*—the opposite of allocation procedures followed in a conventional manufacturing cost accounting system, which "flushes" costs through the accounting records as work progresses. Completion of the manufacturing process or the sale of finished goods triggers recognition of the allocations of materials and conversion costs used rather than the actual uses of those resources as in a conventional cost system. (3)
best attainable standards	Standard costs based on the highest level of efficiency that can be achieved in the production of goods or services. (11)
bill of materials	A document listing all materials that should be used in manufacturing the units included in a job order; takes the place of a materials requisition. (4)
break-even analysis	Analysis of projected cost and volume data designed to show the level of operations, in terms of either dollars or units, at which a firm's total costs for a reporting period will exactly equal total revenues for the period. (16)
budget variance	The difference between actual overhead costs and the costs allowed in the flexible budget for the level of activity actually achieved; also known as *controllable variance.* (13)

buffer stock	The stock of goods held to provide a cushion (or buffer) to keep operations from being interrupted because of lack of units to process. (19)
by-product	A product that emerges from a joint process and whose sales value is relatively insignificant when compared with the sales value of the major products, therefore making it economically impractical to carry out the manufacturing process to produce the by-product independent of the major products (if that were possible). (9)
capacity constrained resource	The resource that constrains (limits) the production capacity of a plant (CCR). (24)
capital-budgeting techniques	Techniques used in deciding whether a firm should invest in a new project or in new equipment. It involves relating the expected return from the project or equipment to the investment required to acquire it. This term is defined more completely in Chapter 20. (3)
capital expenditures budget	A schedule included in a master budget that indicates the expected outlays for plant and equipment during the period covered by the budget. (15)
cash break-even point	The level of operations at which projected cash outflows will equal projected cash inflows. (16)
cash budget	A schedule included in a master budget in which projected beginning and ending cash balances and inflows and outflows of cash are given; typically organized to show beginning cash balance plus projected receipts for the budget period minus projected disbursements for the budget period, to arrive at a projected end-of-period cash balance. (15)
cash inflow after taxes	The inflow of spendable resources after paying taxes on the income generated; calculated by adding depreciation and other long-term asset amortization and noncash expenses to net income after taxes. (20)
cash inflow before taxes	The inflow of spendable resources before deducting income taxes; calculated by adding depreciation and other long-term amortization and noncash expenses to net income before taxes. (20)
change-over costs	The costs associated with changing from the production of one product to the production of another. Such costs are found both in an automated manufacturing environment and in a nonautomated environment. (23)
common costs	Costs of facilities or services associated with the output of two or more operations, products, or services; also known as *joint costs*. (18)
computer-integrated manufacturing (CIM)	Completely automated manufacturing in which all operations are performed by robots controlled by appropriately programmed computers. (3) A manufacturing plant in which the computerized elements of factory automation, such as computer-aided design (CAD) and computer-aided manufacturing (CAM), have been integrated. More recently, CIM has been extended to include people, policies, procedures, information, and business strategy along with the technology. (22)
constraining factor	See *critical factor*.
constraint	Anything that limits the system from achieving higher performances in terms of its goal. (15)

continuous budgeting A moving projection of financial operations for a series of periods immediately ahead. At the end of each period, the portion of the projection associated with that period is removed, and a new projection for the next future period not previously budgeted is added to the series. (15)

contribution margin An amount equal to the difference between sales revenue and variable costs. (14)

contribution-margin ratio The percentage relationship between contribution margin and sales, found by dividing contribution margin by sales. (16)

control account A general ledger summary account that is supported in detail by individual accounts known as a *subsidiary ledger*. (5)

controllable variance See *budget variance*.

conversion costs The sum of direct labor and manufacturing-overhead costs. These are the costs incurred in converting raw materials to finished product. (1)

correlation analysis A technique used to discover and evaluate possible relationships amongst two or more variables, with the objective of predicting future behavior of one or more of the variables. *Caution:* Correlation does not necessarily imply causation. (21)

cost That which must be given up in order to acquire, produce, or effect something. (1)

cost accumulation centers Departments or segments of operations that are the responsibility of specific persons within the organization and for which costs are accumulated. (2)

cost driver The item or activity that causes the incurrence of a specific cost. (23)

cost of goods manufactured The costs attached to goods transferred from the factory to finished-goods inventory. It is total current manufacturing costs adjusted for beginning and ending work in process (WIP) (that is, plus beginning inventory of WIP and minus ending inventory of WIP). (1)

cost of production report Document used in a process-costing system to summarize the flows of units and costs through a process or department. Both units and dollars are accounted for via a four-element equation: Beginning balance + Additions − Removals = Ending balance. (6)

cost of sales The costs attached (allocated) to units of finished product delivered to customers. (1)

cost–volume–profit analysis Analysis of the relationships between either historical or projected costs and the volume of operations; includes break-even analysis but also extends to an analysis of the level of operations required to achieve certain targeted levels of income, the effect that projected changes in operations are expected to have on the break-even level and similar sensitivity issues. (16)

critical factor The primary constraint on the overall level of operations of a firm that determines the starting point for a master budget. In most instances, this is sales; therefore, the sales budget is the starting point for the master budget of most firms. Also called *constraining factor*. (15)

currently attainable standards	Standard costs based on the level of efficiency and production expected to be achieved during the next fiscal period. Such standards allow for normal-spoilage and/or normal-scrap losses as well as expected lost labor time and ordinary equipment failure. Also known as *expected actual standards*. (11)
cycle time	The time required to produce a completed unit. (20)
debit memo	A document stating that the account payable to a vendor is being debited for the return of merchandise or for the amount of an allowance to be made for damaged goods. (4)
decision points	The points in the overall budgeting process at which management must make decisions regarding projected operations to allow the preparation of the master budget to proceed—for example, the decision as to the levels of inventory the firm should attempt to achieve by the end of the budget period. (15)
direct allocation	The allocation of service department (cost-accumulation center) costs directly to producing departments (cost-accumulation centers), with no allocation to other *service* departments. (2)
direct costing	See *variable costing*.
direct fixed costs	The fixed costs that can be directly associated with the implementation of an operating decision. (19)
direct labor	Amounts paid to manufacturing employees who work directly on changing materials to finished products and whose efforts can be economically traced to a particular unit of finished product. (1)
direct labor budget	A schedule in which the amounts of projected direct labor costs for the period(s) are summarized as part of the master budget. (15)
direct labor efficiency variance	An amount equal to the difference between the actual direct labor hours used and the standard hours allowed for the production achieved multiplied by the standard labor rate per hour; also called *direct labor quantity variance*. (12)
direct labor rate variance	An amount equal to the difference between the standard and actual direct labor rates per hour multiplied by the actual number of direct labor hours used during a reporting period; also called *direct labor price variance*. (12)
direct materials	Materials that physically become a part of a finished product that can be feasibly identified with the product, and whose amount can be economically traced to a particular unit of finished product. (1)
direct materials price variance	An amount equal to the difference between the standard and actual prices per unit multiplied by the actual number of units either purchased (preferred treatment) or issued into process. (12)
direct materials quantity variance	An amount equal to the difference between the actual quantity of materials used and the standard quantity of materials allowed to produce a given output multiplied by the standard cost per unit; also called *direct materials usage variance*. (12)

direct materials usage variance	See *direct materials quantity variance*. (12)
dollar days	A measure of inventory control performance as compared to planned inventory; calculated by multiplying the number of days inventory is late (early) by the throughput (cost) that will be realized (incurred early). (22)
economic order quantity (EOQ)	The number of units (order quantity) of a raw material that should be purchased each time an order is placed in order to minimize the total ordering and carrying costs. (3, 19)
equipment performance records	Records evaluating the performance of individual pieces of equipment within an automated manufacturing environment. (23)
equivalent-units divisor	The divisor used in arriving at unit costs in a process costing system. With a first-in, first-out cost-flow assumption, the divisor is equal to units transferred out plus equivalent units in end-of-period work in process minus equivalent units in beginning-of-period work in process. With a weighted-average cost-flow assumption, the divisor is equal to units transferred out plus equivalent units remaining in end-of-period work in process. (6)
equivalent units of production (EUP)	The number of whole units of production that would have been turned out during a reporting period if all cost efforts had been directed only at turning out completed units. This becomes the equivalent-units divisor when using either a first-in, first-out or last-in, first-out cost-flow assumption and is calculated as the units transferred out plus the equivalent units in end-of-period work in process minus equivalent units in beginning-of-period work in process. Sometimes erroneously considered a synonym for any equivalent-units divisor (see *equivalent-units divisor*). (6)
estimated costs	Predetermined costs usually based on historical cost data adjusted for expected changes in operations. (11)
excess capacity	A situation in which a firm has the capability of producing more goods than are currently being produced without expanding its manufacturing facilities. (14)
expected actual standards	See *currently attainable standards*.
expenses	Costs attached to resources and services consumed in generating revenue; sometimes referred to as *expired costs*. (1)
externally imposed constraint	A constraint on the level of operations imposed by the environment in which a firm operates, such as the maximum volume of the firm's product that can be sold at a specified price. (24)
factory ledger	A separate ledger containing manufacturing-related accounts, such as materials, inventory, work in process, finished goods, and manufacturing overhead, and a balancing reciprocal account generally labeled "general ledger account." (5)
factory ledger account	The reciprocal account reflected in the general ledger as a replacement for the balances in manufacturing-related accounts transferred to a factory ledger. (5)

FIFO method of process costing	The cost flow assumption in a process-costing system that assumes that units and the costs assigned to them flow through a production process on a first-in, first-out basis; current period cost(s) per unit are used to value end-of-period work in process. (6)
financial accounting	The accumulation and presentation of financial data for use by investors, creditors, and other external parties. (1)
finished-goods inventory	Manufactured units that have been completed and are being held for sale to customers. (2)
first-in, first-out (FIFO) cost flow assumption	An assumption used in assigning unit costs to goods transferred out or sold and to ending inventories whereby the costs associated with the oldest units in stock are assigned to the first units sold during a reporting period. These costs become cost of sales. That means that the most recent costs per unit will be assigned to the units remaining in inventory. The actual physical flow does not have to be first-in, first-out to use this method of assigning costs. (1)
fixed automation manufacturing system	A conventional assembly-line manufacturing system that includes elements of automation—automated equipment that is single-purpose and not adaptable to new (different) uses. (22)
fixed costs	Costs that in the aggregate remain the same at different levels of operations within some relevant range. (2)
fixed overhead application rate	Budgeted fixed overhead for a period of time divided by the number of units of the activity base (generally direct labor hours) expected to be achieved during that period. The calculation is made for the purpose of establishing an overhead application rate used in both historical and standard cost systems. (17)
flexible automated manufacturing system	A manufacturing system that is completely automated but has flexibility built into it through the medium of alternate computer programs that permit the manufacture of differentiated items in small batches for specific customers or markets. (22)
flexible budget	A budget showing the amounts of costs (and/or revenues) expected to be incurred or realized over a period of time at different levels of activity (measured in terms of some activity base such as direct labor hours, direct labor costs, or machine-hours). A *flexible manufacturing overhead budget* gives the projected costs of various manufacturing overhead items at different levels of activity. (4)
flexible manufacturing overhead budget	See *flexible budget*.
formula relationships	The relationships expected to exist among various budgetary items programmed into the budgetary process. For example, with knowledge of beginning inventory, projected end-of-period inventory, and the amount of sales expected to be achieved, the number of units of finished goods to be produced can be calculated by use of the four-element equation showing beginning balance plus production minus sales equals ending balance. (15)

form utility	Increases in the usefulness of materials and other resources resulting from the conversion of resources into services or products that have different characteristics from the materials and services purchased. (1)
full costing	See *absorption costing*.
functional-expenditure data	In governmental accounting, the amounts of expenditures allocated to various functions performed by a governmental entity. (10)
functional-expenditure-per-unit data	An amount equal to the total expenditures allocated to each function performed divided by the number of functional activity units provided. (10)
functional-unit cost	An amount equal to total costs allocated to each function performed divided by the number of functional activity units provided. (10)
general ledger	A ledger containing the accounts used by a business as part of its double-entry bookkeeping system; contains accounts for all assets, liabilities, owners' equity, income, and expense items required by that system. (5)
general ledger account	The balancing reciprocal account found in a factory ledger when using a split-ledger cost accounting system (see *factory ledger*). (5)
generally accepted accounting practices (GAAP)	Accounting practices that conform to conventions, rules, and procedures that have general acceptability by the accounting profession. (1)
general operating costs	Costs incurred in carrying out the selling and administrative activities of a business. (2)
gross-margin pricing	A pricing procedure that endeavors to realize a price for merchandise that will provide for recovery of the cost of the goods plus a specified margin, in dollars or a percentage calculated on the basis of sales price or on the basis of cost. (19)
gross-margin (profit) variance	The difference between actual gross margins of succeeding periods, or the difference between the projected gross margin and actual gross margin of a reporting period; can be divided into price and volume components. (17)
high–low, two-point method	A way to estimate the fixed and variable components of a semi-variable cost using the differences between the historical amounts for highest and lowest levels of activities (independent variable) and the costs relating to those activities (dependent variable). The variable component per unit of activity is estimated by dividing the difference between the high cost and the low cost by the difference between the high-activity and low-activity amounts. [The activity (independent variable) may be stated in terms of units or some other measure, and it is treated as if it "causes" the dependent variable, cost, to change.] The fixed component then can be estimated as the amount left after removing the aggregate variable component from either the high-level or low-level total cost figures. (11)
historical costs	See *actual costs*.
ideal standards	See *best attainable standards*.

idle-capacity costs A variance attributable to failure to utilize facilities at their practical capacity. Idle capacity may be planned (for future expansion) or unplanned (erroneous demand estimates). (13)

imputed costs Hypothetical or opportunity costs assigned to a product or to an alternative in a decision-making process based on foregone alternative uses of resources. These costs are not entered into accounting records but are useful for cost analysis. (2)

imputed sales value at split-off A value assigned to a joint product that has no sales value at the point of split-off. The assigned amount is calculated by subtracting additional processing costs from the sales value of the product after additional processing, net of selling expenses. That figure is then used with the sales values at split-off of other joint products in allocating joint costs by use of the relative sales value method. Also *called net realizable value.* (9)

incremental contribution margin The additional contribution margin resulting from the sale of one additional unit or group of units; also called *marginal contribution margin.* (14)

incremental income The change in income (revenue) attributed to (a) the addition of one unit of sales or (b) the addition of one item to the firm's resource base; also called *incremental revenue.* (20)

incremental investment The additional investment required to embark on a proposed project such as the addition of equipment or enlargement of facilities. (20)

incremental manufacturing cost The additional manufacturing cost required to produce one additional unit or group of units; also called *marginal manufacturing costs.* (14)

incremental revenue The additional revenue resulting from the sale of one additional unit or group of units; also called *marginal revenue.* (14)

indirect labor Labor costs that are considered to be overhead, that is, amounts paid to manufacturing employees other than laborers working directly on the product (direct labor). (1)

indirect materials Materials used in keeping a factory in operation that do not become a part of the product being produced, or materials used in the product in such small quantities that it is not feasible to trace their costs to the product. (1)

internal constraint A constraint on the level of operations caused by the limited availability of a resource such as machine-time that makes it impossible for the firm to produce as many units as the market will absorb at a specified price. (24)

internal control system The system of documentation and mandated procedures within an organization that is designed to protect physical assets from misuse and to ensure the implementation of managerial directives. (15)

internal rate of return The rate of interest at which the present value of expected cash inflows from a project equals the present value of expected cash outflows. This is the interest rate earned by the project, and it is compared with the cost of capital, stated as a percentage, to determine whether the project

	should be given further consideration. Also called *time-adjusted rate of return*. (20)
inventory	Materials and supplies (including added conversion costs) held by a firm either for use in the production of finished goods or for sale to customers. (1)
investment center	A segment of a corporation whose performance is measured in terms of the relationship of operating results to the resources committed to the segment (investment base). (18)
just-in-time (JIT)	Just-in-time inventory policy: an operating policy that calls for materials, partially processed goods, and finished goods to be delivered to the locations where they are to be processed or sold, at exactly the time they are needed. In a perfect application, minimal inventories would be held in a JIT environment. (3)
job-order costing	A cost-accumulation and cost-allocation system that accumulates the manufacturing costs (materials, direct labor, and overhead) associated with separately identifiable lots of goods as the production process is carried out. (2)
job-order sheet	A form used to accumulate the manufacturing costs (direct materials, direct labor, and applied manufacturing overhead) allocated to a specific lot of goods as it is being produced. (4)
job time card	A form used to accumulate the amount of time that an employee spends working on a particular job on a specified day. (4)
joint costs	The common costs of two or more simultaneously produced products before the point at which the joint products become individually identifiable, accumulated in a joint-processing cost-accumulation center. Also see *common costs*. (9)
joint product	A product produced in conjunction with one or more other products, each earning revenue sufficient to justify joint production. (9)
just in time	See *JIT*. (3)
labor-efficiency variance or labor-quality variance	See *direct labor efficiency variance*. (12)
labor-rate variance or labor-price variance	See *direct labor rate variance*. (12)
lead time	See *manufacturing lead time; total product lead time*. (22)
learning curve	A concept, often presented graphically as a "curve," that projects an expected reduction in the amount of time required to process a unit of product because of the "learning" or "experience" acquired as the processing operation is repeated; also called the *experience curve*. (11)
least-squares method	Regression analysis: a mathematical procedure for estimating the variable and fixed elements of a semivariable cost. It develops an equation (in this book, a *linear* equation) for total cost that minimizes the sum of the squares of the historical deviations from that equation or line. Total pro-

jected cost can then be expressed as a sum of aggregate fixed cost plus the variable cost per unit (the slope of the line) multiplied by the number of units. (11)

leveraged project (investment)
A project financed with borrowed funds. (20)

LIFO method of process costing
A process costing system operating under the assumption that the costs associated with the last units transferred into a process or department will be the first costs transferred out of that process or department. Thus, end-of-period work-in-process inventory is valued via a "layering" of previous periods' costs. (6)

linear programming
A mathematical model used in making operating decisions involving the allocation of scarce resources when the achievement of the operating objective (the objective function) is subject to multiple constraints; requires a quantitative statement of the objective function (maximization of contribution margin or minimization of costs) and of each of the constraints associated with carrying out operations. (19)

long-term decisions
Decisions relating to operations extending over a number of fiscal periods (beyond one year) and generally involving judgments about the acquisition of long-term assets and the amount of production capacity to be provided. (14)

lost units
Units that either disappear through shrinkage or have defects caused by processing that keep them from being transferred to the next process or to finished stock as good units. (8)

machine-hour labor rate
A concept developed by Alexander Hamilton Church that, in effect, treats the machine as a laborer with the cost of operating the machine converted to an hourly rate. (22)

make-or-buy decision
Narrowly, a decision as to whether a particular part or subassembly should be manufactured or purchased from an outside vendor. More generally, any decision concerning internal versus external construction. (19)

management by exception
The technique of managing operations by giving attention only to exceptions from expected goals. In connection with standard costs, this is achieved by giving attention only to the variances from standards. (11)

managerial accounting
The measurement, accumulation, analysis, and presentation of financial data primarily for use by personnel within an entity's organization. (1)

manual manufacturing system
A manufacturing system in which the line employees are the primary work initiators: work is delivered to production employees at their work stations, where they perform the operations for which they are responsible, after which the products are moved to another work station or to a storage area. (22)

manufacturing cell
A plant layout whereby production equipment is arranged so all pieces of equipment required to produce a particular part are grouped together to minimize the movement of semiprocessed units during the production process; sometimes called a *minifactory*. (3)

manufacturing costs	The sum of direct materials used, direct labor costs incurred, and manufacturing overhead applied to production during an operating period. (1, 2)
manufacturing lead time	The time required to completely produce a product (from the time materials are added until the finished unit is ready for shipment). (22)
manufacturing overhead	Costs other than direct materials and direct labor costs that are incurred in keeping a factory in operation. (1)
manufacturing-overhead budget	A schedule included in a master budget in which the projected manufacturing overhead for the budget period is summarized. (15)
manufacturing-overhead control account	The account used to accumulate actual overhead costs as they are incurred during each period. (5)
manufacturing-overhead cost summary account	The account into which various manufacturing-overhead accounts are closed at the end of each period when accounts are maintained in the general ledger or factory ledger for each of the separately categorized overhead cost items. (5)
manufacturing-overhead efficiency variance	See *overhead efficiency variance.*
manufacturing-overhead spending variance	See *overhead spending variance.*
manufacturing-overhead-volume variance	See *volume variance.*
manufacturing resource planning II (MRP II)	A systems planning and control computer program that integrates production and inventory plans into the financial accounting system and permits "what if?" questions of its considerable database. (22)
marginal contribution margin	See *incremental contribution margin.*
marginal manufacturing cost	See *incremental manufacturing cost.*
marginal revenue	See *incremental revenue.*
master budget	A document that consolidates all budgets of an organization into an overall plan, including the projection of a cash flow statement and an operating statement for the budget period and a balance sheet for the end of the budget period. (1, 15)
matching convention	The overall guideline in accumulating and allocating costs that calls for relating costs to the revenues produced by those costs. Costs matched with revenues become expenses on the income statement. (2)
material requirements planning (MRP)	An automated information system using bills of materials, inventory data, and the master production schedule to calculate materials requirements and to generate necessary paperwork. (22)

materials inventory — Materials purchased and held for use in manufacturing finished products or to facilitate the production process. (1)

materials price variance — An amount equal to the difference between the standard and actual prices per unit multiplied by the actual number of units either purchased (preferred treatment) or issued into process.

materials purchases budget — A schedule included in a master budget in which projected materials purchases are shown. (15)

materials requisition form — A form used to indicate the amount and dollar value of materials issued from materials inventory into the manufacturing process. It is a source document for recording the transfer of materials to production. (4)

materials return form — A form used to reflect the amount and dollar values of materials returned from the factory to materials inventory. (4)

maximum inventory level — The largest number of units of an inventory item that a company should ever have in stock; equal to the minimum inventory level plus the economic order quantity. (19)

Microsoft® PROJECT — A computer software program designed to solve network-type problems. Critical paths and slack times are identified, and budget capability links costs with activities. (21)

minimum inventory level — The smallest number of units of an inventory item that a company should ever have in stock, to protect against interruptions of production or loss of sales due to delays in delivery of the item. (19)

model building — The construction of some device (for example, an equation, flowchart, or diagram) that depicts interrelationships among factors that can exist in a real situation. (21)

modified high–low, two-point method — A way to estimate the fixed and variable components of a semivariable cost. Historical cost and activity data are divided into two equal subsets, one containing the higher data points and the other the lower data points. The data in the two subsets are then averaged and used as the high and low points in the high–low, two-point formula. (11)

monetary assets — Cash, or claims to cash, that are fixed in dollar amounts regardless of changes in the level of prices. (18)

multiprocess operation — The division of a factory into sequential processes through which products must pass as they are being produced. Costs (direct materials, direct labor, and manufacturing overhead) are accumulated separately for each process and allocated to the products as they pass through the process. (7)

negative net present value — An amount equal to the excess of the present value of the investment in a project plus the projected present value of cash outflows from the project over the projected present value of cash inflows from the project, all based on a predetermined discount rate. Projects with negative net present values would not be accepted. (20)

net assets — Assets minus liabilities; also *owner's equity*. (20)

net liquid resource inflows	More correctly describes what is generally called *cash inflows*; calls attention to the fact that part of the so-called cash flows may be in the form of increases in short-term receivables, decreases in short-term payables, or increases in other noncash current assets. (20)
net present value (NPV)	The difference between the projected present value of net cash inflows from operating an investment project, discounted at a specified rate, and the present value of the cost of investment in the project. (20)
net-present-value method	A method of evaluating an investment opportunity that compares the present value of the required investment with the present value of projected cash inflows, based on a specified rate of discount. (20)
net realizable value	Generally, a value equal to a product's sales value less its cost of completion and disposal. Here, a value that may be assigned to a joint product or by-product equal to its anticipated sales value less the sum of disposal cost and the cost of processing beyond the point at which the product is removed from the joint process. (9)
net realizable value less normal margin	Generally, a value equal to a product's sales value less the sum of additional processing costs, disposal cost, and normal profit margin. Here, a value that may be assigned to a joint product or by-product, equal to its anticipated sales value less the sum of additional processing costs, disposal cost, and normal profit margin. (9)
net throughput	The difference between revenue and out-of-pocket costs (primarily raw materials). (24)
net-throughput variance	The difference between the amount of net throughput actually realized and the net throughput that could have been realized with perfectly synchronized operations. (24)
net working capital	The difference between current assets and current liabilities at a particular instant in time; often called *working capital*. (20)
nonmonetary assets	Assets other than monetary assets, including assets whose values can increase or decrease due to changes in the purchasing power of the monetary unit (dollars in the United States). (18)
normal-cost system	A cost system in which actual direct materials, actual direct labor, and applied, rather than actual, overhead costs are accumulated and allocated to units produced. (4)
normal-spoilage costs	Costs associated with units that either disappear through shrinkage or are found to be defective that are not in excess of the losses expected to occur on a repetitive basis during the manufacturing process. Such costs are considered unavoidable and are allocated to good units. (8)
normal-spoilage loss	The loss associated with spoiled units that cannot be eliminated on a cost-effective basis and thus is included as a product cost. (5)
normal standards	Standard costs based on the quantity of materials, cost per unit of material, the number of hours of labor, cost per hour of direct labor, and cost per unit of manufacturing overhead that can be expected to be achieved over a longer period of time, such as the length of the business cycle (perhaps three to five years). (11)

no-specific-recognition method — A method of accounting for spoilage losses by eliminating the spoiled units from the equivalent-units divisors so the spoilage loss automatically will be reflected in increased costs per unit; also, the method of accounting for reworking costs when those costs are not removed from work in process. (8)

operating expenses — Expenses incurred in carrying out the selling and administrative expenses incurred during an operating period activities of a business. As used in Chapter 24, the total of all manufacturing expenses (except materials used) plus selling and administrative expenses incurred during an operating period. (*Note:* This special definition is used *only* in Chapter 24.) (1, 24)

operating-expenses budget — A schedule included in a master budget in which projected operating expenses (that is, selling expenses and general and administrative expenses) are shown. (15)

operations research (OR) — Work done in solving management problems, particularly those of a complex nature that can benefit from mathematical or statistical modeling; also called *management science.* (21)

opportunity cost — Cost represented by the value of the best alternative foregone by adopting a particular strategy or employing resources in a specific manner. (1)

optimal production technology (OPT) — Computer software that simulates the production process so bottlenecks can be spotted before they occur. Its objective is to balance the flow of goods through manufacturing operations. (22)

out-of-pocket costs — Incurred costs that are paid for in cash, by giving up other current assets or by the incurrence of current liabilities; also can be thought of as variable costs (that is, costs other than the fixed costs or sunk costs associated with a product or operations). (20)

output measures — The extent to which a company has met its delivery schedules; should disclose the relationships between actual and targeted amounts, to call attention both to a failure to produce goods as needed and to the failure of equipment (and labor) to be idle when scheduled to be idle. (23)

overapplied overhead — The amount by which applied overhead exceeds the amount of actual overhead incurred during a reporting period. (2)

overhead efficiency variance — An amount equal to the difference between standard hours of work produced and actual hours used for that production multiplied by the variable overhead application rate; measures how efficiently the activity base (direct labor hours, machine-hours, raw materials cost, and so forth) was utilized. (13)

overhead rate — See *standard manufacturing overhead rate.*

overhead spending variance — An amount equal to the difference between actual overhead incurred and the costs allowed in the flexible budget for the actual hours worked. (13)

pay-back method — A method of evaluating an investment opportunity that provides a measure of the time required to recover the initial amount invested in a project. (20)

perfect knowledge	An ideal state connected with the use of probability analysis in which the decision maker would know the appropriate action to take and the pay-off(s) associated with that action and thus be able to calculate the value (or cost) of perfect information. (21)
perfectly synchronized operations	The operations of a plant in which the internally constrained resource is being used at as near 100% of its available time as is practically feasible and all other resources are subordinated to the needs of the constrained resource. (24)
period costs	Costs related to the passage of time and not to the products produced. (2)
periodic-inventory method	A system of assigning costs to goods transferred or sold and to ending inventory whereby balances are determined on specific dates by physical count rather than on a continuous basis. (1)
perpetual-inventory method	A system of assigning costs to goods transferred or sold and to inventory on a continuously updated basis so that the balance in an inventory account and cumulative cost of sales is known at all times. (1)
PERT (program evaluation and review technique)	A network-based technique for planning and controlling projects or production that shows precedence relationships among tasks or activities to be completed. Allows the decision maker to focus on critical paths that, if shortened, would hasten completion of the project or decrease production time. (21)
pertinent costs	Costs that will be incurred in the future that are different for alternative courses of action; also called *relevant costs*. (19)
physical-inventory method	See *periodic-inventory method*.
place utility	The addition of usefulness (value) to goods by placing them where they can be conveniently examined and purchased, such as a merchandising business does when it places its goods in counters, on shelves, or in catalogs for customers to examine and purchase. (1)
positive net present value	An excess of the projected present value of liquid resource inflows from a project over the present value of resource outflows for the project plus the present value of the investment required to implement the project, all based on a specified rate of discount. Projects with positive net present values would be considered for acceptance. (20)
predetermined costs	Costs projected (that is, estimated) in advance of operations, based on a knowledge of how the costs are incurred and the causes of those costs. (1)
predetermined manufacturing-overhead application rate	A rate per unit of activity that is used to allocate the approximate amount of overhead costs incurred to units produced during a reporting period; calculated by dividing expected overhead costs by the expected activity base (such as direct labor, direct labor hours, or machine-hours) that is most closely associated with the incurrence of overhead. (2)
price variance	The difference between the actual and standard costs or prices per unit multiplied by the actual number of units; considered a direct materials price variance when used in relation to materials and a direct labor rate

variance when used in relation to labor. Also, the difference between actual sales of one period and budget sales for the same period (or actual sales of one period and actual sales of another period) attributable to a change in price. (12)

prime costs The sum of the costs of direct materials used and direct labor incurred during an operating period. (1)

probability analysis A technique used to assist in decision making that assigns probabilities to the outcomes of various possible courses of action. (21)

process costing A system of cost accumulation and cost allocation in which costs are accumulated for periods of time by processes or departments that produce identical units, and those costs are then allocated to units produced during each reporting period by using unit-cost data calculated for each process or department. (2)

processing performance measures Measures of start-up costs, change-over costs, inventory, and throughput in an automated manufacturing environment. (23)

process-or-sell decision A decision management may be required to make when a market exists for its product in a semifinished state—that is, whether to finish the product or sell it in its semifinished state. (19)

producing department A department (cost-accumulation center) in which work is performed on the product being manufactured; also called *line department*. (2)

product costs Costs allocated to the products being produced. Initially recorded in inventory (asset) accounts, they become an expense (cost of sales) when the product is sold. (2)

production budget A schedule included in a master budget in which production activities for the budgetary period are summarized. (15)

product life cycle The period of time during which a product can be produced and marketed profitably. (20)

profit center A business's responsibility center that has authority to affect both the revenues earned and the costs incurred by the center. Operational effectiveness is evaluated in terms of the amount of profit generated. (18)

profit potential The profit that should be realized from a project or product during an operating period. (20)

purchase order Traditionally, a formal document signed by a purchasing agent and addressed to a vendor (supplier) requesting the vendor to ship the listed goods to the purchasing company. Purchase orders may be automatically generated by computer and electronically transmitted to vendors. (4)

purchase requisition A document generally originated by the materials stores keeper and forwarded to the purchasing department requesting that specified materials be purchased for materials inventory. If inventory records are computerized, a computer program may have the responsibility for initiating purchase orders. (4)

pure-nonprofit enterprises	Service enterprises that realize substantially all of their resources from taxes or voluntary contributions and distribute the services funded by those resources on the basis of need for the services. (10)
pure-profit enterprises	Enterprises financed by owners and creditors that operate for the purpose of producing net income to be distributed to owners on the basis of ownership interests. (10)
pure volume variance	The difference in the expected and actual gross margin of a multiproduct firm that is attributed entirely to the difference in the volume of products being sold. The amount attributable to each product equals the sum of the differences between the quantities of each product expected to be sold (based on projected sales mix and total quantity of products actually sold) and the quantity of each product budgeted to be sold multiplied by the budgeted gross margin per unit for each product. (17)
quantity variance	A variance caused by the difference between the standard quantity allowed for output achieved and actual quantity used multiplied by the standard cost or price per unit; often called *material usage variance* when used in connection with the analysis of direct material variances, or *labor efficiency variance* when used in connection with the analysis of variances in direct labor. (12)
quasi-nonprofit enterprises	Enterprises that have some but not all of the characteristics of pure-nonprofit enterprises. They are financed by contributions and/or taxes but also realize a significant part of their resource inflows in the form of payments (revenues) for services rendered. (10)
quasi-profit enterprises	Enterprises that have some but not all of the characteristics of profit enterprises. They are financed by member contributions but they distribute benefits or services, rather than earnings, to their members. (10)
queuing theory	A branch of probability theory involving waiting lines (often referred to as *queues*), by which the cost of time lost (by personnel or by products) and the cost of additional facilities can be determined accurately. (21)
rate of return on assets	A measure of asset profitability, calculated by dividing net income by total assets. (20)
rate of return on equity capital	A measure of investment performance for owners, calculated by dividing net income by equity capital. (20)
real time	A computer term; refers to the ability to change data and access new information instantaneously without waiting for batch processing. (22)
receiving report	A document prepared by a person in the receiving department indicating the quantities of goods received, along with notations regarding any damage to the goods when they came into the possession of the purchasing company. (With certain approved vendors, goods may not be inspected upon receipt and a receiving record would not be completed.) (4)
recorded costs	Costs recorded in accounting records. (2)
regression analysis	See *least-squares method.*

relative-sales-value method	A method of allocating joint costs on the basis of the aggregate sales value of each of the joint products in relation to the total aggregate sales value of all joint products at the point of split-off. (The numerator in each ratio is the aggregate sales value at the split-off point of the individual product; the denominator is the sum of the aggregate sales values at the split-off point of *all* of the joint products.) (9)
relevant costs	Future costs that are expected to differ for the various alternatives being considered as a decision is being made. They highlight the essential cost differences between alternative courses of action. Also called *pertinent costs*. (1, 14, 19)
relevant range	A range of levels of operations over which aggregate fixed costs and aggregate variable costs can be projected to behave in a linear fashion. (2)
residual income	The income left after deducting a designated amount for the cost of the capital provided to earn income from net income before this deduction. (18)
resource acquisitions measures	Measures of the cost and quality of acquired resources, primarily materials acquired for the production process. (23)
resource utilization measures	Measures of the amount of inventory held in relation to the needs for inventory; the extent to which the production of finished units deviates from sales or production forecasts within an automated or synchronized manufacturing environment. (23)
responsibility accounting	A method of internal reporting that assigns costs to organizational subunits of a firm based on controlability. Each subunit report contains the items they have the ability to control. Therefore they have responsibility for controlling them. (17)
return on equity	See *rate of return on equity capital*.
return on investment	Net income divided by average net assets; also defined as the rate of net sales to investment used to produce those sales multiplied by the ratio of net income to net sales. (18)
revenue center	A corporation's responsibility center that is primarily responsible for generating corporate revenues and whose effectiveness is measured chiefly by the amount of revenues generated. (18)
revenue-producing cost centers	As used in Chapter 10, cost-accumulation centers that provide billable services to an organization's clientele. More generally, a revenue center that also is a cost center. (10, 18)
reworked units	Defective units recycled through certain production processes to correct the defects and thus allow them to pass inspection as good units. (8)
reworking costs	Costs associated with the recycling of defective units through specified production processes to remedy a defective condition. (8)
robotics	The use of mechanical robots to perform various operations in the manufacture of products. (3)

sales budget	A schedule included in a master budget in which projected sales for the budgetary period are shown. (15)
sales mix	The relative composition of various products sold by a firm. *Product mix* (often used as a synonym) is a broader term, for it can relate to the relative composition of products manufactured and/or sold by a firm. (16)
sales mix variance	The variance in gross margin attributed to the difference between the sales mix budgeted and the sales mix actually realized, or the difference between the sales mix of one period and the sales mix of another period. (17)
sales-package contribution margin	The contribution margin of a combination of products based on the expected relative volumes of the individual products to be sold. For example, if a firm manufactures and sells products A, B, and C, in the proportion 3 to 2 to 1, respectively, a sales package would be 3 units of A, 2 units of B, and 1 unit of C, and one weighted-average contribution margin can be associated with the "package." (16)
sales revenue variance	The difference between the actual and budgeted sales revenues for a revenue center, or the difference between the sales revenues of one period and those of another (previous) period; can be divided into two parts— *sales price variance* (change in price times the actual units sold) and *sales volume variance* (change in volume times the budgeted or previous sales price per unit). (18)
sales volume variance	The difference between expected and actual sales that is caused by the change in the volume of sales. (17)
scattergraph method	Used in estimating the fixed and variable components of a semivariable cost. Historical costs and activity data are plotted on a graph, with dollar amounts (dependent variable) along the vertical axis and activity levels (independent variable) along the horizontal axis. The total cost line is then drawn so as to place approximately the same number of data points on each side of the line. The fixed element of the semivariable cost can be determined by reference to the intercept of that line with the vertical axis of the graph. Variable cost per unit of activity can be determined by subtracting the fixed costs from total costs at any activity level and dividing that figure by the number of units of activity associated with that cost. The projected total cost then can be stated as the sum of the aggregate fixed cost plus the variable cost per unit multiplied by the projected number of units of activity. (11)
scrap	Materials coming out of the production process that have no value other than as salvage, such as metal trimmings from stamping operations and spoiled units salvaged for the value of the metal or other materials included in them. (8)
segment cost data	The costs attributed to a segment of a business, including variable costs of the segment plus fixed costs incurred by or on behalf of the segment. (17)
segment of a business	A component of a business whose activities constitute a separately identifiable line of business or class of customer or territory. (18)

semivariable costs	Costs that include both variable and fixed components; also called *semi-fixed costs*. (2)
sensitivity analysis	The process of identifying variations that might occur in projected data in relation to changes in other (key) data. (16)
service department	A department within a business that exists for the purpose of providing services or assistance to other departments. (2)
service enterprises	Enterprises engaged in converting resources into services rather than into finished goods. (10)
service implementation costs	Costs incurred by a business or nonprofit organization in providing services to the organization's clientele; comparable to cost of sales for a manufacturing or merchandising firm. (10)
short-term operating decisions	Day-to-day operating decisions requiring no additional investment in long-term operating assets (operating decisions made within the constraint of the present investment base of the firm). (14, 19)
shrinkage	Spoilage losses that result from shrinkage in the volume of goods being produced—for example, the shrinkage that generally occurs when liquids go through a cooking process. (8)
simulation	A method of studying operational decisions in which a model of the system or process is subjected to a series of manipulations under varying assumptions related to the decisions; can range from simple cost–volume–profit relationships for a single period to the use of complex computer-based models to examine problems involving uncertainty. (21)
simultaneous allocation	A system for allocating service department (cost-accumulation center) costs to producing departments by the use of simultaneous equations that explicitly recognize the services provided to other service departments. Equations developed for allocating the costs of each service department to other service departments are solved simultaneously. The artificial costs resulting from the simultaneous solution are allocated to all departments benefiting from the service department's activities. (2)
specific-recognition method	A method of accounting for defective (lost) units in which the costs associated with the units are separately determined and allocated either to goods units produced or to abnormal-spoilage loss; also, the method of accounting for reworking costs when those costs are removed from work in process and labeled as reworking costs. (Revoking costs removed from work in process are debited either to manufacturing overhead or to abnormal loss for the period.) (8)
split ledger system	A bookkeeping system in which the manufacturing-related accounts are removed from the general ledger and placed in a separate factory ledger. Such an arrangement requires the substitution of a reciprocal factory ledger account in the general ledger to replace the accounts transferred to the factory ledger. A general ledger reciprocal account (general ledger account) is required in the factory ledger to allow that ledger to be maintained as a self-balancing double-entry accounting system. (5)

spoilage costs	The costs of production associated with defective units in excess of amounts recovered from their sales. (8)
spoiled units	Units that are damaged, do not meet specifications, or are otherwise unsuitable for further processing or sale as good output; includes normal as well as abnormal spoilage. (8)
standard cost card	The card or sheet that indicates the amounts of standard costs expected to be incurred to acquire or produce a single unit. (11)
standard costs	Predetermined costs, based on a careful projection of quantity and unit-cost goals, that are expected to be met in the production of goods or services. (11)
standard cost system	A cost-accumulation and cost-allocation system in which manufacturing costs per unit are predetermined and applied to goods as they are produced. Actual costs also are accumulated and compared to standard costs to determine variances. (4)
standard fixed manufacturing-overhead rate	Budgeted fixed overhead for a period of time divided by the number of units of the activity base (generally, direct labor hours) expected to be achieved during that period; used to establish an overhead application rate for both normal and standard cost systems. (13)
standard hours of production	An amount equal to the number of equivalent units of production multiplied by the number of standard hours allowed for the production of each unit; measures the amount of production achieved during a reporting period when using a standard-cost system. (11, 13)
standard overhead application rate	Total manufacturing overhead projected in a flexible budget for the level of activity expected to be achieved divided by the number of units of the activity base (generally, direct labor hours) associated with the projected level of production. (13)
standard variable manufacturing-overhead rate	The total projected variable overhead for a projected level of production divided by the projected activity base (generally direct labor hours) associated with that level of activity. (13)
start-up costs	The costs associated with getting a new product on the production line, including the costs of designing the product and testing its manufacturing feasibility. All costs incurred during total product lead time. (23)
statement of cash flows	A statement showing cash inflows and outflows for a reporting period divided into operating, investing, and financing subsections. (15)
statistical probability analysis	The implementation of probability analysis within the constraints of statistical rules. (21)
step method of allocating service department costs	A method of allocating service department costs that begins by allocating to all other departments (both service and production) the costs of that service department providing the most service to other service departments. The total costs accumulated for each of the other service departments, including those allocated in previous steps, are then allocated on a step basis to all remaining departments (producing departments and service departments that have not yet had their costs allocated) until all service department costs have been allocated to producing departments. (2)

step-variable costs Costs that, in the aggregate, remain fixed over a limited range of operating levels, beyond which they advance a full step upward and again remain fixed over another small range of operating levels. An example would be the additional salary cost when a second supervisor has to be added upon reaching a certain level of operations. (2)

strategic decisions Policy-setting decisions management makes infrequently but that have a great impact on the future operations of a company—for example, the decision to implement a total quality control (TQC) system, or the decision to operate in a JIT manufacturing environment. (23)

subsidiary ledger A supporting ledger, consisting of a group of accounts, that provides a detailed breakdown of the contents of the control account to which it relates. The sum of the balances in the subsidiary ledger accounts will equal the balance in the control account maintained in either the general ledger or the factory ledger. (5)

sunk costs Costs that cannot be recovered regardless of which of the alternate decisions being considered is made. (1)

supporting-service cost centers Cost-accumulation centers that provide services to revenue-producing cost centers; comparable to service-department cost centers for a manufacturing firm. (10)

sustentation costs Costs incurred by a nonprofit organization in sustaining itself; primarily fund-raising costs and certain administrative costs. (10)

synchronous manufacturing A manufacturing control system that focuses on the key constraints and control points in the plant in order to optimize total system performance (rather than individual subsystem efficiency). (23)

targeted net operating income The amount of net operating income a firm wants to achieve during an operating period; typically used to project the amount of sales, in either dollars or units, that will be required to produce the desired operating income. (16)

tax shield The amount of tax benefit associated with a noncash expense, such as depreciation or loss on the disposal of an asset, when cash-flow projections are developed. (19)

technological revolution A period when technological developments occur so rapidly that most equipment becomes obsolete before it has lost its physically productive capability. (20)

Theory of Constraints A theory that postulates that there are identifiable constraints associated with the operations of any business and that management should exercise control over firm operations by identifying those constraints and managing them so as to use the firm's resources most effectively. Also applied to the determination of sales mix. (19, 24)

throughput The extent to which a manufacturing system has generated profit through sales of goods; usually calculated as total sales less materials costs. Where materials represent the only variable cost of production, throughput is equivalent to contribution margin. (22)

throughput speed The length of time it takes a product to move through the manufacturing process and be sold; equal to manufacturing lead time plus the time to sell and deliver (ship) the product. (23)

throughput variance — The difference between the amount of throughput actually realized and the throughput that could have been realized with perfectly exploited and synchronized operation. (24)

time-adjusted rate-of-return method — See *internal rate of return*.

time value of money — The value associated with the use of money over a period of time that causes cash currently held to be worth more than a future claim to cash. (20)

total applied (standard) overhead cost — An amount equal to the standard hours of production achieved multiplied by the standard overhead rate per hour. (13)

total overhead variance — An amount equal to the difference between actual overhead incurred and applied overhead for a reporting period; also called *underapplied or overapplied overhead*. (13)

total product lead time — The time required to design a product, modify or design equipment, conduct market research, and obtain all necessary materials. *Lead time* begins when a decision has been made to accept an order or produce a new product and ends when production commences. (22)

total quality control (TQC) — A manufacturing approach whose ultimate goal is zero defects. To achieve this goal, responsibility for quality is placed on the worker (builder of the product) rather than on the inspector. (22)

traceable fixed costs — Fixed costs that can be directly associated with a specific segment of a business's operations. (14)

trading on the equity — Financing an investment through debt with the intention that the investment will produce a return in excess of the interest to be paid on the debt (see *leveraged project*). (20)

traditional costing — See *absorption costing*.

transfer pricing — The pricing of goods or services transferred from one segment of a business to another. (18)

transferred-in costs — The sum of direct materials, labor, and manufacturing-overhead costs allocated to units in prior departments before the units are transferred to the current processing department. (7)

underapplied overhead — The amount by which actual overhead exceeds the amount of overhead applied to production. (2)

unit cost — The cost associated with a single unit of product; calculated by dividing the aggregate cost of producing goods by the number of units turned out in incurring those costs. (1, 2)

variable costing — A system for accumulating and allocating manufacturing costs that allocates only variable manufacturing costs to the units produced. All fixed manufacturing costs are allocated to the periods in which the costs are incurred. Also called *direct costing*. (2, 14)

variable cost percentage — The percentage relationship between variable costs and sales, calculated by dividing variable costs by sales; also called *variable cost ratio*. (16)

variable costs	Costs that in the aggregate vary directly with changes in the level of operations within a firm's relevant range. Within this range, the variable cost per unit will be constant. (2)
variance	The difference between the actual cost and the cost that was expected to be incurred. (11)
volume variance	An amount equal to the difference between the flexible budget overhead cost for the actual level of production achieved and the overhead applied at that level of production. (13)
waiting line theory	See *queuing theory.*
weighted-average contribution-margin percentage	The contribution-margin percentage expected to be achieved with a projected sales mix; calculated by weighting the dollar unit contribution margin of the products in accordance with the ratios of the numbers of units of each product expected to be sold relative to total units expected to be sold during the reporting period, *or* by weighting the contributed-margin percentages of the products by the ratios of the total sales dollars of each product expected to be sold relative to the total expected sales dollars of all products during the reporting period. (16)
weighted average method of process costing	A method of determining unit costs in a process costing system that averages costs associated with beginning inventory from the prior period with costs of the current period in arriving at the cost per unit to be used in valuing ending work-in-process inventory and goods transferred out of the department or process. (6)
working capital	See *net working capital.*
work-in-process inventory	Partially completed inventory. The work-in-process inventory account is used to accumulate production costs as the manufacturing process is being carried out. (1)
zero-base budgeting	A budget procedure, used primarily by governmental entities, in which managers are required to justify each budgetary expenditure anew, as if the budget were being initiated for the first time, each year rather than basing it on an adjustment of prior-year data. (11)
zero defective goods	A goal of having zero defective units produced by a manufacturing process. The goal is adopted for the purpose of improving quality, reducing costs, and decreasing manufacturing lead time. (3)

Index